The Old English Elegies

ANNE L. KLINCK

The Old English Elegies

A Critical Edition and Genre Study

McGill-Queen's University Press
Montreal & Kingston • London • Buffalo

© McGill-Queen's University Press 1992
ISBN 0-7735-0836-8
Legal deposit second quarter 1992
Bibliothèque nationale du Québec

Printed in Canada on acid-free paper

This book has been published with the help of a
grant from the Canadian Federation for the Humanities, using funds provided by the Social Sciences and
Humanities Research Council of Canada. Publication
has also been assisted by a grant from the University
of New Brunswick.

Canadian Cataloguing in Publication Data

Klinck, Anne Lingard, 1943–
    The Old English elegies
    Includes bibliographical references.
    ISBN 0-7735-0836-8
    1. Elegiac poetry, English (Old). 2. Elegiac poetry,
    English (Old) – History and criticism.
    I. Title.

PR1505.K56 1992   821'.04   C92-090207-3

This book was typeset by Typo Litho composition inc.
in 10/12 Baskerville.

Cover design by Peter Moulding, interior design by
Gwen Burrows.

To Dennis, Mary, and Jenny

Contents

Acknowledgments

Most of this book was written while I was living as a private scholar near Montreal, using the library facilities of McGill University. I would like to thank my husband, Dennis Klinck, for his assistance, and also Leonore Lieblein and Abbott Conway, through whose kindness I was able to use the Interlibrary Loans service. Especial thanks are due to the Interlibrary Loans staff, particularly Karen Bergsteinsson and Maria de Souza.

In 1986 I was supported by a research stipend and other monies from the Social Sciences and Humanities Research Council of Canada, enabling me to visit London and Exeter, where I examined the 1831 British Library Transcript and the Exeter Book itself. Facsimile plates are included here by kind permission of the Dean and Chapter of Exeter Cathedral.

In preparing the Appendix translations from Latin, Welsh, and Norse I was assisted by Peter Blaney at McGill-Queen's University Press, Gwyn Thomas at the University College of North Wales, and Martin Puhvel at McGill University, respectively; any remaining errors are, of course, my own. Helpful pointers to materials outside my own field came from Sarah Westphal, at McGill, and Lauriat Lane, at the University of New Brunswick. The anonymous readers who assessed my manuscript for McGill-Queen's Press and for the SSHRC also made suggestions, many of which I have adopted. The manuscript was typed, with care and accuracy, by Christine Wirta.

Excerpts from the following notes and articles, which I had published previously, are incorporated here passim: "The Old English Elegy as a Genre," *English Studies in Canada* 10 (1984): 129–46; "Growth and Decay in *The Riming Poem*, Lines 51–54," *English Language Notes* 23, no. 3 (1985–86): 1–3; "A Damaged Passage in the Old English *Ruin*," *Studia Neophilologica* 58 (1986): 165–68; "Animal Imagery in *Wulf and Eadwacer* and the Possibilities of Interpretation," *Papers on Language and Literature* 23

(1987): 3–13; *"Resignation*: Exile's Lament or Penitent's Prayer?" *Neophilologus* 71 (1987): 423–30; *"The Riming Poem*: Design and Interpretation," *Neuphilologische Mitteilungen* 89 (1988): 266–79.

Publication of this book has been made possible by support from the English Department and the Faculty of Arts at the University of New Brunswick, and by a grant from the Canadian Federation for the Humanities using funds provided by the Social Sciences and Humanities Research Council of Canada.

Abbreviations

Journal titles are abbreviated according to MLA practice, with the following exceptions:

ZfcP *Zeitschrift für celtische Philologie*
ZfdA *Zeitschrift für deutsches Altertum and deutsche Literatur*
ZfdP *Zeitschrift für deutsche Philologie*

Titles of Old English poetical texts are those to be used by the *Old English Dictionary*; see *ASE* 4 (1975): 213–15, and 8 (1979): 332.

LANGUAGES AND DIALECTS

ae	altenglisch
ags	angelsächsisch
A-S	Anglo-Saxon
eW-S	early West Saxon
lW-S	late West Saxon
ME	Middle English
MHG	Middle High German
MnE	Modern English
nW-S	non West-Saxon
OE	Old English
OHG	Old High German
OI	Old Icelandic
ON	Old Norse
OS	Old Saxon

REFERENCE WORKS

Bosworth-Toller, Toller *Supp*, Campbell *Addenda*
  J. Bosworth, *An Anglo-Saxon Dictionary* (Oxford 1898); *Supplement* by
  T.N. Toller (London 1921); *Addenda* by Alistair Campbell (Oxford
  1972).
Campbell *Grammar*
  A. Campbell, *Old English Grammar* (Oxford 1959).
Concordance, High-Frequency Concordance
  A. diPaolo Healey and R.L. Venezky, *A Microfiche Concordance to Old
  English* (Toronto 1980); R.L. Venezky and S. Butler, *A Microfiche Con-
  cordance to Old English: The High-Frequency Words* (Toronto 1985).
Grein *Sprachschatz*, Grein-Köhler
  C.W.M. Grein, *Sprachschatz der angelsächsischen Dichter, Bibliothek der an-
  gelsächsischen Poesie* 3–4 (Kassel and Göttingen, 1861–64); unter Mit-
  wirkungen von F. Holthausen, hrsg. J.J. Köhler (Heidelberg 1912).
Mitchell *Syntax*
  Bruce Mitchell, *Old English Syntax*, 2 vols. (Oxford 1985).
OE Dict
  Angus Cameron et al., *Dictionary of Old English* (Toronto 1986–).
OE Elegies ed. Green
  The Old English Elegies: New Essays in Criticism and Research, ed. Martin
  Green (Rutherford, Madison, and Teaneck 1983).
SHOEL
  Kenneth Sisam, *Studies in the History of Old English Literature* (Oxford
  1953).
Sievers-Brunner
  Karl Brunner, *Altenglische Grammatik nach der Angelsächsischen Grammatik
  von Eduard Sievers*, 3. Aufl. (Tübingen 1965).

SERIES

CCSL
  Corpus Christianorum, series latina. Turnhout.
EETS
  Early English Text Society Publications. Unless e.s. (extra series) is in-
  dicated, citations refer to the original series.
MGH
  Monumenta Germaniae historica, 500–1500.
PL
  Patrologiae cursus completus, series latina, ed. Jacques Paul Migne (Paris
  1844–64).

EDITIONS AND FACSIMILES OF OLD ENGLISH TEXTS

Page references are given for the Exeter Book elegies, where applicable.

ASPR
  The Anglo-Saxon Poetic Records, ed. G.P. Krapp and E.V.K. Dobbie, 6 vols.
  (New York 1931–53). 3 (*The Exeter Book*): *Wan* (pp. 134–37), *Sea*
  (pp. 143–47), *Rim* (pp. 166–69), *Deor, Wulf* (pp. 178–80), *Wife*
  (pp. 210–11), *Res* (pp. 215–18), *Rid 60, Husb, Ruin* (pp. 225–29).

Baker
  Peter S. Baker, "*Wulf and Eadwacer*: A Classroom Edition," *OEN* 16,
  no. 2 (1983): Appendix 1–8.

Bede
  See *OE Bede*.

B-F, Bliss and Frantzen
  Alan Bliss and Allen J. Frantzen, "The Integrity of *Resignation*," *RES*
  n.s. 27 (1976): 385–402.

BL Transcript
  British Library Additional Manuscript 9067. A pen-and-ink facsimile
  of the Exeter Book made by Robert Chambers (1831).

Co, Conybeare
  J.J. Conybeare, *Illustrations of Anglo-Saxon Poetry*, ed. W.D. Conybeare
  (London 1826): *Rim* (pp. xvi–xxvi), *Deor, Wife, Ruin* (pp. 235–55).

D-B, Dunning and Bliss
  The Wanderer, ed. T.P. Dunning and Alan J. Bliss (London 1969).

Durham Ritual
  Rituale ecclesiae Dunelmensis, Latin text with interlinear OE version, ed.
  Uno Lindelöf with introd. by A.H. Thompson, Surtees Society 140
  (London 1927).

Ett, Ettmüller
  Engla and Seaxna Scôpas and Bôceras, ed. Ludwig Ettmüller (Quedlinburg
  and Leipzig 1850): *Husb* 13–54 (pp. 202–3), *Deor, Ruin, Wife, Wan, Sea,
  Rim* (pp. 211–23), *Rid 60* (pp. 298–99).

Exeter Book facs
  The Exeter Book of Old English Poetry, facsimile with introductory chapters
  by R.W. Chambers, Max Förster, and Robin Flower (London 1933).

Goll, Gollancz
  The Exeter Book, Part I, ed. Israel Gollancz, EETS 104 (London 1895):
  Wan (pp. 286–93).

Gord, Gordon
  The Seafarer, ed. Ida L. Gordon (London 1960).

Gr, Grein
  Bibliothek der angelsächsischen Poesie, ed. C.W.M. Grein, 1–2 (Göttingen

1857–58). 1: *Wan, Sea, Wife, Husb, Ruin, Deor* (pp. 238–50). 2: *Rim* (pp. 137–41), *Res* (pp. 283–85), *Wulf* (p. 369), *Rid 60* (pp. 472–73).

Grein 1857–59 transl
Dichtungen der Angelsachsen stabreimend übersetzt, 2 vols. (Göttingen 1857–59).

Gr, Grein 1865
"Zur Textkritik der angelsächsischen Dichter," *Germania* 10: 416–29. Corrections to *Bibl.*

Grein 1865 transl
"Kleine Mitteilungen 1," *Germania* 10: 305–7. Latin transl. of *Rim.*

Gr-W, Grein-Wülker
Bibliothek der angelsächsischen Poesie von C.W.M. Grein, hrsg. Richard P. Wülker, 3 Bände (Kassel 1881–83; Leipzig 1888–89). 1.2: *Deor* (pp. 278–80), *Wan, Sea, Ruin, Wife, Husb* (pp. 284–311). 2.2: *Res* (pp. 217–23). 3.1: *Rim* (pp. 156–63), *Wulf* (pp. 183–84), *Rid 60* (pp. 218–19).

Im, Imelmann
Rudolf Imelmann, *Forschungen zur altenglischen Poesie* (Berlin 1920). See esp. pp. 421–55 on *Rim.*

Ker, Kershaw
Anglo-Saxon and Norse Poems, ed. Norah Kershaw (later Norah K. Chadwick) (Cambridge 1922): *Wan, Sea, Wife, Rid 60, Husb, Ruin* (pp. 1–57).

Klaeber *Beowulf*
Beowulf and the Fight at Finnsburg, 3rd ed. (Boston 1950).

K-D, Krapp-Dobbie
See *ASPR*, above.

Leo
Heinrich Leo, *Quae de se ipso Cynevulfus (sive Cenevulfus, sive Coenevulfus) poeta Anglosaxonicus tradiderit* (Halle 1857). See pp. 21–27 on *Wulf.*

Les, Leslie
Three Old English Elegies, ed. Roy F. Leslie (Manchester 1961; repr. with corrections 1966): *Wife, Husb, Ruin.*

– *The Wanderer* (Manchester 1966; repr. with additional bibliography, Exeter 1986).

Lindisfarne Gospels, Rushworth Gospels[1] and [2]
The Holy Gospels in Anglo-Saxon, Northumbrian, and Old Mercian Versions, ed. W.W. Skeat (Cambridge 1871–87). Contains parallel W-S, Northumb., and Mercian texts. Northumb. comprises *Lindisfarne* and *Rushworth*[2]; Mercian *Rushworth*[1] (Matthew, Mark 1:1–2:15, John 18:1–3).

Mack, Mackie
The Exeter Book, Part II, ed. W.S. Mackie, EETS 194 (London 1934):

Sea (pp. 2–9), *Rim* (pp. 56–61), *Deor, Wulf* (pp. 82–87), *Wife* (pp. 152–55), *Res* (pp. 164–71), *Rid* 60, *Husb, Ruin* (pp. 190–201).

M-G, Macrae-Gibson
The Old English Riming Poem, ed. O.D. Macrae-Gibson (Cambridge 1983).

Mal, Malone (1933, 1949, 1961, 1966, 1977)
Deor, ed. Kemp Malone. 5 eds.: London 1933–66; Exeter 1977 (posthumous).

Malm, Malmberg
Resignation, ed. Lars Malmberg (Durham and Fife 1979).

OE Bede
The Old English Version of Bede's Ecclesiastical History of the English People, ed. T. Miller, EETS 95–96 (Text; London 1890–91), 110–11 (Introduction and Various Readings; 1898).

Pastoral Care
King Alfred's West-Saxon Version of Gregory's Pastoral Care, ed. Henry Sweet, 2 vols., EETS 45 and 50 (London 1871).

Rushworth Gospels
See *Lindisfarne Gospels*.

Siep, Sieper
Ernst Sieper, *Die altenglische Elegie* (Strassburg 1915): *Deor, Wulf, Sea, Wan, Husb, Wife, Ruin, Rim, Res* (pp. 125–292).

Sweet 1894
An Anglo-Saxon Reader, ed. Henry Sweet, 7th ed. (Oxford 1894): *Wan* (pp. 159–63), *Sea* 1–108 (pp. 171–74); *Sea* 109–24 included in Notes (pp. 222–24).

Th, Thorpe
Codex Exoniensis, ed. Benjamin Thorpe (London 1842): *Wan* (pp. 286–93), *Sea* (pp. 306–13), *Rim* (pp. 352–55), *Deor, Wulf* (pp. 377–80), *Wife* (pp. 441–44), *Res* (pp. 452–59), *Rid* 60, *Husb, Ruin* (pp. 471–78).

Thorpe *Homilies*
The Homilies of Ælfric, ed. Benjamin Thorpe, 2 vols., Ælfric Society (London 1844–46).

Tupper
The Riddles of the Exeter Book, ed. Frederick Tupper, Jr (Boston 1910). Pp. 1–2 on *Wulf*.

Vespasian Psalter (gloss)
The Vespasian Psalter, ed. Sherman M. Kuhn (Ann Arbor 1965).

Wright-Wülker *Vocabularies*
Anglo-Saxon and Old English Vocabularies, ed. T. Wright, rev. R. Wülker, 2 vols. (London 1884).

Plates

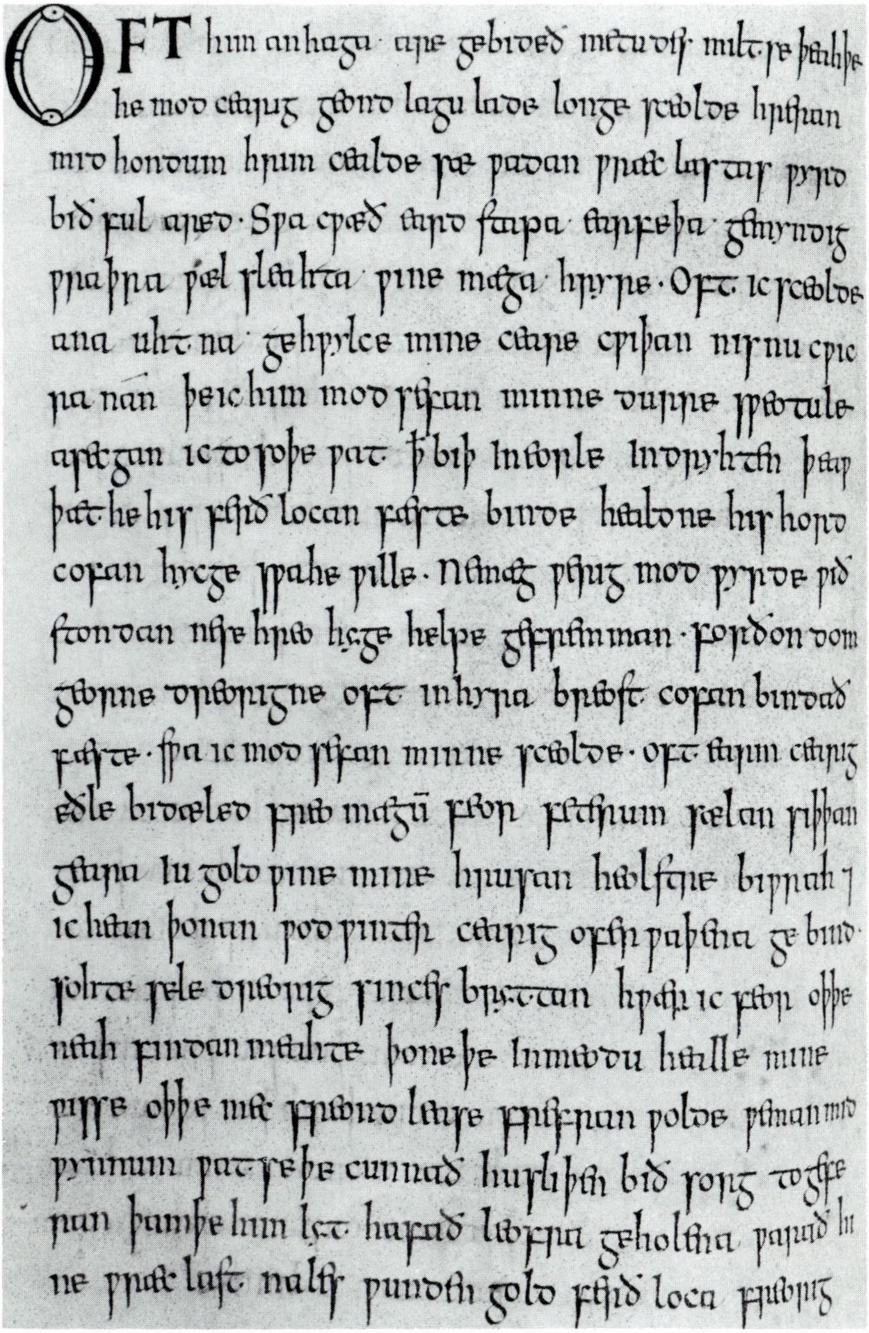

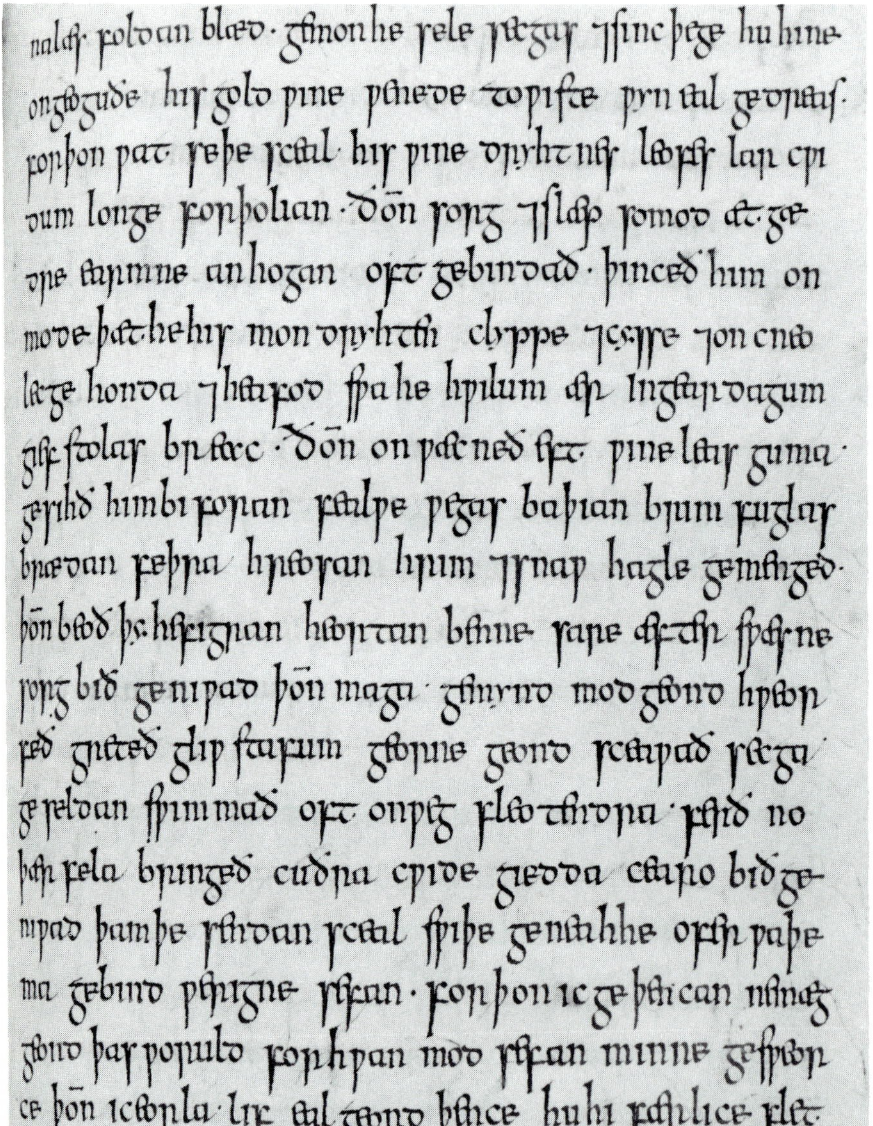
nalas foldan blæd· gemon he sele secgas ⁊ sinc þege hu hine
on geoguðe his gold wine wenede to wiste wyn eal gedreas·
forþon wat se þe sceal his wine dryhtnes leofes lar cwi
dum longe forþolian· ðonne sorg ⁊ slæp somod ætgæ
dre earmne anhogan oft gebindað· þinceð him on
mode þæt he his mondryhten clyppe ⁊ cysse ⁊ on cneo
lecge honda ⁊ heafod swa he hwilum ær in geardagum
gief stolas breac· ðonne onwæcneð eft wineleas guma·
gesihð him biforan fealwe wegas baþian brimfuglas
brædan feþra hreosan hrim ⁊ snaw hagle gemenged·
þonne beoð þy hefigran heortan benne sare æfter swæsne
sorg bið geniwad þonne maga gemynd mod geond hweor
feð greteð gliw stafum georne geond sceawað secga
geseldan swimmað oft on weg fleotendra ferð no
þær fela bringeð cuðra cwide giedda cearo bið ge
niwad þam þe sendan sceal swiþe geneahhe ofer waþe
ma gebind werigne sefan· forþon ic geþencan ne mæg
geond þas woruld forhwan mod sefa min ne gesweor
ce þonne ic eorla lif eal geond þence hu hi færlice flet
ofgeafon modge magu þegnas swa þes middangeard
ealra dogra gehwam dreoseð ⁊ fealleþ· forþon ne mæg
wearþan wis wer ær he age wintra dæl in woruldrice

FOLIO 77A, *THE WANDERER*

pita sceal geþyldig · ne sceal no to hat hiorte · ne to hræð
pyrde · neto pac piga · neto pan hydig · neto forht · neto fægen · neto
feoh gifre · nhæfne gielpes togeorn æn he geare cun
ne · beorn sceal gebidan þon he beot spriced oþþæt
collen ferð cunne gearpe hpider hreþra gehygd hpeor
fan pille · On gietan sceal gleap hæle hugæstlic bið · þonne
ealle þisse populdos pela peste stonded · panu missenlice
geond þisne middan geard pinde bipaune peallas ston
daþ hrime bihrorene hryðge þa eoþas · y oriað þa pin
salo paldend liczað dreame bidrorene duguþ eal cpong
plonc bipealle sume pig fornom · ferede in forðpege sum
ne fugel oþbær ofer heanne holm sumne se hara pulf
deaðe gedælde sumne dreorighleor in eorð scræfe oþþæt
gehydde yþde spa þisne eard geard ælda scyppend oþþæt
burig para breahtma lease eald enta gepeorc idlu stodon
Se þon þisne peal steal pise geþohte · ond þis deorce lif deope
geond þenced frod in ferðe feor oft gemon pæl sleahta
porn ond þas pord acpið · hpær cpom mearg · hpær cpom mago
hpær cpom maþþum gyfa · hpær cpom symbla gesetu · hpær sin
don sele dreamas · eala beorht bune · eala byrn piga · eala
þeodnes þrym hu seo þrag gepat genap under niht helm
spa heo no pære · Stondeð nu onlaste leofre duguþe peal

þurouū hath pryimlicum fyah · sylaf fornoman ascapyr
þe þaspyn pael gyhyn pyrod red messie · 7þaf stan hlewþu ston
maf cnyyrad hyuð hyeorstros hyuye buroed · pyntyrsf yomu
fonþon cemeð nyþed myht ycua norþan onystroed hyyu
hætl yayne hæleþum on andan · tull if tynyroðlic toiþan
nice onystroed þyroa ge ysthyt toþyulo unðsn heoþonū ·
hyshbyð yaoh lathe · hysh byð fyyeoro lathe · hyshbyð mon lathe ·
hyshbyð matz lathe tul hyy toiþan gefstul roel þeonþeð ·
Spa cþæð ynottor onmode gesæt hum rundor æt
rune tul byþ reþelyy 7þytoþe gehtuloeþ neycaul ncfyne
hyy torn toyycthe beoyn ofhyy byeoftum aesþan næn
þe heþsthþa bote cunne toyl myð elne gefymnman yel
byð þam þe hum aye yeceð fyoyne toyæoyn onheþonū
þsh uy tul yeo yast nung ytonoeð :- 7

FELA BIÐ ONFOLD an
fyyið geyxnyia gtongyia gteoyona · þa þa gstst
bsistiro yegad Ingeyicte · yya hyn þyoyivoa
god meotuo meahtum fyið monnum oæleð yx
leð rundor gyfce ystroeð yioe azne ffeoe þaya
æghpyle mot oyyylt yunistroya · oæl onyon nebyð ·

FOLIO 78A, *THE WANDERER* (END)

MÆG ic be me sylfum soð gied wrecan siþas
secgan hu ic geswinc dagum earfoð hwile oft
þrowade bitre breostceare gebiden hæbbe gecunnad
in ceole cearselda fela atol yþa gewealc þær mec oft
bigeat nearo nihtwaco æt nacan stefnan þon he be clifum
cnossað calde geþrungen wæron mine fet forste ge
bunden caldum clommum þær þa ceare seofedun hat ymb
heortan hungor innan slat merewerges mod þæt se mon ne
wat þe him on foldan fægrost limpeð hu ic earmcearig
iscealdne sæ winter wunade wræccan lastum wine
mægum bidroren bihongen hrimgicelum hægl scurum
fleag þær ic ne gehyrde butan hlimman sæ iscaldne
wæg hwilum ylfete song dyde ic me to gomene ganetes
hleoþor 7 hwilpan sweg fore hleahtor wera mæw singende
fore medodrince stormas þær stanclifu beotan þær him
stearn oncwæð isigfeþera ful oft þæt earn bigeal
urigfeþra nænig hleomæga feasceaftig ferð frefran
meahte forþon him gelyfeð lyt se þe ah lifes wyn
gebiden in burgum bealosiþa hwon wlonc 7 wingal hu ic
werig oft in brimlade bidan sceolde nap nihtscua norþan
sniwde hrim hrusan bond hægl feol on eorþan corna
caldast forþon cnyssað nu heortan geþohtas

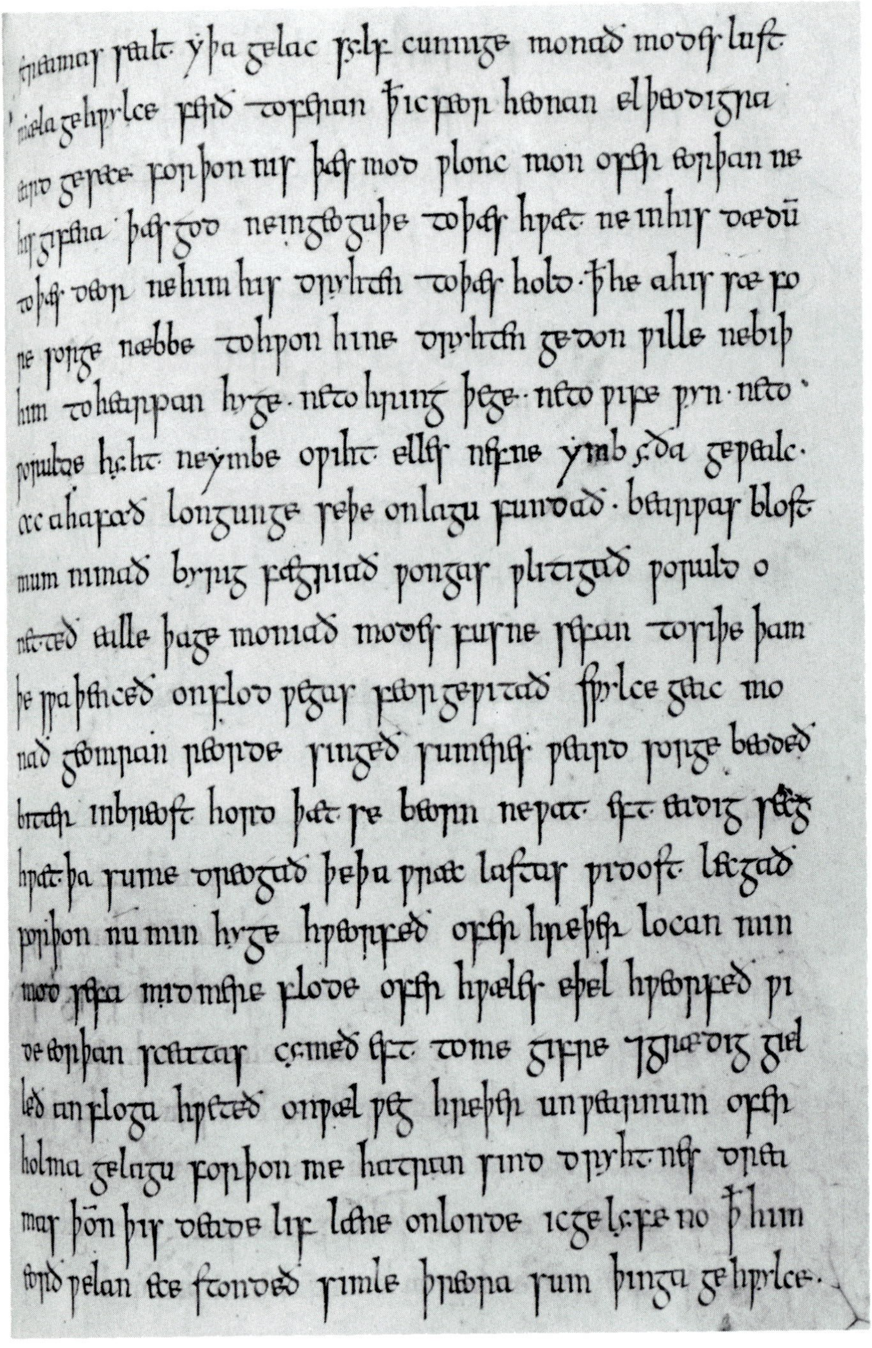

Folio 82a, *The Seafarer*

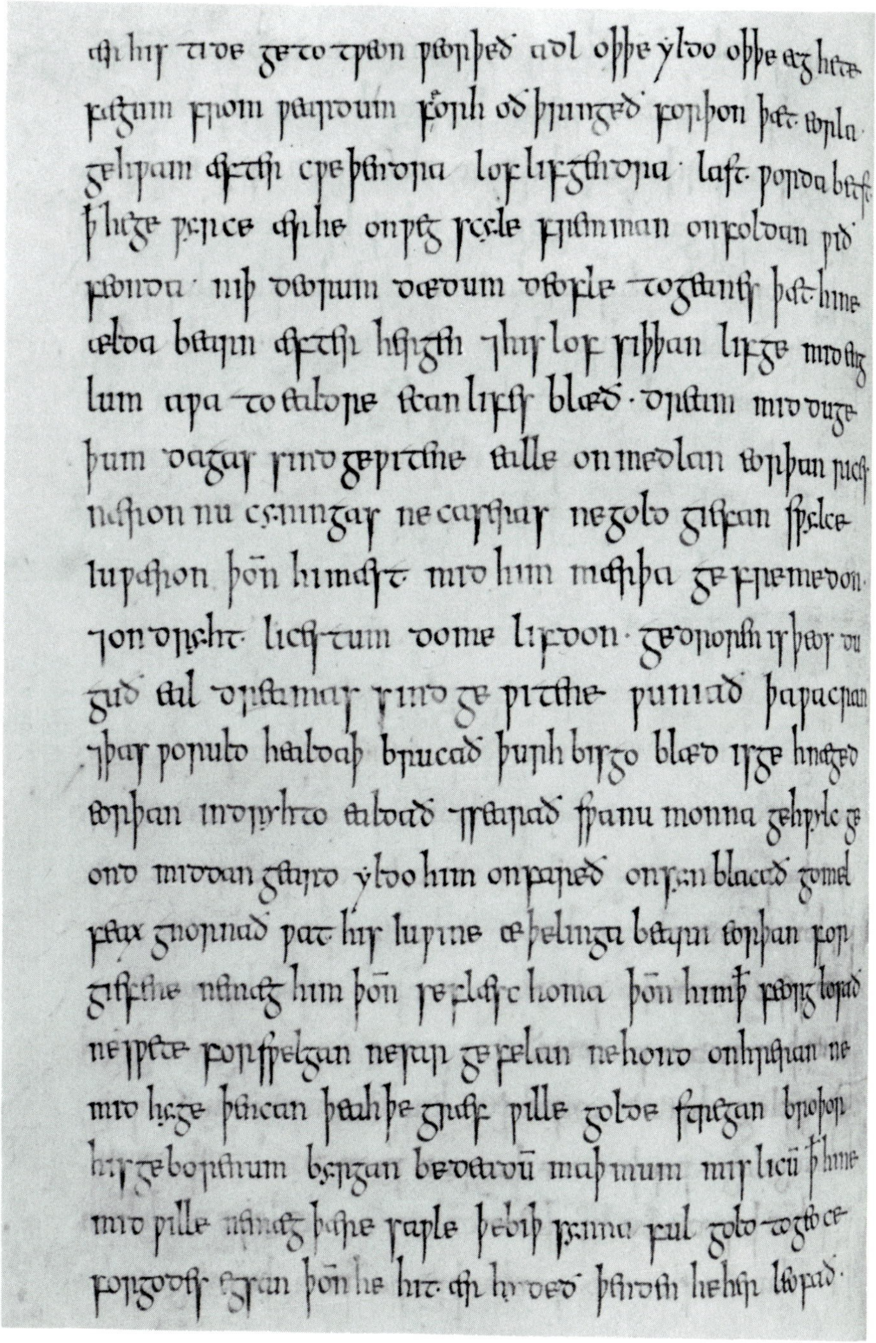

FOLIO 82B, *THE SEAFARER*

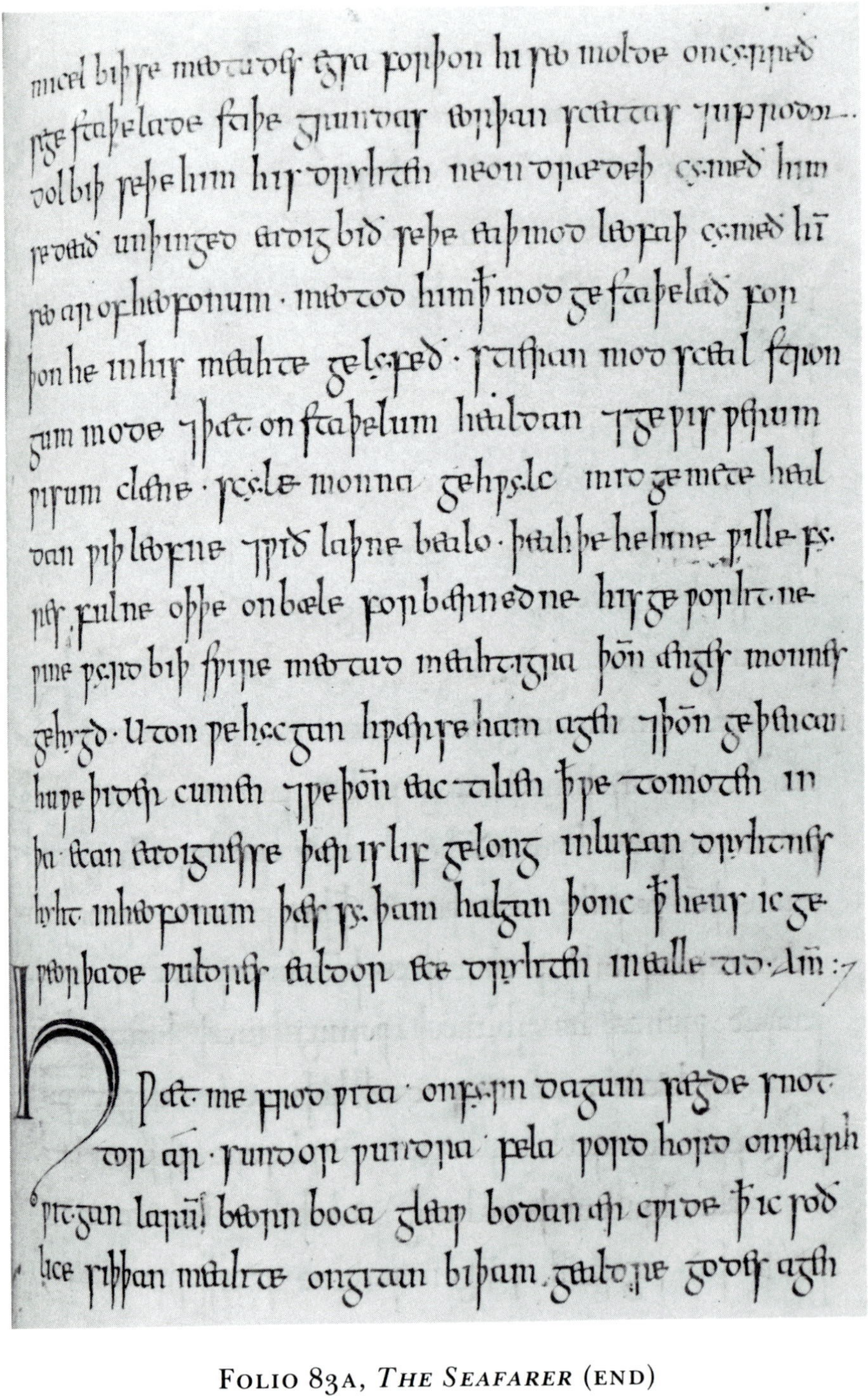

FOLIO 83A, *THE SEAFARER* (END)

hum pilce þon þam þe puldriſ cyning geþoþ inſſegle
humiſ ſæmbel ⁊oniſtun &c un hpylſti egdgum toſſioʒ
ne ſoiþon ſeale monge hreʒun þat he medtude hyne &
hpyle ælda beaþna ſoiplæte idle luſtay laſtelipſſ þ˖n
ne ſiuidiʒe him to liſſa blıſſe ſoiplæte hete niþa ge
hþone ſiʒan inid ſ˖nnid þ˖ſinum þſhe him toþam ſel
lan ince ⁊

Me liſeſ onlah ſeſiſ leohte onyſnah ⁊ſ toþilice
ge tᴐh tillice onyſnah glæd þaſ iᴄqliʒum glinʒed
hiþum blıſſa bleᴅum bloſtma hiþum ſ˖ʒuſ inæt
ſſon ſæmbel ne aleʒon þᴐþh ʒiſſe ʒſſeʒon ſnatʒed
ſaʒum ſic oſſi þonʒum þſinan ʒonʒum liſſe inid
lonʒum leoma ʒtonʒum þa þaſ þaſtinum aſtiliᴄ
ſoiplᴅ onſſnelte uidſti ſiooſtiu aſtiliᴄ ſaᴅ inaʒne
oſſi þuliᴄ ʒiſtay ʒſiʒdon ʒſti ſ˖ſpe inſtiʒdon liſſe
liſiʒdon luſtum ʒlſtiʒdon · ſiuiſti ſiuiad glæd þuih
geſiad inbiuiad þaſ on laʒu ſiuiine laᴅ þaſinie leo
þu nebi glad · haſde ic hᴁnne haᴅ neþaſ me inhᴁl
le gid · þat þaſti ſioſ þpiuiᴅ iuiad oſt þaſti ſinc ge biaᴅ
þhe inſele ſaʒe ſinc ge ſaʒe · þʒnu ʒeþſliᴄe þaioſti
þaſ ic inaʒſti · hoſiſce inᴁ hſtiieᴅon hilde ʒſtiieᴅon
ſaʒuſ ſtiieᴅon ſᴁonᴅon biſſtiieᴅon · ſpa inᴁ hyhti

FOLIO 94A, *THE RIMING POEM*

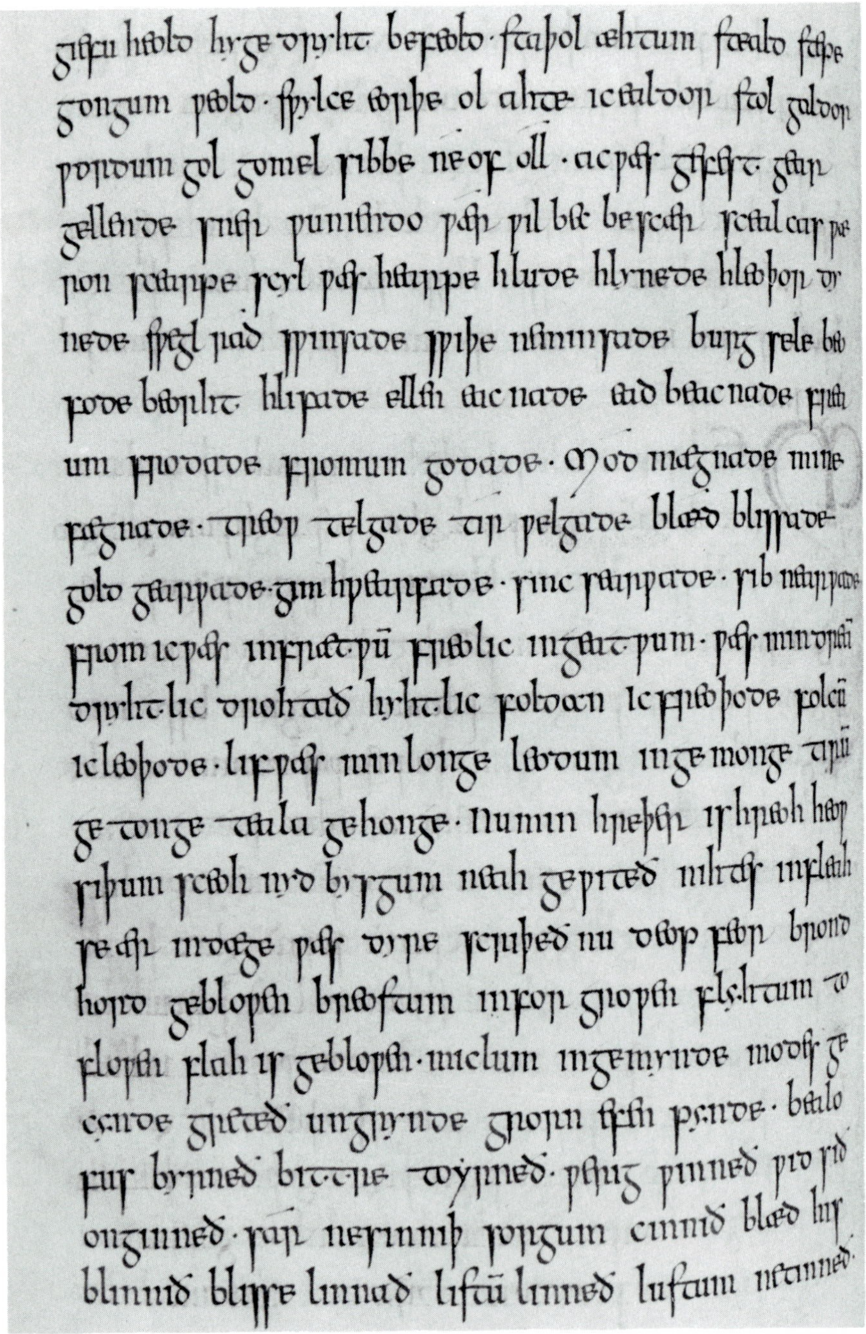

FOLIO 94B, *THE RIMING POEM*

dreamas swa her gedreosað dryhtscype gehreosað· lif her
men forleosað leahtras oft geceosað treowþrag is to
trag· seo untrume genag steapum eatole misþah ond
eal stund genag swa nu woruld wendeþ wyrde sendeþ ⁊ hetes
henteð hæleþe scyndeð wercinge witeð wælgar sliteð
flahmah fliteþ flanmon hwiteð burgsorg biteð bald
ald þwiteþ wræcfæc wriþað wraþ að smiteþ singryn
sidað searofearo glideþ gromtorn græfeþ græft· ha
fað· searohwit solaþ sumurhat colað foldwela feal
leð feondscipe wealleð eorðmægen ealdaþ ellen colað·
me þæt wyrd gewæf ⁊ gehwyrft forgeaf þæt ic grofe græf
⁊ þæt grimme græf flean flæsce ne mæg þonne flan hred
dæg nydgrapum nimeþ þonne seo niht becymeð seo me
eðles onwonn· ⁊ mec her eardes on conn· þonne licho
ma ligeð lima wyrm friteþ ac him wenne gewigeð ⁊ þa
wist geþygeð oþþæt beoþ þa ban an ⁊ æt nyhstan nan· nef
ne se neda tan balawun herge hloten· ne biþ se hlisa
adroren· ær þæt eadig geþenceð he hine þe oftor swenceð
byrgeð him þa bitran synne hogaþ to þære betran wyn
ne gemon morþa lisse þær sindon miltsa blisse hyht
lice in heofona rice uton nu halgum gelice scyldum
biscyrede scyndan generede wommum biwerede wuldre·

FOLIO 95A, *THE RIMING POEM*

MON ge fyrdon geond meodan geftyrð unfynum cenn

þeþe æðelu. nemagon fyrhte apæccan neþum ptan þæh pros fyro geond popl innan fugla 7oeþpa polo hyrhðona popnay pið pæope ſpa pæðſi bibuged þyne beophtan boſm bpim ðyſmeðroe pæl 7 ſpa geſpinz þebiſunium hyþon fnæt·lice geceno pildpa fægan fynum ſnæt mæhnne þon loiroum onſanð ptyrdan eðlſ neoran æſæſi dun rcnafum iſ þæt don panð heſi biuoman hæṫh þæh he·mþþa beano pyſ pæſte pſnay ongepfitum ceþan biſa anſtapan feiſ æðpam fnidio duguda ſftiz buttan dpacan anum þam he ineallte tro 7pnað lopdoþ þuph yfla gehpylc þehe geðenan mæg. ðæt iſ pnæt·lic don pundpum peane hipa gehpylceſ ſpa hæleð fæðad gſt halze guman þæt te ropephſ tunlte pæhe tælzu ge· hyrlceſ bleom bnegoðroe þapa beophtpna gehpylc æð hpæſ æðlicpna opnum lyte opylran beapnu ſpaþeſ doþſ lup blæt bnugda gehpaſ beophtpna 7pceanpa pun opium lyxeð ſte pnætlicpa æðhpylc opnum æðlicpna gið· 7peſſnpa ſnætpum bliceð ſcmle ſellicpna hehaſad pundon gecero milde gemſt pæſt heiſ mon þpæhe

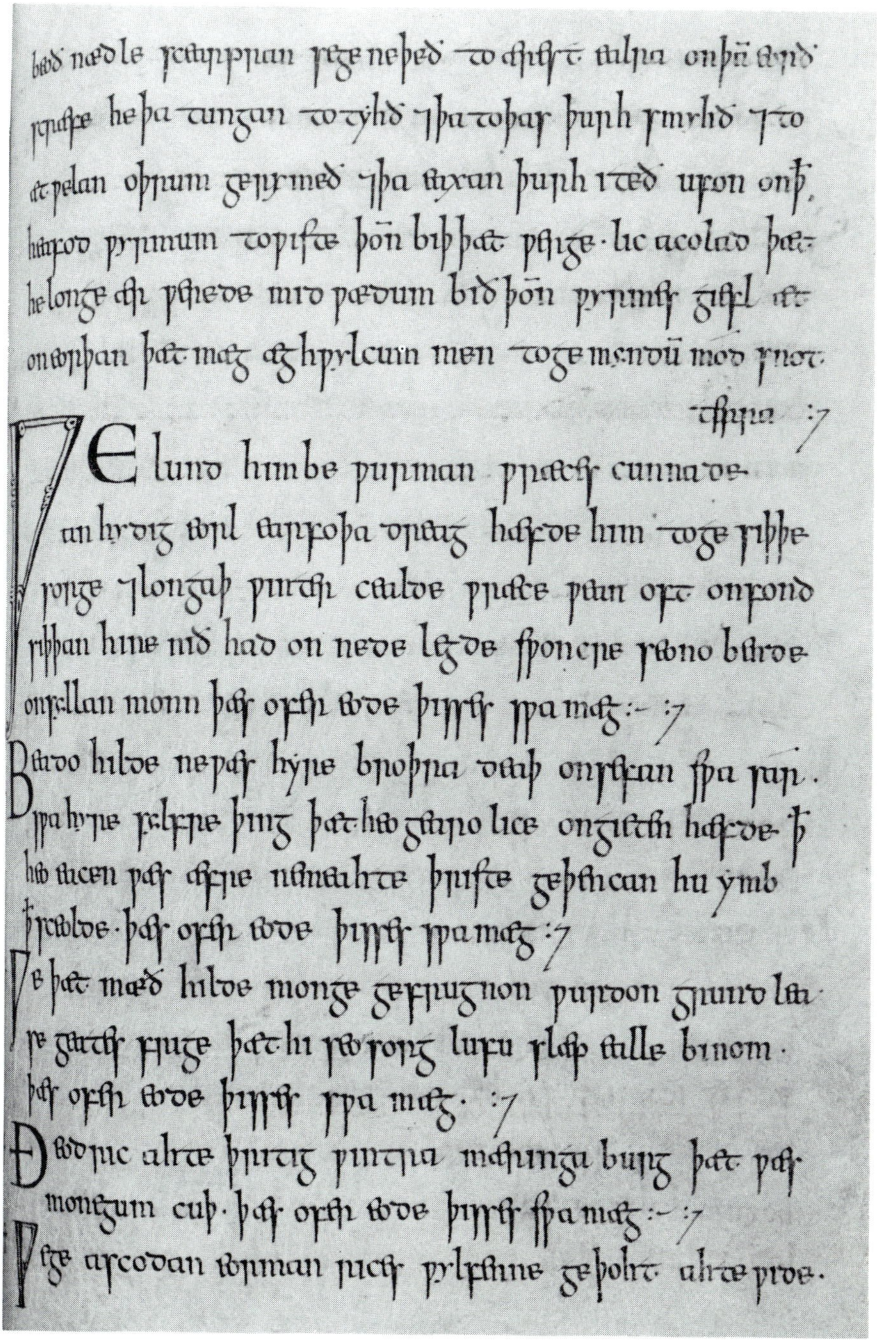
bið nædle scearpran se geneþeð to ærest ealra on þā eorð
scræfe he þa tungan toslyhð ⁊ þa toþas þurh smyhð ⁊ to
ætwelan oþrum gerymeð ⁊ þa eaxan þurh iteð ufon on þ
heafod wyrmum to wiste þon biþ þæt werige lic acolad þæt
he longe ær werede mid wædum bið þon wyrmes giefl æt
on eorþan þæt mæg æghwylcum men to gemyndū mod snot
terra :⁊
WElund him be wurman wræces cunnade
anhydig eorl earfoþa dreag hæfde him to gesiþþe
sorge ⁊ longaþ winter cealde wræce wean oft onfond
siþþan hine niðhad on nede legde swoncre seono bende
on syllan monn þæs ofer eode þisses swa mæg :- ⁊
Beado hilde ne wæs hyre broþra deaþ on sefan swa sar
swa hyre sylfre þing þæt heo gearo lice ongieten hæfde þ
heo eacen wæs æfre ne meahte þriste geþencan hu ymb
þ sceolde · þæs ofer eode þisses swa mæg :⁊
We þæt mæð hilde monge gefrugnon wurdon grundlea
se geates frige þæt hi seo sorg lufu slæp ealle binom ·
þæs ofer eode þisses swa mæg · :⁊
Ðeodric ahte þritig wintra mæringa burg þæt wæs
monegum cuþ · þæs ofer eode þisses swa mæg :- ⁊
We geascodan eormanrices wylfenne geþoht ahte wide ·

Folio 100a, *Deor*

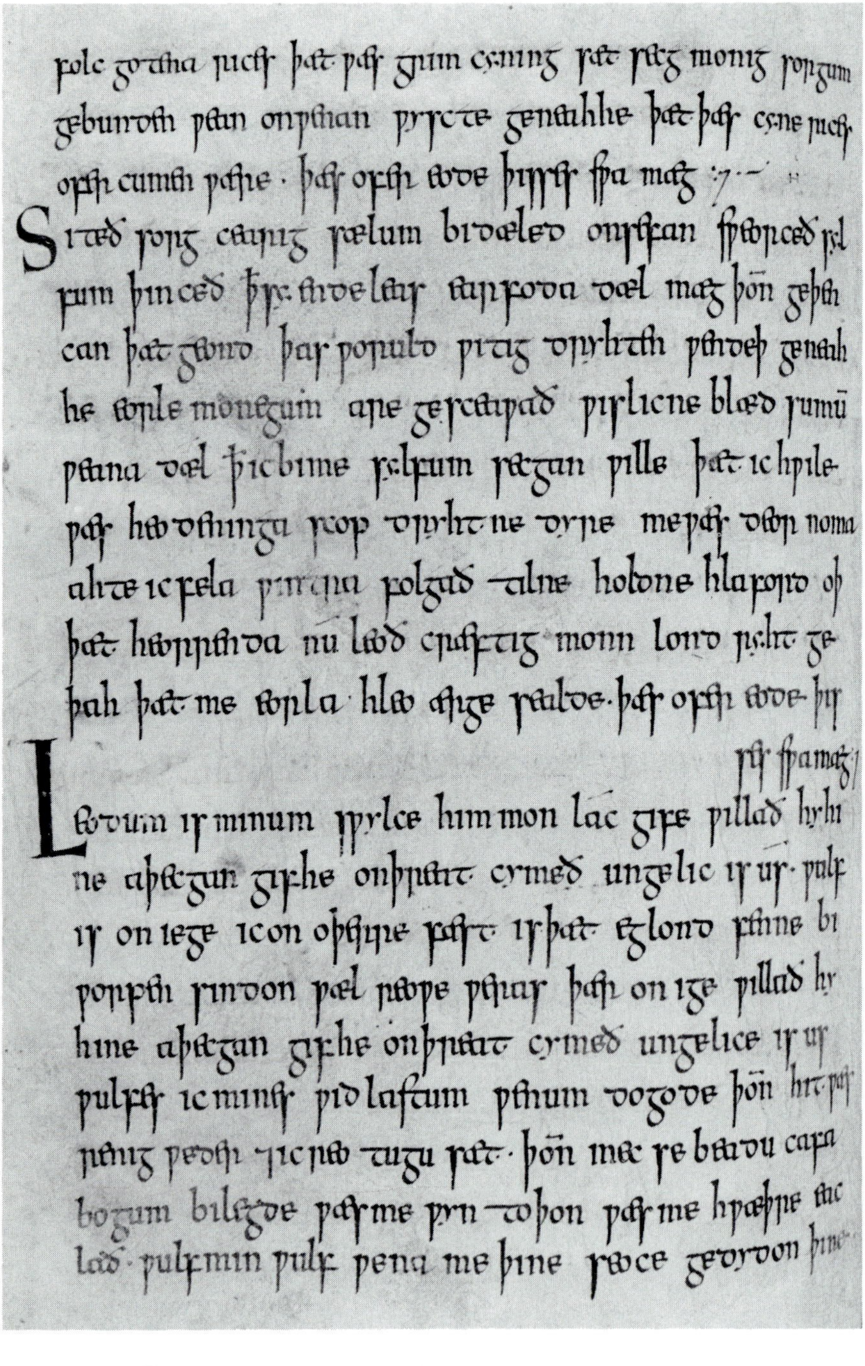
folc gotena rices þæt wæs grim cyning sæt secg monig sorgum
gebunden wean onwenan wyscte geneahhe þæt þæs cyne rices
ofer cumen wære · þæs ofereode þisses swa mæg :7·~
Siteð sorg cearig sælum bidæled onsefan sweorceð syl
fum þinceð þæt sy endeleas earfoða dæl mæg þonne geþen
can þæt geond þas woruld witig dryhten wendeþ geneah
he eorle monegum are gesceawað wislicne blæd sumum
weana dæl þæt ic bi me sylfum secgan wille þæt ic hwile
wæs heodeninga scop dryhtne dyre me wæs deor noma
ahte ic fela wintra folgað tilne holdne hlaford oþ
þæt heorrenda nu leoðcræftig monn londryht ge
þah þæt me eorla hleo ær gesealde · þæs ofereode þis
ses swa mæg
Leodum is minum swylce him mon lac gife willað hy hi
ne aþecgan gif he onþreat cymeð ungelic is us · wulf
is on iege ic on oþerre fæst is þæt eglond fenne bi
worpen sindon wælreowe weras þær on ige willað hy
hine aþecgan gif he onþreat cymeð ungelice is us
wulfes ic mines widlastum wenum dogode þonne hit wæs
renig weder 7 ic reotugu sæt · þonne mec se beadu cafa
bogum bilegde wæs me wyn to þon wæs me hwæþre eac
lað · wulf min wulf wena me þine seoce gedydon þine

FOLIO 100B, *DEOR, WULF AND EADWACER*

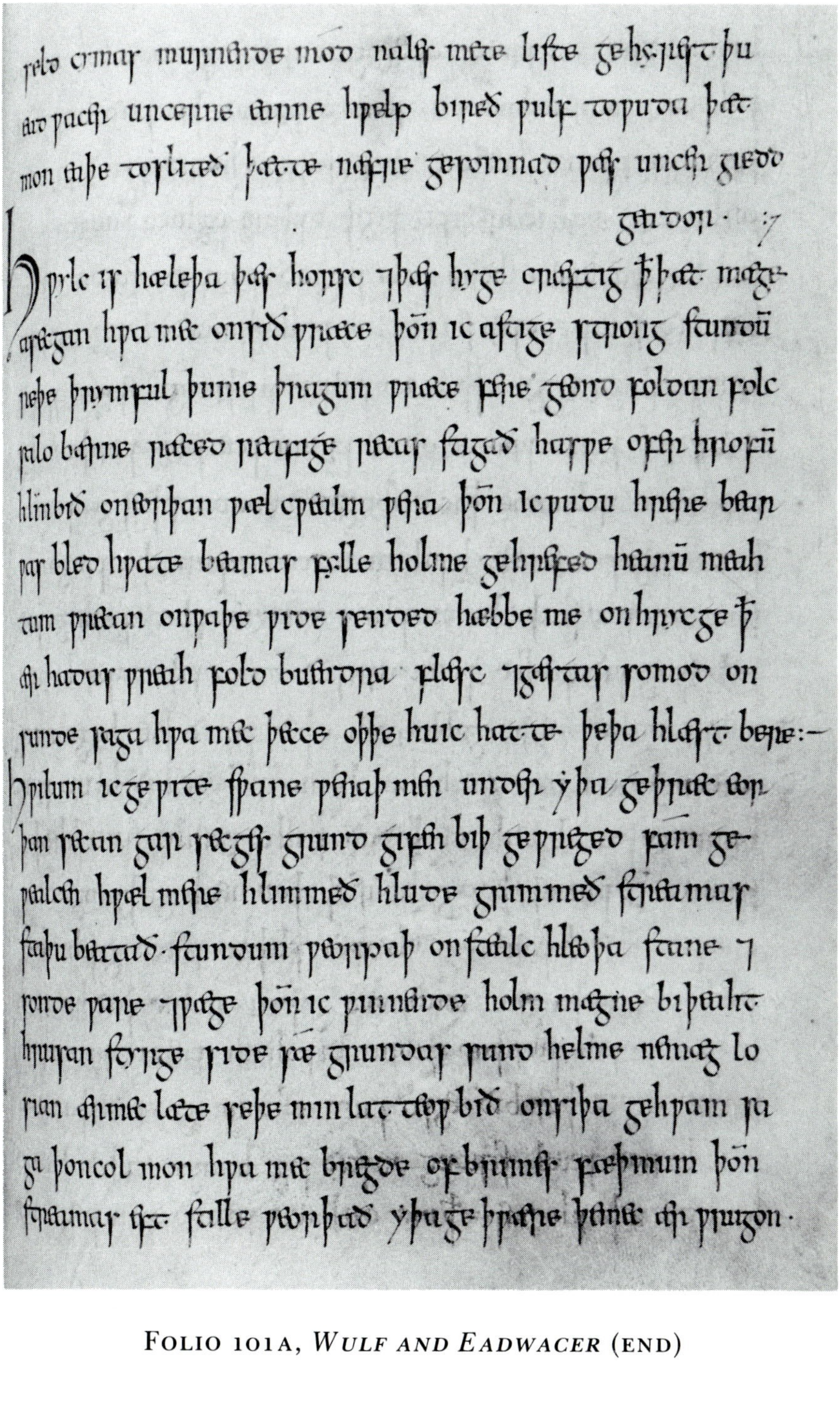

seldcymas murnende mod nales meteliste gehyrest þu
eadwacer uncerne earmne hwelp bireð wulf to wuda þæt
mon eaþe tosliteð þætte næfre gesomnad wæs uncer giedd
geador :7
Hwylc is hæleþa þæs horsc 7 þæs hygecræftig þ þæt mæge
asecgan hwa mec on sið wræce þon ic astige strong stundum
reþe þrymful þunie þragum wræce fere geond foldan folc
salo bærne ræced reafige recas stigað haswe ofer hrofum
hlin bið on eorþan wælcwealm wera þon ic wudu hrere bear
was bledhwate beamas fylle holme gehrefed heanum meah
tum wrecen on waþe wide sended hæbbe me on hrycge þ
ær hadas wreah foldbuendra flæsc 7 gæstas somod on
sunde saga hwa mec þecce oþþe hu ic hatte þe þa hlæst bere:-
Hwilum ic gewite swa ne wenaþ men under yþa geþræc eor
þan secan garsecges grund gifen biþ gewreged fam ge
wealcen hwælmere hlimmeð hlude grimmeð streamas
staþu beatað stundum weorpaþ on stealc hleoþa stane 7
sonde ware 7 wæge þon ic winnende holmmægne biþeaht
hrusan styrge side sægrundas sundhelme ne mæg lo
sian ær mec lete se þe min latteow bið on siþa gehwam sa
ga þoncol mon hwa mec bregde of brimes fæþmum þon
streamas eft stille weorþað yþa geþwære þe mec ær wrugon.

FOLIO 101A, *WULF AND EADWACER* (END)

hrinᵹſ to hæleþum þa he inhtalle peſſ pyræd ᵹpſhꝛoed.
plone þa folmum :⁊

Ic hiſ ᵹeꝺ pꞃece bnne full ᵹomoꞃne minꞃe ſʒlꝼne ſiꝺ
ichæꞇ pꝛeᵹan mæᵹ hpæꞇ ic yꞃmþa ᵹebaꝺ ſiþþan icuppeox
inpſr obþe ſhꝛoſſ no ma þon nu a ic pꞃæ þonn minꞃa
pꞃæc ꞃiþa cꞃiſꞇ minhlaꝼoꞃꝺ ᵹepaꞇ heonan oꝼ leoꝺu
oꝼꞃ yþa ᵹelac hæꝼꝺe ic uhꞇ cænꞃe hpæꞃ min leoꝺ ꝼꞃu
ma londſſ pæꞃe · ꝺa icme ꝼꞃan ᵹepaꞇ ꝼolᵹaꝺ ſꞃan
pꞃe leaſ pꞃecca ꝼoꞃ minꞃe þen heaꞃꝼe · onᵹunnon þ
þæſ monneſ maᵹaſ hycᵹan þuꞃh ꝺyꞃne ᵹeþohꞇ þhy
to ꝺæloſn unc þæꞇ pꞇ ᵹepꞃooſꞇ Inpoꞃulꝺ ꞃuce liꝼꝺon
laꝺ licoſꞇ ⁊mæ lonᵹaꝺe · hꞇ mæ hlaꝼoꞃꝺ min hꞇh
hæꞃꝺ niman alꞇe ic leoþꞃa læꞇ onhiſſum lonꝺ ſꞇe
ꝺe holoꞃa ꝼꞃonꝺa ꝼoꞃþon iſ min hyᵹe ᵹomoꞃ ·
ꝺa icme ꝼul ᵹemæꞇne monnan ꝼunꝺe hæꞃꝺ ꞃæliᵹne
hyᵹe ᵹomoꞃne moꝺ miþſnꞃone moꞃþoꞃ hycᵹꞃoe
bliþe ᵹebæꞃo ꝼul oꝼꞇ pꞇ beoꞇeꝺan þunc neᵹe ꝺæloe
nᵹnmne ꝺeaꝺ ana · opihꞇ ellſſ ſæꞇ iſ þæꞇ onhpoꞃꝼen iſ
nuſſa hiꞇ nopæꞃe ꝼꞃionꝺ ꞃcipe unceꞃ ſæl icꝼeoꞃ ᵹe
nꞃh minſſ ꝼela leoþan ꝼæhꝺu oꞃꝺᵹan helꞇ mæ
mon þunian onpuꝺa buꞃ.ꞃe unꝺꞃ ac ⁊ꞃeo inþa
ſoꞃꝺ ꞃcꞃꝼe · ſalꝺ iſ þeſ ſoꞃꝺ ꞃele ſæl ic ſom oꝼ lonᵹaꝺ.

FOLIO 115A, *THE WIFE'S LAMENT*

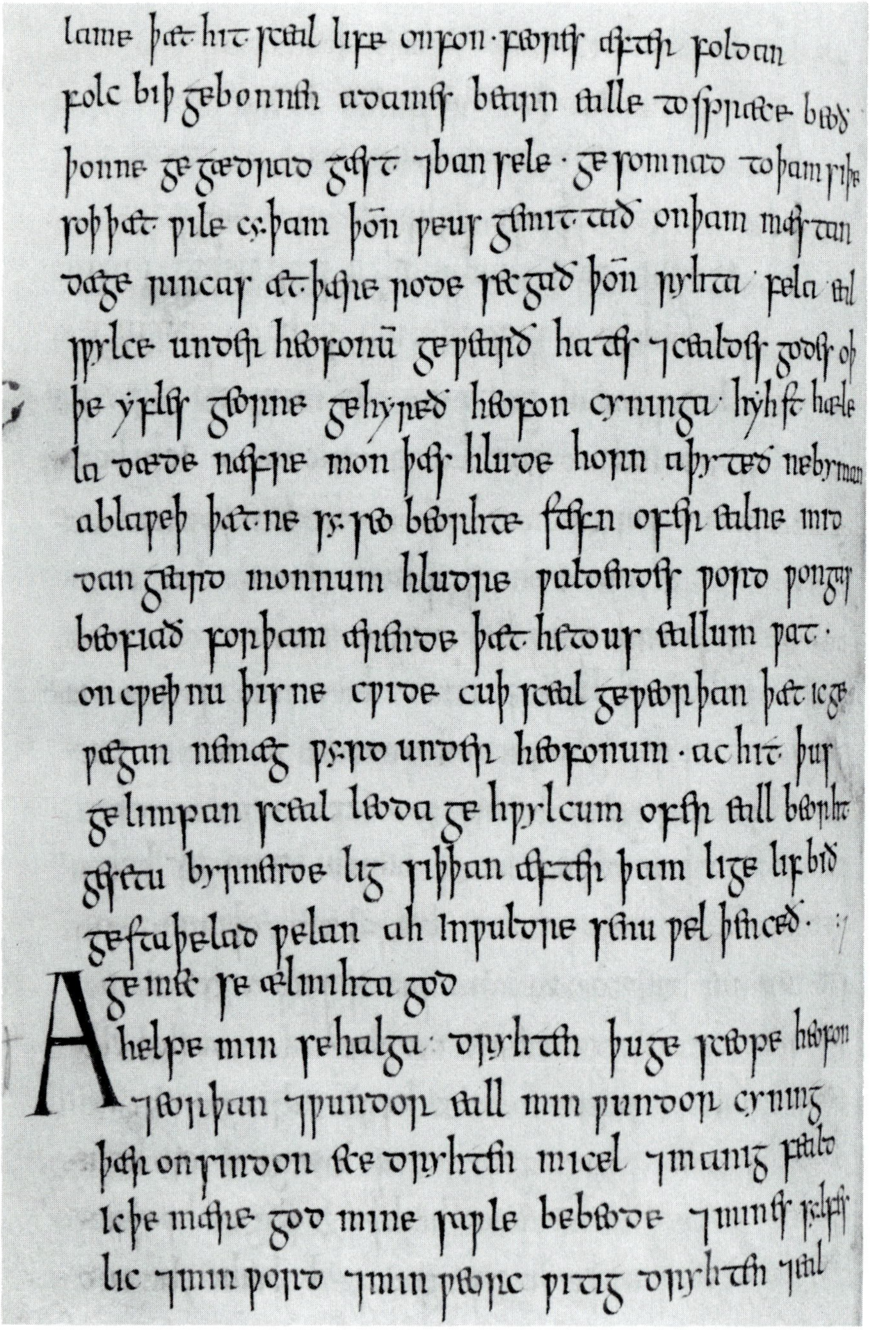

FOLIO 117B, *RESIGNATION*

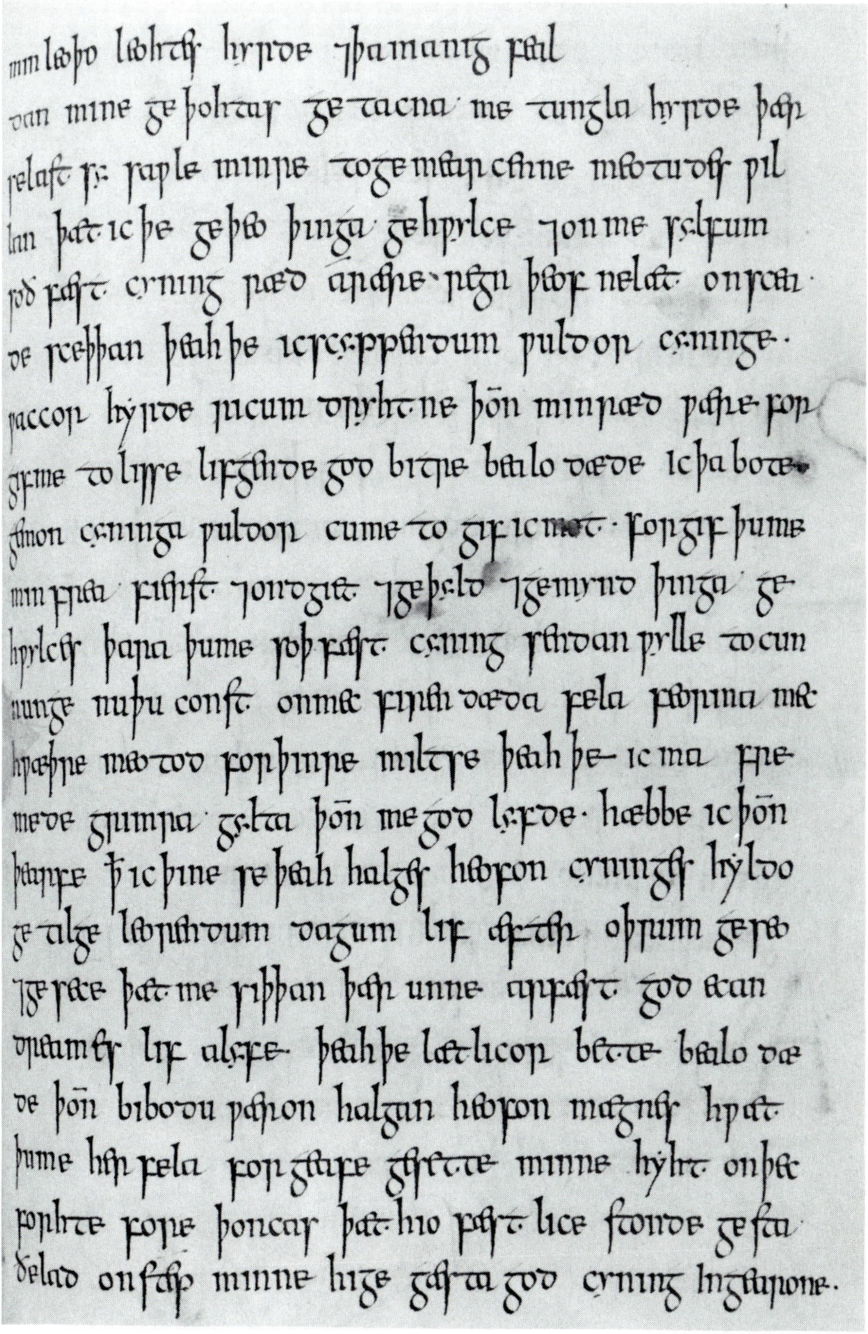

FOLIO 118A, *RESIGNATION*

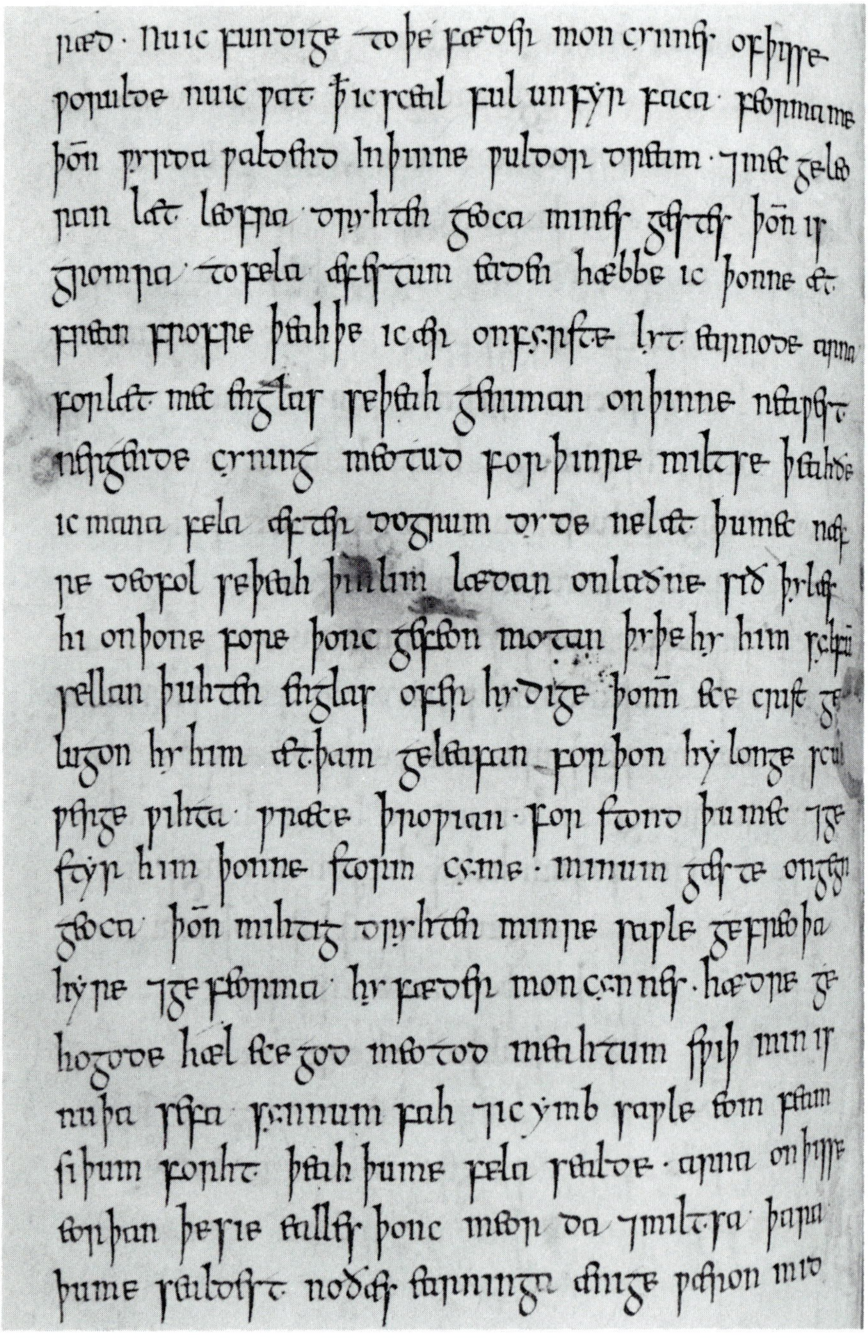

FOLIO 118B, *RESIGNATION*

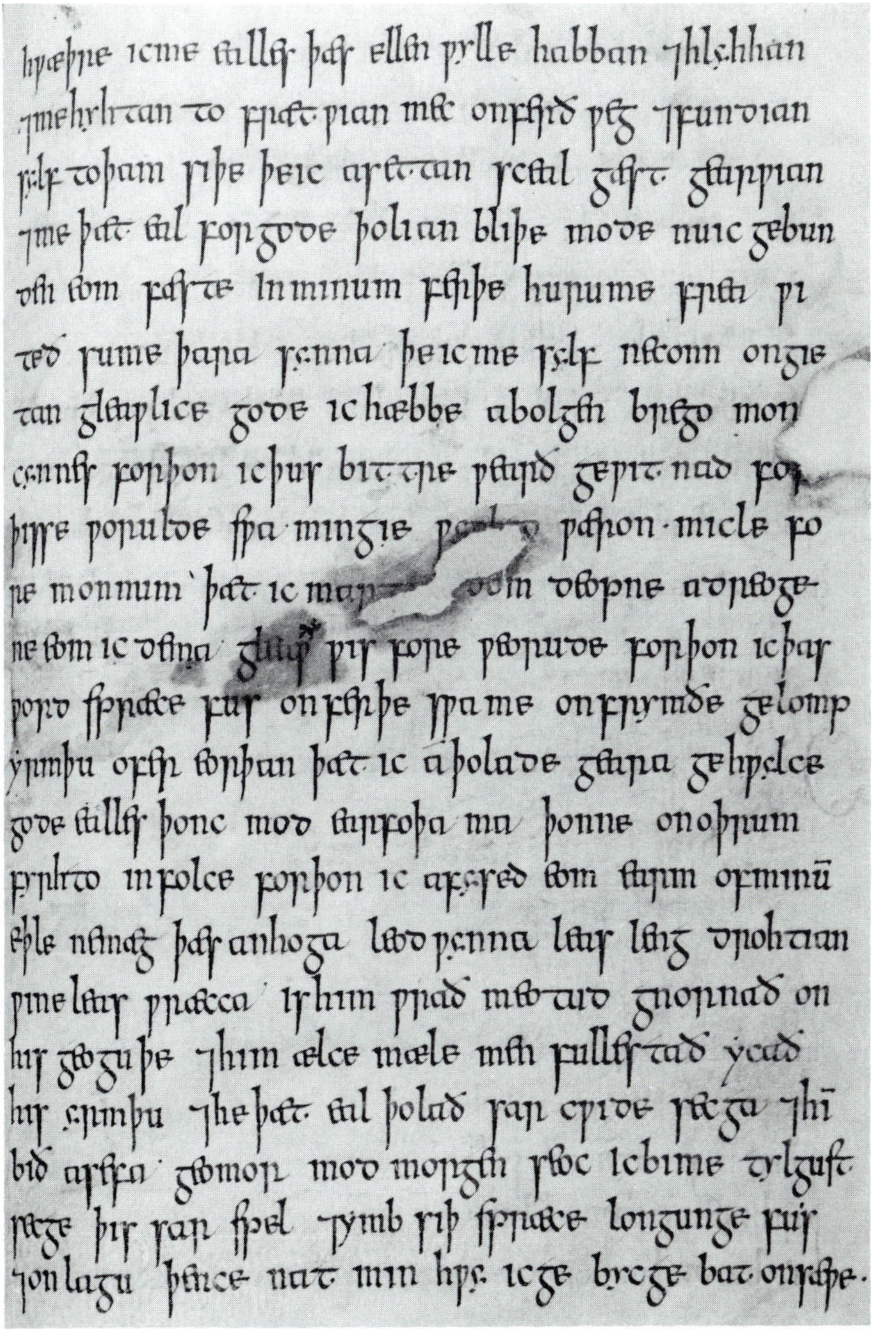

FOLIO 119A, *RESIGNATION*

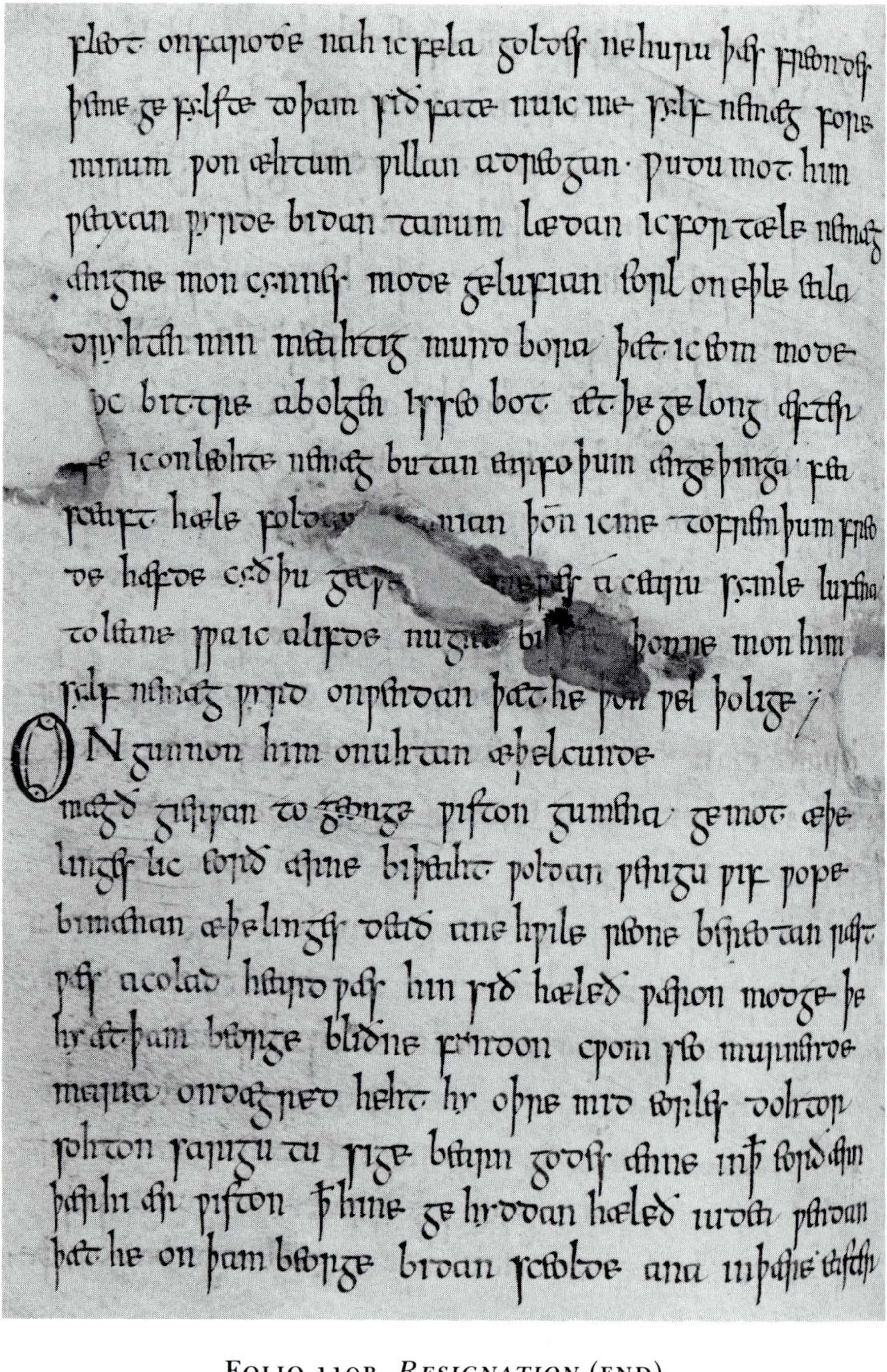

Folio 119b, *Resignation* (end)

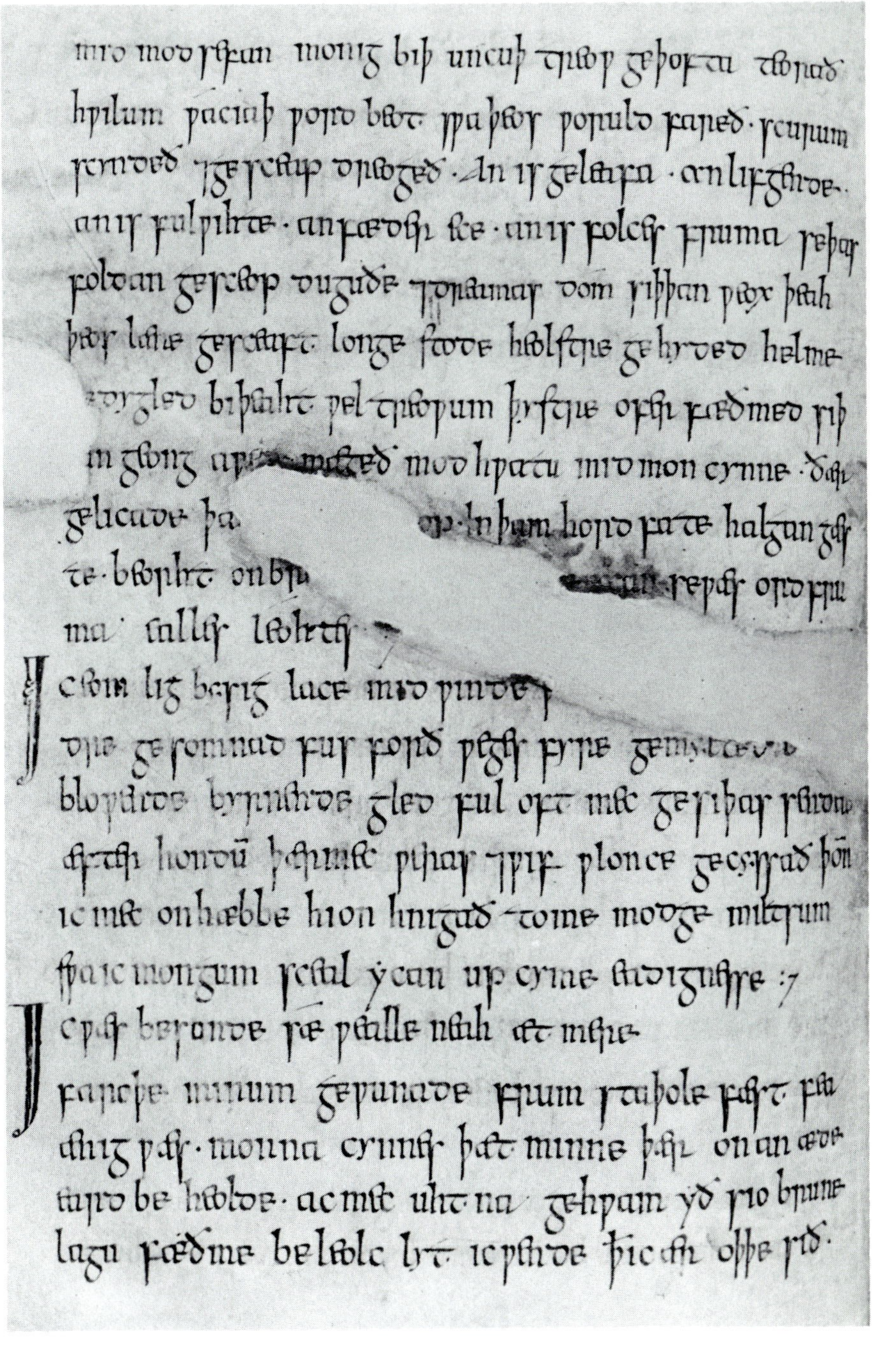

Folio 122b, *Riddle 60*

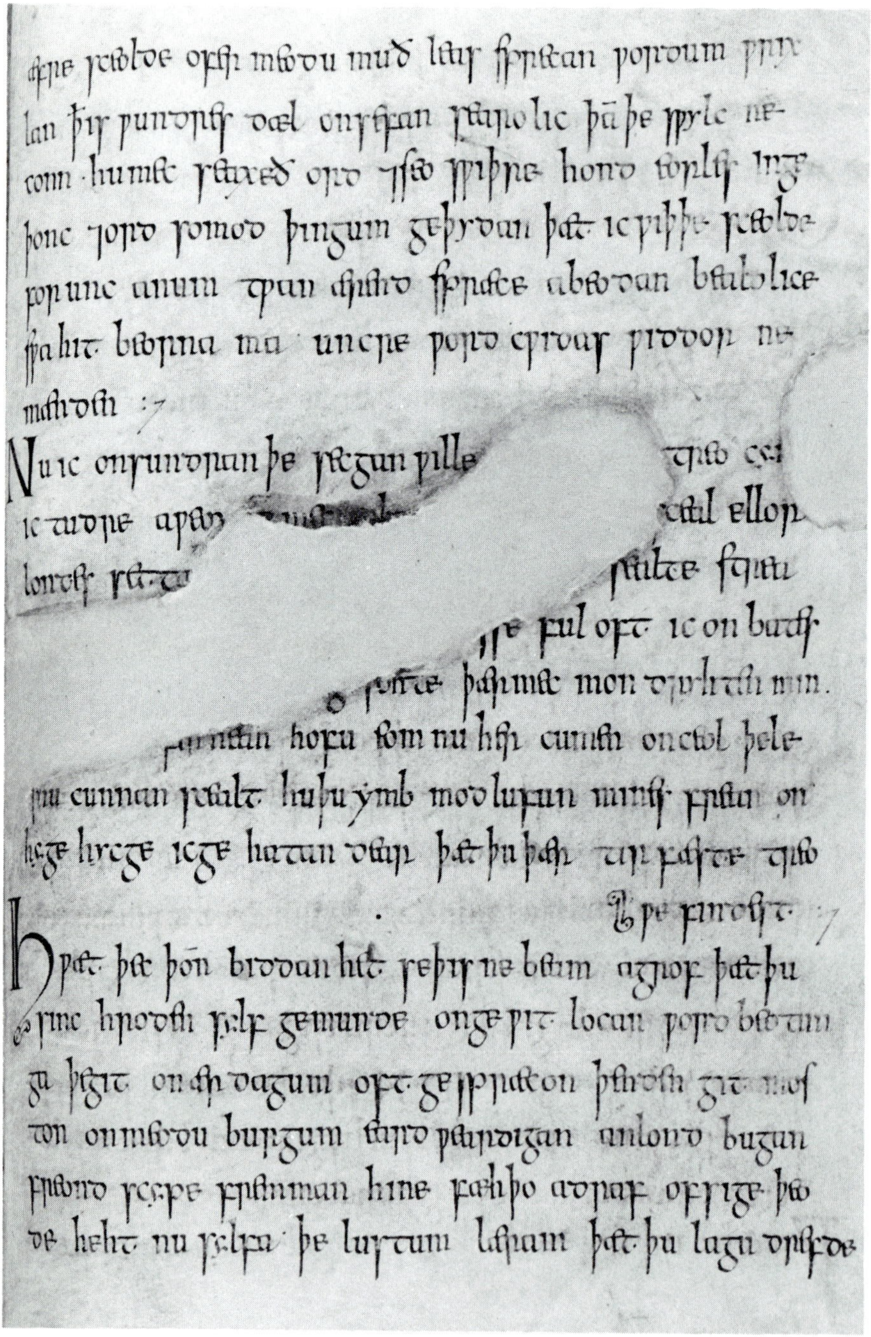

FOLIO 123A, *RIDDLE 60, THE HUSBAND'S MESSAGE*

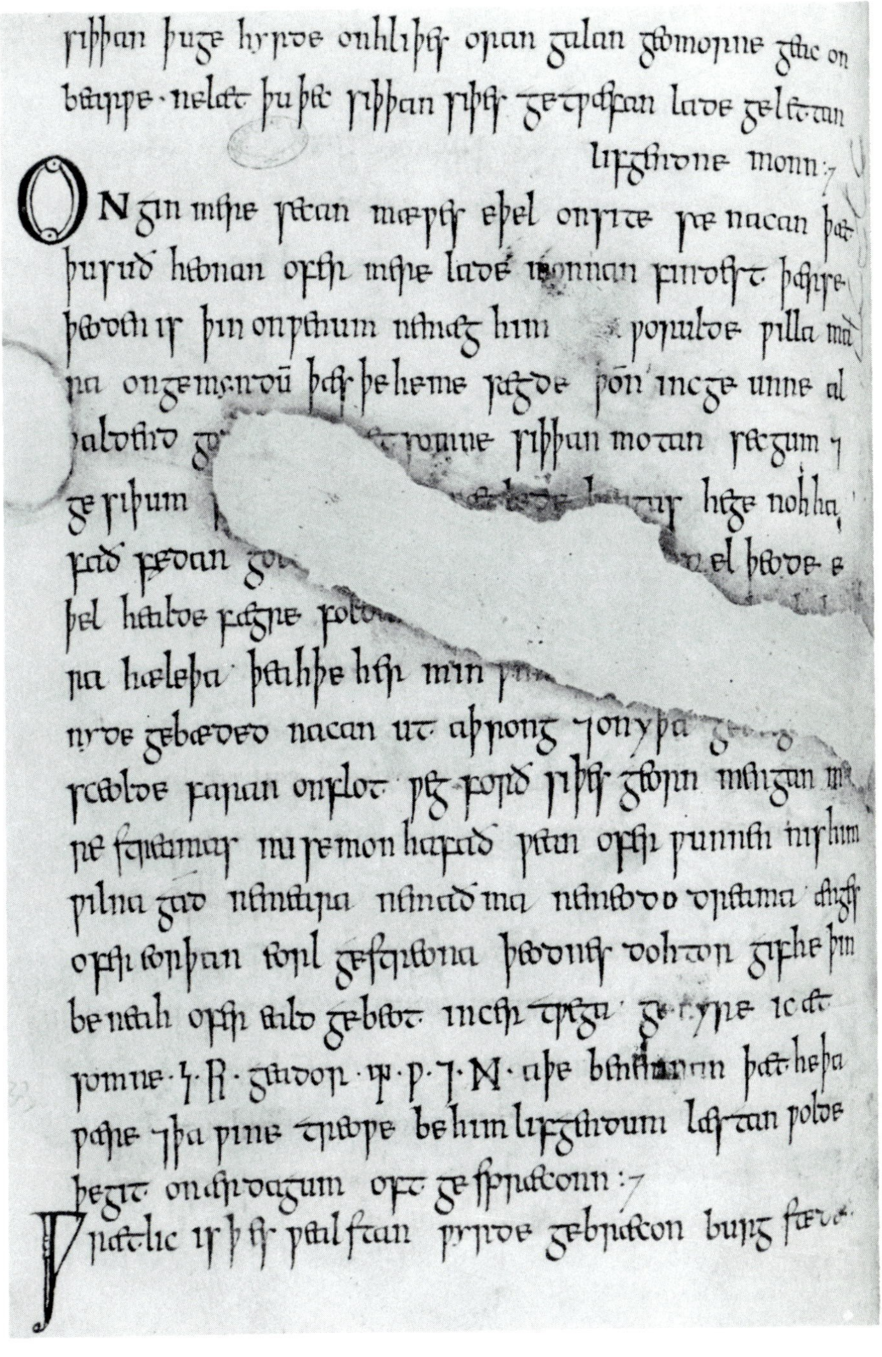

FOLIO 123B, *THE HUSBAND'S MESSAGE*, *THE RUIN*

wurston beornas firea gewrohte hnofas rind gehnorethe
hrunge torras hrim geat torras berofen hrim onli
me scearde scun burge gcrorthe gebrorthe ældo un
deth torone wyrd geap hafað waldstro wyrhtan forþ
wone gelworthe hræro gwre hruyran ofhunro enæc wern
hwda ge wran oft þæs wæg gebad nætham yrnaro wah
nice æfter ofhnum of stonori unwrth frowrnum rad
gwp georwar wræd aht r wurn ge
hwrpth felon gimme
gewrumr wran hw
onþone cwr wærft
wn wunwum brwg mod mo
ne swiwtrne gebrwað hwæt wen Inhwrngwr
wge nor geboro wwll walan wiwrum wurwrum toge
ore bwpht wrhrom burg wrwrom burn wele mornge he
ah borrn gewwuon hwre wwg micel mwwo hwll mornig
wrwrmrmr wull ohwæt þæt onwrwoe wyrwo wwo wwwe
cwrunron walo wroe cwoman walwrgwr swr wwll wor
nom wræg nor wwra wuwroon hrwra wrg wwll wwr twr twr
þolar bwor nawe burg wwll bewwro cwrunron hwrgwr
towrwrwrm wor þon wr hoæu owwngrao yhwr tawron
gwwræ wrgelum wrwwoe hwfwt bwgw nor hwewe

FOLIO 124A, THE RUIN

pong ge cnong gebnocti to bnopgum · þær tu brochin moniz

gleo mod ⁊gold broþht gtroma gefrætþeð plone ⁊pin

gal piz hnypfcū ycan þah onyinc onyflþon onftano gim

mat onftro on æht onfonican fcan · on þar brochtan bung

bnacan picft · fcan hoþu ftovan fqiftim hatæ þfeypp

þroan pylme þcil æll befeeng brophtan boyme þah

þa baþu pachon hat onhneþne · þþeft hyðelic · lecon þonn

gfccan ⌇ refe fcan hatæ fqiti

mat uip þcet hping

mfine hatæ fceþba ba

þu þachon · þonne ⌇

ne fiy cæne lic þing nu⌇

Oft mfe fæfitæ bilæc þnælicu mæple ioff onftna

hþilum uþ ætæah folmum yimum ⁊fiftan yætlðe hol

oum hæbone ypahio hacth þeft yiðþan me onhneþne

hæfood feicave moþan uþ þeþrone onnftano ffaðe

gfþef onð ffngan ellæh volrte hemfe fptæt þeðne

fellan þæboðe þnyþf nat hþæt þæð hþæt ic mæhe ⁊

IC fom hætpo ⁊yctepp Ingongf fçnong ·

fonð niþþf fnom fiftan unfon cuð þave unnoþ þam

be ⁊me þeg yelþa þyhtne ge þypine þincibið on ⌇

FOLIO 124B, *THE RUIN* (END)

Folio 105a, *Riddles 19* (for M rune)

The Old English Elegies

Introduction

This edition has grown out of a deep attachment to Old English poetry that began when I encountered *The Battle of Maldon* long ago and turned it into rather deplorable free verse. I have wanted to deal with the elegies because some of them – most of all *The Wanderer* – speak to me very powerfully. Perhaps essentially I wish not so much to say things about them as simply to let them be: to place them in a literary and scholarly context and at the same time free them from it; to give them to the modern reader as the Anglo-Saxon might have understood them and as we can relate to them now. But inevitably the poems as I present them are the product of my own conditioning and of all the intellectual baggage I bring to the task of scholarship. Philosophically, I share the Anglo-Saxons' Christian view of the world and man's place in it. Methodologically, I have chosen a philological approach, beginning with the establishment of the text. And in my selection of materials which I believe to be related I have assumed the existence of a genre.

In constructing the book, I have placed the Old English texts within their narrower and wider contexts. Starting with the manuscript, and moving outwards to contiguous literatures in other languages, I have tried to trace the lineaments of a kind of discourse which participates in the universal nature of elegy and is at the same time peculiar, unique. My slight acquaintance with the literary theory of the past twenty years has made me aware of the relative and temporary nature of my own knowledge. There have been and will be many other ways than my own of looking at the poems, but I believe my endeavour is still worthwhile, and find the observations of a historian of literary criticism a useful comment on it:

If we can admit ... [that the historical consciousness is open to partial definition], we will implicitly grant two points: (1) a perfectly objective interpretation is possible only if the interpreter is a transcendental being – that is, if he is not human; and (2) the unavoidable given of all cognitive processes – that knowledge, however we may define it, is received through a situated human consciousness that has spatiotemporal location, idiosyncratic colorations, and philosophical and sociopolitical prejudices – this is in itself no excuse to give up the labours of research. ...
(Frank Lentricchia, *After the New Criticism* [1980], p. 207).

Reading the labours of previous workers in the field for the last hundred years and more, I see that fashions in scholarship come and go; that individual writers change their minds, and change them again. Often it has struck me that a critic's final thoughts were not wiser than his first, that a later trend in scholarship was not sounder than an earlier one. But we do profit from the work of our predecessors. Our knowledge of Old English, as a language and a literature, and the influences upon it, has improved through increasingly minute study of the surviving texts. At the present time, the materials which have been assembled for the *Old English Dictionary* project in Toronto and the appearance in recent years of the first really comprehensive study of Old English syntax make a textual study particularly appropriate.

Some reservations have been expressed lately about the very task of editing: should we abandon it altogether? Lee Patterson considers this problem in his essay on the Kane-Donaldson edition of the B-Text *Piers Plowman* (1975; see Patterson 1987, 77–113), and describes the editor's task in this way:

> this examination [of the manuscript evidence] is characteristically governed by two potentially contradictory criteria. One is *difficilior lectio potior*, a principle that assumes that the poetic language of the author is qualitatively different from the prosaic language of the scribes. The other is appropriateness of meaning, which assumes that the poem embodies a "whole structure of meaning" ([Kane-Donaldson] p. 131) that can be made explicit by interpretation. These two criteria correspond in more than a rough way to the two principles by which New Criticism sought to validate the poem as a cultural authority: its radical difference from other discursive forms, and yet its availability to interpretation. In other words, the task of the editor confronted with the mass of lectional evidence is to "read" the evidence as a New Critic would read a poem and to produce as a result of his labors an interpretation that is, in fact, the poem itself. (p. 110)

As Patterson observes, the editor's function assumes that there is an original which can be recovered, an assumption that would be rejected by contemporary poststructuralist thought. It follows from this position that editorial techniques must not be modified but abandoned entirely (p. 111). Patterson asks, "are we prepared to abandon ... [Kane and Donaldson's] commitment to historical understanding per se and accept *Piers Plowman* – and medieval literature in general – as by definition incapable of yielding to editorial ministrations?" (p. 112). The question is rhetorical. As long as there are readers of medieval texts there must be editors too. The present is a time of doubt and self-examination, but, paradoxically, it is also a time when Old English scholars have more aids at their disposal than ever before.

The microfiche *Concordance* and *High-Frequency Concordance* have provided me with a powerful tool not available to earlier editors, since these compilations make possible an examination of words in all their recorded contexts. Some unexpected spellings of particular words must have escaped me in my concordance citations, I hope few. Occasionally, my own investigation of the *Concordance* has led me to differ from the most up-to-date authorities, notably the *Old English Dictionary*, appearing letter by letter as this book is being written, and Bruce Mitchell's massively detailed *Syntax*. The semantics of *cwidegiedd*, "utterance in words," *Wanderer* 55; the force of the verb *magan* in *Deor* 7, etc.; the syntax of *hryre, Wanderer* 7, are a few cases in point. Occasionally, too, on the basis of the possibilities indicated by the *Concordance*, I have suggested a new emendation instead of the received one – *gehwyrft*, "cycle," *Riming Poem* 70, instead of *gewyrht*, "deed" (for MS *gehwyrt*); or rejected one hapax to posit another – *hrostbeam*, "roof support," "vaulting pillar," *Ruin* 31, instead of MS *hrostbeag*, understood as "circular roof-framework."

In large, my versions of most of the poems are those which would be found in other modern editions. However, *Resignation* is here treated as a single, complete poem, rather than two fragments, for reasons explained in Part 1. *The Husband's Message* is regarded as separate from *Riddle 60*, but the latter poem is included so that readers may draw their own conclusions. My treatment of some of the textual cruces has significantly affected my interpretation. Thus, reading (*her*) *heard*, "in his cruelty," in *Wife's Lament* 15 implies an adverse criticism of the husband; understanding *cnyssað* ... (*heortan*) *geþohtas þæt ic hean streamas* ... *sylf cunnige, Seafarer* 33–35, as "my thoughts are agitated because I have personal experience of the sea" makes these lines a reference to the anxiety which mingles with the speaker's eagerness. In cases like these I have excluded other possibilities as less compatible with Old English vocabulary and idiom. In certain instances, though, I have allowed for more than one possible interpretation. And in all these controversies I have tried to present the range of evidence from which different inferences have been drawn.

In detail, my texts of the poems are conservative. As a rule, I have not emended where sense could be made out of the manuscript as it stands, nor where minor variations in spelling appear, for example the occurrence of *e* for *a* or *a* for *e* in inflected endings. In *The Riming Poem*, however, I have been guided by the rhyme-scheme and by the poet's liberties in word-construction and usage – by my understanding of the poem's "whole structure of meaning" – to more extensive emendations, a greater number of nonce-words, and extensions of regular word-uses. Only rarely have I emended to improve the poems' metre, regarding occasional irregularities such as breaches of Kuhn's Law of Sentence Particles (Kuhn 1933, 4–5, 8, and 50) or the occurrence of light verses as metrically possible. Frequently I have found more than one meaning present in a word, and more than one grammatical relationship between the elements of a sentence, which, as Mitchell demonstrates (1980, and *Syntax*, §§ 3789–3803), often relate *apo koinou*, "in common," to different governing or dependent ideas.

Certain aspects of the poems have been dealt with quite briefly, for example the archaeological evidence for the location of the site described in *The Ruin*, a subject which is discussed more fully by Leslie (*Three OE Elegies*, 1961); and the legends lying behind *Deor*, which have been treated extensively in the hypotheses explored by Malone's editions and articles. The thorny problem of dating and dialectal provenance has been given a thorough re-examination. With one or two poems I have felt able to be fairly specific, determining *The Riming Poem* to be tenth-century Northumbrian, on the basis of vocabulary, spelling, and use of rhyme; *Deor* West Saxon and from the Alfredian circle, on the basis of one or two close resemblances to the language of Alfredian works and to the Alfredian Boethius especially. For other poems I have made suggestions, more or less tentatively. In the Glossary I have cited all occurrences of words, listing very frequent word-forms at the end. The statistics which emerge should provide useful evidence of word- and spelling-usage in the various poems.

Inevitably, there is a circularity in the structure of the book, since I begin by grouping the poems as elegies, and then proceed to analyse what makes them, as a group, elegiac. The use of the term "elegy" seemed to me something that had to be addressed immediately, and so I have introduced this issue at the beginning of Part 1, which focuses on the manuscript, rather than leaving it until Part 3, which discusses the genre. One or two other matters have had to be treated in more than one place. The linguistic and orthographical features which may illuminate a poem's provenance are mentioned individually in the Textual Notes, but treated collectively in the section on Date and Dialect in Part 1. The question of the poems' relationship to their sources is treated in broad terms in Part 3, and with reference to specific details in the analysis of individual poems in Parts 1 and 2. Thus, the role of Boethius's *Consolation of Philosophy* arises in connection with *Deor* and *The Wanderer* especially, but also bears upon the elegies collectively, and forms the subject of a section in Part 3.

When offering interpretations of the poems, I have not consciously followed any particular "school," though I have been influenced by my view of them as generically related, and have brought them to bear on one another. The discussion of each poem in Part 1 aims to summarize its structure and distinctive features, and to raise the main critical problems associated with it. I have not hesitated to make value judgements, or to assert that some of the poems are more poetically satisfying than others, and that the reader will probably derive more pleasure from *The Wanderer* or *The Wife's Lament* than from *Resignation*. Nevertheless, as an Anglo-Saxon poem about alienation, *Resignation* can tell us something about *The Wife's Lament*, and as a poem about exile and the search for grace it can shed light on *The Wanderer*, just as those poems, in turn, can illuminate *Resignation*.

In my analysis of the Old English genre, I have found relevant the Graeco-Roman concept of elegy as a semi-lyrical form which came to be associated with melancholy and with lovers' complaints. Undoubtedly, the Old English form had other roots – it has no obvious single source, but I think it probable that Anglo-Saxon poets perceived the parallel between their own melancholy poetry of a personal kind and the Latin genre that Horace (Fairclough 1929, 456–57), echoed by Bede (Kendall 1975, 110), described as suitable for mournful subjects. Ovid's *Letter of Canace to Macareus* offers some interesting parallels with *Wulf and Eadwacer*, and his *Tristia* and *Ex Ponto* collections more scattered resemblances to the Old English poems. These parallels are illustrated in the Appendix, and commented on in Part 3.

Some of the material in this book has already appeared in articles exploring the formal properties of Old English elegy and the poetic function of individual works. The section of "Elegy" as a Classification in Part 1 derives from an earlier discussion of the genre, Klinck 1984. Much of the textual analysis of *The Riming Poem* appears in Klinck 1985–86 and 1988. Some of the commentary on *The Ruin* appears in Klinck 1986. A few of the cruces in *Wulf and Eadwacer* are examined in Klinck 1987a. Some literary arguments for the integrity of *Resignation*, discussed in a more palaeographical framework in Part 1, are presented in Klinck 1987b. More incidental echoes occur here and there throughout the book. Occasionally I have modified my earlier views or substantiated them with further evidence. In general, I have sought in the present book less to explore the literary potential of individual poems than to examine them as discrete manifestations of a common generic impulse, and to move from a close study of the nine texts to a definition of Old English elegy.

PART I

The Poems and the Manuscript

The term "elegy" which I shall be using in this book is inevitably somewhat arbitrary, because the poems considered here are not elegies in the classical sense of compositions in elegiac metre, ἐλεγεῖα, nor in the tradition of the English pastoral elegies modelled on the eclogue and the idyll, such as Milton's *Lycidas*, Shelley's *Adonais*, and Arnold's *Thyrsis*.[1] The Old English poems do have a kinship with later English elegies of a broader kind, for example with Gray's *Elegy*, which treats themes of death and transience in a general way, and even with Tennyson's *In Memoriam*, which, though far longer than the Old English poems, resembles them in consisting of rather various reflections prompted by the need to come to terms with a sense of loss. Since the early nineteenth century, scholars have been applying the words "elegy" and "elegiac" to Old English poetry,[2] and we continue to find them useful, although the genre is a slippery one, and hard to pin down. Perhaps the most widely accepted definition of Old English elegy is that formulated by Stanley B. Greenfield: "a relatively short reflective or dramatic poem embodying a contrasting pattern of loss and consolation, ostensibly based upon a specific personal experience or observation, and expressing an attitude towards that experience" (Greenfield 1966, 143). The characteristic scenery of elegy includes "the sea with cliffs, hail, snow, rain, and storms, plus the meadhall of heroic poetry with its lords, warriors, hawks, horses, and precious cups."[3] Although not intended as a delimitation of a genre, Greenfield's classification of the formulas of exile identifies some of the typical language of elegy (1955, 200–6).

Certainly, a close examination of the individual poems has made me aware how discrete each one in fact is. But, given some reservations, the concept of "elegy" in an Anglo-Saxon context provides us with a convenient locus for particular themes: exile, loss of loved ones, scenes of desolation, the transience of worldly joys. The elegiac themes are presented in a lyrical-reflective mode with characteristic features such as monologue, personal introduction, gnomic or homiletic conclusion, and the ordered repetition of words and sounds, amounting occasionally to refrain or rhyme. These structural features, like the scenic elements, are not peculiar to elegy, and no elegy contains all of them, but the conjunction of several of them in the same poem is distinctive.

The poems included here as elegies are nine: *The Wanderer, The Seafarer, The Riming Poem, Deor, Wulf and Eadwacer, The Wife's Lament, Resignation, The Husband's Message* (to which the immediately preceding *Riddle 60* is sometimes attached), and *The Ruin*, in the order of their occurrence, interspersed with other material, in the Exeter Book.[4] The basic notion of a lament, ἔλεγος,[5] is more or less applicable to all of them, with the significant exception of *The Husband's Message*, where unhappiness is a thing of the past. Some passages from longer works are also frequently referred to as elegies, especially the speech of the Last Survivor and of the Bereaved Father in *Beowulf* (lines 2247–66 and 2444–62a, resp.), and the lament of Guthlac's disciple (*Guthlac* 1348–79); passages of this kind are not included in the present book since they are coloured by and need to be related to their respective narrative contexts.

Although the Exeter Book elegies have commonly been grouped together, there are distinct subcategories among them. *The Wanderer* and *The Seafarer*, like the lesser-known *Riming Poem* and *Resignation*, have close affinities with homiletic literature. In recent years, *Resignation* has been regarded as fragments of two separate poems, a penitential prayer and an elegiac lament.[6] *Deor*, which has strong links with heroic legend, has been categorized with *Widsith* as a *scop* poem.[7] *Wulf and Eadwacer*, *The Wife's Lament*, and *The Husband's Message* are love lyrics.[8] Finally, *The Ruin*, a purely descriptive piece, lacks the monologue form which characterizes the other poems. Those who posit an elegiac genre in Old English disagree about which poems should be assigned to it; thus, *Resignation A* might be excluded as belonging to another genre, *The Husband's Message* as too optimistic, *The Ruin* as too impersonal, and so on. Many would agree with B.J. Timmer (1942), who argues that there is no extant elegiac genre as such, though the elegiac mood is widespread.[9] Amid all this uncertainty, one objective fact remains: the existence of the poems in the same manuscript, the Exeter Book. So a consideration of that work, as an artifact and as an anthology, provides a firm basis for an examination of the poems, their possible relations to each other, and the nature of their genre, which will be discussed more fully later on.

CONDITION OF THE MANUSCRIPT

As we now have it, the Exeter Book is bound with some other materials (the unnumbered, blank first folio plus fols. 1–7), and begins, in an interrupted state, at fol. 8, with *Christ I*. It continues through fol. 130, ending with *Riddle 95*. The folios measure approximately 13.5 × 22 cms. The manuscript is described in detail by Max Förster, in the introductory chapters to the 1933 facsimile edition, and by E.V.K. Dobbie in the *ASPR* collection,[10] so the foliation and other features (such as rulings, dry-point drawings, accent marks, pointing, capitalization) will not be discussed here except as they pertain to the interpretation of the elegies. Towards the end of the book, the folios are increasingly affected by burn damage, apparently caused by a brand falling on the back of the closed book and eating its way in. The burn damage begins on fol. 117a, and starts to obscure the text at fol. 118b, in *Resignation*. Among the elegies, *The Husband's Message* and *The Ruin* are seriously affected. A transcript of the Exeter Book, almost photographic in its accuracy, was made by Robert Chambers in 1831, and is preserved as British Library Additional MS 9067. Because the edges of the burn-holes have crumbled further, or have been obscured by the repairs of 1933, the readings of the 1831 transcript are occasionally valuable. From the way in which Chambers reproduced damaged letters, it is clear that he did not read Old English, but sought to copy exactly what he saw, without interpretation.

DATE AND DIALECT OF THE ELEGIES

The Exeter Book is usually identified with that *micel englisc boc be gehwilcum þingum on leoðwisan geworht* mentioned in the list of donations to the cathedral given by Leofric, Bishop of Exeter from 1050 to 1072. A copy of this list is bound in with the Exeter Book, and the relevant words appear at the bottom of fol. 1b. The manuscript, then, can be no later than 1072; it is generally thought to be about a hundred years earlier. On the basis of the handwriting, Robin Flower concludes that the volume was written "in the West Country early in the period 970–990" (*Exeter Book* facs, p. 90). Assigning a specific date and dialectal provenance to the individual poems is a highly speculative undertaking. Many modern scholars would subscribe to Kenneth Sisam's view that "poems could be produced ... [in] a general Old English poetic dialect, artificial, archaic, and perhaps mixed in its vocabulary" (*SHOEL*, p. 138). Again, considerable doubt has been cast recently on the traditional linguistic tests of date; they provide relative, rather than absolute, evidence, and some of them are more useful than others. In general, metrical data, which are less likely to be subject to scribal changes, are more reliable than syntactic or morphological data unconfirmed by metre. In her evaluation of these tests, Ashley Amos finds that the most reliable is the alliteration of palatal and velar *g*. She is doubtful about those syntactic tests which are easily affected by scribal habits – for example the Lichtenheld test of weak adj. + noun with no preceding def. article, a usage characteristic of *Beowulf*, but also found in the late *Battle of Maldon* (991 or after; lines 47 and 166 are the two unassailable examples).[11] Bruce Mitchell is equally sceptical about the Lichtenheld test (*Syntax*, § 114), although he confirms Campbell's assertion that "the later the verse the less it diverges from the syntax of prose in this matter" (*Grammar*, § 638). However, the traditional tests are supported by John Pope (1981), who observes that "poems known to be late may show a few early features in one category, but lack them in others" (p. 189). R.D. Fulk takes issue with Amos in two articles (1989 and 1990), which vindicate the parasitic-vowel test, regarding the pre-parasiting, monosyllabic scansion of words like *hleaht(o)r*, and the contraction test, regarding the uncontracted, dissyllabic scansion of words like *nean*, as evidence of relatively early composition. It would be unwise to attempt to date or locate any of the elegies on the basis of isolated features, but where the indications are more numerous and relatively consistent it seems legitimate to draw inferences from them.

The poems share the general linguistic characteristics of the manuscript, in which lW-S forms predominate, but which includes some eW-S and Anglian features. Typical Anglianisms which are regular in the manuscript are $\breve{o}$ + nasal in stressed syllables, instead of lW-S $\breve{a}$, and *cwom* for lW-S *com*. The *on* and *om* spellings are too frequent to need illustration. The *cwom* forms occur in *Wan* 92–93 and *Ruin* 25. Although the manuscript mainly has lW-S broken *ea* and *y* as its *i*-mutation, *æld-*, "men," is regularly spelled with *æ*, the *i*-mutation of Anglian retracted *a*; see *Wan* 85, *Sea* 77, *Husb* 3. The form *waldend* for W-S *wealdend* is standard in much Old English poetry, including the Exeter Book, and also common in eW-S prose; it appears in *Wan* 78, *Res* 44, *Husb* 32, *Ruin* 7. Another "Anglianism," which should be regarded as a poeticism rather than a dialectal indicator, is the use of the uncontracted forms of the 2nd and 3rd pers. sg. pres. indic. of verbs; in the Exeter Book these forms are regular. LW-S *y* and *i* far exceed eW-S *ie* in the Exeter Book, but the latter is customarily used in the manuscript when preceded by *g*. EW-S forms appear sporadically as in *stieran* (*Sea* 109), *iege* (*Wulf* 4; cf. *ige*, line 6), *fierst* (*Res* 22; cf. *fyrste*, line 48), pl. *hio* (*Res* 38; cf. *hi*, line 54; *hy*, lines 55 and 57), *sie* (*Res* 67; cf. *sy*, line 11), *sio* (*Rid* 60, 6; cf. *seo*, line 12). Late *ferð* for *ferhð* is regular: e.g. *Wan* 13, 33, 71, 90; *Sea* 26, 37; *Res* 72, 76, 84. A peculiarity of the Exeter Book is the weakened form *sepeah* for *swapeah*, which occurs thirteen times (as in *Res* 29, 49, 52) and is recorded in no other manuscript. The latter, more usual form, occurs seven times in the Exeter Book. See Textual Notes on *Res* 29b. The weak gen. pl. *sorgna* (*Guthlac* 1019; *Precepts* 76 *tornsorgna*; *Wife* 45 *sinsorgna*) is also unique to the Exeter Book.

As a criterion of date, the alliteration of palatal and velar *g*, common in most Old English verse, but absent in *The Battle of Brunanburh* (937 or after) and other late poems, can be cited in *Wan* 22, 35, 52; *Sea* 83 and 92; *Rim* 36; *Deor* 15; *Res* 40, 60, 86; and probably also in *Wan* 73; *Sea* 40, 62, 101; *Res* 46, 74, 78, 92 (incomplete line); *Husb* 23.

Anglian vocabulary occurs here and there in the poems. Among the characteristically Anglian words identified by Richard Jordan in his 1906 monograph, the following appear in the elegies: *alan*, "to bring forth" (*Rim* 23), *grorn*, "grief" (*Rim* 49; cf. W-S *gnornað*, *Sea* 92; *Res* 92), *(ge)leoran*, "to pass away" (*Res* 31 and 45; *Ruin* 7), *nempe/nefne/nemne*, "except" (*Wan* 113; *Sea* 46 and *Rim* 78; *Wife* 22, resp.; cf. W-S *butan*, *Sea* 18). *Næron* (*Sea* 82) is probably equivalent to *ne earon*, "are not," an Anglian verb (Campbell *Grammar*, § 768d). *Oferhydig* (*Res* 56) is regarded by Hans Schabram in his examination of the "pride" words as Anglian (1965, 123–31). In a very detailed study, Franz Wenisch includes the following as Anglian: *acweðan*, "to utter" (*Wan* 91), *blinnan*, "to cease" (*Rim* 53), *gefeon*, "to rejoice in" (*Rim* 6 and 87; *Res* 54), *feter*, "bond" (*Wan* 21), *gefrignan*, "to find out" (*Deor* 14), *forhwan*, "why," conj. (*Wan* 59), *fullestan*, "to support" (*Res* 93; cf. W-S *gefylste*, line 102), *meord* "reward" (*Res* 68), *morþ* = *meorþ*, "reward" (*Rim* 82), *morðor*, "violent death," "crime" (*Wife* 20), *nænig*, "no one" (*Sea* 25), *ofgifan*, "to give up" (*Wan* 61), *rycene*, "quickly" (*Wan* 112), *sceþþan*, "to injure" (*Res* 16), *soðfæst*, "faithful" (*Res* 14 and 24), *symbel*, "feast" (*Wan* 93; *Rim* 5), *tan*, "twig," "lot" (*Rim* 78), *to hwon*, "(to) what," conj. (*Sea* 43), *þreat*, "troop" (*Wulf* 2/7), *winnan*, "to struggle" (*Rim* 51).[12] The heaviest concentration of Anglian words is to be found in *The Wanderer*, *The Riming Poem*, and *Resignation* (mainly *Resignation A*), which are accordingly designated Anglian poems by Wenisch (p. 328). No specifically Anglian words appear in *The Husband's Message* (or *Riddle 60*), and only one each in *Deor* and *Wulf and Eadwacer*. This distribution is interesting, but should not, I think, be taken as decisive without further evidence. As Wenisch admits, Anglian vocabulary is not rare even in lW-S poems.

The features described in the two previous paragraphs would be consonant with a copying of all the Exeter Book poems in West-Saxon territory in the first half of the tenth century, that is, a generation or so before the copying of the Exeter Book itself. For reasons to be explained later, I believe the poems were not all in the same manuscript at that time. Their earlier provenance would have varied as to place and date. Among the elegies, distinctive dialectal features over and above the usual ones in the manuscript are detectable principally in *The Riming Poem*. On the basis of linguistic criteria alone, none of the elegies can be assigned a decidedly early date.

In addition to the more widespread Anglianisms in the Exeter Book, *The Ruin* has some unusual forms: *ældo*, "age" (line 6), for W-S *yldo* (as in *Sea* 70 and 91); *cnea*, "generations" (line 8), for W-S *cneowa*; *þæs*, "this" (lines 9 and 30) for W-S *þes* (*þes* in *Ruin* 1 has probably been altered from *þæs*); *felon*, "reached," "adhered" (line 13), for W-S *fulgon*; *burgræced*, "halls of the city" (line 21), for W-S *-reced*; *hwætred*, "keen-minded" (line 19), for

W-S *hwætræd*; and the curious back mutations *undereotone*, "eaten away" (line 6) and *forweorone*, "perished" (line 7), also containing unstressed *o* for more usual *e*. These forms are probably Anglian, but it is hard to be more specific. The rare back mutations resemble the spellings of the *Vespasian Psalter Gloss* (Campbell *Grammar*, § 210.2, but there is no exact parallel. The form *cnea* is paralleled by two occurrences of gen. pl. *trea*, "trees" – in the Mercian *Vespasian Psalter* and the Mercian-influenced Old English Bede. *Felon* has a parallel *ætfelun* in the former text. *Þæs* for *þes* occasionally appears in Northumbrian glosses. (See Textual Notes on these three words.)[13] Some of the more characteristic Anglianisms are not noticeable, for example smoothing and lack of palatally diphthongized forms (Campbell *Grammar*, §§ 222–33 and 185–89, resp.). The resemblances so far noted are to texts of the late ninth century or after. There are one or two linguistic pointers to an early, pre-ninth-century, date, but they are inconclusive. The poem contains no examples of the (late) construction def. article + weak adj. + noun. The three occurrences of weak adj. + noun (*bradan rices*, line 37; *widan wylme*, line 39; *beorhtan bosme*, line 40)[14] may be significant in a poem of only 49 lines, but this is a doubtful criterion, and the latter two occurrences could be equivalent to *-um* forms. If the poem describes the ruins of Roman Bath, which it is widely held to do, it must have been composed long before the hot baths were completely hidden by silting, as they were by the mid-tenth century.[15]

A specific dialectal provenance can be assigned more confidently to *The Riming Poem*. Equation of *ēa* and *ēo*, and of *-að*, *-eð*, *-ið* in verb endings, are characteristically Northumbrian features (Campbell *Grammar*, §§ 278 and 735b, resp.). *Freaum* (line 32) occurs for *freoum* (this might also be a Mercian form; see Sievers-Brunner, § 297, Anm. 2). The poem rhymes *steald* (for W-S *steold*) and *weold* (line 22), *geseon* and *gefean* (for W-S *gefeon*; line 87); also *-að* and *-ið* (for W-S *-eð* in both; line 53); *-að* and *-eð* (lines 64–65); *-eð* and *-ið* rhymes are linked (lines 51–54). More generally Anglian forms are *onspreht*, for W-S *-eaht*; line 9), *bescær* (for W-S *bescear*; line 26); *bald ald* (with *a* for W-S *ea*; line 63). Some of the poem's off-rhymes can be made more complete by substituting Anglian forms:

bleo(w)um/heowum or *blio(w)um/hiowum*	(MS *bleoum/hiwum*; line 4)
gefegon/wegon	(MS *wægum*, for *wægon*?; line 6)
aweht/onspreht	(MS *aweaht*; line 9)
ger/sner	(MS *gear*; line 25)
grafeþ/hafað	(MS *græfeþ*; line 66)
gewæf/forgæf	(MS *forgeaf*; line 70)
biscerede/generede	(MS *biscyrede*; line 84)

This kind of substitution does not always complete the rhyme: *geteh/onwrah* (MS *geteoh*, = *geteah*; line 2. For Anglian *tēh* see Sievers-Brunner, § 384, Anm. 6). But, still, the poem's rhymes point pretty clearly to an Anglian, most likely Northumbrian, origin. The occurrence of the rare word *alan* (*ol*, line 23), elsewhere recorded only in the *Lindisfarne* and *Rushworth*[2] *Gospel* glosses, is also probably a Northumbrian feature. Other nW-S forms are *neda*, "of necessity," pl. (line 78), with *ē* as the *i*-mutation of *ēa*, for lW-S *ȳ*; also *gerscype*, "noisy conversation" (line 11), *gefæst*, "firm in gifts," and *gellende*, "shrilling" (line 25), with *ge-* for the usual *gie-* of the Exeter Book. The apparently Kentish *wennan/wenne*, "joyfully," for W-S *wynnum/wynne* (lines 7 and 76, resp.) may reflect a scribal idiosyncracy.[16] Possibly some of the poem's rare words have been influenced by Norse: *onspreht* (line 9; ON *sprækr*, "active"), *gerscype* (line 11; ON *gár*, "buffoonery"), *scrifen* (line 13; ON *skrifa*, "to paint"), *scrad* (line 13; ON *skreið*, "shoal or flock"), *leoþu* (line 14; ON *lið*, "ship"), *ol* (line 23; ON *ala*, "to bear," "to feed"), *wilbec* (line 26; ON *víl*, "misery" and *bekkr*, "brook"), *frodade* (line 32; ON *frœða*, "to teach"). All these except *wilbec* have native cognates (see Textual Notes). There are no indications that *The Riming Poem* is particularly early;[17] its language shows some resemblances to the tenth-century Northumbrian glosses. Elsewhere, consistent rhyme is found only in very late Old English verse, especially the Chronicle poems on the death of Alfred Atheling (1036) and of the Conqueror (1086), though it appears much earlier in Anglo-Latin verse, and occasional rhyme is common in Old English poetry. It has been suggested that the form of the poem either influenced or was influenced by Egill Skallagrímsson's *Hǫfuðlausn*, presented at York ca. 948 (see p. 43, below). Such a relationship, though not proven, would be consistent with composition in the north of England prior to or very shortly after that date.

There are several indications that *Resignation* is also comparatively late. One of these is the metrical treatment of the word *frea*, "lord,"[18] which occurs five times in the elegies, once each in *The Wife's Lament* and *The Husband's Message*, three times in *Resignation*. In the first two cases, the word must be given its older, dissyllabic pronunciation in order to provide the verses with the minimum four syllables: *fromsiþ frean* (*Wife* 33), *mines frean* (*Husb* 10). *Resignation* 48a, *æt frean frofre*, is a C-type verse with monosyllabic *frean*. Line 22a, *Forgif þu me, min frea*, could be either A with anacrusis or B, and line 76b, *Huru me frea witeð*, could be either B with resolved second stress or C, dissyllabic or monosyllabic *frea*, respectively, in both lines. Though not particularly significant in isolation, in conjunction with other features the *frea* scansion is suggestive. *Resignation* shows the kind of metrical looseness which becomes increasingly common in late poems.[19] This is especially noticeable in the b-verses. Lines 29b (*þæt ic þine, seþeah*), 34b (*þeah þe lætlicor*), 97b (*ond ymb siþ spræce*) have double alliteration. Line 102b (*þe me gefylste*) has only one stress. In some of the b-verses, as many as five or six syllables precede the first stress: line 48b (*þeah þe ic ær on fyrste lyt*), 52b (*ne læt þu mec næfre deofol, seþeah*), 74b (*ond me þæt eal for gode þolian*). Although the "early" weak adj. + noun construction appears in the genitives *ecan dreames* (line 33) and *halgan heofonmægnes* (line 36), the later usage with def. article occurs in *se ælmiht[g]a god* (line 1) and *þa manigfealdan mine geþohtas* (line 9). In addition to several items of Anglian vocabulary, there are a couple of *n*-less spellings which may be late Northumbrian: *cume* (for *cuman* – unless this is subjunctive; line 21), *stonde* (for *stonden*; line 39); see Campbell *Grammar*, §§ 735 f and i. Again, *þæs* for *þes* (line 89) appears in late Northumbrian texts (Sievers-Brunner § 338, Anm. 4). Most of these Anglianisms occur in the section designated *Resignation A* (to line 69) by Alan Bliss and Allen Frantzen (1976). But three relatively infrequent eW-S spellings (*fierst, hio, sie*; lines 22, 38, and 67, resp.) also appear in this section. Again, the few Anglianisms in the *B* section could be added to, for example by substituting Anglian *gefulleste* for *gefylste* (line 102), which would correct the metre (see Textual Notes). *Resignation* was probably composed no earlier than ca. 900.[20] In the use of language, some divergence is detectable between the penitential prayer and the lament sections. The metrical features commented on are observable in both parts.

In *Deor*, the expected mixture of forms can be found. NW-S spellings occur: e.g. *nede*, "need" (line 5); *seonobende*, "sinew-bonds" (line 6), for *sinobende – seono-* forms are common in poetry. *Wurman*, "serpents" (line 1), for *wyrmum*, shows lW-S rounding of *y* to *u* (Campbell *Grammar*, § 322) and weakening of *-um* to *-an*. The curious *Welund*, presumably from *Welond*, may be related to Mercian *-un* spellings in the pret. pl. of verbs (Campbell *Grammar*, § 735e). Out of the ten other recorded Old English occurrences of this word, eight take the form *Weland*, two *Welond*, both in the Alfredian Boethius. The use of *ofergan* in the figurative sense of "pass away" (in the refrain: lines 7, 13, 17, 20, 27, 42) is Alfredian. Five of the eight other recorded occurrences appear in Alfredian texts, and, out of the remaining three, two are extremely late and one in a glossary. The impersonal *ofercuman* + gen. (line 26) is stylistically similar, and "to overcome" is also one of the meanings of *ofergan*. Neither of these verbs is used in this way anywhere else in Old English verse (see Textual Notes on both words). *Deor*'s resemblance to the Alfredian works in the distinctive use of *ofergan* and *ofercuman*, and in *Welund* for *Welond*, is borne out by the often-noted similarity in theme between this poem and the *Consolation of Philosophy* (see p. 45, below). Thus, resemblances in vocabulary, combined with larger thematic parallels, make it probable that *Deor* originated in the late ninth century or shortly afterwards, in the Alfredian circle.[21] The poem is not metrically irregular, but its unique refrain is the kind of development which is more likely in later verse.

The Wanderer has one or two unusual spellings: gen. sg. *-as* in *giefstolas* (line 44) looks like a late form (Sievers-Brunner § 237, Anm. 1); and *wearþan*, for *weorþan*, (line 64) a Northumbrianism (Campbell *Grammar*, § 278). There are also a few words which probably show Norse influence: *hrimceald* (line 4), corresponding to *hrímkaldr; ferð* in the sense of "crowd" (line 54; see Textual Notes); *hrið*, "snowstorm" (line 102) – all hapax legomena, though the elements of *hrimceald* are familiar. *The Wanderer* contains some characteristically Anglian words, but it is noteworthy that two of these occur in specifically W-S forms unusual in the Exeter Book: *forhwan*, with ă + nasal (line 59), and contracted *acwið* (line 91). These features point to Anglian influence, if not composition in the poem's present form. Assuming a Norse element would preclude an early date and make the late ninth century probable.

Norse influence is also a possibility in *Wulf and Eadwacer*, whose metrical form, varying long lines with short (lines 3, 8, 17, 19) resembles the alternating long and short lines of Norse *ljóðaháttr*.[22] But Charm 9, *For Theft of Cattle* (lines 8–9 and 16–17) provides a native parallel. It has been suggested that *þreat* (line 2/7) may have the Norse sense of "struggle" (*þraut*) or "want" (*þrot*), though Old English "troop" gives quite satisfactory sense (see Textual Notes).

The Wife's Lament, Riddle 60, and *The Husband's Message* lack any very marked indications of a specific provenance. In *Wife* 28 and 36 dat. *actreo* is an Anglianism paralleled in the *Lindisfarne Gospels* (Sievers-Brunner § 129.1, Anm. 2). *Riddle 60* has typically – but not exclusively – eW-S *sio* (line 6), and lW-S *widdor* (= *widor*; line 17). The uncontracted scansion of *frea* in *The Wife's Lament* (line 33) and *The Husband's Message* (line 10) suggests that these are relatively early poems. The same is indicated by the absence of def. article + weak adj. + noun; this construction appears in *Riddle 60* (*seo swiþre hand*, line 12). Weak adj. + noun without article occurs in *fædan gold[es]* (*Husb* 36).

The contraction test applied to *frea* has also been applied to the oblique cases of *heah*.[23] In *The Seafarer*, *þæt ic hean streamas* (line 34b, a C-type verse) shows contracted (i.e. not extremely early) *hean*, along with "early" weak adj. + noun (for another interpretation of the word *hean*, see Textual Notes). *Geomran reorde* (line 53) also uses the weak adj. + noun construction – unless *-an* = *-um*. And the construction appears again in *ecan lifes* (line 79; see Textual Notes). The *u*-spelling in *huilpan*, "curlew('s)"

(*Sea* 21) looks like an early form (Campbell *Grammar*, § 60). Similarly, the *u*-ending in *seofedun* is either early or Mercian (Campbell *Grammar*, § 735e). *Tidege* (= *tiddæge*), "final day" (line 69), appears to have Kentish or Mercian *ĕ* for *ǽ* (Campbell *Grammar*, §§ 164, 168, 169). NW-S *ē* for *ǽ* occurs in *werum*, "pledges," line 110 (Campbell *Grammar*, § 128). See Textual Notes for alternative explanations of *tidege* and *werum*. *Næron* (line 82) is paralleled in Wærferth's translation of Gregory's *Dialogues*, a text showing Mercian influence (see Textual Notes), and may be related to *earun* in the Mercian *Vespasian Psalter* Gloss (Campbell *Grammar* § 768d) and *Life of St. Chad* (in Vleeskruyer 1953, 182).[24] *The Seafarer* contains four instances of Anglian *cald*, "cold" (lines 8, 10, 19, 33), in contrast to W-S *ceald* (line 14; also *Wan* 4, *Deor* 4). But *cald* spellings occur elsewhere in the Exeter Book (*Christ II* 851; *Christ III* 1629; *Phoenix* 17, 59, 67; *Soul II* 15; *Rid 40*, 54) and even in the late *Maldon* (line 91).[25] The cluster in *The Seafarer* may be attributable merely to the thematic importance of the word in that section of the poem. On the basis of the higher proportion of oral formulas, poetic words, and hapax legomena, it has been argued that the first half of *The Seafarer* (to line 64) is older than the second, but these statistics can be changed by a different definition of the terms.[26]

By and large, the alliteration of palatal and velar *g* and the admixture of eW-S forms make it highly unlikely that any of the poems were composed long after 950. Their previous history is much harder to determine. A Northumbrian provenance is suggested by the lexicon and the manuscript forms in *The Riming Poem*. In *The Ruin*, also, unusual forms point to a nW-S, perhaps Mercian, origin. Some distinctive vocabulary in *The Wanderer* makes it likely that there is a strong Anglian, perhaps Northumbrian, influence here too. Less decisively, a few possibly Mercian forms in *The Seafarer* may indicate an origin in that dialect area, and *Resignation* also shows indications of an Anglian element. In *Deor*, one or two peculiarities of usage indicate a West Saxon, specifically Alfredian, background. I would not venture to posit a definite locality for the remaining poems. As regards date, quite possibly some of the elegies, or parts of them, go back a couple of hundred years or more beyond 950, which provides an approximate *terminus ad quem*. Certain dating criteria, in themselves not very trustworthy, can be suggestive if they occur in combination, or are supported by external evidence. Thus, on the basis of such factors as metrical orthodoxy or freedom, metrically attested contractions, syntactic and morphological features (though these last are subject to scribal variation), *The Riming Poem* and *Resignation* can be considered early- to mid- tenth-century; *The Seafarer*, *The Wife's Lament*, and *The Husband's Message* (not necessarily including *Riddle 60*) mid-ninth-century or earlier; with *The Wanderer* and *Wulf and Eadwacer* in between. The Alfredian connection places *Deor* at the end of the ninth or the beginning of the tenth century.

ARRANGEMENT AND FORMAT

The characteristic spellings of the Exeter Book point to a time somewhat earlier than that of the manuscript itself, so the question arises to what extent they reflect the actual copying process. Although Flower supposed more than one scribe (*Exeter Book* facs, p. 83), most scholars agree that the manuscript was written by one hand only.[27] On some pages the lettering is larger and broader, on others smaller and more elongated, but these differences are not very great, and need reflect no more than copying at different times, over a period of months, or longer. Since the scribe sometimes visibly altered letters (e.g. *mæro* to *mære* in *Wan* 100, *þæs* to *þes* in *Ruin* 1), he must have made some morphological changes. I believe that these were relatively few, and that in general he was the "mechanical copyist" that Sisam holds him to be. Sisam bases this opinion on the extreme regularity of the hand combined with the frequent errors (*SHOEL*, pp. 97–98).

There are one or two other features which support this view. Occasionally, a cluster of errors of the same type appears in a particular poem. A conservative treatment of the text reveals that *The Wanderer* is characterized by *n*-errors: omission, faulty insertion, confusion between *n* and another letter. Seven of the eight emendations in the present text involve errors of this kind (lines 14, 22, 24, 28, 59, 89, 102 – in 115 lines).[28] By contrast, the poems which immediately follow *The Wanderer*, *The Gifts of Men* (113 lines) and *Precepts* (94 lines), have one emendation each of this type in the *ASPR* text (lines 66 and 53, resp.). The preceding poem, *Juliana*, has eleven (lines 16, 46, 128, 313, 486, 521, 555, 599, 628, 630, 723; in line 637 the scribe has corrected an *n*-error) in 731 lines. *N*-errors are relatively infrequent in the other elegies. In the texts included here, emendations involving *n*-errors are made as follows: one in *The Seafarer* (line 109 – out of seven emendations in 124 lines), five in *The Riming Poem* (lines 6, 18, 61, 74, 79 – out of 22 emendations in 87 lines; the level of emendation in this difficult poem is high), one in *The Wife's Lament* (line 37) – out of two emendations in 53 lines. But most editors suppose a second *n*-error at line 20; see Text and notes), one in *Riddle 60* (line 15 – out of two emendations in 17 lines), one in *The Husband's Message* (line 21 – out of three emendations in 54 lines). The remaining elegies contain no errors of this type. This peculiarity of *The Wanderer* seems likely to have been a feature of the scribe's exemplar. Another error-cluster, which does not appear in the elegies, is the triple misspelling *fer*(-) for *for*(-), in *Riddles 48, 49,* and *50* (lines 1, 11, and 4, resp.).[29]

Again, punctuation is used more frequently in some poems than in others. Excluding the heavier end punctuation, and points placed on either side of runes, *The Wanderer* has 42 points, *The Seafarer* 21, *The Riming Poem* 32, *Deor* 8 (plus 5 instances of heavier punctuation between stanzas), *Wulf and Eadwacer* 5, *The Wife's Lament* 9, *Resignation* 12, *Riddle 60,* 4, *The Husband's Message* 2 (plus two instances of heavier punctuation between sections), *The Ruin* 11. Except where they are designed to mark off some kind of rhetorical figure, the points coincide with long-line endings, and the more emphatic ones are followed by small capitals. The occurrences of these can be tabulated in the following way (in some cases it is not clear whether a letter is a capital or not):

The Wanderer	10	(lines 6, 8, 15, 39, 45, 66, 73, 88, 97, 111)
	+ 3?	(lines 17, 58, 94)
The Seafarer	1	(line 117)
	+ 1?	(line 47)
	+ A	of final *Amen*
The Riming Poem	2	(lines 33 and 43)
Deor	5	(larger) (lines 8, 14, 18, 21, 28)
Wulf and Eadwacer	0	
The Wife's Lament	2	(lines 9 and 18)
	+ 1?	(line 11)
Resignation	2	(lines 41 and 105)
	+ 2?	(lines 22 and 59)
Riddle 60	0	
The Husband's Message	2	(larger) (lines 13 and 26)
The Ruin	0	

It seems likely that this variation has been affected by the habits of earlier scribes.

Whereas all of the capitals listed above correspond to breaks in thought, only a few of them mark major divisions in the poems: those at *Wan* 58(?), 88, and 111; *Sea* 117; *Rim* 43; while larger capitals perform this function in *Deor* and *The Husband's Message*. One might have expected a point before and a small capital at line 42, at least, in *The Wife's Lament*, which in comparison with *The Wanderer* is very lightly punctuated. In the latter poem, the *sum* series (lines 80b–84) is not marked by rhetorical pointing, in contrast to the *hwær cwom, eala,* and *her bið ... læne* passages (line 92–

93, 94–95a, and 108–9, resp.), which are, although it displays the same kind of anaphora. Within the scribal conventions of the poem, this looks like an unintentional omission.

One or two variations in spelling conventions may also reflect the practice of earlier scribes. Thus, in *The Wanderer* the word *bið* is more commonly spelled with final *ð* (ten times; *biþ* twice), in *The Seafarer* with final *þ* (five times; *bið* once). The verb *willan* in the Exeter Book is regularly spelled with *i*, except at *Guthlac* 593 and in *Resignation*, where the form *wylle* occurs at lines 24 and 70 (see Glossary). These spelling details are slight, but suggestive: they separate *The Wanderer* and *The Seafarer*, while they unite the two halves of *Resignation* at the same time as marking it off from the poems around it.

Distribution of accent-marks (on emphatic syllables) varies in another way – between *The Riming Poem* with 24 in 87 lines and *The Wanderer* with one (*nán*, line 9) in 115 lines. But the scribe shows a preference for certain monosyllabic nouns and adverbs (see Krapp-Dobbie's table, *The Exeter Book*, pp. lxxxii–lxxxviii). In *The Riming Poem*, the accents have the special function of drawing attention to the rhymes and assonances. The triple accentuation of *sǽ*(-) in *The Seafarer* (lines 14, 18, 42) may have a thematic significance.

Variations in error-type, in spelling, and in punctuation reinforce the probability that on the whole the scribe copied without imposing theories or conventions of his own. This makes it likely that he was not actually the compiler. I would agree with Sisam's opinion that "it seems ... the collection was put together by tacking on new items as codices or single pieces came to hand" (p. 97). However, I think it probable that the scribe and the compiler (more than one person may have been involved in the collecting, but for convenience I shall speak in the singular) were contemporaries, the former working at the behest of the latter. This explanation would reconcile Sisam's theory that the Exeter Book was copied from a previous compilation with Dunning and Bliss's objection that "if the scribe had before him a complete exemplar, it would have been easy to arrange the contents into a more systematic order" (edition, p. 3). A revealing detail in *Deor* is the omission of a point before the first occurrence of the refrain, as if the copyist had not recognized it for what it was. Yet the juxtaposition of *Deor* with *Wulf and Eadwacer* seems attributable to the use of refrain in both (in *Wulf* the "refrain" is only a single repetition of two lines, 2–3/7–8), and must represent the choice of a compiler, either at the final stage or earlier. Again, the copyist's failure to point the anaphoras in *Wan* 80b–84, whereas he does so in *Wan* 92–93, 94–95a, and 108–9, suggests his failure to register the rhetorical device on its first appearance in the poem. The scribe, as opposed to the compiler, seems to be responding to material seen for the first time.

It will be useful to see what light can be shed on the elegies by a fuller consideration of the Exeter Book as an anthology. The first half contains a series of long poems on religious subjects. Then follow a variety of shorter works, both religious and secular. In an observation somewhat inconsistent with his stated view of the "generally haphazard" nature of the collection, Sisam subdivides the second part into a section of "shorter didactic poems" (fols. 76b–100a), and "still shorter secular poems" (fols. 100b–end), and argues that the pieces which appear between the riddles at fols. 115ff. form "a patch of collected material that was not digested into the original plan" (p. 291). Among the elegies, *The Wanderer*, *The Seafarer*, and *The Riming Poem* are found in Sisam's section of "shorter didactic poems," *Deor* and *Wulf and Eadwacer* in the section of "secular poems," and the rest in the "undigested" material.

To a limited extent, Sisam's observation is corroborated by the contents of the elegies. Others have perceived an affinity between *The Wanderer*, *The Seafarer*, and *The Riming Poem* as didactic works,[30] and between *Deor* and *Wulf and Eadwacer* as refrain poems, possibly referring to similar legendary material.[31] But there are problems with this account of the manuscript's structure. The catalogue poem *Widsith* falls in the middle of Sisam's "didactic" section; and, if we take out what he regards as undigested material, all of his short poems except *Deor* and *Wulf and Eadwacer* are riddles, and some of them (including *Deor*) have religious content. It is likely that the poems in the part of the manuscript including *The Wanderer*, *The Seafarer*, and *The Riming Poem* were collected at one period, and those in the section containing *The Wife's Lament, Resignation, The Husband's Message*, and *The Ruin* at another. And there may be significance in the proximity, though not juxtaposition, of *Wanderer* and *Seafarer*, *Wife* and *Husband*. But the manuscript arrangement does not encourage us to infer an especially close relationship between these two "pairs." If there was an overall plan for the Exeter Book, it must have been rather vague.

At least, it can be stated that the first half of the anthology (up to fol. 76a) is different in kind from the second. The poems in the former have a certain homogeneity, in that they all treat the lives of various exemplary figures. Similarly, the three bestiary poems (*The Panther, The Whale*, and *The Partridge*) and the two groups of riddles clearly bring together works of the same genre. The likelihood that the compiler obtained these collections ready-made is reinforced by the appearance of the same riddle (*30*) in two places. The remaining poems, including all of the elegies, are more difficult to categorize. In a general way, all of the shorter works in the Exeter Book can be classified as "wisdom literature,"[32] and doubtless the compiler would have regarded them all as edifying or instructive in the very broadest sense. Some of them might be further classified – for example as gnomic poem (*Maxims I*), catalogue poem (*Widsith*), prayer (*Lord's Prayer I*).

The scattering of the elegies among other poems shows that the compiler did not regard them as a distinct group. Also, Sisam is surely right in thinking that they were never grouped together, since there would have been no point in breaking them up again (*SHOEL*, pp. 291–92). This arrangement, or the lack of it, gives the modern scholar pause when defining and describing an elegiac genre. The elegies are placed beside homiletic poems and riddles, and, indeed, contain affinities with both these types of literature – with the former as meditation, and with the latter as evocation of personality, *ethopoeia*.[33] Thus, Dunning and Bliss trace some common preoccupations in *The Wanderer* and the two poems which follow it, *The Gifts of Men* and *Precepts* (edition, pp. 79 and 88–89); Karma Lochrie, in her article on *Resignation* (1986a), detects a common theme in *Judgement Day I*, *Resignation A*, and *B*. *Wulf and Eadwacer*, long regarded as "The First Riddle," is a mysterious, in some ways paradoxical, poem, truly riddle-like. Followed by the riddles, preceded by *Deor*, *Wulf and Eadwacer* has one kind of affinity with the former, another with the latter.

The arrangement of the poems can be revealing for other reasons. In fact, the compiler or one of his predecessors seems to have mistaken *Wulf and Eadwacer* for a riddle, a mistake indicated not just by its position, but by its similar initial capitalization and end punctuation – of the kind given to a series of short poems or to sections in the same (long) poem. The opening of *Wulf* introduces a mysterious *lac*, "gift," which is never really explained, and the close comments that "It is easy to separate what was never joined." These are riddling elements, making the error a natural one. The occurrence of the same error, apparently, in *The Husband's Message* and *The Ruin* is more startling. After the first group of riddles, the Exeter Book contains some rather heterogeneous poems: *The Wife's Lament, Judgement Day I, Resignation, The Descent into Hell, Alms-Giving, Pharaoh, Lord's Prayer I, Homiletic Fragment II, Riddle 30b, Riddle 60, The Husband's Message*, and *The Ruin* (Sisam's patch of undigested material, fols. 115a–24b). Since *The Husband's Message* is divided into three sections with large capitals and characteristic end punctuation – both of the kind used for the riddles and other short pieces – it looks as if someone mistook both this poem and *The Ruin* for riddles (three in the former case). Because of the manuscript presentation, the first editors failed to recognize *The*

Husband's Message as a complete poem, and there is still uncertainty as to whether *Riddle 60* is part of it. (See Textual Notes on *Ic wæs be Sonde* [*Rid 60*] and *Husb* 1.) The openings of both *The Husband's Message* (*Nu ic onsundran þe secgan wille/ ... treocyn*) and *The Ruin* (*Wrætlic is þes wealstan!*) could introduce the kind of marvel that would form the subject of a riddle, though this becomes less true with the second and third sections of *Husband* (beginning *Hwæt, þec þonne biddan het se þisne beam agrof* and *Ongin mere secan, mæwes eþel*, lines 13 and 26, resp.). Both of the poems contain runes: S, R, EA, W, and M confirm the message sent to the wife (*Husb* 50–51 [*ASPR* 49–50]), and the M-rune appears in *Ruin* 23. The enigmatic function of runes is exploited in *Riddles 19, 24, 64,* and *75. The Husband's Message* is not, as a whole, enigmatic, but its runic passage involves secrecy, and perhaps deliberate mystification. I find no particular reason for the inclusion of the M-rune in *The Ruin.* Since the subjects of *Riddle 30* and *60* are both objects made of wood, and *The Husband's Message* features a rune-stave, the compiler must have thought he was putting together a series of tree-riddles at this point. *The Ruin* he presumably thought a riddle because of its opening, its generally descriptive nature, and its rune.

In some ways the elegies, especially *Wulf and Eadwacer*, approach the riddle style, but no careful reader would actually mistake *The Ruin* or most of *The Husband's Message* for riddles.[34] One can only conclude that the compiler was not reading carefully here. The scribe would have been forced to deal with his material quite minutely, but not necessarily to examine it critically. Working long hours, in uncomfortable conditions, over a task he likely found less than fascinating, he might well have regarded his labour with a certain amount of philosophical detachment: his not to reason why. So the compiler's choices in arrangement and the scribe's in punctuation should not be taken as reliable guides to the finer points of the poems, although they are illuminating and reflect some important affinities and distinctions. Though connections can be made between *The Wanderer* and *The Gifts of Men*, it is hard to make them between *The Wife's Lament* and *Judgement Day I*, and even harder between *The Ruin* and the bawdy *Riddle 61*. Again, pointing and capitalization reflect transitions and rhetorical devices detected or copied by the scribe, but he misses significant ones. In *Deor*, where sectional divisions follow the refrain, manuscript pointing and capitalization correspond to the major divisions in the poem; so to a large extent in *The Wanderer*. But in *The Seafarer* and *The Wife's Lament* these scribal indications are less adequate. Manuscript arrangement and presentation of the elegies reflects a variety of stages and techniques, and some oversights, rather than a controlling principle, so as a guide it needs to be used with caution.

INTEGRITY AND INTERRELATIONSHIP OF THE POEMS

In a palaeographical study of the Exeter Book, and of *The Husband's Message* in particular, John Pope has come to the conclusion, first voiced by F.A. Blackburn at the turn of the century, that *Riddle 60, Ic wæs be Sonde*, is part of that poem.[35] As we have seen, the compiler apparently thought *The Husband's Message* was not a complete poem at all, but three riddles, a mistake that reading with any attention will clear up. The relationship between the love-poem and the riddle (if it is a riddle) is more complex. *Ic wæs be Sonde* ends, and the love-poem begins, with a reference to a private communication – a secret – and some object that was originally a plant or tree is the vehicle of communication in both. However, *Ic wæs be Sonde* bears some resemblance to the Latin "Harundo" (reed) riddle. Pope's case hinges on his reading of a word in one of the damaged passages (*Husb* 3), which he believes is *iw*, "yew-tree," not *in*, as it has generally been taken to be. Examination of the manuscript (rather than the facsimile) and the 1831 transcript show that this character cannot be proved to be ᛈ ; it may well be *n* – or another letter. So the palaeographical evidence does not confirm an identical speaker (a yew-wood rune-stave) for the two pieces of poetry. Because of the riddle-type opening in *Ic wæs be Sonde*, the likelihood of "reed(-pen)" as solution, and the inconsistency of these features with the genre and subject of *The Husband's Message*, I regard the two poems as separate, and would attribute their juxtaposition to the similarities noticed by a compiler. For a further analysis of the evidence, see Textual Notes.

If in some cases it is doubtful what constitutes a complete poem, and where that poem actually begins and ends, another problem that arises from a study of the manuscript is the question of whether parts of poems are misplaced or missing because of disarrangement or losses in the folios. Not infrequently, the continuity in thought from one folio to the next is unclear; but actual proof of dislocation is elusive. In the nineteenth century and the early years of the twentieth, Old English poems were commonly regarded as textually corrupt, and lost or misplaced leaves in the manuscript or a predecessor might be one of the explanations. Disarrangement is virtually impossible to prove, but one or two theories of this kind have been advanced. Sir William Craigie (1923–24) argued that the first parts of *The Wanderer* and *The Seafarer* (ending at lines 57 and 64a, resp.) were followed by portions of a poem on the transience of things, and that the second half of *The Seafarer* belonged after the latter part of *The Wanderer*, the mistake arising because "the compiler of the Exeter Book made up the text of each from a defective original with misplaced leaves" (p. 15). In putting forward this theory, Craigie differs from his predecessors who saw Christian interpolation in these poems, only in positing a very specific solution. Some thirty years ago, A.A. Prins (1964) made a similar argument, hypothesizing that there was dislocation between *Wanderer* 65a and b, at the turn from fol. 77a to b, because the scribe "got hold of the wrong page" in his exemplar (p. 241), that the latter parts of *The Wanderer* and *The Exile's Prayer* [*Resignation*] should be switched (*Res* 84ff. forming the conclusion of *Wan*, *Wan* 64bff. that of *Res*), and that the second half of *The Seafarer* was not properly part of the poem.

This kind of scissors-and-paste rearrangement of the poems opens up an endless field of possibilities, but offers no certain, or even very likely, answers. The issue of manuscript losses is more circumscribed. Aside from the preliminary materials bound in with it, the Exeter Book consists of seventeen gatherings, each of which contains a maximum of eight folios. Max Förster concludes from his examination of the manuscript and its discontinuities that Gatherings I, V, IX, XII, and XIV, all of which have lost folios, originally contained eight each, that Gatherings II, XV, and XVI had only seven folios each, and the final, badly damaged, Gathering XVII only five (*Exeter Book* facs, p. 56). The list of losses described by Förster in the 1930s has been added to in the last twenty years: Pope (1969 and 1974) has made a strong case for losses in Gatherings II and XVI, and Bliss and Frantzen (1976), building on Pope's work, have argued for the loss of a folio at the end of Gathering XV, in *Resignation* 69 (after *wære*, at the end of fol. 118). They believe that Gathering XV, like Gatherings II and XVI (if Pope is correct) originally consisted of three double sheets plus two singletons facing in opposite directions, a structure still visible in Gathering VI. However, while the discontinuity Pope detects in Gathering XVI, at *Riddle 70* 4, is marked by problems in sense, concord, and syntax, and in Gathering II, at *Christ II* 556, by faulty metre and a rather abrupt transition, the evidence in *Resignation* is less strong, depending on a violation of Kuhn's Law of Particles, and disparities in language and attitude between *Resignation A* and *B*. Bliss and Frantzen argue that the second half of the outer double sheet has been lost in Gathering XV, and that *Resignation A* and *B* are fragments of two unrelated poems.

Certainly, if all the Exeter Book gatherings originally contained eight folios, this would produce a satisfying uniformity. But it is hard to prove losses from the present appearance of the manuscript. As for the final gathering, its original structure is pretty well guesswork. And there are no obvious physical indications of the losses described by Pope, and by

Bliss and Frantzen – such as the imprint of a knife along the following folio or a sudden increase in the burn damage which affects the last part of the manuscript.[36] I think it possible that Gathering XV originally began with a singleton. Förster, noting that "at present [this singleton] has no fold left" (by which single sheets were secured), suggests as another possibility that the gathering may have begun with a double sheet folded by itself (p. 59).

Though the likelihood of an eight-folio gathering is not to be denied, I believe there are good reasons for adhering to the earlier opinion that *Resignation* is a single poem. I have argued elsewhere (Klinck 1987b) that it does display thematic unity: in its sense of suffering and isolation, its motif of the journey, its desire for the heavenly *bot*. While it is true that there is a concentration of Anglianisms in the first section and the temper of the two parts is different, both of these observations could also be made about *The Seafarer*. Again, the possible Norse loans are concentrated in the first half of *The Riming Poem*. Metrically, *Resignation A* and *B* show similarities (on the metrical objections to line 69, see Textual Notes). In addition, there are some significant collocations which recur:

<blockquote>

Onstep minne hige,
gæsta god cyning,   in gearone ræd.
Nu ic fundige to þe,   faeder moncynnes.   (lines 39a–41)

</blockquote>

<blockquote>

frætwian mec on ferðweg[37]   ond fundian
sylf to þam siþe   þe ic asettan sceal,
gæst gearwian,   ond me þæt eal for gode þolian.   (lines 72–74)

</blockquote>

Not only is the sentiment similar, but there are close resemblances in vocabulary and alliteration which I think unlikely to be coincidental. The resemblance of line 67b (*Þe sie ealles þonc*) to line 86b (*gode ealles þonc*) is especially striking. Verses of the type *–ealles þonc* must be formulaic, but occur in only two other places in the Exeter Book and three times in the rest of the poetic corpus.[38] And the distinctive spelling *wylle*, for *wille*, occurs in both halves of the poem (lines 24 and 70). From the evidence of continuity in the text, then, I think it unlikely that there is a lacuna in the manuscript.[39]

The possibility of a manuscript loss has also been suggested after *Seafarer* 102, although in this case the theory has little currency now. Since lines 103–24, which contain a high proportion of hypermetric verses and the obscure, textually corrupt passage in lines 111–15, are different in these features from the rest of the poem, it was thought by the early editors that they might be part of another poem, with a gap in the manuscript after fol. 82. If there is a loss here, it must be an entire gathering, since line 102 coincides with the end of Gathering X, and both X and XI have eight folios; a gathering containing more would be improbable. In this case, too, there are enough indications of continuity to reject the possibility of an omission: *se meotudes egsa* (line 103) picks up *for godes egsan* (line 101), and line 106, like lines 100–102, speaks of the need to prepare for the end by fearing God (for a fuller discussion of line 103, see Textual Notes).

As I interpret it, the manuscript evidence supports the view that the elegies are preserved in a complete and coherent state, apart from the burned passages and the lines where breaks in metre and sense indicate a small lacuna. On the basis of continuity in the text, I regard *Resignation* as a single poem. *Riddle 60 and The Husband's Message* I find different in subject and therefore separate. It is likely that there are layers of composition in all of the elegies, with certain formulas going back to the prehistoric period, but sorting out "earlier" and "later" elements in the poems is an unrealistic task, so I shall consider them in their present form. There are no indications in the manuscript that any of the elegies might be by the same author, as has been posited for *The Wanderer* and *The Seafarer, The Wife's Lament* and *The Husband's Message*, and sometimes for other poems too.[40] In fact, there are no very strong indications that any of the elegies is even particularly close to another in its provenance. Very broadly, manuscript arrangement suggests some affinities between *The Wanderer, The Seafarer*, and *The Riming Poem*, between *Deor* and *Wulf and Eadwacer*, and between *The Wife's Lament* and *The Husband's Message*. In a still wider sense, the inclusion of all the elegies in the second half of the Exeter Book suggests that they were all regarded as "wisdom literature." The manuscript distinguishes no elegiac genre as such. With this in mind, I will consider more fully later on those features which lead us, looking back from a later age, to categorize the poems as elegiac.

THE WANDERER

Following the long, mainly narrative, poems in the first half of the Exeter Book, the shorter pieces of "wisdom" literature which make up the second half begin with *The Wanderer*. There have been numerous accounts of the poem's structure, and the question of speech boundaries has occasioned considerable disagreement. The relevant points of controversy are discussed in the Textual Notes (see especially notes on lines 6–7, 58ff., 88ff., and 110–15). Along with most modern critics, I regard the poem as a monologue, a form which it shares with all the other elegies except *The Ruin*. Typical, too, is the division into two contrasting halves: the first (lines 1–57) describing the personal experience of the Wanderer; the second (lines 58–115) speaking in more general terms about the transience of earthly power and prosperity. This thematic pattern is fairly closely paralleled in *The Seafarer*, while the meditation on ruins in the second half of the poem resembles *The Ruin*. Lines 111–15 form a hypermetric, gnomic conclusion to *The Wanderer*.

The poem introduces a solitary who, in spite of his sufferings, often receives grace. Once a member of a warrior band, since the death of his lord and friends in battle he has long been an exile, a wanderer on the face of the earth. He laments alone, because there is no one left alive to whom he can speak his heart and he knows that reticence is a virtue. He has sought another lord and another *comitatus*, unsuccessfully. Sometimes, when, worn out with sadness, he falls asleep on a desolate shore, he dreams that he is once more in his lord's hall, only to awaken and find no companions but the seabirds preening their feathers. The contemplation of his unhappy lot brings him to the conclusion that there is nothing on earth to keep him from despair. All men must pass away, just like his own friends. Therefore a man should practise fortitude and the stoic virtues; he will not become wise until he has lived many years. He should reflect how dreadful it will be when the whole world resembles the ruins which may be seen in various places, reminders of an ancient band of warriors who have been slain, their bodies dismembered by carrion beasts; a mighty wall still stands to call to mind that dear company. A wise man contemplating the ruined fortress might well ask "What has become of the glory that was once there?" All the things that we treasure on earth are fleeting. These are the reflections of the wise man (which the Wanderer has become) as he sits apart in meditation. Fidelity and reticence are indeed virtues, but security is to be found only in God.

I have punctuated the entire poem as the Wanderer's monologue with the exception of lines 6–7 and 111, lines 92–96 being treated as a speech within a speech, the words of a hypothetical wise contemplative. This arrangement accords with the thorough study of the poem's speech divisions and of the *swa cwæð* formula (lines 6 and 111) undertaken by Gerald Richman (1982, 469–79; see Textual Notes on lines 6–7). Linking the phrase *on mode* (line 111) with *cwæð*, on the basis of similar expressions elsewhere, rather than with *snottor*, Richman argues that the speaker is thus exonerated of the charge of violating the principle of reticence which he has established earlier (lines 11b–14; cf. also lines 112b–14b), and that

The Wanderer can be seen as "in fact an Old English example of interior monologue" (p. 473).

The syntax of the poem is sometimes a problem, especially in lines 35–57. I have treated *secga geseldan*, "the companions of men" (line 53), and *fleotendra ferð*, "the host of floating ones" (line 54), as having the same referent, the seabirds of line 47. I have not punctuated *secga geseldan* as the object of *geondsceawað* (line 52) denoting the Wanderer's kinsmen (*maga*, line 51), but I believe the ironic application of the term to the seabirds deliberately recalls the human companions whose absence is so keenly felt. Instead of the intelligible speech of men (*cuðra cwidegiedda*, line 55), the seabirds bring merely inarticulate cries. A very similar sentiment is expressed in *The Seafarer*, lines 19b–26.

Few scholars would now regard the "pagan" and Christian elements in *The Wanderer* as separable, or attempt to sort out supposedly original passages from later additions. For theories of this type, see Textual Notes on lines 1–5 and lines 58ff. It is true that a positive religious faith emerges clearly only in the introduction and conclusion, but in the body of the poem there are hints of a broader perspective that will eventually transcend the tragedy which awaits heroes in this world. References to an earthly lord (*goldwine*, lines 22 and 35; *sinces bryttan*, line 25; *mondryhten*, line 41; *maþþumgyfa*, line 92; *þeodnes þrym*, line 95) implicitly suggest by contrast his heavenly counterpart. The Wanderer can think of no reason in *this* world (line 58) why his mind should not grow dark when he contemplates the transitory life of men. And, significantly, it is the *Creator* of men who destroys the fortress in line 85. By the end of the poem, a contrast has been established between the earthly strongholds which pass away and the heavenly *fæstnung* which endures (see Textual Notes on line 115).

The Wanderer has often been linked with *The Seafarer*. But, although the two poems share many themes and motifs (exile, solitude, the wintry sea, the remembered delights of the hall,[41] the contrast between earthly and heavenly values), and have similar structures, all these components were part of the common Old English poetic stock. Linguistically, the two poems diverge. *The Wanderer* has no particularly early forms, and its vocabulary shows evidence of Norse influence and an Anglian, possibly Northumbrian, background, whereas *The Seafarer* contains one or two early or Mercian usages, no Scandinavianisms, and a lower proportion of Anglian words. Conceptually, too, there are significant differences between *The Wanderer* and *The Seafarer*. The latter poem presents an asceticism deliberately sought in order to win wisdom – and grace, but *The Wanderer* describes a solitude imposed by fate not choice (the death of lord and friends, lines 9b–10b and 22–23a); only after the meditation associated with endurance and with the contemplation of loss does a man become wise (lines 64–65 and 88–91) – and realize the need to seek grace. Not until the end of the poem is the active pursuit of grace mentioned (lines 114b–15); at the beginning, the solitary Wanderer has received it many a time (line 1), but has not yet learned to search for it.

In a broad sense, the Wanderer is a pilgrim from this world to the next, but he does not deliberately set out upon this spiritual journey like the speakers in *The Seafarer* and *Resignation*, and the sea-voyage has not the central symbolic significance which it possesses in those poems. The divergence between *The Wanderer* and *The Seafarer* in this respect is pointed out by J.E. Cross (1961a, 71–72). Thus, although the two poems show similar preoccupations, they should not be forced into the same mould, as, for example, in G.V. Smithers's four-part allegorical schema, which he detects in both poems: 1) man's exit from Paradise as an exile; 2) his *peregrinatio* in the world; 3) his death, the end of the world and Judgment Day; 4) his return to the heavenly home (Smithers 1957, 149).[42] At the beginning of the poem, the *eardstapa* (line 6) is a pilgrim without being aware of it; an eschatological significance suggests itself in the scene of ruins described in lines 75–78a, and the Wanderer now knows their message (*hu gæstlic bið/þonne ealle þisse worulde wela weste stondeð*, lines 73b–74); the closing lines assert the permanence of the heavenly *fæstnung*. To a rather limited extent, then, the stages of this pilgrimage can be traced in the poem. Probably the most elaborate interpretation of *The Wanderer* as religious allegory was that proposed by D.W. Robertson, Jr (1951, 18–22), who not only understood the poem as "the advice of ... [a] wise contemplative to his wayfaring and warfaring fellow Christians" (p. 19), a view with which many would concur, but saw some very specific correspondences in detail: the dawn (line 8) in which the Wanderer laments represents the light of God's grace; the burial of his lord (line 23) refers to the rite of baptism, a participation in the burial of Christ; etc.

Another kind of intellectual framework for *The Wanderer* may be found in the notion of *consolatio*, particularly in a Boethian connection. A direct use of Boethius's *De consolatione philosophiae* (ca. 524) was proposed by R.M. Lumiansky (1950, 109–11), who pointed to the contrast between the false felicity of worldly happiness and the true felicity of practising goodness and virtue. Willi Erzgräber, too, sees the *Consolation of Philosophy* as a direct source, perhaps in the Alfredian translation, since the idea of man's subordination to a *fatum* which is overruled by divine *providentia* is central to both (Erzgräber 1961, 61 and 78–79; see also Textual Notes on line 5). And A.D. Horgan relates *Wan* 64–72 especially to Boethius's book 4, prose 6 (see notes on lines 65–72). It is highly probable that the *Consolation* contributed to the nexus of ideas behind *The Wanderer*, but this need not mean that the Old English poet made a deliberate use of it. As noted earlier, there are one or two striking verbal correspondences between *Deor* and the Alfredian Boethius (see also page 45 and notes on *Deor* 1a and 7, below); however, nothing so clear-cut is to be found in *The Wanderer*.

The treatment of meditation as a discipline in the poem has affinities with a Christian tradition going back to St Augustine, and the Wanderer's spiritual progression is exemplary. Gradually, he moves towards the level of understanding which the narrator (or the poet) has achieved.[43] In the course of his development, the Wanderer uses in turn the triad of mental faculties described in Augustine's *De Trinitate*: *memoria* (the narration of personal suffering), *intelligentia* (the contemplation of mutability), *voluntas* (the search for stability in God).[44] By the exercise of this trinity of powers, the image of the divine in man, he ascends towards God. Augustine also defines the last faculty as love. See books 9, 10, and 14 for the triad in its various forms (*PL* 42, cols. 819–1098, esp. cols. 984 and 1048).[45] Again, it cannot be asserted that the poet used the *De Trinitate* specifically, but the ideas expressed there would have formed part of his intellectual background.

Some of the rhetorical passages in *The Wanderer*, notably the *sum* series and the *ubi sunt* motif, have been linked to particular, Christian sources, and James Cross has shown how widespread both were in homiletic writing.[46] But the formulaic, repetitive language of these utterances (lines 80b–84 and 92–96) and of the *her bið ... læne* lines (108–9) probably has world-wide correspondences, and certainly springs from oral, Germanic as well as learned, Christian roots. Norah Kershaw, in her *Anglo-Saxon and Norse Poems*, points out some very far-flung parallels for lines 92–96; lines 80b–84 are reminiscent of references elsewhere to the traditional eagle, raven, and wolf which feed upon the slain; lines 108–9 closely resemble a gnomic pronouncement in the Norse *Hávamál*. The analogues are cited in the Textual Notes on these three passages.

Rather than attempting to separate Germanic and Christian elements in *The Wanderer*, it is more meaningful to see the poem's dichotomies in terms of wordly versus transcendental values. The Wanderer longs for affection and security; at first he seeks them in this world (lines 23b–29a). Perpetual disappointment brings him to the conclusion that there is nothing in *this* world (line 58) to prevent despair. He preaches endurance (lines 65b–72), and reflects that one day all the wealth of the world will lie waste (line 74). Meditation on death and destruction leads to the *hwær cwom* passage, full of passionate regret, and once again to the inescapable fact that all the framework of this earth turns (or "will turn") to nothing (line 110). He advocates endurance once more, but this is no longer enough. It is good and practicable (*til*, line 112) to keep faith and bear one's grief, but well for him (*wel*, line 114) who seeks comfort from the Father in heaven.

The Wanderer has always been a favourite with those who have studied Old English. After a thousand years, its haunting imagery can still recreate for us with a strange intimacy the sensibilities of a vanished heroic world: the solitary who stirs with his hands the ice-cold sea; the dream-hall where the Wanderer lays head and hands on his lord's knee; the seabird "companions of men" who bring the lonely one no familiar speech; the wall wondrously high adorned with serpent shapes; the steed, the rider, the treasure-giver, the shining cups and armour – gone as if they had never been; and, finally, the only fortress that stands.

THE SEAFARER

Along with *The Wanderer*, *The Seafarer* has been the most popular and the most studied of the Old English elegies. At least one modern rendering, Ezra Pound's translation, ranks as a considerable poem in its own right.[47] Like *The Wanderer*, *The Seafarer* presents an ethopoeic exile-figure who narrates his personal experiences in the first half of the poem, and then proceeds to general moral reflections in the second half. Using a conventional formula, closely resembling the opening of *The Wife's Lament* (see note on *Sea* 1–3), the Seafarer introduces the tale of his hardships. In a series of evocative images, he describes how he has suffered cold, hunger, loneliness, and danger on the stormy sea. He repeatedly asserts that the man who enjoys a prosperous life on land has no idea of his feelings (lines 12b–15, 27–30, 55b–57). The speaker's mind is preoccupied with the sea (lines 33b–38). Those like him can have no peace on land; however proud-hearted and successful they are, seafarers are always filled with "longing" (lines 38–47). The burgeoning of life in the springtime impels them to depart (lines 48–52), and the call of the cuckoo admonishes them, presaging sorrow of heart. The speaker longs to go; his spirit ranges far and wide and comes back to him eager and greedy (lines 58–64a). At this point there is a transition to the more impersonal second half of the poem. Using the connective *forþon* (see note on line 27a for the treatment of this word), the narrator declares that the joys of the Lord are warmer to him than this dead life on land (lines 64b–66a). The second half, like that of *The Wanderer*, reflects upon the transience of earthly things, but from a more explicitly religious point of view. Life is unstable, so a man should strive to win eternal glory before he passes away (lines 66b–80a). The world is degenerating, just like the life of each man, who grows old and finally dies (lines 80b–96). It is no use for a brother to place treasures in his brother's grave, for treasure will not redeem the sinful soul (lines 97–102). Great is the power of God, so a wise man will fear the Lord and exercise restraint in his ways, behaving with moderation towards both friend and foe (lines 103–16). This passage of proverbial wisdom includes some typically gnomic lines using hypermetric verses (lines 103 and 106–9; cf. *Wan* 111–15). The poem concludes with a homiletic exhortation: let us consider where we possess a home and how we may come there, striving to win eternal bliss and giving thanks to God (lines 117–24).

Variations in style and attitude in *The Seafarer* led earlier scholars to reject parts of the poem or to treat it as a dialogue expressing different points of view. Whereas lines 1–33a describe the pains of seafaring, much of lines 33b–64a conveys a fascination for the sea. A dramatic, dialogue format, as an explanation for these juxtaposed feelings of fear and longing, was first proposed by Max Rieger (1869, 330–39), who saw in the poem a conversation between an old, disillusioned seafarer and a young enthusiast, assigning lines 1–33a, 39–47, 53–57, 72–124 to the former, and 33b–38, 48–52, 58–71 to the latter. Friedrich Kluge (1883) also regarded the poem as a dialogue, but containing only two speeches, lines 1–33a and 33b–66a, the rest being a later, composite addition. R.C. Boer (1903) related *The Seafarer* to *The Wanderer*, arguing that both had suffered considerable corruption and interpolation; he saw in *The Seafarer* traces of two separate poems: a lament (lines 1–15, 17–22, and 23–24a or 25b–26) and a dialogue (33b–38 and 44–64a), the rest being a later addition of poor quality.

After W.W. Lawrence (1902b) struck a blow against the dialogue theory and vindicated the poem's essential integrity (though only to line 64a! See p. 462), *The Seafarer* came to be viewed as an, at least comparatively unified, monologue. John Pope put forward a "Dramatic Voices" interpretation (1965) arguing for two speeches (1–33a and 33b–102) followed by a conventional epilogue (103–24), but subsequently retracted it (1974). The view that lines 64bff. were a homiletic addition persisted in some quarters (e.g. Wardale 1935, 61), and is obliquely reflected in Jackson Campbell's oral-formulaic argument that the first part of the poem is older than the second (see p. 20, above).

Lines 103ff., which contain much textual corruption and begin a new folio, have been regarded as part of another poem by many scholars, including Thorpe, Ettmüller, Lawrence (p. 471), Kershaw (pp. 18–19), and Krapp-Dobbie (p. xxxix).[48] I have discussed this possibility earlier (pp. 29–30). And Henry Sweet, when he printed *The Seafarer* in the seventh edition of his *Anglo-Saxon Reader*, rejected lines 109ff. because of their corruption (see Sweet 1894, 222).

Many readers will find the moralizing in the second half of *The Seafarer* less attractive than the more picturesque and personal first section. Towards its close, in particular, the poem is faulty. The text is often obscure, and sometimes meaning and syntax break down altogether (especially in lines 111–14). However, there are actually rather close links at all the supposed breaks: the causal clause attaching lines 64b to 64a, the theme of the instability of life uniting 66a and b, the idea of God's *egsa* in line 103 picking up the same word in lines 101–2, the hypermetric-gnomic mode of 106–8 continuing in 109.

Modern scholarship tends to explain the apparent paradoxes in the first half of the poem and the absence of any reference to seafaring in the second by a symbolic reading, whereby the voyage, which may or may not exist on a literal level, has a deeper, spiritual significance. Some have seen the wished-for spring journey, in contrast to the painful winter voyage, as symbolizing the journey of the soul from the trials of this world to the distant glories of the next, an interpretation originating with Levin Schücking in a review of Sieper's *Die altenglische Elegie* (Schücking 1917, 109).[49] For this allegorical reading, see Textual Notes on lines 42–43. The naturalistic view, exemplified by Lawrence (1902b, 466), that the Seafarer is infected with something like John Masefield's "sea-fever," is probably too romantic. A reading which accepts the voyage on a literal level but assigns a spiritual significance to it is Dorothy Whitelock's interpretation of the sea-journey as a *peregrinatio pro amore Dei* (1950; see note, below, on line 38 for Whitelock's view). However, if seafaring is a means of reaching a place of exile (Whitelock, p. 267), an extraordinary weight is attached to the voyage itself. I believe it is possible to interpret the Seafarer's experiences symbolically without actually denying the literal level of the poem. Understood in this way, the Seafarer's life is deliberately strenuous and ascetic; he rejects the illusory blandishments of this world because the joys of the Lord are warmer to him. Symbolically, his voyage is a pilgrimage which he chooses to undertake. Thus, the desire, described in the central portion of the poem, to depart over the sea, is more than a longing to leave this world and travel to the next. Nor is the desired voyage primarily a journey into exile. It is a quest for a transcendental good, a quest which in this poem takes the form of seafaring.

Images of life as a journey, and, more specifically, as a voyage over the sea, must be universal. They are common in patristic writing. Tertullian (early third century) sees the Church as a ship on the troubled sea of the world in his exegesis of Matthew 8.23–27: *quod in mari, id est saeculo, fluctibus, id est persecutionibus et tentationibus inquietatur* (*De baptismo*, chap. 12; in *PL* 1, col. 1323). Cyprian (third century) describes the Christian on his way to the next world as one voyaging home: *Quis non, ad suos navigare festinans, ventum prosperum cupidius optaret ...?* (*De mortalitate*, chap. 26; in *PL* 4, col. 601). Augustine exhorts his readers not to fear the sea of the world with its hostile waves and storms: *Non metuat anima mare hoc magnum, saeculum scilicet, cuius fluctus ac turbines sentimus inimicas saeculi potestates* (*De Cantico novo*, chap. 2; in *PL* 40, col. 680). The theme also appears in Old English homilies: *se rihte siðfæt to ðam ecan life þam ðe lange ær sæton ... on þam unstillum yðum þære sæ þises middaneardes* (*De Nativitate Sanctae Mariae*; in Assmann 1889, 117–18). These allegorical treatments of the sea indicate that the motif was readily available as a Christian symbol, even if none of them exactly parallels *The Seafarer*, where the temptations of this world are associated with the land, in contrast to the sea. The patristic use of the sea as Christian allegory is related to *The Seafarer* by G.V. Smithers (1959, 1–5), John Vickrey (1982, 57–59), Frederick Holton (1983, 208–11), and others.

There are distinct similarities between the journey theme in *The Seafarer* and *Resignation*. However, the Seafarer is actually engaged in a quest in this world, although it leads ultimately to the next, whereas the narrator of *Resignation* is only contemplating a voyage, and his preparation in the first half of the poem is very clearly for his journey to the next world, paralleled in the second half by an unfulfilled desire to undertake a literal voyage (home, if my reading of *Res* is correct; see pp. 55–56, below). In *The Seafarer*, the focus is on the process; in *Resignation*, on the goal. For that reason, the imagery of seafaring is accompanied with a wealth of detail in the one poem, and sketched in a few lines (97b–103a) in the other. The sea has a different function in *The Wanderer*, where it operates as a symbol of desolation. Also relevant to *The Seafarer* is the extended simile at the end of Cynewulf's *Christ II* (lines 850–66), where life is described as a journey in which we ride our "sea-horses" over a perilous sea until we reach safe anchor in the heavenly harbour. But in *Christ II* the voyage is common to everyone; it is not chosen; it does not set the voyager apart from ordinary men.

All of these poems have obviously been influenced by the same traditions, oral Germanic as well as learned Christian. The *Christ II* passage conveys an intrepid eagerness somewhat similar to parts of *The Seafarer*. In another mode, *The Wanderer* resembles *The Seafarer* in using the sea as a place of suffering and loneliness, an idea associated in both poems with the ironic contrast between the seabirds on a wintry sea and the companionship of men in the cheerful hall (*Wan* 45–57, *Sea* 19b–26). The kennings *hwæles eþel* (line 60) and *hwælweg* (line 63; MS *wælweg*; see note) resemble similar expressions elsewhere in the poetry and reflect a "sea" theme in the oral-formulaic tradition. *Hronrad* and *ganotes bæð* occur in *Beowulf* (lines 10 and 1861, resp.), for example. Also typical are words for the cold (*Sea* 8, 10, 14, 19, 33), wintry weather (line 32), and storms (lines 6 and 23). The *Wanderer's* seascapes use similar language: *hrimcealde sæ* (line 4); *hreosan hrim ond snaw, hagle gemenged* (line 48). And the *Christ II* lines refer to *cald wæter* (851), *frecne stream* (853), *windge holmas* (855), *hreone hrycg* (858).

As observed earlier, *The Wanderer* and *The Seafarer* tend to be linked by scholars (see n. 40), but actually there are marked differences between them, and the voyage theme is much more central to the latter poem. Whereas the idea of voyage as quest informs the first half of *The Seafarer* and invites a symbolic, if not fully allegorical, reading, this kind of symbolism is not developed in *The Wanderer*, and, thus, that poem offers less support for an allegorical interpretation.

Structurally, *The Seafarer* is less clearly laid out than *The Wanderer*, perhaps because of textual corruption. However, the various ideas assembled in the second half of the poem can all be related to the Gospel teachings to prepare for the time of reckoning, which will come unexpectedly (cf. especially *Sea* 106), and to lay up treasure in heaven giving up the goods of this world, as expressed in Matthew 19:21 and Luke 18:22, and, more expansively, in Luke 12:20–40 (also Vulg. Psalm 48; 49 in other Bibles; see note on *Sea* 97–102). *The Seafarer* does not speak specifically of heavenly "treasure," but, more literally, of lasting glory (lines 78–79). In a general way, the reference to hoarding or burying treasure in the second half of the poem (lines 97–102) picks up the rejection of the landsman's values in the first half (lines 12b–15, 27–30, 55b–57). The connection is made in lines 66b–67 (*Ic gelyfe no / þæt him eorðwelan ece stondeð*). Again, the contrast in the first half of the poem between the ignorant man who knows nothing of suffering and challenge, and the Seafarer who eagerly embraces them, corresponds to the contrast between the man who is *dol*, "foolish," because he fears not the Lord and death will come to him unexpectedly (line 106), and the one who is *eadig*, "blessed," because he fears the Lord, lives devoutly, and will receive grace (line 107). Although there is no mention of the sea in the second half of the poem, the closing passage speaks of a journey (to the heavenly home, lines 117–18), which reminds us of the voyaging described earlier on.

For all its textual and structural problems, *The Seafarer* is a work of considerable sophistication and power, whose major images and themes operate on two levels, temporal and transcendental. This duality appears not only in the concept of seafaring and the contrast between land and sea, but also in the words for social and moral relationships, such as *dryhten*, *eadig*, *lof*, *egsa*, *oncyrran* (see notes on lines 40a, 55b–56a, 64b–66, 72–80a, 97–102, 103). The ideas in lines 64b–124 are presented in a somewhat disjointed fashion, but the connections are detectable, and, though the poem limps to its final conclusion, it is only after the homiletic development in the second half that the themes which are given such vivid concrete expression in the narrative section of the poem acquire their full resonance.

THE RIMING POEM

Until fairly recently, this poem was usually regarded merely as an eccentric curiosity, of no literary merit.[50] In its consistent use of both rhyme and alliteration throughout, it is unique in Old English, and worthy of attention for that reason alone, but the exigencies of the form compelled the author to use many rare words, perhaps nonce-words, making the poem obscure, and occasionally, when the problem is compounded by textual corruption, almost impenetrable. However, our knowledge of Old English has increased considerably since its first editors, Conybeare and Thorpe, grappled with it over a century and a half ago and frequently found themselves at a loss, and the poem, though difficult, no longer seems as intractable as it once did. Also, recent scholarship, particularly the work of O.D. Macrae-Gibson, who edited *The Riming Poem* in 1983, has gone a long way towards rehabilitating it. Macrae-Gibson's assessment of the poem as "worthy of far higher praise than it usually receives" has been echoed by Karl Wentersdorf, and endorsed by E.G. Stanley, who sees in the combination of stringent rhyme and alliteration a minor mastery comparable to the major artistry of *Pearl*.[51] Not all readers will be equally enthusiastic, and many will find the poem's word-play excessive. But it does achieve a concentration of impressions which is striking, even though it never reaches that fusion of thought and image which marks the more memorable passages in some of the other Old English elegies – and, later, in *Pearl*.

More so than *The Wanderer* and *The Seafarer*, which counterpoise a narrative first half against a reflective second, *The Riming Poem* divides sharply, between lines 42 and 43, into a two-part structure. Parts 1 and 2 evoke precisely opposite moods, which are finally reconciled in the closing lines (from 80 on). The poem contrasts the speaker's former happy and prosperous state with his present bitterness, and links his decline to the corruption of the world generally. In integrating personal experience with this theme, *The Riming Poem* resembles the two other works, and, like them, it moves towards a homiletic close, admonishing us to seek the joy in heaven which will not fade. But the present poem focuses more on sin and corruption than on hardship, like the two others, and its rejection of worldliness is prompted not just by disillusionment, but by disgust.

Whereas in *The Wanderer* and *The Seafarer* the narrator speaks from the standpoint of a retainer, here the persona seems to be a former chieftain or king: he possessed an ancient seat (line 23b) and treated his people kindly (line 40b; see Textual Notes). Thus far, most readers are agreed, though Ruth Lehmann (1970) sees the figure who speaks in the poem as more abstract, perhaps the will of God (p. 440). This is inconsistent, though, with the speaker's bitterness in Part 2 (line 43) and his mortality (lines 70–72a). He is the victim of enmity – his own and other people's – rather than bereavement, like the Wanderer, or loneliness, like the Sea-farer. Wentersdorf perceives the narrator as a ruler who has been forced into retirement because he has more religious devotion than political ability – like Æthelwulf of Wessex (839–56) (1985, 268–70). But the dis-integration described from line 43 on is the product of enmity and re-sentment within as well as without, and, though particularized as a king in Part 1, in Part 2 the speaker, in his confrontation with sin and death, is more like Everyman. If he is the victim of another's treachery in lines 44b–50, the generalized third-person utterance suggests that the malice described is to be attributed to himself as well. Rather than moving from narrative to reflection, Parts 1 and 2 balance two opposing states, the latter in more general terms than the former: innocence and expe-rience, control and vulnerability, harmony and disintegration.

The unusual vocabulary of *The Riming Poem* presents its major difficulty. As well as introducing numerous rare or new words (*getongum*, "hasten-ings," "swift steps," line 8; *gerscype*, "noisy conversation," line 11; *scrad*, "ship," line 13; *sweglrad*, "path of music," line 29; *brondhord*, "secret fire," line 46; *ungepynde?*, "unconfined," line 49; etc.), the poet coins nouns from other parts of speech (*brad*, "open space," line 13; *fleah*, "flight," line 44), forms verbs from nouns (*onspreht*, line 9, from *spræc*, "shoot"), and makes transitive verbs intransitive (*ofeoll?*, "declined," line 24; *beacnade*, "was prominent," line 31; *gearwade*, "was at hand," line 36; *cinnið*, "increases," line 52; *tinneð*, "extends," line 54). These, and other, problem words, var-iously interpreted by scholars, are discussed in the Textual Notes. Al-though sometimes the exact effect intended escapes us, the poet's accumulation of visual and aural images creates an intense evocation of busy prosperity – with blooming landscape (lines 1–4), prancing horses

(7–8), gliding ships (13–14), resounding hall (27–30); and then of frightening decay – secret malice spreading in the heart like a hidden fire (lines 45–50), sin and death entrapping and holding man (lines 65–66), worms devouring him until nothing is left of his earthly being (lines 74–79). After this, the less graphic, and less textually difficult, closing lines come as a relief.

In dealing with the poem's problematic words, I have attempted to produce sense and consistency. Occasionally, this has meant going out on a limb and emending more heavily than I have felt the need to do in the other poems, especially in lines 18, 65 and 79, and in line 26 where a possible emendation is suggested in the Textual Notes. When emending, I have been guided by the techniques visible in the poem as a whole. Thus, I have assumed double a-verse alliteration throughout, and assonance (probably requiring correspondence in vowel-length) but not necessarily full rhyme between the verses.[52] I have rejected some common emendations designed to remove non-standard forms (lines 22 and 53) and to perfect rhymes (lines 63 and 65). Wherever possible, I have sought native derivations for unfamiliar words. A fuller explanation of my rationale in handling the poem is given in my article "*The Riming Poem*: Design and Interpretation" (Klinck 1988).

Various influences on the form and content of the poem have been suggested by scholars. In a general way, the speaker's reversal of fortune and the moral to be drawn from it resemble the story of Job, but there are no correspondences in detail which would mark this as the specific source. *The Riming Poem* has certainly been influenced by Latin accentual verse, and its structures bear a strong resemblance to the trochaic dimeters of some hymns. Thomas of Celano's *Dies irae* (thirteenth century) provides a familiar later example: *dies irae, dies illa,/solvet saeclum in favilla,/teste David cum Sibylla* (lines 1–3).[53] Lines 61b to 69 in *The Riming Poem*, with their four syllables per verse (allowing for resolution, and a more heavily stressed second syllable), are strikingly similar in pattern. This background allows a wide range of possibilities as to date. Anglo-Latin writers had used rhyme since the seventh century, when Aldhelm wrote under the influence of continental and Irish models; James Earl, in his translation and commentary (1985 and 1987) stresses this "hisperic" influence.[54] But rhythmically our poem resembles the vigorously simple contours of accentual, which was gradually taking over from quantitative, Latin verse. Alois Brandl relates the poem to the popularity of leonine rhymes in the Latin verse of the tenth and eleventh centuries and to the growing tendency in the English verse of this period to imitate the Latin *Vierfüssigkeit*.[55]

Norse influence is another possibility, and some of the poem's difficult vocabulary resembles Norse words (see p. 17, above, and Textual Notes). On the basis of its linguistic forms, *The Riming Poem* belongs to the early- to mid-tenth century and the north of England, which gives it the same background as Egill Skallagrímsson's rhyming *Hǫfuðlausn*, presented at York ca. 948 (text in Gordon and Taylor 1957, 112–14). Egill wrote his *Hǫfuðlausn*, "Head-Ransom," as a panegyric to placate his old enemy Erik Bloodaxe, then ruling at York, and save his own life. Egill's poem is the earliest recorded example of "rhyming metre," *runendr háttr*, in Old Norse, just as *The Riming Poem* is the earliest Old English composition to use rhyme throughout. In fact, their verse-forms are strikingly similar; I compare them more fully in Part 3 (p. 238, below). A connection between the two poems is thus very likely:[56] influence could have passed in either direction, or could be attributed to no more than a similar milieu.

In its contempt of the world, *The Riming Poem* offers a familiar medieval moral. Though its two-part structure, ethopoeic voice, and closing wisdom are paralleled in the other didactic elegies, its darker passages have a morbidity which is not precisely elegiac – which is, in fact, in the tradition of the *Soul and Body* poems and of the very late *Grave*.[57] This is especially true of lines 75–77. To a large extent, the poem is a catalogue of images, both heightened and strained by the insistent rhymes; the focus remains on technique, and no real imaginative synthesis takes place. But the form chosen by the author was an extraordinarily demanding one, and it is hardly surprising if the results strike us as over-contrived.

DEOR

Perhaps the most interesting feature of *Deor* is its lyrical form: it is the only surviving poem in Old English with a fully developed refrain. For this reason, I have felt justified in referring to the various sections of the poem as stanzas, though they are very irregular in length, consisting of 7, 6, 4, 3, 7, and 15 lines. No particular model springs to mind. The poem's references to figures known from Scandinavian sources[58] might suggest a Norse background, although these figures belong to the common Germanic stock; Norse strophic poetry has come down to us from the mid-ninth century on. Again, it is possible that the poet was influenced by Latin verse. Rudolf Imelmann in his *Forschungen zur ae Poesie* (1920, 235) suggests Virgil's *Eclogue 8*, which uses repeated lines in a similar way; but this seems too specific. Old English folk poetry itself provides a prec- edent, in the kind of repetition found in the Charms, for example *Ut lytel spere, gif her inne sie/sy* (*For a Sudden Stitch* 6, 12, 15). It has been argued by Morton Bloomfield that *Deor* itself is a sophisticated charm (1964, 534–41). I believe that the form of *Deor* may be regarded as a more developed and more artful use of techniques seen in other Old English poems, and that the poem's design represents a search for lyrical structure detectable in the other elegies too (see Klinck 1984, 134–37).

The stanzaic form of *Deor* is confirmed by the manuscript, which begins a new section, with a large capital, after each occurrence of the refrain. Because there is no refrain, and no sectional division in the manuscript, after line 34, I have not presented lines 28–34 as a separate stanza, although this makes the closing stanza extremely long, and a transition occurs at line 35, where the narrator introduces his own personal history. Apart from the variation in length, each stanza employs the same pattern: laconic statement of misfortune, followed by the consolatory words *þæs ofereode; þisses swa mæg!* (loosely, "That passed over; this will too!"). The pattern is interrupted by the philosophical passage in lines 28–34, which gives additional weight to the closing section. In each of the first five stanzas, the ethopoeic speaker, Deor, refers to some legendary example of suffering which would have been familiar to his audience; in the sixth he speaks of his own, also in a legendary setting.

One other Old English poem uses stanzaic form, the late *Seasons for Fasting* (see *ASPR* 6:xcii–xciv and 98–104), which contains twenty-nine fairly equal sections, mostly of eight lines. This poem does not use refrain. *Wulf and Eadwacer*, the poem immediately following *Deor* in the Exeter Book, displays a tendency towards strophic form, with an irregular pattern of long and short lines and the repetition of lines 2–3 in 7–8. Since *Wulf and Eadwacer* also resembles *Deor* in containing proper names, or epithets, some scholars have drawn the two poems together. Thus, P.J. Frankis (1962) suggests that both refer to the same version of the Norse Heðinn-Hild legend, alluded to in the final stanza of *Deor*, the hero in both being Wulf (*deor* = "animal").

Whereas the other elegies, with the possible exception of *Wulf and Eadwacer*, belong to what the Chadwicks called poetry of a "timeless nameless character" (1932, 1:423), *Deor* is placed firmly in the world of heroic legend. It is full of allusions, and, though Deor himself appears to have been invented specifically for this poem (see Textual Notes, line 37b), all the other characters are stock figures of myth and fictionalized history. Although we can identify most of the personages from other sources, mainly Scandinavian and German, we cannot confidently establish the narratives in the form the poet would have known them. We lack the knowledge which he could have expected of his contemporary audience, for he draws on a body of oral tradition available to us only in scattered and fragmented – and often much later – versions.

If the exact significance of *Deor*'s various *exempla* is obscure, the aim of the poem is clear: it is a consolation. The title used in some German editions, *Deors Klage*, is a little misleading, because the poem comes to terms with misfortune by concentrating on the reminder that it will pass away. Just as Weland, Beadohild, Mæðhild, Ðeodric or his victims, and Eormanric's victims finally saw the end of their suffering, so Deor the narrator, who has been ousted from his position as court *scop*, will see the end of his. There is no overt reference to Boethius's *De consolatione philosophiae* in *Deor*, which operates within a Germanic rather than a classical frame of reference. But, as one of the major medieval works of the consolation genre, and especially as a work which Alfred selected for translation into English, the *Consolation* immediately suggests itself as an influence. Although the Boethian connection has been downplayed recently (by Harris 1987, who prefers to relate the poem to the "Old Testament pessimism" [p. 53] of Wisdom 5:9, *transierunt omnia illa*), most readers will probably see the idea of overcoming misfortune as the dominant theme in the poem. The reflection that, just as one's previous good fortune has passed away, so one's present misfortunes inevitably will too, is a significant theme in Boethius (book 2, prose 3), though it is less central than in *Deor*. In the Alfredian translation, the words *neart þu þeah ungesælig, forðæmðe þa unrotnesse þe þu nu on eart swilce ofergað swa ðu cwist ðæt þa blisse ær dydon* provide an interesting parallel to the refrain of *Deor*, *þæs ofereode, þisses swa mæg.*[59] Both the Alfredian translation of Boethius (but not the original) and *Deor* include Weland and Ðeodric among their examples of mutability. And both speak of God rather than *wyrd* as the author of change. In fact, *witig dryhten* is linked alliteratively with *wendan* (*Deor* 32) in a modification of a more traditional alliterative linkage between *wendan* and *wyrd* (*Wan* 107, *Ruin* 24). This detail may be a reminiscence of an interpolation in the Alfredian Boethius, which notes that some philosophers claim *wyrd* rules the fates of man, but *Ic þonne secge ... þ sio godcunde foretiohhung his walde, næs sio wyrd* (Sedgefield 1899, 32). Whether the poet knew the Latin work at first hand is less certain.[60] It is probable, too, that a consolation genre existed in Germanic poetry independent of influences from Christian-classical culture. Francis Magoun (1942) sees such a genre behind *Deor* and the (tenth- or eleventh-century?) Norse *Guðrúnarkviða I* (in Neckel-Kuhn 1983, 202–6; text and translation included in my Appendix, pp. 288–95, below).

Deor's background in Germanic oral tradition has been the subject of much discussion. Since others have laboured extensively in this field, I have dealt with the legendary background (passim in the Textual Notes) more briefly than the poem's principal editor, Kemp Malone, and have tried to indicate the range of possibilities rather than elaborating a particular hypothesis. Malone's theories, explained in his editions and more fully in a series of articles,[61] are often speculative, and undergo some significant changes over the years, notably between editions 1 (1933), 3 (1961), and 4 (1966). The Weland story, alluded to in stanzas 1 and 2 of *Deor*, is known pretty well from the thirteenth-century Norse *Volsunga saga* and *Þiðreks saga* (for a summary of the relevant material, see Malone's Introduction, editions, pp. 4–7). With stanza 3 we are on much shakier ground. Malone's identification of the names with the characters in some comparatively modern Scandinavian ballads is persuasive, but his assumption that the story alluded to in *Deor* is essentially the same is dubious – especially since his interpretation rests on an emendation (of *monge*, line 14). Again, Malone's insistence upon a Frankish Theodoric for stanza 4 seems idiosyncratic; the weight of scholarly opinion favours Theodoric the Ostrogoth, though it is hard to know whether he is presented as a sufferer or as one who inflicts suffering. The identification of Eormanric with the fourth-century tyrant, later regarded as a contemporary of Dietrich (Theodoric) is certain. And the characters of the final stanza can be identified from other sources, mainly continental, especially the Danish *Gesta Danorum* of Saxo Grammaticus (late twelfth century) and the Icelandic *Skáldskaparmál* by Snorri Sturluson (1222–23?). Malone gives information about all the legendary personages in his Introduction and Glossary of Proper Names (the sections on Geat-Mæðhild and on Ðeodric are altered substantially between editions).

As *Deor* differs from the other elegies in the specificity of its allusions, so its quality of feeling is significantly different. Emotion is controlled by being objectified, and the parallel citation of the various *exempla* serves to this end. The final instance of cruelty or hardship, Deor's loss of his position and *londryht* (line 40), though painful, seems less severe in the light of all the examples which have preceded it. And in linking Deor with Heorrenda, a kind of northern Orpheus, speaker and poet announce their appropriation of a certain reflected glory. Emotional control is achieved by a tightness and economy both of form and of content. The repeated intervention of the stoic refrain imposes its own stringency, and a wealth of narrative is compressed into 42 lines. There is no cry of despair as in *Wulf and Eadwacer* and *The Wife's Lament*, no urgency as in *The Husband's Message*, none of *The Ruin's* indulgence of the imagination or *The Riming Poem's* bravura, and the tight structure leaves little room for the expansive meditations of *The Wanderer* and *The Seafarer*; only lines 28–34 allow for something of this. The author of *Deor* combines lyrical form and heroic content with a carefully modulated understatement, and the poem which emerges displays a poise that is impressive.

WULF AND EADWACER

Probably no work composed in Old English has occasioned as much scholarly disagreement as *Wulf and Eadwacer*. Variously regarded as a riddle, a charm, a *Frauenlied*, a funeral lament, a canine or lupine story,[62] it continues to puzzle its readers. The poem is ostensibly a lament by a female speaker (indicated by the feminine *reotugu*, "mournful," line 10) addressed to an absent Wulf. This much can be stated as a fact. Whether the poem should be taken at face value is another question. Some passages, especially the impassioned lines 13–15, indicate that it should. Other passages – lines 1 and 18–19, which are restrained and cryptic – suggest a certain distancing of the speaker from her material. Nothing in the poem, though, encourages us to regard it as merely trivial. So if it is a riddle it must be a serious one, and it is probably not a canine love-story, a wen charm, or a complaint about a misplaced passage of verse.[63] In addition to the diversity of proposed solutions, another objection to the riddle theory is that no particular riddle-subject is being pointed to. In the genuine riddles a distinct object or creature is always present, although it is sometimes hard for the modern reader to identify. Also, a riddle typically focuses on the marvellous nature of the creature's physical being, not on his or her psychological situation, as here (see Klinck 1984, 133, and Part 3, p. 228, below). Again, this preoccupation makes it unlikely that the poem is a charm, although it resembles the Charms in its incantatory repetitions: of lines 2–3 in lines 7–8, and of the word *wulf*.

In the light of these considerations, it seems reasonable to treat *Wulf and Eadwacer* as a lament, of a deliberately enigmatic kind. The use of animal words like *wulf* and *hwelp* contributes in large part to the poem's enigmatism – and resembles the personification of the non-human in the Riddles. If the poem is neither a riddle nor a joke, it is hard to believe that the characters really are animals. Peter Orton (1985, 223–58) believes that we have here an anthropomorphic piece about wolves, but he is at a loss to explain the purpose of such a poem (p. 256). I have argued elsewhere (Klinck 1987a) that not only *wulf* and *hwelp*, but *dogode* ("followed like a dog"? see Textual Notes on line 9), *bogum* ("shoulders"), and *tosliteð* ("tears apart") are also animal terms, that this language is markedly disparaging, and that it colours though it does not negate the grief expressed in lines 13–15 (p. 11). My analysis of *lac*, "gift," "sacrifice?" and *apecgan*, "take, consume," links these words also with the animal imagery (Klinck 1987a, 4–6). I believe that this explanation fits in with the nature of the poem as an erotic "woman's song," like *The Wife's Lament*, expressing intense and ambivalent feelings. This type of half-mocking animal imagery would be less appropriate to a mother's lament for her son. Thus, *Wulf and Eadwacer* should be understood "as a love poem, essentially serious, though infused with irony ... – a poem whose lamenting voice acquires a cutting edge from its distinctive use of 'brutal' imagery" (Klinck 1987a, 13).

Much about the poem remains uncertain, notably the number of characters and their relationship to one another. Probably the most widely held view is still that put forward by Henry Bradley in 1888: "The speaker ... is ... a woman ..., Wulf is her lover ... and Eadwacer ... her tyrant husband" (p. 198). The love triangle accounts well for the tensions in the poem, but at least one eminent critic believes there are two characters and no more, the woman and Wulf (Greenfield 1986, 5–14). However, most scholars see the *hwelp* of line 16 as the speaker's child. Again, *Eadwacer* is sometimes regarded as an epithet of Wulf. The name, though, "Property-watcher," suggests a rôle opposite to a wolf's. And is the *beaducafa* ("the battle-bold one," line 11) Eadwacer, Wulf, or yet another person? In dealing with these problems in the Textual Notes, I have attempted to represent the range of opinions without hopelessly confusing the reader.

As I understand it, the poem contains four characters: the narrator, the fugitive Wulf, Eadwacer – who has some kind of guardianship over the speaker which includes a sexual relationship – and the woman's child. The poem opens with the mystifying statement "It is to my people as if one gave them a gift." If my interpretation of *apecgan* (line 2/7) as "take, consume" (see Textual Notes) is correct, the gift is Wulf, who is likely to be slaughtered by the speaker's people if they catch him. In the "refrain" she voices her desperate anxiety, and alienation ("It is different with us") – perhaps from her people, but more powerfully with regard to Wulf, from whom she is separated, each on an island fastness. In weeping rain she sits and weeps. The *beaducafa* embraces her, and his lovemaking brings both pleasure and pain. She pines for her Wulf. Suddenly (as I read the syntax of lines 16–17), she addresses another person: "Eadwacer! The wolf is carrying our wretched [emending to *earmne*, line 16] cub to the forest." The poem ends with another cryptic pronouncement: "That is easily torn apart which was never joined, our story together."

I have referred earlier (pp. 23–26, above) to the significance of *Wulf and Eadwacer*'s position between *Deor* and the Riddles – a placing which may reflect two sorts of affinities, perceived at two stages of the compilation of the Exeter Book anthology. Like *Deor*, *Wulf and Eadwacer* is markedly lyrical in form and displays a tendency to strophic structure (more fully realized in the former poem), with the repetition of lines 2–3 and the intervention of single verses at lines 3, 8, 17, and 19, a shape which W.W. Lawrence thought indebted to Norse *ljóðaháttr* (1902a, 251). Possibly, too, *Wulf and Eadwacer*, like *Deor*, makes allusion to Germanic legends (see Textual Notes on *Eadwacer*, line 16a; also Frankis's arguments for a connection between *Deor* and *Wulf*, p. 44, above), though I believe that in this case the characters are likely to have been created specifically for the poem. In its brevity, its cryptic style, and its use of animals, *Wulf and Eadwacer* resembles the Riddles. Indeed, the poem's riddling quality is an essential ingredient, although it has far greater cogency as a love-lament. As Alain Renoir observed nearly thirty years ago (1965, 160–1), to an extent the poem's capacity to move us stands apart from its precise meaning. *Wulf and Eadwacer* is an intense evocation of longing and despair, a passionate outburst that is nevertheless controlled by objectifying irony and an enigmatic reticence.

THE WIFE'S LAMENT

Like *Wulf and Eadwacer*, *The Wife's Lament* has fascinated and perplexed generations of modern readers, has met with a lively critical interest and occasioned much discussion, but has never found a consensus of interpretation. Most scholars accept that the narrator of the poem is female; a few, arguing that a woman's love-lament would not occur in the context of Anglo-Saxon heroic verse, have thought that the speaker who has lost his lord is actually a man, rather than a woman separated from her husband.[64] But the sex of the speaker is pointedly established by the feminine inflexions of the first two lines, which cannot be explained away without doing violence to the poem (see Textual Notes). Another group of critics, influenced by the narrator's dwelling place in an "earth-cave" (*eorðscræf*, lines 28 and 36; *eorðsele*, line 29), have thought she was a dead person.[65] The woman's isolation, though, is the product of her husband's alienation (lines 25b–26; see notes) and his kin's plotting (lines 11–12), the result of which is a separation in this world (*þæt wit gewidost in woruldrice/lifdon laðlicost*, lines 13–14a) and the overturning of vows of fidelity to the death (lines 21b–25a). Some readers believe that the grove dwelling under an oak-tree among *bitre burgtunas*, "bitter enclosures" (line 31), was formerly the site of heathen worship,[66] and it has even been suggested that the speaker is not a woman at all but a cast-off heathen deity addressing her converted priest.[67] It is very likely that the location was intended to evoke superstitious associations or lingering memories of heathen practices. The sacred places of early European peoples were often groves, especially oak groves.[68] But unless we read the unlikely form *herheard* meaning "temple-dwelling" in line 15 (see note), there is no explicit reference to paganism in the poem.

If it is accepted that the narrator of *The Wife's Lament* is a living woman lamenting her confinement in the wilderness and her separation from a living husband,[69] the underlying situation is established, but much in the poem remains uncertain. It is tempting to reconstruct the events which lie behind the banished wife's unhappy plight. Some see a feud among the husband's kin which drove him into exile, whereupon his wife went into exile too, only to be banished to the earth-cave by her husband – or someone else, either from hostility or for her own protection.[70] A further theory holds that the villain of the piece is the "young man" of line 42, who had designs on the wife in her husband's absence, and meeting with no success falsely accused her to her husband of adultery, so that she was banished to the cave.[71] All of this is very speculative.

In order to make sense of the poem at all one is forced to make certain assumptions, to accept certain possibilities and reject others. In general, I have tried to minimize the narrative background, and have preferred readings which are well established for Old English vocabulary and do not require emendation. Thus, I exclude a third person from the poem, and I regard it as a hypothesis only – one of two alternatives postulated by the wife (lines 45b–47a) – that the husband is in enforced exile. On the basis of normal sequence, I find a pluperfect sense questionable for *ongunnon* (line 11), which is often treated as referring back to an earlier stage in the narrative. My understanding of the relations between husband and wife hinges on reading *her heard* (line 15), where I take *heard* as the adjective "cruel" applied to the husband, and on translating *mines felaleofan fæhðu* (line 26) as "the enmity of my very dear one." The more favourable view of the husband, initiated by W.W. Lawrence (1907–8, pp. 388–89), and advanced by many scholars, including Leslie (Introduction, pp. 6–7), involves a treatment of the phrasing in these lines which I find hard to justify (see Textual Notes). The same is true of Lawrence's "mindful of death" as a translation of *morþor hycgend[n]e* (line 20; see notes on lines 19–21a).

After a conventional opening of the "elegiac" type (lines 1–5), the narrator of the poem declares that her present troubles began when her husband went abroad (lines 6–7a) – for unspecified reasons. She set off to seek *folgað*, a place in someone's household (see note on lines 9–10) because she was left friendless and forlorn, a *wineleas wræcca*. The man's kin began to plot to keep husband and wife as far apart as possible (lines 11–14a) – again, for unspecified reasons. It is possible that the husband's original departure was brought about by this plotting, but the poem's arrangement suggests that the *dyrne gepoht* of the kinsmen is a later thing (see note on lines 11–12). The husband then cruelly commands his wife to be seized (line 15). This command may be conveyed from a distance, since there is no mention of his return. No one intercedes on his wife's behalf because she has "few friends in this country" (line 16) – either her husband's territory or somewhere she has unsuccessfully sought protection. She has the unhappy experience of finding the man who had seemed so compatible to her hiding his thoughts under a cheerful de-meanour and contemplating some dark crime (lines 18–21a; see notes). It is not clear whether she actually sees him at this time or merely recollects and imagines, in her awareness of his cruelty. She laments that their love and their vows are broken (lines 21b–25a); she must endure far and wide the enmity of her beloved (lines 25b–26). She is commanded to dwell in a cave in the woods, a dismal place, where, afflicted with "longing," she compares her own wretched state with the happier lot of lovers who are united (lines 27–41). Here she reflects that the "young man" – her hus-band, not a third party – must have a hard heart and trouble under his cheerful demeanour (lines 42–45a), whether he enjoys good fortune (lines 45b–46a) or ill (lines 46b–50a). The latter possibility she elaborates on, imagining for her husband a situation reminiscent of her own (lines 47b–52a). The poem ends with a cry that speaks for all unhappy lovers: "Woe to him who must with longing wait for his dear one!"

The structural divisions of the poem are less clearly defined than they are in some of the elegies, notably *The Wanderer, The Seafarer,* and *The Riming Poem,* where we have two contrasting halves: personal and general, or past and present, the second section leading to a homiletic and escha-tological close. *The Wife's Lament* divides into three major sections rather than two, and its preoccupations are different, but the same kind of movement is detectable. The first four or five lines introduce the poem; line 5, which speaks of a life of suffering, could be regarded either as the end of the introduction or the beginning of the narration. This section consists of a series of events which may be, but are not undoubtedly, in chronological sequence. At line 29 there is a shift from narrative to de-scription and reflection, though this line is closely linked to the preceding. Here the speaker elaborates on her present situation. This second major section ends at line 41. She then turns her attention to her husband (or, as some think, to general observation), and for the rest of the poem speaks in the third person. The poem's closing sentence (lines 52b–53) is im-passioned in tone but gnomic in format. The pattern of the poem, then, moving forward in time and outward from the self, can be seen to resemble that in the three elegies mentioned above.[72] Also, both introduction and conclusion draw on established formulas and closely resemble *The Seafarer* and *The Wanderer*, respectively, in these features (see notes on these lines).

Each of the events related in lines 6 to 28 is presented as the cause of suffering. Because it is the effect that is emphasized, the relationship of these events to one another in time is not entirely clear. The adverb *ærest* (line 6) at least makes it certain that the departure of the husband (*min hlaford*) was the beginning of a series of woes. The word *ða* (lines 9 and 18) can be either adverb or conjunction, and embraces the meanings "after" and "at the same time," as well as allowing a sense of causality. Conjunctive order is possible in line 9 and evident in line 18 (see notes), giving us the meaning "after" shading into "because." "Then" (i.e. after the husband's departure) is the most natural translation of the first *ða*, but "when" cannot be excluded. The latter translation would make the plotting of the kin definitely subsequent to the wife's search for *folgað*, protection in someone's household. Line 15, which I understand as the husband's order to have his wife seized, looks like the next link in the chain of events. His action in doing this made his wife aware of a previously unknown aspect of his character and made her heart sad. Lines 27–28 form the last link in the chain and bring us up to the present situation: "(Finally,) I was commanded to dwell in this earth-cave."

Another difficulty which the modern reader encounters is that the poem's utterances bear relationships to each other which are not always adequately expressed by modern punctuation. A temporal and causal relationship is present in *forþon* line 17, and possibly in *ða* line 9, both to what precedes and to what follows. In the second and third major sections of the poem, where the mode is reflective, extended periods occur whose inner structure is quite complex (lines 33b–41 and 42–52a). It is possible to subdivide them, for example after line 36 and line 45a, but to do so reduces their impressive cumulative effect. In the second period, lines 45b–47a virtually depend on both the preceding and the following statements (see note on lines 47b–52a).

Though *The Wife's Lament* displays some important structural affinities with *The Wanderer* and *The Seafarer*, its subject links it with the love poems: *Wulf and Eadwacer* and *The Husband's Message*. In fact, many scholars have found the resemblances to the latter poem more than accidental and have seen *The Husband's Message*, which looks forward to the reunion of a separated couple, as a sequel to *The Wife's Lament*. For reasons explained more fully in the section on that poem (pp. 58–59), I find such a connection very unlikely: the two pieces are totally different in tone and mode, and the shared motifs are probably traditional (see also note on

Wife 21b–23a). But the three love poems do form a subgroup among the elegies, and in the extant corpus of Old English poetry their subject is unusual. This is especially true of the two poems with female narrators, which seem to belong to a category of "women's songs" better known to us from somewhat later medieval literature, Latin and vernacular.[73] It has been suggested that such songs derive from a popular rather than an aristocratic background, and certainly *Wulf and Eadwacer* is metrically atypical. However, apart from the irregular line 24, the poetics of *The Wife's Lament* are very much in the mainstream of Old English tradition. In its impassioned intimacy, though, the poem is distinctive, and very close to *Wulf and Eadwacer*; in both, a suffering woman laments her confinement and her separation from the man she loves. Since the details and the language of the two poems differ, there is little reason to posit a more direct connection between them.

In the past, many scholars believed that *The Wife's Lament* arose from some oral story known to the contemporary audience, and attempts were made to identify a saga background for the poem, sometimes in conjunction with *The Husband's Message* (see p. 59, below), sometimes independently. Theories of the second type usually relate *The Wife's Lament* to later medieval tales of wronged wives. Thus, Grein (*Bibliothek* 1:363) suggested the story of Genoveva (who was obliged to live in hiding in a cave after being falsely accused of adultery);[74] Svetislav Stefanovíc (1909, 428–31) favoured Crescentia, who, as a result of the same accusation, was sent to the woods to die; Edith Rickert (1904–5, 365–76) proposed the tale of Constance in the version attached to the wife of Offa I, who was banished after an accusation of witchcraft. Though the possibility of a background in oral saga cannot be denied, there is no specific mention of either adultery or witchcraft in the poem. Also, the characters are unnamed, which suggests the poet did not wish to particularize.

More recent scholarship has not much concerned itself with the question of a saga background. But many different contexts for understanding the poem have been proposed. As noted by Alain Renoir (1975), *The Wife's Lament* can be related to "a Germanic tradition of suffering women," including Guthrun (see my Appendix, pp. 288–303, below), Hildebrand's wife in the *Hildebrandslied*, Brynhild in *Helreið Brynhildar*, Beadohild in *Deor* and *Vǫlundarkviða*, as well as Wealhtheow, Freawaru, and Hildeburh in *Beowulf*. A background in folktale has also been posited, relating the poem to the folktale type in which a woman marries a supernatural being and loses him by breaking a taboo (Fitzgerald 1963). Although there is nothing overtly homiletic in the poem, many critics place it in a Christian context. Renoir suggests it may have conveyed the Christian message that

God puts down the mighty (1977b). Again, it has been proposed that the poem relates to the test of female consort sometimes undergone by monastics (Dunleavy 1956), and that it arises from the same background as the letters written to Boniface by nuns (Schaefer 1986). One or two scholars, linking the poem with *The Husband's Message*, have found in it a developed allegory representing the love between Christ and his Bride, the Church (see pp. 59–60, below).

Whatever framework we find for interpreting *The Wife's Lament*, it remains something of an enigma. The speaker's feelings, not the events of her life, nor even in any exact sense her physical surroundings, are the focus, and this makes the poem both highly evocative and at the same time tantalizingly laconic and elliptical. Probably the poet intended to mystify; the woman's circumstances are disturbing largely because they are strange and undefined. Although not a riddle, *The Wife's Lament*, like *Wulf and Eadwacer*, has a riddle-like allusiveness and indirection. Much of the poem's language refers not to action but to attitude, or the environment which creates and symbolizes it: the repeated word *geomor*, "sad" (lines 1, 17, 19, 42); the wife's love for her husband juxtaposed with his hard-heartedness (lines 18–21a and 26) or with his suffering (lines 49–51a); the oppressive hills and valleys which hem the speaker in (lines 30–32a); the earth-cave mentioned three times and always alliterating (lines 28–29 and 36); the phrases which express "utter longing" (*eal ... oflongad*, line 29; *ealles þæs longaþes*, line 41); the sense of weariness and alienation concentrated in line 29. Words for "longing," which combines desire, suffering, and anxiety (see note on *Sea* 47a) form a leitmotiv, appearing in lines 14, 29, 41, and finally in line 53, where *langoþ* is linked with *leof* in the poem's summation. The banished wife longs for her loved one, and the intensity of her suffering is vivid, but its ultimate causes remain obscure.

RESIGNATION

Critical interest in *Resignation* has grown in recent years, as different approaches to it have been developed. Having affinities with two separate genres, the penitential prayer and the exilic lament, the poem poses certain problems. The failure to reach an editorial consensus on an appropriate title reflects this. Thus, in the nineteenth century, Thorpe called it "A Supplication," while Grein included it, untitled, in his section of "Hymnen und Gebete." Sieper entitled it "Klage eines Vertriebenen." Krapp-Dobbie, drawing on the sentiment of the last two lines, name it "Resignation," now its conventional title. Alois Brandl's "Gebet des Vertriebenen" (1908) and Mackie's "The Exile's Prayer" allude to both of the poem's aspects.

The issue of the poem's integrity has been discussed above (pp. 28–29), and the objections raised to line 69 (providing evidence for a missing folio) are discussed in the Textual Notes. Scholars have long been aware that *Resignation* contains two kinds of subject matter which are, to a certain extent, separable. Interestingly, when Levin Schücking chose to include the poem in his anthology (*Kleines ags Dichterbuch*, 1919), he selected the second part only, from line 78b on, although his introduction makes clear that he regarded this piece as only a portion of the whole. He comments that "der busspsalmartige Beginn" moves into a personal lament in the manner of "der elegischen Lyrik" (p. 21). More recently, A.A. Prins (1964) thought that the part of the poem beginning at line 84 did not properly belong with what preceded it (see pp. 27–28, above). It will be noticed that the divisions perceived by Schücking (after line 78a) and Prins (after line 83) are different from that detected by Bliss and Frantzen (after line 69). In fact, the poem moves rather gradually from the prayer mode to the narrative mode, and formulaic introductions characteristic of the latter occur at lines 83b, 89b, and 96b. A brief return to the prayer mode takes place at lines 108b–111a, where the speaker expresses his desire for the heavenly *bot* in terms reminiscent of lines 20b–21.

Like *The Seafarer*, *Resignation* speaks of a voyage (lines 97b–104), although in this case the journey is never realized because the narrator is too poor to buy a passage. Doubtless influenced by his symbolic interpretation of *The Seafarer* (see p. 37, above), although he does not specifically make a connection, Schücking observes that the motif of the voyage in *Resignation* should be understood symbolically (p. 22), and this view is adopted by Krapp-Dobbie, who state that "The poem deals not with an actual exile from wordly prosperity, but with spiritual dejection, and the mention of the sea-journey ... is evidently to be taken symbolically" (p. lx). Seen in this way, the voyage represents the journey of the soul, for which the speaker longs and is preparing, but for which he feels ill equipped. He never actually tells us what his destination is, but if the journey is symbolic it is that mentioned earlier, in lines 41–42a, *Nu ic fundige to þe, / fæder moncynnes, / of þisse worulde*. As Marie Nelson explains, the journey over the ocean is thus "the voyage of the soul after death," "a voyage to the heavenly *patria*."[75]

Some forty years ago, E.G. Stanley proposed a somewhat different interpretation of the poem, and applied to it what might be called the "realistic" reading of *The Seafarer*, whereby the voyage is undertaken in a perfectly literal sense as a *peregrinatio pro amore Dei* (see p. 37, above; and Stanley 1955). As Bliss and Frantzen point out (1976, 402), there are some inconsistencies involved in this type of interpretation. In particular, it seems strange that the speaker should wish to go into penitential exile if he is an exile already. For this reason they believe that he is not, although lines 88b–89a appear to indicate this (see Textual Notes). In my article *"Resignation*: Exile's Lament or Penitent's Prayer?"* (Klinck 1987b), I have suggested that understanding the voyage symbolically as the death journey, and literally as a voyage out of exile and back home, obviates these inconsistencies and brings the second part of the poem into line with the first. The speaker's poverty (line 101) and loneliness (lines 102 and 106b–8a) are then the natural consequences of his exile plight. Differences in tone between the two parts of the poem remain: the first emphasizes the narrator's awareness of God's grace (lines 19, 33–34a, 51a, 66b–68) and his own sin (25b–26a, 27b–28a, 34b–36a, 51b–52a, 64b–65a); the second dwells upon his hardships and miseries (81b–82a, 85b–87, 111b–13). But we are told that he is suffering a just punishment (78b–81a).

Structurally, *Resignation* employs a two-part framework, like *The Wanderer*, *The Seafarer*, and *The Riming Poem*, though the transition between the two parts is more gradual. In using the motif of the voyage as a symbol of the soul's quest, the poem exemplifies the same pattern as *The Seafarer*, but in reverse: here, the spiritual meditation precedes the image in which it finds concrete expression. Critics have tended to find the lament section more evocative than the prayer which precedes it. Schücking (1919) describes it as "psychologisch von hohem Reize" but believes it can only be understood fully with reference to a specific character in some well-known narrative (p. 21). Bliss and Frantzen perceive *Resignation B*, rather modernistically, as a psychological study in self-pity which is unique in Old English (pp. 400–402). They reject the usual comparisons with *The Wanderer* and *The Seafarer*. Undeniably, *Resignation* has some defects. The first part is very repetitive, and the second fails to develop its suggestive images of the longed-for boat and the flourishing tree that counterpoint the speaker's misery; the poem's ending, which merely admonishes the unfortunate to make the best of a bad job, is a let-down. But, whatever the poem's inadequacies, it benefits from being read as a unified whole, an interesting, though not entirely successful, attempt to integrate two different poetic forms: the prayer of a penitent and the lament of an exile.

THE HUSBAND'S MESSAGE

In the main, *The Husband's Message* is a straightforward poem, neither arcane nor philosophical, but a combination of accidents makes it quite a puzzle for the modern reader. We cannot be sure where the poem begins, what has been lost in the damaged passages, who the speaker is, or exactly what the poet intended by the runes. The resemblance of the poem's opening, "Now I want to tell you privately about this species of wood," to the preceding riddle, which describes an object designed to convey "a message for us two alone" (line 15), has given rise to considerable speculation as to whether this piece is a genuine riddle or actually the opening of the lyric which follows it. As explained above (p. 27), and in the notes on *Ic wæs be Sonde* (*Riddle 60*), I find the greater weight of evidence in favour of separating the two rather than treating them as a single poem, and would attribute their juxtaposition to a compiler's noticing their similarity. Since there is a significant body of counter-opinion, I have included the text of *Ic wæs be Sonde* along with *The Husband's Message*.

The problem is further complicated by the damaged state of the text. The poem consists of a message from a prince (*þeoden*, line 29) who, after being driven away from his own people (lines 19b–20a), has made a new life for himself (lines 44b–47; K-D 43b–46), and now summons his lady, a prince's daughter (line 48; K-D 47), to whom he was betrothed long ago (lines 15b–16 and 54, K-D 53) to join him abroad (lines 26–8). Lines 2–8a describes the history of the messenger who is bringing this summons. Unfortunately, this passage coincides with a large burn-hole in the manuscript, and so much has been lost that it is impossible to be sure whether the messenger, also the poem's narrator, who has often travelled over the sea (lines 6–8a) and has now come in a ship (lines 8b–9a) is a human emissary or the personified rune-stave ("this wood [which the prince] engraved," line 13), which conveys to the lady a guarantee of her lord's fidelity (lines 50–4; K-D 49–53).

I have attempted no large reconstructions of the damaged passages (lines 2ff. and 33ff.) myself, but have cited some representative ones – as suggested by the standard editions, and also by John Pope in his palaeographical article (1978, 42–63). In describing the manuscript indications where the text is missing, I have tried not to be influenced by previous opinions. Of course, this is a very tricky business, when one is attempting to define the exact shape of a fragmentary letter and to estimate how many letters would have fitted into a given space. In line 3, I find Pope's *iw* reading, based on the appearance of the facsimile, unconfirmed by the manuscript itself, while in line 37 both the manuscript and the British Library Transcript confirm an *-ed* before *elþeode*, and not the *n* or *r* seen by Leslie. In line 30, the erasure has space for about three letters, and my restoration *ofer* supposes that the word was incorrectly written. None of the suggestions made for the missing word after *yþa* in line 42 (K-D 41) seems to me to fit the manuscript traces exactly. As for the erased letter in *ge–yre* (line 50; K-D 49), I restore *gehyre*, but I believe the marks on the parchment suggest that the scribe actually wrote *genyre* – in error.

The vexed question of the narrator's identity is to some extent bound up with that of the poem's beginning. Those who regard the narrator as a rune-stave, a view which has recently been associated with Pope's restoration *Iw mec ælde hataδ* ("'Yew' men call me") in line 3 (1978, 59), usually treat *Ic wæs be Sonde* as a part of *The Husband's Message*.[76] A non-human speaker would be unique among the elegies, but this poem, which is not elegiac in the usual sense of the word, is rather distinctive in the group anyway; also, the use of the runic cryptogram (lines 50–51; K-D 49–50) resembles the enigmatism of the Riddles, in which personification of an object is the rule. Again, *Wulf and Eadwacer* is very much like a riddle and *The Wife's Lament* is enigmatic, so there is a certain overlap in technique between the genres.

Whether the narrator is human or non-human, *The Husband's Message* is a love-lyric of a rather formal kind. It is designed to evoke, not the feelings of the speaker, but those of the lord towards his lady: his fidelity, his confidence in the strength of the vows they made together, his urgent desire for her, all mediated by the messenger's ceremonious deference. It is not actually clear from the poem whether the pair are married – as the conventional modern title implies – or only betrothed. Lines 15b–19a, which speak of vows often repeated during an earlier life together, could apply to either situation. *The Lover's Message*, Mackie's name for the poem, would be an equally suitable title.

Because of the resemblance between the situation in this poem and that in *The Wife's Lament*, where also a woman is separated from her husband, some scholars are inclined to link the two. The poems introduce the speaker and the subject in a similar way (see notes on *Husb* 1 and 2); in both works the husband departs over the waves (*Wife* 6–7a; *Husb* 41–44a; K-D 40–43a); both speak of *fæhδu/fæhþo* (*Wife* 26; *Husb* 19, resp.); in both reference is made to repeated vows of loyalty made in the past (*Wife* 21b–23a; *Husb* 15b–16 and 54; K-D 53). Thus, it has been argued that the poems form "a diptych of elegy and consolation" (Howlett 1978, 7). But the similarity derives from a circumstance common in heroic life and poetry, and from a conventional structure and diction (see p. 11, above, and Part 3, pp. 226–30, below). The divergences between the two poems in mode and content are major. In its evocation of the speaker's misery, *The Wife's Lament* conveys an intensely personal emotion quite different from anything in *The Husband's Message*. The present poem is not an impassioned outcry, but a stately and measured address. The narrator of *The Wife's Lament,* in her loneliness, thinks of lovers who share their bed (*Wife* 33b–34), while the lord in *The Husband's Message* declares through his intermediary his greatest happiness will be that he and his wife should distribute treasure together (*Husb* 30–35a). In *The Wife's Lament* the husband, either directly or through a representative, has banished his wife to the woods, whereas in *The Husband's Message* he has left her involuntarily and remained committed to her. These discrepancies make it extremely unlikely that the two poems were intended to be taken together, or that they refer to the same story, about two lovers who experience a period of separation (*Wife*), to be united at last (*Husb*).

The proponents of a shared narrative background believe the poems arise from some tale which would have been common knowledge among their contemporary audience. The idea was first suggested by Christian Grein (1880, 10) and developed by Moritz Trautmann (1894, 222–25). Others have subsequently attempted to identify the story. Rudolf Imelmann related both poems to his lost "Odoaker-Dichtung" (1907a, esp. 38); see note on *Wulf* 16a. A.C. Bouman proposed the Sigurd legend, the wife being Guthrun (1962, 41–91). *The Husband's Message* has also been related separately to a legendary background. W.H. Schofield suggested that perhaps we have here an early version of the tale told by Marie de France in her lay [*Chevrefoil*], where Tristan carves a message on a piece of wood and leaves it for Isolt (1906, 201–2). See p. 53 above, for similar suggestions about *The Wife's Lament.*

It is possible that some narrative, known to the Old English poets' contemporaries, lies behind each poem, but since there is no way of establishing with any probability what it might be, speculation in this direction is unhelpful. I find it significant that neither *The Husband's Message* nor *The Wife's Lament* uses names drawn from legend – unlike *Deor.* This makes it highly probable that in these poems, as in most of the other elegies, a situation and characters are created strictly for the purposes of the poem, though with a stronger dramatic element in the love poems than in the didactic elegies. See also p. 49, on *Wulf and Eadwacer.*

A different kind of background is supposed by those scholars who have read the poems as religious allegory. M.J. Swanton sees behind both the relationship between Christ and his Bride the Church, which in *The Wife's Lament* "yearns for the re-establishment of a previous union"; in *The Husband's Message* Christ responds by reaffirming their eternal pledge of faith (1964, esp. 289–90). W.F. Bolton, relating both poems to the exegesis of bride and bridegroom in the Song of Songs, suggests that the two are "symmetrical halves of a single poem" (1969, esp. 348–50). R.E. Kaske (1967) and Margaret Goldsmith (1975) treat *The Husband's Message* (including *Ic wæs be Sonde*) separately as Christian allegory using this kind of symbolism (see notes on *Ic wæs be Sonde* and *Husb* 50a).

The allegorical readings are subject to the same objection as those which relate the poems to Germanic legend: that we really have very little to go on in the text. While some of the elegies – *The Wanderer, The Seafarer, The Riming Poem, Resignation* – have an overt homiletic purpose, the love poems do not. This makes it much harder to justify finding a religious symbolism behind the imagery. In *The Seafarer* and *Resignation* it is natural to find this symbolism because the journey motif is explicitly given a spiritual force (*Sea* 63–66a; *Res* 72–74a). But in *The Husband's Message* and *The Wife's Lament* nothing specifically invites us to think in religious terms.

Of all the problems confronting the modern reader, the interpretation of the runic message has prompted the most diverse and the most ingenious solutions. As I explain in the Textual Notes, the most convincing method is to regard the runic characters as words – the rune-names, not letters. Treating the runes as the letters of the lord's name seems reasonable, but there is no obvious name the letters would render – in any order, and some of the suggestions made in the past now seem fairly preposterous. Ernst Kock's theory (1921, 122–23) that we have here the elemental oath-guarantors – heaven, earth, and man – is the one, of many, that has been the most widely adopted. It involves regarding *sigelrad*, "sun-path," as a kenning, and *earwynn*, "earth-joy," as a periphrasis (for "earth"), but remains the explanation that fits in the most neatly and does the least violence to the runes and their context.

As a poem, *The Husband's Message* is perhaps less interesting, and certainly less complex than *The Wife's Lament* and *Wulf and Eadwacer*. But it does speak feelingly of the bond between the two lovers, which has endured time and distance. Although the poem's language is formal, the energy of the lord's appeal makes itself felt in the eager imperatives *ne læt, ongin, onsite* of lines 24–27. The firm reassurance of the poem's refrain-like close is also conveyed more subtly by the confident indicative *findest* in the clauses of indirect statement and purpose in lines 12 and 28 (see Textual Notes).[77] And the poem has some haunting details: the sad-voiced cuckoo (which also appears in *The Seafarer*) summoning to the voyage (line 23), the fugitive compelled by necessity to push his boat out into the sea (line 41; K-D 40). While it lacks the imaginative range of some of the other elegies, *The Husband's Message* is an accomplished poem. Perhaps calling it an "elegy" is misleading, but in structure and motifs it clearly belongs within this group, although it differs markedly from the others in its optimistic tone.

THE RUIN

In many ways *The Ruin* appears the easiest of the elegies, lacking the ambiguities of *The Wife's Lament* and *Wulf and Eadwacer*, the puzzles of *The Husband's Message*, the allusions of *Deor*, and the moral complexities of the didactic poems. Yet *The Ruin* has its problems too. Being the last of the elegies in the Exeter Book, it has suffered the most from the burning, and substantial portions of the text are irretrievably damaged, so that the total effect of the poem is lost to us. Perhaps the missing sections would have provided some more clues to guide us in interpreting the poem and deciding whether it is description merely, as it seems to be on the surface, or whether a more profound symbolism is to be found in the ruined city, its splendour gone. As far as we can see, the overall pattern consists of an alternating movement between past and present, the poet dwelling increasingly on the past,[78] until, in the second half of the poem, his attention remains fixed there. This shifting movement culminates in the impressive period beginning at line 31b, which piles phrase on phrase up to the climactic and comprehensive *on þas beorhtan burg bradan rices* (line 37). Thereafter the syntax becomes simpler and the sentences shorter, as the focus narrows to a contemplation of the marvellous baths.

The *Ruin* poet creates the impression of describing an actual scene, present to the eye of the narrator. Although there is no ethopoeic evocation of a character, as in the other elegies, the sense of an onlooker, a real eyewitness, is strong. It is conveyed by the repetition of the demonstrative "this" (lines 1, 9, 29, 30, 37) as well as by the visual details, unusually specific for Old English poetry (*ræghar ond readfah*, "hoary with lichen and stained with red," line 10; *gebond / weall walanwirum*, "bound the wall together with strips of wire," lines 19–20; *þæs teaforgeapa tigelum sceadeð*, "this red arch is coming away from its tiles," line 30). The poet tries to render in his traditional language features of an unfamiliar architecture, and this very precision sometimes makes interpretation difficult. Certainly, the poem reads like a description of an actual site. In the middle of the nineteenth century, Heinrich Leo (1865) and John Earle (1870–73) independently came to the same conclusion: that the subject of *The Ruin* was Roman Bath. The stone structures, with their domes and arches and hot baths, must be Roman – though it has been pointed out that Anglo-Saxon ruins could be imposing too, [79] – and Bath, with its red stonework, its great circular pool (*hringmere*, line 45), and especially its hot springs, fits the picture; other sites have been proposed, less convincingly.[80] The abandoned Roman cities and forts which dotted the landscape must have made a powerful impression on the Anglo-Saxon mind, and they have found a place in the common stock of poetic formulas and themes. Close resemblances to *The Ruin* appear in the opening of *Maxims II*: *Ceastra beoð feorran gesyne,* / *orðanc enta geweorc, þa þe on þysse eorðan syndon,* / *wrætlic weallstana geweorc* (lines 1b–3a; cf. *Ruin* 1–2 and 16).

Although the poet was probably inspired by a particular, Roman, scene, in the typical manner of Old English verse he universalizes and Germanicizes it, and his evocation of feasts and battles long ago is much like that in other poems, including *The Wanderer*. Whether he regarded the vanished glories of the fallen city with nostalgia only or with criticism too is an open question. It has been suggested that on the moral level the city is not Bath but Babylon, as that city appears in the Apocalypse of St John (Keenan 1966). In the text as it now stands there is no explicit indication that this moral is to be drawn. *Wlonc ond wingal*, "proud and flushed with wine" (line 34) is the kind of phrase that the Anglo-Saxon homilist would use to condemn the luxurious worldling; in *The Seafarer* (line 29) it is associated with thoughtlessness and ignorance, at least. Here in *The Ruin*, however, there is nothing else to indicate that the *beorn monig* (line 32) to whom it is applied may be essentially sinful. There are one or two other phrases which may have evoked by association the idea of the wrath of God. The *woldagas*, "times of pestilence" (line 25) may have suggested the plagues inflicted on Egypt in Exodus 7–11 and on the sinful world in Apocalypse 9. Some of the language used to describe the collapse of the city resembles that in Cynewulf's account of the destruction of the world by fire in *Christ II*: *Wongas hreosað,* / *burgstede berstað* (lines 810b–11a; cf. *Ruin* 2 and 31). In *The Wanderer* the connection between ruins and the end of the world is quite clear: a wise man, when he looks at the windswept walls, will think how dreadful it will be when all the world is laid waste (lines 73–77). Both poems, and also *Maxims II*, describe the ruins as *enta geweorc* (*Wan* 87, *Ruin* 2), and the same term denotes the hilt of the magic sword in *Beowulf* (*enta ærgeweorc*, line 1679), on which is engraved the destruction of the giants in the Flood. An *enta geweorc* would be perceived not just as the marvellous work of those with superhuman powers, but also as the product of the pagan past. Again, *The Ruin* may be indebted to works like Gildas's *De excidio et conquestu Britanniae* (ca. 540), in which the destruction of a civilization is God's punishment for sin, as well as to devout but less condemnatory works in the *de excidio* tradition such as Venantius Fortunatus's *De excidio Thoringiae* (569–70) and Alcuin's *De clade Lindisfarnensis monasterii* (793).[81] The fate of the city in *The Ruin* is an exemplification of the theme *sic transit gloria mundi*. Beyond that, there are hints of a further message, but the moral stays at the level of overtone and suggestion.

Unlike the pattern in *The Wanderer* and *The Seafarer*, the movement towards the close of *The Ruin* is not eschatological but retrospective. Whereas the poet begins with a confrontation of the ruined wall, he turns with increasing frequency to a progressively more vital past, until, after line 32a, he ceases to mention present decay, and loses himself in admiration of the city as it once was. It remains true that the glory of this world passes away, but in *The Ruin*, unlike the other two poems, the evocation of that glory takes pride of place. It is on this note that the poem ends, so far as we can tell from a badly damaged text, as the poet wonders at the splendid amenities of the city and its baths. The effect is to de-emphasize the elegiac theme and bring another theme to the fore: the triumph of the human imagination.

NOTES

1 The material in the first section of Part 1 is largely derived from the beginning of my article "The OE Elegy as a Genre." See Klinck 1984, 129–30.

2 Probably the first person to use this terminology is W.D. Conybeare, in 1826, who adds *The Wife's Lament* (he calls it "The Exile's Complaint" and thinks it the utterance of a man) to the OE materials assembled by his brother. Conybeare describes this poem, along with the *Metres of Boethius*, as rare examples of "compositions of an elegiac character" in OE. See *Illustrations of A-S Poetry*, p. 244.

3 I quote from Herbert Pilch (1964, 211), who gives a very detailed composite account of the genre's structure and imagery.

4 Unless otherwise indicated, citations of these poems refer to my own texts, citations of all other OE poems to *ASPR*. Where my own lineation differs, Krapp-Dobbie's *ASPR* line numbers are included in parentheses.

5 Interestingly, many ἐλεγεῖα, including all of the earliest ones, were not laments. A.E. Harvey (1955) suggests that the elegiac form may have originated in a lament – as the ancients claimed it did – providing that this was of a gnomic and consolatory rather than an impassioned kind (p. 171). I discuss the classical idea of elegy more fully in Part 3.

6 Following Alan Bliss and Allen J. Frantzen (1976). They divide the text at the end of fol. 118b (after *wære*, line 69), supposing a missing folio. Lars Malmberg's edition of the poem (1979) follows Bliss-Frantzen.

7 See Eliason 1966.

8 This remains the prevailing view, but there is a heavy weight of counter-

opinion. Allegorical interpretations of *Wife* and *Husb* have been put forward by M.J. Swanton (1964), R.E. Kaske (1967), et al. The theory that the narrator of *Wife* was a man who had lost his lord was last proposed by Jerome Mandel (1987, 152–55). Though no longer regarded as "The First Riddle," *Wulf* continues to perplex, and has been interpreted as a mother's, instead of a mistress's, lament. See, most recently, Suzuki 1987. The various interpretations to which the poems have given rise are considered more fully below.

9 Timmer finds only *Wulf* and *Wife* to be elegies "pure and simple" (pp. 35–36). The fairly recent *OE Elegies* ed. Green (1983), an anthology of essays by various hands, treats all of the works incorporated in my own study except *Rim*. That poem is included in the elegiac group by its most recent editor, O.D. Macrae-Gibson (1983); see his edition, p. 1.

10 A palaeographical investigation of the manuscript has recently been undertaken by Patrick Conner (1986), who divides it into three booklets on the basis of such features as type of ruling, formation of *s* and *y*, treatment of initial capitals, and distribution of dry-point drawings.

11 See Amos 1980, esp. 30–49, 101–2, 112–28, and 167–70.

12 Wenisch 1979. See *Index zu den ae Wörtern* for the relevant sections.

13 Cecilia Hotchner (1939) asserts that there are only three nW-S characteristics in the poem (*æ* in *ældo*, line 6; *eo* in *undereotone* and *forweorone*, lines 6–7; *ē* in *hwætrēd*, line 19), and that these forms are "probably Kentish, or less plausibly, Mercian"(p. 86). The occurrence of *ĕ* for *ǣ*, accompanied by *æ* for *e* (*þæs*, *burgræced*) resulting from confusion between the two sounds, could reflect the Kentish *ǣ* > *ĕ* change. This would mean either a relatively late date for the poem, or an intermediate copying stage. On the *ǣ* > *ĕ* change, see Campbell *Grammar*, §§ 288–92.

14 In referring to these two constructions, I exclude adj. + noun preceded by the demonstrative *þes*, and also adjectives in the comparative, because these are always declined weak.

15 On the archaeological evidence for an early date, see Leslie *Three OE Elegies*, pp. 26–28. Leslie also discusses the dialect features of the poem and concludes it is probably Mercian (pp. 31–34). However, he suggests that *Wife* and *Husb* have the same dialectal provenance, whereas I find that the dialectal forms in *Ruin* are much more distinctive. Leslie assigns an eighth-century date to all three poems, and believes that *Ruin* precedes the middle of that century (pp. 34–36).

16 E.G. Stanley (1984, 450–52) argues that these are not Kentish spellings, but forms of the word *wenn*, "excrescence". See also Textual Notes.

17 Cf. Macrae-Gibson: "there are no diphthongal forms where metre requires two syllables, and weak adjectives occur only after demonstratives" (edition, p. 2).

18 This test, involving contraction after loss of intervocalic *j*, is useful because the word cannot be proved to occur in dissyllabic form in the datable late texts. However, it is rejected by Edwin Duncan (1986), who argues that the syllabicity of *frea* was dependent on its syntactic context and was not affected by chronological factors (see esp. pp. 93–95). Duncan's statement that *"frea* was monosyllabic unless it occurred as the second element of a compound or as a separate word following a possessive pronoun" (p. 101) is, as he admits, a generalization which does not cover all cases, though it does trace an interesting tendency. I would question Duncan's treatment of *frea* in *Maldon* 16 and 184 and in *Res* 22 as necessarily dissyllabic, and of *sip-frean* (sic) in *Wife* 33 as a compound (see pp. 97 and 98–99, resp.). R.D. Fulk rejects the test on the argument that *frea* derives not from a *j*-stem but from a *w*-stem **frawan-* (1990, 13–16).

19 Malmberg, who scans "a fair number" of the verses with one stress only, sees this as a feature suggesting a late date for *Res A* (edition, pp. 4–5); he finds a lower proportion of light verses in *Res B*, and, accordingly, thinks it earlier (p. 7). I regard the metrical features of the two parts as similar.

20 Thomas Bestul (1977) suggests that *Resignation* was inspired by "the great interest in personal confessional prayer stimulated by the Benedictine reform of the tenth century." However, such an inspiration for the poem would push the date of composition right up to the time of copying the manuscript itself.

21 Kemp Malone, who does not suggest an Alfredian connection, thinks ca. 900 a possible date; he thinks it likely that the poem was originally Anglian, but does not exclude the possibility of composition in West Saxon. See his first edition of the poem (Malone 1933, p. 22; unchanged in the 5th ed., Malone 1977). The relationship of Boethius to *Deor* and other OE elegies is considered in Part 3, pp. 233–34, below.

22 The resemblance was first pointed out by Eduard Sievers, in his *Altgermanische Metrik* (1893, § 98).

23 The test has been criticized as unreliable because reconstructed dissyllabic forms appear in late texts. In fact, occurrences of these forms are very rare: one in the poetry (*þone heahan dæg, Gloria I*, 27) and four elsewhere: *heaha, heahan, heohan, hiehe* (*Concordance* H011:96 and 97, H015:222, and H019:159, resp.). For a vindication of the contraction test in words involving intervocalic *h*, see Fulk 1990, pp. 5–9 and 15–16. *Gloria I* dates from the late tenth century. See *The A-S Minor Poems* (*ASPR* 6), pp. lxix–lxxviii.

24 Ida Gordon, who sees Celtic elements in the poem, suggests "West Mercian" composition or inspiration, but this seems too specific. As regards date, she proposes the mid-ninth century, or a little earlier, because of the resemblance to Mercian homiletic texts of the ninth century. See her edition, pp. 31–32.

25 Wenisch 1979 classifies all the former as Anglian, not distinguishing between

the three *Christ* poems or the various riddles; *Maldon* he regards as definitely southern. See p. 328.

26 See Campbell 1960 and O'Neil 1960.

27 See Dobbie, *The Exeter Book* (*ASPR* 3), p. xiii; Sisam *SHOEL*, p. 97; Dunning-Bliss, *The Wanderer*, p. 4.

28 Most editors make an insertion before *mine* in line 27, assuming confusion over this word, a larger error of the same type. See Textual Notes.

29 Sisam thinks it is also possible that this cluster, on fol. 113a, "represents an exceptional lapse into the scribe's forms" (p. 98), but reproduction of a peculiarity from an earlier exemplar is a more plausible explanation of this aberration.

30 For example, Emily Grubl groups them together in her *Studien zu den ags Elegien* (1948, 77–80). She does not include *Resignation* in her study. Though placed in another part of the manuscript, *Res* displays some similarities to *Wan*, *Sea*, and *Rim*.

31 See A.C. Bouman's article on *Wulf* (1949), repr. in Bouman 1962, 93–106. Also P.J. Frankis (1962) on *Deor* and *Wulf*.

32 The term used by T.A. Shippey in his *OE Verse* (1972, 67) and *Poems of Wisdom and Learning in OE* (1976, 1). The notion of wisdom literature as a category going back to Old Testament and Near Eastern traditions is the subject of Elaine Tuttle Hansen's *The Solomon Complex: Reading Wisdom in OE Poetry* (1988), though she finds that the elegies, with the exception of *Deor*, are not central to the OE wisdom canon (p. 6).

33 The term *prosopopoeia* can be applied to the personification of a non-human entity in the riddles and elsewhere. For definitions of the two terms by Latin and Greek authors, see the study of rhetoric by Heinrich Lausberg (1973:1, §§ 820–29).

34 Noting the runes and the placement among the riddles, Fritz Hicketier (1889) suggested that these poems, and *Wife* too, should be regarded as riddles, but his view has never found much support.

35 Pope 1979, 25–65. The first half of this essay is concerned with possible losses in the Exeter Book, and Pope's findings are summarized on pp. 64–65, "Contents of the Exeter Book by quires." Part 2, pp. 42–63, deals with *Husb*.

36 The singleton lost in *Christ II* would have dropped out leaving no trace. The half-sheet in *Riddle 70* (fragments of two riddles) would have been cut out; a stub is clearly visible here, exactly like that of the preceding singleton. Probably something has been lost at the beginning of the next, and final, gathering. This would explain both the somewhat heavier burn damage and the absence of a knife-mark. In the case of *Resignation*, the half-sheet woud have fallen off at the fold. No stub is visible, and the folios are now too tightly bound to examine their condition at the spine.

37 Emended to *forðweg* by Bliss-Frantzen et al. See Textual Notes.

38 *Jul* 593b *sægde ealles þonc* and *Fort* 97a *Forþon him nu ealles þonc* in the Exeter Book. Elsewhere, *Gen* 238b *and sædon ealles þanc*, *Beo* 2794b *frean ealles ðanc* (a closer parallel), and *And* 1150b *Gode ealles þanc* (identical with *Res* 86b). For the occurrences of *þanc/þonc* in the poetic works, see *Concordance* THoo1:294–96, and THo15:314–16.

39 Marie Nelson (1983) accepts the idea of a lost folio, but believes the remaining fragments are part of the same poem. See esp. p. 133. This is a possibility, but the resulting poem would be very long for this part of the manuscript.

40 W.J. Sedgefield (1922, 32) thought that *Wan* and *Sea* were by the same author. Similarly G.V. Smithers (1957, 152–53). W.F. Bolton (1969), taking up Swanton's theory (1964) that *Wife* and *Husb* are based on the allegorical interpretation of the Song of Songs, suggests that the two poems are really one. It was argued by Rudolf Imelmann in a series of studies culminating in his *Forschungen zur ae Poesie* (1920) that *Wan*, *Sea*, *Wife*, *Husb*, and *Wulf* were all fragments of a lost composition about a continental Saxon Odoaker (Eadwacer), and that *Deor* and the Franks Casket showed allusions to this work.

41 For the idea of the sea as an "anti-hall" in both poems, see note on *Sea* 5b.

42 For this kind of schema in patristic writings cf. Gustav Ehrismann (1909), who relates *Sea* to the human drama of expulsion from Paradise, wandering in the world, and final return to the heavenly home, as exemplified in didactic writings, Latin and vernacular (pp. 218–30). Smithers adds another stage (no. 3) to the "drei Stufen" defined by Ehrismann (p. 218).

43 See Osborn 1975 and 1978.

44 See Doubleday 1969 and Selzer 1983; also Fichte 1985 for a criticism of this approach.

45 Translated in McKenna 1963, 269–313 (books 9–10) and 411–49 (book 14).

46 See Cross 1958–59 (on lines 80b–84), and 1956 (on lines 92–96).

47 Pound translated lines 1–99a. His "howlers" have fairly recently been vindicated by Fred C. Robinson (1982), who argues that he had a better knowledge of OE than is supposed.

48 Kershaw 1922, Krapp-Dobbie, and others have thought they were following Lawrence (1902b) in rejecting only lines 103–24, but actually Lawrence regarded lines 64bff. as a homiletic addition, and lines 103ff. as part of a different text.

49 This idea of the death-journey is influenced by the interpretation of Ehrismann (1909). Cf. Smithers 1957 and 1959, and see n. 42, above. Ehrismann sees in the Seafarer the aspirations of the pious ascetic.

50 Cf. Mackie 1922: "He [the poet] is intent upon a jingle and is careless of sense" (p. 508).

51 Macrae-Gibson 1973, 65; quoted by Wentersdorf 1985, 266. See also Stanley

1984b (review of Macrae-Gibson's edition), esp. p. 527. James Earl finds the subject matter of the poem unremarkable, but is impressed by the poet's ingenuity: "his real 'theme' ... is the poetic language itself, which in his hands is very rich" (1987, 195).

52 Earl 1985 refers to *Rim*'s "extremely strict double-alliterative pattern" (p. 31), and notes that as well as exact rhymes the poem has grammatical rhymes with consonantal variation, like *gearwade, hwearfade* (1987, 187). His own ingeniously free translation (included in Earl 1985 and 1987) attempts to reproduce *Rim*'s elaborate patterning and linguistic boldness.

53 Text as in Raby 1953, 448. Earlier, and closer to home, is a (seventh-century?) Anglo-Latin poem, from which Earl 1987 quotes as the most striking example of the kind of Latin hymnody which influenced *Rim*: *sancte sator, suffragator/ legum lator, largus dator,/iure pollens, es qui potens,/nunc in aethra firma petra* (in Dreves, Blume, and Bannister 1886–1922, 51:299).

54 The word derives from the elaborately obscure Latin of the poems collectively known as the *Hisperica Famina*, composed in Ireland in the seventh century (edited in Herren 1974). Earl defines "hisperic," with reference to *Rim*, as a term applied to "playfully erudite poetic obscurantism, both formal and linguistic – that is, poetry of intense and intentional difficulty, in both the composing and the deciphering" (1987, 189).

55 See his *Geschichte der ae Literatur* (Brandl 1908, 1081). Cf. also Ernst Sieper's observation, in his book on the elegies, that "sich der Verfasser von dem rhythmischen Schema der lateinischen Gedichte – bewusst oder unbewusst – leiten lass und einer regelmässigen Abwechslung von betonter und unbetonter Silbe zustrebt" (1915, 247).

56 This connection was first made by Grein, in the introduction to his Latin translation of *Rim* (1865), though he actually attributes the poem to Cynewulf. Earl refers in passing to *Hǫfuðlausn* as "an uncanny but probably unrelated analogue" (1987, 189). He does not explain his assumption that the two poems are unrelated.

57 This poem, which may be as late as the early twelfth century, is not usually included in the OE collections. Conybeare offers it as a "Norman-Saxon Fragment on Death" (1826, 270–3). The text is also printed in Schröer 1882. Alvin Lee (1972) includes a section on *The Grave* in his chapter on the elegies, where he characterizes the poem as "an almost gloating description of the confinement of the grave and the imminent putrefaction of the human body to be placed in it" (p. 155).

58 Mainly the Poetic or Elder *Edda*, the *Skáldskaparmál*, the *Volsunga saga*, and the *Gesta Danorum*. More specific references to these and other analogues are made in the Textual Notes. A parallel translation of the *Volsunga saga* is available in the edition cited (Finch 1965). For an English version of the *Gesta Danorum*,

see Finch 1979. The *Poetic Edda* is translated in Hollander 1962. And *Skáld-skaparmál* is included in Snorri's *Prose Edda* (sometimes called the Younger *Edda*), translated in Brodeur 1929, 87–240.

59 Cf. the Latin: "Quodsi idcirco te fortunatum esse non aestimas, quoniam quae tunc laeta videbantur abierunt, non est quod te miserum putes, quoniam quae nunc creduntur maesta praetereunt" (Stewart, Rand, and Tester 1973, 188).

60 See Markland 1968 and Bolton 1972 for arguments contra and pro. Bloom-field denies any connection with the Latin or OE Boethius, and observes that the theme "just as good times will give way to bad times so bad will also give way to good" is a commonplace (1986, 277).

61 See Malone:

1934a; repr. in 1959, pp. 158–63
1934b; repr. in 1959, pp. 116–63
1936
1937a
1939; repr. in 1959, pp. 164–67
1942.

62 There have been various solutions to the supposed riddle: Cynewulf (Leo 1857), riddle (Trautmann 1883), the Christian preacher – Wulf being the Devil (Morley 1888), the two stones of a mill (Patzig 1923). For the charm theory, see Fry 1971, and cf. Bloomfield's interpretation of *Deor* (1964 and 1986; mentioned pp. 43–44, above, and Part 3, n. 9, below). *Wulf* has been linked with *Wife* as an erotic "woman's song" in a popular rather than aris-tocratic tradition by Malone 1962 and Davidson 1975. The poem is read as a mother's lament for her son by Frese 1983, Osborn 1983, and Suzuki 1987; facetiously as a story about a romantic female dog by Sedgefield 1931; and, more seriously, as an anthropomorphic study of a family of wolves by Orton 1985.

63 For the last theory, see Eliason 1974.

64 See Schücking 1906; Bambas 1963; Stevens 1968; Mandel 1987, 152–55; more tentatively, Rissanen 1969.

65 See Lench 1970; Tripp 1972, who also interprets *Wan* and *Sea* in this way; Johnson 1983.

66 For example, Davis 1965, 303–4; Wentersdorf 1981, 509.

67 Doane 1966, 88–9.

68 Tacitus in his *Germania* (AD 98) noted that the sacred places of the Germanic tribes were woods and groves: *lucos ac nemora consecrant* (chap. 9; text and transl. in Hutton and Peterson 1970, 144 and 145). In his epic on the Civil War (written AD 60–65), Lucan describes the felling by Julius Caesar of a grove sacred to the Gauls, an ancient, terrifying place, where the gods were worshipped with *barbara ritu* (*Pharsalia* 3.399–425; text and transl. in Duff

1928, 142–4 and 143–5). The most ancient oracle of Zeus was located in the grove at Dodona in Epirus; cf. *Odyssey* 14.327 (text and transl. in Murray 1919, 2:56–8 and 57–59), where it is said that Odysseus had gone to Dodona to learn the will of the god from the lofty oak, ἐκ δρυὸς ὑψικόμοιο.

69 It has been suggested that the husband or lord has died. See, resp., Bouman 1962, 43–60; Rissanen 1969, 98–99.

70 For a reading which assumes a narrative background of this type, see Curry 1966, 189–92. The various permutations and modifications of this hypothetical plot-line are mentioned in the Textual Notes on lines 9–15. Leslie assumes a somewhat simpler plot, without a journey into exile by the wife. See his Introduction, pp. 5–7.

71 It is mainly the earlier scholars who saw this triangle and intrigue in the poem. The theory originated with Grein in a footnote to his translation (1857–59, 1:256). See also, with variations, Roeder 1899, 113–19; Stefanovíc 1909, 428–29; and Sieper's edition, pp. 217–25. And cf. Short 1970, who argues that the wife is punished for eloping to a lover. Others think she may have been accused of practising witchcraft. See Wülker 1885, 226; Davis 1965, 303–4 and note.

72 A somewhat different account of the poem's movement is offered by Barrie Ruth Straus (1981), who uses speech-act theory to argue that *Wife* is an energetic depiction of personal experience and that this energetic, personal mode continues in the last section – which she regards as a curse.

73 See Malone 1962 and Davidson 1975.

74 Evidence for the legend is very late. It is found in *L'Innocence Reconnue ou Vie de Sainte Geneviève de Brabant* ca. 1638 by René de Cérisier.

75 See Nelson 1983, esp. 134, 135, and 141.

76 Peter Orton 1981, who treats *Husb* as the utterance of a rune-stave, thinks that *Ic wæs be Sonde* is not necessarily a part of it and does not include this piece in his analysis of the poem.

77 I cannot agree with Alain Renoir, who argues that the poem may be less optimistic than has been supposed, and points out that the tales of Sigurd, Hildebrand, and other Germanic heroes who went away from their women do not have happy endings (1981, 74–75).

78 I have suggested that the first damaged section, beginning at line 12, may focus on the remaining impressiveness of the crumbling buildings, rather than on the decay of the preceding lines (Klinck 1986b).

79 By R.I. Page, in his inaugural lecture at Cambridge (1985, 22–24).

80 Hadrian's Wall (Herben 1939), and Chester (Dunleavy 1959).

81 For the texts of these three Latin works, see, resp., Mommsen 1898, 25–85; Leo 1881, 271–75; Dümmler 1881, 229–35. The Gildas text is also included in Winterbottom 1978, 87–102 (transl. pp. 13–79); see esp. 96–99 (transl. pp. 25–29). For translations of the Fortunatus and Alcuin texts, see Calder and Allen 1976, 137–46.

PART II

Texts and Textual Notes

In the texts of the poems, emended forms are indicated by italics, restorations by square brackets. Manuscript abbreviations (7 for *ond*, þ for *þæt*, ~ for word endings including *m* or *n*) are silently expanded. Where letters and words are missing because of damage to the manuscript and no restoration is suggested, the mark – is used to estimate every possible letter or letter-size space. Three asterisks (* * *) are used to indicate suspected lacunae which are not actually visible in the manuscript or which are of unspecified length.

All emendations incorporated in the major editions are cited in the textual apparatus: that is, those in most of the separately published editions of individual poems and also in the seminal collections of the nineteenth and twentieth centuries. Ettmüller's and Grein's texts are cited fully because of their historical importance, but since they are not based on an examination of the manuscript, their suggestions do not always correspond to MS indications in the damaged passages.

Other commentaries are cited in the textual apparatus only if their suggestions have been subsequently incorporated in one of the major editions or in the present. Minor orthographical changes and obvious accidental errors made by the editors are ignored. Footnote suggestions are omitted unless subsequently adopted. Editorial variations in word division are not regularly cited in the apparatus, but where they produce different interpretations are commented on in the notes.

Emendations in the following editions and commentaries are cited below the texts:

WORKS GIVEN COMPLETE CITATION*	WORKS GIVEN OCCASIONAL CITATION
Conybeare (*Rim, Deor, Ruin*)	Conybeare 1826 (*Wife*)†
Thorpe	Leo 1857
Ettmüller	Grein 1861
Grein	Grein *Sprachschatz* 1861
Grein-Wülker	Rieger 1861
Gollancz (*Wan*)	Grein 1865

---

* See List of Abbreviations for the contents of collected editions.

† The Conybeare texts of other elegies are cited fully. In this case, W.D. Conybeare's text, added posthumously to those assembled by J.J. Conybeare, is full of misreadings of the MS, which are ignored here.

Tupper (*Wulf*)
Sieper
Imelmann (*Rim*)
Kershaw
Malone 1933 (*Deor*)
Mackie
Krapp-Dobbie
Gordon (*Sea*)
Leslie 1961 (*Wife, Husb, Ruin*)
Malone 1961 (*Deor*)
Leslie 1966 (*Wan*)
Dunning-Bliss (*Wan*)
Malmberg (*Res*)
Baker (*Wulf*)
Macrae-Gibson (*Rim*)

Rieger 1869
Sievers 1884
Sievers 1885
Sievers 1886
Hicketier 1888
Kluge 1888
Herzfeld 1890
Bright 1891
Bülbring 1891
Holthausen 1893
Kögel 1894
Sweet 1894
Trautmann 1894
Kluge 1897
Kluge 1902
Holthausen 1907b
Holthausen 1908
Klaeber 1909
Holthausen 1912
Holthausen 1913
Sisam 1913
Schücking 1919
Holthausen 1921
Holthausen 1930
Klaeber 1935
Malone 1936
Sisam 1945
Holthausen 1953
Bliss-Frantzen 1976
Wentersdorf 1985

THE WANDERER

"Oft him anhaga   are gebideð,
metudes miltse,   þeah þe he modcearig
geond lagulade   longe sceolde
hreran mid hondum   hrimcealde sæ,
5   wadan wræclastas: wyrd bið ful aræd."   (MS aręd)
    Swa cwæð eardstapa,   earfeþa gemyndig,
wraþra wælsleahta,   winemæga hryre.
    "Oft ic sceolde ana   uhtna gehwylce
mine ceare cwiþan;   nis nu cwicra nan
10   þe ic him modsefan   minne durre
sweotule asecgan.   Ic to soþe wat
þæt biþ in eorle   indryhten þeaw
þæt he his ferðlocan   fæste binde,
healde his hordcofan,   hycge swa he wille.   (MS healdne)
15   Ne mæg werig mod   wyrde wiðstondan,
ne se hreo hyge   helpe gefremman.
Forðon domgeorne   dreorigne oft
in hyra breostcofan   bindað fæste.
Swa ic modsefan   minne sceolde
20   oft earmcearig,   eðle bidæled,
freomægum feor   feterum sælan,
siþþan geara iu   goldwine *minne*   (MS mine)
hrusan heolstre biwrah   ond ic hean þonan
wod wintercearig   ofer *waþema* gebind,   (MS waþena)
25   sohte seledreorig   sinces bryttan
hwær ic feor oþþe neah   findan meahte

4b   Th   *hrimcalde* (also Ett)
5b   Th   *aræd* (also all eds.)
12a   Ett   *on* (also Gr)
13a   Ett   *ferðcofan*
14a   Th   *healde?*, in fn. (Gr *healdne*; other eds. *healde*)
22b   Th   *miñe* (Gr, Gr-W *mine*; other eds. *minne*)
23a   Ett   *heolster* (also Gr, Gr-W, Goll, Siep, Ker)
        Ett   *biwreah*
24b   Th   *waþema* (also all eds.)

þone þe in meoduhealle   mine wisse,
oþþe mec *freondleasne*   frefran wolde,   (MS freond lease)
weman mid wynnum.   Wat se þe cunnað
30 hu sliþen bið   sorg to geferan
þam þe him lyt hafað   leofra geholena.
Warað hine wræclast,   nalæs wunden gold,
ferðloca freorig,   nalæs foldan blæd;
gemon he selesecgas   ond sincþege,
35 hu hine on geoguðe   his goldwine
wenede to wiste: wyn eal gedreas.
Forþon wat se þe sceal   his winedryhtnes
leofes larcwidum   longe forþolian.
Ðonne sorg ond slæp   somod ætgædre
40 earmne anhogan   oft gebindað,
þinceð him on mode   þæt he his mondryhten
clyppe ond cysse   ond on cneo lecge
honda ond heafod,   swa he hwilum ær
in geardagum   giefstolas breac.
45 Ðonne onwæcneð eft   wineleas guma,
gesihð him biforan   fealwe wegas,
baþian brimfuglas,   brædan feþra,
hreosan hrim ond snaw   hagle gemenged.
Þonne beoð þy hefigran   heortan benne,
50 sare æfter swæsne;   sorg bið geniwad
þonne maga gemynd   mod geondhweorfeð:
greteð gliwstafum,   georne geondsceawað –
secga geseldan   swimmað *eft* onweg,   (MS oft)

27b Ett *mine mæð wisse*
Siev 1885 *minne wisse* (also Goll)
Kluge 1888 *mildse wisse*
Kluge 1902 *miltse wisse* (also Siep)
Klaeb 1909 *min mine wisse* (also Ker, K-D)
Les *me mine wisse*
D-B *minne myne wisse*
28a Th *freondleasne* (also all eds.)
29a Gr *wenian* (also Gr-W, Goll, Siep, Ker, D-B)
44b Th *-stoles?*, in fn. (*giefstoles* adopted by Ett, Goll)
46b Bright 1891 *wægas* (also D-B)
50a Th *sare æfter swæfne* (Ett *sar æfter swefne*)
52a Siep *gligstafum*
53b Th *swimð eft?*, in fn. (Leslie *swimmað oft*; other eds. *swimmað eft*)

fleotendra ferð   no þær fela bringeð
55   cuðra cwidegiedda;   cearo bið geniwad
    þam þe sendan sceal   swiþe geneahhe
    ofer waþema gebind   werigne sefan.
    Forþon ic geþencan ne mæg   geond þas woruld
    forhwan *modsefa* min   ne gesweorce   (MS mod sefan minne)
60   þonne ic eorla lif   eal geondþence,
    hu hi færlice   flet ofgeafon,
    modge maguþegnas.   Swa þes middangeard
    ealra dogra gehwam   dreoseð ond fealleþ.
    Forþon ne mæg wearþan wis   wer ær he age
65   wintra dæl in woruldrice.   Wita sceal geþyldig;
    ne sceal no to hatheort,   ne to hrædwyrde,
    ne to wac wiga,   ne to wanhydig,
    ne to forht, ne to fægen,   ne to feohgifre,
    ne næfre gielpes to georn,   ær he geare cunne.
70   Beorn sceal gebidan   þonne he beot spriceð
    oþþæt collenferð   cunne gearwe
    hwider hreþra gehygd   hweorfan wille.
    Ongietan sceal gleaw hæle   hu gæstlic bið
    þonne ealle þisse worulde wela   weste stondeð,
75   swa nu missenlice   geond þisne middangeard
    winde biwaune   weallas stondaþ,
    hrime bihrorene.   Hryðge þa ederas;
    woriað þa winsalo.   Waldend licgað
    dreame bidrorene;   duguþ eal gecrong,
80   wlonc bi wealle.   Sume wig fornom,
    ferede in forðwege;   sumne fugel oþbær
    ofer heanne holm;   sumne se hara wulf
    deaðe gedælde;   sumne dreorighleor

59   Gr   *modsefa min ne* (also all eds.)
64a   Th   *weorþan* (also Ett, Gr, Goll, K-D)
72a   Ett   *hwiðer*
74a   Ett   *eall* (also Gr, Goll, Les)
       Gr-W   *ealre* (also Siep, Ker, K-D, D-B)
76a   Ett   *biwawne* (also Gr, Gr-W, Goll, Siep, Ker)
77b   Gr   *hryðgeað ederas*
       Gr 1865   *hryðge þa ederas*
78a   D-B   *woniað*
81a   Ett   *on* (also Ker)
82a   Ett   *heahne* (also Gr)

in eorðscræfe   eorl gehydde.
85 Yþde swa þisne eardgeard   ælda scyppend,
oþþæt burgwara   breahtma lease
eald enta geweorc   idlu stodon.
Se þonne þisne wealsteal   wise geþohte
ond þis *deorce* lif   deope geondþenceð,   (MS deornce)
90 frod in ferðe,   feor oft gemon,
wælsleahta worn,   ond þas word acwið:
'Hwær cwom mearg? Hwær cwom mago?   Hwær cwom
                      maþþumgyfa?
Hwær cwom symbla gesetu?   Hwær sindon seledreamas?
Eala beorht bune!   Eala byrnwiga!
95 Eala þeodnes þrym!   Hu seo þrag gewat,
genap under nihthelm   swa heo no wære!'
Stondeð nu on laste   leofre duguþe
weal wundrum heah,   wyrmlicum fah.
Eorlas fornoman   asca þryþe,
100 wæpen wælgifru,   wyrd seo mære.
Ond þas stanhleoþu   stormas cnyssað;
hrið hreosende   *hrusan* bindeð,   (MS hruse)
wintres woma,   þonne won cymeð,
nipeð nihtscua,   norþan onsendeð
105 hreo hæglfare   hæleþum on andan.
Eall is earfoðlic   eorþan rice;
onwendeð wyrda gesceaft   weoruld under heofonum.
Her bið feoh læne,   her bið freond læne,
her bið mon læne,   her bið mæg læne.
110 Eal þis eorþan gesteal   idel weorþeð."
    Swa cwæð snottor on mode;   gesæt him sundor æt rune.
"Til biþ se þe his treowe gehealdeþ;   ne sceal næfre his torn to
                    rycene
beorn of his breostum acyþan,   nemþe he ær þa bote cunne,
eorl mid elne gefremman.   Wel bið þam þe him are seceð,
115 frofre to fæder on heofonum,   þær us eal seo fæstnung stondeð."

89a Th *deorce* (also all eds.)
99a Ett *fornomon* (also Ker)
102a Th *hreð-* [*hreosende*, as compound]?, in fn. (Ett *hreðe hreosende*)
102b Th *hrusan*?, in fn. (Gr, Gr-W *hruse*; other eds. *hrusan*)
115b Ett *fæstung* (by error?)

THE SEAFARER

Mæg ic be me sylfum   soðgied wrecan,
siþas secgan,   hu ic geswincdagum
earfoðhwile   oft þrowade.
Bitre breostceare   gebiden hæbbe,
5   gecunnad in ceole   cearselda fela,
atol yþa gewealc,   þær mec oft bigeat
nearo nihtwaco   æt nacan stefnan
þonne he be clifum cnossað.   Calde geþrungen
wæron mine fet,   forste gebunden,
10   caldum clommum,   þær þa ceare seofedun
hat' ymb heortan,   hungor innan slat
merewerges mod.   Þæt se mon ne wat
þe him on foldan   fægrost limpeð,
hu ic earmcearig   iscealdne sæ
15   winter wunade   wræccan lastum,
winemægum bidroren,
bihongen hrimgicelum;   hægl scurum fleag.
Þær ic ne gehyrde   butan hlimman sæ,
iscaldne wæg.   Hwilum ylfete song
20   dyde ic me to gomene,   ganetes hleoþor,
ond huilpan sweg   fore hleahtor wera,
mæw singende   fore medodrince.
Stormas þær stanclifu beotan,   þær him stearn oncwæð
isigfeþera,   ful oft þæt earn bigeal
25   urigfeþra.   Nænig hleomæga

8a   Ett   *cnossade* (also Gr, Gr-W)
9a   Sweet 1894   *wæron fet mine* (also Siep)
10b   Ett   *ceara*
11a   Sweet 1894   *hate* (also Mack)
13b   Th   *fægnost*, as MS reading (also Ett, Gr)
16   Th   indicates verse missing before *winemægum* (also Ett, Siep)
       Ett   *wynnum beloren*, supplying a-verse, in fn. (Gr, Gr-W *wynnum biloren*)
       Mack   omission marks in b-verse
19b   Ett   *ylfetes*
21a   Siep   omits *ond*
25   Th   indicates verses missing between *urigfeþra* and *nænig* (also Ett, Gr-W)
       Mack   prints *nænig hleomæga* as 25a and omission marks in b-verse
25b   Gr   *ne ænig* (also K-D)

feasceaftig ferð   *frefran* meahte.   (MS feran)
Forþon him gelyfeð lyt,   se þe ah lifes wyn,
gebiden in burgum,   bealosiþa hwon,
wlonc ond wingal,   hu ic werig oft
30   in brimlade   bidan sceolde.
Nap nihtscua,   norþan sniwde,
hrim hrusan bond,   hægl feol on eorþan,
corna caldast.   Forþon cnyssað nu
heortan geþohtas   þæt ic hean streamas,
35   sealtyþa gelac   sylf cunnige;
monað modes lust   mæla gehwylce,
ferð to feran   þæt ic feor heonan
elþeodigra   eard gesece;
forþon nis þæs modwlonc   mon ofer eorþan,
40   ne his gifena þæs god,   ne in geoguþe to þæs hwæt,
ne in his dædum to þæs deor,   ne him his dryhten to þæs hold,
þæt he a his sæfore   sorge næbbe,
to hwon hine dryhten   gedon wille.
Ne biþ him to hearpan hyge   ne to hringþege –
45   ne to wife wyn   ne to worulde hyht –
ne ymbe owiht elles   nefne ymb yða gewealc,
ac a hafað longunge   se þe on lagu fundað.
Bearwas blostmum nimað,   byrig fægriað,
wongas wlitigað,   woruld onetteð;
50   ealle þa gemoniað   modes fusne,
sefan to siþe,   þam þe swa þenceð,
on flodwegas   feor gewitað.
Swylce geac monað   geomran reorde,
singeð sumeres weard,   sorge beodeð
55   bitter' in breosthord.   Þæt se beorn ne wat,
esteadig secg,   hwæt þa sume dreogað   (MS eft eadig)

26b   Gr *felian*
        Gr 1865 *frefran* (also Siep, Ker, Mack, K-D, Gord)
32a   Ker *band*
34b   Th *heah-[streamas]*?, in fn. (Ett *heahstreamas*)
46a   Ett *ohwiht*
49a   Gr *wlitigiað*?, in fn. (adopted by K-D)
51a   Th *feran to siþe* (also Ett, Gr)
52b   Th *gewitan*?, in fn. (Ker *gewitað*; other eds. *gewitan*)
56a   Th *est-[eadig]*?, in fn. (adopted by Ett, Gr-W, Ker, Mack, K-D)
        Gr *sefteadig* (also Gord)

þe þa wræclastas   widost lecgað.
Forþon nu min hyge hweorfeð   ofer hreþerlocan,
min modsefa   mid mereflode,
60 ofer hwæles eþel   hweorfeð wide,
eorþan sceatas;   cymeð eft to me
gifre ond grædig,   gielleð anfloga,
hweteð on *hwælweg*   hreþer unwearnum,   (MS onwæl weg)
ofer holma gelagu;   forþon me hatran sind
65 dryhtnes dreamas   þonne þis deade lif,
læne on londe.   Ic gelyfe no
þæt him eorðwelan   ece stondeð;
simle þreora sum   þinga gehwylce
ær his tidege   to tweon weorþeð:
70 adl oþþe yldo   oþþe ecghete
fægum fromweardum   feorh oðþringeð.
Forþon þæt eorla gehwam   æftercweþendra
lof lifgendra   lastworda betst,
þæt he gewyrce   ær he onweg scyle,
75 fremman on foldan   wið feonda niþ,
deorum dædum   deofle togeanes,
þæt hine ælda bearn   æfter hergen,
ond his lof siþþan   lifge mid englum
awa to ealdre,   ecan lifes *blæd*,   (MS blæð)
80 dream mid dugeþum.   Dagas sind gewitene,
ealle onmedlan   eorþan rices;

61a   Ett   *ofer eorþan sceatas* (also Gr-W)
      Gr   *geond eorþan sceatas*
63a   Th   *hwæl-[weg]*?, in fn. (Gr *wælweg*; other eds. *hwælweg*)
63b   Th   *hweþer*, as MS reading (also Ett)
67a   Gr   *eorðwela*
67b   Ett   *stondað* (also Gr-W, Siep, Ker, Mack, K-D, Gord)
68b   Ett   *gehwylcum*
69a   Gr   *tiddæge*?, in fn. (Ker, Mack, Gord *tiddege*)
      Gr *Sprachschatz   tid aga* (adopted by Gr-W, K-D)
72a   Gr   *Forþon þæt is eorla gehwam*
      Holt 1921   *Forþon þæt bið eorla gehwam* (also K-D)
      Gord   *Forþon bið eorla gehwam*
75a   Sisam 1913   *fremum* (also K-D, Gord)
77a   Ett   *ealda*
79b   Th   *blæd* (also all eds.)

næron nu cyningas   ne caseras
ne goldgiefan   swylce iu wæron,
þonne hi mæst mid him   mærþa gefremedon,
85   ond on dryhtlicestum   dome lifdon.
Gedroren is þeos duguð eal;   dreamas sind gewitene.
Wuniað þa wacran   ond þas woruld healdaþ,
brucað þurh bisgo.   Blæd is gehnæged;
eorþan indryhto   ealdað ond searað;
90   swa nu monna gehwylc   geond middangeard:
yldo him on fareð,   onsyn blacað,
gomelfeax gnornað;   wat his iuwine,
æþelinga bearn   eorþan forgiefene.
Ne mæg him þonne se flæschoma   þonne him þæt feorg losað
95   ne swete forswelgan,   ne sar gefelan,
ne hond onhreran,   ne mid hyge þencan.
Þeah þe græf wille   golde stregan
broþor his geborenum –   byrgan be deadum –
maþmum mislicum   þæt hine mid wille,
100   ne mæg þære sawle   þe biþ synna ful
gold to geoce   for godes egsan,
þonne he hit ær hydeð   þenden he her leofað.
Micel biþ se meotudes egsa   for þon hi seo molde oncyrreð;
se gestaþelade   stiþe grundas,
105   eorþan sceatas   ond uprodor.
Dol biþ se þe him his dryhten ne ondrædeþ;   cymeð him se deað
    unþinged.

Eadig bið se þe eaþmod leofaþ;   cymeð him seo ar of heofonum.

82a   Th perhaps *ne syndon nu*, fn. (Ett *ne sindon nu*)
        Gr *nearon* (also Gord)
        Gr-W *ne aron* (also Siep, Ker, Mack)
94b   Ett *feorh*
97a   Ett *ac þeah þe*
        Ker *þeah he*
98b   Rieger 1869 *bycgan* (also Gr-W)
99b   Th *he ne?*, in fn. (adopted by Gr-W)
        Ett *wat ic þæt he mid nylle*
        Gr *him ne?*, in fn. (adopted by Siep, Mack)
        Sisam 1945 *ne wile* or *nile* (Gord *nille*)
102   Gr *þam þe hit ær hydeð*
        Ett text ends here

Meotod him þaet mod gestaþelað   forþon he in his meahte
        gelyfeð.
Stieran *mon* sceal strongum mode,   ond þaet on staþelum
        healdan,   (MS mod)
110 ond gewis werum,   wisum clæne.
Scyle monna gehwylc   mid gemete healdan
wiþ leofne ond wið laþne   * * * bealo,
þeah þe he hine wille fyres   fulne * * *
oþþe on bæle   forbærnedne,
115 his geworhtne wine.   Wyrd biþ *swiþre*,   (MS swire)
meotud meahtigra   þonne ænges monnes gehygd.
Uton we hycgan   hwær *we* ham agen   (MS se)
ond þonne geþencan   hu we þider cumen,
ond we þonne eac tilien   þæt we to moten,
120 in þa ecan   eadignesse
þær is lif gelong   in lufan dryhtnes,
hyht in heofonum.   Þæs sy þam halgan þonc
þæt he usic geweorþade,   wuldres ealdor,
ece dryhten   in ealle tid. Amen.

108a Th   *meotud*, as MS reading (also Gr)
109a Th   *mon* (Gr-W *mod*; other eds. *mon*)
111b Gr   *mod gemete healdan*
112   Th   omission marks before *bealo* (also Gr, Gr-W, K-D, Gord)
      Holt 1908   *wiþ leofne lufan* (also Ker, Mack)
113   Th   omission marks after *fulne* (also Gr, Mack, K-D)
      Gr   *þeah he*
      Gord   *he ne* instead of *he hine*
115b Gr   *swiðre* (also Gr-W, Siep, Ker, Mack; K-D, Gord *swiþre*)
117b Th   *we* (also all eds.)

THE RIMING POEM

Me lifes onlah   se þis leoht onwrah,
ond þæt torhte geteoh,   tillice onwrah.
Glæd wæs ic gliwum,   glenged hiwum,
blissa bleoum,   blostma hiwum.

5   Secgas mec segon,   symbel ne alegon,
feorhgiefe gefegon.   Frætwed *wægon*   (MS wægum)
wicg ofer wongum,   wennan gongum,   (MS wic)
lisse mid longum,   leoma getongum.
Þa wæs wæstmum aweaht   world onspreht,

10   under roderum areaht,   rædmægne oferþeaht.
Giestas gengdon,   gerscype mengdon,
lisse lengdon,   lustum glengdon.
Scrifen scrad glad   þurh gescad in brad;
wæs on lagustreame lad,   þær me leoþu ne biglad.

15   Hæfde ic heanne had;   ne wæs me in healle gad

2a   Gr   *getah* (also Gr-W, Siep)
2b   Ett   *onwreah* (also M-G)
3b   Gr   *niwum* (also Gr-W, Siep)
4a   Ett   *bliwum* (also Gr, Gr-W)
4a-b   Siev 1884   *bleowum ... heowum* (Siep, Im *bleowum ... hiwum*; M-G *bleoum ... heowum*)
5a-b   Ett   *sægon ... alægon* (also Gr, Gr-W)
6a   Ett   *feohgiefe gefægon* (also Gr, Gr-W; Siep, Im, K-D *feohgiefe gefegon*)
6b   Gr   *frætwed wægon* (also Gr-W, Siep, K-D, M-G; Mack *frætwed wægun*)
    Siev 1886   *frætwe wegon* (Im *frætwe wægon*)
7a   Gr   *wicg* (also Gr-W, Siep, Im, Mack, K-D, M-G)
7b   Ett   *wena on gongum*
    Gr   *wrennan gongum* (also Gr-W)
    Siep   *wrænsan gongum*
    Im   *wenan gongum*
8a   Ett   *lis*
8b   Siev 1886   *gehongum* (also Siep, Im, K-D)
9b   Ett   *woruld aspreaht*
    Gr   *woruld onspreaht* (also Gr-W; Siep *woruld onspreht*)
9a-b   Siev 1886   *... wæstmum awæht, ofer woruld onspræht* (Im *wæstm aweaht, ofer world onspreht*)
10b   Gr   *radmægne* (also Gr-W)
11b   Ett   *gepscipe*
13a   Siep   *scufen scrad opglad*
14b   Im   *mec*
15a   Co   *hælde*
    Ett   *heahne* (also Gr)

þæt þær rof weord rad.   Oft þær rinc gebad
þæt he in sele sæge   sincgewæge.
Þegnum *geþwære*   *þeoden* wæs ic *mære*;

(MS geþyhte þenden; mægen)

horsce mec heredon,   hilde generedon,
20   fægre feredon,   feondon biweredon.
Swa mec hyhtgiefu heold,   hygedryht befeold,
staþolæhtum steald,   stepegongum weold,
Swylce eorþe ol   ahte ic – ealdorstol,
galdorwordum gol,   gomelsibbe ne *ofeoll*.   (MS of oll)
25   Ac wæs gefest gear,   gellende sner,
wuniendo wær,   wilbec bescær.
Scealcas wæron scearpe,   scyl wæs hearpe,
hlude hlynede,   hleoþor dynede,
sweglrad swinsade,   swiþe ne minsade,
30   burgsele beofode,   beorht hlifade,
ellen eacnade,   ead beacnade,
freaum frodade,   fromum godade,

16a   Th   *word*
       Ett   *weorud* (also Gr, Gr-W, Siep; M-G *werod*)
18a   Co   omission marks after *geþyhte*
18a-b Ett   *þegnum geþyhte, þenden wæs ic mægenhyhte*
       Gr   (*sincgewægel*) *þegnum geþyhte. Þunden wæs ic myhte* (also Gr-W, Siep, Mack)
       Siev 1886   *þegnunge þege, þenden wæs ic wege* (Im *þegnum geþæge. þenden wæs ic wæge*)
       K-D   *þegnum geþyhte. Þenden wæs me mægen*
       M-G   *þegnum geþyhte – þenden wæs ic in mægen*
20b   Ett   *feondum* (also Gr, Gr-W, Siep, Im)
21b   Ett   *higedryht* (also Gr, Gr-W)
22a   Ett   *steold* (also Gr, Gr-W, Siep, Im, K-D)
22b   Gr   *stepegengum*
24a   Ett   *gealdorwordum*
24b   Gr   *gomen sibbe* (also Gr-W, Siep, K-D)
       Im   *gomel sibb* (also M-G)
       Ett   *ofol* (also Gr, Gr-W, Im, Mack)
25a   Siev 1886   *geffest ger* (Siep, Im, Mack *geffest gear*)
25b   Ett   *snear* (also Gr, Gr-W)
26a   Co   *wuniende* (also Ett)
29b   Holt 1913   *swiþo* (also Siep)
30a   Ett   *bifade* (also Gr, Gr-W)
31b   Co   *eacnade*
       Gr   *weacnade* (also Gr-W, Siep)
32a   Gr   *flodade* (also Gr-W, Siep)
32b   Gr   *fremum* (also Gr-W)
       Holt 1913   *freomum* (also Siep)

       mod mægnade,   mine fægnade,
       treow telgade,   tir welgade,
35   blæd blissade,
       gold gearwade,   gim hwearfade,
       sinc searwade,   sib nearwade.
       From ic wæs in frætwum,   freolic in geatwum;
       wæs min dream dryhtlic,   drohtað hyhtlic;
40   foldan ic freoþode,   folcum ic leoþode;
       lif wæs min longe   leodum in gemonge,
       tirum getonge,   teala gehonge.
        Nu min hreþer is hreoh,   *heofsiþum* sceoh,   (MS heow siþum)
       nydbysgum neah.   Gewiteþ nihtes in fleah
45   se ær in dæge wæs dyre.   Scriþeð nu deop *in feore*
                                    (MS deop feor)

       brondhord geblowen,   breostum in forgrowen,
       flyhtum toflowen.   Flah is geblowen,
       miclum in gemynde.   Modes gecynde
       greteð ungrynde   grorn, *ungeþynde*,   (MS efen þynde)
50   bealofus byrneð,   bittre toyrneð.
       Werig winneð,   widsið onginneð,
       sar ne sinniþ,   sorgum cinnið,

33b   Ett   *myne* (also Gr, Gr-W)
35   Co   omission marks before *blæd blissade*
35b   Ett   *bleo glissade* (also Gr, Gr-W)
       Th   omission marks after *blæd blissade* (also Siep, Im, Mack)
43b   Co   *heoh-*
       Ett   *heof-* (also Gr, Gr-W, Siep, K-D)
       Im   *hreow-*
44b   Co   *gewited nihtes infleah*
       Ett   *gewitod nihtes infleah* (also Gr, Gr-W)
45a   Th   *deor*, in fn. (adopted by Siep, Mack)
45b   Ett   *deop fyre* (also Gr, Gr-W)
       Holt 1913   (*deor ...*) *deope þeor* (Siep *deope nu þeor*)
       Holt 1930   *deop in feore* (also K-D, M-G)
       Mack   *deop ond feor*
46a   Ett   *brondhord is geblowen*
49   Co   *greteð ongrynde grorn ofen þynde* (Ett *græteð on grynde grornofen þynde*)
49b   Th   *grorn efen wynde* (also Im; Gr *grorn efen winde*)
       Gr 1865   *grorn efen þynde*
       Siev 1886   *grorn oferþynde* (also Mack)

blæd his blinnið,   blisse linnað,
listum linneð,   lustum ne tinneð.

55 Dreamas swa her gedreosað,   dryhtscype gehreosað.
Lif her men forleosað,   leahtras oft geceosað.
Treowþrag is to trag,   seo untrume genag.
Steapum *steaðole* misþah,   ond eal stund genag.   (MS eatole)
Swa nu world wendeþ,   wyrde sendeþ
60 ond hetes henteð,   hæleþe scyndeð.
Wercyn gewiteð,   wælgar sliteð,   (MS wen cyn)
flahmah fliteþ,   flan *man* hwiteð,   (MS mon)
burg sorg biteð,   bald ald þwiteþ,
wræcfæc wriþað,   wraþ að smiteþ,
65 *singryn* sidað,   *searo feor* glideþ,   (MS singrynd; sæcra fearo)

53b	Ett	*blis seo*
	Ett	*linnið* (also Gr, Gr-W, Siep, Mack, K-D, M-G)
	Im	*linneð*
54	Ett	*linnið ... tinnið*
54b	Co	*cinneð*
55b	Co	*dryht scyre*
57b	Im	*gehnag* (also Mack)
58a	Ett	*steaðole* (also Mack; Gr, Gr-W, Siep *staðole*)
58b	Ett	*gehnah* (also Gr, Gr-W, Siep; M-G *genah*)
	Kluge 1897	*gehnag* (also Im, Mack)
59a	Ett	*woruld* (also Gr, Gr-W, Siep)
60a	Gr	*hendeð* (also Gr-W, Im)
60b	Ett	*hæleþas scendeð*
	Gr	*hæleþ gescendeð* (also Gr-W, Siep)
	Schück 1919	*hæleþe scendeð* (also Mack)
61a	Co	*wer cynge witeð*
	Ett	*wercyn gewiteð* (also Gr, Gr-W, Siep, Im, Mack, K-D)
62b	Co	*man* (also Ett, Gr, Gr-W, Siep, Im, M-G)
63a	Ett	*borh sorh*
	Gr	*borgsorg* (also Gr-W, Siep, Mack, K-D)
	Im	*borg sorg* (also M-G)
64a	Gr	*wræc sæc writeð* (also Gr-W; Siep *wræc sæc wriþeð*)
64b	Ett	*smiðað*
65a	Ett	*syngryn* (also Gr, Gr-W, Siep)
	Schück 1919	*singryn* (also Im, Mack, K-D, M-G)
	Gr	*sideð* (also Gr-W)
65b	Ett	*searo fearo* (Mack *searafearo*; other eds. *searofearo*)
	Ett	*glidaþ* (also Siep, Im)

gromtorn græfeþ,　　græf hæft hafað,　　(MS græft; hæft not in MS)
searohwit solað,　　sumurhat colað,
foldwela fealleð,　　feondscipe wealleð,
eorðmægen ealdaþ,　　ellen cealdað.　　　　　　　　(MS colað)

70　　Me þæt wyrd gewæf　　ond gehwyrft forgeaf　　　(MS gehwyrt)
　　þæt ic grofe græf,　　ond þæt grimme græf
　　flean flæsce ne mæg,　　þonne flanhred dæg
　　nydgrapum nimeþ,　　þonne seo neaht becymeð　　　(MS neah)
　　seo me eðles ofonn,　　ond mec her eardes onconn,
　　　　　　　　　　　　　　(MS on fonn; heardes)

75　　þonne lichoma ligeð,　　lima wyrm friteþ,
　　ac him wenne gewigeð,　　ond þa wist geþygeð,
　　oþþæt beoþ þa ban　　* * * an,
　　ond æt nyhstan nan,　　nefne se neda tan

66a　　Ett　grorn torn (also Gr, Gr-W, M-G; Siep, Im grorntorn)
66b　　Ett　græft hæft hafað
　　　　Gr　græft ræft hæfeð (also Gr-W)
　　　　Holt 1913　græft cræft næfeð (Im græft cræft ne hafað; M-G græft cræft hafað)
　　　　Siep　omission marks between græft and hafað (also Mack, K-D)
　　　　Went 1985　græf hæft hafað
68a　　Co　fold fela
　　　　Ett　folcwela
68b　　Co　feondscire
　　　　Ett　freondscipe – by error?
69b　　Ett　cealdað (also Gr, Gr-W, Siep, Im, Mack, M-G)
70b　　Ett　gewyrc
　　　　Gr　gewyrht (also all eds.)
71b　　Ett　geræf (also Gr, Gr-W)
　　　　Siev 1886　scræf (also Siep, Mack, M-G)
72a　　Ett　fleon (also Gr, Gr-W, Siep, Im)
72b　　Co　ðon flah hred dæg (Ett þonne fleah hred dæg)
73b　　Ett　neaht (Im niht; other eds. neaht)
74a　　Ett　ofonn (also all eds.)
74b　　Ett　mec her eardes (Gr me her eardes; other eds. mec her eardes)
75b　　Ett　limu (also Gr, Gr-W, Siep)
　　　　Gr　þigeþ (also Gr-W, Siep, Mack)
76a　　Gr　and him (also Gr-W)
　　　　Gr　wynne (also Gr-W, Siep, Im)
76b　　Co　gehygeð
77b　　Co　omission marks after an indicating loss of a verse (also Th)
　　　　Ett　omission marks between ban and an (also Siep, Im, Mack, K-D)
　　　　Gr　gebrosnad on an (also Gr-W)

hælepum her *gehloten.*   Ne bið se hlisa adroren.

(MS balawun; gehlotene)

80 Ær þæt eadig geþenceð;   he hine þe oftor swenceð,
    byrgeð him þa bitran synne,   hogaþ to þære betran wynne,
    gemon morþa lisse,   *þær* sindon miltsa blisse   (MS her)
    hyhtlice in heofona rice.   Uton nu, halgum gelice,
    scyldum biscyrede,   scyndan generede,
85 wommum biwerede,   wuldre generede,
    þær moncyn mot,   for meotude rot,
    soðne god geseon,   ond aa in sibbe gefean.

79a   Co   *balawan herge* (*hlotene*)
      Ett   *balawum si her* (Gr, Gr-W, Siep, Im *balawum her*)
      Holt 1953   *helepum her*
      Ett   *gehloten* (also all eds.)
79b   Ett   *aþroten* (also Gr, Gr-W, Siep)
      Mack   *abroten*
81b   Ett   *ne hogað*
      Gr   *hycgað* (also Gr-W, Siep)
82a   Ett   *ne gemon*
      Ett   *myrða lissa*
      Gr   *meorða lisse* (also Gr-W, Siep, Im, Mack)
82b   Ett   *blissa*
      Gr   *þær* (also Gr-W, Siep, Im, K-D)
84a   Ett   *bescerede*
      Gr   *biscerede* (also Gr-W)
84b   Co   *scyndum* (also Ett)
85b   Co   omits this verse; prints omission marks
      Ett   *geferede*
      Gr   *geherede* (also Gr-W, Siep, Im)
87b   Ett   *a* (also Gr)
      Ett   *gefeon* (also Gr, Gr-W, Siep)

DEOR

Welund him be wurman   wræces cunnade,
anhydig eorl,   earfoþa dreag;
hæfde him to gesiþþe   sorge ond longaþ,
wintercealde wræce,   wean oft onfond,
5   siþþan hine Niðhad on   nede legde,
swoncre seonobende   on syllan monn.
Þæs ofereode;   þisses swa mæg!

Beadohilde ne wæs   hyre broþra deaþ
on sefan swa sar   swa hyre sylfre þing,
10   þæt heo gearolice   ongieten hæfde
þæt heo eacen wæs;   æfre ne meahte
þriste geþencan   hu ymb þæt sceolde.
Þæs ofereode;   þisses swa mæg!

We þæt Mæðhilde   monge gefrugnon:
15   wurdon grundlease   Geates frige,
þæt hi seo sorglufu   slæp' ealle binom.
Þæs ofereode;   þisses swa mæg!

Ðeodric ahte   þritig wintra
Mæringa burg.   Þæt wæs monegum cuþ.
20   Þæs ofereode;   þisses swa mæg!

1a   Co *Weland*, as MS reading (also Th, Ett, Gr, Gr-W, Siep)
    Rieger 1861 *be wornum* (Gr-W *be warnum*)
    Kögel 1894 *be wurnan* (also Siep)
3a   Ett *gesiðe*
6a   Gr *swoncre seonobenne* (also Gr-W)
6b   Ett *unsyllan*
10a   Th *þa?*, in fn. (adopted by Ett)
11a   Siep *eacenu*
14a   Rieger 1861 *We þæt be Mæðhilde* (Siep *We be Mæðhilde*)
14b   Malone 1936 *mone gefrugnon* (also Mal 1961)
16a   Th *hī* (Ett, Gr, Gr-W, Siep, Mack *him*)
16b   Th *ealne*, in fn. (adopted by Ett, Gr)

We geascodan   Eormanrices
wylfenne geþoht;   ahte wide folc
Gotena rices.   Þæt wæs grim cyning.
Sæt secg monig   sorgum gebunden,
25 wean on wenan,   wyscte geneahhe
þæt þæs cynerices   ofercumen wære.
Þæs ofereode;   þisses swa mæg!

Siteð sorgcearig   sælum bidæled,
on sefan sweorceð,   sylfum þinceð
30 þæt sy endeleas   *earfoða* deal.   (MS earfoda)
Mæg þonne geþencan   þæt geond þas woruld
witig dryhten   wendeþ geneahhe,
eorle monegum   are gesceawað,
wislicne blæd,   sumum weana dæl.
35 Þæt ic bi me sylfum   secgan wille,
þæt ic hwile wæs   Heodeninga scop,
dryhtne dyre;   me wæs Deor noma.
Ahte ic fela wintra   folgað tilne,
holdne hlaford,   oþþæt Heorrenda nu,
40 leoðcræftig monn,   londryht geþah
þæt me eorla hleo   ær gesealde.
Þæs ofereode;   þisses swa mæg!

21b Ett *Eormenrices*
25b Co *wigsete*
29   Co *sweonceð ... þenceð*
30b Co *earfoða* (also all eds.)
33b Gr *gesceapað*
37b Co *nama* (also Ett)
39b Co *oððe ðæt*

WULF AND EADWACER

Leodum is minum   swylce him mon lac gife.
Willað hy hine aþecgan   gif he on þreat cymeð.
  Ungelic is us.
Wulf is on iege,   ic on oþerre.
5 Fæst is þæt eglond,   fenne biworpen.
Sindon wælreowe   weras þær on ige.
Willað hy hine aþecgan   gif he on þreat cymeð.
  Ungelice is us.
Wulfes ic mines widlastum   wenum dogode,
10 þonne hit wæs renig weder,   ond ic reotugu sæt,
þonne mec se beaducafa   bogum bilegde –
wæs me wyn to þon;   wæs me hwæþre eac lað.
Wulf, min Wulf,   wena me þine
seoce gedydon,   þine seldcymas,
15 murnende mod,   nales meteliste.
Gehyrest þu, Eadwacer?   Uncerne *earmne* hwelp   (MS earne)
  bireð wulf to wuda.
Þæt mon eaþe tosliteð   þætte næfre gesomnad wæs,
  uncer giedd geador.

1   Siep omission marks before line 1
3   Leo *ungelice* (also Siep)
4a   Siep *Wulf min is on iege*
5   Siep *fæste*
9   Hicketier 1888 *hogode* (also Tupper, Baker)
     Siep omits *wenum*
10a Siep *wæs hit reonig* (omits *þonne*)
11a Siep *me se beaducafa* (omits *þonne*)
13a Bülbring 1891 *Min Wulf, min Wulf* (also Tupper)
16   Holt 1893 *earmne*
     Siep *earone*
     Mack *eargne* (also Baker)
18   Grein *gesomnod*
19   Herzfeld 1890 *gæd* (also Siep)

THE WIFE'S LAMENT

   Ic þis giedd wrece   bi me ful geomorre,
   minre sylfre sið.   Ic þæt secgan mæg
   hwæt ic yrmþa gebad   siþþan ic up weox,
   niwes oþþe ealdes,   no ma þonne nu.
5   A ic wite wonn   minra wræcsiþa.
   Ærest min hlaford gewat   heonan of leodum
   ofer yþa gelac.   Hæfde ic uhtceare
   hwær min leodfruma   londes wære.
   Ða ic me feran gewat   folgað secan,
10   wineleas wræcca   for minre weaþearfe.   (MS wręcca)
   Ongunnon þæt þæs monnes   magas hycgan
   þurh dyrne geþoht   þæt hy todælden unc,
   þæt wit gewidost   in woruldrice
   lifdon laðlicost,   ond mec longade.
15   Het mec hlaford min   her heard niman.
   Ahte ic leofra lyt   on þissum londstede,
   holdra freonda;   forþon is min hyge geomor,
   ða ic me ful gemæcne   monnan funde
   heardsæligne,   hygegeomorne,
20   mod miþendne,   morþor hycgende
   bliþe gebæro.   Ful oft wit beotedan
   þæt unc ne gedælde   nemne deað ana,
   owiht elles.   Eft is þæt onhworfen.
   Is nu   swa hit no wære
25   freondscipe uncer.   *Sceal* ic feor ge neah   (MS seal)

3b   Co   *upaweox* (Ett *up awox*; Siep, Mack, Les *up aweox*)
10   Co   *wrecca* (also Ett)
12b   Ett   *todældon*
15b   Gr   *her eard* (also Siep, Les)
         Gr 1865   *herheard* (also K-D)
18a   Ett   *þæt*
20b   Th   *hycgendne* (also Ett, Gr, Gr-W, Mack, K-D, Les)
21b   Co   *beotedon* (Ett *beotodon*)
24b   Ett   inserts *nið todælde* as b-verse after *wære*
         Siep   omission marks between *nu* and *swa* (also K-D)
         Les   *is nu fornumen* as a-verse
25b   Th   *sceal* (also all eds.)

mines felaleofan   fæhðu dreogan.
Heht mec mon wunian   on wuda bearwe,
under actreo   in þam eorðscræfe.
Eald is þes eorðsele;   eal ic eom oflongad.
30   Sindon dena dimme,   duna uphea,
bitre burgtunas   brerum beweaxne,
wic wynna leas.   Ful oft mec her wraþe begeat
fromsiþ frean.   Frynd sind on eorþan,
leofe lifgende   leger weardiað,
35   þonne ic on uhtan   ana gonge
under actreo   geond þas eorðscrafu,
þær ic *sittan* mot   sumorlangne dæg,   (MS sittam)
þær ic wepan mæg   mine wræcsiþas,
earfoþa fela,   forþon ic æfre ne mæg
40   þære modceare   minre gerestan,
ne ealles þæs longaþes   þe mec on þissum life begeat.
A scyle geong mon   wesan geomormod,
heard heortan geþoht,   swylce habban sceal
bliþe gebæro   eac þon breostceare,
45   sinsorgna gedreag,   sy æt him sylfum gelong
eal his worulde wyn,   sy ful wide fah
feorres folclondes   þæt min freond siteð,
under stanhliþe,   storme behrimed,
wine werigmod   wætre beflowen,
50   on dreorsele;   dreogeð se min wine
micle modceare;   he gemon to oft
wynlicran wic.   Wa bið þam þe sceal
of langoþe   leofes abidan!

26b	Co	*fæhða* (also Ett)
27b	Th	*r[ecte] wudu*, in fn. (Ett *wudubearwe*)
28a	Siep	*actreowe*
29a	Co	*cald* (also Ett)
30b	Gr	*dune*
35b	Ett	*ane*
36a	Siep	*actreowe*
37a	Co	*sittan* (also all eds.)
41	Co	*ðæs longa ðæs* (Ett *þæs longaðes þæs*)
43b	Co	*swylc* (also Ett)
47b	Th	*þær?*, in fn. (adopted by Ett)
50b	Holt 1908	*wine min* (adopted by Siep)

RESIGNATION

Age mec se *ælmihtga* god! (MS ælmihta)
Helpe min se halga dryhten! Þu gesceope heofon ond eorþan,
ond wundor eall, min wundorcyning,
þær on sindon, ece dryhten,
5 micel ond manigfeald. Ic þe, mære god,
mine sawle bebeode ond mines sylfes lic,
ond min word ond min weorc, witig dryhten,
ond eal min leoþo, leohtes hyrde,
ond þa manigfealdan mine geþohtas.
10 Getacna me, tungla hyrde,
þær selast sy sawle minre
to gemearcenne meotudes willan,
þæt ic þe geþeo þinga gehwylce,
ond on me sylfum, soðfæst cyning,
15 ræd arære. Regnþeof ne læt
on sceade sceþþan, þeah þe ic scyppendum
wuldorcyninge waccor hyrde,
ricum dryhtne, þonne min ræd wære.
Forgif me to lisse, lifgende god,
20 bitre bealodæde. Ic þa bote gemon,
cyninga wuldor, cume to, gif ic mot.
Forgif þu me, min frea, fierst ond ondgiet,
ond geþyld ond gemynd þinga gehwylces
þara þu me, soþfæst cyning, sendan wylle
25 to cunnunge. Nu þu const on mec
firendæda fela. Feorma mec, hwæþre,
meotod, for þinre miltse, þeah þe ic ma fremede
grimra gylta þonne me god lyfde.
Hæbbe ic þonne þearfe þæt ic þine, seþeah,
30 halges heofoncyninges, hyldo getilge,
leorendum dagum, lif æfter oþrum

---

1 Th, Gr, Gr-W, Siep omit
2a Th *ahelpe* (also Gr, Gr-W, Siep)
3b Th *wuldorcyning* (also Gr, Siep)
4a Gr *þe þær* (also K-D, Malm)
17b Gr *wacor* (also Siep)

geseo ond gesece, þæt me siþþan þær
unne arfæst god ecan dreames,
lif alyfe, þeah þe lætlicor
35 bette bealodæde þonne bibodu wæron
halgan heofonmægnes. Hwæt þu me her fela
* * * forgeafe. Gesette minne hyht on þec,
forhte foreþoncas, þæt hio fæstlice
stonde gestaðelad. Onstep minne hige,
40 gæsta god cyning, in gearone ræd.
Nu ic fundige to þe, fæder moncynnes,
of þisse worulde, nu ic wat þæt ic sceal
ful unfyr faca, feorma me þonne,
wyrda waldend, in þinne wuldordream,
45 ond mec geleoran læt, leofra dryhten,
geoca mines gæstes. Þonne is gromra to fela
æfestum eaden, hæbbe ic þonne
æt frean frofre, þeah þe ic ær on fyrste lyt
earnode arna. Forlæt mec englas, seþeah,
50 geniman on þinne neawest, nergende cyning,
meotud, for þinre miltse, þeah ðe ic mana fela
æfter dogrum dyde. Ne læt þu mec næfre deofol, seþeah,
þin lim lædan on laðne sið,
þy læs hi on þone foreþonc gefeon motan,
55 þy þe hy him sylfum sellan þuhten,
englas oferhydige, þonne ece Crist;
gelugon hy him æt þam geleafan. Forþon hy longe scul[on],
werge wihta, wræce þrowian.
Forstond þu mec ond gestyr him, þonne storm cyme
60 minum gæste ongegn. Geoca þonne,
mihtig dryhten, minre sawle;
gefreoþa hyre ond gefeorma hy, fæder moncynnes,
hædre gehogode; hæl, ece god,
meotod meahtum swiþ. Min is nu þa
65 sefa synnum fah, ond ic ymb sawle eom

34b Gr *þeah þe ic lætlicor*
37a Th omission marks indicating verse missing *after* forgeafe
    Gr *hroðra forgeafe*
    Gr-W omission marks in a-verse *before* forgeafe (*also* Siep, Mack, K-D, Malm)
55b Gr *þuhton*

feam siþum forht,   þeah þu me fela sealde
arna on þisse eorþan.   Þe sie ealles þonc,
meorda ond miltsa   þara þu me sealdest.
No ðæs earninga   ænige wæron mid.

70   Hwæþre ic me ealles þæs   ellen wylle
habban, ond hlyhhan,   ond me hyhtan to,
frætwian mec on ferðweg,   ond fundian
sylf to þam siþe   þe ic asettan sceal,
gæst gearwian,   ond me þæt eal for gode þolian

75   bliþe mode,   nu ic gebunden eom
fæste in minum ferþe.   Huru me frea witeð
sume þara synna   þe ic me sylf ne conn
ongietan gleawlice.   Gode ic hæbbe
abolgen, brego moncynnes.   Forþon ic þus bittre wearð

80   gewitnad for[e] þisse worulde,   swa min *gewyrhto* wæron
                               (MS mingie wyrhto)
micle fore monnum,   þæt ic mart[ir]dom
deopne adreoge.   Ne eom ic dema gleaw,
wis fore weorude.   Forþon ic þas word spræce,
fus on ferþe,   swa me on frymðe gelomp

85   yrmþu ofer eorþan,   þæt ic a þolade
geara gehwylce –   gode ealles þonc –
modearfoþa   ma þonne on oþrum,
fyrhto in folce.   Forþon ic afysed eom
earm of minum eþle.   Ne mæg þæs anhoga,

90   leodwynna leas,   leng drohtian,
wineleas wræcca.   Is him wrað meotud.
Gnornað on his *geohþe*;   (MS geoguþe)

66a   Gr   *nalles feam siþum forht* (also Gr-W, Siep)
69b   B-F 1976 *ænige wæron.* / *Mid* * * * (adopted by Malm)
72a   Th   *forðweg* (also Gr, Siep, Malm)
           Gr 1865   *ferðweg*
80a   Th   *fore* (also Gr, Gr-W, Siep, Mack)
80b   Th   *gewyrhto* (also Gr, Mack, K-D, Malm)
81b   Th   *martyrdom* (also Gr)
83b   Th   *sprece* (also Gr)
86b–   Th   *godes ealles* / *þoncmod earfoþa* (Gr-W, Mack *gode* etc.)
  87a   Gr   *godes ealles* / *wonn modearfoþa* (Siep *gode* etc.)
92   Klaeb 1935   *geohþe*
           Gr omission marks throughout b-verse (also Gr-W, Siep, Mack)

ond him ælce mæle   men fullestað;
ycað his yrmþu;   ond he þæt eal þolað,
95   sarcwide secga,   ond him bið a sefa geomor,
mod morgenseoc.   Ic bi me tylgust
secge þis sarspel,   ond ymb siþ spræce,
longunge fus,   ond on lagu þence.
Nat min * * *
100   hwy ic gebycge   bat on sæwe,
fleot on faroðe.   Nah ic fela goldes,
ne huru þæs freondes   þe me gefylste
to þam siðfate,   nu ic me sylf ne mæg
fore minum wonæhtum   willan adreogan.
105   Wudu mot him weaxan,   wyrde bidan,
tanum lædan.   Ic for tæle ne mæg
ænigne moncynnes   mode gelufian,
eorl on eþle.   Eala, dryhten min,
meahtig mundbora,   þæt ic eom mode [s]eoc,
110   bittre abolgen.   Is seo bot æt þe
gelong æfter [li]fe.   Ic on leohte ne mæg
butan earfoþum   ænge þinga,
feasceaft hæle,   foldan [w]unian.
Þonne ic me to frempum   freode hæfde,
115   cyðþu gecwe[me],   me wæs a cearu symle
lufena to leane;   swa ic alifde nu.
Giet bið þæt *selast*,   þonne mon him sylf ne mæg
                                               (*selast* not in MS)
wyrd onwendan,   þæt he *þonne* wel þolige.   (MS þon?)

---

93   Th omission marks indicating verse missing after *mæle*
97b   Th *sprece*, in fn. (adopted by Gr)
99   Th omission marks through 1½ verses (also Gr-W, Siep, Mack, K-D)
        Gr *nat min sefa sarum geswenced*
        Malm omission marks through ½ verse
110   Th *bitre* (also Gr)
111a   Gr *gelong æfter laðe*
115b   Th *wæs a cearu symle* (also Gr, Gr-W, Siep)
117a   Gr *Grimlic bið þæt*
        Holt 1912 *selast* (also Siep, Mack, K-D, Malm)
118b   Th *þōn* (all eds. *þonne*)

IC WÆS BE SONDE (RIDDLE 60)

Ic wæs be sonde,   sæwealle neah,
æt merefaroþe,   minum gewunade
frumstaþole fæst.   Fea ænig wæs
monna cynnes   þæt minne þær
5   on anæde   eard beheolde;
ac mec uhtna gehwam   yð sio brune
lagufæðme beleolc.   Lyt ic wende
þæt ic ær oþþe sið   æfre sceolde
ofer meodu   muðleas sprecan,
10   wordum wrixlan.   Þæt is wundres dæl,
on sefan searolic,   þam þe swylc ne conn,
hu mec *seaxes* ord   ond seo swiþre hond,   (MS seaxeð)
eorles ingeþonc   ond ord somod,
þingum geþydan   þæt ic wiþ þe sceolde
15   for unc anum *twam*   ærendspræce   (MS twan)
abeodan bealdlice,   swa hit beorna ma
uncre wordcwidas   widdor ne mænden.

1a   Th   *sande* (also Ett, Gr)
5a   Ett   *anede*
9a   Gr   *ofer meodubence* (also Mack, K-D)
        Gr 1865   *ofer meodudrincende* (also Gr-W)
12a   Th   *seaxes* (also all eds.)
15a   Th   *twam* (also all eds.)
17b   Ett   *widor*
        Gr   *mændon*

THE HUSBAND'S MESSAGE

Nu ic onsundran þe   secgan wille
————————— treocyn   ic tudre aweox.
I[n] mec æld——————————   ———— sceal ellor londes
setta[n] —————————   ———————————c

5   sealte strea[mas]   ——————————————————sse.
Ful oft ic on bates ————————   ——————————— gesohte
þær mec mondryhten   min —————————
ofer heah *hafu.*   Eom nu her cumen   (MS hofu)
on ceolþele,   ond nu cunnan scealt

10   hu þu ymb *modlufan*   mines frean   (MS modlufun)
on hyge hycge.   Ic gehatan dear
þæt þu þær tirfæste   treowe findest.
Hwæt, þec þonne biddan het   se þisne beam agrof
þæt þu, sinchroden,   sylf gemunde

15   on gewitlocan   wordbeotunga
þe git on ærdagum   oft gespræcon,
þenden git moston   on meoduburgum
eard weardigan,   an lond bugan,
freondscype fremman.   Hine fæhþo adraf

20   of sigeþeode.   Heht nu sylfa þe
lustum *læran*   þæt þu lagu drefde,   (MS læram)
siþþan þu gehyrde   on hliþes oran
galan geomorne   geac on bearwe.
Ne læt þu þec siþþan   siþes getwæfan,

25   lade gelettan,   lifgendne monn.

2a   Gr *ymb treocynn* (Gr-W *ymb treocyn*)
        Mack *ymb þisum treocynne*
4   Gr *sette siðfæt ofer*
6   Gr *bates bosme sohte* (Les *bates bosme* ——————————— *gesohte*)
7b– Gr *min onsende, / heah hofu*
  8a
8a   Siev 1885 *hafu* (adopted by Les)
9b   Gr *sceall*
        Gr 1865 *scealt*
10a   Th *modlufan,* as MS reading? (also all eds.)
11a   Siep *on hyge þin hycge*
21a   Th *læran* (also all eds.)

Ongin mere secan,   mæwes eþel,
onsite sænacan,   þæt þu suð heonan
ofer merelade   monnan findest
þær se þeoden is   þin on wenum.
30 Ne mæg him [ofer] worulde   willa * * *
mara on gemyndum,   þæs þe he me sægde,
þonne inc geunne   alwaldend god
——————— ætsomne   siþþan motan
secgum ond gesiþum   s[inc gedælan],
35 næglede beagas.   He genoh hafað
fædan gol[des],   ——————————   (MS fędan)
———————ed elþeode   eþel healde,
fægre fold[an]   —————————————————
————— [hold]ra hæleþa,   þeah þe her min win[e]
40 ——————— ———————
nyde gebæded   nacan ut aþrong,
ond on yþa ge————g—   [ana] sceolde

30a   Ett   *on worulde* (also Gr-W, Mack, Les)
        Ker   *-n worulde*
        Gr   *to worulde*
30b– Ett *willa mara / beon on gemyndum*
 31a Gr   *willa gelimpan / mara on gemyndum* (also Mack, K-D, Les)
        Siep willa * * * / *mara on gemyndum* (also Ker)
33a   Ett *þæt git ætsomne?*, in fn. (adopted by Gr, Mack, Les)
34b   Gr   *sinc brytnian* (also Les)
        Kluge 1897 *sinc gedælan* (also Siep, Mack)
35   Th   *ætlede beagas*, as MS reading (also Ett)
36a   Ett *fættan goldes?*, in fn. (adopted by Gr-W, Siep; Mack *fettan goldes*)
        Gr   *feohgestreona, fættan goldes*, as a complete line
(36b–)Ett *þeah þe he on elþeode?*, in fn. (Gr *þeah he on elþeode*)
 37a Siep *þeah þe he feorran wunie / and mid elþeode*
        Mack omission marks followed by *mid elþeode*
        Les   *geond elþeode*
(38b–)Ett *wlancra hæleða?*, in fn. (Gr *him fela þegniað / wlancra hæleða*)
 39a
39b   Ett *winedryhten?*, in fn. (adopted by Gr)
42a   Th   *gong, reading* MS *geong* (also Ett)
        Gr   *begong*
        Gr 1865 *geong* (also Gr-W, Siep, Ker, Mack, K-D)
        Traut 1894 *gelagu* (also Les)
42b   Ett *ana sceolde* (also Gr, Mack, Les)
        Siep *anred sceolde*

faran on flotweg, forðsiþes georn,
mengan merestreamas.　　Nu se mon hafað
45　wean oferwunnen; nis him wilna gad,
ne meara, ne maðma, ne meododreama,
ænges ofer eorþan eorl gestreona,
þeodnes dohtor, gif he þin beneah.
Ofer eald gebeot incer twega
50　ge[h]yre ic ætsomne ᚻ·ᚱ geador,
ᚹ·ᛈ ond ᛗ aþe benemnan
þæt he þa wære ond þa winetreowe
be him lifgendum læstan wolde
þe git on ærdagum oft gespræconn.

50a　Th　*gecyre*, as MS reading (also Ett, Gr, Gr-W, Ker, K-D)
　　　Traut 1894　*gehyre* (also Siep, Mack, Les)
50b–　Th　prints runes (also Mack, K-D); other eds. transliterate
　51a　Gr　*D* for final rune (also Ker)
　　　Gr-W　*M(D?)*
　　　other eds.　*M*
54b　Th　*gespræcon* (also Ett, Gr, Gr-W, Siep, Ker, Mack)

THE RUIN

Wrætlic is þes wealstan!   Wyrde gebræcon;
burgstede burston,   brosnað enta geweorc;
hrofas sind gehrorene,   hreorge torras,
hringeat berofen,   hrim on lime;   (MS hrim geat torras berofen)
5 scearde scurbeorge,   scorene, gedrorene,
ældo undereotone.   Eorðgrap hafað
waldendwyrhtan,   forweorone, geleorene,
heard gripe hrusan,   oþ hund cnea
werþeoda gewitan.   Oft þæs wag gebad,
10 ræghar ond readfah,   rice æfter oþrum,
oftstonden under stormum.   Stea[p], geap gedreas.

1a Siep   *þæs* (also Ker, Mack)
1b Ett   *wyrde gebrecum*
    Gr   *wyrðige bræcon*
    Gr 1865   *wyrde gebræcon*
2a Ett   *burgstedas*
2b Ett   *brosniað*
3b Co   *hreos getorras*
    Gr   *hreoðge torras*
    Gr 1865   *hreorge* etc.
4a Co   *hrimgeat berofen* (Ett *hrymgeat behrofen*)
    Th   *hrimge (hrimige)? berofne*, in fn. (Gr *hrimge edoras berofene*)
    Gr 1865   *hrungeat-torras berofen* (also Gr-W)
        or   *hrungeat berofen* (also K-D, Les; Mack *hrungeat ✶ ✶ ✶ berofen*)
    Kluge 1897   *hringgeat berofen*
    Siep   *hrumge berofene*
5a Ett   *scurbeorga*
5b Siep   *scorene sind gedrorene*
6a Co   *under Eotene*
    Ett   *under Eotonum*
    Gr   *underetene*
7a Siep   *waldend and wyrhtan*
7b Ett   *forweorene* (also Gr)
8b Ett   *cneowa?*, in fn. (adopted by Siep)
    Gr   *cneo*
    Gr 1865   *cnea*
9a Th   *gewiton*, in fn. (adopted by Ett)
9b Ett   *þes* (also Gr)

Wu[n]að giet s[e]————————   ——————[n]um geheapen.

(MS wo–að)

Felon [i]———————————   ———————————[e]
grimme gegrunde[n]   ———————————————

15 ——————————r[e] scan   heo———————————————
——————————————g orþonc   ærsceaft ————————
——————————————g—— lamrindum beag.
Mod mo[nade   m]yneswiftne gebrægd;
hwætred in hringas   hygerof gebond

20 weall walanwirum   wundrum togædre.
Beorht wæron burgræced,   burnsele monige,
heah horngestreon,   heresweg micel,
meodoheall monig,   mondreama full;   (MS ᛁ dreama)
oþþæt þæt onwende   wyrd seo swiþe.

25 Crungon walo wide;   cwoman woldagas.
Swylt eall fornom   *secgrofra* wera.   (MS secg rof)
Wurdon hyra wigsteal   westenstaþolas.
Brosnade burgsteall,   betend crungon,
hergas to hrusan.   Forþon þas hofu dreorgiað,

30 ond þæs teaforgeapa   tigelum sceadeð,
hrostbeames rof.   Hryre wong gecrong,   (MS hrost beages)
gebrocen to beorgum,   þær iu beorn monig,
glædmod ond goldbeorht,   gleoma *gefrætwed*,   (MS gefrætweð)
wlonc ond wingal,   wighyrstum scan;

35 seah on sinc, on sylfor,   on searogimmas,
on ead, on æht,   on eorcanstan,

12a   Les   *worað*, as MS reading
12b   Ett   *geheawen* (also Gr, Les)
12a–b Kluge 1897   *Wunað giet se weallstan wæpnum geheawen* (Mack *wonað* etc.)
18b   Mack   *myne swiftne*
18a–b Les   *mod monade, myne swiftne gebrægd*
24a   Ett   *oð þæt onwende*
26a   Ett   *ealle*
26b   Th   *weras*, in fn.
      Ett   *secgrofe weras*
      Holt 1907b   *secgrofra* (also K-D, Les)
29b   Gr   *dreorgað*
30a   Co   *þæs teafor geapu* (also Th, Gr-W; Ett, Gr 1865 *þas teafor geapu*; Gr *þas teaforgeapu*)
31a   Gr 1865   *hrof* (also Gr-W, Ker, K-D, Les)
33b   Co   *gefrætwed* (also all eds.)
      Ett   *gleame*
36b   Siep   *eorcnanstan*

on þas beorhtan burg   bradan rices.
Stanhofu stodan;   stream hate wearp,
widan wylme.   Weal eall befeng
40   beorhtan bosme,   þær þa baþu wæ[r]on,
hat on hreþre.   Þæt wæs hyðelic.
Leton þonne geotan   [l] ———————————
ofer h[arn]e stan   hate streamas,
un[d]——————————   ——————————
45   [o]þþæt hringmere   hate ———————
———————————————   þær þa baþu wæron.
Þonne is ——————————————
——————————re   þæt is cynelic þing
hu se ———————————   ——————— burg ———

39b   Th   *ealne?*, in fn. (adopted by Ett)

THE WANDERER

1–5 The poem's introduction, like its conclusion, refers to God's grace (*are*, lines 1 and 114). For the common early view of these lines as a later interpolation see Bernhard ten Brink: "The epic introduction ... as well as the close, may be additions of a later time; because in them is expressed a Christian sentiment and view of life, with a distinctness quite absent from the body of the poem" (ten Brink 1877; tr. Kennedy 1883, 61). Sieper takes this supposed interpolation through line 7 (pp. 196–201). The integrity of *Wan* was defended by W.W. Lawrence (1902b, 460–80). Later opinion has varied as to whether lines 1–5 should be assigned to the narrator or the Wanderer; see note on lines 6–7, below.

1a The meaning of the word *anhaga*, which recurs in the form *anhogan* in line 40, is clear enough, essentially "one who is alone." *Spearwa anhoga* glosses *passer solitarius* in the *Lambeth Psalter* 101.8 (Lindelöf 1909, 159). However, the derivation of the word in its two forms has been disputed, the *a*- form resembling *haga*, "enclosure" (see Holthausen 1934, 147), and the *o*- form *hogian*, "to think" (see Gordon 1954, 3). Thus, the etymological meaning might be "one who is enclosed, or encloses himself, alone" or "one who meditates alone." Both Leslie and Dunning-Bliss think it likely that the two forms originally developed separately and then fell together; as the latter suggest, close similarity in meaning would facilitate this. The word, in its two forms, is recorded twelve times – all except the Psalter gloss in poetry. See *Concordance* A012:288 (*anhaga-*) and 293 (*anhoga-*).

1b In line 70 *gebidan* clearly means "wait." Here *gebideð* could mean either "awaits" or "experiences." Gollancz ("wisheth for") and Kershaw ("is ... looking for") take the word in the former sense, but the poem's more recent editors, Leslie and Dunning-Bliss, favour the latter. Both point out the echo of *are gebideð* (line 1) in *are seceð* (line 114) and the contrast between the passive reception of grace at the beginning of the poem and the active search for it at the end; see Leslie, p. 24, Dunning-Bliss, pp. 81–82. The meaning "experiences" is further supported by the adversative *þeah þe*; the Wanderer experiences grace "although" he must suffer on the wintry sea. However, the various uses of *gebidan* – "wait for," "live to see," "live through," "endure" – all embody a notion of the duration of time. Thus, although in this context the word is most closely rendered by "experiences," it conveys also the sense of enduring through hardships until grace is granted. For the occurrences of the word in its immediate context, see *Concordance* G005:207–14 and 268–75 (*gebid-*); G007:50–51 (*gebyd-*).

5b Earlier editors saw a personification of *Wyrd*, "Fate," here. Leslie and Dunning-Bliss, following B.J. Timmer (1941, 24–33 and 213–28, esp. 220–23), interpret the word simply as "man's lot." Willi Erzgräber, among other scholars, sees in the poem the Boethian notion of a *fatum* which is subject to divine Providence (1961, 57–85, esp. 78–79). Finding a degree of personification in the various references to *wyrd* in *Wan* (lines 5, 15, 100, 107) need not imply an evocation of Northern deities, but merely a poetic presentation of fatalism. Whether a force or an event, *wyrd* is associated with death and disaster. Cf. note on *Ruin* 24.

MS *arᵹd* is regularly printed as *aræd* – possibly equivalent to *anræd*, "resolute" (thus, with a query, Toller *Supp*), accented on the prefix, or more probably meaning "appointed" (thus Leslie and Dunning-Bliss) and accented on the second syllable. As Dunning-Bliss point out, the latter is less regular metrically, but has parallels elsewhere, e.g. *Beowulf* 183b *Wa bið þam ðe sceal* and, close in phrasing as well as metre, *Maxims I* 191 *geara is hwær aræd*.

6–7 Both Leslie and Dunning-Bliss treat these lines as the narrator's, with the Wanderer's monologue beginning at line 1 and continuing at line 8, the narrator interposing again at line 111 (also lines 88–91, Dunning-Bliss), an arrangement which follows the structural analysis of R.M. Lumiansky (1950, 104–12). Most of the earlier editors favoured a different arrangement, commencing the Wanderer's utterance at line 8, marking another speech later, usually at line 92, and giving lines 111–15 to the narrator. Stanley B. Greenfield argued for a monologue extending from line 8 to line 110; he noted that *Sea* and *Wife* provide parallels for beginning a lament with a first-person formula (1951, 451–65, esp. 455–6; endorsed in Greenfield and Calder 1986, 282–85). Greenfield subsequently noted that he was "inclined to yield" to the other position (1970, 113–16).

The issue of speech boundaries in *Wan* has been investigated fairly recently by Gerald Richman, who concludes that "the *swa*-clauses in *The Wanderer* [lines 6 and 111] would refer back to the previous speech material and forward to new material, thus supporting the interpretation of the poem as a single monologue" (1982, 469–79, esp. 479). For the structural divisions of the poem, see also notes on lines 1–5, above, and lines 88ff. and 110–15, below.

7b For parallelism with *earfeþa* and *wælsleahta*, one would expect the gen. pl. *hryra*, dependent on *gemyndig*. The form *hryre* has been construed as acc. object. Thus Ernst Kock opened the Wanderer's soliloquy at line 7b, and made *hryre* object of *cwiþan*, in apposition to *ceare* (1918, 78). Walther Fischer argued that *hryre* was the object of *cwæð*, line 6 (1935, 299–302). However, the construction of the sentences is smoother if *hryre* is treated as dat. object of *gemyndig*, following Toller *Supp* and Leslie – though Bruce Mitchell is unwilling to treat *hryre* in this way; see *Syntax*, § 65 and fn. 6, § 204 fn., § 1413; and Mitchell 1975, 14–15, where he speculates "Is it possible ... that *hryre* is in fact a levelled form of an aberrant genitive singular *hryran*?" Treating *hryre* as a dat. dependent on *gemyndig* makes it parallel in sense, though not in grammar, to *earfeþa* and *wælsleahta*. It is noteworthy that the form *hryre* is considerably more common than the other inflexions, and that the gen. pl. *hryra* is unrecorded. Although *gemyndig* is regularly used with gen. (and occasionally with acc.), there are two other instances of a construction with dat.: *gemyndige ... Cristes bebodum and ðæra apostola lare* in an Ælfric homily for Pentecost (Thorpe 1844–46, 1:312) and *gemindig minum naman 7 þines* in a late OE life of St Margaret (Herbst 1975, 77). The clear linking of gen. and dat. in the second example refutes Mitchell's objection that *hryre* in *Wan* 7b cannot be dative because of the genitives which precede it (*Syntax*, § 204 fn.) Kershaw's explanation of *hryre* as "a loose causal or comitative instrumental" (though rejected by Mitchell) is also plausible; so Dunning-Bliss: "causal or comitative dative." For the occurrences of *hryre* see *Concordance* H024:286–96 (*hryr-*) and R006:305 (*ryr-*).

8 Grein, Grein-Wülker, Gollancz, Sieper, Kershaw, and Krapp-Dobbie commence the Wanderer's speech at this point. Of these editors, only Kershaw indicates the close of this speech. See note on line 29b, below.

12b *Indryhten* = "noble." A rare word. Here, as in *Rid 43* 1, and *Rid 95* 1, the word seems to be a part of the traditional heroic vocabulary and used with a general sense of approbation. Dunning-Bliss, who believe that the Wanderer does not speak his mind because he has no worthy confidants – "the great ones of the earth have gone and only the foolish remain," deny that *indryhten* necessarily conveys approval (Introd., pp. 84–6), and gloss it as "aristocratic."

14a MS *healdne* has been almost universally emended to *healde*, subjunctive, parallel to *binde* (line 13). Another intrusive *n*, universally emended out, appears in *deornce* (line 89).

15a *Werig mod* is sometimes printed as a compound adjective, here used substantivally. Thus Thorpe, Gollancz, Kershaw, and Leslie. Parallelism with *se hreo hyge* supports treating *werig* as adjective and *mod* as noun. But the sense is little affected by the choice between compound adj. or adj. + noun. *Werigmod* is clearly a compound epithet at *Wife* 49.

16a *Hreo* suggests a more turbulent state of mind than *werig*. In his note on line 16, Leslie associates the word with sadness and grief, but Dunning-Bliss point out that *hreo[h]* means something more like "fierce," and make a link between this line and line 112, where the noun *torn* has similar connotations.

17b A masculine noun must be understood with *dreorigne*, either *hyge* from line 16 (Leslie) or *modsefan* in line 19 (Dunning-Bliss). *Dreorig*, which only rarely has its etymological meaning of "bloodstained," has been understood in most contexts as "sad." However, Karl Wentersdorf argues that the word has a stronger meaning, "anguished" (1975, 288). Similarly, *OE Dict* takes the meaning as suffering or causing "anguish, grief, horror, or misery."

20a *Earmcearig* = "wretched and sad." The compound is recorded only here and in *Sea* 14. Cf. *modcearig* (line 2), "sad at heart," and *wintercearig* (line 24), "desolate as winter" (Leslie).

22b Most editors emend to *minne* in keeping with the concept of a single lord. Mitchell argues that the pl. cannot be excluded either here or in lines 35–36 (1967, 139–49). However, the form *wenede* in line 36 is more likely to be sg. than (subjunctive) pl., and artistically the remembrance of one lord is more affecting than that of a series. Only one lord figures in the immediately following section of the poem, the dream passage, lines 37–44.

23a Ettmüller emended *heolstre* to *heolster* in order to supply a subject for "buried." As Kock argued (1904, 227), the text can be accepted in its unemended form with *ic* understood, *heolstre* being dat., and *hrusan* gen., "in the darkness of earth." The poem's more recent editors have followed Kock. The Dunning-Bliss suggestion that *hrusan* might be construed as nom. here and *hruse* as acc. in line 102 if both are taken as late OE levelled endings seems too tolerant of anomalous forms.

24a The first element of *wintercearig* has sometimes been interpreted in the sense "year," giving the meaning "sad with old age." Thorpe, Grein *Sprachschatz*, Grein-Köhler, and Bosworth-Toller give translations along these lines. Others, including Leslie and Dunning-Bliss, take *winter* in its literal sense with implications of desolation. See also note on *earmcearig* (line 20a), above.

24b MS *wapena* is universally emended to *waþema*. The phrase *waþema gebind* recurs in line 57a. There is dispute as to whether "the binding of the waves" refers to a covering of ice or merely an expanse of water. Dunning-Bliss favour the former, Leslie the latter. Elsewhere the word indicates either a unit of measure (as in *þreo gebind æles* in a charter, Robertson 1956, no. 86) or some kind of constriction. It glosses *strictura* and *tenacitas ventris* (constipation); see Wright-Wülker *Vocabularies*, col. 113, line 21 (*gebynd*) and col. 232, lines 32–33 (*gebind*), resp. *Isgebind(e)*, "the bond of ice," occurs in *Beowulf* 1133. The context in *Wan*, however, appears not to call for frozen waves: the Wanderer speaks of rowing in line 4 and of dull waves with seabirds bathing in lines 46b–47a. *Gebind* here, then, may indicate no more than a gathering together – of a large body of water. For the occurrences of the word, see *Concordance* G005:308–9 (*gebind*; *gebynd* is not listed).

25a *Seledreorig* = "sad over (i.e. at the loss of) a hall." This compound, like *selesecgas* in line 34, is unique. The earlier editors printed *sele dreorig*. Fischer (1935, 299–301) suggested that the two elements should be taken together as a compound adjective modifying an implied *ic*, and rejected the interpretation of it as two words – both Grein's "[Ich] suchte eines Schatzespenders Saal im Kummer" (1857–59 transl 1:252) which treated *bryttan* as a gen. dependent on *sele*, and Rudolf Jacobsen's explanation of *sele* and *bryttan* as parallel acc. objects of *sohte* (1901, 62n.). Wentersdorf (1975, 289–90) argues that *sele-* means "times, seasons" here, and translates the compound "anguished (*or* grieved) by the [troubled] times"; cf. note on line 17b, above. This translation is improbable, since the medial vowel of *sele* (sometimes *sæl*) is short; in *sæl*, "time, season," it is long.

27b If *mine* = *myne*, the MS *mine wisse* is metrically unusual because the first syllable of *mine* is short. *Mīne*, "my people," has been proposed independently by John Pope (1966, 82–83) – "might know of my (people)" – and by K.R. Brooks (1968, 158) – "knew my people." Pope notes that "know a person" would be expressed by *cunnan* not *witan*. The Pope-Brooks reading has the advantage of avoiding emendation, but the sense of knowing (i.e. feeling) concern for the speaker is more satisfactory than that of knowing, or knowing of, his people. Many have accepted Klaeber's emendation to *min mine wisse*, "felt love for me" or "took (kind) thought of me," on an analogy with *Beowulf* 169 *ne his myne wisse*, understood by Klaeber as "nor did he (God) take thought of him [Grendel]" (1909, 254). Various other suggestions have been made, several retaining *mine* in the sense of "thought," "purpose," or "love" and inserting another word to improve the metre. Leslie, objecting to Klaeber's proposal on metrical and syntactic grounds, suggests *me mine wisse*, "feel love for me." Dunning-Bliss: *minne myne wisse*, "would know my thought" (Introd., p. 63). They question the existence of *mine/myne* as "love" in OE, but Leslie points to *wifmyne* in *Genesis* 1861 (the word refers to Pharaoh's desire for Sarah). Of the emendations, Leslie's is the smoothest, but the line can be accepted unemended as "would feel concern" with "for me" implied. The phrase then forms an A verse with short first stressed syllable.

In the form *myne* the word occurs six times in the poetry meaning "care, concern" (a feeling which might be positive or negative). Cf. also ... *þam mannum þe habbað ænigne myne to Gode* in Ælfric's Homily for the Sunday after Ascension (Pope 1967–68, 1:383). See *Concordance* M025:56.

28a MS *freond lease* involves another *n* error. Universally emended to *freondleasne*.

29a For a possible transition of speakers after this verse, see the following note.

Several editors, including Dunning-Bliss, emend MS *weman* to *wenian* because of the appearance of that word (*wenede*) in line 36. This emendation was first made by Grein, but in his corrections to his edition he returned to the MS form (Grein 1865, 421). (Grein-) Wülker even thought it possible that the MS reading was *wenian*. Dunning-Bliss note three other places where the scribe wrote *m* for *ni* (*Christ* 361, *Guthlac* 696, *Juliana* 128). However, all of these involve the same element: *nied*. Since "entice" makes perfectly good sense here, emendation is unnecessary.

29b The shift from the first to the third person here has led some scholars to see a change of speaker. Kershaw ends the Wanderer's speech at line 29a, though she admits that later points are a possibility (see Introd., p. 2, and text). Krapp-Dobbie claim to adopt this point for closing quotation marks (Introd., p. xxxix), but their text has none – here or elsewhere – for the first speech. Regarding the poem as a debate between the narrator and the Wanderer, W.F. Bolton assigns lines 1–7, 29b–57, 64–91, and 111–15 to the former (1969, 7–34).

31b The noun *gehola* is related to *helan*, "to conceal." Grein *Sprachschatz* glossed it as "celator, tutor, Berger?" (also Grein-Köhler). Julius Zupitza found support for this translation in Ælfric's account of the Seven Sleepers: *we beoð þine geholan and ealne weg þine midsprecan* (Skeat 1966 [1881–1900], 1:524); and in the gloss *gehala vel geruna* for *sinmistes vel consecretalis* (Wright-Wülker *Vocabularies*, col. 110, lines 21–22). See Zupitza 1890, 279–80. However, as Dunning-Bliss note (Introd., p. 59), these two uses point to a meaning "confidant" rather than "protector." Leslie glosses "close friend." Campbell *Addenda* deletes Bosworth-Toller's "protector" and supplies "friend, confidant."

32a *Warað* = "occupies," i.e. "occupies his mind." In this line the word is commonly translated "is his portion." Gollancz: "His portion is the exile's track"; Eilert Ekwall: "exile falls to his lot" (1924, 134–35); Leslie: "exile claims him." But Kershaw translates "His thoughts are full of homeless wanderings, lit. '(The thought of) his exile possesses him'" (Notes); Dunning-Bliss: "exile pre-occupies him" (Introd., p. 70).

34a *Selesecgas* (a hapax legomenon) = "retainers." Cf. *seledreorig* in line 25. Leslie suggests that, like *seldguma* and *selepegn* (*Beo* 249 and 1794, resp.), the word refers to men of lower rank. But in this passage in *Wan* the speaker seems to be thinking of those who participate in the festivities of the hall, i.e. his companions. Cf. *secga geseldan* in line 53. Grein and Grein-Wülker printed *sele, secgas*, but compounds in *sele-* are well attested. Grein 1865 corrected to *selesecgas* (p. 421).

35b–36a For the possibility of construing this as pl., see note on line 22b, above.

37a The verb *wat* has no obvious object. Various solutions to this problem have been proposed. Kershaw, followed by Dunning-Bliss, takes *wat* here as a repetition of *wat* in line 29 and believes that "the object is to be inferred from the preceding passage" – i.e. lines 30–31. Leslie argues that the object of *wat* is the statement in lines 39–44; similarly Mitchell (1968b, 178–82). Walter Sedgefield believed that *wat* was used absolutely (1922, p. 154). Leslie rejects this solution on the grounds that *witan* cannot be used in this way. But since there is no evident stated object, the verb should be interpreted in a general way as "understands" – without an explicit object, but referring back to *wat* in line 29, and with the following lines, 39–44, an exemplification of the statement in lines 30–31 *hu sliþen bið sorh to geferan* ...

37–57   The syntax of this passage has been very variously interpreted. Krapp-Dobbie place periods after lines 40, 44, 48, 50a, 53a, 53b, 55a, and 57; Leslie after lines 44, 48, 50a, 55a, and 57; Dunning-Bliss after lines 38, 48, 52, and 57.

Both the latter editions point out that conjunctive order, with the verb at the end of the clause, indicates *Đonne/þonne* means "when" in lines 39 and 51, resp. *Đonne/Þonne* in lines 45 and 49, resp., as Dunning-Bliss observe, is followed by demonstrative order, with the verb immediately following, which suggests that in these instances the word is the adverb "then." In their treatment of the entire passage Dunning-Bliss follow Mitchell 1968b, 187–91. Noting that "the appearance of four *þonne*-clauses within 20 lines strongly suggests correlation" (Introd., p. 20), they punctuate lines 39–48 and 49–52 as two sentences displaying "a chiastic pattern in which each of the subordinate clauses, *ðonne sorg ond slæp* and *þonne maga gemynd*, describes the dreams of the Wanderer, and each of the principal clauses, *ðonne onwæcneð eft* and *þonne beoð þy hefigran*, describes his waking experiences" (Introd., p. 21). Lines 46 and 52 are regarded as in asyndetic coordination with the *þonne* clauses which precede them (p. 19).

Dunning-Bliss's argument is attractive, and some kind of correlation is certainly felt between the series of *þonne*'s, but perhaps not the strictly grammatical one which they perceive. Both lines 41ff. and 45ff. gain greater emphasis if *þinceð him on mode* (line 41a) is taken as the principal clause of the sentence beginning at line 39, and *Đonne onwæcneð eft ...* (line 45) as that of the next – making three sentences for Dunning-Bliss's two. With the syntax of lines 45 and 46 understood in this way, the clauses in line 52a and b can be treated – again, for reasons of emphasis – as principal, rather than subordinate and parallel to line 51. Syntactically, this handling of the entire passage resembles Kershaw's, though her punctuation differs at the following points: semicolons after lines 38, 53; comma after line 50a; periods after lines 51, 52.

For a useful caveat about the inevitable distortion which occurs when OE texts are forced into the mould of modern punctuation, see Mitchell 1980, 385–413.

40a   For the word *anhoga/anhaga*, see note on line 1a, above.

41–44   This passage evidently refers to a ceremony in the hall. L.M. Larson commented that the reference was to the formal reception of the retainer into the lord's *comitatus* (1908, esp. 461, n. 11). The same theory was elaborated at greater length by Frederick Tupper, who cited

Maxims I 67–68 (*Hond sceal heafod inwyrcan, hord in streonum bidan,* / *gifstol gegierwed stondan, hwonne hine guman gedælan*) and *A Journey Charm* 23bff. (*si me wuldres hyht,* / *hand ofer heafod* ...) as allusions to the same Germanic ceremony of "commendation," whereby a retainer pledged service and a lord protection and rewards (1912, 97–100). The gesture of placing head and hands on the knee certainly seems to have the implication of submission on the one side and protection on the other, but *hwilum* (*Wan* 43) indicates that the ceremony took place on more than one occasion (see Leslie, Notes), so it cannot have been the initiation specifically. More probably a ritual enactment of the bonds and obligations between lord and man took place at times of formal gift-giving – as implied by *giefstolas breac.*

42b Grein-Wülker, followed by Sieper and Kershaw, read, erroneously, MS *læge,* and printed *lecge* as an emendation.

43b *Swa* is commonly translated "as when," which makes good sense but is rejected by Mitchell because unparalleled (1968b, 182–87; see also *Syntax,* §§ 2608 and 3285). In his 1968 article Mitchell offers several possibilities, mostly with "because," which is not convincing here. His first suggestion, "just as," is the most persuasive of his alternatives. The translation "as when" is vigorously defended by Dunning-Bliss, who state that "Here literary considerations must outweigh linguistic arguments." Leslie also understands the conjunction in this way.

44b *Brucan,* usually accompanied by a genitive, occasionally takes a dative or accusative. Some see *giefstolas* here as acc. pl. Thus Bosworth-Toller. But since the passage refers to one lord, one throne seems more appropriate. Cf. note on line 22b, above. Thorpe suggested emending to *giefstoles,* a suggestion adopted by Ettmüller and Gollancz – and by Campbell *Addenda.* However, as Klaeber pointed out (1906, 300–301), *-as* does occur as the gen. sg. termination (in comparatively late texts; see Sievers-Brunner § 237, Anm. 1) and should be so regarded here, making emendation unnecessary. Klaeber's further suggestion that *he* in line 43 refers to the lord and not his retainer is less persuasive (1929, 229), although it is regarded as a possibility by Mitchell (1968b, 182–187).

46b *Wegas* = *wǣgas,* "waves," with long vowel. Gollancz translated "ways." But, as well as being supported by the metre, "fallow waves" is found elsewhere in the poetry: *on fealone wæg* (*Gifts of Men* 53) and *fealewe wægas* (*Andreas* 1589). Most editors have not felt the need to emend, but

Dunning-Bliss, following J.W. Bright (1891, 161), print *wægas*; they argue
that the scribe "would no doubt have written *wægas* if he had understood
the word correctly."

49–53 For the syntax of this passage, especially the *þonne* clauses, see
also note on lines 35–57, above.

In line 51, it is possible to take either *maga gemynd* or *mod* as the subject
of *geondhweorfeð*. Because *greteð* and *geondsceawað* (line 52) have no other
expressed subject, Leslie thinks the three verbs are parallel, sharing the
same subject, *gemynd*. However, this produces a strained translation:
"when recollection of kinsmen pervades his imagination, comes to it (the
imagination) joyously, eagerly surveys it." Leslie's further identification
of *secga geseldan* (line 53) with the imagination, "the companion of men,"
is also a rather forced image. Dunning-Bliss, too, treat the verbs as parallel,
but regard *mod* as the subject, and translate "when his imagination calls
his kinsmen to mind one by one, greets them joyfully, gazes at them
eagerly" (Introd., p. 22), a very free rendering of *maga gemynd mod geondhweorfeð*, which they render more literally as "his imagination visits every
part of his memory of his kinsmen"; this interpretation, like Leslie's,
involves a strained use of metaphor. The image of a memory moving
through a mind is more natural than the converse, and the subject of
greteð and *geondsceawað* can be taken to be an implied *he*, just as in lines
22b–23a it is an implied *ic*. The object of these verbs is to be inferred
from *maga gemynd*. Some editors, including Krapp-Dobbie, treat *secga
geseldan* as the object of the verbs in line 52. Leslie regards the phrase as
the object of *geondsceawað* and as a reference to *mod*.

Peter Clemoes (1969), who, like Dunning-Bliss, takes *mod* as the subject
of the verbs in lines 51–52, sees these lines as exemplifying the patristic
notion of the mind's ability to range beyond the confines of the body, and
compares the passage to *Sea* 58–64a. Cf. also an earlier article by Vivian
Salmon (1960). And see note on *Sea* 58–62.

Translate lines 51–52: "... when the memory of his kinsmen moves
through his mind: he greets it with utterances of joy, scans it eagerly."
See note on line 52a, below, for *gliwstafum*.

50a The simplest way to treat *sare* is as an adjective applied to *benne*, but
it is also possible to construe the word as an adverb or as the noun *sar* in
the dative case. Both Leslie and Dunning-Bliss adopt the adjectival interpretation.

50b Dunning-Bliss differ from other editors in punctuating this verse

and also the similar line 55b as parentheses, with dashes. But this punctuation unnecessarily complicates the syntax. The parallelism between the
two verses is preserved if each is punctuated as a principal clause followed
by a subordinate clause which serves to expand and explain it.

52a Since the first element of the hapax legomenon *gliwstafum* has the
meanings "music," "mirth," here the idea of sounds of joy seems appropriate. However, Salmon, relating the passage to shamanistic practices,
understands the word to convey the idea of music specifically: "with music
runes" or "with magic songs" (1960, 8). The second element, *stæf*, "written
character, letter," appears to have weakened in meaning to "expression,
indication." Thus, the compound presumably means something like "with
utterances of joy." Leslie and Dunning-Bliss translate simply "joyfully"
(Bosworth-Toller: "joyously"), and cite as parallels *arstafum* (*Rid 26* 24)
and *sarstafum* (*Guth* 234); these seem to mean "with marks of kindness"
and "with cruel words," resp.

53–54 The linking of *secga geseldan* with what follows rather than with
what precedes is structurally more persuasive. Ettmüller, Grein, Grein-
Wülker, Sieper, Kershaw, and Dunning-Bliss punctuate in this way. Such
a punctuation allows lines 54–55a to be perceived as a variation of
line 53. The referent of *secga geseldan*, "companions of men," has often
been taken to be the kinsmen of line 51. Thus Kershaw translates freely:
"His warrior comrades again melt away [emending *oft* to *eft*, line 53], and
as they vanish their spirits bring no familiar greetings to his ear." Translations of this type depend upon a metaphorical understanding of *swimmað*
(line 53) and *fleotendra* (line 54). But, as W.J.B. Owen (1950) argued, and
as the OE *Concordance* confirms, there is no evidence that the verbs could
be used in these senses in the A-S period; see Owen 1950. Similarly, it is
very doubtful if *fer(h)ð* could be used for "spirit" in this concrete sense,
as Ekwall pointed out (1924, 135). However, Owen's objection to the
metaphorical interpretation of *swimman* and *fleotan* can also be made to
his own "realistic" interpretation of these verbs as references to sailors on
a ship (a modification of Sedgefield 1922, 154–55), since his explanation
demands unrecorded transferred senses for *swimman* and *fleotan*. For the
occurrences of these disputed words in their immediate contexts, see
Concordance Fo06:294–97 (*ferhð-*) and Fo07:8, 10–11, 13 (*ferð-*); Fo08:241,
282–86 (forms of *fleotan*); G033:48 (*geswummen*) and G042:159 (*giswom*);
S030:319, S032:236–38, S033:118, 149 (forms of *swimman*); S033:273–
74 (*swym-*).

Graham Midgely (1959) regards *secga geseldan* as the seabirds mentioned
in line 47, with *fleotendra ferð* understood as "a group or troop of floating

ones." His handling of the passage incorporates G.V. Smithers's interpretation of *ferð* with this meaning as a Norse borrowing (1951–52, 84–85). Midgely's explanation is adopted in its essentials by Dunning-Bliss, who substitute "minds" for "troop." This identification of the *secga geseldan* with the seabirds has the advantage of bringing out a parallelism between the present passage and lines 45–48, and a resemblance with *Sea* 18–22. Nevertheless, an allusion to the vision of kinsmen should not be excluded. On one level the "companions of men" are seabirds, but on another they are a reminder of the illusory vision which vanishes, just as the birds swim away. Mitchell argues that in fact *secga geseldan* can be taken *apo koinou* with both what precedes and what follows it (1980, 396).

In connection with seabirds the meaning "troop" for *ferð* is more appropriate than "minds, spirits," and as a Scandinavianism is supported by the hapax legomena *hrið* (*Wan* 102) and *hrimceald* (*Wan* 4), corresponding to ON *hrið* and *hrímkaldr*, resp. (see Smithers). The resemblance to the cognate OE *fyrd*, which occurs as *ferd* or *færd* in Anglian texts (Campbell *Grammar*, § 193a) would have been perceived by the listener. Smithers is followed by Campbell *Addenda*, who gives the gloss "crowd." Taken as the subject of *bringeð*, *ferð* should be sg., not neuter pl. "minds, spirits." Dunning-Bliss explain their pl. as the rendering of a distributive sg. – each "floating one" having one mind only. Leslie's treatment of lines 53b–54a as a parenthetic comment on a hallucination – "the minds of seafarers often swim away" – is unconvincing.

Oft in line 53b is usually emended to *eft*. The idea of the birds swimming away *again* or *back* is more pointed than that of their swimming away *often*, though it might be argued that the Wanderer uses the word *oft* to indicate that his experiences are repeated (as in lines 1, 8, 17, 20, 40). The MS reading is retained by Midgely and Leslie.

Translate lines 53–55a: "The companions of men swim away again; the host of floating ones brings there no familiar speech(es)." See also the following note.

55a This phrase is commonly understood as "familiar sayings." Both elements of the hapax *cwidegiedd* have the sense of "utterance," the former embodying the notion of rational words, the latter of narrative whether sung or spoken. Dunning-Bliss conceive the first element to exclude the idea of song which may be present in *giedd*; they translate "spoken utterances" (see Introd., p. 44), a rendering which is followed by *OE Dict*. But more significant is the emphasis of both elements on *meaningful* utterance. Midgely's "speeches or songs expressing thoughts" (1959) is more exact. As he observes, the point is that the birds make "mere noise." For the occurrences of *cwide*, see *Concordance* C014:147 (*cwed-*);

Co15:120–34 (*cwid-*), 186 (*cwude*), 189–204 (*cwyd-*). For *giedd*, see note on *Wulf* 19.

57a For *waþema gebind*, see note on line 24b, above.

58ff. Line 58 begins the contrasting second half of the poem, now generally regarded as a continuation of the Wanderer's monologue – but numerous other accounts of the poem's structure have been offered. R.C. Boer saw lines 58–87 as an interpolation between two passages uttered by different speakers (1903, esp. 4–6). Sieper regarded lines 58ff. as a homiletic addition of a composite nature (pp. 196–201); similarly W.A. Craigie (1923–24, 15), who attributed the addition of this section to a mistake caused by misplaced leaves in the scribe's original. A.A. Prins (1964, 241–46) believed that *Res* 84–end rightly forms the sequel to *Wan* 57. For the Craigie and Prins theories, see also Part 1, pp. 27–28, above. Pope argued for a second speaker beginning at this point and continuing through line 110 (1965, 164–73), but retracts this argument in favour of the monologue interpretation (1974, 75–76). Bolton has the Wanderer taking up the debate from the narrator at this point; see note on line 29b, above.

58–59 Grein's omission of the final *n* from MS *mod sefan* has been generally accepted. The scribe seems to have thought the phrase was accusative with *ne* the inflectional ending rather than the negative: he writes *mod sefan minne*. This would make *modsefan* the object of *gesweorce*, "darken," with the subject an unexpressed "I" or "it." Since the verb is elsewhere intransitive, an intransitive use is more probable here: "I cannot think why in this world my mind should not grow dark" (adopting Grein's emendation).

Scholars disagree as to whether the Wanderer's mind does or does not grow dark. Lumiansky argues that it does not grow dark, because of the Christian wisdom which the Wanderer has acquired (1950, 106). Ida Gordon takes issue with Lumiansky and asserts that the Wanderer *is* saddened (1954, 6). J.E. Cross adopts a similar position (1961, 67). Leslie finds significant the placing of *geond þas woruld* outside the subordinate clause (thus making the phrase modify *geþencan*) and the emphasis on the alliterating *þas*: "the discussion of the wanderer's state of mind [is confined] to the evidence of this world alone." But Dunning-Bliss assert that *geond þas woruld* "obviously belongs with the following clause"; also, "think in this world" instead of "why in this world" sounds a little forced. Mitchell points out that the subjunctive *gesweorce* can be translated either as "does not become dark" or "may not [or "shall not"] become dark," and comments: "the mere fact that the wanderer can think of no reason why he does, may, or will not despair can scarcely be accepted as proof that he eventually does" (1968a, 57–59). Dunning-Bliss state that the wording "leaves open the question ..." and quote Mitchell. In the context of the following lines, which paint a gloomy picture of decay, a darkening of the Wanderer's mind is appropriate, but, as Leslie notes, *þas* hints at a broader context – which emerges at the end of the poem.

62 One or two scholars have ended the Wanderer's speech at this point. Thus Bernard Huppé closed at line 62a what he saw as the first of "two contrasting and complementary pagan monologues" and commenced at 62b a Christian "bridge passage" extending through line 87. See Huppé 1943, esp. 529–30.

64a MS *wearþan* has been emended to the usual *weorþan* by several editors, including Krapp-Dobbie, but interchange between *ea* and *eo* does occur – it is especially characteristic of Northumbrian texts (Campbell *Grammar*, § 278) – so the MS form should be allowed to stand here.

65a A hypermetric verse in a gnomic context. Cf. the hypermetric group at the end of the poem, lines 111–15. Prins thinks the text corrupt here, and suggests that 65a was originally a complete, though not perfect, line (1964, 240–41).

65b–72 This passage, as a call for moderation, has been compared with admonitions in Wulfstan, especially his *De Baptismate*: *Ne beon ge ofermode ne to weamode ne to niðfulle ne to flitgeorne ne to felawyrde ne ealles to hlagole ne eft to asolcene ne to unrote. And ne beon ge to rance ne to gylpgeorne ne færinga to fægene ne eft to ormode* ... See VIIIc in Bethurum 1957, 184. The resemblance was first pointed out by Klaeber 1913, 259. Elizabeth Suddaby, who comments that *to fægen* "seems at first sight out of place," suggests that Wulfstan is here warning against an unstable temperament and that the *Wan* passage contains a blurred reflection of the same idea (1954, 465–66). Cf. also *Ne ænig man to hlagol sy ne færinga to fægen ne eft ne beo to ormod*, Homily Xc in Bethurum, p. 205. Leslie, who regards the *Wan* lines as an injunction to moderation, comments that they embrace "both Christian teaching ... and the nobler of the heroic virtues" (Introd., pp. 13–15).

However, Mitchell argues that all of these passages use the device of meiosis, whereby an admonition not to be too ... really means that the quality in question should be avoided altogether. See Mitchell 1968b, 191–98, and *Syntax*, §§ 1142–43, and cf. also *Res* 27b–28. This argument works well for most of the epithets; for *fægen*, "joyful," it is more dubious. In the case of *gielpes to georn*, the addition of *ær he geare cunne* indicates that a *gielp*, "boast," based on self-knowledge is justifiable. The following lines, 70–72, further clarify this. Dunning-Bliss's "foolish self-glorification" for *gielp* in this instance (Introd., pp. 54–58 – on *gielp* and *beot*) is therefore too pejorative. Their translation of *fægen* as "servile" here is supported only by the description of Cerberus's reaction to Orpheus in the Alfredian Boethius, *ongan onfægnian mid his steorte* [*fægnian* in another MS] (Sedgefield 1899, chap. 35, p. 102), but this can be rendered literally "began to show gladness with his tail." Bosworth-Toller translate the word in this way. A.D. Horgan (1987, 44) renders it "prosperous," relating it to *ne longa felicitate luxurient* in Boethius (*Consolation*, book 4, prose 6; in Stewart, Rand, and Tester, p. 366) and to *feohgifre*. Mitchell's "over-confident" for *fægen* here is more plausible, though "over-" is conveyed by *to* rather than inherent in the adjective itself. For the uses of *fægen, fægnian, fægnung, fægenness*, see *Concordance* F001:93 (*faegen*); F001:100–101 (*fagen-*); F002:269–72 (*fægen-*); F002:313–24 and F003:1–7 (*fægn-*); F004:220 (*fegne*).

The entire passage is related by Horgan to God's assignment of good and ill fortune according to men's capacities. But the emphasis here is on the avoidance of faults, not on the divine wisdom as in Boethius 4.6. In fact, the whole passage can be regarded as a call for self-control. Some of the qualities referred to, i.e. elation and eagerness to make a boast, are not totally undesirable; others are, and the modifying *to* can be explained as understatement in those cases.

Hrædwyrde, "hasty of speech" (line 66), is a hapax legomenon, but is paralleled by *felawyrde*, "talkative," in Wulfstan VIIIc, quoted above, and by *fægerwyrde*, "fair of speech," and *wærwyrde*, "careful of speech" (*Precepts* 12 and 57, resp.).

As Dunning-Bliss observe, *cunne* in line 69 "is best taken as absolute," but its implied object, as indicated by the repeated *cunne* in line 71, is *hwider hrepra gehygd hweorfan wille* (line 72). Mitchell 1980 suggests that the *cunne* clause may be linked *apo koinou* with both lines 69a and lines 70–72 (p. 407).

The context clearly indicates the meaning "wait" for *gebidan* (line 70). In line 1, the word means "experience" (see note).

Collenferð (line 71) is glossed by Bosworth-Toller as "fierce-minded, bold of spirit"; by *OE Dict* as "brave, bold-spirited; proud; audacious"; Grein *Sprachschatz* and Grein-Köhler relate the verb to OHG *quellen*, "swell." The adjective is a poetic term, applied to warriors in a context of approbation, and found in apposition to *anhydige, ellenþriste, cene, ellenrofe*. In view of these rather general connotations, Dunning-Bliss's "ready for action" is probably over-precise. For the occurrences of *collenfer(h)ð* (once as *collenfyrhþ*), see *Concordance* C006:202–3.

73b *Gæstlic* is more common in the form *gastlic*, both normally meaning "spiritual" as opposed to "corporeal." The *a*- spelling is rare in poetry but extremely frequent in homiletic prose; the *æ*- spelling is more characteristic of poetry. Smithers argues that in the present instance the word "clearly means 'awesome' ... and not 'spiritual' or 'mysterious'" (1957, 141). Such a meaning is supported by a single occurrence of the verb *gæstan*, "terrify" (*Juliana* 17). Leslie and Toller *Supp* gloss *gæstlic* in *Wan* 73 "terrible," Dunning-Bliss "terrifying." Campbell *Addenda* cites this usage in a late homily: *mycel stefne 7 gastlic* (Warner 1917, 85). As Smithers points out, lines 73–74 allude to the fear associated with the end of the world. However, it is not unreasonable to see also in the word *gæstlic* here its more general sense of "spiritual, immaterial." Kershaw gives "mysterious" in her translation, and tentatively suggests in her notes that the word may imply "'a spiritual time' in contrast to *þisse worulde*."

74a MS *ealle* is emended by some editors, including Leslie, to *eall*, in agreement with *wela*. Others, including Krapp-Dobbie and Dunning-Bliss, emend to *ealre*, in agreement with *þisse worulde*. However, the MS reading can be accounted for as it stands. The most likely explanation is a pl. adj. with a collective sg. noun, as in *ealle folc hine beweop* (Ælfric's *Life of the Maccabees*, in Skeat 1966 [1881–1900], 110), *ealle þreat gecorenra lareowa* (OE Bede, Miller 1890–91, book 4, chap. 19, p. 310), *ealle wisdom heora* (rendering *omnis sapientia eorum* in the *Cotton Tiberius* and *Arundel Psalter* glosses 106.27; Campbell 1974 and Oess 1910, resp.); with the last cf. *ealle wisdomas* in another gloss (*Cotton Vitellius*, Rosier 1962). The use of *ealle* in *Wan* 74a can alternatively be explained as an adverb. Cf. also *ealle eorðan ymbehwyrft utan ymblicggan* in the prose section of the verse *Solomon and Saturn* (Menner 1941, 170). In late OE texts, presumably post-dating *Wan, ealle* seems to be becoming an indeclinable form and frequently shows lack of concord. See, passim, *High-Frequency Concordance, ealle*, E003:1 – E005:629.

76a *Biwaune = biwawene*, past participle of *biwawan*, "blow upon."

77b The early editors took the hapax *hryðge* as an allusion to the ruinous state of the buildings, relating the word to *hrīðian*, "to shake, have a fever." Grein emended to a verb form, *hryðgeað ederas*, but restored *hryðge þa ederas* in his corrections (Grein 1865, 421). The connection between *hryðge* here, *hrīð* in line 102, and ON *hríð*, "snow, snow-storm," was pointed out by William Strunk, who translated *hryðge*, "snow-covered" (1903, 72–73). Kock argued for "storm-beat" (1918, 78). Leslie glosses "exposed to storms" (also Campbell *Addenda*); Dunning-Bliss "snow-swept." That the idea of snow, as well as storm, is embodied in *hryðge* is indicated by the way in which *hrīð* is used in line 102, and also by the mention of hoar-frost in the present line along with the linking of hoar-frost with snow in line 48. Cf. note on *ferð* (line 54), above, the meaning of which is also illuminated by a Norse usage.

The basic sense of *edor* is "fence" or "enclosure." Kock translates "yards" here (1918, 78); Leslie "precincts." But in the present instance the word seems to mean something more like "buildings" (Dunning-Bliss's translation), a usage which is similar to that in the formulaic *in under edoras* (*Genesis* 2447 and 2489; *Beo* 1037 – spelled *eoderas*). The word is also used metaphorically in the poetry for "lord" or "prince" as protector.

78a "Wander" does not make sense for *woriað*. Some such extended meaning as Grein *Sprachschatz* "rollen in Trümmern umher" (also Grein-Köhler) or Bosworth-Toller "totter (are ruinous)" fits the context. Leslie's "moulder" is further from the usual sense of the word. Dunning-Bliss reject these extended meanings, and emend to *woniað*, "decay," citing the occurrence of *wonað* in a similar context in *Ruin* 12, where Leslie *Three OE Elegies* prints *worað*. In fact, damage to the manuscript makes it impossible to tell whether the letter in that poem is *n* or *r*; in the present text the word is emended to *wunade*. See note on *Ruin* 12a.

80b–84 In their enumeration of the fates of the corpses of the slain, these lines have both traditional Germanic and Christian parallels. Wülker believed that this passage referred to a variety of ways of death: "im Kriege, auf Seefahrten, auf der Jagd, durch Krankheit oder durch Alter" (1885, 206). His interpretation was influenced by Thorpe's footnote suggestion that *fugel* (line 81) meant a ship, an identification now largely abandoned, although Krapp-Dobbie find it plausible. Wülker's explanation was refuted by James Bright, who pointed out that these lines referred to death in battle, and that the *fugel* was a bird of prey, citing similar references to carrion creatures attendant on battle in *Judith* 205–7, *Maldon* 106–7, *Brunanburh* 60–65. See Bright 1898, pp. 176–77 (also paginated as 351–53). The difficulty with the notion of a bird carrying off a man is obviated by assuming that this is done piecemeal.

As Bright explained, the *sumne* clauses are to be understood as distributive of the *sume* clause which precedes them. Other kinds of *sum* series are to be found elsewhere in OE poetry, especially *The Gifts of Men* and *The Fortunes of Men*. The significance of the *sum* series in *Wan* has been discussed by Cross, who rejects the "beasts of battle" derivation and proposes instead a Christian, homiletic inspiration, citing parallels in OE, Latin, and Greek prose (1958–59, 75–100). See, for example, *Blickling Homily* 7: *awecceaþ ealle þa lichoman of deaþe, þeah þe hie ær eorþe bewrigen hæfde, oþþe on wætere adruncan, oþþe wildeor abiton, oþþe fuglas tobæron, oþþe fixas toslitan* ... (Morris 1874–80, 95; noted by Klaeber 1913, 259). Cross's contention that the *Wan* passage alludes to the doctrine of the resurrection of the body, though fragmented, is challenged by G.H. Brown (1978), who relates the motif here to pictures of a single "thematic" bird and beast (one representing many) sharing human carnage.

In line 83a, Leslie suggests two possible renderings for *deaðe gedælde*: "dismembered at death" or "got ... as his share at the death." Dunning-Bliss's "handed over to death" is the more usual translation. The expression occurs twice, in the infinitive, in *Andreas* (lines 955 and 1217), where it is a periphrasis for "kill." The idea of the separation of body and soul at death may also lie behind the usage here, so that the *Wan* verse could mean both "separated (his body from its vital force) at death" and "gave (his body) to death as its portion."

Dreorighleor (line 83b) is usually understood as "sad-faced." Dunning-Bliss prefer "with tear-stained cheeks" (Introd., p. 46); Wentersdorf "with agonized looks" or "with ill-fated looks" (1975, 288) – see note on line 17b, above; *OE Dict* "with grief-stricken or tearful countenance."

86 *Burgwara* = gen. of *burgware/-waras*, "inhabitants." A collective fem., *-waru*, "community," is also found, as well as weak masc. forms, nearly always in the pl. Ekwall, taking *-wara* as nom. pl. fem., suggested "cities" rather than "inhabitants" (1924, 135), a suggestion which is approved by Krapp-Dobbie. However, the word does not elsewhere denote buildings as distinct from people. *Burgwara* is probably dependent on *breahtma*, but, as Leslie notes, may be in asyndetic co-ordination: "deprived of inhabitants, of sounds." For the occurrences of the word, see *Concordance* B019:214–18 and 263–75.

88ff. At this point, the speech beginning at line 92 is introduced. Most scholars now regard the entire passage as part of the Wanderer's monologue. Thus Leslie, who sees line 92ff. as the utterance of an imaginary figure introduced by the Wanderer and characterized by "this-wordly wisdom" (Introd., p. 18). Huppé commenced the second of two monologues at line 88 (1943, pp. 526–29); see note on line 62, above. Dunning-Bliss consider lines 88–91 to be the narrator's words, with the Wanderer then speaking directly again.

88b *Wise geþohte* is probably best regarded as instrumental adj. + noun. Thus Bosworth-Toller, citing under *geþoht*; also Gollancz and Kershaw. Leslie and Dunning-Bliss gloss as adverb + verb. Though possible, this construction involves an uncalled-for tense change from this line to the following.

89a MS *deornce* is an obvious error – universally emended to *deorce*.

92–96 The *ubi sunt* passage, placed in the mouth of the contemplative described in lines 88–91, represents a medieval commonplace which also has wider affinities. Bright noted *Metres of Boethius* 10.33 (*Hwær sint nu þæs wisan Welandes ban ...?*) and *Christ and Satan* 36b–37 (*Hwær cwom engla ðrym / þe we on heofonum habban sceoldon?*), along with several instances in classical Latin and one in Greek (1893, 94). Kershaw cited examples of similar rhetorical phrasing in Norse, Homeric Greek, Hebrew, and Sanskrit. Cross designates fourteen OE passages as examples of the formula, the most characteristic source being Isidore of Seville's *Synonyma de lamentatione animae peccatoris* (early seventh century): *Dic ubi sunt reges? ubi principes? ubi imperatores? ubi locupletes rerum? ubi potentes saeculi? ubi divites mundi? quasi umbra transierunt, velut somnium evanuerunt. Quaeruntur, et non sunt* (*PL* 83, col. 865). *Wan*'s use of *cuman*, instead of the verb "to be" usual in the Latin versions of the motif, has a precedent in Pseudo-Augustine *Sermo LVIII ad fratres in eremo*: *ubi ergo abierunt illa omnia? ubi pompa, ubi schemata, ubi exquisita convivia?* (*PL* 40, col. 1341), translated in *Blickling Homily* 8 *Ac hwyder gewiton þa welan* ... See Cross 1956, esp. 26 and 39. Cf. also *Sea* 82–85 *næron nu cyningas* ... Although most editors continue the speech commencing at *Wan* 92 through line 110, the rhetorical expressions associated with the *ubi sunt* motif come to an end at line 96, indicating that the wise contemplative's words end at this point. Leslie closes quotation marks here.

93a The sg. *cwom*, instead of pl. *cwomon*, is probably to be attributed to parallelism with *cwom* in the three preceding exclamations.

93b *Seledreamas*, usually understood as "joys of the hall," is translated by Wentersdorf "joyful times of the past" (1975, 291). See also note on line 25a, above.

98 Uncertainty as to the nature of the wall and its markings has occasioned a good deal of critical speculation. Assuming that the wall was part of an Anglo-Saxon wooden structure, W.H. French (1952) argues that the serpentine shapes were created by the channels of wood-boring beetles and their larvae. Christopher Dean (1965) suggests that the structure is the enclosing wall of a barrow erected as a monument by the Wanderer himself. But in line 87 the ruins are described as *enta geweorc*, a phrase that in *Ruin* 2 and *Maxims II* 2 is applied to what are clearly Roman ruins. Tony Millns (1977) believes that the serpentine motif is composed of Roman herring-bone masonry and to an Anglo-Saxon suggested a memorial of the dead. The exact nature of the serpent shapes is impossible to determine, but in all probability they refer to some kind of decoration on a Roman structure.

100b Cf. *Ruin* 24b *wyrd seo swiþe*. Though glossing *wyrd* as "course of events," Leslie sees a personification in *Wan* 100. Dunning-Bliss believe that this phrase means "the quest for the glorious destiny of death in battle" (Introd., p. 73). But *mære* could well have the sense of "notorious" rather than "glorious" here, as in its application to Barabbas in the *Lindisfarne* and *Rushworth*[1] *Gospel* glosses on Matthew 27:16 (Skeat 1871–87, 231), and to Grendel in *Beo* 103 and 762. *Wyrd* would then be used in the sense of a destructive force rather than an event. See also note on line 5b, above.

101a The word *stanhleoþu* could refer to either stone walls (Leslie) or rocky slopes (Dunning-Bliss: "stony slopes," i.e. slopes strewn with stones, Introd., pp. 65–66), or to both.

102a *Hrið* is a hapax legomenon, but can be explained from the Norse word, which means "storm" or "snowstorm." The rest of the line indicates that here the storm also brings snow which covers the earth. Cf. note on *hryðge* (line 77), above.

102b Most editors accept Thorpe's emendation to acc. *hrusan*, though Dunning-Bliss think it may be possible that MS *hruse* is a late acc. form. See note on line 23a, above.

103a Although Leslie cites *dægredwoma* and *dægwoma*, "harbinger of day," in support of his "harbinger" for *woma*, assuming "a semantic shift ... from voice or noise announcing something to the act of announcement itself," there is no evidence that the simplex could mean anything other than "a resounding noise" – here, the raging wind of winter.

107a The pl. *wyrda* here has been seen as a reference to the three Norns of Scandinavian mythology. Thus Edith Wardale (1935, 59). Leslie and Dunning-Bliss understand *wyrda gesceaft* as "ordered course of events." *Wyrd* and *onwendan* are linked alliteratively elsewhere; cf. esp. *Ruin* 24 *oþþæt þæt onwende wyrd seo swiþe*. For the concept of *wyrd*, see note on line 5b, above.

108–9 A proverbial utterance with an ON parallel in *Hávamál* 76 and 77: *Deyr fé, deyja frœndr, / deyr sjálfr it sama*. See *Edda* 1 (Neckel-Kuhn 1983, 29). In line 109b *mæg* very likely means "woman," though most translate "kinsman." The former word is quite common in poetry, and here would provide a better balance with *mon* in the a-verse.

110 *Gesteal* is a rare word which seems to mean some kind of supporting structure. Bosworth-Toller: "constitution, frame." Gollancz: "structure." Leslie: "framework," citing *þan toþa þa tunga to spæce gesteal ys* in the Leechdoms (Cockayne 1866, 3:102). Dunning-Bliss: "foundation," on an analogy with *wealsteal* in line 88 (Introd., pp. 66–67).

110–15 The earlier editors closed at line 110 the speech beginning at line 92. Lawrence and Greenfield end the enclosing monologue as well at this point (Lawrence 1902b, 471–77; Greenfield 1951, 464–65; Greenfield and Calder 1986, 284). Line 111 is obviously spoken by the narrator. The following lines are now usually assigned to the Wanderer, but earlier practice treated them as the concluding frame. Some justification for regarding them in this way is provided by the hypermetric form which lines 112–15 share with line 111. However, symmetry with the opening lines and with the earlier *swa cwæð* utterance argues for giving the conclusion, like the introduction, to the Wanderer. See also notes on lines 1–5 and lines 6–7, above.

115b *Fæstnung* here probably suggests "fortress" as well as "security." It is found as a gloss on *munimentum*, "fortification." Cf. also Proverbs 18:10 *Turris fortissima nomen Domini*. For the various occurrences of *fæstnung*, see *Concordance* F003:312–15, and F007:27–28 (*festnung*-).

THE SEAFARER

1–3 For the use of *mæg* (line 1) here, cf. *Wife* 2 and the refrain in *Deor*, and see note on *Deor* 7. In its introduction of a personal narrative, the opening of *Sea* has close affinities with that of *Wife*, and also resembles *Wan* 8–9a, *Deor* 35, and *Res* 96b–97.

Earfoðhwile could be construed either as acc. obj. of *þrowade*, or as dat. of attendant circumstances, varying *geswincdagum*, with *þrowade* used absolutely. The latter would call for a comma at the end of line 2.

5b The unique compound *cearselda*, "abodes of care," is now widely accepted. Klaeber (1924, 124) objected that the notion was "too far-fetched," and suggested *cearsiða* or *cearsælða* (the latter proposed by Ettmüller in a fn.), both, presumably, meaning "unhappy experiences." The "anti-hall" image in the word *cearselda* is also implicit in the contrast between the cries of the seabirds and the cheerful voices of men, lines 19b–22. For the idea of the "anti-hall" here, in *Wife*, and in *Beowulf* 2450–62a (the Father's Lament), see Kathryn Hume (1974, 70–71). Cf. also Brian Green on *Wan*: "Implicitly, the sea is a hall in which Wyrd is 'lord'" (1976, 444).

6b The verb *bigitan*, "to obtain, to seize," is sometimes used figuratively, with an inanimate subject, in the poetry. Cf. especially *Wife* 32 and 41, and see the entry in Campbell *Addenda*: sense 6, "where the subject is not personal, of strong, painful agencies."

Þær, punctuated in the present text as "where," could also be translated as "there." See Mitchell *Syntax*, § 2527.

8a Early editors emended *cnossað* to *cnossade*, which would bring the tense into line with *bigeat* (line 6). A similar shift occurs in *Beo* 1921b–23 *næs him feor þanon / to gesecanne ... / Higelac Hrepling, þær at ham wunað*. Gordon suggests that the use of the present in *cnossað* "is probably to mark the habitual nature of the action."

The verb *cnossian*, evidently related to *cnyssan*, "strike, beat upon," occurs only here. Cf. the use of the latter verb in line 33. Gordon prefers "dashes by the cliffs" to Bosworth-Toller's "strikes on rocks"; similarly Mackie: "beating along the cliffs." Whether the collision is with the cliffs themselves or with the waves beside them, the situation is certainly hazardous. *OE Dict* glosses the infinitive "to toss, pitch; or perhaps to strike, clash."

8b Editors usually begin a new sentence here. However, D.R. Howlett (1975) and P.R. Orton (1982a, 255–56), for different reasons, advocate placing the period at the end, instead of in the middle, of line 8. Howlett argues that this gives symmetry between lines 1–8 (prologue) and 117–24 (epilogue); Orton that the traditional punctuation breaches Kuhn's Law of Sentence Particles, whereby an unstressed particle (*wæron*, line 9) must fall in the first metrical dip of the clause. Sweet, in his *Reader*, had also placed the period at the end of line 8 (1894, 171). Such a punctuation attaches *calde geþrungen*, "oppressed by cold," to the ship rather than to the Seafarer's feet, and is thus less realistic, although not impossible. Mitchell *Syntax* (§ 3947) advocates taking *calde geþrungen apo koinou* with both, and finds the application of Kuhn's Law in such cases overly dogmatic.

9a   As Gordon notes, in an a-verse with single alliteration, the second lift usually alliterates only if it is the more strongly accented word. Sweet's *wæron fet mine* (1894, 171) would correct this. But the possessive is ordinarily less stressed than other adjectives; also, if the initial *e* is original in MS *efteadig secg* (line 56; commonly emended), that verse shows a noun alliterating in preference to its preceding adjective.

10b   The Seafarer's lamentations are transferred to his personified "cares." Holthausen's emendation from *seofedun*, "lamented," to *seomedun*, "weilten," is unnecessary (1935, 7). The *u* of the ending is an early or Mercian form; see Campbell *Grammar*, § 735e.

11a   *Hat* has occasionally been emended to *hate*, in agreement with *ceare* (line 10), but the omission of the *e* can be explained as an elision before the following vowel; thus Gordon, Cf. *Sea* 55 and *Deor* 16.

14a   See note on *Wan* 20a; the word *earmcearig* is recorded only in these two places.

16   There is only one verse here, so it is likely that something has been lost. Ettmüller supplied *wynnum biloren* to make an a-verse. Another possibility – since this line continues the *w*-alliteration of the previous – is that the poet accidentally composed an extra verse.

17a   *Hrimgicelum* is a hapax legomenon constructed on the same lines as *isgicel*, "icicle."

18–22   For the contrast between the seabirds and the speaker's absent boon-companions, cf. *Wan* 45–48 and 53–55a, and see notes on *Wan* 53–54 and 55a. The swan, gannet, curlew, and seagull are named in the present passage. A sharper parallelism between the birds' cries and the sounds of the hall is achieved by placing the heaviest punctuation at the end of line 19, as in the earlier editions; this pairs off *gomene* and *hleoþor*, *sweg* and *hleahtor*, *mæw* and *medodrince*. However, beginning the new sentence with *Hwilum ylfete song* (thus Kershaw, Krapp-Dobbie, Gordon) has the advantage of linking the swan with the other birds. Since the word *ylfetu* is found in both strong and weak forms, both "the song of the swan" and "the swan sang" are theoretically possible translations; the former is preferable because the other sounds are expressed by phrases, not clauses.

U for *w* in *huilpa(n)* is probably an early spelling (Campbell *Grammar*, § 60). The word is recorded only here in OE, but the connection with Dutch *wulp* or *wilp* and Scots *whaup*, "curlew," was pointed out by A.E.H. Swaen (1907, 387). On the identification of the species, see also the following note.

23 The a-verse is hypermetric. The rest of the poem's verses of this type appear in the latter part of *Sea* (lines 103 and 106–9). Gordon thinks it possible that the half-line was originally *storm stanclifu beot.*

Mitchell comments that the second *þær* in this line may mean either "there" or "where" (*Syntax*, § 2527), but correlation with *þær* in line 23a and continuity with lines 24–25a support "where," introducing parallel subordinate clauses in 23b and 24b.

Stearn is probably the tern, its modern etymological equivalent, though Margaret Goldsmith, who attempts to identify the various birds mentioned in *Sea*, observes that the Anglo-Saxons appear not to have made the same distinctions between the species as are made at the present time (1954, esp. 234). Goldsmith takes *stearn* as some kind of gull, perhaps the kittiwake, since terns are not winter birds or cliff birds.

24b Since *earn*, "eagle," is masc., *þæt* must be the pronoun object of *bigeal*; in this compound, found only here, the prefix makes the verb *giellan* transitive: "cried out at (the storms)." See Bosworth-Toller on *be-/bi-/big-*. "Cried around the rocky cliffs," Gordon's alternative translation (*Notes*), is less in accord with other uses of the prefix. *Þæt* must refer in a rather general way to the tumult which the eagle cried as if in response to, just as the tern "answered" the storms (*him ... oncwæð*, line 23b). For the kind of sound conveyed by *giellan*, which occurs in line 62 (*gielleð*), see note on lines 58–62.

25 Almost certainly corrupt: the line lacks alliteration and *urigfeþra*, "wet-feathered," nearly repeats "icy-feathered" from the previous a-verse. Some of the earlier editors indicate a lacuna here.

Various emendations have been suggested to provide alliteration. Grein altered *nænig* to *ne ænig* in the b-verse; similarly Holthausen: *ænig* here and *ne* before *meahte* in line 26 (1908, 248). But it is the a-verse which is the more suspect. Kluge offered *heaswigfeþra* instead of *urigfeþra* (1888,

130), Goldsmith *hyrnednebba* (1954, 234–35). Neither of these emendations can be more than conjectural.

26b MS *feran* does not make sense. *Frefran*, suggested by Grein 1865 (p. 422) in preference to his earlier *felian*, has been widely accepted, though Grein-Wülker retained the MS reading. Cf. *Wan* 28, where the solitary seeks a lord who *mec ... frefran wolde*.

27a For reflexive *him* see note on line 106.

The connective *forþon*, which functions as both adverb and conjunction, occurs several other times in the poem: lines 33, 39, 58, 64, 72, 108 (probably not in line 103; see note). Although the word normally means "therefore" or "because," its meaning in *Sea* has been disputed, since these meanings do not always seem to fit. Nicolas Jacobs (1989) argues that the illogical use of this connective reflects an ambivalence on the part of the poet towards his subject. One solution to the logical problem is to suppose an adversative use. But Max Rieger's "aber" for *forþon* here and in lines 33, 39, 58, and 72 (1869, 339, n.) is hard to support. Marjorie Daunt (1918) quoted five supporting OE illustrations of what she believed to be an adversative sense. Her examples may be explained, though, as uses of a rather loose connective. Thus, Alfred translates *sed* by *forþæm* in the *Pastoral Care*, but the word actually renders the whole clause *sed inter haec sciendum est* (see Sweet 1871, chap. 1, pp. 164–65, and *PL* 77, col. 47, resp.). Again, in the Blickling Homily for Palm Sunday *Þa he þa geseah þæt hie nænige bote ne hreowe don noldon, ah hie for þon heora yfelum þurhwunedon ..., for þon*, translated "nevertheless" by Morris, could be "accordingly" (see Homily 6 in Morris 1874–80, 79). E.A. Kock argued that a concessive use of ON *fyrir þvi* supported the existence of a similar usage for the corresponding word in OE (1918, 75–76). The discussion pro and contra an adversative or concessive OE *forþon/forþæm/forþi* is summarized by Mitchell *Syntax* §§ 3081–84; he concludes that the case for such a usage is not proven.

As W.W. Lawrence pointed out, *forþon* occurs in the *Lindisfarne* and *Rushworth*² *Gospel* glosses where other OE versions have *soðlice* or a similar word (1902b, 465). For example, in Mark 16:4, *Corpus* and *Hatton* have *soðlice*, *Lindisfarne* and *Rushworth*² *forþon* (see Skeat 1871–87, 130 and 131). O.S. Arngart (formerly Anderson) believes that all the *forþon*'s except in line 103 can be translated "therefore" (1979, 251–52). But "therefore" really cannot be made to fit all the occurrences.

Some of the uses of *forþon* can profitably be treated as correlative: line 33 with 39, and line 58 with 64 (see Gordon, Notes, on lines 39 and 64). This treatment gives the construction "For the following reason thoughts now strike upon my breast [i.e. agitate me] ...: because there is no man so proud of heart ..." (lines 33bff.); and "For the following reason my spirit turns ...: because the joys of the Lord are warmer to me ..." (lines 58ff.). The use of this correlation in *Sea* 58 and 64 is pointed to by S.O. Andrew (1940, § 37). Cf. also A.D. Horgan, who finds not only these two examples of the correlative use, but also a third, implied, correlation between *forþon* in line 72 and another unexpressed *forþon*, "because," between line 80a and b (1979, 45–46).

It seems best to render *forþon* variously according to the context. Only one instance (line 108) is clearly marked as the subordinating conjunction by conjuctive word order. Translate: "therefore" (line 72), "because" (lines 39, 64, 108), "for the following reason" (lines 33 and 58), "indeed" (line 27).

27b–28a Kershaw, Krapp-Dobbie, and Gordon argue that *agan* functions as an auxiliary, like *habban*, here, and cite the *Sermo Lupi ad Anglos* in support: *Ne þrælas ne moton habban þæt hi agon on agenan hwilan mid earfeðan gewunnen* (see Bethurum 1957, 262). But Mitchell *Syntax* (§ 743) is dubious about this periphrastic use of *agan*. Though it is possible to translate *agan* as an auxiliary in these particular cases ("has experienced" and "have obtained," resp.), the sense does not demand it. Translate: "he who possesses the joy of life, having remained in cities." Similarly, the Wulfstan passage may be translated: "what they possess ..., won with toil." Kluge's emendation to *gebideð* (1888, 130) is unnecessary.

29a The word *wingal*, "flushed with wine," occurs also in *Daniel* 116 (*Þa onwoc wulfheort* [Nebuchadnezzar], *se ær wingal swæf*), where it is clearly pejorative, and, in the same formula *wlonc ond wingal*, in *Ruin* 34 (applied to the inhabitants of the city in its glory), where there are no other obvious indications of an unfavourable meaning but the word may convey a criticism. The second element, *gal*, "wanton, lascivious," certainly has a bad connotation. Cf. *symbelgal* (*Judgement-Day I* 79), *medugal* (*Daniel* 702 and *Judith* 26), *meodugal*, *-gales* (*Fortunes of Men* 52 and 57). In all of these examples the *-gal* words indicate wanton self-indulgence. See also *Concordance* G001:87–90, 97, 99–101, 135–50 for *gal* as a simplex and as the first element of compounds. In *Sea*, the word *wingal* suggests a heedless delight in earthly pleasures.

33b–34 For the meaning of *forþon* see note on line 27a.

The transition, beginning at line 33b, from the hard life on the wintry sea to an intense desire to undertake a voyage (lines 36–38) led to the supposition that the poem was a dialogue, with a change of speaker here.

Thus Rieger (1869, 334–39) et al., and, more recently, John Pope (1965, 173–86). Certainly, a shift in attitude occurs at line 33b. Lawrence saw in this a compelling antithesis between the sea's fascination and its hardships (1902b, 466), a view dismissed as anachronistically modern by Anderson (1937–38, 7), who, regarding the seafaring as symbolic, sees a transition to a different kind of voyage here: "he [the Seafarer] is longing to leave the cliffs and rocks of time and set out for the distant glories of eternity" (p. 15). Recent scholarship has understood the seafaring, whether literal or not, as a representation of a spiritual pilgrimage. Accordingly, Greenfield sees lines 33bff. as a spiritual turning-point where "the seafarer's insight becomes for him a kind of conversion to the Christian *via*" (1981, 207). J.P. Vickrey (1982) sees here a transition from a sinful to a penitential state, both described in symbolic terms. But, though line 33b introduces a change of emphasis, from the Seafarer's suffering on the sea to his desire for it, this need not indicate a change of heart if he is seen as one who deliberately seeks an ascetic life.

Cnyssað ... heortan geþohtas could be translated either as "thoughts agitate my heart" or as "the thoughts of my heart agitate (me)." The verb is generally understood as conveying the urge to set out on a voyage. Kershaw translates "thoughts are making my heart to throb, until of my own accord I shall venture ... ," Mackie "there press thoughts upon my heart that I myself should explore ...," Gordon "the thoughts trouble my heart now that I myself am to venture ..." Mitchell (1968a, 59–63) interprets the passage along the same lines but rejects as unsupported Gordon's rendering of separated *nu ... þæt* by "now that" and prefers Kershaw's "until." Jacobs 1989 is undecided between two different meanings for *cnyssað*: "trouble, disturb," and "excite" (pp. 106–7). In fact, this verb suggests distress rather than eagerness. Literally the word means "strike or dash," metaphorically "afflict" or "crush." See Bosworth-Toller, and *Concordance* Coo6:158–63, and Goo8:24–27; *OE Dict* under *cnyssan* renders this passage "my heart thoughts oppress [me] so that I ..." *Cnyssan* is used of temptations, but not, apparently, of wholesome desires. Cf. *ðæt hine ne cnysse sio wilnung ðæt he sciele monnum lician* in the *Pastoral Care* (Sweet 1871, chap. 19, p. 140). Since the Seafarer's longing is not this kind of temptation, it seems best to translate the lines differently: "my thoughts agitate me in that (i.e. "because") I have experience of the seas," Bosworth-Toller's use I(1)c of *þæt*, introducing a noun clause subject of the verb (*cnyssað*) as a further explanation of a noun in the main clause (*geþohtas*). If treated in this way, the transition at line 33b from the preceding passage is less abrupt. The general sense of lines 33b–43 is then that the Seafarer has troubled thoughts (lines 33b–34a) while he wishes to go to sea (lines 36–38) because there is no one (lines 39–41) who cannot be fearful about such a voyage (lines 42–43).

Hean (line 34b) is usually understood as "high," i.e. "deep," applied to *streamas*, but it has been suggested independently by Vickrey (1982, 75) and John Richardson (1983) that the word means "humble" and applies to *ic*, indicating the speaker's spiritual state. The traditional application of the word "high" to the sea tends to support the conventional interpretation, although, as Richardson points out, the weak form of the adjective, if in agreement with *streamas*, is unusual. Thorpe suspected that *hean streamas* was an error for the compound *heahstreamas*. With *hean streamas* cf. the alliterative formula *heah holm* in *Christ and Satan* 17, *Wan* 82 (*heanne holm*), and *Azarias* 123 (*hea holmas*). If original, *hean*, "high," in the weak form may point to a comparatively early date of composition for *Sea*.

35b The emphatic *sylf* here has been taken to mean that the speaker has not undertaken this voyage before. Thus, advocating a dialogue interpretation, Wülker (1885, 210) and Pope (1965, 173–86); also, for different reasons, Anderson (1937–38, 19). The word is usually translated "myself," but has sometimes been rendered differently, to avoid the implication that the speaker has not yet voyaged. Kershaw gives "of my own accord," a translation also advocated by Greenfield, arguing that the word *sylf* indicates the voyage of exile is now actively sought rather than passively endured (1969, 218). Retracting his "dramatic voices" theory, Pope argues for translating *sylf* "alone" (1974, 78–80). Greenfield later suggests "for myself," with *sylf* indicating a new, fuller awareness (1981, 205–7). Mitchell *Syntax* (§ 474) comments that there are "lexicographical difficulties" with "alone" but that the meanings of *sylf* "merge into one another."

In accordance with the interpretation put forward in the previous note, *sylf* can be understood in its usual sense as emphasizing that the speaker's experience is very personal: his knowledge of the sea has not been gained at second hand; he has made and continues to make trial of the sea, its perils and its hardships.

36–37a If lines 33b–35 are understood as describing the Seafarer's agitation of heart because he knows the pains and perils of seafaring (see the two previous notes), lines 36–37a, expressing the urge to undertake the voyage, introduce another idea and thus constitute an enumeration, not a variation.

38 The speaker's desire to seek "the land of foreigners" is taken by Dorothy Whitelock (1950) as evidence that the poem is about voluntary exile undertaken as a *peregrinatio pro amore Dei*. G.V. Smithers understands the phrase *elþeodigra eard* as the heavenly home, *elþeodige* being good Christians who are *peregrini*, "aliens," in this world (1957, esp. 145–48 and 151; also 1959). But too much emphasis is placed on the voyage itself for it to be merely the means to a place of exile (Whitelock), and one would expect some further indication if *elþeodigra eard* is to be understood strictly allegorically (Smithers). However, the voyage and the destination certainly have more profound implications, since there is no one so proud-hearted (*modwlonc*, line 39) and successful (lines 40–41) that he is not concerned about his sea-voyage and what God will do with him (lines 42–43). The voyage to the land of strangers far away represents a journey into the unknown, both physically and spiritually, and the longing for it indicates the desire of the aspiring soul for something beyond the familiar satisfactions of this world. Cf. note on lines 42–43, below.

39 Lines 39ff. refer to all those who go seafaring (literally or figuratively) and the speaker by inclusion. The powerful mingling of anxiety and yearning which emerges from the following passage gives weight to a symbolic interpretation of *sæfore* (line 42). R.F. Leslie's fairly recent argument that the *modwlonc mon* (line 39) resembles the thoughtless land-dwellers of lines 12b–13a and 27–28a fits in with the description of success in life in lines 40–41 but not with the assertion that such a man, however successful, will have a care about his sea-voyage and his fate (lines 42–43); see Leslie 1983, 103–4.

40a Since the hypothetical man described here is a retainer rather than a lord, "good in gifts" probably means "prosperous in gifts received"; material gifts are referred to but spiritual gifts are inevitably suggested; cf. the contrast between the man's earthly and heavenly lord (lines 41 and 43, resp.). Greenfield comments on the use of word-play in the poem (1954, esp. 18–20).

42–43 L.L. Schücking suggested that *sæfore* was to be understood as "nicht nur das Leben des frommen, sondern auch das Leben als Weg zur Ewigkeit und in diesem Sinne auch ... der Tod" (1917, 109). Cf. also Anderson (1937–38, 15). Schücking and others cite *Bede's Death Song* and *An Exhortation to Christian Living* as expressing comparable sentiments. The same second element occurs in *sæfore*, "sea-journey" and *neidfaerae*, "necessary journey" (*BDS* 1). Cf. also *Uncuð bið þe þænne / tohwan þe þin drihten gedon wille, / þænne þu lengc ne most lifes brucan* (*Exhort* 60b–62). Leslie's argument that line 42 refers merely to the *modwlonc mon's* fear of drowning (Leslie 1983, 104; see also note on line 39, above) diminishes the larger implications conveyed by *ofer eorþan* in line 39 and *a* here. The *sæfor* represents not so much a death journey as a spiritual quest, which is undertaken only by adventurous souls – in contrast to the land-dwellers of lines 12b–13, 27–28a, and 55b–56a.

Vickrey, who interprets the voyage here as a penitential discipline, argues that *sorg* refers to present sorrow not anxiety concerning the future (1982, 72–74), but line 43 points to the latter. Cf. also line 47. For the theory that this *sæfor* is a different one from that described in lines 1–33a, see also note on lines 33b–34, above.

44–46 Lines 44–45 describe, in a heroic context, typical earthly pleasures, so it is appropriate that *wif* (line 45) should have its broader sense of "woman," whether a wife or not.

Since *ymb yða gewealc* cannot meaningfully be construed with *hyht*, "pleasure," it is best to treat line 45 as parenthetic with the phrases in line 46 dependent on *hyge*, "thought." Gordon punctuates in this way.

47a Although Gordon rejects the meaning "longing" here, it is in keeping with the general tenor of this part of the poem that *longung* should mean both "anxiety" and "yearning." Thus Greenfield (1966, 158). Longing for a voyage is also expressed in *Res* 98, *longunge fus*.

48–49 The verbs here have given rise to some discussion. Because the use of *niman* with the dative/instrumental is unique, some have thought it might be an error. Kershaw tentatively suggests *blostmiað* for *blostmum nimað*; Stanley supposes that *blostmum* is an error for *blostman* (1962, 57). Eilert Ekwall justifies the usage, comparing it to such expressions as *tearum geotan, gledum spiwan, streamas weorpað stane* (1924, 135). Cf. also the use of *læden* + dat., "bring forth branches," in *Res* 106. Toller *Supp* cites *Sea* 48 under sense VIII(6a) of *niman*: "to get on, develop, flourish," which is a variant of VIII(6) "to move oneself, go, proceed." The *Sea* usage can also be related to Toller *Supp*'s sense I(3) "take hold, get rooted" as in *þonne nimeþ þæt feax to, 7 seo sealf genydeð þæt hyt weaxeþ* in the *Medicina de Quadrupedibus* (5.11; in die Vriend 1984, 250–1). The OE corresponds to Latin *capillos fluentes continet et cogit crescere*, "(the salve) holds the falling hair together and makes it grow," but since OE *to* cannot mean "together" the subject must be *feax* and the meaning "the hair takes," *to* having a figurative sense of motion. Again, the intrans. use of *niman* with a dat. or instr. in *Sea* 48 has probably been influenced by the use of *onfon*, "receive," plus dat. For the uses of *(ge)niman*, see *Concordance* Go23:257–99 (*genam-*, *genæm-*); G024:30 (*genemað*), 66 (*geneom-*), 190–258 (*genim, geniom-*), 306–21 (*genom-*); G025:1–16 (*genum-*), 32–33 (*genym-*); G041:299–301 (*ginim-, giniom-*); N002:231–52 and 298–324 passim (*nam, naman*); N003:1–135 passim (*naman*); N007:318 (*nieme*); N008:231–312 (*nim-*), 320–24 (*niom-*); N010:56–59 (*nom*), 89–114 passim (*noman*), 134–35 (*nomon*), 319–20 (*num-*); N011:92–102 and 111 (*nym-*).

Afægrian occurs as a transitive verb and the past participle *fægeredre* glosses *falerata* (Napier 1900, no. 5309). Other uses of *wlitigian* are transitive or absolute. (See *Concordance* W17:89–90 and 104–8). Gordon treats both verbs as transitive; Kershaw only *fægriað*. Against a transitive usage, Phyllis Whittier (1968) argues that the woods (*bearwas*) do not beautify the dwellings (*byrig*) and meadows (*wongas*), but only themselves. Also, the parallelism between the verses is more consistent if all the verbs are treated as intransitive, with *niman* taking the dat./instr. Thus Ekwall (1924, 135); also Mackie. Translate: "Groves take on blossoms, towns become fair, plains grow lovely, the world is in motion."

Onetteð is understood by J.E. Cross (1959) as "hastens to its end," a reference to the homiletic notion that the world *crescit ut cadat*. Somewhat similarly, N.F. Blake (1962) suggests that the reawakening of plant life in spring evokes the resurrection of man before the Judgment. Such an interpretation involves reading this part of the poem in the light of the eschatological preoccupations of the second half.

50–52 Technically, *fusne*, "eager" (line 50), could be an adjective in agreement with *sefan*, "heart" (line 51). But a *modes fusne sefan*, "a heart eager of mind," is rather odd, so *fusne* should be understood as an adjectival noun, parallel to *sefan*, meaning "the one eager of mind." Mitchell (1985) observes that *sefan* could be not only acc., but, alternatively, gen. and parallel to *modes* ("eager of mind, of heart") or dat. belonging to *siþe* ("to a journey for the heart"). But the latter two constructions involve a more contorted syntax. The meaning of *mod* and *sefa* in this context is much the same. *Þam* (line 51) is most naturally taken as an indefinite pronoun, referring to any person who thinks in a particular way, though, as Mitchell notes, it could refer to *sefan* ("for a heart which thinks ...") or *siþe* ("to a journey by which [unexpressed subject] thinks ...").

Nearly all editors emend to *gewitan* in line 52, an infinitive dependent on *penceð*, "intends ... to go." However, it is possible to retain MS *gewitað* as an Anglian spelling of *gewiteð*; see Campbell *Grammar*, § 735b.

Translate these lines: "All these things admonish the eager of mind, (urge) the heart to a journey, for him who thinks thus, who departs far on the paths of the flood."

53–55a For the sad voice of the cuckoo prompting to the voyage, cf. *Husb* 21b–23: *þæt þu lagu drefde, / siþþan þu gehyrde on hliþes oran / galan geomorne geac on bearwe*. The idea is evidently a traditional one. In *Sea* the cuckoo is seen both in its more common English role as the bird (here the "keeper") of summer, and as the presager of care. The gloomy implications are developed further than in *Husb*, where they are confined to the word *geomor*. Sieper (pp. 70–77) regarded the association of the cuckoo with sadness as probably of Celtic inspiration, citing its occurrence in the Llywarch Hen poems [see *Claf Abercuawg* in the Appendix, pp. 268–75, below], although he found it also in Slavic and Baltic folklore. Gerhard Dietrich notes that the cuckoo's call as an ill omen is also documented in German folk tradition (1966, 21). In other A-S sources the cuckoo has pleasant associations, as in *Guthlac* 744 and in Alcuin's *Versus de cuculo* and *Conflictus Veris et Hiemis* (texts in Dümmler 1881, 249–72). J.D. Pheifer notes that in the *Conflictus*, which he thinks may have been composed by an Irishman in Alcuin's circle, Hiems has a negative and Ver a positive view of the cuckoo (1965, 282–84). The characterization of the cuckoo's voice as "sad" has also been explained as indicating a change in tone as spring moves into summer. Thus C.W. Kennedy believed that the harsh call was a summons to sailing on the calmer seas of summer (1936, 26–27). It is doubtful, though, that the cuckoo's voice, whether in spring or summer, can be described as harsh, though it might be considered plaintive. Whatever its origin, the association of the cuckoo's call with sadness, as well as with the pleasantness of summer, is appropriate here, where the wished-for voyage is also the object of fear and anxiety.

55b–56a MS *eft eadig* is almost universally emended. Thorpe's *esteadig* requires the least adjustment, though one might expect the emphatic adjective to alliterate. Grein's *sefteadig* is adopted by Gordon. Vickrey 1989 suggests retaining the MS reading and translates it as "the warrior, retainer prosperous in turn" (p. 152). He understands it as referring, not to the same hypothetical land-dweller mentioned in lines 12b–13 and 27–28a, but to this rich man's "successor and spiritual heir," an explanation which is ingenious, if a little over-complicated.

Leslie (1959/68, 259–61) commented on the triple antithesis whereby lines 55b–57 parallel the two previous contrasts between the fortunate land-dweller and the Seafarer. However, Greenfield (1966, 156) believes that the good fortune in the present instance is transcendental and renders *esteadig* "filled with (Divine?) grace." Influenced by this interpretation, Leslie more recently has seen the *esteadig secg* as a type which may include the Seafarer, who envisages a journey into exile but does not yet know what it will involve (Leslie 1983, 107). But since the language of the three passages (*Sea* 12b–15, 27–30, 55b–57) is markedly similar, it is probable that the present lines also refer to the heedlessly prosperous land-dweller. Thus, there is a play on *eadig* here and in line 107, where it means "blessed." Cf. note on line 40a, above, and Greenfield 1954, 18–20.

58–62   For the translation of *forþon*, see note on line 27a, above.

The flight of the soul described in these lines has been related to pagan and Christian ideas. Vivian Salmon (1960), who finds both here, traces in this and the immediately following passage the shamanistic concept of the free-ranging soul. Peter Clemoes (1969) believes that this part of *Sea* was influenced by a passage in Alcuin's *De animae ratione liber* which presents the mind's ability to think of absent things as a flight over land and sea. Both Salmon and Clemoes find, respectively, the same ideas in *Wan* 50b–57. F.N.M. Diekstra sees the soul's flight in *Sea* as "an additional *peregrinatio* metaphor, supplementing that of the sea journey" (1971, esp. 433). *Eorþan sceatas* (line 61) must be taken as the object of the preposition *ofer*, since *hweorfeð* cannot take a direct object. Cf. Mitchell *Syntax*, § 1174.

Sieper thought that the word *anfloga*, "lone flier" (line 62), referred to the cuckoo. He is followed in this by Gordon, and by Orton, who argues that *gielleð* need not necessarily convey a strident sound (1982b, 453–54). But the uses of *giellan* do suggest shrillness of sound: it is applied to a harpstring (*Rim* 25), spears in flight (*For a Sudden Stitch* 9), the cries of certain animals and birds (e.g. *Sea* 24, *þæt earn bigeal*) – all quite different from the soft call of the cuckoo. For the occurrences of *giellan*, see *Concordance* G020:285 (*gellende*); G040:201 (*giell-*); G041:197–98 (*gill-*); G052:21–22 (*gyl-*).

Smithers (1959, 20–22) translates *anfloga* "flier against," i.e. "assailer," and understands it as a "disease-bringing malign influence," something like a valkyrie, which leads to death; he takes *gifre and grædig* (line 62a) with *anfloga*, not *hyge* (line 58). Both Smithers and Salmon (1960, 6) associate this part of the poem with the Norse belief in the free-ranging *hugr*.

If the passage is seen as an especially vivid and concrete expression of the Seafarer's desire to go to Sea, *anfloga* can, accordingly, be understood as the speaker's spirit which ranges over land and sea like a bird. Thus Salmon (1960, 1–6), Clemoes (1969, 62–73), Diekstra (1971, 433–46), et al. *Gifre and grædig* refers to *hyge*, but also applies to *anfloga*. Both of these adjectives, basically meaning "greedy," are often used in violent or destructive contexts (cf. *Genesis* 792b–93a *Gesyhst þu nu þa sweartan helle/ grædige and gifre*). Gordon translates *gifre* "full of fierce longing" (Glossary).

The soul's sharp cries (*gielleð*) are appropriate to this "fierce longing"; they also evoke the bird-cries mentioned before (lines 19b–24).

63a Smithers (1957, 137–40) argues for the retention of the MS reading, *wælweg* (commonly emended to *hwælweg*), signifying the journey of the soul to the abode of the dead. For the voyage in lines 33b–64a as a journey of death, see notes on lines 33b–34 and 42–43, above. Stanley has also suggested retaining the MS form, and translating it as "ocean-way" (from *wǣl*, "deep pool") but allowing "way of slaughter" (from *wæl*) as a subsidiary meaning (1962, 57–58). And A.D. Horgan favours retaining *wælweg* in the sense of "deadly sea" (1979, 45–46). The usual emendation has the advantages of giving double alliteration, recalling *hwæles eþel* (line 60), and forming a poetic compound of a well-attested type; cf *hranrad/hronrad*.

64b–66 Line 64b, which introduces the explicit moralizing, is often regarded as the major transition of the poem. If *forþon* is translated "because" and taken as correlative with *forþon* in line 58, lines 64b–66a can be seen as a bridge between the narrative-descriptive first half and the homiletic second half of the poem. See note on line 27a, above, for the treatment of *forþon*.

Earlier scholars tended to regard the second half of *Sea* as a later addition. Thus, Friedrich Kluge, who put forward a modified version of Rieger's dialogue theory, took the original poem to line 66 only, and found indications of reworking in lines 64b–66a (1883, 322–27).

On londe (line 66) has the double meaning of "on land" (as opposed to "at sea") and "on earth" (as opposed to "in heaven"). The end of this sentence contains the final reference to seafaring, with obvious spiritual implications here, and to the contrast between the ignorant life on land and the strenuous quest of the voyage at sea.

67 With the reflexive *him*, cf. lines 27 and 106. MS *stondeð* is generally emended to *stondað*, but can be explained as an Anglianism. Cf. note on *gewitað*, line 52, and see Campbell *Grammar*, § 735 c.

68–69 MS *tide ge* has been variously interpreted and emended. Grein printed *tidege* in his *Bibliothek* but suggested *tiddæge* as an alternative. In his *Sprachschatz* he glossed *tidege* "terror temporis constituti (mortis)?" but also entered *ær his tid aga?* as a possible emendation, glossing *agan* "praeterire." This emendation is adopted by Grein-Wülker and Krapp-Dobbie. Smithers (1959, 12–13) sees eschatological implications in *tidege*, which he understands as "His (God's) awesome time." Similarly Stanley (1962, 58–

59): "fearful hour." However, this would be more likely to take the form *egetid*. Bosworth-Toller glosses *tidege*? "fear of a time, fear of the time of death." The occurrence of the word *tiddæg*, meaning "life-span," in *Genesis* 1165 (*þa his tiddæge / under rodera rum rim wæs gefylled*) supports the existence of that word here. Although Kershaw, Mackie, Gordon, and Campbell *Addenda* all give *tiddege* (= *tiddæge*), the MS reading can be retained as a form of the word with simplified *d*. *Ě* for *æ* is a characteristic of (late) Kentish and some Mercian texts, especially the mid-ninth-century *Vespasian Psalter* gloss; see Campbell *Grammar*, §§ 164, 168, 169.

To *tweon* was emended to *to teon* by William Strunk (1903, 73) and *to teone* by Holthausen (1920, 25), both in the sense of "ruin." But, as Klaeber pointed out (1927, 354–55), the MS reading makes good sense and means "becomes uncertain"; he cites for comparison Pseudo-Wulfstan *he is tweo-gendlic þysse worulde wela* (Homily 49, *Larspell*, in Napier 1883, 263). *His* refers forward to *fægum fromweardum* (line 71) – any man.

Translate: "Always, in every case, before his final day one of three things makes (life) precarious ..."

71a *Fromweard*, "turned away," "departing" (i.e. from this life), functions as an adjectival noun here.

72–80a *Forþon* = "therefore" here. See note on line 27a, above. *Lof* is used in two senses in this sentence: the praise that comes from men, and the glory that is conferred in heaven. Gordon comments in her Notes on how traditional Germanic ideas are Christianized here. *Ecan lifes* shows a possibly conventionalized use of the "early" wk. adj. + noun construction without preceding def. article. Cf. *ecan* and *halgan* in *Res* 33 and 36, resp.

The syntax of this passage is rather complicated, and has been emended to avoid the awkwardness of an infinitive (*fremman*, line 75) dependent on *gewyrce*, a construction not found elsewhere. For occurrences of *ge-wyrc(e)an* see *Concordance* G037:78 (*geweorcaþ*), 83 (*geweorht*), 108 (*gewerc-*), 255 (*gewirc-*); G038:261–309 (*geworht-*); G039:257–78 (*gewyrc-*). Sisam read *fremum* (dat. pl.), "beneficial actions," parallel to *deorum dædum*, and inserted *biþ* between *þæt* and *eorla gehwam* (1912–13, 336). Sisam's solution, which involves rather heavy emendation, is adopted by Krapp-Dobbie, and, in a slightly modified form, by Gordon. Kock (1918, 76) suggested *fremme*, parallel to and varying *gewyrce*. If the MS reading is retained, the construction can be explained by understanding *biþ* or an equivalent verb in line 72, and treating lines 74 and 75 as parallel in thought, both expanding *þæt* (line 72), the former by a clause, the latter by an infinitive phrase; the *þæt* clause at line 77 forms the object of both *gewyrce* and *fremman*.

80b–85 J.E. Cross (1957, 29–30) relates this passage to the *ubi sunt* motif and believes that lines 82–83 have their ultimate source in Isidore's *Synonyma de lamentatione animae peccatoris*; see note on *Wan* 92–96. Cf. also the phrasing in Pseudo-Wulfstan *hwær syndon nu þa rican caseras and þa cyningas þe jo wæron ...? hwær is heora ofermedla ...?* (Homily 49, *Larspell*, in Napier 1883, 263). A similar sentence occurs in the Vercelli variant of this sermon (Homily X, in Szarmach 1981, 15).

A verb in the present tense seems to be called for in line 82. The MS reading is sometimes emended to *nearon* (thus Gordon, after Grein) or *ne aron*, which would be Anglian equivalents of *sindon* (see Campbell *Grammar*, § 768d), but *næron* can be accepted as a variant of *nearon*. Cf. *hweþre næron na ungemæccan þam, þe þa foretacnu doð* in Gregory's *Dialogues* (book 1, chap. 12; in Hecht 1900–1907, 90), translating *signa tamen facientibus dispares non sunt* (*PL* 77, col. 213). Also *þine fotswaþe ... næron oncnawene* for *vestigia tua non cognoscentur* in the *Lambeth Psalter* gloss (76.20; in Lindelöf 1909–14). With *mid him* (line 84), "among themselves," which MnE finds superfluous, cf. the reflexive *him* in lines 27, 67, and 106.

87–90 Cf. Wulfstan: *... hit is on worulde a swa leng swa wacre. Men syndon swicole, 7 woruld is þe wyrse* (Homily V, in Bethurum 1957, 137). Cross relates this part of the poem to the concept of the deterioration of the world in its sixth and last age (1962, esp. 2). For the parallel between the aging of each man and that of the world, see Smithers (1959, 10), who observes that Hrothgar's Sermon (*Beo* 1724b–68), *Sea*, *Wan*, and *Rim* all "use the contrast between man's flourishing and careless youth and his miserable old age to reinforce the eschatological ideas that accompany it." Martin Green points out resemblances between the ideas in this part of *Sea* and those in apocryphal apocalypses, especially the Book of Baruch: the instability of man's life, the aging of the world like a man, the inversion of the natural order in the relationship between the weak and the strong; see Green 1975, esp. 507–9.

92b–93 *Forgiefene*, with single *n*, indicates the plural form, so *iuwine* and *bearn* must also be pl. Sweet emended to *forgiefenne* (1894, 174). The possibility of this error is less likely than in the similar *iuwine mine*, usually emended to *minne*, in *Wan* 22. In that poem there is consistent reference to one lord, whereas here rulers have recently been mentioned in the pl. (line 82).

97–102 The reading and interpretation of this passage have been disputed. Lines 97–99 look like a reference to the custom, originally pagan but surviving into the early Christian period, of burying grave goods.

Sisam 1945 rejects the notion that the passage reflects the survival of a pagan custom, and prefers to see in it an echo of Psalm 48, on the inefficacy of riches at the time of death and the inability of any man to redeem his brother's soul by giving a ransom to God. Gordon follows Sisam in this regard. However, the first part of this passage may well be seen as a comment on a Germanic custom from a Christian point of view. Michael Cherniss argues that gold (line 97) and treasure (line 99) are the concrete expression of worth and the equivalent of glory: "The honour and glory which a warrior has won in his lifetime and which, from a heroic point of view, 'will go with him' (i.e., 'remain his possession in death') cannot save his soul from God's Judgment" (1968–69, esp. 148).

Geborenum (line 98) = "born brother"; the noun is implied. Since the syntax of lines 97–99 is hard to follow, various emendations have been proposed. From Thorpe on, many editors have supposed a negative in line 99b. Grein printed *hi ne* (for *hine*), but suggested *him ne* as a possibility. Rieger (1869, 338), followed by Grein-Wülker, emended *byrgan* (line 98) to *bycgan*, and *hine* (line 99) to *he ne*, translating "mit toten Schätzen erkaufen, dass er nicht auch sterben müsse." Daunt 1916 emended line 99 to *maþmas mislice, þe hine mid wille* and translated "... will bury with the dead man various treasures which he (the living man) wishes (to be) with him." Sisam (1945, 316) emends *wille* (line 99) to *ne wile* or *nile* and translates "... bury (him) beside the dead with all kinds of treasures, – *that* will not go with him." Gordon prints *nille* and follows Sisam in her translation, taking *þæt* as the subject of *nille* and treating the latter as a modal verb expressing futurity. Cherniss (1968–69, 149) also treats line 99b in this way, but reads *wille*, rejecting Sisam's emendation.

It is possible to explain the syntax without emendation if line 98b is regarded as parenthetic, *maþmum mislicum* as varying *golde*, and *broþor* as the implied subject of *wille* (line 99). Translate: "Although a brother will strew with gold the grave for his born brother – bury him among the dead –, with various treasures, which he (the living brother) wishes (to go) with him ..." Krapp-Dobbie translate along these lines and note that "an elliptical style seems to be typical of this part of the poem" (p. 297, Notes).

For godes egsan (line 101b) encompasses the meanings "instead of the fear of God" and "in the face of the fear of God," the latter referring to the awesome presence of God on Judgment Day, an idea which is taken up in the following lines.

103 The commencement of a new gathering here, along with the mediocre quality of the rest of the poem and the high proportion of hypermetric lines – including this one – led some earlier scholars to believe that lines 103–24 were not originally part of the same text. Thus Lawrence 1902b, 471. Following Thorpe's supposition of a missing leaf, Ettmüller and some other editors ended the text at line 102. R.D. Stevick (1965) thinks it possible but unlikely that part of the MS is actually missing here, and suggests that the defects in the latter half of *Sea*, esp. in lines 103–24, are evidence of an unfinished composition. The close connection in thought between lines 101–2 and line 103 makes a gap in the MS at this point highly improbable. But, as Pope notes, "It is by no means impossible that *The Seafarer* was partially recast from time to time before it reached the Exeter Book" (1978, 33). In this sense, the material in lines 103–24 may be of a different and later provenance.

Gordon takes *hi ... oncyrreð*, "turns itself," as "will turn aside," and cites Apocalypse 20:11 *a cuius conspectu fugit terra*; Cross (1961, 549) questions whether this meaning is present. But, just as line 101b can embrace two meanings, so *for þon hi seo molde oncyrreð* can mean both "before which the world will turn away" and "before which the world changes"; the latter sense alludes to the dependency of the changing world on God and ties in with lines 104–5. The relationship between line 103a and the following verses is the most meaningful if *þon* is taken to refer specifically to *egsa*, rather than functioning as part of the more general term *forþon*.

106 This begins a group of hypermetric lines (106–9). Line 106 closely resembles *Maxims I* 35 *Dol biþ se þe his dryhten nat, to þæs oft cymeð deað unþinged*. For the insertion of the reflexive *him*, which is redundant from a modern point of view, cf. lines 27, 67, 84.

109–10 MS *mod* is almost universally emended to *mon*. Cf. *Maxims I* 50 *Styran sceal mon strongum mode*. The verb "to be" is implied in line 110. Mackie translates 110a "and constant towards men," but *werum* probably = *wǽrum*, "pledges," with nW-S *ē* for *ǽ* (see Campbell *Grammar*, § 128), since this would give the long syllable which usually accompanies a stress; also, the other items which require discipline are qualities, not people. Because of the difference in vowel length, a play on words is unlikely. However, Charles Dahlberg (1982) sees not two but three meanings here; he argues that the primary meaning is *wĕrum*, "weirs," in the sense of "restraints," and sees in the passage an admonition against a loose tongue influenced by Benedictine rules against talking.

Lines 109–24 were omitted by Sweet in his *Reader* on the grounds that the text became corrupt after line 108 and could not have formed part of the original poem (see Sweet 1894, 222, Notes).

111–15a Textual corruption makes this passage obscure. Both sense and metre indicate a lacuna between *laþne* and *bealo* in line 112. Most editors print omission marks here. Line 113 is also faulty; Mackie and Krapp-Dobbie print *þeah þe hine wille fyres* in the a-verse and *fulne* followed by omission marks in the b-verse. Gordon prints *fyres fulne* in the b-verse, but places daggers before both lines 112 and 113. Line 114, where the a-verse contains only one stress, may well be defective too.

Various emendations and restorations have been proposed. Holthausen supplied *lufan* after *leofne* in line 112, transposed *wille* to the end of line 113 to correct the alliteration, and inserted *seon* after *bæle* in line 114 (1908, 248). Klaeber follows Holthausen, but substitutes *gedon* for *seon*, taking it with both *fyres fulne* and *forbærnedne*, in the sense of "cause to be wrapped in fire, to be burned up," and cites references to funeral pyres in *Beo* 1116 and 2126 (1932–33, 341–42). Holthausen's *lufan*, adopted by Kershaw and Mackie, completes the sense and makes a neat antithesis between line 112a and b. Whereas Klaeber understands lines 113–15a as paying one's last respects to a dead friend, Kemp Malone interprets these lines in an inimical sense: if a friend is so false one would like to give him pagan burial – i.e. damn him eternally – one must still do him no wrong; Malone reads line 112 as *wiþ leofne ond wiþ laþne gelice bealo*, and adopts Klaeber's version of the following lines (1937, 214–15). Gordon understands the passage as expressing the vain desire to save a friend from the fires of Hell, and emends *hine* (line 113) to *ne*. Unlike most editors, she places a comma, instead of a period, after line 115a, thus making lines 113–15a dependent on lines 115b–16.

The problem is that while line 112a introduces two relationships, friendly and hostile, only one of these is developed in lines 113–15, whether these lines are understood as expressing duty to a genuine friend or punishment for a false friend. Possibly the original text also developed the other half of the comparison. Although the sentiment is entirely Christian, lines 113–14 allude to cremation, seen as destruction rather than honour. Cf. lines 97–102.

Translate: "Every man shall act with restraint towards both friend and foe * * * evil, although he wishes him full of flame, or burned on the pyre, the friend that he has made."

117–24 The *uton* exhortation, which ushers in the final section of the poem, is especially characteristic of the prose homilies, where it may occur throughout, though the ending is a favourite position. Cf. Wulfstan's *Sermo Lupi ad Anglos: And utan gelome understandan þone miclan dom þe we ealle to sculon, 7 beorgan us georne wiþ þone weallendan bryne hellewites, 7* *geearnian us þa mærða 7 þa myrhða þe God hæfð gegearwod þam þe his willan on worolde gewyrcað.* God ure helpe, amen (Homily XX in Bethurum 1957, 275; see also the variants on pp. 260 and 266). The closing passages of VI, VII, VIIIc, Xc, XIIIc, XV, and XXI in Bethurum's collection also use exhortations with *utan*. Cf. too the final section of *Rim* (lines 80–87), where the last sentence begins, with *uton*, at line 83b. The ideas of taking thought (*geþencan*, line 118), striving (*tilien*, line 119), and giving thanks (*þonc*, line 122) are also characteristic; cf. the closing sentences of *Vercelli Homily* 11 (Szarmach 1981, 21), where *geþencen*, *þancien*, and *tilien* occur. In lines 117–18, the phrasing recalls the journey theme in the first half of the poem.

119b *We to moten* is virtually identical in sense to *we þider cumen* (line 118). *To* is adverbial, and the verb of motion is unexpressed.

124 The closing line reflects the Latin formula *qui vivit et regnat ... per omnia secula seculorum*. *In ealle tid* should probably be taken *apo koinou* with both *þonc* and *geweorþade*. The final *amen*, which is not metrically part of the poem, again indicates the closeness of this section to the prose homilies. Although a closing *amen* is not infrequent in religious poems, among the elegies only *Sea* is given this formal indication that the poem is regarded as a sermon or prayer. *Vainglory*, which immediately follows *Sea* in the Exeter Book, also ends in this way.

THE RIMING POEM

1–2 Bosworth-Toller takes *þæt geteoh* as a noun, on an analogy with *sulhgeteogo*, "plough-implements" (*gegaderie [man] ealle his sulhgeteogo*, in the charm *For Unfruitful Land*, line 48), but, from the form of the adjective, *-geteogo* is more likely to be fem. (sg. or pl.) than acc. pl. neut. The noun is unrecorded elsewhere. It is more probable that the form in *Rim* is a variant of *geteah*, "drew forth"; the preterite in *-eoh* also appears in the *OE Bede ... þa twa mægða Norðhymbra ... in ane sibbe 7 in an folc geteoh 7 geþwærade* (4.166; in Miller 1890–91, 19). Translate: "To me he granted life who revealed this light, and drew forth the bright one [the sun], fairly revealed [it]."

Very probably line 2 never contained a perfect rhyme, seeing that the verbs *geteon* and *onwreon* belong to different classes, though a termination in *-eah* for both is possible, class I contracts frequently taking class II preterite terminations in lW-S (Campbell *Grammar* §§ 739–40). Restoration of the rhyme by emendation to *getah* (Grein *Sprachschatz* suggests "doctrina, disciplina?"; Sieper emends but treats as a verb) is unsupported elsewhere, no forms *tag/tah* or *getag/getah* being recorded. Macrae-Gibson emends *onwrah* to *onwreah* to improve the rhyme, following Ettmüller.

For the forms of *(ge)teon*, see *Concordance* G033:283 (*geteag*), 284–86 (*geteah*), 307 (*geteh*); G034:41–42 (*geteoh*); T001:95 (*taeh*), 192 (*tæh*), 255–59 (*teah*); T002:4 (*teh*), 141–42 (*teoh*).

6b–8 MS *wægum* (line 6) was emended to the verb *wægon* by Grein; also MS *wic* (line 7) to *wicg*, "horses." *Wennan* (line 7) has been variously emended, but can be accepted without emendation as equivalent to *wyn-num*, "joyfully." See Sedgefield 1921, 61. The form *wenne* (= *wynne*) occurs at line 76, and also in the *Kentish Psalm* (*Psalm 50*) 80 and 157. E.G. Stanley, however, rejects the idea of a Kenticism in *Rim* 7 and 76, and prefers to derive the word from *wenn*, "excrescence," translating it "(over) hummocks" here and "pustule" in line 76 (1984, 450–52).

Getongum (line 8) as a noun is unrecorded elsewhere, but an adjective *getonge* occurs at line 42. Both are probably associated with the adjectives *getang*, "close to, in contact with," and *getenge*, "pressing upon, assailing," and also with the verb *(ge)tengan*, "to hasten after." The word *getang* in *Andreas* 138 *corðor oðrum getang* could be either the strong preterite of a similar verb or the adjective.

Translate: "Adorned horses carried [me] over the plains, joyfully in their journeys, pleasantly on the long ways, with hastening of their limbs," taking *longum* (line 8a) as a substantival adjective referring to *gongum* (line 7), rather than as an epithet of *getongum* (line 8b).

9 MS *onspreht* is glossed by Bosworth-Toller as "enlivened" on the basis of ON *sprækr*, "active," but no verb *(on)spreccan* is recorded elsewhere in OE. Very possibly this is a nonce-word coined from OE *spræc*, "shoot" (glossing *sarmentum* in Wright-Wülker *Vocabularies*, 2:119.48) and meaning "sprouted" in the sense of "full of growth."

10 *Rædmægen* is a compound not found elsewhere, but the elements "counsel" and "force" are readily comprehensible. Translate *rædmægne oferþeaht* "covered over by wise power" – in both a literal sense (varying and expanding *wæstmum aweaht*, line 9), and a symbolic sense.

11–12 The first element of the hapax legomenon *gerscype* (line 11) is obscure, but the context suggests a word associated with conviviality. A plausible translation is "noisy talk," on the basis of the verb *gyrran*, "to make a loud noise," *ger-* being a nW-S spelling ("garrio," *ic gyrre,* Ælfric's *Glossary,* in Zupitza 1880, 214). The resemblance was noted by Grein in his *Sprachschatz,* but he glosses the word, spelled *gerscipe,* as "joculatio?" In his Supplement to Grein-Köhler, Holthausen cites ON *gár,* "buffoonery." Mackie translates "talk"; Mackie 1922, "chatter."

Glengdon (line 12), which is usually a transitive verb, seems here to be used intransitively, and to mean not "adorned," but "were adorned."

13–14 These lines are difficult, but *wæs on lagustreame lad* (line 14) is a clear reference to a voyage. *Scrad,* otherwise unrecorded, appears to be related to *scriþan,* "to glide," and to mean "that which glides" – here, a ship. Bosworth-Toller cites ON *skreið,* "a shoal, flock." For *scrifen,* on an analogy with ON *skrifa* in the sense of "to paint," Bosworth-Toller postulates "painted," a meaning unique in OE. The word is best explained as the past participle of *scrifan* in the common meaning of "to appoint." Thus Mackie 1922 (p. 512) and edition.

Gescad (line 13) has been interpreted by some as "strait" (Grein 1865 transl: "divortium"). Etymologically the word means "a division" and this topographical interpretation would contrast well with *in brad,* but *gescad* never has this concrete sense in OE, where it means either "distinction, difference" or "discernment, right judgment" – probably also its meaning here. For the occurrences of *gescad/gescead,* see *Concordance* G028:55–100.

Leoþu (line 14) is another hapax. Either "ship" or "voyage" would fit the context; the former is supported by ON *lið,* "ship," the latter by OE *liðan,* "to sail."

Translate the two lines: "The appointed ship glided with good steering into the open; (my) journey was on the ocean stream, where the voyage/ship did not betray me."

16 *Weord* = W-S *werod.* Back mutated forms of this word are common. The syncope of unstressed *o* is paralleled in other words, e.g. *world* for *woruld/worold* (line 9). The form *weord* seems to be Northumbrian (see Sievers-Brunner, § 113b on *world* and Anm. 4 on *weorod*).

18 This line, which lacks the usual rhyme, and does not, as it stands, make sense, must be corrupt, and various emendations have been proposed. The organization of this part of the poem into two-line units makes a rhyme in *-æge* or *-ege,* linking line 18 with line 17, likely. Sievers 1884 suggests *þegnunge þege, þeodne wæs ic wege*; Holthausen 1913, *(sincgewege) þegnum geþege. Þenden wæs ic wege* ... However, no such adjectives as *(ge)þege* and *wege* (or *[ge]þæge* and *wæge*) are recorded. Wentersdorf 1985, who

sees an omission caused by haplography, proposes the following reconstruction: *Þenden wæs ic [on myhte, / folgoð wæs fægen, fysede ic] mægen*,
"So long as I was [in power, my retainers rejoiced; I made ready] the
army ..." (p. 272). Krapp-Dobbie cautiously emend only by substituting
me for *ic*: (*sincgewæge*) *þegnum geþyhte. Þenden wæs me mægen* ...; Macrae-
Gibson, by inserting *in* between *ic* and mægen. But *geþyhte*, unrhyming
and elsewhere unknown, is probably a mistake (though it is glossed by
Bosworth-Toller as "good, advantageous," citing *þyhtig*, "strong"). An
emendation which provides rhyme in line 18, and assonance, with which
the poet seems sometimes to have been satisfied, between lines 17 and 18,
is *Þegnum geþwære, þeoden wæs ic mære*, "Mild to thanes, I was a renowned
prince."

21 The first element in *hygedryht* is to be related to *hiwan/higan*, "members
of a household" (see Bosworth-Toller), rather than to *hyge*, "mind" – as
in Earl 1987's "a thoughtful or intent troop" (p. 192). Translate "band of
household retainers."

22a Both these words are hapax legomena. The elements of *stapolæhtum*,
"something fixed" and "possessions," indicate "landed estates." *Steald*
(= *steold*) is probably the preterite of a class VII verb *stealdan*, elsewhere unrecorded in OE but related to Gothic *gastaldan*, "to possess." The
word is commonly emended to *steold*, but *ēa* for *ēo* is a feature of some
Northumbrian texts (Campbell *Grammar*, § 278b).

23 *Ōl* must be the preterite of the very rare class VI verb *alan*, found
elsewhere only in the *Lindisfarne* and *Rushworth*[2] *Gospels*, where it glosses
"parent" (confusing it with *pariunt*): *byrgenna ðaðe ne foedað vel ne alað vel
adeauæð* (Luke 11:44). The existence of the word is substantiated by ON
ala, "to bear; to feed." Translate: "According as the earth brought forth
I possessed – an ancient seat."

24 MS *ofoll* is emended by Grein to *ofōl*, the preterite of a hypothetical
compound *ofalan*, "to decline." This makes a perfect rhyme with *gōl*, but
is lexically dubious. *O(f)fēoll* seems more likely (cf. the single *f* in *gefest*,
line 25), though here *offeallan* would have to be taken intransitively as "to
fall away," rather than in its transitive sense found elsewhere, "to fall
upon."

Grein emends MS *gomel sibbe* to *gomen sibbe*, translating "laetitia pacis
non decrescebat" (Grein 1865 transl). Krapp-Dobbie follow Grein, ob-

serving "If *gomel* is retained, *sibbe* must be emended to *sibb*, a nominative" (p. 312, Notes). Macrae-Gibson emends to *gomel sibb*, following Imelmann. But *gomelsibbe* can be taken as a compound in the dative case, with "I" the implied subject of the verb: "I did not fail in old-established friendship."

25 *Gefest* = *gieffæst*, "strong in gifts," with nW-S *e* for *ie* and *æ*, resp., and simplified *f*.

26 This remains the most impenetrable line in the poem. Earl 1987 fancifully interprets *wilbec bescær* as "I distributed will-books" (i.e., book-land) (pp. 192–93). The mysterious *wilbec* has been variously emended, and has been explained as it stands with recourse to *bec*, "brook," and ON *víl*, "misery": "durans pax rivum lamentationis amputavit" (Grein 1865 transl). The metaphor of severing a stream is very forced. Also, the preterite singular vowel in *bescær* is short, whereas a long vowel is desirable here. At this point, the reader or listener is expecting a series of nouns with predicative epithets, following the pattern of *gefest gear* and *gellende sner*. *Wuniendo wær* could continue this pattern (rather than being the subject of *bescær*), and it seems more likely that the words lying behind *wilbec bescær* also did. *Wynlic gestær*, "(my) history (was) joyful," would fit. *Stær*, but not *gestær*, is recorded elsewhere.

29 *Sweglrad* = "the path of music" – i.e., the instrument. Macrae-Gibson, citing *sigelrad* in *Husb* 50 [*ASPR* 49], argues for "the heavens, seen as the place of the sun's course," and takes *hleopor* as the subject of *minsade* (p. 45, Notes). But in one or two other instances *swegl*, usually meaning "heaven" or "sun," means "music," notably in the compound *sweglhorn*, a musical instrument. Probably this usage has been influenced by *sweg*, "sound."

30 *Beofode*: "trembled," i.e. vibrated with the sound.

31 *Beacnade*: "was a beacon, was striking." Emended by Grein to *weac-nade*, but it is possible to derive an acceptable meaning from *beacnian*, "to make a sign."

32 *Freaum* = W-S *freom*, dat. pl. of *freo*, "free, noble"; *frea*, "lord," is not found in the plural. *Frodade* is a hapax, but obviously related to *frod*, "wise," and ON *frœða*, "to teach." Both *frodian* and *godian* are here intransitive. Mackie 1922 takes an unexpressed *ic* as the subject of both verbs, but since the speaker does not refer to himself elsewhere in this passage, the verb can be taken in an impersonal way (thus Krapp-Dobbie and Macrae-Gibson). Translate: "There was wisdom among the nobles; there was wealth among the strong."

35 Half of the line is missing. Probably the scribe forgot the b-verse when he made the transition to a new MS line, *blæd blissade* falling at the end of the previous. Among conjectured restorations, Ettmüller suggests *bleo glissade*, Wentersdorf 1985 *bliss wissade*.

36–37 J.J. Conybeare translated *Gold gearwade ... sinc searwade* "Gold was at hand ... silver was artificially wrought" (p. xxi). Although *sinc* is inadequately conveyed by "silver," an intransitive rendering of the two verbs fits well with the context, paralleling *hwearfade* and *nearwade*. *Gyrwan* is elsewhere almost exclusively transitive, but an intransitive use appears in the Alfredian translation of St Augustine's *Soliloquies*: [*Treowu*] *grenu wexað and gearwað and ripað* (Carnicelli 1969, 53). Grein 1865 transl assumes *ic* as the subject for both verbs: "aurum paravi ... thesaurum machinatus sum." Mackie 1922 translates "I furnished gold ... treasure did treachery" (p. 513), and similarly in his edition ("I provided gold," etc.). A sinister interpretation of *syrwan*, which means "to act with craft, to contrive" in both good and bad senses, is inappropriate in this optimistic section of the poem (the contrary is argued by Macrae-Gibson 1973, 69). It seems probable that the word is here used intransitively, with an emphasis on the meaning of the simplex, similarly to *glengdon* (line 12), *ofēoll?* (line 24), *beacnade* (line 31), and means "was cunningly made."

40 Grein 1865 transl renders *folcum ic leopode* "populis cantavi." This is very strange, though *galdorwordum gol* (line 24) touches the same theme. In line 40, however, the rhyme will be defective if *lēopode* has a long syllable. Though the poet allows off-rhyme, he seems to pair vowels of the same length. Also, the only support for a verb *lēopian*, "to sing," is *Guthlac* 391–93: *woð oþer / ne lythwon leoðode, þonne in lyft astag / ceargesta cirm*. Bosworth-Toller's citation of these two instances is corrected by Toller *Supp*, which supplies instead *līðian*, "to unloose, release." In her 1979 edition of the Guthlac poems, Jane Roberts follows Toller; see pp. 143 (Notes), 206 and 207 (Glossary). However, Toller's translation, which makes the word identical in meaning to *gelīðian*, does not fit either of the two passages well. Macrae-Gibson translates "gave grace to" but gives no infinitive. Sievers 1886 argues for a verb *līþian*, "to lead," analogous to OS *lithōn* (p. 349). But the verb *līþian*, "to be, become, or make mild," would fit both contexts excellently. For an example of *līþian* with a dative of the person in the homiletic prose, see *He his folc gegladode and lipegode him* (Assman 1889, 95). For the sentiment, compare *leodum lipost, Beowulf* 3182. *Leopode,* then, in *Rim* 40 and *Guth* 392, would be derived from a variant of *liðian* with short vowel, probably influenced by *geliðian.* Translate: "I was mild to the people."

41–42 *Getonge* = *getang,* "in contact with." See note on lines 6b–8, above. One would expect *long* and *getong,* but the poet may have supplied forms in *-e* for the sake of rhyme. *Gehonge* is otherwise unrecorded. Grein translates line 42 "gloriae dedita, narrationum studiosa" (1865 transl), taking *teala* as the gen. pl. of *talu,* "tale," but the adverb "well" is much more probable. Mackie 1922 renders "familiar with glory, well devoted to it" (p. 515; also in his edition); Lehmann 1970, taking the connection with *hōn* in the same way, "touching on glory, inclined to good" (p. 445); Macrae-Gibson, "resting on glory, indeed firmly attached to it" (p. 47, Notes). *Gehonge* may also be influenced by *behongen/behangen,* "hung about with," which moves into the sense of "adorned" (e.g. *helmum behongen,* "adorned with helmets," *Beowulf* 3139 – of the funeral pyre). Translate: "My life was long among the people, associated with glory, fairly adorned."

43 Ettmüller emends MS *heowsipum* to *heofsipum,* "times of lamentation," a reading which has been accepted by most editors. Mackie retains the MS, explaining it rather forcedly as "disasters of various hues," and considering Ettmüller's emendation "very probable" (Mackie 1922, 514). Macrae-Gibson also retains the MS, commenting "The *heow* whose *sip* is clearly a journey of departure are to be seen as the same that were an emblem of rejoicing in 3–4" (p. 48, Notes).

44 *Fleah,* "flight," is unique. Grein emends to *gewitod nihtes infleah,* taking *gewitod* as a noun "conditio" and *infleah* as the verb, "effugit" (1865 transl). The suggestion is rejected by Sievers 1886, who argues for retention of the MS, interpreting *fleah* as a noun (p. 350). The poet appears to have coined it from pret. sg. 1 and 3 of *fleogan.*

45 This line has been variously emended to improve the rhyme and the sense. Mackie offers "... *deor. Scripeð nu deop ond feor,*" translating "(he who in the day had been) bold. There wanders now deep and far (a burning secret disease)." See also Mackie 1922, 514–15. *Dēor,* "brave," makes a good antithesis with *in fleah* (line 44), but the long vowel is unlikely to have been paired with the short one in *fēore,* "far." Sievers 1886 suggests *dēore ... fēore,* the dat. sg. of *feorh* (p. 350), a suggestion which is expanded to *deore ... in feore* by Holthausen 1930 (p. 40), and adopted in the latter form by Krapp-Dobbie and Macrae-Gibson. This gives both rhyme and acceptable sense, but the spelling *dyre* can be retained. Translate lines 44b–46a: "He who previously, in the day, was illustrious now departs by night in flight. There moves deep within his being a hidden, spreading fire." *Dyre*, "precious," is probably here also suggestive of *deor*, "brave." Cf. *Deor* 37.

45b–47a The word *brondhord* and the meaning of its context have occasioned considerable critical discussion. *OE Dict* regards it as "of uncertain meaning," and cites all the following interpretations as possibilities. James Cross (1962, 11–15) suggests translating the word by "rusted (burned) treasure," meaning a sin which has changed the speaker's life; this sin is most likely covetousness, which is frequently represented by burning (*bealofus byrneð*, line 50). Claus Schaar (1962) proposes "a diseased thought" – avarice, taking *hord* in its metaphorical sense of "thought." Margaret Goldsmith (1967), also adopting the interpretation "burning avarice," translates "burning contagion from a corroding hoard," seeing in these lines a reference to the sin which torments the soul in its damnation. Macrae-Gibson, who sees parallelism between *gewiteþ ... in fleah* (line 44) and *Scripeð ... flyhtum toflowen*, interprets *brondhord* as the speaker's self-destructive delight in his gold, which has now gone, *se* (line 45) referring to *brondhord* (1973, 81–82; edition, pp. 48–50, Notes). However, there is no need to see a reference to actual treasure, or the lust for it, here. As *wordhord* means "hoard of words," *brondhord* can mean "hoard of fire," i.e. a hidden fire, *hord* being "that which is stored and hidden." Judging by the eight other hapax compounds in *-hord* (see *Concordance*, Reverse Alphabet, RA01:290), the word could readily be combined with another to suit the context. Here, the image is one of a fire that is covered, imperceptible to the eye, but spreading. It is also an image of evil as a disease. That the Anglo-Saxons did not distinguish sharply between physical and spiritual ailments is seen, for example, in the Seafarer's suffering (*Sea* 2b–4) and in the arrows of the Devil mentioned in Hrothgar's Sermon (*Beowulf* 1741b–47).

48b–49 *Gecynde*, "nature," is the object of the verb *greteð*; the subject is *grorn*. This word, along with the related verb *grornian*, is a less common, Anglian equivalent of *gnorn* (and *gnornian*).

MS *efen pynde*, a hapax legomenon, is interpreted by Grein as "like a cistern" ("cisternae instar," 1865 transl). Krapp-Dobbie treat *efenpynde* as an adjective, a reading which is followed by Lehmann 1970, who translates "equally penned in" (p. 445). Sievers 1886 emends to the adjective *ofer-pynde*: "Der Schmerz ... wird dem aufgestauten Gewässer verglichen, das den Damm übersteigt" (p. 352). The context, in lines 45b–50, requires a word suggestive of something unconfinable. A possibility is *ungepynde*, parallel to and varying *ungrynde* in the a-verse. Translate: "The mind's nature is attacked by a bottomless, unrestrained bitterness; it burns murderously, spreads savagely."

52–54 *Sinniþ* (line 52a) is taken as a noun by Grein (also Grein-Wülker): *sarne sinniþ*, who is followed by Bosworth-Toller: "continued enmity or trouble." But parallelism and rhyme suggest a verb, like the others ending in *-inniþ/-eð/-að* in lines 51–54. Sievers 1886 argues for a meaning "ceases," deriving from an original sense of "move along" ("einhergehen") which developed into "strive after," "go beyond," and "go away" (p. 352). There are three other possible occurrences of this verb: *ne ic me eorðwelan owiht sinne* (*Guthlac* 319), *fægerro lyt ... idesa sunnon* (*Genesis* 1852–53), *Hra weorces ne sann* (*Andreas* 1277); all of these are translated "care for" by Bosworth-Toller. Seeing that ON *sinna* has the meanings "travel," "go with, side with," "care for, heed," it is possible that in OE the central meaning was "be favourable to, give consideration to," merging into "stop for." The *Lindisfarne Gospels* translation of Latin *sinite*, "permit," slang "leave," by *forloetas vel blinnað*, (Luke 22:51) suggests that the glossator may have been influenced by OE *sinnan*, which happens to sound like the Latin verb, and that *sinnan*, "have a care for," and *blinnan*, "cease," had an overlap of meaning.

Cinnið (line 52b) is a hapax legomenon. It is usually interpreted as an intransitive verb related to *cennan*, "bring forth," and meaning "increase." See Sievers 1886, 353. Grein 1865 transl equates it with *cinan*, "to crack, break apart": "anxietatibus hiscit." *OE Dict*: "of uncertain meaning: perhaps 'to gape', or perhaps intransitive form of *cennan* 'to teem.'"

Tinneð (line 54) is unrecorded elsewhere. It has been derived from *tinnan*, "stretch," on the basis of *tinde bogan, tetendit arcum*, a gloss on Psalm 36:14 (*The Blickling Homilies*, in Morris 1880, 261). Thus, Bosworth-Toller translates *lustum tinneð* "does not joyfully extend." Holthausen 1910b suggests "burn or glow," on an analogy with *ontendan*, "kindle," and MHG *zinnen*, "burn": "er glüht nicht vor lust," an interpretation which is accepted by Mackie 1922 (pp. 515–16; also edition) and by Krapp-Dobbie. Some support for the meaning "extend or grow" is offered by the occurrence of a verb *tennað* in *Fortunes of Men* 4, where it expands on *cennað bearn* (lines 2–3). Very likely *tennað*, "make to grow" (?), is another transitive usage, along with *tinde*, "stretched," while *tinneð*, "grows" (?) is intransitive. The poet's usage would then parallel his handling of *cinnan*.

For a further discussion of the verbs in this passage, see my note (Klinck 1985–86), where I argue that *cinnið* and *tinneð* are "intransitive uses, perhaps coined by the poet, of normally transitive verbs, and [that] both ... present the condition of man, the decline of his glory and increase of his sorrow, in terms of the processes of nature."

Linnað (line 53b) is usually emended to *linnið*, but *-að*, as well as earlier *-ið*, is common for W-S *-eð* in Northumbrian texts (Campbell *Grammar*, § 735b).

Translate lines 52–54: "Grief gives no quarter; it increases in cares. A man's glory ceases, declines in joy, is cunningly deprived of it, does not grow in delight."

57 Elsewhere *trag* means "evil." Grein translates "sluggish" ("segne," 1865 transl), on an analogy with German cognates such as *träge*, "indolent."
Genag = gehnag.
Translate: "The time of good faith is too unreliable; being feeble, it declined."

58 Ettmüller emends MS *eatole* to *steaðole*, an emendation adopted by several editors, but not by Krapp-Dobbie or by Macrae-Gibson. The MS reading, "It went grievously ill with the eminent," makes sense, but the emendation *steaðole* gives the usual double alliteration in the a-verse. The only other lines without this feature are 77 and 79, both containing other irregularities. Translate: "It went ill with the high seat, and every hour declined."

61a "The race of men passes away." Conybeare prints *wer cynge witeð*, following the MS spacing, but mistaking *n* for *r* in the first word. Ettmüller's *wercyn gewiteð* (also reading the MS as *wer*) is adopted as an emendation by most editors. Macrae-Gibson keeps *wencyn*, translating "the kindred of joy."

62 Most editors, with the exception of Macrae-Gibson, print *flah mah*, but *flahmah* can be a substantival adjective meaning "the treacherously evil one." *Mān*, "crime," the obvious correction of MS *mon*, is printed without comment by Ettmüller. *Hwitan* is glossed "to make white, to polish" by Bosworth-Toller, referring to this passage, *hwitian*, "to be, become, or make white," being the verb that occurs elsewhere. It is probably unnecessary to extend the meaning "whiten" to "polish," since the trimming of the arrow would involve whitening it by exposing the bare wood. Macrae-Gibson, citing a reference to the function of a *sweord-hwita* in Alfred's laws, takes the word as meaning to put into good condition, and translates "the arrow is fletched" (p. 52, Notes).

63 *Burg sorg* is usually emended to *borgsorg*, "anxiety that comes from debt," in order to improve the internal rhyme which characterizes these verses, but "sorrow frets the city" is an acceptable reading, and the poet's rhymes are often inexact.

In the second verse, the two adjectives function as abstract nouns: "old age cuts off boldness" (Grein 1865 transl "audaciam senectus exscindet?"). Macrae-Gibson relates *þwiteþ* to the use of *aþwitan* to translate *frustrare* and interprets as "obstruct" or "bring to nothing" (p. 52, Notes).

64 *Wræcfæc* is probably a compound, "time of misery," though sometimes treated as two words. *Wriþað* = *wridað*, "flourishes." The proposed emendations are unnecessary. A form in *þ* occurs in *Weox þa ... and wriþade mægburh Semes, Genesis* 1702–3a.

Smiteð probably means "smites" (= "breaks") rather than "smears" (= "defiles") here, though the latter is possible. In either case, the word makes sense, and provides off-rhyme with *wriþað*, making emendation to *smiþað* (Ettmüller) superfluous.

65 Emendation of MS *singrynd* to *syngryn* (Ettmüller) gives the meaning "the net of sin." Mackie 1922 retains the MS and translates "constant grief" (p. 517). In his edition he emends to *singryn* with the same translation; similarly Krapp-Dobbie and Macrae-Gibson. But probably *sin-* = *syn(n)-* here, making a compound found twice elsewhere in homiletic contexts: *... mæg se bisceop ... þæs mannes syngrina ... geliðian* (Bethurum 1957, 238), and *... þæt us deofol ... ne mæge ... mid syngrinum gehremman* (Ure 1957, 81–82).

MS *sæcra fearo* does not make sense. The first element is usually emended to *searo*, "deceit, treachery," following Ettmüller. Mackie, emending to *searafearo*, translates "the indirect path is treacherous," on the basis of *faru*, "a going" (see also Mackie 1922, 516 and 517), an interpretation which is approved by Krapp-Dobbie (who print *searofearo*). However, this necessitates a very free rendering of *glideþ*. Macrae-Gibson takes *fearo* as "ship(s)" on an analogy with *fær* (p. 53, Notes). The verse might be emended instead to *searo feor glideþ*, which gives partial rhyme between *searo* and *feor*.

Translate: "The net of sin spreads wide; cunning creeps far."

66 *Gromtorn* is emended to *grorn torn* for the sake of internal rhyme by Ettmüller and others, some taking it as a compound. But the MS reading, kept by Mackie and Krapp-Dobbie, and its off-rhyme are acceptable.

MS *Græft hafað* is a defective verse. Various words have been supplied. Ettmüller's *hæft*, which can mean both "imprisonment" and "prisoner," makes good sense and maintains the internal rhyme. Elsewhere *græft* means "sculpture" not "grave." Omission of the final *t*, proposed by Wentersdorf (1985, 273–74), gives a more probable form and internal near-rhyme with *hæft*.

Translate: "Fierce resentment burrows deep; the grave keeps its prisoner."

67 *Solað*, "becomes foul," related to *sōl*, "filth," is a hapax legomenon, but a similar word and sentiment occur in *Hat acolað, hwit asolað, Latin-English Proverbs* 3.

Bosworth-Toller translates the a-verse "The armour or implement that was bright grows rusty," in accordance with Grein 1865 transl "armatura candida polluitur," but, in view of the proverbial parallel, a more literal translation is appropriate: "Cunningly white grows soiled."

69 MS *colað* is emended to *cealdað* for the sake of rhyme by Ettmüller and most later editors.

70 MS *gehwyrt* is usually emended to *gewyrht* (following Grein). But *gehwyrft*, "a turning," is probable (*hwyrft* is the usual form), and supported by *on geares gehwyrftum*, rendering *in anniversariis*, in a gloss on the *Regularis Concordia* ("De consuetudo monachorum," line 1158; in Logeman 1891, 446).

Translate: "Fate wove for me and the cycle of time apportioned ..."

71a Sievers 1886 proposes to emend *græf* to *scræf* in order to avoid the repetition (p. 354), but the poet several times uses the same word to make a rhyme (lines 1–2, 3–4, 46–47, 53–54, 57–58, 84–85), though not elsewhere within the same line.

72 *Flean* = *fleon*

73 MS *neah* is emended to *neaht* by Ettmüller and subsequent editors.

74 Ettmüller's emendation of MS *on fonn* to *ofonn*, from *ofunnan*, "to begrudge, deny," is generally accepted. His *eardes* for MS *heardes* gives vowel alliteration, but the usual translation, "deprives" (Grein 1865 transl "habitatione privat") for *onconn* is a far cry from the meaning of *oncunnan* elsewhere – "to accuse." Wentersdorf 1985 reads *herheardes*, citing *Wife* 15 (where he reads *herheard*, "pagan sanctuary"), and translates "will accuse me of idolatry" (pp. 290–92). But *eardes* can be taken like *landes*, "by land," or *nihtes*, "by night," and *onconn* as "assails" (or "will assail"), as in *oncuðon hie me butan scylde*, where *oncuðon* renders *impugnabant* in the *Pastoral Care* (see Sweet 1871, chap. 46, p. 355, and *PL* 77, col. 91). For the occurrences of *oncunnan* in their contexts see *Concordance* O004:99–101.

Translate: "(the night) which will deprive me of my native country and assail me here in my homeland."

75 Grein emends *friteþ* to *þigeþ* to give the line rhyme. He is followed by several editors, including Mackie. Lehmann 1970 suggests *frigeð*, "seeks out" (pp. 444, and 448, note), but *fricgan* means "to ask." Quite possibly, the poet was satisfied with assonance at this point. *Lima* is probably a late spelling of *limu* (Sievers-Brunner, §§ 44, Anm. 7, and 237, Anm. 5).

76a For *wenne*, see note on lines 6b–8, above. Conybeare, Thorpe, and Ettmüller read as *wen* + neg.

77 This line is defective. Grein suggests *oþþæt beoð þa ban gebrosnad on an*, a reconstruction accepted by some editors but not generally adopted; Wentersdorf 1985, *oþþæt beoð þa ban gebarod on an* (p. 275). Macrae-Gibson defends the MS: "this representation of the final reduced state of man ... by a half-line reduced almost to nothing, if indeed a scribal error, must be one of the happiest in the history of poetry" (p. 54, Notes).

78–79 Line 79, which is unusual both in its alliterative pattern and in its lack of rhyme, is very problematic, and numerous suggestions have been made for emending MS *balawun*, *gehlotene*, and *adroren*. Most editors take *balawun* as equivalent to *bealwum*. Ettmüller emends to *balawum*. Mackie, Krapp-Dobbie, and Macrae-Gibson retain the MS reading. Holthausen makes several different proposals aimed at introducing *h*-alliteration, including *heleþum* for *balawun* (1953, 150). The conservative emendation of MS *gehlotene* to *gehloten* (Ettmüller) is adopted by many editors. Kluge 1897 emends to *gehroren* to give rhyme with the b-verse (p. 149). Conversely, Mackie 1922 emends the b-verse to *abroten*, "destroyed" (p. 518; also edition). Lehmann 1970 reads *hælepum her gehloren* (pp. 444 and 448–49). Wentersdorf 1985 finds an omission here similar in kind to that which he sees in line 18; in the present case he supposes a lacuna between two words ending in *-sa*, and offers as a possible reconstruction: *Ne bip se hlisa [abroten/peah pe lif forloren, worulde lissa] adroren*, or alternatively *.../ponne lif forloren ...* (pp. 276–7).

Among these suggestions, *hælepum* seems a reasonable substitution for *balawun*. The configuration of consonants and vowels is similar, and the word provides suitable alliteration. Emendation of the non-rhyming *gehloten(e)* and *adroren* is more dubious, since the words make sense and there are other places in the poem where assonance replaces rhyme. Translate: "... except the inescapable lot appointed for men. That fame will not be diminished." The allusion appears to be to the Last Judgment.

82 *Morpa* = *meorda*, "rewards." This spelling is unique, but the word is an Anglianism. Some forms occur with *ð/p*. See *Concordance* Mo12:267–68. The MS reading is sometimes emended to *meorpa*, following Grein.

MS *her* in the b-verse is emended to *pær* by Grein, making the clause refer more clearly to heaven. Most editors accept this emendation, but Mackie and Macrae-Gibson retain *her*, and begin a new sentence.

83b–87 For the conventional homiletic close beginning with *uton* cf. *Sea* 117–24 and note.

DEOR

1a Elsewhere in OE the name of the famous elvish smith of Germanic legend appears eight times as *Weland-* and twice as *Welond-*, both in the Alfredian Boethius, 19.46 (see *Concordance* Wo06:10 and 106). The earlier editors print *Weland* as the MS reading; (Grein-) Wülker argues that the MS letter is actually an *a* with open top. Later editors take it as the *u* which it clearly is, though some emend to *a*. In view of the limited occurrences of the name, and of the spelling *un* for *on* or *an* substantiated in other words, the MS reading should be accepted.

Wurman is usually regarded as a form of *wyrmum*, "serpents." A derivation from *wurma*, "purple dye," makes little sense. Since the reference is so obscure, some have emended. Grein, while printing *bewurman* in his text, later suggests "*be wimman* (= *wifman*)?" (Grein 1865). Max Rieger emends to *be wornum*, "in abundance" (1861, 82); Rudolf Kögel to *be wurnan*, "with pains" (1894, 101). Other emendations have also been suggested. Frederick Tupper argues that *wurman* refers to the name of the Scandinavian tribe, the Wurmas, to which Niðhad, the persecutor of Weland, belonged (1911–12, 266), but the place-name evidence on which this argument is based is tenuous. Malone sees *wurman* (*wyrmum*) as a metaphorical reference to swords with their damascened serpent-shapes (editions, pp. 6–7). Similarly Robert Kaske (1963), who regards the snake as Weland's hallmark, so that *be wurman* means "among the products of his craft, all marked with serpents." But, since there are no other examples in OE of this synedochic usage of *wyrm*, it is better to take the word in its literal sense. Perhaps, in the version of the legend represented here, although not in the other recorded versions, Weland was placed in a snake pit.

1b   The word *wræces* here could mean either "exile" or "torment" or both.

5–6   The preposition *on* (line 5) here follows its object, *hine*, and falls into the a-verse. *Hine ... on* is varied in line 6b by *on syllan monn*. This reading is more satisfactory metrically and syntactically than taking *nede* as the object of *on* and placing the latter in the b-verse, which is done by some of the early editors, including Conybeare, Ettmüller, and Grein-Wülker. In line 6b, *onsyllan* is treated as a single word, "unhappy," by Conybeare and Thorpe, and emended to *unsyllan* by Ettmüller.

There is dispute as to the nature of the "supple sinew-bonds" which Niðhad placed on Weland. In the (tenth- or eleventh-century?) Norse version of the story Vǫlundr is hamstrung by his captor Niðuðr: *Svá var gǫrt at skornar vóro sínar í knésfotom* (*Vǫlundarkviða*, connecting prose between stanzas 17 and 18; earlier, he was bound: *vissi sér á hǫndom hǫfgar nauðir / enn á fótom fjǫtur um spenntan* (*Vǫlundarkviða*, stanza 11. See Neckel-Kuhn 1983, 116–23). The resemblance between the OE and the Norse is noteworthy, especially in the use of *nede/nauðir*, "constraints," as virtually equivalent to "fetters." In the OE text, *seonobende* could refer to bonds either made of sinews or applied to the sinews. The former would be unusual, but there is a precedent in the binding of Samson with *septem nerviceis funibus necdum siccis*, Judges 16:7 (see Dickins 1915, 72, n. 6; Jost 1961, 86–87). If the *Deor* allusion refers to hamstringing, then the bonds must be metaphorical and "supple" a transferred epithet. This is how Malone interprets the lines in his earlier editions; in his 1966 edition he adopts Jost's argument (see editions, p. 6). Certainly, the OE text, taken alone, does not suggest hamstringing. But the motif of the supernatural lame smith, which appears also in Hephaestus/Vulcan, is obviously ancient. At any rate, emendation to make the mutilation explicit (as in *swongre seonobenne*, suggested by Grein in a footnote), is unjustifiable.

For the Weland story, see also note on lines 8–13, below.

7 The refrain of the poem has been variously translated. Syntactically, *þæs* and *þisses* can be described as genitives of respect, a usage not found elsewhere in OE with *ofergan*, though *Deor* 26 *þæt þæs cynerices ofercumen wære* is similar. Because of the peculiarity of this construction, Mitchell *Syntax* would explain the former usage as "genitives of point of time from which" ("It passed away from that; it can from this"), and the latter as an ellipsis with subject *wea* understood (§§ 1404–7). The subject of *ofereode* and *mæg* is left unstated; line 12b, *hu ymb þæt sceolde*, is similarly elliptical.

Taking the verbs in line 7 impersonally, W.W. Lawrence translates "That passed over; this likewise may!" and paraphrases in a "free but interpretative rendering" favoured by L. Whitbread (1947, 20), "old troubles have passed away and present ones may" (1911–12, 24–29). Malone glosses *magan* here "MAY, be able, be possible; *by litotes*, will" (Glossary), and translates "that passed; this will pass too" (Introduction, p. 1), an interpretation which might be supported by the *Lindisfarne Gospels* use of *magan* + infin. to render the Latin fut. indic (see Matthew 21:38 and 28:7). P.J. Frankis denies that suffering is turned to happiness in the poem's various *exempla*, and sees the refrain as implying no more than the passing of life itself (1962, 171–2). However, most scholars find a definite reassurance in the refrain.

Line 7b is usually understood as a reference to the speaker's own situation, but some, notably Morton Bloomfield (1964), who reads the poem as a kind of sophisticated charm, believe it to be addressed to some other contemporary misfortune. Again, some scholars regard the unstated subject as a person. Theodor Grienberger finds in the line an assertion of the range of Deor's art as a minstrel: *"þæs (þæt) ofereode þisses (ic secgan) mæg* 'von dem, was sich begeben hat (oder auch was vorüber gegangen ist) davon kann ich Kunde geben'" (1921, 399), a treatment of the genitives which is syntactically dubious. Knud Schibsbye (1969) proposes "'a man (and the sufferer mentioned in the preceding lines is an instance) managed to survive in that (i.e.: the misery described), so may a man (Deor for one) in this (i.e. the misery described towards the end of the poem).'" However, the verb *ofergan* is not elsewhere recorded with the meaning "survive."

Certain translations, including Burton Raffel's "That passed, and so may this" (1964, 57–58), suggest a possible optative force in *mæg*, like the modern "may this pass away!" Mitchell *Syntax* states categorically "*magan* + infinitive does not express a wish in OE" (§ 1013). Strictly, none of the occurrences of *magan* in OE render the modern optative "may," but there are contexts, including *Deor*, in which a wish, as well as a possibility, is indicated. Thus, *Magon we þonne gehycgan (hu mycel 7 hu diorwyrþe sio on-sægdnes bið)* in *Vercelli Homily* 14 (Szarmach 1981, 30) closely resembles *we micle nydþearfe habbað þæt we ... geþencen* and *Uton þonne ... geþencan* in the same work (pp. 29 and 31, resp.), and *Deor* 31ff., *Mæg þonne geþencan ...,* is very comparable. The introductory formula *Mæg ic wrecan/secgan*, versions of which are used in *Sea* 1 and *Wife* 2, could be translated "I want to say" or "I will say," as is indicated by the variant found in *Deor* 35, *Þæt ic bi me sylfum secgan wille. Mæg*, then, in the *Deor* refrain, expresses something stronger than possibility; it indicates what is desired and expected. For occurrences of the pres. indic. of *magan*, see *Concordance* M001:126–29 (*maeg, maege, maegi, maegon*), 139–43 (*maga*), 143–65 (*magan*), 181–207 (*mage*), 220–324 (*magon*); M007:41–200 (*mæg*); M010:321–24 (*meg, megan*).

Ofergan has the following meanings: 1) "pass over" (literal), 2) "over-whelm" (literal and figurative), 3) "overcome," 4) "transgress," 5) "pass on or away" (figurative). The various senses are enumerated more fully (in six categories) by Bosworth-Toller. The context and the absence of a direct object point to sense 5 in *Deor* (Bosworth-Toller and Toller *Supp*'s v). Eight other examples of this usage are recorded: two in the Alfredian Orosius and *Pastoral Care*, one in the Alfredian Boethius, the very late OE *Rood Tree*, the C *Chronicle* entry for 1053, and a glossary – rendering *excederet* (the last placed in a different category by Bosworth-Toller). The preponderance of Alfredian uses is striking, and suggests a background for the composition of *Deor*, presumably, like the Orosius, from the Alfredian circle rather than the king's own hand (see Liggins 1970 and Bately 1970; and cf. Part 1, pp. 18–19, above). In these various occurrences of *ofergan* as "pass on or away," the subject is a state of being, not a person, which makes a similar usage probable here: literally, "it passed over with regard to that." The line also implies as a subsidiary meaning sense 3 – "overcame" (cf. the use of *ofercuman* in line 26) – although one would expect an accusative rather than a genitive with this usage. For the occurrences of *ofergan*, see *Concordance* O001:172–75 and 210–15.

For the interpretation of the refrain in its final occurrence, see note on line 42, below.

8–13 Cf. *Vǫlundarkviða* stanza 36: *nu gengr Bǫðvildr barni aukin* (Neckel-Kuhn 1983, 123). Beadohild was raped by Weland as part of his vengeance on Niðhad, her father. This revenge is depicted on the front panel of the early-eighth-century Franks Casket, which shows Weland standing in his smithy, with Beadohild and her maid approaching, and the bodies of Niðhad's sons lying under the anvil. For a detailed description of the casket panel and its bearing on *Deor*, see Whitbread 1956. Beadohild became the mother of the hero Widia – the consolation implied in *Þæs ofereode*. He is mentioned in *Widsith* 124 and 130 (as Wudga), and in *Waldere II* 8–9, where he is identified as *Niðhades mæg* and *Welandes bearn*. Viðga also figures in the thirteenth-century *Þiðreks saga*.

14   There are two cruces here: the question of whether MS *mæð hilde* is one word or two, and the interpretation and possible emendation of *monge*.

Scholarly opinion is now overwhelmingly in favour of reading the woman's name *Mæðhilde*, following Thorpe. The earliest scholars, Conybeare and Wilhelm Grimm ([1829] 1957, 22–24), saw no person here and interpreted the line as a reference to the destruction of battle. Grein-Wülker, Mackie, and others, following Grein, understand *þæt mæð Hilde* as "the violation of Hild." Grein *Sprachschatz* posits a neuter noun *mæð*, "violatio?" on the basis of ON *meiða*, "to hurt, maim," but without support in OE, and equates Hild with Odila, raped by Erminrikr in the *Þiðreks saga*. The only OE neuter noun of this form means "a mowing of hay," "hay," "hayfield," and occurs exclusively in agricultural contexts. See *Concordance* M001:136; M010:20; M013:209. Grein-Köhler repeats Grein, but Holthausen's Supplement suggests the emendation *mæðel*. Although the name *Mæðhild* is unique in OE, the first element is paralleled in the masculine name *Mæðhelm* in the *Liber Vitae* (Sweet 1885, 156). The existence of relatively modern Scandinavian ballads about the lovers Gaute/Gauti and Magnild/ Magnhild makes an allusion to a similar pair in *Deor* highly probable. Various other ways of interpreting the half-line and/or emending the problematic *mæð* have been suggested, but none has been widely accepted.

Malone 1933 reads *monge* as dative of an (otherwise unrecorded) *mong*, "love-commerce" (p. 8). Malone 1961 emends to *mōne*, "moans," in accordance with his new interpretation in the light of the Scandinavian ballads. See editions, pp. 8–9, and Malone 1936, where he explains that Geat's wife lies in bed bewailing the love of a water-demon which will prove fatal to her. However, the reading "moans" (acc. pl.) involves unnecessarily emending the text, puts a strain on the syntax, and is justifiable only by the dubious assumption that the story alluded to in *Deor* is essentially the same as the one in the modern ballads. Although the word order is unusual, the unemended text makes perfectly good sense if *monge* is understood as *monige*, in apposition to *we*. See Klaeber 1948; he here retracts his earlier suggestion that *monge* might be emended to *mān* or *mōd* (Klaeber 1906, 284). Taking *þæt* as a demonstrative pronoun, translate: "Many of us have heard about the business of Mæðhild."

15 *Frige* was taken by Conybeare as the nom. pl. of *freo*, "free men, nobles," and the words understood along the lines of "Geat's men became homeless." Conybeare was followed by W. Grimm ([1829] 1957, 22–24), Grein, Brandl (1908, 975–76), and Sieper. However, the impossibility of translating *grundleas* ("bottomless," as in "bottomless pit") in this way precludes this interpretation of the text. Among modern critics, only J. Anderson (1983, 210) has interpreted the word *frige* like Conybeare. Since Thorpe's translation "courtships", *frige* has usually been identified with *weres frige* (*Juliana* 103, *Elene* 341) and *weres frigum* (*Christ I* 37), the "embraces" or "love" of a man. This is how Malone interprets the word in his 1933 edition. Reinterpreting the stanza in the light of the Scandinavian material, Malone 1936 treats *frige* as gen. sg. of "wife," on the basis of one other definite instance of *freo* as "woman" – *Genesis B* 457. He translates: "the lamentations [reading *mone*, = *māne*, line 14] ... of Geat's lady grew boundless," (pp. 254–55). Whitbread, treating *Geates* as an objective rather than a subjective genitive, translates: "her passion for Geat [instead of the usual "Geat's passion"] grew boundless" (1940–41, 382). Tupper (1911–12), who equated Hild with Beadohild and saw in the stanza an allusion to Niðhad's (the Geat's) grief for his sons, slain by Weland, took *frige* as an expression denoting parental, rather than sexual, love, but this view has found little support.

Identifications of Geat have variously treated the name as signifying a member of a tribe, a divinity, or a particular person (Conybeare et al. equated Geat with "the Goth," i.e. Dietrich/Theodoric). The second view is influenced by the occurrence of the name "Geat" in the mythical sections of the A-S genealogies (for a list of these, see Klaeber *Beowulf*, pp. 254–55), and by Odin's inclusion of Gautr among his names in *Grímnismál*, stanza 54 (see Neckel-Kuhn 1983, 68). Accordingly, Kemble thought Geat to be Odin (1849, 1:370–72); S. Stefanovic (1910) suggested an incestuous relationship between Odin and one of his Valkyrie daughters. Lawrence (1911–12, 32–40) identified (the) Geat with Heðinn, who is enamoured of Hild in Saxo, book 5 and in *Skáldskaparmál*, chap. 62 [50]. See, respectively, *Gesta Danorum* (late twelfth century), in Knabe and Hermann 1931, 131–34, and *Edda Snorra* (1222–23?), in Jónsson 1931, 153–55. Though the connection with this stanza in *Deor* is highly speculative, the name Heðinn has a definite counterpart in the later reference to the Heodenings (see note on line 36b, below). N. Eliason (1965) finds in the third stanza of *Deor* an allusion to an incest story originally involving the

wife of the legendary Offa and her father, and subsequently transferred
to Offa's son (Ongengeat). Of the many attempts to identify the shadowy
Geat and (Mæð)hild, Malone's is the most plausible, but the content of
the story known to the *Deor* poet remains irrecoverable.

16 This line has frequently been emended. Thorpe prints *hī* and *ealle*,
but adds "r[ecte] *ealne*" in his apparatus. He translates: "so that from him
hapless love all sleep took." The authenticity of the MS reading is vindicated by Stefanovic (1910, 398), who points out that *beniman* can take
an acc. + instr. construction, and that *slæp* can be read as *slæpe* with final
e elided before the *e* of *ealle*. Cf. *Sea* 11 and 55. *Hi* could be either sg.
("her") or pl. ("them"), but if Mæðhild is regarded as the main subject of
the stanza, and as a victim, like Weland in stanza 1 and Beadohild in
stanza 2, the sg. is more appropriate.

18 Most scholars have regarded Ðeodric here as Theodoric the Ostrogoth, who ruled in Italy from 493 to 526, metamorphosed in continental
legend into Dietrich von Bern, who spent thirty years' exile at the court
of Attila before he was able to win his kingdom. There is dispute as to
whether the thirty years for which Ðeodric *ahte* represents the historical
rule or the fictitious exile. If Ðeodric is another victim figure, the latter
would seem to be indicated. *Waldere II* 8–10 speaks of Widia's release of
Ðeodric from captivity (*of nearwum*). The mention of Eormanric in the
next stanza, who in later tradition takes the place of Odoacer, Theodoric's
historical foe, suggests that the two persons are already in some way
associated in the mind of the *Deor* poet. The fragments of the OHG *Hildebrandslied* (ca. 800) do not mention Eormanric, but refer to Dietrich's
flight from Odoacer, accompanied by many men, including Hildebrand
(*Forn her ostar giweit, floh her Otachres nid – / hina miti Theotrihhi enti sinero
degano filu*, lines 18–19; the poem is printed in Dickins 1915, 78–84).
Hildebrand speaks of how he spent sixty summers and winters in exile,
presumably with Dietrich (*Ich wallota sumaro enti wintro sehstic ur lante*,
line 50). The unhistorical connection with Eormanric first appears in the
late-tenth-/early-eleventh-century *Quedlinburg Annals*: [*Ermanricus*] *Theo-
doricum ... patruelem suum, instimulante Odoacro, patruelo suo, de Verona pul-
sum, apud Attilam exulare coegit* (Pertz 1839, 31).

Some critics, including Frankis (1962, 161–63), see Ðeodric not as the
victim of exile but as the wielder of tyrannical power. The ecclesiastical
view of Theodoric as the Arian heretic responsible for the deaths of
Boethius, Symmachus, and Pope John I would accord with this interpretation. This view is reflected in the Alfredian Boethius, in Wærferth's

translation of Gregory's *Dialogues*, and in the *OE Martyrology*. In the last two, Theodoricus/Ðeodric is hurled into hell by Pope John and Symmachus. See *Dialogues* (Hecht 1900, 305–6); *Martyrology* (Herzfeld 1900, 84).

Further, the use of the word *ahte*, "possessed," usually indicates some kind of control. Sedgefield 1922 wonders if *ahte* should be emended to *ehte*, "persecuted" (p. 141). M. Ashdown suggests "had held and then held no more" – i.e. Ðeodric's good fortune came to an end (1929, 327), but the context gives no indication of such a pluperfect usage. E. Ekwall believes that here and in line 23 *ahte* means "held as a usurper" (1934, 81). Klaeber 1948, supporting the exile theory, argues that *ahte* could mean merely "dwelled in" here (pp. 124–25). Since external evidence exists for both Ðeodric's tyranny and his exile, and since the figure in the *Deor* stanza itself might parallel either the victims of the previous allusions or the tyrant Eormanric of the following one, either interpretation is viable.

Unlike the majority of scholars, Malone rejects the identification with Theodoric the Goth in favour of a Frankish hero. In edition 1 (1933) he identifies Ðeodric with the son of Clovis who reigned from 511 to 534. Edition 4 (1966) modifies this position, so that Ðeodric "answers to the young Sigiwald of Gregory of Tours who was given the name Theodric when he came to be thought of as the son ... of the Frankish king of that name" (p. 41). The Gregory reference is in the *Historia Francorum*, book 3, chap. 13 (see Krusch and Levison 1951, 110). Malone's arguments for a Frankish Theodoric are discussed more fully in the following note.

19a The "Mærings" appear to be linked with the Ostrogoths in three medieval sources. In the ninth- or tenth-century inscription on the runic stone from Rök in Sweden, Þiaurikr is designated *skati Marika*, "lord of the Mærings (?)"; in the Latin prologue, composed in the later tenth century, to Notker's OHG translation of Boethius, Theodoric is described as *regem mergothorum et ostrogothorum* (Piper 1882, 1:3); and in the twelfth-century Regensburg gloss *Gothi Meranere* a similar identification of the tribes seems to be made (see Müllenhoff 1860–65, 415). The "city of the Mærings" might well be Ravenna, Theodoric's capital, or possibly Verona, the site of his victory over Odoacer in 489 – the "Bern" of legend. If the reference is to Ðeodric's exile, the place must be some indefinite spot in Hunnish territory where Ðeodric sojourned with his followers. J. Anderson's "fortress of basil flowers" (*mæringc* occurs once as a plant name) is improbable (see Anderson 1983, 209).

Whereas *Mæringas* is commonly understood as "famous ones," "glorious ones," from *mære*, Malone renders the word "borderers," from *mearc*. The Mærings, he argues, were originally Visigoths, who came in south German tradition to be associated with Meran in the Tyrol. His Frankish Ðeodric, in the shape of the Wolfdietrich of MHG poetry, was brought up (in exile) at the house of the faithful Berchtung von Meran. In the twelfth-century *Kaiserchronik*, Wolfdietrich, here the grandfather of Dietrich von Bern, is himself Prince of Meran: *ain vurste was dô ze Merân,/gehaizen was er der alte Dieterîch*, lines 13840–41 (Schröder 1895, 1:331). For Malone's exposition of his theory of the development of the Frankish Theodoric into an exile-and-return hero, see Malone 1934b, 76–84. It is, however, quite possible that the name Meran was imported into the Wolfdietrich story from the traditions surrounding the Ostrogothic Dietrich; see Heinzel 1889, 68–70.

21b–23 Ermanaricus the Goth (died ca. 375) is presented by his contemporary Ammianus Marcellinus as ... *bellicosissimi regis ... vicinis nationibus formidati* (book 31, chap. 3; Rolfe 1972–82, 3:396. Later writers speak of his brutality, especially in his savage execution of Sunilda/Svanhild (Jǫrmunrekk's wife in Norse tradition). See Jordanes's mid-sixth-century *Getica*, chap. 24 (Mommsen 1882, 91–92). For the Scandinavian sources, see *Guðrúnarhvǫt*, stanza 2 (Appendix, p. 296, below), based on *Hamðismál*, stanza 3 (Neckel-Kuhn 1983, 269), *Skáldskaparmál*, chap. 51 [42] (Jónsson 1931, 131–33); and the later thirteenth-century *Volsunga saga*, chap. 42 (Finch 1965, 75–76). The *Quedlinburg Annals* describe Ermanaricus as *astutior in dolo, largior in dono* (see also note on line 18, above). The Anglo-Saxons likewise regarded him with a mixture of admiration for his munificence (his gift of a weighty gold ring, *Widsith* 89–92) and horror at his cruelty and treachery (*wraþes wærlogan*, *Widsith* 9; *searoniðas ... Eormenrices*, *Beowulf* 1200b–1201a).

26 Literally "that it might be overcome with respect to that rule." *Cynerice* here, though usually glossed as "kingdom," makes better sense if taken in its more abstract meaning of "kingly power." Eormanric's people would wish to be rid of him, but not to be conquered. Whitbread makes this point, but understands the syntax differently: "'that (this part) of their kingdom [i.e., their king] should be overcome' ... [an] elliptic partitive construction" (1943, 369). Taking *cynerice* as "rule" is a simpler solution. The construction with a genitive is rare, but a possible analogue exists in *wuldorfæst ys 7 micel cristenra manna god þæs wuldorge———ces [wuldorgeworces* supplied by editor] *nane mennisce searwa ofercuman ne magon*, from the *Life of St. Christopher* (Rypins 1924, 75). It is characteristic of the *Deor* poet's style to use an impersonal verb with its effective subject contained in an oblique case or adverbial phrase, as here, in the refrain, and in line 12.

28–34 The view of some earlier scholars that these lines might be a Christian interpolation has long been rejected. Lawrence argued for the integrity of the text (1911–12, 27–28). The subject could be taken as the sorrowful man of line 28, with *sorgcearig* functioning as a substantival adjective. Schücking 1919 attributes a conditional force to lines 28–30, indicated by the inverted word order of *siteð sorgcearig* (p. 32). Treated in this way, these lines would modify lines 31–34. Following Schücking, Malone prints the whole passage as one sentence. But Mitchell *Syntax*, who quotes this and two other possible examples, is very sceptical about the existence of the inverted conditional clause in OE (§§ 3681–82), and most editors punctuate as two sentences, placing a period after line 30.

35 This point marks a shift in the thought of the poem, but there is no MS indication of a break – as there is, by the use of end punctuation and capitalization, after the refrain in lines 7, 13, 17, 20, and 27. The refrain is absent here. Most editors, therefore, print lines 35–42 continuously. Malone prints them as a separate section.

36b The Heodenings must be the "people of Heoden"; cf. *Widsith* 21: *Hagena [weold] Holmrygum and Heoden Glommum. Skáldskaparmál* 62 [50] tells the story of Heðinn's (Heoden's) elopement with Hǫgni's daughter Hild and of the ensuing endless battle in which Hild always brings to life the slain warriors (Jónsson 1931, 153–55). Saxo Grammaticus tells another version of the story (Knabe and Hermann 1931, 131–34). Deor does not appear in the Hild story – or elsewhere in heroic literature.

37b Whereas the other proper names in the poem belong to heroic legend, Deor seems to be an imaginary figure. The name is recorded several times in A-S documents; in Kentish and Mercian contexts it appears as *Diar(a)* and *Diera*. See Searle 1897, pp. 164 and 166; also Birch 1885–87, nos. 209, 210, 226, 241, 242, 327, 442, 497, 507. As used in the poem, *Deor* may be an epithet or nickname. It probably means "bold," but there is clearly also a play on *dyre*, "dear," in the a-verse. Frankis, who connects this poem with *Wulf and Eadwacer*, understands the b-verse as "My name was an animal" – i.e. "Wulf" (1962, 172–74). W. Bolton, who also takes *deor* as "animal," finds this statement disparaging (1972, 227), but the tone of the lines does not suggest this kind of self-criticism. The use of the past tense has provoked some discussion. Lawrence thought that the name was an appellation given to the speaker while he was skald among the Heodenings (1911–12, 40–42); others have attributed the past tense merely to the past nature of the events described (thus Grienberger 1921, 406). Whether an epithet or a regular proper name, "Deor" reflects the speaker's respected status at the court of the Heodenings – a status which he no longer enjoys.

39b Heorrenda corresponds to Hjarrandi, the father of Heðinn in *Skáld-skaparmál*. In the roughly contemporary MHG *Kudrun*, Hôrant is a minstrel who charms Hild on behalf of his lord Hetel. As in the Norse version, Hild is abducted from her father (Hagen), and a battle results, but in this case ends in reconciliation. See *Kudrun*, books 5–8 (Bartsch 1965). Evidently, Heorrenda was a legendary minstrel with fabulous powers. Deor's own prowess is implied by associating him with such a figure.

42 While *þisses* here, as elsewhere in the poem, refers to a present misfortune – probably Deor's loss of his position as court *scop* – the use of *þæs* must be different here. In contrast to earlier references to misfortune overcome, *þæs* here refers to the speaker's past happiness. This is the generally accepted view, but some scholars express disagreement or qualifications. Bloomfield takes *þæs* as alluding to the misfortune just described, which has passed away (1964, 537); Jerome Mandel believes that the final *þæs* "can refer as easily to Heorrenda's good fortune as it can to Deor's ill fortune" (1977, 8). For the interpretation of the refrain, see note on line 7, above.

WULF AND EADWACER

1 The enigmatic nature of this line, most commonly translated "It is to my people as if one gave them a gift," has led some scholars to believe that the opening of the poem has been lost. Henry Bradley regarded the poem as a "fragment," but did not elaborate (1888, 198). Fritz Hicketier suggested a lacuna of 1½ lines before line 1 (1888, 571–72); Ruth Lehmann a loss of 2 lines (1969, 164); W.W. Lawrence an omission of 2 lines between lines 1 and 2 (1902a, 251).

Heinrich Leo, in accordance with his strained interpretation of the poem as a charade on the name *Cynewulf*, treated *leodum* as *leoðum*, "limbs," in the sense of the parts of a word (1857, 22) – an emendation which never found much acceptance. Among more recent critics, only N. Eliason, who interprets the poem as a playful complaint about the separation of two related passages of poetry, has regarded *leoðum* as a possibility (1974, 229).

Lac, in the b-verse, is most frequently understood as "gift," with specific reference to Wulf, who forms a kind of gift to the *wælreowe weras* on the island (line 6). Some regard the "gift" as the speaker herself; thus J. Adams (1958, 3); also J. Fanagan (1976, 134). The word *lac* has also been translated as "battle"; e.g. by Gustav Budjuhn, who set the poem in a hunting context and found both "battle" and "game" appropriate [as in *gelac*] (1916, 258). Donald Fry, arguing that the poem is a charm, translates *lac* "medicine," as in three glosses (1971, 255–56). As pointed out by A. Cameron and A. diPaolo Healey, the meaning "battle" is based on a misinterpretation of *laces* in *Guthlac B* 1034 (1979, 96). A contextual study of the uses of *lac* shows that it always has the central meaning of "offering"; frequently the word refers to a sacrifice to a deity, occasionally to a message, and possibly to a medication or potion (a meaning cited by Bosworth-Toller but deleted by Toller *Supp* as merely a shortened form of *lacnung*). For the various occurrences and forms, see *Concordance* Loo1:69–111 and 127–32. After an evaluation of "battle," "message," and "game" as possibilities, Peter Baker concludes that "gift" is the only appropriate meaning in this context (1981, 5:40–41). However, "sacrifice" can be taken as a subsidiary meaning – though Baker argues that this usage would demand a more ceremonious verb.

2/7 This sentence can be construed either as a statement or a question. Mitchell *Syntax* observes that "The order VS is not peculiar to questions," and that the context must be our guide (§ 1645). *Willað* contains an element of futurity here, but should not be regarded as simply a modal forming the future tense; it also carries a sense of intention (cf. Mitchell *Syntax*, §§ 1023–24 and 1997). Continuity with line 1, which presents a hypothesis, favours interpreting line 2/7 as a prediction. *Hine* in line 2 lacks an antecedent, but when the sentence recurs in line 7, it is clear that the reference is to Wulf.

The verb *aþecgan* is very rare. Clearly, it is related to the much more common *þicgan*, "to take," often used of food. This connection has led to two, opposite interpretations: 1) "receive" (i.e. welcome), 2) "consume" (i.e. destroy). In his examination of verbs in -*þecgan*, Baker comes to the conclusion that they mean either literally "give to eat," or metaphorically "serve," the latter being extended to "kill" in *Genesis A* 2002 *ecgum ofþegde*. He favours the metaphorical "kill" in *Wulf*, but believes the literal meaning is also present. See Baker 1981, 5:42–43 and 45; also edition, p. 5. The literal "give food to" was also suggested by Bradley (1888, 198). However, rather than treating forms in -*þecg*- and -*þeg(d)*- as parts of a weak causative verb related to but distinct from *þicgan*, it is more consistent with the evidence to explain these forms as variants of *þicgan* without semantic distinction (unless in the prefixes). Weak forms of *þicgan* in *þe(c)g*- can thus be added to weak forms of this verb in *þig(d)*- (for the latter, see Campbell *Grammar*, § 749). All of Baker's examples can more simply be translated "take" or "consume(d)." Such a meaning also fits the present context, and picks up the idea of *lac* (line 1). For the various forms of -*þecgan*, see *Concordance* A018:317 (*aþe(c)g*-); THoo5:287 (*þegde* – once) and 308 (*þegeð* – twice); Ooo2:91 (*oferþecgan* – once; an emended form; MS *oferþegcan*). -*þecgan* is discussed more fully in Klinck 1987a.

Some scholars have interpreted *on þreat cymeð* in the light of ON *þraut*, "struggle," or *þrot*, "want lack" – notably Lawrence, who regarded the poem as a translation from ON (1902a, 255–58) and rendered the phrase "come[s] into heavy straits." But, since such a meaning is elsewhere unrecorded in OE and the translation theory is doubtful, there is no reason to avoid the regular OE meaning of *þreat*, "host, troop." The absence of a final *e* in *þreat* makes it unlikely that the word is dative, as some have taken it to be – for example, Arnold Davidson (1975, 25 and 27). Thus, the translation "if he comes in (i.e. with) a troop" is less probable. Rudolf Imelmann's emendation to *in þreate* (1907a, 24) is not justified. The abstract meaning "violence" may also be present.

Translate: "They intend to kill him if he comes into their troop."

3/8 This verse, like lines 17 and 19, stands alone as an isolated half-line, an arrangement which gives the poem a quasi-strophic structure emphasized by the repetition of lines 2–3 in lines 7–8. Lawrence saw an imitation of Norse metre in the use of these short lines (1902a, 251).

The adverbial form *ungelice* in line 8, as distinct from the adjective *ungelic* in line 3, is probably a scribal variant without semantic significance, though Harry Kavros finds in the change an increasing sense of entrapment and passivity (1977–78, 83–84).

Ungelic(e) is us, "It is different with us," has been variously interpreted. Some scholars take *us* as a reference to the speaker and her husband (not Wulf). Thus Lehmann, who finds a distinction between the plural here (*us*) and the dual in lines 16 (*uncerne*) and 19 (*uncer*), the dual being reserved, she believes, for the woman and Wulf (1969, 159 and 163). Others see in *us* a reference to the speaker and her people – e.g. Terrence Keough, who translates "It is unlike us," meaning it is unlikely that the speaker's people will accept Wulf (1976, 554–55). Stanley B. Greenfield, who believes Wulf and Eadwacer are the same person, takes the line to refer to the speaker and her husband/lover, the difference being that she, unlike her people, would welcome Wulf (1986, 11). Baker believes that in line 3 *us* refers to the speaker and her husband, who are different from Wulf, but in line 8 to the speaker and Wulf, who are different from each other (1981, 5:44–46). In fact, the last interpretation can well be applied to both occurrences of the line. Since line 4 states that the speaker and Wulf are on two separate islands, and line 9 also refers to their separation (and its effect on the narrator), *Ungelic(e) is us* can reasonably be taken to be a reference to this separation, and, along with the preceding line, an expression of the speaker's despair about Wulf and herself.

4a The words "wolf" and "wolf's head" are associated with outlaws. If captured, an outlaw's head could immediately be struck off like a wolf's, *lupinum enim caput geret a die utlagacionis sue, quod ab Anglis vulves heved nominatur*; see *Leges Edwardi Confessoris* 6.2a, in Liebermann 1903–16, 1:631. The *Leges EC* are post-Conquest (regarded by Liebermann as mid-twelfth century) but incorporate earlier material.

Lawrence (1902a, 255–58) saw *iege* (also *ige*, line 6) as an indication of Norse influence (cf. ON *ey*). *Ea* is the usual form of the simplex, but *i(e)g-* and *eg-* are common in compounds – cf. *eglond*, line 5.

5 *Fæst* = "secure" in the sense of "inaccessible" – because surrounded by fen. Cf. Hicketier: "unzugänglich ist jenes Eiland" (1888, 572). Toller *Supp* understands the word as "fortified," sense IV of *fæst*. Sieper emends to the adverbial form, *fæste*, making the word modify *fenne biworpen*.

6b For the form *ige*, see note on line 4a.

Imelmann emended to *her on ige*, finding it more likely that the *wælreowe weras* should be on the speaker's island (1907a, 20); this suggestion is adopted by Wesley Mattox (1975, 33, n. 1, and 37).

9 *Widlastum* has sometimes been taken as an adjective applied to *wenum* – "far-ranging" – but the word *widlast* in its three other occurrences appears to be a noun: *widlast wrecan* (*Genesis* 1021), *Wadað widlastas* (*Andreas* 677), *Widlast ferede/rynestrong on rade* (*Riddle 19* 6–7) (Bosworth-Toller cites the occurrences in *Wulf* and *Genesis* as adjectives); cf. the use of *wræclast*, "path of exile." *Widlast* is, therefore, best interpreted as a noun, "wide track," "far journey."

Dogode is a hapax legomenon of uncertain provenance and meaning. Grein glossed the infinitive "*pati?*" (also Grein-Köhler), and Bosworth-Toller renders it "to bear, suffer" (Campbell *Addenda* deletes). Max Rieger translated "habe [hatte?] ich lange Weile," relating the verb to *dogor*, "day" (1869, 216–17). Lehmann suggests a connection with Scots *dow*, "to fade" (1969, 160–61). Mattox offers "I was bound in cares," on an analogy with Middle Dutch *duwen*, "squeeze" (1975, 38). At least as likely as these various proposals is a connection with late OE *docga*, "dog," recorded twice in place names as *doggene* and once, as a gloss on *canum*, in the gen. pl. *docgena*; see *OE Dict*, and *Concordance* D008:232 and 286. *Docgena* occurs in the gloss on Prudentius's *Peristephanon*, book 5, and refers metaphorically to torturers as "curs." For the variation between *g* (*dogode*) and *cg* (*docgena*), cf. *sceagode* and *sceacgede*, "comosus," in Wright-Wülker *Vocabularies* (col. 206, line 9, and col. 380, line 14, resp.).

Hicketier's emendation to *hogode* (1888, 578–79) has been accepted by many. *OE Dict* gives "**dogian*: of uncertain meaning; has been emended to *hogode*." But this raises some syntactical problems. A dative object for *hycgan/hogian*, "think (about the far journeys ...)" is supported elsewhere only in *agenum hicgean welan*, a very literal rendering of *propriis studere divitiis* in the OE gloss on Defensor's *Liber scintillarum* (Rhodes 1889, 158). A genitive object (Hicketier construes *hogode* with *Wulfes*) is found only as a substantival adjective or pronoun anticipating a clause: *Hycgað his ealle, /hu ge hi beswicen!* "Think of it ...," *Genesis B* 432–33. However, one would expect a dative object with a verb *dogian*, "to follow (like a dog)," on an analogy with *fyl(g)ian*.

Translate the line: "I followed the far journeys of my Wulf in (my) hopes."

10 This and the following line can be punctuated as one or as two sentences. If a period is placed after line 10, it is possible, though not necessary, to take the *beaducafa*, "battle-bold one" (line 11) as Wulf, visiting the speaker between his "far journeys." However, the repetition of *ponne* at the beginning of lines 10 and 11 suggests that the two are parallel statements, both dependent on *dogode* (line 9); in this case, the *beaducafa* must be another person, since Wulf is absent. See Baker 1981, 5:46 and 48.

Renig, "rainy," also suggests *reonig*, "mournful," though Sieper's emendation to the latter word is uncalled for. *Reotugu* is a hapax legomenon, but clearly related to *reotian*, "to lament." The word is usually translated "weeping," and a link between the woman and sympathetic nature is obviously intended in the OE. Baker believes that the adjective conveys the sound of the woman's complaints; he prefers to translate "wailing" (1981, 5:47; edition, p. 8).

11b   For the syntax of line 11, see the previous note.

This phrase is usually taken as a reference to sexual intercourse. One or two have understood *bog* as "branch," giving the translation "put branches around me." Thus Mackie: "gave me shelter"; cf. also Campbell *Addenda*. *OE Dict* gives "upper arm ... sometimes regarded as ... [involving] a euphemism for sexual intercourse," but notes the other translation. Apart from the usage in *Wulf*, the word occurs in the sense of "shoulder" as a gloss on *lacertus* and *armus*, and with specific reference to a ram, horse, ox, or beast for slaughter – but not to a human being. For this reason, Peter Orton argues that *se beaducafa* must be an animal (1985, 233–36). The use of *bogum* in *Wulf* accords with the animal imagery in terms of which the male figures in the poem are depicted; thus, the effect in the OE is rougher than its usual translation "laid his arms about me." For the occurrences of *bog* "shoulder of an animal" (also spelled *bogh, boh, boog*), see *Concordance* B016:231, 247–49, 251–53, and 286.

12   *To þon* is usually translated "to an extent" or "to a degree." But when the phrase is used in this manner it precedes a clause: "to the extent that ..." See Bosworth-Toller and Toller *Supp*, *se* V3, with prep. *to*; also Mitchell *Syntax* §§ 2889–2904, esp. 2895. The phrase here, therefore, probably means simply "joy in that." Thus Bosworth-Toller, under usage Ia of *wyn(n)* (with the preposition *to*), citing several other examples. Cf. also *to þon gefegon* in the *OE Bede*, book 5, chap. 17, p. 464 (Miller, the editor, translates "rejoiced at this," p. 465). For occurrences of *to þon*, see *Concordance* TH015:120–282, passim.

Lað may be construed as either adjective ("hateful," "displeasing") or noun ("pain," "annoyance"). The latter makes a more exact parallel with *wyn*. But the distinction is not felt in the OE.

The loose alliteration of *w* and *hw* led Ferdinand Holthausen to suspect the integrity of the line and to suggest ways of regularizing it; see Holthausen 1893, 188, and 1914, 77. However, the metre of the poem is in other ways irregular, and the loss of *h* before a consonant also occurs in *wælreowe* (line 6).

13   The a-verse is lacking a syllable according to strict metre. Karl Bül-bring proposed *Min wulf, min wulf* (1891, 157); Holthausen *Wulf, min Wulf, la!* (1893, 188); Imelmann *Wulf se min Wulf* (1907a, 14). More recent critics accept the line as the most dramatic example of the poem's metrical licence.

Wena ... þine is commonly understood as "my expectations of you" – i.e.

my anxious awaiting of you; cf. line 9. Osborn (1983, 177) regards the *wenum/wena* in both occurrences as experienced by Wulf, who, "even in emotional stance ... is presented as active" in contrast to the speaker's passivity.

14b *Seldcymas* = "rare visits." Taken literally by most scholars, but very likely an understatement. Baker parenthetically characterizes the word as "doubtless litotes for 'never coming'" (1981, 5:48). Cf. Mackie's translation "thy constant absence." Cf. also (*Reste he ðær) mæte weorode*, "(he remained there) with a small company," meaning "alone," of Christ placed in the tomb, *Dream of the Rood* 69. Hicketier's "coming into the house" (1888, 579) is theoretically possible but contextually less appropriate.

15b This form of *metelist* can be categorized either as nom. pl. (thus Baker, edition, p. 7) or dat. sg. The latter assumes an ellipsis: "(It was) not through lack of food." Though sometimes taken as a hypothetical cause of distress, the reference to lack of food seems rather pointless unless the woman has actually suffered this hardship; cf. P.J. Frankis (1962, 172, n. 3).

16a Now usually punctuated with a question mark at the end of the verse. Leo placed the question mark after *þu*, taking *Eadwacer* in opposition to *uncerne earne hwelp* (1857, 24–25). Similarly Grein in his edition; in his textual corrections he placed the question mark after *Eadwacer* (Grein 1865, 428). Max Rieger (1869, 217–18) punctuated line 16 as a single sentence, and this punctuation, along with the early identification of *hwelp* and *Eadwacer*, has recently been revived by Orton (1985, 228–33); see the following note on line 16b. Hicketier, taking *Eadwacer* as vocative (now the standard interpretation), pointed out that the word could as well be a man's name as a wolf or dog's, and noted that Auðawakrs [Odoacer] was the name of the first king of Italy (1888, 580–82).

This resemblance led Imelmann to develop his elaborate theory that *Wulf, Wife*, and *Husb* were fragments of a lost composition about another Odoacer – a Saxon king of the fifth century [Adovacrius]. Imelmann's theory, first explained in his *Die ae Odoaker-Dichtung* (1907a), was expanded in subsequent publications (1907b, 1908, 1920), which brought forward other OE elegiac poems as evidence for the existence of an Odoacer saga. A connection between *Wulf* and the better-known Odoacer, the enemy of Theodoric the Ostrogoth (OE Ðeodric), is proposed by A.C. Bouman (1949), who ties in the poem with the Weland story and with *Deor*. Lehmann also argues for a connection, of a different kind, with this

Odoacer (1969, 154–57). But since the poem contains no specific indication of the tale's being common knowledge (for example, the use of a formula like *we gefrugnon*), and since there is no proof that Eadwacer = Odoacer, it is best to regard the figure as imaginary.

The name is usually translated "property-watcher," and sometimes regarded as an epithet rather than a proper noun. Thus Adams, who applies the term to Wulf, and denies the existence of a second man in the poem (1958, 2). Translated in this way, *eadwacer* has a certain appropriateness as indicating some kind of possession or guardianship of the speaker or the *hwelp* (line 16b). Greenfield also understands the word as an epithet of Wulf but translates "the guardian of ... [my] happiness (1986, 12). *Eadwacer/Edwacer* is elsewhere recorded a few times as a proper name: in two charters (see *Concordance* E008:204); in a Latin life of Oswald and on two coins in the British Museum (see Searle 1897, 189).

There are some pointers in the poem to indicate that Eadwacer is a person separate from and contrasting to Wulf. If Eadwacer is being addressed here, it is reasonable to suppose that he is distinct from the man or animal *wulf* (line 17) referred to in the third person in the course of the address. Also, a "wolf" and a "watcher" fulfil mutually antagonistic rôles. Hence the usual view that the former is the speaker's fugitive lover and the latter her husband. Eadwacer might also be a guardian rather than a husband. Baker regards him as a kind of gaoler (Wulf being the husband from whom the speaker is separated), who has used the woman sexually (1981, 5:49–50). Keough believes that Eadwacer is not the third person in a sexual triangle, but simply a representative of the woman's tribe (1976, 556–57). Fanagan's view of Eadwacer as lover, Wulf as husband, is less probable (1976, 134–35). The exact nature of the relationship is undefined in the poem, but the use of the name *Eadwacer* suggests a socially recognized authority figure, in contrast to *Wulf*, a name which has connotations of outlawry (see note on line 4a, above). Probably Eadwacer is identical with the *beaducafa* of line 11a, about whose embraces the speaker has mixed feelings.

16b The word *hwelp*, "young animal," is taken literally, in its sense of "young dog" or "young wolf," by scholars before Bradley 1888, and by a few after, notably Walter Sedgefield (1931), who reads the poem as a canine love-story, and, more seriously, by Orton 1985, who argues that the poem is about a family of wolves. Some modern scholars treat the image as a metaphor: for a wen (Fry 1971, 253), a passage of poetry (Eliason 1974, 230), the relationship between the speaker and Eadwacer (Fanagan 1976, 135, and Greenfield 1986, 11); Baker finds this last a possibility (1981, 5:50). However, most interpreters understand *uncerne ... hwelp* as the child of two people, either linking it with Wulf because *hwelp* means an animal (e.g. Lehmann 1969, 162–63), or with Eadwacer because of the disparaging nature of the term (e.g. Davidson 1975, 28–30, and Mattox 1975, 35). Probably the referent of *uncer(ne)* in the present instance and in the next sentence (line 19) is the same. Probably, too, a parallelism is intended between the fates of the two things possessed by "the two of us": the *hwelp* carried off by a wolf to the forest, and the *giedd* which is easily torn asunder. Hence, the relationship with the fugitive lover is likely to lie behind both, and the child to be his.

MS *earne* has been variously emended to *eargne* ("cowardly"), *earmne* ("wretched"), and *earone* ("swift"). The word was accepted by Grein *Sprachschatz*, without emendation, as the accusative of *earu/earo* (Grein-Köhler queries the unemended form). Bradley, also accepting the MS form, proposed a derivation from *earg/earh* (1888, 198), but later approved Holthausen's emendation to *earmne* (Holthausen 1893, 188, and Bradley 1893, 390). The choice between these explanations is largely determined by the interpretation of the contex: "swift" being a likely epithet for "dog" (now discredited), "cowardly" for Eadwacer's child, and "wretched" for Wulf's.

17 The third isolated half-line. See note on line 3/8.

Bireð could be either present or future. Although the image conveys the action of an animal rather than a man, the word-play must be deliberate and the man Wulf also intended. The audience/reader is not told if the wolf carries off the whelp to tend it or to devour it, but the occurrence of the verb *toslited* in the next sentence, though applied to something else, is suggestive of a wolf's rending and tearing. Mattox believes that this word indicates the child will be slaughtered (1975, 39–40). Also, whether MS *earne* is understood as *eargne* or *earmne*, the adjective precludes a cheerful attitude towards the child and its situation. Johan Kerling's inference that "Wulf will bring the child to safety" is, therefore, unlikely (1980, 140–43). The child is lost to the speaker and Eadwacer; either it will share Wulf's precarious life or it will be destroyed.

18 The object of *toslited*, "tears apart," is *þæt*, anticipating *uncer giedd geador* in the next line, and the concept, therefore, an abstract one. Nevertheless, the verb contributes to the animal imagery running through the poem by suggesting the action of a savage beast. See notes on lines 16b and 17.

The pronouncement made in this line refers obliquely to Christ's words about marriage in Matthew 19:6, *Quem Deus coniugit, homo non separet.* James Spamer sees this allusion as the speaker's repudiation of her marriage with Eadwacer (1978, 143–44). But the observation could as well apply to the doomed nature of the woman's non-marriage with Wulf. Thus Keough (1976, 557–58) and others.

19 For the use of isolated half-lines, see note on line 3/8.

The verb *tosliteð*, "rends apart," suggests a violent end for *uncer giedd geador*, "the story of us two together"; for the referent of this phrase, see notes on lines 16b and 18. Georg Herzfeld suggested that possibly *giedd* should be emended to *gæd*, "fellowship" (1890, 66n.), a suggestion which was adopted by a few but is now generally rejected. Because of the enigmatic nature of the poem, some scholars have translated *giedd* in this context as "riddle"; e.g. Adams 1958, 4–5; Davidson also regards this as a possibility (1975, 25–26 and 30). Rieger rendered *giedd* "Rätselwort" (1869, 217–18). Although the word *giedd* is used once elsewhere to refer to a riddle: *Nu me þisses gieddes/ondsware ywe* (*Riddle 55* 14b–15a), what it actually means in this case, as in general, is "story, tale." A *giedd* is an utterance of narrative and instructive nature; it may or may not be musical, or in verse form. For the occurrences of the word in its various contexts, see *Concordance* G009:124 and 183; G040:109, 112–13, 115, 187–88; G050:258–59, 261. The use of *giedd* as one of the OE designations for elegy is discussed in Part 3, pp. 244–45, below.

THE WIFE'S LAMENT

1–2 The earliest editors of *Wife* failed to recognize that the feminine endings of *geomorre* and *minre sylfre* established the female identity of the speaker. W.D. Conybeare missed their significance entirely; Thorpe, in a footnote, suggested emending *minre sylfre* to *minne sylfes*. Ettmüller pointed out that a woman was speaking, and accordingly entitled the poem *Wreccan Wifes Ged*. These feminine inflexions make any argument in favour of a male speaker improbable. Levin Schücking proposed deleting lines 1–2 as a later addition and opening the poem with an exclamatory *Hwæt!* in line 3 (1906, esp. 447), but returned to the more usual view of the poem in his *Dichterbuch* (1919, 18–21). Rudolph Bambas, also advocating a male speaker, suggests that either some introductory lines have been omitted or that the crucial feminine forms are scribal errors (1963, esp. 304). Martin Stevens proposes emending *sið* to *siðe*, taking it as a fem. noun, and understanding *geomorre* as an adverb, with double *r* merely a spelling variant (1968, esp. 73–82). Jerome Mandel (1987, 152–55) follows Stevens. For a refutation of Stevens's arguments, see Mitchell 1972, 222–34, and Mitchell *Syntax*, § 1175.

Like *Sea*, *Wife* opens with a conventional "elegiac" introduction. Cf. also *Deor* 35, *Res* 96b–97, and *Husb* 1.

3b   Many editors, including Leslie, emend to *aweox*. Sievers (1885, 516) regarded this emendation as necessary on metrical grounds. But if *up* is unstressed and the first accent falls on *ic*, we have a regular B-type verse of the same pattern as *oþþæt ic aweox*, *Rid 9* 10.

5   Fritz Roeder (1899, 113) took *wite* as the verb, "find fault with," and *wonn* as a noun, "darkness, melancholy," translating "immer werde ich tadeln das Düster meiner Unglückspfade." Schücking (1906, 438), relating *wite* to Gothic *witan*, "auf etwas sehen," emended *wonn* to *worn*, and translated "immer steht mir vor Augen die Fülle meiner Misgeschicke." He prints *wonn* in his *Dichterbuch* (1919, 19). A better sense is achieved by treating *wonn* as the preterite of *winnan*, here used as a perfect, "have suffered," like *gebad* (line 3), with *wite* the noun, "torment." Thus most editors, including Leslie. Bosworth-Toller cites this transitive usage of *winnan* as sense B II and gives several examples. In *Guthlac* 469 and *Genesis* 1014 the expression *wite winnan* seems to have the meaning of paying the penalty.

6–8   Most scholars have interpreted these lines as a reference to the husband's flight or banishment, and have associated them with lines 11–12, which refer to the kin's plotting to separate him from his wife. However, Svetislav Stefanovíc (1909, 403–7) found no evidence here for the assumption that the husband was in enforced exile. Similarly Fritz Schulze (1969, 69–70), and Douglas Short (1970, 590), who suggests that the conduct of warfare or foreign policy has called the husband abroad.

The use of the words *hlaford* and *leodfruma* here, along with *frean* (line 33) and *wine* (lines 49 and 50) might be taken as evidence that the lament was uttered by a man who had lost his lord. But husbands are regularly referred to as their wives' "lords" in OE. See Toller *Supp* sense II (2)b of *hlaford*: "The master of a wife, a wife's lord and master, the husband." Cf. also the use of similar oath formulas for bride and for retainer in two legal texts, *Be Wifmannes Beweddunge* and *Swerian* (in Liebermann 1903, 442–45 and 396–99, resp.) In *Wife*, references to the speaker's "lord" can be explained partly by this social and legal background, and partly by the conventional idiom of OE poetry which was designed to celebrate the male world of the *comitatus*.

Uhtceare is the sleeplessness that comes from grief and anxiety (cf. *uhtna gehwylce, Wan* 8), but when taken in conjunction with *Wife* 33b–36 the word can be seen to contain an element of sexual deprivation in this context.

9–10 Stefanovíc links lines 9–10 with lines 11–14, and finds it possible, though not obligatory, to translate *ða* "when" (1909, pp. 405–6). In fact, the delayed verb in line 9 may indicate conjunctive order, but the construction is clearer in line 18 (see note). Most editors, but not Leslie, treat lines 9–10 as independent of the following lines, with *ða* meaning "then." See also p. 52, above.

Folgað, which is derived from *folgian* in the sense of "serve," has the meaning "service (of a master)," "place" (in someone's service; cf. Grein-Köhler "Amt, Gefolgschaftsdienst"), "retinue," "household," "area of authority." Deor says that he had a *folgað tilne*, "a good place" (*Deor* 38). Schücking read these lines in *Wife* as a statement that the (male) speaker attached himself to a second lord after the first's departure (1906, 439–41). Roeder (1899, 115), followed by Leslie and others, supposed it was the husband's retinue which the wife went to seek. If she was looking for her husband specifically, though, one would expect her to say so. Klaeber suggests that *folgað* here means "exile" (1935, 39). Karl Wentersdorf understands the word as "exile, refuge, asylum," an extension of its use in the sense of "security," and believes it refers to the cave where the speaker is living (1981, 496–98). But the word *folgað* always indicates some kind of social setting. See *Concordance* F010:236–39 (*folgað-*) and 259–61 (*folgoð-*); also Bosworth-Toller and Toller *Supp.* In this case, the wife's search for *folgað* aims to remedy her situation as a *wineleas wrœcca*, a forlorn person, if not an exile specifically. Probably *folgað* refers to the protection afforded by a large household (thus Malone 1962, 113). In view of her present plight, the narrator must have failed to find it (as believed by Schulze 1969, 70), or else failed to keep it. Short (1970, 592–93) argues that the wife went to a lover, but this is reading too much into the text.

11–12 Most, although not all, critics believe that *þæs monnes magas* are the husband's kin. Such a view avoids the unnecessary complication of introducing another character here. Thus Schücking; see the previous note. Also Thomas Davis, who thinks that the husband was banished for murder and that line 11 refers to the kin of the slain man (1965, 301–2). However, the question arises why the kin should try to separate the married pair if they are already apart. Many scholars have taken *ongunnon* as a pluperfect, referring to a time previous to the husband's departure, the cause of which was the kin's plotting. Rudolf Imelmann translated:

"Das hatten des Mannes Geschlechtsgenossen zu ersinnen begonnen," and explained: "ihr Gatte hat sie verlassen müssen, gezwungen durch die Feindschaft seiner Verwandten" (1907a, 27). Leslie punctuates lines 9–10 as dependent on lines 11ff., which appears to link lines 11–12 with the immediate, not the more remote, past, but in his Introduction (p. 5) suggests that the husband's departure was brought about by the kin's plotting. If the reader is to preserve the narrative sequence, lines 11–12 must be understood as describing the kin's intention to keep the pair apart, rather than to part them initially. Mitchell *Syntax* doubts that "one simple past tense in a series of past tenses can – with no contextual or grammatical hint – interrupt the narrative flow and disrupt the obvious time sequence by referring further back in time" (§ 644; see also Mitchell 1975, esp. 24).

14 The indicative endings in *lifdon* and *longade* show that these verbs represent the result of the kin's plotting, whereas *todælden* (line 12) reflects their purpose. *Laðlicost*, "most hatefully," means both "unpleasantly" and "with mutual resentment." The wife still longs for her estranged husband, but her feelings towards him are ambivalent.

15 Like *ongunnon* (line 11), *het* has sometimes been explained as a pluperfect. See note on lines 11–12, above. The syntactic objections to this treatment weigh heavily against Leslie's view that the line refers to the wife's adoption of a new land when she married (reading *her eard*; see Leslie's Introd., pp. 5–6). Schulze's argument that the wife has not been banished but merely left behind (1969, 67–68) rests on an unconvincing sense for *hatan*: "to allow," rather than "to command." Others believe the line indicates that the husband ordered his wife into exile (thus J.A. Ward, 1960, 28).

Thorpe and Ettmüller regarded "Herheard" as the lord's name, but later scholars have found this implausible. Grein's emendation of MS *her heard* to *her eard* simplifies the syntax, but deprives the verse of suitable alliteration; it is unlikely that the adverb would take the stress in preference to the noun. Grein later suggested *herh-eard* (1865, 422), meaning "grove-dwelling," which in the "Nachträgliche Verbesserungen" to his edition he relates to *wuda bearwe* (line 27) and to OHG *haruc*, "lucus," and glosses in his *Sprachschatz* as "habitaculum in nemoribus" (similarly Grein-Köhler). Grein's suggestion is adopted by Krapp-Dobbie. But the OE *he(a)rg/hearh*, "heathen temple," "idol," has a definite pejorative sense and is not recorded in precisely this spelling (see *Concordance* Ho02:19 (*haerg-*); Ho10:78 (*hærg-*); Ho12:271–73 (*hearg-*), 273 (*hearh-*); Ho17:308–12 and 321–22 (*herg-*); Ho18:11 and 23–24 (*herg-*), 64 and 70–80 passim (*herig-*). Toller *Supp* gives the emended form *hearh-eard* in Grein's sense with a query, and also cites this line under *heard* as an alternative possibility. Moritz Trautmann's suggestion that the word *herheard* means "sanctuary" in the sense of "refuge" (1894, 222–25) is not substantiated elsewhere in OE. Later scholars have found a specifically pagan significance in the word. Thus A.N. Doane (1966, 86–88). Also Wentersdorf (1981, 509), who finds it in *Rim* 74 also (generally emended to *her eardes* to provide alliteration; see note).

Since the existence of a word *herheard* is dubious and there are problems with emending to *her eard*, it seems best to read *her heard*, along with Kershaw and Mackie: "My lord commanded, cruel, to seize me here." As Leslie observes (Notes), this interpretation involves an unusual separation of adjective and noun. *Heard* is almost felt as an adverb if the sentence is construed in this way. The most natural referent for *her* is *þissum londstede*, "this country," a place which may or may not be the husband's own territory but is clearly alien to his wife.

16–17 In support of his argument for taking *het* (line 15) as a reference to an earlier time, Leslie comments that the wife uses the verb *ahte* in the preterite tense (Introd., p. 6). But she goes on to state in the present tense that her heart is sad. Her grief is attributable to causes which began in the past: a lack of friends and a hostile husband. *Lyt* is probably to be taken as a typical OE understatement. CF. *Wan* 31. *Forþon*, "therefore," introduces a new principal clause, but the statement made in it applies both to what precedes and what follows. See the following note; also Mitchell *Syntax*, §§ 3789–3803, on *apo koinou* constructions.

18 Leslie begins a new sentence here. But conjunctive word-order, with the pronouns immediately following the conjunction and the verb delayed, indicates that the clause introduced by *ða* is dependent on line 17b. See Andrew 1940, §§ 4 and 16. In addition to its temporal force, *ða* contains a causal element in this instance (cf. Mitchell *Syntax*, § 3156). *Funde* is indicative, not subjunctive; see Campbell *Grammar*, § 741, and Mitchell *Syntax*, § 2564. Stefanovíc (1909, 410–11) interpreted the verb in a concrete sense as "met," "found after a search," but the more abstract sense "realized (that he was)," "found to be" is probable here. For the circumstances involved and the translation of lines 18ff., see the following note.

19–21a The noun *gebæro/-u* (line 21) occurs as both fem. sg. and neut. pl. See Bosworth-Toller and Toller *Supp*. Here it is usually construed as some kind of instrumental sg. In this case, if *bliþe* modifies *gebæro* there is a lack of concord between adj. and noun. Leslie suggests a rather complicated explanation in his Notes. But *bliþe gebæro*, "a cheerful demeanour," can better be explained as acc. sg. or pl. (as in line 44), object of *funde* (line 18), and parallel to the epithets in lines 19–20a. Treating the phrase in this way makes the form grammatically regular, and enables *hycgende* (line 20), which has been widely emended to *hycgendne*, to be accepted unchanged as a modifier of *gebæro*. The personification involved in this treatment of lines 20b–21a resembles that in *Sea* 10b.

The attributes described in these lines need not be regarded as a complete account of a man's personality, but as a reflection of his attitude and behaviour in particular circumstances. Since *bliþe gebæro* is at variance with the other epithets, some editors, including Krapp-Dobbie, separate it from them by a period, and link it to *ful oft wit beotedan* (line 21b), thus making *bliþe* nom. pl. in agreement with *wit*. But the recurrence of the same phrase in line 44 makes it probable that a parallel is intended between the two passages, especially in view of the additional resemblance between *geomormod, / heard heortan geþoht* (lines 42b–43a) and *heardsæligne, hygegeomorne*. For these reasons, it is likely that the *gemæcne monnan* of line 18 and the *geong mon* of line 42 are the same person: the husband, who is assuming a cheerful demeanour but concealing unpleasant thoughts. Other explanations – Imelmann's seducer (1907a, 28–29), Short's lover (1970, 597) – must invent a hypothetical rôle for the extra character.

Some critics, following W.W. Lawrence (1907–8, esp. 388–89), see the husband in a relatively favourable light, and understand *morþor hycgend[n]e* as "mindful of death." But, though *morþor* need not always mean "murder," it always carries a sense of evil or violence, and never refers to death in a general sense. For the similar words *morð* and *morþor*, see *Concordance* Mo22:167 (*mord-*), 219 (*morth-*), 221–38 (*morð-*). The man, then, is brooding upon some evil intention. It has been argued that this enmity is directed towards the tribe of the man he has supposedly slain (Davis 1965, 302), or his own kin (Lee Ann Johnson 1971, 499–500; Wentersdorf 1981, 513). His wife, though, is the most obvious target, and it is she who laments. Cf. also notes on lines 15 and 26.

Since *funde* can mean "realized" rather than "met" (see note on line 18), and there is no other indication that the speaker rejoined her husband, he may still be far away when he manifests cruelty towards his wife, and has her seized (line 15) and confined in a cave (lines 27–28). In that case, she is perhaps thinking of his earlier behaviour when she speaks of *morþor hycgende / bliþe gebæro*.

Translate lines 18–21a: "... since I found the man full suited to me hard in his fortune, sad of mind, concealing his intention: a cheerful demeanour contemplating a crime."

21b–23a The closest point of resemblance between *Wife* and *Husb* occurs here. Cf. *Husb* 15b–16 (and 54) *wordbeotunga* / *þe git on ærdagum oft gespræcon*. The recurrence of *beot-*, *oft*, and the dual pronoun in connection with the couple's past vows is noteworthy. Though some scholars argue that the two poems belong together (see Part 1, pp. 58–60, above), it may well be that a "lovers' vows" theme, like the better-documented exile theme, was widespread and traditional.

24 This line is abnormally short, and it looks as if part of one of the verses has been lost. Various fillers have been supplied. It is possible, though, that the poet deliberately took this metrical liberty for dramatic effect. Cf. the three-syllable verse at a moment of intense emotion in *Wulf* 13a.

25b The early editors printed *feor geneah*, "far enough," which gives satisfactory sense. Grein 1865's *feor ge neah*, "far and near," makes the assertion more sweeping and has been adopted by subsequent editors.

26 Leslie comments that the word *fæhðu* must refer to a vendetta in which the husband is involved rather than to hostility towards his wife. The word is common in the poetry and also the laws; it means "feud" or "enmity," certainly something much more serious than dislike. In the present context, "suffer enmity" is a more straightforward rendering of *fæhðu dreogan* than "suffer the consequences of a feud (involving other parties)." Cf. *Godes yrre bær, Beowulf* 711. *Fæhðu* here suggests a rift between husband and wife amounting to a feud. For the occurrences of the word, see *Concordance* F003:21–25.

27–29 The person, *mon*, who has commanded the woman to dwell in her cave in the woods could be either the husband directly or some agent(s) acting on his instructions.

Line 28a is probably to be read as a type-A verse with weak first foot. A C-type verse would require dissyllabic *treo*, which is unlikely. Sieper emends to *actreowe*, the regular WS form, here and in line 36a. Loss of *w* in the inflected cases of *treo* occurs in the Northumbrian *Lindisfarne Gospels* and other Anglian texts (see Sievers-Brunner, § 129.1, Anm. 2). With dat. sg. *-treo* here and in *Wife* 36, cf. gen. pl. *cnea* in *Ruin* 8 and see note.

The cave under an oak-tree has been interpreted as a place associated with pagan worship (Doane 1966, 88–89; Wentersdorf 1981, 509), a barrow (Leslie; Lench 1970, 17–19), or an underground dwelling of a traditional Germanic type (Harris 1977, 204–8). Those who read *herheard niman* in line 15 regard the meaning of that line and lines 27–28 as the same. *Her heard niman*, the reading of the present text, indicates the seizure of the woman for the purpose of confining her within the cave. Others see the actions of lines 15 and 27 as quite separate. See note on line 15, above.

Again, whereas most scholars regard the wife as banished from human company, some believe that she has been sent to this isolated spot for her own protection from the feud in which her husband is thought to be involved (Harris, 204–5; Wentersdorf, pp. 498 and 509).

The circumstances of the speaker's confinement in an *eorðscræf* or *eorðsele* (the former word appears in the pl. in line 36) have been adduced in support of the theory that she is actually dead: a barrow-wight (Lench), a revenant (Raymond Tripp 1972, 356–60), or "suffering ... the terrors of a purgatorial afterlife" (William Johnson 1983, 78). *Eorðscræf* commonly, but not always, means "grave." See Bosworth-Toller, Toller *Supp*, and *Concordance* E014:232–34. *Eorðsele* is recorded twice elsewhere, *Beo* 2410 and 2515, where it applies to the dragon's barrow. Doane (1966, 88–89) regards the location in *Wife* as one dedicated to the worship of a female deity (the speaker). Davis believes that the narrator is thought to be a witch and for that reason is forced, by unidentified persons, to inhabit a place with pagan associations (1965, 303–4, n.).

Whether the place is an excavated chamber or a natural feature, it is certainly grim and strange; prominence is given to its antiquity (*eald*), to the, perhaps significant, oak-tree above it (see pp. 49–50, above), and to its wild setting (lines 30–32a). Possibly such a place would evoke frightening suggestions of pagan religion or magic for the A-S audience. The near repetition of line 28 in line 36 gives the alliterating words *actreo* and *eorðscræf/-scrafu* special emphasis.

31 *Burgtunas* = "fortified enclosures." The word is recorded as a proper name in charters (see *Concordance* B019:201, 205, and 261–62), and survives in names like Burton and Broughton. The "bitter enclosures overgrown with briars" may be the remains of an abandoned settlement. Leslie suggests that the poet is perhaps thinking of an ancient earth-work.

32b–33a The departure of the speaker's lord here becomes an active source of torment. Cf. line 41, and see note on *Sea* 6b. The metre requires an archaic dissyllabic pronunciation of *frean* in line 33a, as in *Husb* 10b.

33b–36 These lines are now generally perceived as an expression of the speaker's sexual loneliness. They were taken by early editors as an allusion to dead friends. Thus Thorpe, translating *lifgende* "once living." Matti Rissanen suggests emending *lifgende* to *licgende*, and translates "The friends are in the ground, the loved ones lying dead, they dwell in the tomb" (1969, esp. 95). But, if *on eorðan* is understood as "on earth" and *leger* as "bed," rather than "grave," the passage can be seen to contrast the good fortune of lovers who keep their bed together with the situation of the speaker, who paces alone in the small hours. *Uhte* here (and more indirectly in line 7) is the time when lovers are abed, not just a time of solitary sleeplessness as in *Wan* 8. For the use of *freond* meaning "lover," cf. *Maxims II* 43b–44a *Ides sceal dyrne cræfte, / fæmne hire freond gesecean.* The word is applied to the husband in line 47.

Whatever the exact nature of the woman's subterranean dwelling, the fact that she can walk around it indicates it is larger than the usual grave. The pl. *eorðscrafu*, which varies the sg. in line 28, also suggests a certain spaciousness. Leslie thinks the place is a chambered barrow. Cf. note on lines 27–29, above.

The masc. form *ana* is emphatic, and can be used instead of the fem. where a fem. identity has already been established. See Campbell *Grammar*, § 683, and cf. note on lines 1–2, above.

37–41 The punctuation of these lines varies, and word-order is not decisive (cf. note on line 18, above). Krapp-Dobbie place a period before line 37 and a semicolon before line 39b. But the parallelism between and the cumulative effect of these clauses and the *þonne* clause in lines 35–36 is better rendered by treating the entire passage, beginning at line 33b, as a single sentence. Leslie punctuates in this way.

37b With *sumorlangne dæg*, "summer-long day," suggesting time drawn out to the greatest possible length, cf. *winterstunde*, "winter hour," in *Genesis* 370, which is used to precisely the opposite effect.

42–47a For the punctuation of these lines in relation to lines 47b–52a, see the following note.

The interpretation of this passage presents the main crux of the poem. Both syntax and reference are controversial. Taking the subjunctives of lines 42, 45, and 46 as expressing a wish, Grein regarded this section as a curse on the person who had alienated the husband by making false accusations against his wife (1857–59, 1:256, n.). However, the existence of such a person is doubtful. Many scholars have seen lines 42ff. as a generalization of the gnomic type. Lawrence found here "one of those moralizing incursions ... of which the Anglo-Saxons were so fond" (1907–8, 389). Thorpe had translated "Ever must a young man be sad of mind ..." Leslie points out gnomic parallels elsewhere, observing that *sceal* is used "to list fundamental qualities," *scyle* "to indicate desirable qualities" (Notes). In fact, because of the sense of necessity or obligation inherent in the meaning of *sculan*, the functions of indicative and subjunctive tend to overlap, as in *Sea* 109–11 (cited by Leslie), and the present instance. Though the gnomic form is detectable in *Wife* 42–43, the combination of qualities described – trouble and hardness of heart along with a cheerful demeanour – seems specific to a particular person in a given situation, the husband, as presented earlier, in lines 18–21a, with the difference that the earlier passage focuses on his evil intentions, this on his unhappiness. Cf. note on lines 19–21a, above. Greenfield understands the reference of lines 42ff. in this way, but has modified his earlier view of them as a mild curse (1953, 907–12; 1966, 167–68). It has been argued by Schücking (1906, 445) and others that the *geong mon* of line 42 is the speaker (whether male or female), but this is unlikely, even if *geong mon* means a young person of either sex, because the speaker displays neither an unyielding heart nor a cheerful bearing. The passage, then, can be read, not as a curse, but as a pronouncement, introduced in the gnomic style, on the situation of the husband: he must always be sad, full of care in spite of his cheerful appearance.

The syntax of the two *sy* clauses in lines 45b–47a is also problematic, and the words *æt him sylfum gelong* may have virtually opposite meanings. Thus, these clauses may express complementary wishes: "let all his joy in the world be furnished by himself alone; let him be outlawed far and wide ..." Again, they may be alternative hypotheses: "whether it be that all his joy in the world is at his own disposal, or whether it be that he is outlawed far and wide ..." The first translation, treating the verbs as optatives, turns the passage into a curse. The second, treating them as conditional constructions, permits a milder interpretation. If the guilty third person posited by Grein and others is excluded, the latter is more likely, since lines 45b–47b then apply either to any "young person," or, more probably, to the husband, whom the wife evidently still loves and misses.

45a Gen. pl. *sinsorgna* is a weak form. Though rare, this is not unique.

Cf. *Guthlac* 1019–20 *sorgna ... hatost* and *Precepts* 76 *tornsorgna ful*; also *arna Res* 49 and 67; and see Campbell *Grammar*, § 617.

46b–47a *Feorres folclondes* does not refer to the young man's own territory from which he is outlawed, as assumed by Wentersdorf's "banished far away from his distant estates" (1970, 610), but to the "distant country" where he is imagined to be at present. See Mitchell *Syntax*, § 1399; the construction is a genitive of place. A technical meaning for *folclond* in the sense of land that reverts to the community is not required here. Since *sy ful wide fah* presents a hypothesis merely, it cannot be asserted that the husband actually has been banished. See note on lines 6–8, above.

47b–52a In this passage, the woman is clearly speaking of her husband, whom she refers to by the affectionate terms *freond* (cf. line 33), and *wine* (lines 49 and 50). *Þæt*, "in that," might introduce the reason why she should wish a third person condemned to banishment: because "my friend" is suffering (thus Roeder 1899, 114, et al.). But more probably the *þæt* clause expands on the situation of the husband if he is outlawed far and wide. See note on lines 42–47a.

Lines 47bff. are obviously continuous with what precedes them, but the preceding clauses introduced by *sy* can depend on both lines 42–45a and lines 50b–52a. For this type of *apo koinou* relationship, see Mitchell 1980, esp. 412; also *Syntax*, §§ 3789–3803. In fact, the whole passage from line 42 to 52a can be treated as a single periodic sentence, a reflection on the predicament of the husband. Whatever his circumstances are, he is bound to be unhappy, whether he is fortunately placed (lines 45b–46a), or whether he is an outlaw in exile (lines 46b–47a).

The wife goes on to imagine him in a vague dismal location. Kershaw wonders: "Is it a cave on the coast, to which access can be obtained only by water, or a flooded ruin?" (Notes). Rissanen suggests that the features of the scene point to the husband's death by drowning (1969, 98). Wentersdorf, emending *siteð* to *siðeð* (line 47) and understanding *-sel(e)* as *sæl* (line 50), translates: "voyaging in stormy weather beneath rocky cliffs, covered with frost, drenched by the sea, and in dire straits" (1970, 610). But the scene is not presented realistically and need not be regarded as an actual spot; the elements of rocky slope, storm, hoar-frost, proximity to water, and a "dreary hall" form a composite of traditional elegiac motifs (cf. *Wan* 46–48 and 75–77, *Sea* 29b–33a, *Ruin* 3–4). Also, the place is described in terms which recall the wife's own dwelling – a gloomy chamber enclosed or dominated by rock, as she imagines for her husband an unhappiness like her own.

With *werigmod* (line 49) cf. *werig mod* (*Wan* 15) and see note.

52b–53   The poem ends in a gnomic pronouncement with the characteristic *bið*, both "is" and "shall be," used for assertions of general truths.
Cf. the sentence beginning *Wel bið þam þe* which forms the final 1 ½ lines
of *Wan*. The statement in *Wife* applies to all who must long for a dear
one, more specifically to the speaker herself – and also to her husband,
whom she imagines as equally lonely.

Grein 1865 suggested emending *of* to *on*, giving "in or with longing."
But "from longing" expresses the reason for the wife's state of mind as
she waits.

RESIGNATION

1   This line, which is metrically incomplete, occupies part of the space
between *Res* and the previous poem in the MS. Editors before Mackie
assign it to neither poem, and commence their text with *Ahelpe*, regarding
the initial capital of *Age*, which extends through the next line of the MS,
as the first letter of *(a)helpe*. No verb *ahelpan* is recorded elsewhere. MS
ælmihta is supported elsewhere only by *ælmihtne* in *Dan* 195, which forms
a metrically inadequate verse and which is emended by Krapp-Dobbie
and others to *ælmihtigne*. Holthausen 1935 suggests expanding *Res* 1 to
Age mec se eca ælmihtga god (p. 9).

3   *Wundorcyning* is a self-explanatory hapax legomenon. The repetition
of *wundor* is awkward but may well be deliberate. Thorpe, followed by
Grein and Sieper, emends to *wuldorcyning*.

4   The relative pronoun *þe* is understood; Grein, along with Krapp-
Dobbie and Malmberg, inserts it at the beginning of the line. Mackie begins
a new clause, taking *micel ond manigfeald* (line 6) as substantival adjectives
forming the subject of the verb. Mitchell *Syntax* §§ 2305–9 discusses absence of the nominative relative pronoun, observes that, apart from uses
with the verb *hatan*, examples are few, and finds "some plausibility" in
editorial emendations. He does, however, cite eleven instances (including
the present), which is enough to validate the construction.

8a   To improve the metre, Holthausen 1907b suggests emending to *ond
leoþo min eal* (p. 201), Holthausen 1935 to *ond eal min leoþocræft* (p. 9).

11–12 Instead of taking the verb *gemearcenne* in the unique sense of "observe" (Thorpe, Mackie, Malmberg), it can be treated impersonally, and the dative *sawle minre* can be understood *apo koinou* with both *selast* ("best for my soul") and *gemearcenne* ("point out to my soul"). Mitchell *Syntax* discusses numerous examples of the *apo koinou* construction in OE (§§ 3789–3803), though he does not mention this one. Translate: "where it should be best to point out to my soul the will of God."

13a "That I may prosper before thee." Cf. *fela riccra manna geðeoð Gode*, in Ælfric's *Dominica Tertia post Epiphaniam Domini* (Thorpe *Homilies* 1:130), and ... *ðe Gode geþugon þurh gehaltsumnysse his beboda*, in his *Sermo de Sacrificio in Die Paschae* (Thorpe *Homilies* 2:280). In all three places, the verb includes the idea of serving or pleasing God.

15b–16a The word *regnþeof*, "mighty thief" – here a reference to the Devil – is recorded elsewhere only in *Exodus* 539, in the pl., *regnþeofas*. The present passage is an allusion to Christ's comparison of the Devil to a thief who comes in the night (Matthew 24:43 and Luke 12:39).

16b Although Grein-Wülker and Sieper place a comma after *scyppendum*, treating it as a noun, the *-um* inflection indicates that the participial force of the word is strong. The form also occurs in the *Benedictine Rule*; see *Concordance* S010:54.

17b *Waccor* = *wacor*, "more weakly." The spelling with double *c* also occurs in the *Laws of Edgar* 4:1.5a (Liebermann 1903–16, 1:208).

19a *Lisse* here has the sense of "remission." For this usage, see also *Lisse ic gelyfe leahtra gehwylces*, glossing [*Credo in*] *remissionem peccatorum*, *The Creed* 54 (*ASPR* 6:80). For the construction *Forgif me to lisse*, "Grant me remission," see Bosworth-Toller under sense I 5 (F1) of *to*: "with verbs of making, appointing, being, accounting, naming, and the like, where often the preposition now has no representative." *Forgif* also means "forgive" (my bitter sins) here.

20b As in lines 110b–11a, the *bot*, "remedy," is the joys of the afterlife. The idea of a *bot* provided by God also appears in *Christ I* 152b–53a, which resembles the phrasing of *Res* 110b–11a.

21b The syntax is better if *cume* is understood as a weakened form of *cuman* ("if I may come to [it]"), though a case could be made for pres. subjunctive ("that I come to it, if I may") dependent on *gemon*. Klaeber 1935, taking *cume* in the former way, comments on the weakened ending here and in *stonde* (= *stonden*), line 39 (pp. 36–37). The feature may be merely scribal, but it accords with a late date and possibly Northern provenance for the poem. See Part 1, p. 18. *To* is adverbial, with *þa bote* implied.

25a *To cunnunge*: "to try me," rather than "(for me) to experience."

26b The basic sense of *feormian*, "to give food to," yields two possible meanings here: "sustain" and "receive as a guest." Since in this passage the narrator is speaking of the conduct of his present life in this world, the former meaning is preferable.

27b–28 In saying that he committed "*more* grievous sins than God permitted," whereas God permits none, the speaker is using the understatement characteristic of OE poetry, here in the form of meiosis. See Textual Notes on *Wan* 65b–72.

29b *Seþeah* = *swa þeah*, "nevertheless." The second alliteration on *þ* is irregular. This spelling, which suggests a weakened pronunciation, is characteristic of and peculiar to the Exeter Book, although the usual *swa þeah* also occurs. For the various forms, sometimes printed as one word, sometimes two, see *Concordance* S015:49 (*seþeah*; twelve occurrences, all in Exeter Book); S027:183–85 (*suaðeah*) and 223 (*suæðæh*); S031:73–93 (*swaþeah/swaðeah*) and 94 (*swaþeh*); S032:141 (*sweþeah*); THoo3:86 (*sua ðeh*); THoo6:95–127 (*swa þeh/swa ðeh*, passim; *suae/suæ ðeh*, pp. 96 and 122, resp.); *High-Frequency Concordance* TH043, *þeah*, pp. 5–9 (seven occurrences of *swa þeah* in Exeter Book, passim; *se þeah*, p. 8, in *Rid 4* 7); Tho43–044, *þeah*, pp. 1–233 (no occurrences of adverbial *se þeah*; in Psalter glosses *se þeah* ... translates *qui licet* ..., pp. 220–21).

31a *(Ge)leoran* is a characteristically Anglian word (Jordan 1906, 44: "das wichtigste Merkmal des anglischen Wortschatzes"). Cf. line 45a.

31b These words have been interpreted as "another way of life" (Mackie's translation). Stanley 1955 states explicitly that the reference is to life on earth: "Only thus is the full significance of *siþþan*, 'the life hereafter,' brought out: it stands in opposition to the new way of life on earth" (p. 457). But *æfter oþrum*, "after (this) other one," is most naturally taken to refer to this life on earth, as opposed to the next life in heaven. Then, in line 32b, *siþþan* is equivalent to *æfter oþrum* and *þær* refers specifically to *lif* in the previous line. Malmberg interprets line 31b as a reference to the heavenly life.

33b Cf. line 36a and see note on *Sea* 79b.

34b–35a The subject *ic* is understood (cf. line 37). Grein inserted it before *lætlicor*. Line 34b, like line 29b, has double alliteration, not normally found in a b-verse.

37 The beginning of the a-verse is missing, though there is no gap in the MS. Grein inserts *hroðra*, which supplies the necessary alliteration.
Ic is understood before *sette*, as before *bette* (line 35).

38b–39a Malmberg takes *hio* as nom. sg. fem., referring to *hyht*, but no feminine forms of this noun are recorded. The pronoun must be nom. pl. masc., referring to *foreþoncas*, and *stonde* must be a weakened form of *stonden*. See note on line 21b, above. For occurrences of *hyht*, see *Concordance* H019:162 (*hieht*); H020:124–61 (*hiht-*); H030:126–55 (*hyht-*).

39b–40 *Onstep* is a hapax legomenon, but clearly related to *stepan/stipan*, "to exalt." *Ræd* is translated by Mackie as "benefit," by P.L. Henry as "plan" (1966, 178). The concept embraces both: "what is best" (for me).

42b A verb of departing is understood.

43a *Unfyr* = *unfyrn*, "before long." Cf. *Andreas* 1371 (*þa þe ...*) *unfyrn faca feorh ætþringan*. The word is also associated with coming death in other contexts. See *Concordance* U003:250–51. If *unfyrn faca* is a fixed formulaic expression, the spelling here may possibly be explained as *n*-loss between two consonants (Campbell *Grammar* § 477.5).

43b *Feorma* must here mean "receive," but probably also embraces the idea of "sustain," which is in line with the desire for support expressed in *gesette* (line 37) and *onstep* (line 39).

45a See note on line 31a, above.

45b In *leofra dryhten*, "lord of the beloved ones," the gen. pl. must refer to the blessed – unless the *r* is merely a scribal error and the reading should be *leofa dryhten*, "dear lord."

46b–47a   It is uncertain whether we should read *æfestum*, "maliciously," Thorpe's and Mackie's interpretation, or *æfestum*, "to the pious one," following Klaeber 1935 (p. 37). The latter's argument for a contrast between the virtuous man (*æfestum*) and his foes (*gromra*) is fairly persuasive. *OE Dict* cites under "malice" but also allows "pious." *Eaden*, "allotted," is emended by Holthausen 1894 to *eacen*, "increased" (p. 195).

49a   With the weak gen. pl. *arna* here and in line 67, cf. *Wife* 45 *sinsorgna*.

49b–52   For *sepeah* (lines 49 and 52) see note on line 29b, above. *Æfter* (line 52) here has the sense of "during" associated with its spatial meaning of "along." Line 51a repeats line 27a.

56a   Schabram characterizes *oferhygd-* words as Anglian, in contrast to W-S *ofermod-* words; the former are much more common in the poetry (see Schabram 1965, 123–29).

57b   Textual lacunae caused by burn holes begin to appear from this folio (118b) on. The final letters of *sculon* are missing, in a hole at the end of an MS line, but the context makes this restored form certain.

63a   *Gehogode* has virtually an active sense here: "thinking." Cf. *gelyfed*, "believing," a very common expression, especially characteristic of Ælfric's prose. See *Concordance* G021:172–76. *Hædre* has previously been interpreted as "anxiously," on an analogy with *Sol and Sat* 62: *hige ... hædre wealleð*. But the B MS of that poem reads *hearde*, and in *Res* the form *hædre* can more convincingly be treated as "brightly," the adverb derived from *hador*, "bright." Taken in this way, *hædre gehogode* refers to the soul's state after, rather than before, divine assistance. Translate: "Father of mankind, protect it and sustain it [my soul], pure in thought."

63b   *Hæl* is probably the imperative "save," unless the adjective "whole," in agreement with an implied *sawle*, is read as *hæl'*, with final *e* elided before a vowel. (Cf. *Sea* 11 and 55; *Deor* 16).

66a   Thorpe suggests in a footnote, but does not print in his text, *faum* for *feam*, and translates "for its hostile courses fearful." Grein, followed by Grein-Wülker and Sieper, emends to *nalles feam siþum*, to improve the sense. Krapp-Dobbie suggest the possibility of taking *feam* as *fægum*. But *fea*, "few," can be understood as "some." Mackie translates the verse by "sometimes afraid."

67   For the weah gen. pl. *arna*, see note on line 49a.

69   Regarded by Bliss and Frantzen as the ending of the fragment *Resignation A*. They suggest that a pronoun is missing, and object to line 69b on metrical grounds, altering the earlier lineation to make *mid* ... begin another line, which breaks off at this point (pp. 389–90). If *mid* is given a stress (like *to* in line 71), the verse is type E. Though it violates Kuhn's Law of Particles, whereby the sentence particle *wæron* ought to be stressed since it is postponed from the first metrical dip of the clause, examples of metrical irregularity are not infrequent in *Res* (see notes on lines 29b, 34b, 102b). And see Mitchell *Syntax*, § 3947 for some reservations about Kuhn's Law. Also, although Bliss and Frantzen deny the parallel, the use of the adverbial *mid* in this line is similar to that of *to* in line 21 (see Klaeber 1935, 36–37). In Malmberg's text, which follows Bliss-Frantzen, *mid* ... forms line 70, and subsequent lines are therefore numbered one ahead of *ASPR* and the present text. The issue of *Resignation*'s integrity has been discussed more fully in Part 1, pp. 28–29.

71b   Bliss and Frantzen take this phrase to mean "trust in myself" as opposed to in God, and find this attitude sharply different from that expressed earlier, in what they regard as a separate poem (p. 394). However, even if the phrase is interpreted in this way, the speaker's having confidence in himself does not preclude his having faith in God, but would be the result of God's grace (*ealles þæs*, line 70, referring to *meorda ond miltsa*, line 68). But *me* in line 71b can quite naturally be interpreted as a dative of interest, here used reflexively, and *to* as adverbial. Thus, under *hyhtan*, Bosworth-Toller translates these words "I will have courage, and laugh and look forward with hope." *Me* in lines 70 and 74 is used in much the same way.

72–73   Thorpe and Grein emend *ferðweg* to *forðweg* (MS reading restored by Grein 1865); also Bliss-Frantzen (pp. 398–99) and Malmberg, rejecting the notion of penitential pilgrimage seen in the word by Stanley 1955 (pp. 460–61). *Ferðweg*, "the way of the soul," is a hapax legomenon, but readily comprehensible. What is meant is the journey from this world to the next, which can begin in a spiritual preparation in this world, but need not necessarily imply a journey of exile undertaken as a penance. *Frætwian*, "adorn," here has the sense of "equip." For the sentiment in lines 72b–73, compare lines 41–42a.

75b   *Gebunden* seems here to have the sense of "committed, obliged." Cf.

We beoð mid Gode sua micele suiðor gebundne, translating *tanto apud Dominum obligatiores sumus* (*Pastoral Care*, chap. 117, p. 23). Mackie translates literally "bound"; Bliss and Frantzen render "now that I am in firm control of my spirit" but comment that this is "conjectural" (pp. 398 and 399).

80a The top of the *r* in *for[e]* and possibly a following *e* are burned away at the end of an MS line.

80b–81 Ms *gie wyrhto* contains a superfluous *i*, probably by scribal error. The *ir* in *martirdom* is lost, but BL Transcript preserves part of these missing letters. Bliss and Frantzen point out that in this instance the word had the general sense of "suffering" rather than its strict ecclesiastical sense, and cite for comparison *Guthlac* 470–72: ... *him god wolde / þonc gegyldan / ... þæt he martyrhad mode gelufade* (p. 399).

84 A.A. Prins argues that from this point on the poem should rightly form the conclusion of *Wan*. See Part 1, p. 28, above.

85b–87 Editors up to and including Mackie treat *þonc* as the beginning and not the end of a line. Thorpe, Grein, and Schücking 1919 emend *god* to *godes*, understanding lines 85b–86 as "I was deprived of every good." Grein-Wülker, followed by Mackie, reads the following a-verse as *þoncmod earfoþa*, "brooding over my hardships" (Mackie). But *gode ealles þonc* is very similar in expression to *Þe sie ealles þonc* (line 67b), as is pointed out by Klaeber 1935, who notes too that line 87 requires *m*-alliteration, and therefore the compound *modearfoþa*. Klaeber's interpretation of line 87 as "more than in the case of other people" (p. 37) is persuasive (as against Krapp-Dobbie's "more than in previous years"; similarly Bliss-Frantzen, and Malmberg, who take *oþrum* as sg.). Klaeber 1935 also offers the possible emendation *ma þonne oþre*. In accordance with their view that the speaker here is unrepentant, Bliss and Frantzen regard line 86b as ironical (p. 400, footnote), but if the speaker is seen as devout, there is no inconsistency in his thanking God for trials as well as consolations.

88b–90 *Forþon*, a connective which can imply various relationships (see note on *Sea* 27a), must here introduce an example rather than a cause of *modearfoþa*. *Afysan*, "hasten," which is used both transitively and intransitively, often contains a sense of eagerness, and is here interpreted in that way by Stanley 1955 (p. 459, n. 2), Bliss-Frantzen (p. 398), and Malmberg. However, such an interpretation is inconsistent with *earm*. Mackie's "I have been driven in wretchedness from my home" fits the context better. By translating *ic afysed eom* with "I feel impelled to depart," Bliss and

Frantzen are able to deny that the speaker is at present in exile (p. 402), which is the most natural interpretation of these lines. Switching to the third person in line 89b generalizes the situation, but does not negate its applicability to the speaker himself. The self-explanatory hapax *leodwynna*, "joys of the people," must mean the joys collectively experienced by a social group, from which the speaker is cut off.

Þæs (line 89) = *þes*. The position of the word makes a demonstrative masculine ("this solitary," "the solitary") more natural than a semi-adverbial neuter genitive ("For that the solitary cannot ..."). On the latter, see Mitchell *Syntax*, § 3115. *Þæs* for *þes* occurs in Northumbrian texts (Sievers-Brunner, § 338, Anm. 4); see note on *Ruin* 1a.

92   This line is metrically incomplete and almost certainly corrupt. Klaeber 1935 emends *geoguþe* to *geohþe*, noting that the same error occurs in *Beowulf* 2793 (p. 37). Since there is no other reference in *Res* to the speaker's youth and line 43a suggests that he is old, *geohþe* makes considerably better sense.

93–94a   The most straightforward interpretation of these lines is as a reference to physical needs. Klaeber 1935, who finds *fullestað* out of keeping with the context, suggests emending to *hine ... eful(e)siað*, "slander ["lästern"] him" (p. 37). But if *mæle* is taken as "meal," *fullestað*, "give aid to," indicates a giving of food. This is Sieper's understanding of the passage: "nimmt Gabe er / der Mahlzeiten jede" (p. 291). This interpretation of *mæle* makes it possible to treat line 94a, "his miseries increase" (with intransitive *ycan*), as independent of line 93, and to avoid the inconsistency of the translation "every time men help him they increase his miseries," which can only be explained in, rather modern, psychological terms. These lines, then, are a simple statement that the exile is oppressed by poverty and dependent on handouts.

Fullestan is regarded by Wenisch (1979, 170–75) as an Anglian word, in contrast to W-S *fylstan*. For the coexistence of the two forms, see Sievers-Brunner, § 43, Anm. 4. Cf. also note on line 102b, below.

96b   Stanley 1955 takes *bi me* as "for my own sake" (pp. 458–59), but "about myself" is more natural, and in accordance with similar expressions in the opening lines of *Sea* and *Wife*.

97b–98   Cf. *Sea* 47 *ac a hafað longunge se þe on lagu fundað*.

99   Sense and metre indicate that most of this line is missing. Grein expands to *nat min sefa sare geswenced*; Mackie suggests *nat min sefa sarum* *gebysgad* (appendix B, p. 245). As Krapp-Dobbie point out, "confident reconstruction of so large a gap is hardly possible."

100 Possibly *gebycge bat* means "buy a passage" rather than "buy a vessel"; the former is argued by J.E. Cross, (1974, 93–97). In either case, the speaker is destitute, and therefore unable to pay for the voyage he desires – probably a voyage *home* rather than into penitential exile.

102b This verse is metrically irregular. It is most naturally read with only one stress. If *me* is stressed, the verse must be taken as type A with anacrusis and alliteration on the second, instead of the first, lift. Holthausen 1907b suggests *þe gefylste me* (p. 201), which produces a type-B verse. As Malmberg comments, "It is tempting to assume that *gefylste* has been substituted in the transmission for *gefulleste*" (p. 27, Notes), producing a C verse. Cf. *Beowulf* 2668 ... *feorh ealgian; ic ðe fullæstu*, and *fullestað* in *Res* 93b. It is also possible, though, that weakened verses of this type were acceptable in later OE.

106b Bliss and Frantzen see *tæle* as subjective, equivalent to the *sarcwide* of line 95a, and translate both as "wounding speech" (pp. 398 – translation, and 400 – notes); they comment "Kindness is interpreted by the speaker as *sarcwide secga*" (p. 399). According to this interpretation, the calumny exists only in the narrator's mind. But it is more plausible that the calumny is real. It may refer to the abuse of strangers in the present, but it may also refer to the narrator's own *eþel* in the past and suggest a reason for his expulsion.

109 The initial *s* of *seoc* is burned away.

110b–11a See note on line 20b, above.

111 The hole in the MS allows room for two letters before *-fe*; [*li*]*fe* is the generally accepted restoration. For *on leohte*, Bliss and Frantzen suggest "in happiness" (p. 400); Malmberg interprets the phrase as a reference to "the light which surrounds God in Heaven, here seen as extending to earth to encompass all Christians" (p. 28, Notes). Both cite *Christ* 1463: *þæt þu on leohte siþþan, / wlitig, womma leas, wunian mostes*. But *on leohte* can be understood without reference to the *Christ III* passage as "in the world," i.e., in the light of life. This interpretation is suggested by E.A. Kock (1920).

113b The beginning of *-unian* is burned away. *Wunian* fits the sense. However, Krapp-Dobbie, because of the size of the space left in the MS, prefer *gewunian*.

114–16 Although the hole in the MS here is rather large for two letters, *gecwe[me]* fits the sense. These lines are usually interpreted as an assertion that in return for love towards strangers the narrator received only sorrow. Thus, Klaeber 1935 translates "wenn ich gegen Fremde Liebe, angenehme Vertrautheit hatte (empfand), war (mir) immer Kummer als Lohn meiner Freundlichkeiten" (p. 38). But it is more idiomatic to take *hæfde* as "received" and *to* as "from, on the part of" (see Bosworth-Toller and Toller *Supp* under sense I[5]h). *Lufena* is probably gen. pl. of the rare *lufen*, "hope." The sense must be that the only friendship or kinship the speaker could have was among strangers, and this was virtually none at all. Translate: "When I had to obtain my friendship from strangers, the pleasant sense of community, I always had sorrow in return for my hopes; thus I have been living now."

117 *Þæt* is very faint because of a stain on the MS. The word *selast* is suggested by Holthausen 1912 (p. 88) to complete the sense and supply the alliteration.

118 The MS appears to have *þon*, not *þōn*, but the parchment is stained here.

IC WÆS BE SONDE (RIDDLE 60)

In the MS this is presented as the second of six short pieces between *Homiletic Fragment II* and a collection of riddles. In all six, light initial capitalization and end punctuation correspond to the scribe's treatment of short poems. The first piece is another version of *Rid 30*, pieces 3, 4, and 5 constitute a single poem, *The Husband's Message*, and piece 6 is *The Ruin*. The compiler seems to have thought that all six were riddle-like, the last two involving the use of runes, which is often enigmatic (*Ruin* 23 contains the *M* rune). See Part 1, pp. 25–26, above. Thorpe printed the first three pieces (i.e. *Rid 30*, *Ic wæs be Sonde*, *Husb* 1–12) as riddles, and pieces 4–5 (*Husb* 13–54) as "A Fragment." Subsequent editors have mostly treated *Ic wæs be Sonde* and *Husb* separately, as riddle and lyric, respectively, the riddle being solved as "reed-pen."

The solution "reed-flute" was proposed by Franz Dietrich (1859, 477), who pointed out the resemblance to the *Harundo* riddle of Symphosius (ca. 400):

Dulcis amica dei, ripae vicina profundae,
Suave canens Musis; nigro perfusa colore,
Nuntia sum linguae digitis signata magistri

(Text as in Ohl, 1928, 36). On the whole, the similarity is of rather a general kind, but lines 1–2a of *Ic wæs be Sonde* are particularly reminiscent of *ripae vicina profundae*. The OE piece is more expansive, and it deals with the object described as the instrument of writing rather than music, whereas both uses are present in the Latin poem.

The fact that *Ic wæs be Sonde* 14b–17 express a sentiment similar to that in *Husb* 1 raises the possibility of a connection. This was first suggested by Joseph Strobl, who believed that *Husb* presented the solution, "rune-stave," to the preceding riddle (1887, 55–56). Subsequently, F.A. Black-burn (1901) argued that the supposed riddle was actually the opening of *Husb*, the whole being the speech of a rune-stave. This position has sub-sequently been adopted by a number of scholars, including Ralph Elliott (1955) and John Pope (1978, 42–63). The latest editor of the Exeter Book Riddles, Craig Williamson, treats *Ic wæs be Sonde* as one, though he gives some weight to the alternative possibility (1977, 315–20). Williamson thinks both "reed-pen" and "rune-stave" possible solutions. By and large, the emphasis on the speaker's watery home coupled with the resemblance to the Symphosius riddle militates against including the poem in *Husb* and points to the traditional solution: "reed" or "reed-pen." It is unlikely that this object can be the speaker in the following poem (which contains nothing that looks like a reference to a reed), as argued by Margaret Goldsmith, who sees *Ic wæs be Sonde* + *Husb* as "a dark allegory of divine love, 'spoken' by the Reed representing the word of God" (1975, esp. 263). The placing of *Husb* immediately after *Ic wæs be Sonde* is probably to be attributed to the compiler's impression that the two were on similar sub-jects. *Ic wæs* is a common riddling opening. It also occurs in *Rids 14, 56, 65 (... wæs ic), 72, 74*, and *92*. The case for and against the inclusion of *Ic wæs be Sonde* in *Husb* is summarized in Part 1, p. 27, above.

Æt merefarope (line 2) = "beside the sea-waves." The compound occurs also in *Andreas* 289 and 351. Leslie notes that the description of the en-vironment in lines 1–7a here could refer to "the brackish water of a coastal marsh," a typical habitat for reeds (1968, 453).

MS *meodu* (line 9) gives a very light verse and is commonly emended, but can be accepted as it stands as an A3 type.

Þingum geþydan þæt ... (line 14) has the meaning "compelled, with the design that ..." Both concrete and abstract uses of *geþywan*, "to press," are involved. *Þingum* is used instrumentally, in Bosworth-Toller's sense I(10) of *þing*: "an object, a purpose."

Widdor (line 17) shows lW-S consonantal doubling before *r* (as in *widdra*) – here extended to the *-or* ending. See Campbell *Grammar*, §§ 453–54.

THE HUSBAND'S MESSAGE

1–12 On the sectional divisions of *Husb* in the MS and the question of continuity between this poem and the preceding riddle, see the previous and following notes. Lines 1–12 are printed by Thorpe as a riddle and are excluded from Ettmüller's text of *Husb*.

Because burn damage affects this part of the text and many words have been lost, the lineation is uncertain and editorial arrangement varies. Kershaw does not attempt to put lines 1–8a in metrical form, and prints according to the MS lineation, her verse text beginning with line 8b. Mackie prints lines 1–4 as in the present text, but places *-sse* at the end of line 6a and prints *ful* to *gesohte* as 6b–7. Krapp-Dobbie print this passage as follows:

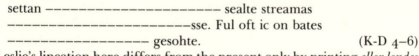

settan –––––––––––––––––––– sealte streamas
–––––––––––––––––––––––sse. Ful oft ic on bates
––––––––––––––––– gesohte.   (K-D 4–6)

Leslie's lineation here differs from the present only by printing *ellor londes* as part of 4a.

1 The reference to a private communication is thought by some to indicate continuity with *Ic wæs be Sonde*. However, the formal affinities of this line point to the introduction of a separate poem of the "elegiac" type. Cf. *ic ... secgan wille* with *Mæg ic ... secgan* (*Sea* 1–2) and *Ic ... secgan mæg* (*Wife* 2), and contrast the typical riddling openings *Ic eom, Ic wæs,* and *Ic seah*.

2 The damage to the manuscript begins to affect *Husb* at this point. A 3½-cm. gap occurs after *wille*, and another gap, at the margin, after *treocyn*, so that possibly this word has lost an inflectional ending. The initial letter of the word after *wille* cannot have been an ascender, since there is enough of the parchment left to have preserved the upstroke. Both Mackie's *ymb þisum* [*þissum?*] *treocynne* and Pope's *of hwylcum treocynne* (1978, 48 and 57) fit the spaces and give satisfactory sense. It is unclear from the fragmentary state of the MS whether the speaker is a human messenger referring to the rune-stave (*treocyn*) and his own personal history (*ic tudre aweox*), or whether the rune-stave is speaking about itself – as Pope's restoration would make explicit; see the following note.

Peter Orton (1981, 49), who finds resemblances to the Riddles in *Husb*, notes that *Ic ... aweox* occurs as an opening formula in *Rids 73* and *88*. But cf. *Wife 3 siþþan ic up weox* and the previous note. In *Husb*, as in *Wife*, the narrative formula, with verbs of saying, takes precedence. Citing Kuhn's Law of Sentence Particles, Orton argues that *ic*, as an unstressed particle occupying the first metrical dip of the clause, must introduce a new sentence here. But the law is not universally applicable; see Mitchell *Syntax*, § 3947, and cf. notes on *Sea* 8b and *Husb* 49.

3 The words before and after *mec* are partially destroyed. In the former, the tops of an *i* and of what may be an *n* can be detected. BL Transcript has what appears to be the upper half of *in*. This is the word printed by most editors, though Pope (1978, 48) argues that the second letter is actually *wynn*, and the word *iw*, the yew-tree. He restores line 3a as *Iw mec ælde hata ð*, "' yew' men call me" (1978, 57). Because of a mark on the parchment, it looks as if the crucial letter is shaped like the top of a ⟩. But if the page is held to a light and the letter magnified, it can be seen that the curve to the left is not part of the letter. From what remains it is possible that the scribe wrote either *n* or ⟩ – or some other character. After *mec*, the top of *e*, the upstroke of *l*, and the horizontal top of *d* are visible. The initial *a* is just barely detectable when the page is held to a light. One cm. further on, the top of an upstroke is visible, probably beginning the next word; from this point the gap extends another 4 cms. to *sceal*. Leslie, who ends the verse-line with *sceal*, suggests *In mec ælda bearn ærende sceal*, understanding *in* as "in my [the messenger's] charge" (Notes). Pope: *Iw mec ælde hata ð. Ac ic sceal ellor londes*. He regards this as a hypermetric line.

4–5 The final letter of *settan* is partially destroyed, but the restoration is certain. After *settan*, there is a gap of 7 cms. followed by a *c* (confirmed by facsimile and BL Transcript though now obscured in MS), and then *sealte streamas*. Only traces of the tops of the last three letters of *streamas* remain, but this is obviously the word called for. 1⅜ cm. further on, the upstroke of an ascender is visible, after which the gap extends for another

7 cms. to -*sse*. The spaces here are so large that all restorations must be highly conjectural. Pope offers as a possibility *settan sipas mine, ponne mec sealte streamas/on flot fergað frean to lisse* (1978, 57). But the inclusion of *settan* and *sealte streamas* in a single line (thus Grein, Grein-Wülker, Krapp-Dobbie, as well as Pope) gives too little accommodation to the words likely to have been lost. Also, the double alliteration of *sealte streamas* in a b-verse would be irregular, even if the line were hypermetric as Pope suggests (p. 60). The present text prints *sealte streamas* as an a-verse (along with Leslie), and assumes a generous spacing for the following words; the missing parchment would have room for about twenty-five letters, but this would make an abnormally heavy b-verse for this poem.

6–7 At this point, the burn hole extends from the left edge of the page inwards and the beginnings of the next two MS lines are missing. Measuring from the margin, the space before *gesohte* is approximately 6½ cms. long, and that before *ofer* 2⅞ cms. Leslie's *bosme* is a plausible restoration to complete line 6a. For 6b he offers *byrig þær gesohte* (Notes). Pope suggests for these two lines *Ful oft ic on bates stefne burgstede þær gesohte / þær mec mondryhten min gelædde* or ... *min getæhte* (1978, 52–53, 57, 60).

To meet the objection that a rune-stave is unlikely to describe itself as having frequently travelled on a ship, Pope argues that the wooden messenger could previously have been shaped into "a useful object of some sort that the lord had taken with him on earlier expeditions" (p. 53). Orton believes that the rune-stave is to be regarded as generic, rather than individual and short-lived (1981, 45). Leslie finds the speaker's reference to his "lord" here and elsewhere inconsistent with "the limited and temporary nature of a rune-stave" (Introd, p. 14) – this kind of personified-retainer relationship is characteristically used in the Riddles, especially in connection with weapons.

8 "Over the high dwellings" (MS *hofu*) appears not to fit the nautical context; possibly a scribe mistook the rare *hafu*, "seas," for the more common *hofu*.

9 The pronoun *þu* is understood. This construction, which postpones the subject to the following clause, is only slightly more elliptical than that in lines 8 and 20, where the object of the previous clause becomes an unexpressed subject. Correction of the verb to *sceal(l)*, in agreement with a previous *ic* (line 6), as by Grein and Mackie (Notes), is unnecessary.

10 The b-verse preserves an archaic dissyllabic pronunciation of *frean* and may be an indication of early composition; cf. *Wife* 33 *fromsiþ frean,* and see Part 1, n. 18. For the designation of the husband as the speaker's "lord," see note on lines 6–7, above.

11b–12 Kershaw thinks it possible that *Paris Psalter* 100.6 *hwær ic tirfæste treowe funde* is borrowed from the present line, but the words may well be formulaic and traditional. *Husb* uses the indicative (*findest*). Mitchell *Syntax* (§ 2014), citing *Husb* 11–12 among other examples, observes that the indicative is used "after verbs and verb groups which imply some element of volition or purpose" when the *result* is stressed. *Findest* occurs in similar circumstances in line 28.

13 The occurrence of *Hwæt* at the beginning of this line, has led at some stage in the compilation of the Exeter Book to the impression that this was the beginning of a new poem. See Part 1, pp. 25–26, above. Following the indications provided by the end punctuation after line 12 and the capitalization of *hwæt*, Thorpe printed this section as a new piece. Ettmüller treated it as the opening of a fragment, and placed omission marks above this line. However, the sense is clearly continuous with the preceding. E.A. Anderson (1973) has argued for a change of speaker, from messenger to rune-stave here, but has subsequently modified this position, to view the entire poem as the speech of a messenger (1975).

16 Repeated in line 54.

18b Some editors have printed *an lond* as a single word. Thus Moritz Trautmann, who translates "Nachbarland" or "Land, das man besitzt" (1894, 216–17). Similarly Sieper. The alliteration indicates that *an* is emphatic. It can be treated as a separate adjective, with the meaning "one and the same" here.

19b–20a Cf. the use of *fæhðu* in *Wife* 26, and see note. The separation of the pair of lovers resembles the situation in *Wife*, but whereas in that poem an estrangement has taken place, here it is a physical separation only.

20b For the omission of the pronoun subject, see note on line 9; the pronoun object is also understood: "(He) bids (me) inform you." *Sylfa*, in apposition to the unexpressed *he*, is an unusual, but not unparalleled weak form. See Mitchell *Syntax*, § 472.

23 The motif of the sad-voiced cuckoo summoning to a voyage appears also in *Sea* 53. In the present instance, one or two scholars, proposing an allegorical interpretation, have related the motif to the voice of the turtle-dove seen as a symbol of spiritual renewal in the Song of Songs. See R.E. Kaske (1967, 58–59) and W.F. Bolton (1969, 345). Friedrich Schubel (1973) rejects a Celtic provenance in favour of this specifically biblical derivation, which he also relates to *Sea*. The cuckoo is so common in European literature and lore that a widespread folk background is probable. See note on *Sea* 53–55a.

26 Final punctuation at the end of line 25 and capitals at the beginning of line 26 indicate another sectional division in the MS, lines 26–54 being presented as a separate poem. See Part 1, pp. 25–26, and notes on *Ic wæs be Sonde* (*Rid 60*) and *Husb* 13.

27b–28 Indicative *findest* here could be regarded as evidence of a consecutive (result) clause, not a final (purpose) clause, but, in view of the strong element of purpose in lines 26–27a, is probably better taken as final. The indicative emphasizes that the contemplated goal will actually be achieved. See Mitchell *Syntax*, §§ 2803 and 2992, and cf. note on lines 11b–12, above.

30 There are erasure marks between *him* and *worulde*, and space for about three letters in the erasure. Traces remain of the last of these; the final upward flourish suggests the right-hand side of an *r*, not an *n*. The present text supplies *ofer*. Possibly the scribe made the erasure because he had omitted one of the letters – and then forgot to rewrite the word. Some editors, including Leslie, supply *on*, but Krapp-Dobbie print simply *Ne mæg him worulde*, commenting that "the person who made the erasure probably knew what he was doing" (Notes).

The line is also metrically defective – unless *mara* is included in the b-verse, making 31a incomplete. Grein's *gelimpan*, which fits sense and metre, is adopted by Krapp-Dobbie and Leslie.

32b–43 Kershaw does not put in verse-form, but prints according to the MS lineation from *-waldend* to *georn*.

33 Burn damage now begins to affect the text on the verso of fol. 123. Excluding space for the final *d* of *god* (only part of the horizontal stroke remains) and the missing initial *a* of *ætsomne*, a gap of 2½ cms. intervenes between these words. Ettmüller's *þæt git* would fit, but is, of course, conjectural.

34–35a Alliteration and the preservation of the downstroke make initial *s* virtually certain for the word after *gesiþum* – probably *sinc*. From this *s* to *næglede* a gap of 4½ cms. intervenes. The lower portions of the first four letters of *næglede* are destroyed, and also those of the first three letters of *beagas*, but these words are still legible. In all probability, a word meaning "to dispense" (treasure) follows *sinc*.

36a The top of the *l* in *goldes* and the *-des* are missing, but the restoration is highly probable. *Fædan* is sometimes emended to *fættan*, since the formula *fættan golde(s)* appears in *Beowulf* 1093, 2102, and 2246. *Fædde beagas* occurs in *Beo* 1750. Both words mean "adorned." *Fæd(an)* is the past participle of **fæn*, forms of which occur as glosses on Latin *pingere*. See *Concordance* A004:88 (*afæd, afægde*); F001:93 (*faedun, faehit*); F004:221 (*fegð*) and 226 (*feidon?*); G012:57 (*gefegað*). The use of the weak adjective here may reflect early composition (see Part 1, p. 19) or may be merely traditional.

36b–37 The final *d* of the word before *elþeode* is preserved. Before this, the top of an *e* can just be detected if the page is held to a light (not an *n* or *r* as Leslie thinks). This is confirmed by BL Transcript. A gap of 7½ cms. occurs between *gol-* (in *goldes*) and this *-ed*. Leslie supplies *geond* immediately before *elþeode*, and comments that line 36b probably either opened a clause dependent on *genoh hafað* or began a new statement (Notes). Various, very conjectural, restorations have been proposed. Pope suggests *fędan goldes, feohgestreona,/þæt he mid elþeode eþel healde* (1978, 59).

38–39a In *foldan* only the bottom of the *a* and the merest trace of the *n* remain. The burn damage then extends to the right edge of the page. But towards the end of this MS line the tops of three ascenders are visible. The position of the last two of these and the need for an adjective alliterating on *h* indicate that the partially missing word ending in *-ra* is in fact *holdra*, first suggested by Trautmann (1894, 214 and 218). Excluding space for the final *-an*, the extent of the gap from *foldan* to *holdra* (i.e. to the second ascender) is 7⅞ cms. Again, any restoration must be extremely conjectural. Leslie suggests *him fela þenian sculon / (holdra hæleþa)*. Pope (1978, 59): *nalæs he þær fea teleð / (holdra hæleþa)*. It is also possible that the missing portion, which is rather long for a b-verse in this poem, included some unstressed element(s) at the beginning of line 39a – as indicated in the present text.

39b–40 Only a trace of the final *e* in *wine* is preserved. Excluding space for this, a gap of approximately 6½ cms. extends to the right-hand margin. Editorial arrangement varies, since the space is very long merely to complete the line after *wine* and very short to supply an entire missing line. Krapp-Dobbie print in the former way, Leslie in the latter – also the text given here. The metre and alliteration of the words following the lacuna show that they constitute both halves of a new line. Pope solves the problem by supposing the scribal omission of a word in line 39b and putting *wine* into line 40a. He restores thus: (*peah þe her [herra] min / wine*) *leas gewat of wicstede* (1978, 59 and 61). This illustrates another possibility, but it depends on an emendation (*herra*), and is, of course, very doubtful.

42 Most of the upper part of the word following *yþa* is destroyed. But it is clear that the word begins with *ge*; then follow perhaps three letters (the remaining portion of the first looks circular), another *g*, and a trace of another letter. Trautmann's *gelagu* (1894, 214 and 218), adopted by Leslie, does not exactly suit the indications between *e* and *g*. Pope's *gebelg*, "swell" (1978, 59 and 61–62), which elsewhere means "anger," fits here, but does not account for the letter after *g*. See *Concordance* G005:124 for occurrences of the noun *gebelg*. Many editors, including Krapp-Dobbie, print *geong*, a less common form of *gang*, "course, path." The adjective *ana*, alliterating with *yþa*, is a likely restoration for the 2-cm. space between *ge–––g–* and the margin.

47 The word *ne* is understood before *ænges*. The idea "he has no lack of any noble treasures in the world" subsumes the specific examples of treasures and delights given in the previous line.

48 Kershaw, following Thorpe, punctuates this as the beginning of a sentence, but the meaning is surely that the husband will lack for nothing if he enjoys (*beneah* + gen.) his wife. Most editors punctuate accordingly.

49 Most scholars understand *gebeot* as the betrothal vow, but Blackburn, taking the word in its militant sense of "threat," regards it as a reference to the feud which earlier separated the lovers and translates the line "In spite of the old threat against you both" (1901, 11). Since the vow of fidelity is the subject of the immediately following lines and *twega* is most naturally construed as a subjective genitive, the usual interpretation of *gebeot* is much more probable.

As a preposition governing *gebeot*, *ofer* permits a variety of translations. Thorpe translates "after"; Grein *Sprachschatz* "against" ("zuwider laufend"); similarly Blackburn's "in spite of" and Bosworth-Toller's "contrary to the old promise" (cited under *gebeot*); Trautmann (1894, 219) "in addition to" ("zu dem"); also Kershaw and Mackie; Rudolf Imelmann (1907a, 37) "according to" ("gemäss"); Leslie (Notes and Glossary) "concerning." Unless *gebeot* is understood as "threat," it is hard to fit "against, in spite of" into the context. The speaker expects a reinforcement, not a contradiction, of the old vow of plighted troth, so "in addition to" (Bosworth-Toller's sense II(8)β) seems the most suitable translation; "according to" and "concerning" are also possible, and may be regarded as part of the meaning here. Anderson (1975, 290) takes *ofer* with *genyre* (line 50) as "superimpose on" (the old vow). But there is no support elsewhere in OE for such a treatment of *genyr(w)e*; see the note following.

Line 49 is sometimes treated as closing, sometimes as opening a sentence. Krapp-Dobbie punctuate in the former way, Leslie in the latter. Both constructions give acceptable sense. Orton (1981, 49, and 55, n. 31) notes that by Kuhn's Second Law of Sentence Particles, if a verse-clause opens with a dip it must contain a particle, and that *ofer* at the beginning of a sentence forms a dip with no particle. But cf. note on *Husb* 2, above. In fact, although a period is placed before *ofer* in the present text, it is possible to take line 49 *apo koinou* both with what follows and with what precedes. See Mitchell *Syntax*, §§ 3789–3803, on *apo koinou* constructions (which he finds widespread in OE although he does not cite this particular example), and 3947.

50a The middle consonant in *ge–yre* has been erased. Early editors – also Kershaw and Krapp-Dobbie – printed *gecyre*, usually understood as *gecyrre*, "turn"; Kershaw derives from *ceosan*, "choose." However, as Jakob Schipper noted in his collation of Thorpe's edition with the MS (1874, 335), the remaining traces of the letter look more like *n*, making *genyre*. Trautmann also saw the MS in this way, reading *genyre* as *gehyre* with partially erased *h* (1894, 218–19). In fact, the top of the left-hand stroke curls very slightly towards the left – suggesting an *n*.

R.E. Kaske (1964) argued strongly for *n* on the basis of an ultraviolet examination, and subsequently used this reading in his allegorical interpretation, which regards the narrator of *Rid 60* + *Husb* as the Cross conveying a message from Christ to his Church (1967, esp. 44–50). But, as Kaske 1964 admits, there are phonological, semantic, and syntactic

objections. It is unlikely that a *w*-less *genyre* (= *genyrwe*), meaning "I constrain into unity" (*ætsomne*) or "I constrain to declare" (*benemnan*, line 51)
would occur. Apart from the doubtful *nierodon* where medial *o* seems to
have absorbed *w*, the only support for the form is a late gloss *geniered*,
and the sense would be unparalleled. *(Ge)nirwan/-ian*, basically meaning
"to constrict," is used both literally and figuratively, always with a sense
of confinement or repression, and does not occur with an infinitive of
purpose. See *Concordance* G024:151 (*genier-*) and 269 (*genirw-*); G025:34–
38 (*genyr-*); N007:318 (*nierodon*); N009:1 (*niorwedon*) and 15–16 (*nirew-*,
nirw-). Stanley B. Greenfield (1972, 172) argues for a concrete meaning
"constrict," i.e. crowd together the letters on the rune-stave, but this also
supposes *genyrwan* + infin. Trautmann's *gehyre*, "I hear" (adopted by
Mackie, Leslie, and others), followed by an acc. + infin. construction,
makes excellent sense and regular syntax. Probably the scribe erased an
n written in error, and failed to write in the correct letter.

50b–51a In the runic passage, some kind of guarantee of the husband's
betrothal vow is obviously given, but the question of what precisely the
runes represent has occasioned much debate. The runic characters in
these lines are *S, R, EA, W,* and either *M* or *D*. Resemblance between the
last runic letter and the *M* rune in *Ruin* 23 makes *M* probable. Max Förster
observes that when the runes in the Exeter Book are pointed individually
(as here) the scribe means them as separate letters or words, not as letters
combined into a word (*Exeter Book* facs, 62, n. 21). Therefore, interpretations of the latter kind, which construe the runes as the letters of a
name, are inherently less probable. Thus Fritz Hicketier (1889, 363–65):
Dwears, a name elsewhere unknown, or *Sigeweard* (*S* for *Sige* + *W, EA, R,
D*); Imelmann (1907a, 40): *Eadwacer*, with the vowels given only once and
the *S* and *C* rune confused (cf. note on *Wulf* 16a); Bolton (1969, 340):
smearw, "oleum" (a reference to *oleum effusum nomen tuum* in the Song of
Songs [Cant. 1:2]). Trautmann's suggestion (1894, 214 and 220) that the
runes represent elements in the names of oath guarantors is somewhat
more plausible; he prints *SigeRed, EadWine,* and *Monn* in his text.

The most convincing explanations of the runes are those which follow
the lines of Ernst Kock's proposal, treating the letters as rune-names: *S,R*
= *sigelrad*, "sun's road," i.e. heaven; *EA,W* = *earwynn*, "earth's joy," i.e.
lovely earth; *M* = *monn*, "man." Kock (1921, 122–23) regards these things
as elemental guarantors, and translates, reading *gecyre*: "I place together
Heaven, Earth, and Man, / confirming by an oath ..." Ralph Elliott (1955)
also uses the rune-names, but takes *ear*, the name of the *EA* rune, in its
sense of "sea" rather than "earth," and understands the runes as a tele-

scoped message: "Follow the *sun's path* across the *ocean*, and ours will be *joy* and the happiness and prosperity of the bright *day*" (reading the final rune as *D*), or "Follow the *sun's path* across the *sea* to find *joy* with the *man* who is waiting for you" (my italics). This explanation involves reading a considerable amount into the runes. Goldsmith (1975, 251–52 and 259) treats these lines in a similar way, but understands the passage as an allegorical one – a summons to the life after death. Williamson also accepts Elliott's rune-names, but understands them as forming a riddle with the solution "ship," which he relates to the runic puzzles in *Rids 19* and *64*; in *Husb* the ship is perhaps a conveyance to the next world (1977, 316). Peter Nicholson (1982) argues that the *S* rune here and in stanza 16 of the *Rune Poem* stands for *segl*, "sail," not *sigel*, "sun," its usual name, and renders the message: "Take the path across the sea to find the joy of the earth with the man to whom you were betrothed" (p. 318). Allowing for the substitution *segl* for *sigel*, Nicholson's is the most straightforward among those which explain the runes as an abbreviated message.

However, Kock's explanation, adopted by many scholars, including Leslie, has the advantage of fitting the syntax and requiring no separate expansion of the runes into a message. Reading *gehyre*, translate: "I hear sun's path (heaven), earth's joy (earth), and man (the husband) all together declare by oath that he would keep the pledge and the oath all his life ..." For a discussion of runes, see Maureen Halsall's edition of the *Rune Poem*, especially the notes on stanzas 16 (*sigel*) and 29 (*ear*) (1981, 133–34, and 160–62).

54   Repeats line 16. The double *n* in *gespræconn* is a spelling variant, and many editors emend to *gespræcon*. Leslie notes a similar orthographical doubling in *Christ* 1198 *cwenn* and *Finnsburg* 38 *gebærann* (emended to *gebæran* by Krapp-Dobbie). Cf. also the slight variation in the "refrain" of *Wulf: ungelic/-e* (lines 3 and 8).

THE RUIN

1a   The space between *þ* and *e* in the MS makes erasure of an earlier *þæs* probable. Cf. lines 9 and 30. Some editors, including Leslie, see traces of an original *æ* here. In addition to the common "Anglianisms" of OE poetry, *Ruin* contains several distinctive spellings, of which this is one. *Þæs* for *þes* occasionally appears in Northumbrian texts: the *Lindisfarne* and *Rushworth²* *Gospels* and the *Durham Ritual* glosses. See Sievers-Brunner, § 338, Anm. 4. Cf. also *Res* 89.

1b "Fates broke (it)." The syntax would be smoother if these words were understood as "broken by fate," but *gebræcon* for *gebrocen* is highly unlikely. Although in his text Ettmüller takes this verse with the following and emends to *Wyrde gebrecum / burgstedas burston*, in his notes he suggests alternatively taking line 1b with the preceding verse and emending to *wyrde gebrocen*. Most editors retain the MS reading. There is no need to treat *wyrde* as a personification, since the meaning "disastrous event" for *wyrd* is common in OE.

4 MS *hrim geat torras berofen* (4a) is obviously corrupt, and probably the result of confusing this verse with the preceding (*hreorge torras*) and the following (*hrim on lime*). Various emendations have been proposed, of which the most widely accepted has been Grein's *hrungeat berofen* (1865), "the barred gate removed," with the first element in the compound corresponding to MnE "rung." However, *hrung* is recorded only once in OE (*hlodan under hrunge*, *Rid* 22 10), whereas compounds in *hring*- are well attested. The compound *hringgeat*, printed by Kluge 1897 could refer to a gate in an arched or circular structure. Cf. *hringmere*, "circular pool" (line 45). *Hringeat*, with simplified *g*, permits a smaller emendation.

5 The word *scur*, "shower," can refer to a scattering of missiles (e.g. *flana scuras*, *Jud* 221), as well as rain, hail, etc. (as in *scursceade*, *Gen* 813). The hapax *scurbeorge* has the double meaning here. Thus, the "mutilated storm-protections" encompass the *hrofas*, *torras*, and -*geat* of the preceding lines.

6 *Ældo*, "age" (lW-S *yldo*), is another spelling especially characteristic of Anglian texts. Aside from this usage in *Ruin*, forms of this word in *æld*- are recorded principally in the *OE Bede, Lindisfarne Gospels, Rushworth¹ ᵃⁿᵈ ² Gospels* and the *Durham Ritual*. See *Concordance* Æ005:89–90.

Editors before Grein understood MS *under eotone* (for *underetene*, "eaten away") as "under the Jutes." The unique spelling shows an irregular back mutation of *e*, where the *o* in the following syllable is probably merely orthographical. -*on(e)* for *en(e)* in the past participle is found in *Rushworth²* (see Sievers-Brunner, § 366, Anm. 4); analogical extensions of back mutation are especially characteristic of the Mercian *Vespasian Psalter* gloss (see Campbell *Grammar*, § 210.2).

7a There is disagreement as to whether the elements of this verse should be regarded as a compound, a construction which Krapp-Dobbie find "highly unusual." But *w(e)aldend* is frequently used as an epithet – of the Deity – and in the dative *wealdendgode* (*Paris Psalter* 56.2 and 67.16) must be the first part of a compound. The same form, *w(e)aldend*, occurs as a zero-plural noun in *Wan* 78, *waldend licgað*. The epithets *w(e)aldend* and *wyrhta* are frequently found as a pair, applied to God, so it would be natural for an OE poet to use them jointly. For the various forms of this word and its compounds, in their immediate contexts, see *Concordance* W001:106–21; W003:276–91.

7b Both of these forms are unique. *Forweorone*, "decayed," seems to be a variant of the strong past participle *forweren(e)*, to which it bears exactly the same relationship as *-eotone* (line 6) to the usual *-etene*. The form *forworen* is also recorded. However, the usual form of this past participle and its derivatives is the weak *forwered-*.

Similarly, *geleorene*, "passed away," is a strong form of what appears elsewhere as a weak verb. J.E. Cross (1957) vindicates the MS reading as opposed to Sievers-Brunner's *forworene, gelorene* (§§ 382, Anm. 3; 384, Anm. 3), pointing to the derived nouns *geleornis* and *geliornis* in support of a strong past participle with this diphthong. Franz Wenisch cites one other example of a strong past participle, but without the diphthong: *loren*, in the OE *Martyrology*, where other MSS have *ferde* (1979, 175).

For the various forms of *(ge)leoran*, see *Concordance* G020:47–51; L008:102–8 and 184. For forms related to *forweorone*, see F016:263, 279–81, and 294. *(Ge)leoran* is an Anglian word. See Jordan 1906, 44–46. Also Wenisch 1979, 175–81 (in the section *Gemeinanglisches Wortgut*).

8 Kluge 1897 emended *cnea* to *cneowa*. But a parallel to this contracted form is to be found in *trea* (= *treowa*). See *þara trea acyrfe 7 lafe oððe fyre forbærnde wæron*, OE *Bede* 3.16, p. 224. The form *trea* is also recorded in *swe swe in wuda trea*, glossing *quasi in silva lignorum*, *Vespasian Psalter* 73.5. Cf. dat. sg. *actreo* in *Wife* 28 and 36.

9 *Gewitan*, as Mitchell shows (1965, 44–46), is best taken as pret. indic. The OE use of the present form to signify both present and future allows for a sense of futurity in this sentence: "The grip of earth holds (and will hold) the mighty builders ... until a hundred generations of the race of men have passed away." Mitchell points to a similar construction in *Christ* 1002–6: *þæt fyr nimeð* [future] *... oþþæt eall hafað ældes leoma ... for-bærned*.

For the form of *þæs* see note on line 1a.

10a Conybeare, Thorpe, and Ettmüller took *ræghar* and *readfah* as names of persons. The first element of *ræghar*, a hapax legomenon, is derived by Grein-Köhler from *rah*, "roe," by Bosworth-Toller from *ræge*, "she-goat." More plausibly, Kershaw suggests a derivation from *ragu*, "lichen," giving "hoary with lichen" for the compound (pp. 55 – transl., and 178 – notes). This suggestion is accepted by Mackie, Krapp-Dobbie, and Leslie, and by Campbell *Addenda*.

Readfah, "stained with red," might be taken to indicate a mottled effect, the basic meaning of *fah* being "variegated." Thus Leslie, who takes it to refer to orange lichen (p. 69 – notes). But it is probable that in this case the word refers to the dominant colour of the building materials. Cf. line 30, where *teaforgeapa*, "red arch," is associated with *tigelum*, "tiles."

11a The past participle *ofstonden*, "having endured," could agree with either *wag* (line 9b) or *rice* (line 10b), but sense demands the former: the wall endured while the dispensation of men changed.

11b As Leslie observes, the poet "has a penchant for asyndetic parataxis" (p. 70 – Notes). Cf. lines 5b and 7b. For the association of the two adjectives, "prominent" and "broadly curved," cf. *Sol and Sat* 415a *seomað steap and geap, Max II* 22b–23a *Gim sceal on hringe / standan steap and geap*, and *Gen* 2558 *Strudende fyr steapes and geapes. Geap* here has sometimes been taken as a noun meaning "curved structure"; however, the gloss cited in support of this is probably intended to translate *curvus*, corrupted into *cornas*. See Wright-Wülker *Vocabularies* 1:274.

12a The damage to the manuscript makes it impossible to tell whether the medial consonant of *wo–að* is *n* or *r*. The vowel before this consonant is also unclear; BL Transcript confirms *o*. The transcript reads *wonað*, but the upcurl finishing the left downstroke of the *n* is not present, so the letter could be part of an *r*. Also, the left stroke of the "*n*" is very slightly longer than the right, and a faint line connects it to the mark indicating the burn edge, as if Chambers was not sure whether the letter in the MS was complete or not (cf. BL Transcript rendering of *harne*, line 43). *Wonað* is the reading printed by most editors. Grein-Wülker prints *wonað*, but gives *wenað* as the actual MS reading. Without explanation in his notes, Leslie prints *worað*, which he glosses as from *worian*, "to moulder." But *worian* means "to move in an erratic way." In *Wan* 78, *Woriað þa winsalo*, "the wine-halls totter," the normal usage of this word is extended. Leslie comments on the similarity between the two passages in his edition of *Wan* (p. 83 – Notes), and glosses the word in the same way. But the following adverb *giet* makes both *wonað* (= *wanað*, "decays") and *worað*, however its meaning is extended, unlikely. These words would indicate a contrast between the ruin's present and its former state, whereas *giet*, "yet, still," indicates some kind of continuity. *Wunað*, "remains," printed by Kluge 1897, gives the sense demanded by the adverb: "Still ... [the monument] remains." That *wonað* may have been an error for *wunað* is suggested by the occurrence of the reverse error at *Phoenix* 72, where *wuniað* is written for *waniað/woniað*.

A word beginning with *se-* follows *giet*. The tall *e* after *s* indicates that a short or descending letter immediately follows. Very likely the word is *seo*, as Leslie suggests.

12a–b A burn-hole of 5 cms. follows, up to *-num geheapen*. The letter after the gap could be either *n* or *r*, but the former is confirmed by BL Transcript, which has a clear *n* here, complete with the upcurl finishing the left downstroke. Kluge 1897's reconstruction *wunað giet se wealstan wæpnum geheawen* would fit the space, but *se-* is almost certainly not a complete word.

Ettmüller's emendation *geheawen*, "hewn," has been adopted by some editors, since *gehypan* and *geheapian*, "to heap," are weak elsewhere. Grein-Wülker and Krapp-Dobbie print *geheapen*. In view of *forweorone, geleorene* (line 7b), the MS reading should be retained here as another strong form of a commonly weak verb.

13a *Felon* = *fulgon*, from *feolan*, "to get to," "to stick to" – in both literal and figurative senses. "Persisted," "have persisted" would accord well with "remains" in the previous line. For the form, cf. *ætfelun* (glossing *adhaeserunt*), *Vespasian Psalter* 101.6. Nineteenth-century editors, and Krapp-Dobbie, read *fel on* (i.e. *feoll on*) for MS *felon*, but scribal practice would attach the preposition *on* to the following and not the preceding word.

The beginning of another word, possibly the letter *i*, follows *felon*. Then there is a gap of 9½ cms., after which part of another letter is visible (ending the word before *grimme*). Leslie may be right in seeing "the distinctive top hook" of a low *e* in this letter. But there is no sign of the middle horizontal stroke which one would expect.

14a *Grimme gegrunde[n]* should be placed at the beginning of this line in view of the double alliteration and the number of words probably lost in the preceding gap. The final *n* is almost obliterated, but the reconstruction is virtually certain.

14b–15a A gap of 8¾ cms. follows *gegrunden*, after which fragments of the lower portions of possibly two letters are visible, forming the end of a word before *scan*. BL Transcript has what is clearly the long stroke of an *r* (it is not long enough for the other descenders), followed by the bottom of another letter, not a descender; it could be a low *e*. Holthausen 1912 favours *-re*, and offers *hædre scan heofontungol* as a possible reconstruction. Leslie suggests *-rð*.

15 As Leslie notes, *heo*, coming at the end of MS line, could be part of an incomplete word (hence Holthausen's *heofontungol*).

The earlier editors printed *scan heo* in the a-verse, but the preceding space left by burn damage is large enough to accommodate the b-verse of line 14 as well as part of the following a-verse.

15b–16 The damage here extends to the left edge of the page. Calculating from the left margin, a gap of 9¾ cms. follows *heo*. Earlier editors printed *orþonc ærsceaft* in the a-verse. Krapp-Dobbie and Leslie place the former word in the a-, the latter in the b-verse, which is more consistent with the size of the preceding gap. Mackie's arrangement of the words in mid-line leaves indeterminate where the verse division occurs.

17 Again calculating from the margin, a gap of 7¼ cms. follows *ærsceaft*, which completes the preceding MS line. One cm. before the initial *l* of *lamrindum*, the lower portion of a *g* is visible, and then the base of another letter, not a descender, forming the end of a word – probably in the a-verse, with *lamrindum beag* in the b-verse.

Lamrindum is a hapax legomenon, but its elements, "earth or clay" and "rinds or crusts," are readily comprehensible. The phrase is usually understood as a reference to the crumbling of the ruin. Thus, Leslie explains that it "sank beneath encrustations of mud." The intention of this damaged passage is now irrecoverable, but if *wunað(?) giet* (line 12a) marks some kind of a turn in thought, to the capacity of the buildings to survive, a theme with which *felon* interpreted as "have persisted" would accord, these lines are likely to express admiration of the construction, an idea which is present in the better-preserved lines 18–20; the word *orþonc* (line 16), whatever its precise meaning here (Leslie takes it as a noun, "monument of skill"), undoubtedly expresses admiration for the builders' ingenuity. In view of these contextual clues, *lamrindum beag* looks like a reference to the way the buildings were made. *Beag*, "bent" (intrans.), will then be a verb relating to the curvature of the structures. Cf. *hringeat* (?), line 4; *geap*, line 11; *hringas*, line 19; *teaforgeapa*, line 30; *hringmere*, line 45. *Lamrindum* probably refers to a covering of tiles, as in *þæs teaforgeapa tigelum sceadeð* (line 30). Cf. also a *Rushworth*[1] gloss on *figuli*, "potter('s)": *tigle vel lamwyrhte* (Matthew 27:7, p. 229), and the Psalter gloss *lamsceal* for *testa*, "potsherd" (Psalm 21:16; in Oess 1910 and Rosier 1962).

18 Counting from the left margin, a gap of 3 cms. intervenes between *mo-*, which falls at the end of the previous MS line, and *-yne*. Only the lower part of the *y* is preserved. Leslie's conjecture *monade* for the first word, though a little short for the space left, is very plausible. For the other, Holthausen 1912 suggests *cyneswiftne*; Leslie *myne swiftne*, citing *Riming Poem* 33 *mod mægnade, mine fægnade*. Remains of the letter before *y* (two dots, merely) could be part of an *m*. Also, Leslie's *myne* provides the necessary alliteration. He translates "the mind suggested, stimulated a swift purpose," "stimulated" rendering *gebrægd* (pp. 72 – Notes, and 80 – Glossary). However, the verb *(ge)bregdan*, "to move sharply," "to brandish," "to weave," "to trick," is not found elsewhere in this sense. Accepting Leslie's reconstruction, but taking *myneswiftne* as a compound adjective and *gebrægd* as a noun, one can translate "the spirit instigated a keen-minded device" – i.e. conceived an especially clever idea. A noun *gebregd*, with literal meaning "sharp movement" and figurative "clever trick" appears in *Phoenix* 57–58a *ne wintergeweorp ne wedra gebregd / hreoh under heofonum*, and in *Fortunes of Men* 70b–71a *tæfle cræft, / bleobordes gebregd*. The two instances are cited under separate meanings by Bosworth-Toller: "tossing" – neut., and "cunning" – masc., respectively. Cf. the glossing of *astutia* by *gebregd(e)* (Meritt 1957, 65). Also *gleobeames gearobrygda list*, referring to deft movement in playing the harp, *Gifts of Men* 50.

For the occurrences of *(ge)bregdan* and *gebregd*, see *Concordance* B017:91–101 and 127–29; B018:39, 48, and 301–2; G006:166–67, 180–82, 221–22, and 317.

19-20 This sentence, beginning at line 18, refers to the ingenious construction of the buildings. Line 20, MS *weall walan wirum*, resembles *wirum bewunden walan* (*Beo* 1031; emended to *walu* by Krapp-Dobbie, *wala* by Klaeber), and the gloss *walana wira* (describing two strips of raised ornamentation, 1 Kings 7:24) and *wala* (*vibices*); see, respectively, Meritt 1945, 46, item 6 and n. 2, and Napier 1900, 116, item 4487. In view of these parallels, the element *walan* here must mean "strips," and not "foundations" as suggested by Grein *Sprachschatz* (on the basis of *wyrtwalan* glossing *radices*) and accepted by subsequent editors. For a discussion of *wala*, "ridge," see Meritt 1941, 331–39; also Campbell *Addenda*. Further, the connection between *wala(n)* and *wir* in two other places indicates that it is these elements which should be treated as a compound, and not *weallwalan*. This reading gives a D-type verse, *weall walanwirum*, with resolved stress in the second lift. Translate: "with wondrous art the stout-hearted one ingeniously bound the wall together with strips of wire into circular structures." For *hringas*, cf. *hringmere*, line 45. The *walanwirum* are metal cramps. See Leslie's note on *wirum* (p. 72). The top of the *h* in *hygerof* is burned away, but the reading is certain.

21b *Burnsele* = "halls with running water"; i.e. bath houses. The word is a hapax legomenon but its meaning is clear.

22a *Horngestreon*, "horn-treasure," is usually interpreted as "abundance of horn-like structures" – perhaps a reference to the arches which so impress the narrator. *Horn-* has often been rendered "pinnacles." Leslie prefers "gables." Although *horngestreon* is a hapax, compounds in *-gestreon* are common. As a rule, the second element refers to treasure in the ordinary sense. But *bocgestreon*, "library," i.e. a treasure consisting of books, in the *OE Bede* (5.18, p. 466), resembles the usage in *Ruin*.

23b The rune which forms the first element of the compound *mondreama* could be either *M* or *D*, but sense and alliteration demand *M(on)*.

24b "Fate the irresistible," fate here being that which brings disaster. Cf. line 1b. There is, however, more justification for seeing a degree of personification in the present passage. The variation between "disastrous event" and "force of disaster" also appears in *Wan* (see note on *Wan* 5b): *Wyrd bið ful aræd* (line 5b), *Ne mæg werig mod wyrde wiðstondan* (line 15), *wyrd seo mære* (line 100b), *onwendeð wyrda gesceaft weoruld under heofonum* (line 107). Cf. also *Sol and Sat* 444b–45 *wyrd seo swiðe, / eallra fyrena fruma, fæhðo modor*, where personification is explicit. And see B.J. Timmer on *wyrd* (1941, 24–33, and 213–28).

25 The a- and b-verses imply, without actually asserting, death by warfare and pestilence, respectively. *Cringan*, "fall," and *wæl*, "corpse" or, collectively, "corpses," are both associated with death in battle. The pl. noun is found elsewhere only in *Beo* 1042 *ðonne walu feollon. Wol* means "pestilence," but often in a figurative sense, especially in compounds. See *Concordance* W017:235–37 and 261; W018:173–80.

26b Earlier editors understood *secgrof* as a noun, "host of men," and Bosworth-Toller lists the word accordingly, citing OHG *ruaba*. Holthausen's *secgrofra* (1907b) avoids this dubiously attested hapax. The adjective *secgrof*, "sword-brave," is also unique, but compound adjectives in *-rof* of this type are very common, e.g. *æscrof, beadurof, guðrof, heaðorof*. Holthausen's emendation is adopted by Krapp-Dobbie and Leslie.

27a The usual interpretation of *wigsteal* as "place for warfare" is rejected by Mackie (1925, 92), who argues instead for "place of idols." In his edition, Mackie returns to the conventional view, translating "battlements." Mackie's earlier interpretation is accepted by Karl Wentersdorf in his textual study of the poem (1977, 174).

27b *Westenstaþolas*, "waste places," is sometimes printed as separate adjective and noun (thus Krapp-Dobbie), but, since the first element lacks the inflectional ending, it is best treated as a compound.

28b The participial noun *betend*, "those who repair," may be compared with *feormend*, "those who take care of," in *Beo* 2256b *feormynd swefað*.

29b *OE Dict* suggests as an alternative possibility that *dreorgiað* here may mean "are falling down," from *dreosan*, instead of "are desolate," from *dreorig*.

30–31a *Þæs teaforgeapa* has been variously interpreted. *Þæs* is understood as "its" by Thorpe and others, but *hofu*, to which it would refer, is plural. Ettmüller emends to *þas*, in agreement with *geapu*, Conybeare's emendation. However, *þæs* for *þes* in line 9, and probably line 1, makes it virtually certain that the same usage occurs here. The rare *teafor-*, though other derivations have been proposed for it, is generally taken to refer to red colouring, since it glosses *minium*; see Wright-Wülker *Vocabularies* 1:34. Since *teafor-* is uninflected after *þæs*, it must be the first element of a compound. The form *-geapa* may be either a weak masc. noun (unknown elsewhere) or an adjective. Bosworth-Toller's emended form *geapu*, "expanse" (translated by others "arch," "pinnacle[s]," etc.) is deleted by Campbell *Addenda*. Krapp-Dobbie reject an adjectival usage, arguing that *-geapan* would be required to agree with *hrostbeages*; Leslie suggests that *-geapa* is an adjective modifying *(h)rof*. But, in accordance with the appositive technique of OE verse, *teaforgeapa* may well be a substantival adjective, "this red-arched (thing)." Mackie's "this arch of red stone" renders the sense, and is accepted by Campbell *Addenda*, although he allows for the possibility of an adjectival usage.

MS *hrost beages rof* is also problematic. *Hrost* (MnE roost) is extremely rare in recorded OE, but its use for "roof-framework" or the like, in OS, illuminates its meaning. The early editors, along with Sieper and Mackie, interpret MS *rof* as the adjective "brave." This yields, literally, "the roof-framework, brave in its ring," loosely translated by Mackie as "the roof-work, strong and circular." Grein's *hrostbeages hrof* (1865), is adopted by Krapp-Dobbie and Leslie. The compound *hrostbeages* is rendered by Bosworth-Toller "the woodwork of a circular roof." But *beag*, unlike *hring*, is nowhere found in an architectural sense; the former word is used exclusively for (circular) personal ornaments – occasionally in extended or figurative senses; see *OE Dict*. For occurrences of *beag*, see *Concordance* B001:29 and 240–41; B002:37–52; B005:33–34, 61, 71, 200. The word, variously spelled, also occurs as the second element in compounds beginning with *coren-, drihtin-, earm-, heafod-, heals-, herut-, rand-, sig-, sweor-, ufer,* and *wuldor-*. The existence of *hrostbeag* must be regarded as doubtful. Another possibility is *hrostbeames (h)rof*, "the ceiling of the roof support"; i.e. the inner vault above a pillar.

Translate: "and this red arch is coming away from its tiles, the ceiling of the pillared vault."

31b This is sometimes interpreted as "fell to the earth," but *(ge)cringan* is never followed by an accusative in this way. For occurrences of this verb, see *Concordance* C008:153; C010:55–56; G008:101–4. Thus, neither *(h)rof* in the previous verse, nor *hryre* in the present can be the subject of the verb. The former is Mackie's interpretation (placing a period after *sceadeð*), the latter Leslie's. Further, although Latin *ruina* is found in the sense of "ruined building(s)" OE *hryre* seems not to be. In the possible parallel *ne timbreð he no healle ac hryre* (*Pastoral Care* 49, p. 383) translating *non habitaculum sed ruina fabricatur*, *hryre* may well have been felt as "destruction." For the different uses of this word, see *Concordance* H024:286–96; R006:305. The subject of *gecrong* must be *wong*, in the sense of "place" – with any buildings that may be there. Cf. *Christ* 810b–11a *Wongas hreosað, / burgstede berstað*. A unique compound *hryrewong*, "place of ruin," is possible, but rather unlikely. Translate: "the place collapsed in ruin."

32a *To beorgum* = "into mounds." The mounds are created by piles of fallen masonry.

33b Leslie explains *gleoma* as the dative sg. of a unique feminine *u*-stem noun *glimu/gleomu*; such a word would mean much the same as the usual masc. *glæm*, "brightness." But a gen. pl. instrumental is more probable. Though rare, this construction has parallels: Mitchell *Syntax* cites four other examples (§ 1394). The word is understood in this way by Krapp-Dobbie and others. This interpretation could apply to a fem. *gleomu*.

Alternatively, *gleoma* could be related to the word *gleam* (with falling together of *eo* and *ea*; see Campbell *Grammar*, § 278), recorded only in *Gen* 12 *Hæfdon gleam and dream* (joy and mirth).

MS *gefrætweð* is an obvious error for *gefrætwed*. The word is emended by Conybeare and subsequent editors.

34a For the formula *wlonc ond wingal*, see note on *Sea* 29a.

36b In *eorcanstan*, "jewel," the sg. is used with pl. sense. This poeticism provides a simpler explanation than J.E. Cross's suggestion that *eorcanstan* is a metaphor for the city itself (1955, 204–5).

37b The weak adjective *bradan* may be an indication of early composition. See Part 1, p. 16.

38b–39a Either "the stream hotly gushed up in a wide surge," or "the stream gushed up (with) heat, a wide surge." *Weorpan*, "to throw," is here used intransitively with a dative. Cf. *Beo* 2582a *wearp wælfyre*, and *Maxims I* 183 *teoselum weorpeð*. Leslie comments, while citing the *Beo* parallel, that "*hate* cannot be an adverb ... since *weorpan* is never used intransitively without a following preposition" (p. 75 – Notes). But the adverb is indistinguishable in this construction from the dative-instrumental which forms it.

39b *Weal* is explained as *wæl*, "deep pool," by Stewart Baker (1963), but most regard it as the enclosing wall of the bath.

40b The lower parts of the ƿ and *r* in the final word are burned away, but the verb *wæron* is obviously what is required.

41b On the grounds that the verse has only one stress, Holthausen suggests emending to *þæt wæs hyðelic þing* (1935, 10). But the verse can be scanned with a second stress on *-lic*.

42b A gap of 5½ cms. intervenes between the beginning of the word after *geotan*, and *ofer*. The top of an ascender, now covered by the repair patch, is visible in the facsimile and BL Transcript at the edge of the burn. An *l* here would supply the alliteration in the b-verse. Leslie, who detects part of a curve, takes the letter for *þ*.

43a The lower parts of *f* and *r* in *ofer* are burned away; *harne* is very unclear and the bottom of the *r* is lost. In BL Transcript the *r* looks quite like the medial consonant in *wo–að* (line 12), but in the present case the left downstroke is clearly continued to the line marking the burn-edge.

44–45   A gap of 9¾ cms. intervenes between the letter after *un*-, and *-þþæt*. A fragment of this letter, possibly the horizontal stroke of a *d*, is just visible. Part of the missing *o* in *oþþæt* is preserved by BL Transcript. The size of the gap suggests that the rest of line 44 has been lost after *un[d]-*. The bottom of a descender is all that remains of the letter beginning the word after *hate*. Kluge 1902 reconstructs *ungesewene yldum oþþæt, / Hringmere haten* ..., taking *hringmere* as a proper noun. But the word is certainly *hate* (probably, "hot") and not *haten* ("called"). *Hringmere*, "circular pool," is a hapax formed on the same principle as *hringpytt*, "circular pit," and *hringsetl*, "circus." Placing *hate* in the b-verse (Krapp-Dobbie and Leslie) accords with the size of the following gap, 9¾ cms. from the remains of the descender to *þær*. Possibly the word after *hate* is *streamas*, as Krapp-Dobbie suggest.

46b   MS spacing and the repetition of line 40b indicate that these words belong to the b-verse. The lower part of the *þ* in *þær* is burned away.

47–48   Since the width of the right-hand margin varies, and the burn damage here extends beyond it, nearly to the edge of the page, the length of the missing portion of text can be estimated only roughly – perhaps 10½ cms. Although many of the earlier editors printed *þæt is cynelic þing* in the a-verse, Mackie, Krapp-Dobbie, and Leslie place these words in the b-verse, which is more probable – on the basis of MS spacing and of similar utterances elsewhere; cf. *(ac) þæt wæs god cyning* (*Beo* 11b and 863b), and *þæt wæs geomoru ides* (*Beo* 1075b).

49   MS *huse* is printed continuously by Krapp-Dobbie and by the earlier editors, sometimes in the compound *þinghuse*. The final *e* is covered by the repair patch but can be seen when held to a light. Mackie and Leslie print *hu se*, which would make sense as the opening of an explanatory clause after *þæt is cynelic þing*.

After *hu se*, the burn damage extends to the edge of the page, obscuring the end of the poem. Only the word *burg* is visible (top of *b* and *g* burned away), the first word, apparently, of a concluding short MS line written on the right-hand side, in the space between this poem and the next. Perhaps 8 cms. of text has been lost before *burg* and 3 cms. after, allowing room for closing punctuation and margin. Fragments of the lower portions of two or three letters are detectable after *burg*. Leslie sees traces of *str-*.

PART III

The Nature of Elegy in Old English

The delineation of genre has not been one of the major preoccupations of recent literary analysis. Nor have I attempted to bring this part of my book into line with recently influential trends in literary criticism by deconstructing the notion of genre, or by showing how genre operates as a vehicle for the implementation of a particular social and political hegemony. I doubt that in the long term the usefulness of this volume will be diminished by these omissions. The notion of genre, of the class of works to which a particular text belongs, is always an important concept, although there are periods of history when it is not usually in itself an object of study. In fact, the medieval period was such a time, and one of our difficulties in dealing with an Old English elegiac genre is the absence of any explicit contemporary guides to it. To define and explain this type of poetry I have rather eclectically drawn on certain theorists whose insights seemed apropos, although the objects of their investigations might be a quite different body of literature.

Calling these nine poems elegies is a retrospective classification which relates them to a universal literary mode. As Tzvetan Todorov puts it, in the preface to his study of "the fantastic," genres are the links by which a work "se met en rapport avec l'univers de la littérature" (1970, 12). He adds that generic classification is neither complete nor exclusive, observing "On devrait dire qu'une œuvre manifeste tel genre, non qu'il existe dans cette œuvre," and "une œuvre peut ... manifester plus d'une catégorie, plus d'un genre" (p. 26).[1] My own generalizations about elegy in Old English begin by assuming both of these provisos. Similarly perceptive and useful is Joachim Heinzle's insistence that a genre which is more than a mere taxonomic convenience should be a part of a writer's consciousness and influence his creative choices; for these reasons Heinzle discards the medieval German *Mären* genre as defined by Hanns Fischer (Heinzle 1978, esp. 122–25).[2] If we are to apply "elegy" to Old English in a meaningful way, we should be able to demonstrate that the Anglo-Saxon "elegists" intended to produce poems of a particular sort, even if such poems are never explicitly classified by them; Heinzle notes that the absence of a generic term may be attributable merely to the "gattungspoetologischen Desinteresse des Mittelalters" (p. 123).

Todorov's theory allows for a plurality of genres applicable to any particular work. I find this approach attractive, and would offer it as a response to those who prefer to classify certain Old English elegies as "wisdom literature," "consolation," "scop poetry," "debate," "Frauenlied," etc. (cf. Part 1, p. 12, above). It seems to me that there is no single answer to the question "What kind of poem is this?" The notion of genre is defined more narrowly by René Wellek and Austin Warren (1948) as "a grouping of literary works based, theoretically, upon both outer form (specific meter or structure) and also upon inner form (attitude, tone, purpose – more crudely, subject and audience)" (p. 241), although, presumably, a given text could belong to more than one grouping of this kind. E.D. Hirsch's idea that there is for every work an "intrinsic genre," the author's notion of exactly the kind of work he intended this particular example to be (1967, esp. 86–88), is thought-provoking, and probably in a sense true, but it is a restrictive and exclusive use of the term "genre" – and quite different from the one I am using here.

As I apply the term, I intend a particular historical manifestation which corresponds to a transhistorical tendency; the distinction is much like that made by Alastair Fowler (1983) in his study of genres, between *kind*, with formal features, and *mode*, which is not defined by formal structures (see esp. pp. 74 and 106–11) – although I prefer not to confine myself to Fowler's terminology and I would take issue with his theory that the *mode* originates in the historical *kind*; I am inclined to believe that the reverse is true. The view advanced by Fowler that genre features exist in families is also congenial to Old English elegy: collectively, the group of features defines the family, but no single feature need be shared by all its members (p. 41).[3]

When Todorov refers to generic linkage with the universe of literature, he is speaking of relating items to already existing works, but, of course, relationships will also exist with works not yet conceived, and between which the authors perceive no connection. I suggested such links between Old English and later English elegy at the beginning of Part 1. They may be more than simply modal links, extending sometimes to the shape of a poem (or a piece of prose) as well as its subject and temper. If "elegy" is understood in a narrow sense, either as "composition in elegiac metre" or "lament for the dead,"[4] these Old English poems are not elegies, though both the narrower definitions may influence our perception of them and I believe have a bearing on the Anglo-Saxon perception of such poems – as will appear later. But if, in its broadest sense, elegy is a literary form which conveys a meditation upon absence, loss, or transience, Old English elegy can be seen as a particular manifestation of that form.

The genre in Old English must have been variable and changing, but I shall present it in static terms, because the chronology of the works is uncertain. Thus, one cannot in practice apply to Old English Hans Robert Jauss's theoretically interesting view of the evolution of a genre as a progressive reshaping of the horizons of expectation which leads on the one hand to ossification in stereotypical works and on the other to the formation of a new genre (Jauss 1972).[5] The limited number of the Old English elegies and the uncertainty of their dates makes it virtually impossible to trace an evolutionary pattern among them.[6] Also, the Old English genre has produced no identifiable successor in Middle English. In form it tends towards the lyric that emerges later, but its characteristic vocabulary and motifs disappear.[7]

GENERIC THEMES

The essential element of elegy as it is found in these Exeter Book poems is the sense of separation: a distance in time or space between someone and their desire. A similar sense of the gulf between what is and what might be is pointed to by Schiller, in his Romantic definition, as fundamental to the elegiac *Empfindungsweise*: "sadness may derive ... [in] elegy only from [an] enthusiasm awakened by the ideal."[8] The feeling appears at its most unqualified in *The Wife's Lament* and *Wulf and Eadwacer*. Alain Renoir has commented on its centrality in both poems (1965, on *Wulf*; and 1975, on *Wife*). But it is central in the other elegies too. The object of desire may be an individual, as in the two "women's songs" and in *The Husband's Message*, or a collectivity, as in the other poems. In these latter, the speaking voice expresses its separation from an ordered society of men. This is true even in *The Ruin*, where no central character is created and the voice is no more than that. In *The Wanderer, The Seafarer, The Riming Poem*, and *Resignation*, the ordered human society is juxtaposed with an eternal order, the desire for which transcends all feelings of human loneliness. Significantly, the four poems which express this dual sense of separation are all constructed in two parts, and the least successful of the four is the one in which the mundane anticlimactically follows the transcendental. Longing that springs from unsatisfied desire is the product of separation, and pervades all the poems, *The Wife's Lament* and *Wulf and Eadwacer* most painfully, *The Husband's Message* with hope for reunion. Also, feeling is more mediated in that poem because the expectant one is replaced by his messenger, whether human or inanimate, as the speaking voice.

In the close-knit tribal society depicted by Old English poetry, separation from the person or persons to whom one belongs deprives not only of companionship but of one's entire function in the world. One's lord, whether liege-lord or husband, and friends, that is "loved ones," "kin," provide an enveloping security. Thus, the sense of separation which in a modern setting might arise from a multiplicity of situations characteristically takes the form of exile. Nearly all the central characters in the elegies are exiles of one kind or another. The Wanderer is left forlorn after the death of his lord and comrades; the Seafarer voyages over the sea because "the joys of the Lord are warmer to him than this dead life"; the ruler in *The Riming Poem* seems to have been driven out by treachery; Deor has been ousted from a prestigious position at court; the speaker and her lover in *Wulf and Eadwacer* are isolated on separate islands; the Wife has been banished to a cave in the woods; the Husband was driven overseas by feud; the penitent in *Resignation* longs to travel Home.

In *The Ruin*, instead of the dislocation of exile, and in addition to it in *The Wanderer* and *The Seafarer*, we find the dislocation brought about by death and time. The Wanderer has experienced this directly, but also creates the experience in an imaginative and generalized way, as does the Seafarer. The voice in *The Ruin* speaks impersonally, but through visual detail and the repeated use of the word "this" (lines 1, 9, 29, 30, 37) evokes the presence of an observer, who imaginatively identifies as his fellow the *beorn monig* feasting long ago in the now ruined hall, and thus makes the loss of the city his own.

STRUCTURE

The sense of separation which gives rise to the elegies is overcome in various ways in the different poems. In *The Wife's Lament* and *Wulf and Eadwacer* the speaker anticipates no end to her pain, but she comes to terms with it by externalizing it as the focus of speech moves away from the self towards a final gnomic generalization. The turn takes place at *Wulf* 16, with a shift to direct address, and at *Wife* 42, with a change to a more impersonal utterance. The same kind of conclusion is used at the end of *Resignation* (lines 117–18), but here it falls very abruptly after a first-person statement of the speaker's troubles, and since the ending offers no more than endurance in this world it appears inadequate after the desire previously expressed for *bot* in the next (*Res* 20b–21a and 110b–11a). A progress towards consolation is fundamental to *The Wanderer, The Seafarer, The Riming Poem*, and *Deor*. In the first three poems it corresponds to an eschatological movement from personal suffering, through meditation on transience, to a contemplation of the eternal. In *Deor* a consolatory movement is accomplished within each stanza, with cumulative force, so that the poem becomes a kind of incantation, effecting the removal of an ill by a repeated formula, applied to past cases and now urged as a confident remedy for the present.[9] *The Ruin* uses a movement towards the past, instead of away from it; here separation is progressively replaced in the course of the poem by wonder at the marvels of a past civilization. In *The Husband's Message* it is the power of pledged fidelity which bridges the distance between the married, or betrothed, couple. The messenger affirms his lord's continuing love, urging the lady to let no one keep her from her journey to reunion (lines 24–25), and the close of the poem seals the pledge with a reiterated reference to the vow "which you two often spoke in the past."

There are a number of formal features associated with elegy in Old English, but none of them is essential. The openings of *The Seafarer* and *The Wife's Lament* point to a convention whereby a fictitious persona proposes to give an autobiographical account of himself and his woes, and the same convention is visible, less prominently, in *Deor* 35 and *Resignation* 96b–97a. The sententious ending, which may be an extended homiletic admonition (*Wan, Sea, Rim*) or a laconic bit of gnomic wisdom (*Deor, Wulf, Wife, Res*) is common. A two-part structure, balancing contrasting halves, characterizes the longer, didactic elegies, that is *The Wanderer, The Seafarer, The Riming Poem*, and *Resignation*. To a varying degree, the theme of the poems is marked by verbal repetition. This sometimes extends to an entire line, as in the refrain of *Deor*, lines 2–3 and 7–8 of *Wulf, Husband* 16 and 54 (K-D 53). In other poems, a key word, phrase, or motif is repeated: *ar* at the beginning and end of *The Wanderer* (see Part 1, p. 33, above); words for "longing in *The Wife's Lament* (lines 14, 29, 41, 53) and the reiteration of "cave(s) under an oak-tree" (*Wife* 28 and 36); the contrast between the Seafarer and the ignorant land-dweller in lines 12b–15, 27–30, 55b–57 of that poem; and, less pointedly, *Þe sie ealles þonc* and *gode ealles þonc* in *Resignation* 67 and 86. In *The Riming Poem*, a sustained rhyming inflexion serves to contrast the past tense in lines 28–37 with the present in lines 50–69 (interrupted by another rhyme at 57–58). In *The Ruin*, repeated assonance highlights the contrast between splendour and decay, especially in lines 3–11.[10]

VOCABULARY

Certain turns of phrase are also typical. In addition to the usual heroic vocabulary about lord and retainers, feasting and entertainment in the hall, the giving of treasure, a few motifs predominate. Words expressing wretchedness, sorrow, dreariness and woe, or longing and expectation, or absent brightness and joy are thematic in all the poems. In several of them, words for the self combine with verbs of intention and narration in the introduction of the speaker. He proposes to tell (*secgan wille, Deor* 35 and *Husb* 1; *secgan mæg, Wife* 2; *Mæg ... secgan, Sea* 1–2; *secge, Res* 97; cf.

sceolde ... cwiþan, Wan 8–9); he speaks "about myself" (*Sea* and *Wife* 1; *Deor* 35; *Res* 96); he will narrate a story, *giedd wrecan* (*Sea* and *Wife* 1). In contrast to the epic *ic gefrægn/hyrde* or *we gefrunon/hyrdon*, announcing what is well known and public,[11] the formula which characterizes elegy signals a private revelation. Like the riddle, it emphasizes a personal identity, but with reference to mental and verbal faculties (*mæg, wille; secgan, wrecan*), whereas the characteristic riddle formula introduces its speaker with *ic eom* or *ic wæs*,[12] a difference which reflects the elegy's preoccupation with psychology, as opposed to the riddle's with physical being.

The elegiac ideas of separation,[13] disintegration, the hostility of the natural elements all find expression in fixed images. People are isolated by water: by the sea (*Wan, Sea, Wife, Res, Husb*), by fen (*Wulf* 5), or in some vaguer way (*wætre beflowen, Wife* 49). They are afflicted by cold (*Wan, Sea*; metaphorically, Weland in *Deor*), and by hunger (*Sea, Wulf*). The Wanderer and the penitent in *Resignation* represent themselves as persons "enclosed" or "meditating" alone, *anhagan* (*Wan* 1 and 40; *Res* 89; see note on *Wan* 1a). The latter and the banished Wife use the formula *wineleas wræcca*, "friendless outcast" (*Wife* 10; *Res* 91; cf. *wineleas guma, Wan* 45). *Wræc* and *wræce* (nom. *wracu*), the suffering of an exile, literal or metaphorical, is the condition of Weland, Deor's first example of misfortune (*Deor* 1 and 4). It is also the condition of those separated from God, like the fallen angels (*Res* 58) and the sinner (*Res* 91).[14] The Wanderer and the Seafarer follow an exile's path or paths, *wræclast(as)* (*Wan* 5 and 32; *Sea* 15 and 57), while the Wife speaks of her "painful experiences" or "journeys of exile," *wræcsiþas* (*Wife* 5 and 38; the word embraces both meanings). The Wanderer is "wretched, deprived of my homeland," *earm-cearig, eðle bidæled* (*Wan* 20); the narrator of *Resignation* "driven wretched from my homeland," *afysed ... earm of minum eþle* (*Res* 88b–89a; see note).

Deprivation expressed by verb forms in *bi-* is recurrent. The Wanderer is deprived of his homeland (*Wan* 20); the dead of joy (*Wan* 79); the Seafarer of kinsmen-friends (*Sea* 16); the lovers Geat and Mæðhild of sleep (*Deor* 16); the typical unfortunate of good times (*Deor* 28). The adjective *leas*, "without," "deprived of," is similarly frequent, in compounds like *freondleas* (*Wan* 28) and *wineleas*, and also as a simplex: the buildings of an ancient fortress are "without the sounds of their inhabitants" (*Wan* 86); the cave in the woods is "a dwelling without joy" (*Wife* 32); the unhappy solitary is "without his people's joy" (*Res* 90).

In those poems which meditate on the destruction of a society, words for falling are characteristic, applied to the descent of snow and hail, the death of men, the collapse of buildings, as well as to passing away in an abstract sense and the decline of the world in general. In *The Wanderer, The Seafarer, The Riming Poem,* and *The Ruin,* words of this type appear repeatedly, especially *hreosan, dreosan,* and *feallan,* but also *cringan* of buildings and men, *(h)nigan* ("to bow down") and *hnægan* ("to bring low") – both words applied to social and moral qualities. Interestingly, *The Ruin,* where explicit moralizing is absent, uses the "falling" motif in exclusively concrete senses (*hreosan,* line 3; *dreosan,* lines 5 and 11; *cringan,* lines 25, 28, 31), whereas *The Riming Poem,* the most arrestingly figurative of the group, uses it only in metaphorical ones (*hreosan,* line 55; *(h)nigan,* lines 57 and 58; *feallan,* line 68; *dreosan,* lines 55 and 79). In *The Wanderer* and *The Seafarer,* the descent of obliterating snow (*hreosan* in *Wan* 48, 77, 102; *feallan* in *Sea* 32) becomes an emblem of mortality (*hryre, Wan* 7; *dreosan* in *Wan* 36, 63, 79 and in *Sea* 86; feallan *Wan* 63; *cringan, Wan* 79; *hnægan, Sea* 88).

Forms of *hreosan* appear in proximity to *hrim,* "rime" (*Wan* 48 and 77; *Ruin* 3–4) and to *hrið,* "snowstorm" (*Wan* 102). Rhyming inflexions of *hreosan* and *dreosan* are paired in *Riming Poem* 55, and occupy the same sentence in *Ruin* 3–5. More elaborate word-links, whose associations go beyond the requirements of the context, appear in *Wanderer* 101–5, *Seafarer* 23a and 31–33, *Wife* 48. The resemblances between these passages suggest that the words *stanclif, stanhlip, storm, hrim, hrið, hruse, hægl, nipan, niht, cnyssan, beotan,* belong to a "bad-weather" theme, which, like the "exile" theme, is one of the topoi of elegy. Another probably lies behind the alliterating *geac* and *geomor* (*Sea* 53; *Husb* 23), referring to the plaintive note of the cuckoo which is the summons to a voyage. Close similarity in vocabulary (*longung, lagu, fundian/fus*) indicates that "longing for a voyage" in *Seafarer* 47 and *Resignation* 98 is similarly traditional. Other motifs marked by characteristic vocabulary are the "binding" of sorrow (*Wan* 39–40; *Deor* 24),[15] and the association of loneliness with *uhte,* the earliest morning (*Wan* 8; *Wife* 7 and 35; cf. *Res* 96 *mod morgenseoc*). Less sharply defined in terms of vocabulary, but probably also traditional, is the contrast between the lonely sea with its crying birds, and the companionable hall with the voices of men (*Wan* 41–55a; *Sea* 18–26).

Gnomic pronouncements with *sceal* and *bið* are characteristic of the larger category of wisdom poetry, and convey the generalizations whereby many of the elegies deal with the particular by placing it in the context of the universal, often through the medium of the weightier, more solemn, hypermetric line. Pronouncements with *sceal,* expressing what is felt to be desirable or obligatory, occur in *Wanderer* 65b–74 and 112b–14a; *Seafarer* 109–11; *Wife's Lament* 42–45a (see note on *Wife* 42–47a). *Bið* statements, which express what is and will be (the use of *beon* as opposed to *wesan* often indicates futurity) appear in *Wanderer* 112a and 114b–15; *Seafarer* 44–47, 100–102, 103, 106, and 107; *Riming Poem* 77 and 79b; *Wife's Lament* 52b–53; *Resignation* 117–18.

ORAL GERMANIC SOURCES

As far as I can see, the combination of features which characterizes the elegies cannot be traced to any one dominant source. Various influences have contributed, oral and literary. It was suggested by Levin Schücking (1908) that the elegies arose from a *Totenklagelied*, a suggestion endorsed by Sieper (p. 6). No early Germanic funeral laments are recorded. But judging from the evidence of *Beowulf* we can deduce that two kinds of utterances were formally associated with funerals. One was a lamentation voiced by a woman at the funeral pyre, as by Hildeburh over her son and brother (*Ides gnornode, /geomrode giddum, Beo* 1117b–18a) and by a nameless woman over Beowulf (*giomorgyd [Ge]at[isc] meowle ..., Beo* 3150). This type of lament fits into a widespread tradition of the impassioned display of grief at funerals, especially by women.[16] The other type of funeral song is the stately eulogy uttered by warriors riding around Beowulf's burial mound. This description in *Beowulf* resembles Jordanes's account (mid-sixth century) of the rite performed around Attila's body (ca. 453),[17] and also has culturally very wide parallels persisting to the present day. The first kind of funeral song has a later counterpart in strophes 3–11 of *Guðrúnarkviða I* (see Appendix, pp. 288–95, below), but here the focus has shifted to the recitation of others' troubles as a kind of consolation. It is possible that the women's songs of mourning mentioned by the *Beowulf* poet would have resembled *The Wife's Lament*. But, of course, none of the Old English elegies is occasioned by the death of a named individual. Neither is any of them conceived as a tribute to an individual, so a background in funeral eulogy is unlikely. It is quite feasible, though, that narration by a real person of his own woes would have developed into a genre of lament by fictitious persons, which is what we see in some of the elegies. Early evidence supports this kind of origin rather than the "dramatic monologue ... by a figure from a known heroic story" postulated by Joseph Harris largely on the basis of Eddic poetry (1983, 48). Procopius records (ca. 550) that, besieged, and suffering severe hardship, Gelimer, sixth-century king of the Vandals in North Africa, asked for a harp (κιθάρα) to accompany a certain song which he had composed on his present misfortune (ᾠδή τις αὐτῷ ἐς ξυμφορὰν τὴν παροῦσαν πεποίηται).[18] Similarly, Hrothgar in *Beowulf* is described as chanting his own history to the harp: *gyd awræc, /soð and sarlic* (*Beo* 2108b–9a); the formulaic vocabulary is that of the elegiac introduction which I have described earlier. Unfortunately, songs of this type are lost to us. However, it seems reasonable to infer that some of the traditional language of the elegies is descended from a genre of autobiographical oral poems, originally chanted to the harp, which narrated the speaker's misfortunes, rather than from a genre of death-poems, specifically.

CHRISTIAN SOURCES: THE HOMILETIC ELEGIES

Many scholars see a background of Christian belief and doctrine behind the elegies. In three of the poems – *The Wanderer, The Seafarer, The Riming Poem* – the problem of loss and change is solved in an explicitly religious way, by pointing at the poem's close to the reassurance of a permanence beyond this life, a *fæstnung* which the virtuous man can expect to win. The speaker in *Resignation* hopes for this too, although the poem's structure expresses it less satisfactorily. In *Deor* the emphasis is somewhat different; the speaker reflects in the sixth stanza that both good and bad fortune depend on the dispensation of God, in his wisdom, and that both are liable to change. *The Ruin's* treatment of the theme of transience presents no overtly Christian perspective, but the vocabulary of the poem, with expressions like *enta geweorc, burgstede burston* and *hryre wong gecrong, woldagas, wlonc ond wingal*, would evoke the use of this language in other contexts where a definite moral is drawn (see Part 1, pp. 62–63, and note on *Sea* 29a). Unless the remaining poems, the love lyrics, are interpreted allegorically, as Christian exegesis has traditionally interpreted the Hebrew love poetry in the Song of Songs,[19] they cannot be regarded as the vehicles of a specifically religious message. It is always possible that there are associations and implications which the modern reader does not know, but the love poems appear to speak in entirely secular language, whereas the didactic poems invite the audience/reader to interpret the narrative in a spiritual, more or less symbolic, way. The nature and extent of the symbolism varies from poem to poem; it is most fully realized in *The Seafarer* and *Resignation*, where the desire to undertake a voyage is emblematic of the soul's yearning.

All of the elegies as we have them, though containing earlier elements, are the products of a Christian society, composed by and designed for people with Christian beliefs. This need not mean that they must instruct in a narrowly theological sense. Even if the authors of the poems in their present form were all persons in the religious life, as the copiers almost certainly were, they might have exercised their talents in secular as well as devotional directions. The presence of several bawdy riddles in the

Exeter Book suggests that some monastics did.[20] It seems best, then, to consider the homiletic elegy a particular development of the form, seen in *The Wanderer*, *The Seafarer*, *The Riming Poem*, and *Resignation*, rather differently in *Deor*, and obliquely in *The Ruin*. All of these works have been influenced by the application of specifically Christian values to the problem of social alienation. *Deor*'s use of exampla to draw a moral resembles the sermon technique, but the hortatory tone is missing; in *The Ruin*, the resemblance to homiletic works forms a kind of subtext, which never surfaces in actual moralizing.

The theme of wordly insecurity common to all this subcategory of the elegies finds its expression in references to death (*Wan* 7, 22b–23a, 61, 78–87, 99–100; *Sea* 68–71, 94, 106; *Rim* 56, 61?, 73b–74; peripherally in *Deor* 8; *Ruin* 6b–7, 25–29a), bodily decay (*Sea* 94–96; *Rim* 75–77), ruins (*Wan* 73–105; *Ruin* 1–11, 27–32a), moral corruption (*Sea* 100–101; *Rim* 56–57, 64–65; *Res* 27b–28, 34b–36a, 51b–52a, 64b–65a, 76b–78a, 80b–81a), the decline of the world (*Wan* 62b–63, 73–74, 106–10; *Sea* 80b–90; *Rim* 55, 59, 69), the power of *wyrd* (*Wan* 5, 15, 100, 107; *Sea* 115; *Rim* 59, 70; *Res* 118; *Ruin* 1, 24). *Wyrd* as the agent of change – under the control of God – is implicit in *Deor* 32, where *witig dryhten* replaces *wyrd*, the word that formulaic tradition would evoke in association with *wendan*, with which it is linked elsewhere (*Wan* 107; *Rim* 59; *Ruin* 24; also *Maxims I* 8b–9a). In *The Wanderer*, *The Seafarer*, and *The Riming Poem*, pessimistic themes lead to, in *Resignation* are preceded by, a statement of religious commitment. *The Seafarer* and *The Riming Poem* close with a peroration typical of prose sermons, using the *Uton* ..., "Let us ...," formula (*Sea* 117; *Rim* 83b), urging the listener to take thought (*geþencan*, *Sea* 118; *Rim* 80; cf. *Deor* 31), and strive to win the eternal reward. *Geþencan*, *tilian*, and *þonc*, and the final *in ealle tid, Amen* are characteristically homiletic vocabulary (see notes on *Sea* 117–24). *The Seafarer* ends, as *Resignation* begins, with the language of prayer.

In their attitudes and motifs, these elegies show the influence of a learned, written tradition in which certain Christian Latin works figure prominently. They may or may not have been direct sources. Also, this strand of influence is very closely interwoven with others. The poems in this group have been influenced by works like Alcuin's verses (composed in or shortly after 793) addressed to the surviving monks of Lindisfarne on the sack of their monastery;[21] his poem forms a series of variations on the *sic transit gloria mundi* theme. But there are also formulaic indications of a Germanic background for this theme, in the resemblance between the *Her bið feoh læne, her bið freond læne* passage in *The Wanderer* and the *Deyr fé, deyja frœndr* lines in *Hávamál* (see note on *Wan* 108–9). The same mingling of influences occurs in the treatment of the exile theme in these religious elegies; it suggests man's exile from Paradise, as stated at the beginning of Alcuin's poem, but the formulaic language is Germanic, secular – and probably pre-Christian. Again, this group of the elegies, especially *The Ruin*, resemble not only Alcuin's but also other Latin works in a *de excidio* tradition, notably Venantius Fortunatus's poem (written in 569–70) on the destruction of Thuringia, which takes the form of a letter from Queen Radegunde to her kinsman Amalfrid.[22] Alcuin's and Venantius's poems are somewhat longer than the Old English elegies (240 and 172 lines, respectively), but they offer some parallels in detail, as well as in general theme, to their Old English analogues. The opening of the *De excidio Thoringiae* speaks of vaulted chambers (*cameris*, line 6) and lofty roofs which used to shine with gold (*ardua quae rutilo nituere ornato metallo ... fulgida tecta*, lines 7–8) – all now destroyed by fire. Similarly, *The Ruin* describes bright arched structures, now crumbling (lines 21–22a and 30–31a). The *De clade Lindisfarnensis monasterii* opens with the wretchedness of exile (*miseras terras exul adibat inops*, line 2), as does *The Wanderer* (lines 2b–5). However, in their thematic development, the nature of their allusions, and the persona adopted, the Alcuin and Venantius poems are quite different from the Old English pieces.

The voyage theme in *The Seafarer* and *Resignation* recalls the common patristic metaphor of the troubled sea of this world (see Part 1, pp. 37–38, above), and at the same time represents a particular form of the theme of separation by water which appears in the secular as well as the religious elegies. The *ubi sunt* pasages in *The Wanderer* and *The Seafarer* are characteristic of sermons and homiletic works, and the motif has its early medieval *locus classicus* in Isidore of Seville, but the theme also has other parallels (see notes on *Wan* 92–96; *Sea* 80b–85). And there are both Christian and Germanic echoes in the "ways of death" described in *The Wanderer*, reminiscent both of sermons on the resurrection of the body and renderings of the beasts-of-battle theme in the poetry (see note on *Wan* 80b–84). In his thought-progression, the persona in *The Wanderer* draws on the faculties of memory, intelligence, and will, the threefold capacity of the soul as defined in Christian philosophy, and especially by Augustine in his book on the Trinity (see Part 1, p. 34, above), but there is no particular resemblance between the actual wording of the poem and the relevant passages of Augustine's work.

THE RÔLE OF CONSOLATION: BOETHIUS

Most of these elegies embody a movement towards reassurance, towards the assertion that the separation from what is loved in this world is not permanent (*Deor*) or will be transcended by a union in the next (*Wanderer*,

Seafarer, Riming Poem). In fact, Stanley B. Greenfield sees consolation as a basic component of elegy in Old English (1966, 143; see Part 1, p. 11, above).[23] However, the "pattern of loss and consolation" defined by Greenfield is not fulfilled in all of the elegies, even in this group. *The Ruin* provides no solution to the problem of transience, but shifts the emphasis away from it. *Resignation* expresses a yearning for the next world which is never more than a fervent prayer. Among the love poems, *The Wife's Lament* and *Wulf and Eadwacer* offer no amelioration; *The Husband's Message* looks forward with bright hope, so it is inappropriate to speak of consolation.

Where consolation is a major element, it is natural to look to Boethius's *Consolation of Philosophy* (ca. 524), as it was interpreted by the Christian Middle Ages.[24] Boethius's long, mainly prose, work, with its distinction between true and illusory happiness and its insistence on spiritual rather than material good, which is necessarily transient, provides a likely background of thought for the homiletic elegies and can be identified as an influence on *Deor*. Not only are there one or two resemblances in detail to the Alfredian version which can hardly be fortuitous (see Part 1, pp. 18–19 and 45, above), and a general similarity in the citing of legendary examples, but the attitude of philosophical detachment towards misfortune which marks *Deor* and distinguishes it from the emotional involvement in the other homiletic poems resembles very closely the teaching of Philosophy to Boethius. However, as short lyric poem *Deor* is very different from the Latin work, and its allusions are Germanic instead of classical. The Boethian idea of a Fate which is ultimately subject to the control of divine Providence (book 4, prose 6) is a possible influence not only on *Deor* but on all the other elegies in this group, and may have contributed to their idea of *wyrd*, especially in *The Wanderer* (see Part 1, pp. 33–34, above, and note on *Wan* 5b). I do not find it probable, though, that the elegies were collectively inspired by Boethius, as suggested by Leslie Whitbread (1970), who posits this origin even for the love lyrics (he does not consider *The Riming Poem*).[25]

CHRISTIAN LATIN SOURCES: LITERARY FORMS AND RHETORICAL THEORY

These connections between the elegies dealing with social themes and the Christian Latin literature of the early Middle Ages appear in concept and motif rather than poetic structure. In the latter respect there are no very exact models, although structural parallels of a general kind and resemblances in certain formal features exist. In a general way, the movement from exampla towards a conclusion resembles the techniques of Latin sermons and homiletic poems. In broad terms, it is possible to trace the same progression from exile and hardship to an optimistic expectation of a better life to come in *The Wanderer* and Alcuin's *De clade Lindisfarnensis monasterii*; some would see the Wanderer's exile in the allegorical terms which are clearly laid out at the beginning of Alcuin's poem.[26] Again, the Old English poems use rhetorical devices which are defined and classified in the standard medieval treatises, like Isidore of Seville's *Etymologiae* (early seventh century). But whether, for instance, the poets actually thought of themselves as using Isidore's *ethopoeia*[27] when they created a fictitious persona it is impossible to say. It is the names, rather than the devices, which are an importation from Graeco-Roman rhetoric. We notice, at any rate, that the elegies in the homiletic group show a more conspicuous use of such devices than the love poems: for example, homeoteleuton extending to rhyme in *The Ruin* and *The Riming Poem*, antithesis in *Wanderer* 32–33 and *Seafarer* 19b–22, anaphora and parallelism in *Wanderer* 66–69, 80b–84, 92–96, 108–9. Some of these, and numerous other, devices are listed in Bede's *De Schematibus et Tropis* (written in 701–2), explained – not always as we should define them – and illustrated from Holy Writ.[28]

The relationship of these elegies to Christian Latin learning is not specific to their poetic genre, but defines the much larger category of homiletic literature which elegy overlaps. Though the themes of social-homiletic elegy – death and change – have been deeply affected by a foreign, learned tradition, they have not actually originated in it. The areas of influence can be identified, but we can only guess at the course this influence took. We cannot know the extent to which the individual poets themselves read Anglo-Latin writers of the early period like Bede, or, closer to their own time, Alcuin and the continental authors of the Carolingian renaissance, or earlier continental writers like Fortunatus and Isidore, or Augustine and the Church Fathers. The ideas of these men and their fellows were widespread currency, and their vocabulary is reflected in Old English prose. Where a poem actually translates a Latin original, a first-hand knowledge can be assumed, but as far as we know none of the elegies is a translation (*Riddle 60*, sometimes regarded as part of *The Husband's Message*, seems to be based on a Latin enigma; see Textual Notes). It is quite conceivable that some of the poets were ignorant of Latin, and that Latin learning was transmitted to them through the medium of Old English prose.[29] This may be the case with the vocabulary and theme of *Deor*; perhaps it is less probable with the conspicuous and extensive rhetoric in *The Wanderer*.

LATIN ELEGIAC POETRY

While Christian Latin learning provides a background of ideas for one branch of Old English elegy, Latin poetry, pagan and Christian, offers a parallel for the genre as a whole, and for the other branch of it – the love lyric. Of course, there is no counterpart in Old English for the elegiac couplet: a hexameter followed by a pentameter, the latter composed of two hemistichs, each containing two and a half feet. But in broad terms the Old English elegies, which add touches of rhyme and refrain to the common Germanic metre, display a form which mediates between stichic and strophic verse as the classical elegiac mediates between the hexameter and the lyric strophe (see Klinck 1984, 130 and 137). Again, there is a resemblance in spirit between the lyric-reflective mode of the Old English poems and much Latin elegy. The characteristic poetic forms of Old English elegy can be seen to fulfil a similar need. Also, Latin elegiacs offer more parallels in subject matter than the pastoral poems (composed in hexameters) of Virgil and the Greek bucolic poets like Theocritus and Bion who have provided a model for English pastoral elegy (see Part 1, p. 11, above).

Etymologically, the term ἐλεγεῖα, "poem in elegiac couplets," is derived from ἔλεγος, "sad song," originally accompanied by the flute. The earliest recorded Greek elegies, by Archilochus (ca. 680–ca. 640 BC) celebrated battle or carousing or attempted to console. Callinus and Tyrtaeus also wrote martial elegiacs. Other subjects of early elegy included the loss of amorous youth (Mimnermus), and, in the next century, public exhortation (Solon). The elegiac couplet was also used for epigram and funerary inscription – commemorative rather than mournful. In Roman writers the form was often used for the expression of melancholy – but not exclusively so. In his poem on the death of the elegiac poet Tibullus, Ovid personifies the metre as *flebilis ... Elegeia*, "tearful Elegy" (*Amores* 3.9:3; text and translation in Showerman 1921, 480–85). In his *De Arte Poetica*, Horace avers that it was first used for mournful subjects, *querimonia* (lines 75ff.; text and translation in Fairclough 1929, 456–57).[30] This view of the elegiac metre was taken over by early medieval writers. Isidore observes that it is the form which is appropriate to the unfortunate and to sad subjects,[31] and Bede, echoing Horace, calls it suitable for the complaints of the unhappy (*huius modulatio carminis miserorum querimoniae congruit, De arte metrica* 1.10; in Kendall 1975, 110). It is significant that the two *de excidio* poems by Fortunatus and Alcuin, respectively, were both composed in elegiacs. The more educated Anglo-Saxon poets would have been aware of this view of the Latin metre. It would, then, be natural for them to think of their own compositions on themes of loss and longing, death and change, as generically related to Latin poems defined as elegiac in terms of metre. The Old English *Phoenix*, one of the long poems in the first half of the Exeter Book, paraphrases a Latin work in elegiacs, the *De ave phoenice* attributed to Lactantius (ca. 240–ca. 320 AD). Though *The Phoenix* is not one of the elegiac group defined in terms of the themes, structure, and vocabulary described at the beginning of this chapter, as a poem on the death and rebirth of the sacred bird, which medieval Christians saw as an allegory of the Resurrection, *The Phoenix* bears a significant relationship to the poetry of separation in Old English, especially to those poems which look forward with hope for a lasting union.[32] Among the pagan authors, the elegies of Ovid, one of the better-known Roman poets in Anglo-Saxon times, are a probable, and those of Propertius a possible influence on Anglo-Saxon poets.[33] Latin love elegy, which is often very voluptuous, seems in general fairly remote from the Old English mode. And the city sophistication of these poets, their "urbanity," is unlike anything in Old English. But Ovid's *Heroides*, mournful poems cast in the form of letters from various legendary personages to their absent lovers, and his *Tristia* and *Epistulae ex Ponto*, the two collections which arose out of his exile at Tomis on the Black Sea, display some interesting resemblances to the Old English poems in depicting the sufferings of the expatriate or of the star-crossed lover. A poignant motif in both *The Wanderer* and some of the poems from Ovid's exile is the vivid presence to the mind's eye of absent objects of affection, a reminder which intensifies pain (*Wan* 41–57; *Tristia* 3.4b:9–15; *Ex Ponto* 3.7:33–34; see Appendix, pp. 262 and 266, below). It seems reasonable to conclude that the Anglo-Saxon "elegists" were influenced, not necessarily at first hand, by the Latin elegiac mode, in pagan and Christian authors. The formal connection between the Latin and Old English poems is less an imitation or inheritance than a parallel development of poetic structures to express themes of longing and loss.

More specific connections between the Old English elegies and classical poems are hard to prove. Rudolf Imelmann was of the opinion that the saga of Eadwacer, which he saw as the narrative background, took its poetic form in the elegies (he does not include *The Riming Poem* and *Resignation*) from *Heroides* 18 and 19, the letters of Hero to Leander and Leander to Hero, respectively, along with influence from the story of Dido and Aeneas as told in Virgil's *Aeneid* 1 and 4, and, formally rather than thematically, from Virgil's *Eclogues* (see especially Imelmann 1920; the very elaborate theory is summarized on p. 237). Helga Reuschel (1938) suggested that the *Heroides* and the two collections of poems on

Ovid's exile collectively provided the inspiration for the elegies. Such a thoroughgoing dependency is unlikely, but there are definite thematic and stylistic parallels.[34] It is possible, too, that *The Wife's Lament* and *Wulf and Eadwacer* were influenced by the letters of unhappy women in the *Heroides*, but not necessary to postulate the latter as a principal source. There are some noteworthy similarities between *Wulf and Eadwacer* and *Heroides* 11, the letter of Canace to Macareus (see Appendix, pp. 254–61, below) – the tyrannical guardian-figure, the illicit love, the infant carried off to the woods to be torn asunder by wild beasts – although there appears to be no incest in the Old English poem; its interpretation is, of course, problematic, and the situations in both poems can be related to widespread folk motifs.

RHYME, REFRAIN, STROPHE: THE QUESTION OF OLD NORSE INFLUENCE

As a group, the Old English elegies cannot be derived from Latin verse forms. But one of them, *The Riming Poem*, shows the influence of the rhymed verse used in Latin hymns, and in the same respect resembles the mid-tenth-century Norse *Hǫfuðlausn* by Egill Skallagrímsson (see Part 1, pp. 42–43, above). Whether one poem influenced the other or both arose from the same milieu, the resemblance is striking. *Hǫfuðlausn* is a *drápa*, a heroic lay consisting of stanzas interspersed with the occasional shorter stanza serving as a refrain. The Old English piece does not divide into strophes like its Norse companion, which is composed in a modified version of the four-line-stanza *fornyrðislag*, "old lore," metre used for most Eddic verse. But *The Riming Poem* does make frequent use of two-line units joined by fourfold rhyme linking two pairs of a- and b- verses, and this kind of quadruple rhyme forms a consistent pattern in *Hǫfuðlausn* (there are one or two exceptions). Rhythmically, too, the poems are similar: *Hǫfuðlausn* is composed in lines of two alliterating verses, each verse containing two stressed and two (occasionally three) unstressed syllables; *The Riming Poem* uses similarly short, strongly accented verses, and shows a similar tendency towards an octosyllabic line, especially in lines 61–69.

Two of the other elegies resemble the strophic structures of Old Norse verse: *Deor* in its stanzas and refrain, *Wulf and Eadwacer* in its use of a long followed by a short line (2–3, 7–8, 16–17, 18–19). This pattern in the latter poem resembles the elements of the *ljóðaháttr*, "song metre," stanza, which consists of two units of long + short lines; the proverbial *deyr fé, deyr frœndr, /deyr sjalfr at sama* lines from *Hávamál* (stanza 76; repeated on 77) form the first half of a *ljóðaháttr* stanza. Although it is not impossible that these two Old English poems were directly influenced by Old Norse, their probable dates (*Wulf and Eadwacer* ninth century: *Deor* late ninth – early tenth century) and their West Saxon dialect make this unlikely, whereas *The Riming Poem* seems to be a little later in date and is strongly Anglian in language. The features in which *Deor* and *Wulf and Eadwacer* resemble Norse strophic poetry also appear elsewhere in Old English, notably in the Charms. For example, *A Sudden Stitch* repeats *Ut lytel spere, gif her inne sy* (lines 6, 12, 17) as *Deor* repeats its refrain; *Theft of Cattle* uses a short line with double alliteration (*and fere ham þæt feoh*, line 9) like *Wulf and Eadwacer* (lines 3, 8, 17, 19). And the Charms contain many lines with a high number of unstressed syllables – again like *Wulf and Eadwacer*. Thus, these two elegies can be related to an Anglo-Saxon tradition of popular poetry. As noted above, all of the elegies, to a varying degree, impose a structure created by significant repetitions. With allowance made for some foreign influence, this technique can be perceived as a more sophisticated development of native songs and incantations, rather than an importation from abroad.

Although there may be influence from Old Norse poetry, and there are certainly affinities, we look in vain for a specifically elegiac model. The Norse poems which might fall into this category are more vehement in their grief; they are immediately inspired by a death and are written not just in sorrow but in anger. Also, the dramatic element in the Eddic poems is very strong. Chronologically, all the Norse examples we have are later than the Old English poems. There are generic relationships with aspects of elegy, though. The recitation of woes in *Guðrúnarkviða I* resembles the form of *Deor* as a kind of incantatory consolation; as depictions of women's sorrows, the Guthrun poems are like *Wulf and Eadwacer* and *The Wife's Lament*. Both these kinds of resemblance suggest a shared heritage – in the narrow context Germanic, but in a broader frame of reference universal. Only with *The Riming Poem* is a direct connection likely, and even here we do not know that an actual borrowing from Old Norse took place. Also, *Hǫfuðlausn* is a praise poem, not an elegy, so the resemblance is strictly one of verse-form. Egill's *Sonatorrek*, the lament for his sons (ca. 960), is too late to have been an influence – and differs markedly in style and mood; in verse-form it uses *kviðuháttr*, alternating half-lines of three and four syllables.

CELTIC ANALOGUES

It is probably no coincidence that the body of foreign poetry which comes closest in spirit and imagery to Old English elegy was also composed in

Britain, at approximately the same time. Whereas Christian and classical Latin poetry offer similarities of intent and motif but no really close and extensive parallels in detail, and Norse verse uses its own developments of the Germanic alliterative long line in defiant Eddic and skaldic laments, Old Welsh contains a significant body of elegiac poetry which strikes some of the same chords as Old English elegiac verse. Like Old English poetry, Old Welsh (preserved in Middle Welsh manuscripts) portrays the kind of heroic milieu that existed in the sixth and seventh centuries. Though composed later, perhaps in the ninth century, it arises out of the events of that period. Generically, the Old English elegies on social subjects, as distinct from the love poems, have much in common with the Welsh verse which springs from the social disruptions of that age. Various poems and passages are preserved, associated with Urien Prince of Rheged (eastern Galloway), with Llywarch Hen ("Llywarch the Old"), who has lost all his twenty-four sons in battle, with Heledd, sister of Cynddylan Prince of Powys and Lord of Pengwern (Shrewsbury), who has seen her family killed and their home destroyed. These are historical, though fictionalized, figures. There are strong resemblances between the meditations on ruins in the Old English elegies and Welsh *de excidio* or *encomium urbis* poems like *Edmyg Dinbych* (*The Praise of Tenby*), Heledd's lamentations in *Stafell Gynddylan* (*The Hall of Cynddylan*), the series of stanzas in *Yr Aelwyd Hon* (*This Hearth*; Appendix, pp. 276–79, below).[35] Similarities between this last poem and *The Ruin* struck W.D. Conybeare long ago, and he included a translation of the former in his edition (pp. 250–51). Like Llywarch, Heledd, and the nameless speaker in *Claf Abercuawg* (*The Sick Man of Abercuawg*; Appendix, pp. 268–75, below), the personae in the Old English poems have lost their place in society. In all of these Welsh poems, as in their Old English analogues, the joyful meadhall where warriors are rewarded with largesse is counterpoised against the same scene devastated by battle, or in ruins, or against a single figure, whose loneliness and hardship form a poignant contrast to the festivity and splendour from which he is removed.

In temper and motif, the two poetic traditions contain much that is identical, and it is natural to attribute this identity to their closeness in place, time, and social background. Some kind of intercourse between the invading and the indigenous linguistic communities must have occurred, but the literary resemblances are not of the narrow kind that would make importation of the tradition from Old Welsh a very persuasive hypothesis. It has been argued by Herbert Pilch (1964) that the Old English genre has actually been created on an analogy with a Welsh genre now known to us only through *Claf Abercuawg*, which, unlike the other Welsh poems, he places in the same category of "nameless" and "placeless" poetry as most of the Old English elegies (he supposes the place-name "Abercuawg" to have been invented; see Pilch, pp. 213–14). Along with the obvious similarities, there are some major differences, though. Like his Old English counterparts, the Sick Man is an "outcast" or "exile," a *difro* (stanza 13). The Welsh poem emphasizes the speaker's pitiful physical plight – his sickness, his dilapidated dwelling – whereas the Old English persona, even when physically afflicted (*Sea* 8b–12a) or impoverished (*Res* 101b–4), is much more concerned with a psychological, spiritual condition. In *Claf Abercuawg*, as in other Old Welsh poems, personal statement is combined with observation of nature and moral comment: three of the principal ingredients of Old English elegy. But in the latter the three components are presented in a more integrated way. The didactic element, where it is explicit, is central. Again, the natural environment functions as the outward embodiment of a state of mind, whereas in the Welsh poetry it has a quite separate existence which conveys the indifference of the natural world to the feelings of men. The contrast is noteworthy in the way the two traditions treat the cuckoo motif, which Sieper thought must be a Celtic loan (see note on *Sea* 53–55a). In *The Seafarer* and *The Husband's Message* the cuckoo's call in the springtime corresponds to the heart's impulse; in *Claf Abercuawg* the voices of the spring cuckoos are instinct with exuberant life – precisely the opposite of the speaker's depressed and morbid state. Only in *Resignation* 105–8a, where the speaker juxtaposes his miserable self with a flourishing tree, does the technique characteristic of Welsh verse appear. Again, the epigrammatic, punning style, whereby apparently unconnected personal statements and gnomic utterances on nature and morals are linked, is the concomitant of the exacting Welsh verse-form, which has no replica in Old English. Pilch suggests (p. 220) that the occurrence of structured repetition in the shape of refrain or rhyme in the Old English poems is an attempt to recreate the form of the Welsh *englynion* (stanzas) with their intensive repetition and word-play. But in fact there is much less resemblance to the stanzaic structures of Welsh than to those of Norse, and the greater difference in language and metre would have made Welsh a harder source to borrow from.

The Old English poems, then, are rather distant from the Welsh poetry of the period in form, but close to it in subject. In addition to the resemblance in the specifically elegiac themes of transience and isolation, there are some other similarities in treatment and attitude, which can be related to the Celtic context in Ireland as well as Britain. Celtic monasticism, as practised in Ireland, was a shaping influence on Anglo-Saxon Christianity through seventh-century figures like Bishop Cuthbert, with his yearning for an anchorite's simplicity and seclusion. The influence of Old Irish verse associated with the hermit Culdees (*cultores dei*, in Irish *célé de*) has been traced by P.L. Henry (1966, esp. 29–66), who relates Old English elegiac poetry to a penitential genre in Irish and Welsh. Although Henry finds the genre more distinct and developed in Old English than the evidence really warrants, the correspondence between the desire to leave the world expressed in *The Seafarer* and *Resignation* with the sentiments of Celtic, especially Irish, asceticism, is significant. The connection in the motif of the voyage is undeniable, even if one doubts that the two Old English poems are about penitential pilgrimage in a literal sense like some Celtic pieces. For example, an Irish poet expresses his desire "to advance as a pilgrim / Over the great waves of the joyous sea" (early-tenth-century? text and translation in Henry, pp. 63–66); and a Welsh poet declares "My mind is (bent) on a journey, / Intending to go to sea; / A beneficial design" (Old Welsh; text and translation in Henry, pp. 86–87; no date suggested). This type of poetry is not elegiac, however, since the spiritual integration which is the object of desire in elegiac poetry has already been achieved. The tensions which mark Old English poetry on similar themes are absent. Again, in the nature poetry of the Culdees there is no tension with the natural environment: "The songs of the bright-breasted ring-doves, a beloved movement, the carol of the thrush, pleasant and familiar above my house" (tenth century; see Jackson 1971, 68–70; for complete Irish text see Meyer 1901). Here the narrator, affectionately describing his hermit's hut, is almost effaced into the scene, in contrast with Old English elegy, which subordinates the scene to the speaker's own spiritual condition, or Welsh elegy, which suggests his alienation from it.

SOURCES AND ANALOGUES: CONCLUSION

Finding sources for the Old English elegies leads us to the three major cultural and linguistic areas bearing upon Anglo-Saxon England: Latin, Celtic, and Germanic. It is probable that the form originated in the continental period, as an autobiography with mournful content. Typically, the situation which gives rise to regret or longing is one of exile; it may also be caused by the destruction of the group to which the speaker belonged. Again, these situations, which are often expressed in formulaic language, must go back to the prehistoric, that is the preliterate, period. A social background is to be found in the clash of nations and tribes. Precisely the same situations and the same social background occur in the context of early Welsh verse, the foreign literature with which Old English elegy shows the closest affinity. The resemblance can be explained by the similarities between the Germanic and Celtic cultures, but, since the two literatures were in such close proximity, borrowing of theme and motif in both directions would be natural. There is no evidence, though, that Old English literature borrowed from Welsh in the systematic way it sometimes borrowed from Latin and the relationship between conquerors and conquered would not encourage it. The didactic poetry which reflects an ascetic ideal has been influenced, directly or indirectly, by the kind of monasticism that developed in Ireland. In its explicitly Christian content, elegy draws on Latin learning; again, in the absence of actual translation it is hard to know how directly. Borrowings of this kind are not genre-specific and have only a vague relationship to poetic form. It is probable, though impossible to prove, that the poets were influenced by classical and Christian Latin elegy as a mode. The elegiac couplet was not a metre they could imitate, but some Anglo-Saxon poets must have been aware of its association with melancholy and with love poetry. They may have been influenced by the classical elegists' treatment of love, especially un-happy love, and by Ovid's poems on his own exile. In so far as Old English elegy is formally distinguished from other Anglo-Saxon poetry, the dis-tinction lies in a sophisticated and deliberate use of repetition and echo as a structuring device. It is possible that this technique was influenced by Old Norse poetry, which is in strophic form, but, in view of relative chronology and the occurrence of the technique at a cruder level in other Old English poems, this feature may well be a native development, moving in the direction of the strophic structures found in other literatures – and in Middle English. Only with *The Riming Poem* can we be reasonably certain that foreign influence – in this case Latin hymnody – was a shaping factor.

AUTHORSHIP OF THE ELEGIES

In my analysis of Old English elegy, I have tried to avoid assumptions about its authors. What we know about them is minimal. The poems are preserved in a collection donated by a cleric to his church. They were certainly read, and almost certainly copied, by persons in the religious life. Some of the authors obviously had a devotional intent. Some, I would say, did not. It is convenient to treat the author of each poem as a single individual, but in some sense their authorship is composite. Formulas, themes, and probably large passages of poetry have been used and reused, modified, shifted around. The "author," then, is the hypothetical person who put the poem together in its present state – allowing for subsequent orthographical changes and copying errors. In practice it might be hard to distinguish between authors and copyists (cf. R.M. Liuzza, 1987, esp. 14), though there is evidence that at the final stage the Exeter Book was copied rather mechanically. But it is impossible to avoid the concept of an authorial figure, or to dispense with the notion of authorial intention. As noted in Part 1 (p. 30, above), there is no particularly strong evidence that any two or more of the elegies were composed by the same person.

THE "WOMEN'S SONGS"

I regard it as probable that the authors were members of religious houses, simply because of the circumstances of copying and preserving manu-scripts in Anglo-Saxon England. However, I do not exclude the possibility that some of the authors were women. This possibility suggests itself especially in the case of the two "women's songs." A recent critic has postulated a background for *The Wife's Lament* in female monasticism – though interpreting the poem in a devotional rather than an erotic con-text.[36] But a capitulary of Charlemagne prohibiting nuns from writing *winileudos*, "poems to a friend," i.e. "love poems" (*Capitulare generale anni 789*, § 3; in Pertz 1835, 68), is an interesting bit of evidence for this practice on the Continent which suggests it existed in England too. We cannot assume, though, that *The Wife's Lament* and *Wulf and Eadwacer* were com-posed by female authors; there are plenty of examples of male poets expressing their empathy with suffering women.[37] It is noteworthy that *Wulf and Eadwacer* diverges from the other elegies in metre and vocab-ulary. In its use of varying line-lengths, a heavy number of unstressed syllables, the irregular verse 13a, *Wulf* resembles the popular poetry found in the Charms. Though the poem is on a conventional elegiac subject, none of the conventional formulas appear – associated with exile, sepa-ration by water, bad weather, mental or physical affliction. Words like *apecgan, dogode, reotugu, bogum* (of a human) are unusual, and seem to have a different source from the normal poetic stock. For these reasons, it is very probable that *Wulf and Eadwacer* comes from a popular back-ground, rather than the aristocratic tradition to which most Old English poetry belongs. The diction and metre of *The Wife's Lament* are more conventional, but it is entirely possible that this poem too, as woman's song, was influenced by another tradition.

DESIGNATIONS FOR "ELEGY" IN OLD ENGLISH

There is no evidence that the Anglo-Saxons possessed a specific word, like "elegy," to denote the kind of poetry I have been describing. Probably they would not have used a term more precise than *giedd* to refer to their elegiac poems. This word, along with its compounds, appears in *Wanderer* 55, *Seafarer* 1, *Wulf* 19, *Wife* 1. *Giedd*, which cuts across the modern distinctions between song and speech, fact and fiction, prose and verse, means a relatively extended utterance, of an artistic kind, with a narrative content and an instructive or exemplary value. The word *giedd* is proverbially associated both with poetic entertainment and with wisdom: *Maxims I* tells us that *Gleawe men sceolon gieddum wrixlan* (line 4) and that *Wæra gehwylcum wislicu word gerisað, /gleomen gied ond guman snyttro* (lines 165–66).[38] *Giedd* is applied to utterances as varied as riddle (*Rid 55* 14) and biblical parable; for example in the *Rushworth² Gospels* John 10:6, where *proverbium*, "parable" in the King James Bible, is translated *soðcwide vel gedd*. As the *Concordance* shows (see note on *Wulf* 19, p. 177, above), *giedd* occurs in glosses and in poetic and Northumbrian texts. Its usage can be delimited with reference to *leoð*, "song," and *spell*, "account." The former refers to a specifically musical or poetic utterance (as in *leoðwisan geworht*, "composed in verse" – applied to the contents of the Exeter Book; see Part 1, p. 13, above). The latter, like *giedd*, refers to a narrative, but the concepts of exemplary significance and artistic shaping are not inherent.[39] Both *leoð* and *spell* are used of elegiac utterances (*fusleoð*, *Guthlac* 1346; *sorhleoð*, *Dream of the Rood* 67 and *Beo* 2460; *sarspel*, *Res* 97). But *giedd* is the favoured term.[40] It also appears in *Beowulf* 1118, 2108, 2446 (in apposition to *sarigne sang*), and 3150. No Old English simplex exists which combines the idea of artistic narrative with personal observation or with sadness and longing. So these three elements are linked by compounding and word-juxtaposition, providing the characteristic elegiac collocations of *soð*, *sylf*, *sar*, and *sið* with *geomor* and *giedd*.

A DEFINITION OF OLD ENGLISH ELEGY IN ITS LITERARY CONTEXT

In selecting the texts for the Appendix, I have tried to provide examples of elegiac poems from the three cultures with which the Anglo-Saxons were in contact. It is quite possible that none of the works chosen was an actual source; only the Ovidian poems definitely predate the Old English elegies. But, in their different ways, all of these foreign poems represent literary forms of elegy which the Anglo-Saxon poetic community would have been aware of. Some of its members would have known of elegiacs in Latin, of Welsh *englynion*, and, from the ninth century on, of Norse strophes. They would have known the typical motifs, and some, at least, of the legendary and mythological characters.

Reference to these, and other, foreign analogues also helps to define Old English elegy by what it is not, as well as by what it is. It does not use the intensive repetition and word-play of Welsh *englynion*, the elaborate kennings of skaldic verse, the learned mythical allusions in Norse and Latin poetry. It does not dramatize a precise moment in time, like the Guthrun poems and *Heroides* 11. In its evocation of sadness and longing, it has developed a frame of reference all its own, with a typical vocabulary and a mode that ranges between the lyric and the reflective. It has not developed a distinctive metre, but it reflects an awareness of lyric poetry in other languages, and popular songs in its own. This influence is felt in the imposition of strophic structures on the stichic form of the traditional heroic verse. If I may, finally, offer my own attempt at defining the genre: Old English elegy is a discourse arising from a powerful sense of absence, of separation from what is desired, expressed through characteristic words and themes, and shaping itself by echo and leitmotiv into a poem that moves from disquiet to some kind of acceptance.

NOTES

1 Todorov regards the different genres as originating in different kinds of speech acts via a series of transformations. See also Todorov transl. Berrong 1976–77, 159–70.

2 Heinzle sums up his criticism of Fischer's demarcation in this way: "Selbstverständlich lassen sich die Texte entsprechend klassifizieren, aber diese Klassifizierung ist rein formallogischer Art, besagt nichts über die Kräfte, die den Prozess der poetischen Produktion tatsächlich bestimmt haben – und ist damit nich geeignet, 'historische Wesenserkenntnis' zu vermitteln" (p. 125).

3 Fowler notes that this "theory of family resemblance ... [was] invented by Dugald Stewart ... [and] developed by Wittgenstein in a famous analogy between language games and games in general" (p. 41).

4 It is in this latter sense that Peter Sacks (1985) understands the term in his study of English elegy from the Renaissance to modern times; he sees elegiac poems as performing "the work of mourning" and consolation, and reflecting "the myths and ceremonies associated with that work" (p. 326). Though his approach is very different from Todorov's, Sacks also shows the influence of speech-act theory in his view of the genre as performative.

5 See Jauss transl. Bahti 1982, 76–109, esp. 88–89. Jauss derives this description from his observation of medieval Romance literature, for example the evolution from *chanson de geste* to *roman arthurien* to the novella genre of the *Decameron*.

6 Joseph Harris sees a "development ... from heroic story to psychology and general life patterns and on to allegory and homily, "with *Wulf* at one end and *Sea* at the other," but he adds warily: "I am speaking of a typological development and not of the dates of surviving texts or even their actual relative chronology" (Harris 1983, 50).

7 The moralistic strain in OE elegy is the most obvious survivor – as in the thirteenth-century *Worldes blis ne last no throwe* and *Were beth they biforen us weren* (in Brown 1932, 80 and 85, resp.).

8 "So darf bey der Elegie die Trauer nur aus einer, durch das Ideal erweckten, Begeisterung fliessen." Schiller is here speaking of a "mode of feeling" (*Empfindungsweise*) rather than a genre. See his *Über naïve und sentimentalische Dichtung*, in Wiese and Koopman 1962, 450; transl, Elias 1966, 126. Schiller's essay appeared in 1795.

9 I would endorse Morton Bloomfield's view that *Deor* uses the charm form (1964, 534–41), but not his assumption that the poem was actually composed by a minstrel named Deor (1986, 275).

10 Assonance here emphasizes the same kind of appositive technique that Fred C. Robinson (1985) makes the subject of his study of *Beowulf*.

Sieper notes two kinds of repetition, associated with closure (the "refrains" of *Deor, Wulf, Husb; Ruin* 40 and 46 – this last seems to me less significant), and opening (*Wan* 11, 29, 37; *Sea* 12 and 55; *Wulf* 4, 9, 13; *Wife* 15 and 27).

11 See *Beowulf* 1–2, *Andreas* 1, *Exodus* 1, *Daniel* 1, *Phoenix* 1, *Juliana* 1, *Partridge* 1, *Rids* 45, 48, and 67: 1; with the introductory exclamation *Hwæt!* in *Beo, And, Ex,* and *Jul*. Other opening formulas are more characteristic of the Riddles; see the next note. The *Hwæt, we gehyrdon/gefrunon* formula can also be used at point of transition within poems (*Genesis* 939, *Fates of the Apostles* 23 and 63, *Elene* 364, 670, 852, *Christ* 586, *Solomon and Saturn* 179; the last example uses the sg., *ic*).

In a recent study of these formulas, Ward Parks (1987) considers their orality rather than their epic quality; he sees them as reflections of an oral frame of mind, even in the context of written transmission.

12 See *Rids* 5, *14, 17, 18,* 20, 24, 25, 27, 30, 56, 60, 62, 71, 72, 74, 79, 80, 81, 92, 95. *Ic seah*, introducing an interesting object, is also common (*Rids 13, 19, 29, 34, 36, 37, 38, 42, 51, 52, 53, 55, 59, 64, 68, 75, 76, 87*). Their introductory use of the riddlic and the elegiac form, respectively, is one of the reasons for separating *Riddle 60* and *The Husband's Message* (see Textual Notes).

13 This concept embraces, but is not confined to, the theme of exile as classified in formulaic terms by Stanley B. Greenfield (1955). He divides the formulas into those associated with status (e.g. *wineleas wræcca, earm anhaga*), deprivation (past participles like *bereafod* and *bedæled*), state of mind (adjectives such as *hean, earm, geomor, -cearig*), and movement in or into exile (with the word *wræclast*).

14 Cain is described as a *wineleas wrecca* (*Gen* 1051); Nebuchadnezzar in his bestial state as a *wundorlic wrœcca* (*Dan* 633); Satan in Hell is condemned to "follow the paths of exile," *wadan wrœclastas* (*Sat* 120). The use of this kind of imagery in the context of OE biblical epics and saints' lives, specifically in *Andreas* 290–314, *Guthlac* 1346b–79, and *Christ and Satan*, is commented upon by Leonard Frey (1963). In such passages, these and other poems partake of the elegiac quality which is most sustained in the elegies themselves.

15 Cf. the association of *sorh* and *bend* in *Juliana* 624b–26. The binding of frost and cold (*Wan* 102; *Sea* 9 and 32) is a more widespread idea, found, for example, in *Beo* 1133 (*isgebind*), 1609 (*forstes bend*), *Maxims I* 74b–75a (*inbindan/ forstes fetre*). In these three contexts it is not particularly elegiac.

16 Margaret Alexiou observes that in the archaic Greek period praise of the dead was traditionally assigned to the men, lamentation to the women (1974, 105).

Schücking derives the OE elegy from a *sorhleoð* or *sarig sang* (he regards this as a technical term) uttered by one of the mourners at a funeral and lamenting his own bereavement; he places the lamentations of Hildeburh and the nameless *meowle* in this category, and regards the Lament of the Last Survivor and the Father's Lament (*Beo* 2247–66 and 2444–59, resp.) as derived from it. See Schücking 1908, 7–12.

17 See Jordanes, *Getica* 49.256–57; in Mommsen 1882, 124. Jordanes's *History of the Goths* is translated in Mierow 1908; see pp. 80–81 for this passage. Also excerpted in Gordon 1960, 110–11.

18 Ὑπὲρ τῶν πολεμῶν, *Histories of the (Vandal) Wars* 4.6:33; text and translation in Dewing 1916, 262–63.

19 Interpretations of this type have been applied to *Husb* by R.E. Kaske (1967) and Margaret Goldsmith (1975); to *Husb* and *Wife* jointly by M.J. Swanton (1964) and W.F. Bolton (1969). See Part 1, pp. 59–60, above. *Wulf* has not, as far as I know, been explained in this way, but a kind of allegorical solution to the poem as religious riddle was proposed long ago by Henry Morley, who argued that the speaker was the Christian preacher and Wulf the Devil (1888, 224–26).

20 *Rids 25, 42, 44, 45, 54, 61, 62.*

21 *De clade Lindisfarnensis monasterii*; text in Dümmler 1881, 229–35; translation in Calder and Allen 1976, 141–46.

22 *De excidio Thoringiae*; text in Leo 1881, 271–75; translation in Calder and Allen 1976, 137–41.

23 J.E. Cross defines *The Wanderer* as belonging to the genre of *consolatio* found in Christian and classical Latin works (1961a, 63–75). Among the homiletic elegies, *Deor* especially can be classified in this way.

24 Text and translation in Stewart, Rand, and Tester 1973. Boethius is known to have been a Christian, but his *Consolation*, which takes the form of a Socratic

dialogue and is steeped in Plato and classical philosophy, shows no more than an enlightened monotheism.

25 Whitbread suggests that *Wife* and *Husb* represent "somewhat confused attempts ... at a dramatic treatment of the Orpheus legend as told by Boethius (III, met. 12)." For *Wulf* he suggests a possible link with Boethius's tribute to his suffering wife (book 2, prose 4). See Whitbread 1970, 176–79.

26 See Smithers 1957, 148–49.

27 *Ethopoeiam vero illam vocamus, in qua hominis personam fingimus ...*, and *Ethopoeia est, cum sermonem ex aliena persona inducimus ... Etymologiae* 2.14:2 and 2.21:32, resp.; in Lindsay 1911. See Lausberg 1973, 1, §§ 820–29 for other definitions of *ethopoeia*.

28 Bede lists seventeen schemes: prolepsis, zeugma, hypozeuxis, syllepsis, anadiplosis, anaphora, epanalepsis, epizeuxis, paronomasia, schesis onomaton, paromoeon, homeoteleuton, homeoptoton, polyoptoton, hirmos, polysyndeton, dialyton; and thirteen tropes: metaphor, catachresis, metalepsis, metonymy, antonomasia, epitheton, synecdoche, onomatopoeia, periphrasis, hyperbaton (including hysterologia, anastrophe, parenthesis, tmesis, synchysis), hyperbole, allegory (including irony, antiphrasis, enigma, charientismos, paroemia, sarcasm, asteismos), homeosis (including icon, parable, paradigm).

Jackson Campbell (1966) cites a string of rhetorical figures he finds in *Wan*, including a number of the above and some others (pp. 198–201); he assumes that "any Old English poet ... who could read Latin at all" (p. 192) would have used these quite consciously.

29 Alfred's well-known comments about the widespread illiteracy in England when he came to the throne (in 871) and the scarcity of men who could read their service-books in English or translate a composition out of Latin should make us wonder whether all clerics were fully conversant with Latin, even in more auspicious times. His own efforts aimed at providing access to Latin learning in translation. See the Preface to the *Pastoral Care*, in Sweet 1871–72, 2–3.

30 Horace adds that the elegiac metre was subsequently used (in votive epigrams) to express granted prayer (*voti sententia compos*, "sentiment fulfilled in its wish"). C.O. Brink (1971, 166–67) notes that he has deliberately excluded contemporary narrative and amatory elegy. It was assumed in ancient times – by Horace and others – that elegy began as lamentation, but we lack the evidence to support this. It has been argued by Denys Page (1936, 206–30) that a body of early Doric threnodies in elegiac metre existed, of which Andromache's lament in Euripides' play (*Andr* 103–16) is the only survivor, but many scholars doubt that the elegiac metre was originally used for lament. See Bulloch 1985, 33–34; also Part 1, n. 5, above.

31 *Elegiacus autem dictus eo, quod modulatio eiusdem carminis conveniat miseris. Te-*

rentianus hos elegos dicere solet, quod clausula talis tristibus, ut tradunt, aptior esset modis. See *Etymologiae* 1.39:14–15; in Lindsay 1911. This passage is related to Isidore's sources by Jacques Fontaine (1959, 167).

32 *The Phoenix* would fit into Peter Sacks's view of elegy as rooted in the fertility rites associated with death and rebirth, the re-emergence of light, etc. See Sacks 1985, 33–34; also n. 4, above.

33 Ovid is often quoted. The (hexameter) *Metamorphoses* were well known. Of his poetry composed in elegiacs, the *Ars Amatoria* and *Fasti* were available to the Anglo-Saxons, probably the *Amores*, and possibly the *Epistulae ex Ponto*. We lack evidence for the *Heroides* and the *Tristia*, but it is likely that the Anglo-Saxons at least knew *about* them. For the use of the *Heroides*, *Tristia*, and *Ex Ponto* by continental writers of the Carolingian renaissance and later, see Dorothy Robathan (1973, 192–93). For citations of Ovid in Anglo-Latin writers, see J.D.A. Ogilvy (1967, 210–13); the verbal parallels which he notes are not always conclusive. Ogilvy cites two echoes of Propertius in Alcuin (p. 229), which he finds not "overwhelming proof of knowledge." But one of them strikes me as significantly close: with P. *Elegies* 4.1:23 (*saginati lustrabant compita porci*, "[the blood of] fattened swine purified the crossroads"; in Butler 1912, 264), cf. A. *Carmina* 49.9 (*competa lustrat*, "he examines the crossroads" – of the cock looking for food; in Dümmler 1881, 262).

34 A more incidental connection between OE poetry and classical Latin verse is made by Peter Martin, who argues that motifs like the binding of frost (he understands *Wan* 24 and 57 *waþema gebind* in this way), the bridging of ice, and the icicles on the person of the Seafarer (*Sea* 17) derive from classical writers including Virgil and Ovid – for example the description of Scythian winter in *Tristia* 3.10 (Martin 1969, 375–90). Of course, the A-S poets did not need to turn to Latin to observe the effects of cold.

35 *Edmyg Dinbych* is edited with translation and notes in Williams 1972, 155–72; translation in Calder et al. 1983, 57–59. *Stafell Gynddylan* is in Williams 1953, 35–37; translation in Calder, 56–57.

36 Ursula Schaefer (1986) sees this poem in the light of Boniface's correspondence with nuns as a reflection of the need for a friend to provide good counsel and prayer.

37 In a feminist approach to these two poems, Marilynn Desmond calls for their recuperation into the corpus of women's literature, on the grounds that in the context of anonymous composition "the gender of the author becomes insignificant ..., the gender of the speaker ... all-important" (1990, 583). *Wife* and *Wulf* are also related to women's songs, in the sense of poetry about though not necessarily by women, by Lois Bragg (1989), who associates them with later medieval lyrics written in various languages.

38 This passage is quoted by Barbara Raw, who, noting the use of the word *giedd* in *Sea* and *Wife*, theorizes: "It is possible that this word referred to a specific literary genre, the speech of a fictitious character talking of the wisdom which springs from personal experience" (1978, 18). She adds that melancholy is characteristic of the *giedd*. Except when qualified, though, the semantic field of *giedd* is broader than this.

39 Ida Masters Hollowell believes "that *gied* probably had its origin in cult song and magic formulas" (1980, 586). She regards Widsith as a *woðbora*, a kind of seer "closely associated with his *gied*, a formally constructed piece, composed in alliterative lines, and often associated in Old English with wisdom" (p. 585).

40 In his attempt to distinguish between different kinds of oral performance, Jeff Opland comes to the conclusion that *leoð* originally designated an unaccompanied performance of a ritual kind, whether sung or spoken, whereas a *song* could be accompanied (as in *hearpsang*), and that *giedd* was to some extent synonymous with both words. His analysis is devoted mainly to establishing the meaning of *leoð*, and he notes that he has not had the benefit of a complete concordance to OE. See Opland 1980, 246–49.

APPENDIX

Some Analogues

Latin:	*Heroides* 11
	Tristia 3.4b
	Epistulae ex Ponto 3.7
Old Welsh:	*Claf Abercuawg*
	Yr Aelwyd Hon
Old Icelandic:	*Sonatorrek*
	Guðrúnarkviða I
	Guðrúnarhvǫt

*HEROIDES 11: CANACE MACAREO**

Publius Ovidius Naso (Ovid)

Siqua tamen caecis errabunt scripta lituris,
    oblitus a dominae caede libellus erit.
dextra tenet calamum, strictum tenet altera ferrum,
    et iacet in gremio charta soluta meo.
5   haec est Aeolidos fratri scribentis imago;
    sic videor duro posse placere patri.
Ipse necis cuperem nostrae spectator adesset,
    auctorisque oculis exigeretur opus!
ut ferus est multoque suis truculentior Euris,
10   spectasset siccis vulnera nostra genis.
scilicet est aliquid, cum saevis vivere ventis;
    ingenio populi convenit ille sui.
ille Noto Zephyroque et Sithonio Aquiloni
    imperat et pinnis, Eure proterve, tuis.
15   imperat heu! ventis, tumidae non imperat irae,
    possidet et vitiis regna minora suis.
quid iuvat admotam per avorum nomina caelo
    inter cognatos posse referre Iovem?
num minus infestum, funebria munera, ferrum
20   feminea teneo, non mea tela, manu?
O utinam, Macareu, quae nos commisit in unum,
    venisset leto serior hora meo!
cur umquam plus me, frater, quam frater amasti,
    et tibi, non debet quod soror esse, fui?
25   ipsa quoque incalui, qualemque audire solebam,
    nescio quem sensi corde tepente deum.
fugerat ore color; macies adduxerat artus;
    sumebant minimos ora coacta cibos;
nec somni faciles et nox erat annua nobis,
30   et gemitum nullo laesa dolore dabam.
nec cur haec facerem poteram mihi reddere causam
    nec noram quid amans esset; at illud eram.

---

* The *Heroides* (ca 10 BC) are edited in Palmer 1898 (repr. 1967). For the text with facing
translation, see Showerman 1921.

HEROIDES ("HEROINES") 11: CANACE TO MACAREUS

If my writing is lost, hidden by blots, the letter will have been smeared by the blood of its slain mistress. My right hand holds the pen, my other hand a drawn sword, and my paper lies spread out in my lap. This is the picture of Aeolus's daughter writing to her brother; in this way, it seems, I can please my severe father.

I might wish that he were present as a witness of my death, and that the work were finished before the eyes of its instigator! As he is fierce and far more savage than his East Winds, he would have looked dry-eyed on my wounds. To be sure, living with the cruel winds has some effect; he becomes like his people in mood. He rules over Notus, Zephyr, and Sithonian Aquilo, and over your wings, wild East Wind. Alas, he rules the winds but not his own swelling wrath, and the kingdom he possesses is smaller than his own faults. What use for me to approach heaven by my ancestors' names and be able to count Jupiter among my kin? Is the sword that I hold in my woman's hand any less deadly? – my funeral gift, no natural weapon for me.

Oh Macareus, I wish that the hour which made us one had arrived later than my death. Why ever, brother, did you love me more than a brother, and why was I to you what a sister ought not to be? I too glowed, and just as I had heard of felt some god in my burning heart. My colour had fled my face; wasting had come upon my limbs; with unwilling mouth I took little food. Sleep was not easy, a night was a year to me, and I would utter groans though afflicted with no pain. I could give myself no reason why I should do these things, nor did I know what a lover was; but that is what I was.

Prima malum nutrix animo praesensit anili;
    prima mihi nutrix "Aeoli, "dixit, "amas!"
35   erubui, gremioque pudor deiecit ocellos;
    haec satis in tacita signa fatentis erant.
    iamque tumescebant vitiati pondera ventris,
    aegraque furtivum membra gravabat onus.
    quas mihi non herbas, quae non medicamina nutrix
40   attulit audaci supposuitque manu,
    ut penitus nostris – hoc te celavimus unum
    visceribus crescens excuteretur onus!
    a, nimium vivax admotis restitit infans
    artibus et tecto tutus ab hoste fuit!
45   Iam noviens erat orta soror pulcherrima Phoebi,
    denaque luciferos Luna movebat equos.
    nescia quae faceret subitos mihi causa dolores,
    et rudis ad partus et nova miles eram.
    nec tenui vocem. "quid," ait, "tua crimina prodis?"
50   oraque clamantis conscia pressit anus.
    quid faciam infelix? gemitus dolor edere cogit,
    sed timor et nutrix et pudor ipse vetant.
    contineo gemitus elapsaque verba reprendo
    et cogor lacrimas conbibere ipsa meas.
55   mors erat ante oculos, et opem Lucina negabat –
    et grave si morerer mors quoque crimen erat,
    cum super incumbens scissa tunicaque comaque
    pressa refovisti pectora nostra tuis,
    et mihi "vive, soror, soror o carissima," aisti;
60   "vive nec unius corpore perde duos!
    spes bona det vires; fratris nam nupta futura es.
    illius de quo mater et uxor eris."

61 Showerman: *fratri*

The first to have an inkling of my trouble was my nurse, with her old woman's perception; it was my nurse who first said to me, "Daughter of Aeolus, you are in love!" I blushed, and cast my eyes down in shame to my lap. This was enough for a tacit sign of my confession. And then the weight of my defiled womb began to grow, and my secret burden weighed upon my failing limbs. What herbs and medicines did my nurse not bring to me, and apply with audacious hand – this is the only thing I have concealed from you – so that the burden growing deep within my vitals might be driven forth. Oh, only too tenacious of life, the child withstood the arts applied to it and was safe in its shelter from its foe.

Now it was the ninth time that the lovely sister of Phoebus had risen, and the tenth time that the Moon was driving her bright horses. Unrealizing what cause it was that gave me sudden pains, I was unskilled, a new soldier in my labour. I did not hold back my cries. "Why are you betraying your crime?" said my old nurse, and knowing my trouble closed my wailing mouth. Unhappy girl! What was I to do? Pain forced out my groans, but fear and my nurse, and shame itself, forbade them. I stifled my groans, caught back the words that were slipping out, and was forced to swallow my own tears. Death was before my eyes, and Lucina [goddess of birth] refused to help – and if I should die death too would be a heavy crime, when bending over me you parted my clothing and my hair and, pressing my bosom with your own, gave me warmth again, and said to me, "Live, sister, oh dearest sister! Do not destroy two lives in one body! Let good hope give you strength, for you shall be your brother's bride. Of him who made you a mother you shall also be the wife."

Mortua, crede mihi, tamen ad tua verba revixi,
et positum est uteri crimen onusque mei.
65 quid tibi grataris? media sedet Aeolus aula.
crimina sunt oculis subripienda patris.
frondibus infantem ramisque albentis olivae
et levibus vittis sedula celat anus,
fictaque sacra facit dicitque precantia verba.
70 dat populus sacris, dat pater ipse viam.
iam prope limen erat – patrias vagitus ad auris
venit, et indicio proditur ille suo!
eripit infantem mentitaque sacra revelat
Aeolus; insana regia voce sonat.
75 ut mare fit tremulum, tenui cum stringitur aura,
ut quatitur tepido fraxinus icta Noto,
sic mea vibrari pallentia membra videres;
quassus ab inposito corpore lectus erat.
inruit et nostrum vulgat clamore pudorem
80 et vix a misero continet ore manus.
ipsa nihil praeter lacrimas pudibunda profudi;
torpuerat gelido lingua retenta metu.
Iamque dari parvum canibus avibusque nepotem
iusserat, in solis destituitque locis.
85 vagitus dedit ille miser – sensisse putares,
quaque suum poterat voce rogabat avum.
quid mihi tunc animi credis, germane, fuisse –
nam potes ex animo colligere ipse tuo,
cum mea me coram silvas inimicus in altas
90 viscera montanis ferret edenda lupis?
exierat thalamo. Tunc demum pectora plangi
contigit inque meas unguibus ire genas.

76 Showerman: *fraxina virga*

Dying, believe me, nevertheless I revived at your words, and gave birth to the guilty burden of my womb. But what reason was there to rejoice? Aeolus sat in the middle of his hall. My sins must be removed from my father's eyes. My diligent old nurse concealed the child with leaves and branches of silvery olive and with light ribbons, did pretended sacrificial rites, and uttered words of prayer. The people made way for the sacrifice; even my father made way. And now the threshold was near – when to my father's ears came the crying of a child, and he was betrayed by the evidence that he himself gave! Aeolus seized the baby and laid bare the false sacrifice. The palace resounded with his cries of rage. Just as the sea shivers when touched by a light breeze, as the ash is tossed when struck by the warm South Wind, thus you might see my pale limbs shudder. My bed shook as I lay upon it. My father rushed in, published my disgrace with loud voice, and scarcely kept his hands from my wretched face. In my shame I uttered nothing but sobs; icy fear had tied my frozen tongue.

And then he had ordered his little grandson to be given to the dogs and birds of prey, and abandoned in the wilderness. The wretched baby began to cry – you would think that it knew, and with what voice it could appealed to its grandfather. What kind of feelings do you think I had then, brother – you can gather from your own, when before my eyes my hostile father carried the child of my womb to the deep woods, to be devoured by mountain wolves? He left the room. Then at last it was that I beat my breast and drove my nails into my cheeks.

Interea patrius vultu maerente satelles
   venit et indignos edidit ore sonos:
95 "Aeolus hunc ensem mittit tibi" – tradidit ensem –
   "et iubet ex merito scire quid iste velit."
scimus, et utemur violento fortiter ense.
   pectoribus condam dona paterna meis.
his mea muneribus, genitor, conubia donas?
100 hac tua dote, pater, filia dives erit?
tolle procul, decepte, faces, Hymenaee, maritas
   et fuge turbato tecta nefanda pede!
ferte faces in me quas fertis, Erinyes atrae,
   et meus ex isto luceat igne rogus!
105 nubite felices Parca meliore sonores,
   amissae memores sed tamen este mei!
Quid puer admisit tam paucis editus horis?
   quo laesit facto vix bene natus avum?
si potuit meruisse necem, meruisse putetur –
110 a, miser admisso plectitur ille meo!
nate, dolor matris, rapidarum praeda ferarum!
   ei mihi! natali dilacerate tuo!
nate, parum fausti miserabile pignus amoris!
   haec tibi prima dies, haec tibi summa fuit.
115 non mihi te licuit lacrimis perfundere iustis,
   in tua non tonsas ferre sepulcra comas.
non super incubui, non oscula frigida carpsi.
   diripiunt avidae viscera nostra ferae.
Ipsa quoque infantis cum vulnere prosequar umbras
120 nec mater fuero dicta nec orba diu.
tu tamen, o frustra miserae sperate sorori,
   sparsa, precor, nati collige membra tui,
et refer ad matrem socioque inpone sepulcro,
   urnaque nos habeat quamlibet arta duos.
125 vive memor nostri, lacrimasque in vulnera funde,
   neve reformida corpus amantis amans.
tura rogo placitae nimium mandata sororis
   tu fer; mandatum persequar ipsa patris!

127–28 Showerman; *tu, rogo, dilectae …/perfer*

Meanwhile a guard of my father's came with sorrowful face, and uttered these unworthy words: "Aeolus sends this sword to you" – he handed me the sword, "and commands you to know by your desert what this weapon means." I know, and will bravely use the violent sword. I will put my father's gift in my breast. Is it with presents like these, my begetter, that you endow my marriage? Is it with a dowry like this, father, that your daughter shall be rich? Take far away, deceived Hymen [god of marriage], your wedding torches, and with frightened foot flee this cursed dwelling! Bring for my wedding torches the ones you bear, dark Furies, and with that fire light my funeral pyre! Marry happily, my sisters, and with a better Fate, but still be mindful of me whom you have lost!

What crime did the little boy commit, given so few hours of life? By what deed did he, scarce fully born, injure his grandfather? If the child could have deserved death, let it be thought that he deserved it. Oh wretched baby! He is punished for my crime. Son, your mother's grief and prey of ravening beasts! Alas for me! Torn to pieces the day of your birth! Son, wretched token of my too unblest love! This was your first day, this your last. It was not permitted that I should shed the proper tears for you, nor carry shorn locks to your tomb. I have not bent over you, nor taken a cold kiss. Greedy beasts are tearing the child of my own entrails.

I too with my death-wound will follow the shades of my child, and will not long have been called a mother or bereaved. But you in whom your wretched sister had vain hope, gather, I pray, the scattered limbs of your son, bring them to their mother, place them in a shared grave, and let one urn, however meagre, hold us both. Live, mindful of me, shed tears on my wounds, and as a lover do not shun your lover's corpse. Will you bring incense for the pyre at the behest of your too pleasing sister; I myself will perform the behest of my father!

*TRISTIA 3.4B**

Ovid

Proxima sideribus tellus Erymanthidos Ursae
  me tenet, adstricto terra perusta gelu.
Bosphoros et Tanais superant Scythiaeque paludes
(50)   vix satis et noti nomina pauca loci.
  5 ulterius nihil est nisi non habitabile frigus.
    heu, quam vicina est ultima terra mihi!
  at longe patria est, longe carissima coniunx,
    quicquid et haec nobis post duo dulce fuit.
(55) sic tamen haec adsunt ut quae contingere non est
  10   corpore sunt animo cuncta videnda meo.
  ante oculos errant domus, urbsque, et forma locorum,
    acceduntque suis singula facta locis.
  coniugis ante oculos, sicut praesentis, imago est.
(60)   illa meos casus ingravat, illa levat.
  15 ingravat hoc, quod abest; levat hoc, quod praestat amorem
    inpositumque sibi firma tuetur onus.
  vos quoque pectoribus nostris haeretis, amici,
    dicere quos cupio nomine quemque suo.
(65) sed timor officium cautus compescit, et ipsos
  20   in nostro pone carmine nolle puto.
  ante volebatis, gratique erat instar honoris,
    versibus in nostris nomina vestra legi.
  quod quoniam est anceps, intra mea pectora quemque
(70)   adloquar, et nulli causa timoris ero.
  25 nec meus indicio latitantes versus amicos
    protrahet. oculte si quis amabat, amet.
  scite tamen, quamvis longe regione remotus
    absim, vos animo semper adesse meo.
(75) et qua quisque potest aliqua mala nostra levate;
  30   fidem proiecto neve negate manum.
  prospera sic maneat vobis fortuna, nec umquam
    contacti simili sorte rogetis idem.

---

* The *Tristia* (ca 9–10 AD) is edited in Luck 1967–77. For text with facing translation, see Wheeler 1924.

TRISTIA ("SORROWS") 3.4B

The land closest to the constellation of the Erymanthian [Great] Bear holds me, a land seared with gripping cold. Then there are the Bosporus, the Don, the marshes of Scythia, and a few names in a region scarcely even known. Beyond there is nothing but uninhabitable cold. How close to me is the very edge of the world! But my homeland is far away, far away my beloved wife, and whatever was sweet to me after these two. Yet in a way these things are present, although I cannot touch them bodily: they are all visible to my mind's eye. My home, the city, and the appearance of places pass before my eyes; each happening with its scene comes to me. Before my eyes is the image of my wife, as if she were really here. It is she who both increases and lightens my misfortunes. She makes them worse because she is not here; she lightens them because she offers her love and supports with steadfastness the burden laid on her. You also are fixed in my heart, friends, whom I wish I could mention, each one by name. But cautious fear holds me back from that obligation, and I think that you yourselves would not wish to be included in my poem.

Once you wished it, and it was like a welcome honour to have your names read in my verses. But since it is risky I will address each one within my heart and be a cause of fear to no one. My verse will give no token to bring to light my hidden friends. If anyone loved me in secret, let him love me now. But know, in however far-removed a region I am, that you are always present in my heart. Relieve my sufferings in whatever way each of you can; do not deny an outcast a faithful hand. So may fortune remain kind to you, and may you never meet with the same fate or make the same request.

*EPISTULAE EX PONTO 3.7**

Ovid

Verba mihi desunt eadem tam saepe roganti,
    iamque pudet vanas fine carere preces,
taedia consimili fieri de carmine vobis,
    quidque petam cunctos edidicisse reor.
5 nostraque quid portet iam nostis epistula, quamvis
    charta sit a vinclis non labefacta suis.
ergo mutetur scripti sententia nostri,
    ne totiens contra quam rapiens amnis eam.
quod bene de vobis speravi ignoscite, amici:
10   talia peccandi iam mihi finis erit.
nec gravis uxori dicar, quae scilicet in me
    quam proba tam timida est experiensque parum.
hoc quoque, Naso, feres: etenim peiora tulisti.
    iam tibi sentiri sarcina nulla potest.
15 ductus ab armento taurus detrectat aratrum,
    subtrahit et duro colla novella iugo.
nos, quibus adsuevit fatum crudeliter uti,
    ad mala iam pridem non sumus ulla rudes.
venimus in Geticos fines; moriamur in illis.
20   Parcaque ad extremum qua mea coepit eat.
spem iuvat amplecti – quae non iuvat inrita semper,
    et fieri cupias siqua, futura putes:
proximus huic gradus est bene desperare salutem,
    seque semel vera scire perisse fide.

---

* The *Ex Ponto* (ca 13 AD) is edited in Lenz 1938. For text with facing translation, see
Wheeler 1924.

LETTERS FROM PONTUS 3.7

I am making the same petition so often that words fail me, and now I am ashamed that my empty prayers are without an end. I think that the same song is becoming a weariness to you and that you have all learned by heart what I request. You already know what my letter conveys, although the paper has not yet been broken open from its bonds. Therefore let the intent of my writing be changed, so that I shall not swim so many times against the current that carries it away. Forgive me for hoping well of you, friends; now this will be an end for me, who have trespassed so many times. I will not be called a burden to my wife, who, indeed, is as timid as she is honourable towards me, and little venturesome. You will endure this too, Naso, for you have borne worse. No load can be felt by you now. The bull led from the herd refuses the plough, and draws back his unaccustomed neck from the hard yoke. I, whom Fate made used to cruel treatment, have long been experienced in all ills. I came to the lands of the Getae; let me die there. Let my Fate take to the limit the course which she has begun. It helps to cherish a hope, even if the hope is of no avail and always vain. If you long for something to happen, let yourself think it will come to be. The next step is to despair completely of salvation, and for the first time to know with sure conviction that you are lost.

25   curando fieri quaedam maiora videmus
        vulnera, quae melius non tetigisse fuit.
    mitius ille perit subita qui mergitur unda
        quam sua qui tumidis brachia lassat aquis.
    cur ego concepi Scythicis me posse carere
30   finibus et terra prosperiore frui?
    cur aliquid de me speravi lenius umquam?
        an fortuna mihi sic mea nota fuit?
    torqueor en gravius, repetitaque forma locorum
        exilium renovat triste recensque facit.
35   est tamen utilius, studium cessare meorum,
        quam quas admorint non valuisse preces.
    magna quidem res est quam non audetis, amici.
        sed si quis peteret, qui dare vellet erat.
    dummodo non nobis hoc Caesaris ira negarit,
40   fortiter Euxinis immoriemur aquis.

We see that some wounds get worse when they are treated, which it would have been better not to touch. The man who sinks right away beneath the water dies a gentler death than he who tires out his arms in the swelling waves. Why did I imagine that I could be free of the Scythian lands and enjoy a kinder country? Why did I ever hope for any mitigation of my lot? Was this the kind of fortune I had come to know as mine? Oh, I am tortured worse, and the repeated image of places renews my unhappy exile and makes it fresh. But it is better for the efforts of my friends to cease than for the prayers they have brought to be of no account. The affair which you dare not broach is a serious one, friends. But if anyone should make the request, there would be someone willing to grant it. If only Caesar's anger does not deny me this, I will die bravely by the waters of the Euxine sea.

*CLAF ABERCUAWG**

1
Goreiste' ar fryn a erfyn fy mryd,
A hefyd ni'm cychwyn.
Byr fy nhaith; diffaith fy nhyddyn.

2
Llym awel, llwm benedr biw.
Pan orwisg coed tegliw
Haf, terydd glaf wyf heddiw.

3
Nid wyf anhyed; miled ni chadwaf;
Ni allaf ddarymred.
Tra fo da gan gog, caned!

4
Cog lafar a gan ddydd.
Gyfrau eichiawg yn nolydd Cuawg.
Gwell corawg na chybydd.

5
Yn Aber Cuawg yd ganant gogau
Ar gangau blodeuawg.
Cog lafar, caned yrhawg.

6
Yn Aber Cuawg yd ganant gogau
Ar gangau blodeuawg.
Gwae glaf a'u clyw yn fodawg.

7
Yn Aber Cuawg cogau a ganant.
Ys adfant gan fy mryd
A'u cigleu nas clyw hefyd.

* This text of *Claf Abercuawg* (late ninth century?) uses modernized spelling, mainly as in Ford 1974, 66–74. The standard edition is Williams 1953: text, pp. 23–27; notes (in Welsh), pp. 160–75.

THE SICK MAN OF ABERCUAWG*

1

My mind implores to go and sit on a hill, but I cannot set off. My journey's short; my dwelling-place desolate.

2

The wind is sharp, the cowherds bare. When the trees put on fair summer colour, I am extremely ill today.

3

I am not sprightly; I do not keep a host; I cannot move about. Let the cuckoo sing while it will!

4

A loquacious cuckoo sings at daybreak a loud song in the meadows of Cuawg. A prodigal is better than a miser.

5

In Abercuawg cuckoos sing on flowery branches. Loquacious cuckoo, let it sing awhile.

6

In Abercuawg cuckoos sing on flowery branches. Woe to the sick man who hears them constantly.

7

In Abercuawg cuckoos sing. It is bitter to my mind that those who heard them do not hear them too.

* Some of the stanzas are very obscure and the translation is uncertain.

8

Neus endewais i gog ar eiddorwg bren.
Neur laeswys fy nghylchwy:
Edlid a gerais neud mwy.

9

Yn y fan odduwch llon ddar
Ydd endewais i lais adar.
Cog fan, cof gan bawb a gar.

10

Cethlydd cathl fodawg; hiraethawg ei llef,
Taith oddef tuth hebawg;
Cog freuer yn Aber Cuawg.

11

Gorddyar adar, gwlyb naint;
Llewychyd lloer, oer dewaint.
Crai fy mryd rhag gofid haint.

12

Gwyn gwarthaf [bre, gwlyb] naint, dewaint hir.
Ceinmygir pob cywraint.
Dylywn pwyth hun y henaint.

13

Gorddyar adar, gwlyb gro.
Dail cwyddid; difrid difro.
Ni wadaf, wyf claf heno.

14

Gorddyar adar, gwlyb traeth.
Eglur nwyfre; ehalaeth
Ton. Gwyw calon rhag hiraeth.

15

Gorddyar adar, gwlyb traeth.
Eglur ton tuth ehalaeth.
Angred ym mabolaeth,
Carwn be'i caffwn etwaeth.

16

Gorddyar adar ar Edrywy ardd.
Ban llef cwn yn niffaith.
Gorddyar adar eilwaith.

8

I listened to a cuckoo on an ivy-clad tree. My clothing has become slack: my grief for those I loved is greater.

9

I listened to the voice of the birds above the mighty oak. Loud cuckoo, everyone remembers what he loves.

10

Singer of a constant song; its cry is full of longing; wandering its movement like a hawk's; loud-voiced cuckoo in Abercuawg.

11

Loud are the birds, wet the brooks; the moon shines brightly, the dead of night is cold. My mind is sore because of the pain of sickness.

12

Hilltops are white, brooks wet, long the dead of night. Every curiosity is admired. I have the right to the reward of sleep in old age.

13

Noisy are the birds, wet the shingle. The leaves fall; the exile is dejected. I do not deny it, I am sick tonight.

14

Noisy are the birds, wet the shore. Bright is the sky, very broad the wave. A heart is withered by longing.

15

Noisy are the birds, wet the shore. Bright is the wave with its broad motion. What was loved in youth, I would love to have it again.

16

Noisy are the birds on high Edrywy. Loud the baying of dogs in desolate places. Noisy are the birds again.

17
Cyntefin: cain pob amad.
Pan frysiant cedwyr i gad,
Mi nid af; anaf ni'm gad.

18
Cyntefin: cain ar ystre.
Pan frys cedwyr i gadle,
Mi nid af; anaf a'm de.

19
Llwyd gwarthaf mynydd, brau blaen onn.
O ebyr dyhepgyr ton
Pefr. Pell chwerthin o'm calon.

20
Ys im[i] heddiw pen y mis
Yn y westfa ydd edewis.
Crai fy mryd; cryd a'm dewis.

21
Amlwg golwg gwyliadur
Gwnelid syberwyd segur.
Crai fy mryd; clefyd a'm cur.

22
Alaf yn ail, mail am fedd.
Nid eiddun dedwydd dyhedd.
Amaerwy adnabod amynedd.

23
Alaf yn ail, mail am lad.
Llithredawr llyry, llon cawad,
A dwfn rhyd. Berwid bryd brad.

24
Berwid brad anfad ober.
Bydda[w]d dolur pan burer:
Gwerthu bychod er llawer.

25
Peridor pair i enwir.
Pan farno Dofydd, ddydd hir,
Tywyll fydd gar; golau gwir.

17

Early summer: every growth is lovely. When warriors hasten to battle, I cannot go; a wound will not allow me.

18

Early summer: fine on the borderland. When warriors hasten to the field of battle, I cannot go; a wound afflicts me.

19

Grey is the mountain peak, fragile the tips of the ash. From estuaries a bright wave flows. Laughter is far from my heart.

20

It is the end of the month for me today in the lodging which he has left. Sore is my mind; fever has seized me.

21

Clear is the sight of the guard. Idleness allows a man to be noble. Sore is my mind; sickness wastes me.

22

Cattle in cowsheds, mead in the bowl. The fortunate one does not long for discord. Patience is the girdle of knowing.

23

Cattle in cowsheds, beer in the bowl. Slippery are the paths, fierce the shower, and deep the ford. The mind brews treachery.

24

Treachery brews a wicked deed. There will be pain when it is purified, the selling of little for much.

25

A cauldron will be prepared for the wicked. When the Lord judges, on that long day, dark will the false be; bright the true.

26

Cerygl yn ddyrch mad, cyrchyniad cewig.
Llawen gwyr odduwch llad.
Crin calaf, alaf yn eiliad.

27

Ciglef don drom ei tholo.
Fan y rhwng gra[ea]n a gro.
Crai fy mryd rhad lledfryd heno.

28

Osglwg blaen derw, chwerw chwaeth onn;
Chweg efwr, chwerthiniad ton.
Ni chel grudd gystudd calon.

29

Ymwng uchenaid a ddynaid arnaf
Yn ol fy ngorddyfnaid.
Ni ad Duw dda i ddiriaid.

30

Da i ddiriaid ni ader,
Namyn tristyd a phryder.
Nid adwna Duw ar a wnel.

31

Oedd macwy mab claf, oedd goewin gynran
Yn llys fre[e]nin.
Boed gwyl Duw wrth eddein.

32

O'r a wneler yn nerwdy
Ys diriaid yr a'i dderlly;
Cas dyn yman, cas Duw fry.

26

Chalices are raised, the attacker ready. Cheerful are men over beer. Withered is the reed, the cattle in cowsheds.

27

I have heard the heavy-thudding wave loud between the gravel and the pebbles. Sore is my mind from dejection tonight.

28

Bushy is the top of the oak, bitter the taste of the ash; sweet the cow-parsnip, laughing the wave. The cheek cannot hide the heart's pain.

29

Often a sigh comes upon me, as is habitual with me. God allows no good to the unfortunate one.

30

No good is allowed to the unfortunate one, only sadness and anxiety. God does not undo whatever he does.

31

The sick man was a young man once, a bold warrior in the king's court. May God be gentle with the outcast.

32

Whatever may be done in an oratory, wretched is he who reads it; hated by man here, hated by God on high.

*YR AELWYD HON**

1

Yr aelwyd hon a'i goglyd gawr –
Mwy gorddyfnasai ar ei llawr
Medd a meddwon [yn] eiriawl.

2

Yr aelwyd hon, neus cudd dynad –
Tra fu fyw ei gwercheidwad.

....

3

Yr aelwyd hon, neus cudd glesin –
Ym myw Owain ac Elphin
Berwasai ei phair breiddin.

4

Yr aelwyd hon, neus cudd callawdr llwyd –
Mwy gorddyfnasai am ei bwyd
Cleddyfal dyfal diarswyd.

5

Yr aelwyd hon, neus cudd cain fieri –
Coed cynneuawg oedd iddi:
Gorddyfnasai Reged roddi.

6

Yr aelwyd hon, neus cudd drain –
Mwy gorddyfnasai ei chyngrain
Cynwynas cyweithas Owain.

7

Yr aelwyd hon, neus cudd myr –
Mwy gorddyfnasai babir
Gloyw a chyfeddau cywir.

* This text of *Yr Aelwyd Hon* (late ninth century?) uses modernized spelling mainly as in
  Ford 1974, 114–17. For an unmodernized text, see Williams 1953: text, pp. 18–19; notes
  (Welsh), pp. 143–48.

THIS HEARTH*

1

This hearth, which greyness covers – more habitual on its floor were mead and petitioning mead-drinkers.

2

This hearth, nettles hide it – whilst its guardian was alive ...

3

This hearth, borage hides it – in the time of Owain and Elphin its cauldron boiled prey.

4

This hearth, grey lichen hides it – more accustomed was it with furious, fearless sword-strokes about its food.

5

This hearth, fair briars hide it – it once had burning logs: Rheged was accustomed to giving.

6

This hearth, thorns hide it – its warriors would have been more accustomed to the favour of generous Owain.

7

This hearth, ants hide it – more accustomed was it to rush-candles and loyal drinking-companions.

* Written about the ruined hall of Urien, Prince of Rheged. Urien ruled in Rheged (now the eastern half of Galloway) in the sixth century. Owen and Elphin were his sons.

8
Yr aelwyd hon, neus cudd tafawl –
Mwy gorddyfnasai ar ei llawr
Medd a meddwon [yn] eiriawl.

9
Yr aelwyd hon, neus cladd hwch –
Mwy gorddyfnasai elwch
Gwyr ac am gyrn cyfeddwch.

10
Yr aelwyd hon, neus cladd cywen –
Nis eiddigafai anghen
Ym myw Owain ac Urien.

11
Yr ystwffwl hwn, a'r hwn draw –
Mwy gorddyfnasai amdanaw
Elwch llu a llwybr arllaw.

8

This hearth, dock-leaves hide it – more habitual on its floor were mead and mead-drinkers petitioning.

9

This hearth, where a pig roots – more accustomed was it to the joyful shouting of men and carousing around the mead-horns.

10

This hearth, where a chicken roots – in the lifetime of Owain and Urien, want did not afflict it.

11

This column, and that one there – more habitual around them were the joyful shouting of the host and a pathway to the bestowing of gifts.

SONATORREK*

Egill Skallagrímsson

1

Mjǫk erum tregt   tungu at hrœra
eðr loptvægi   ljóðpundara.
Era nú vænlegr   um Viðris þýfi,
né hógdrœgt   úr hugar fylgsni.

2

Era auðþeystr   þvíat ekki veldr
hǫfuglegr,   úr hyggju stað
fagnafundr   Friggjar niðja
ár borinn   úr Jǫtunheimum.

3

Lastalauss   er lifnaði
á Nǫkkvers   nǫkkva bragi.
Jǫtunshals   undir flota
Náins niðr   fyr naustdyrum.

4

Þvíat ætt mín   á enda stendr,
sem hræbarmr   hlynjar markar.
Era karskr maðr   sá er kǫggla berr
frænda hrørs   af fletjum niðr.

5

Þó mun ek mitt   ok móður hrør
fǫður fall   fyrst um telja.
Þat ber ek út   úr orðhofi
mærðar timbr   máli laufgat.

---

* For MS variants, textual problems, and emendations in *Sonatorrek* (ca 960), see Helgason 1961, 29–38, and Turville-Petre 1976, 27–41.

*LOSS OF SONS**

1

It is very difficult for me to move my tongue or set in motion the balance of song. There is now little hope of Odin's plunder [poetry]; it is not easily drawn from the heart's hiding-place.

2

It does not flow easily from the mind's abode – heavy grief stands in the way – the joyful finding [the mead of poetry] of Frigg's kinsfolk brought long ago from the realm of giants.

3

Blameless was that gift when it came to life on [the Dwarf] Nǫkkver's ship [poetry]. The sea, poured from wounds in the Giant's [Ymir's] neck, flowed beneath Nainn's boat-shed door [the cliff where Egill's sons are buried].

4

For my line stands at its end, like the dead trunk of the forest maple. It is not a happy man who carries out of his house the limbs of his kinsman's corpse.

5

But first I will relate my mother's death and my father's fall. I will bring out of the temple of words [mouth] proud timber bearing leaves of speech [for a eulogy].

* Composed after the death of Egill's son Bǫðvarr by drowning in a shipwreck. His son Gunnar had died of fever shortly before.

Explanations of obscure names, allusions, and kennings are added in the translation. The meaning is often uncertain.

6

Grimmt várum hlið   þat er hrǫnn um braut
fǫður míns   á frændgarði.
Veit ek ófullt   ok opit standa
sonar skarð   er mér sjár um vann.

7

Mjǫk hefr Rán   ryskt um mik;
em ek ofsnauðr   at ástvinum.
Sleit marr bǫnd   minnar ættar,
snarran þátt   af sjǫlfum mér.

8

Veiztu ef sǫk   sverði of rækak
var ǫlsmiðr   allr tíma.
Hroða varbrœðr   ef vega mættak
fœra ek andvígr   Ægis mani.

9

En ek ekki   eiga þóttumk
sakar afl   við súðbana,
þvíat alþjóð   fyr augum verðr
gamals þegns   gengileysi.

10

Mik hefr marr   miklu ræntan.
Grimmt er fall   frænda at telja,
síðan er minn   á munvega
ættar skjǫldr   aflífi hvarf.

11

Veit ek þat sjalfr   at í syni mínum
vara ills þegns   efni vaxit,
ef sá randviðr   røskvask næði
unz her-Gauts   hendr of tœki.

12

Æ lét flest   þat er faðir mælti,
þótt ǫll þjóð   annat segði;
ok mér upp helt   um herbergi
ok mik afl   mest um studdi.

6

Grim was the gap which the wave broke open in my father's family-enclosure. Empty and open wide I know my son's place stands, the breach which the sea made for me.

7

Rán [the sea-goddess] has shaken me very hard; I am cut off from dear friends. The sea has severed the bond of my family, a stout strand of my very self.

8

You know that if I could pursue the offence with the sword, the alesmith [the foam-brewing sea-god] would be at the end of his days. If I were able to wield arms I would go fighting against Ægir, sworn brother of the storm, and his wife [Rán].

9

But I felt that I had not the strength to fight against the sea that kills ships. For an old man's helplessness will appear before the eyes of all.

10

Much has the sea torn from me. It is cruel to tell the death of my kin, since the shield of my family passed away from life down the road to bliss.

11

I know myself that no bad man would have come to maturity in my son if that shield-tree [warrior] had been able to grow to his prime before the hands of Odin took him hence.

12

He always valued most what his father spoke, though everyone else said otherwise. He supported me in my householding and was the chief stay of my strength.

13
Opt kemr mér   mána bjarnar
í byrvind   brœðraleysi
hyggjumk um,   er hildr þróask,
nýsumk hins   ok hygg at því:

14
Hverr mér hugaðr   á hlið standi
annar þegn   við óðræði.
Þarf ek þess opt   of þvergǫrum
verð ek varfleygr   er vinir þverra.

15
Mjǫk er torfyndr   sá er trúa knegum
of alþjóð   Elgjar galga
því at niflgóðr   niðja steypir
bróður hrer   við baugum selr.

16
Finn ek þat opt   er fjár beiðir
....

17
Þat er ok mælt   at enginn geti
sonar iðgjǫld   nema sjalfr ali
enn þann nið   er ǫðrum sé
borinn maðr   í bróður stað.

18
Erumka þokt   þjóða sinni
þótt sérhverr   sátt um haldi
Burr er Bileygs   i bœ kominn
kvánar son   kynnis leita.

19
En mér fannsk   í fǫstum þokk
hrosta hilmir   á hendi standa.
Máka ek upp   jǫrðu grímu
rýnnis reið   réttri halda,

20
Síz son minn   sóttar brími
heiptuglegr   úr heimi nam,
þann er ek veit   at varnaði
vamma varr   við vámæli.

13

My mind, the breeze of the giant, often recalls the loss of my brother. I think of it when battle grows fierce. I look all around for him, and wonder this:

14

What other thane will stand boldly by my side in violent battle? I often need this in the face of those who come against me. I grow cautious and flee as friends grow fewer.

15

It is very hard to find anyone I can trust among all the people of Odin's gallows [Yggdrasil, the world-tree]. He who accepts compensation in money for the slain body of his brother evilly casts down his kin.

16

I often find it so when he asks for money ...

17

It is said too that no one gets compensation for his son unless he himself brings forth yet another son, who will be in the place of the other, a man born in his brother's stead.

18

The company of men is disagreeable to me, although each one keeps the peace. My son, the child of my wife, has come into the castle of Odin the Poor-Sighted, to seek his kin.

19

It seemed to me that the god who brews ale [Ægir] was standing relentlessly opposed to me. I cannot hold up my head erect, the chariot of thought,

20

Since the deadly fire of sickness took my son from the world, him who I know shunned evil speech, wary of faults.

21

Þat man ek enn   er upp um hóf
í goðheim   Gauta spjalli,
ættar ask,   þann er óx af mér
ok kynvið   kvánar minnar.

22

Átta ek gott   við geirs dróttinn;
gerðumk tryggr   at trúa hánum
áðr vinátt   vagna rúni,
sigrhǫfundr   um sleit við mik.

23

Blótka ek því   bróður Vílis,
goðjaðar   at ek gjarn sék.
Þó hefr Míms vinr   mér um fengnar
bǫlva bœtr   ef hit betra telk.

24

Gáfumk íþrótt   ulfs um bági
vígi vanr   vammi firrða
ok þat geð   er ek gerða mér
vísa fjandr   af vélundum.

25

Nú er mér torvelt;   Tveggja bága
ok Nara nipt   á nesi stendr.
Skal ek þó glaðr   með góðan vilja
ok óhryggr   Heljar bíða.

21

I still remember when the friend of the Gauts [Odin] raised up to the home of the gods the ash-tree of my family, which grew from me and from my wife's stock.

22

I possessed the favour of the lord of the spear [Odin]; I grew trusting to believe in him, until the friend of chariots, the ruler of victory, broke friendship with me.

23

It is not because I am eager that I sacrifice to Odin, protector of the gods and brother of Vilir. Yet Odin, friend of Mimir, has granted me compensation for my ills, if I take better account.

24

The enemy of Fenriswolf [Odin], the god used to battle, gave me the flawless art of poetry and the wits to point out dissemblers as foes.

25

Now it is hard for me. [Hel,] the sister of Nari and Odin's enemy [Fenriswolf], is standing on the headland [where Egill's sons are buried]. Yet glad and with good will, undejected, I shall await Hel [the goddess of death].

GUÐRÚNARKVIÐA IN FYRSTA*

Guðrún sat yfir Sigurði dauðom. Hon grét eigi sem aðrar konor, enn hon var búin til at springa af harmi. Til gengo bæði konor ok karlar at hugga hana; enn þat var eigi auðvelt. Þat er sǫgn manna, at Guðrún hefði etið af Fáfnis hjarta ok hon skilði því fugls rǫdd. Þetta er enn kveðit um Guðrúno:

1
Ár var þatz Guðrún   gorðiz at deyja
er hon sat sorgfull   yfir Sigurði.
Gerðit hon hiúfra   né hǫndom slá,
ne kveina um   sem konor aðrar.

2
Gengo jarlar   alsnotrir fram,
þeir er harðz hugar   hána lǫtto.
Þeygi Guðrún   gráta mátti,
svá var hon móðug,   mundi hon springa.

3
Sáto ítrar   jarla brúðir
gulli búnar,   fyr Guðrúno.
Hver sagði þeira   sinn oftrega
þann er bitrastan   um beðit hafði.

4
Þá kvað Gjaflaug,   Gjúka systir:
"Mik veit ek á moldo   munar lausasta.
Hefi ek fimm vera   forspell beðit,
þriggja dœtra,   þriggja systra,
átta brœðra,   þó ek ein lifi."

5
Þeygi Guðrún   gráta mátti;
svá var hon móðug   at mǫg dauðan
ok harðhuguð   um hrer fylkis.

* For textual variants and glossary to *Guðrúnarkiða in Fyrsta* (tenth or eleventh century?), see Neckel-Kuhn 1983, 201–6, and 1968, resp.

THE FIRST LAY OF GUTHRUN

Guthrun sat over the dead Sigurd. She did not weep like other women, but she was ready to burst with grief. Both women and men went to her to cheer her, but it was not easy. They say that Guthrun had eaten [the dragon] Fafnir's heart and that she understood the speech of birds. This is a lay about Guthrun.

1

Once, Guthrun was prepared to die, as she sat grieving over Sigurd. She did not lament, nor wring her hands, nor wail like other women.

2

Very wise earls went to her to relieve her hard heart. But Guthrun was not able to weep. She was so incensed she could have burst.

3

Adorned with gold, the exquisite wives of the earls sat by Guthrun. Each one related her own woe, the bitterest that she had endured.

4

Then Gjaflaug, Gjúki's sister, spoke: "I know that I am the most joyless person on earth. I have endured the loss of five husbands, three daughters, three sisters, eight brothers, yet I alone live."

5

Nevertheless Guthrun could not weep, so incensed was she at her husband's death, and hard of heart over the prince's body.

6

Þá kvað þat Herborg,   Húnalanz drótning:
"Hefi ek harðara harm   at segja.
Mínir sjau synir   sunnan lanz,
verr inn átti,   í val fello;

7

Faðir ok móðir,   fjórir brœðr,
þau á vági   vindr of lék,
barði bára   við borðþili.

8

Sjálf skylda ek gǫfga,   sjálf skylda ek gǫtva,
sjálf skylda ek hǫndla   helfor þeira
þat ek alt um beið   ein misseri,
svá at mér maðr engi   munar leitaði.

9

Þá varð ek hapta   ok hernuma
sams misseris   síðan verða.
Skylda ek skreyta   ok skúa binda
hersis kván   hverjan morgin.

10

Hon œgði mér   af afbrýði,
ok hǫrðom mik   hǫggom keyrði.
Fann ek húsguma   hvergi in betra,
enn húsfreyjo   hvergi verri."

11

Þeygi Guðrún   gráta mátti,
svá var hon móðug   at mǫg dauðan
ok harðhuguð   um hrer fylkis.

12

Þá kvað þat Gullrǫnd,   Gjúka dóttir.
"Fá kanntu, fóstra,   þótt þú fróð sér,
ungo vífi   annspjǫll bera."
Varaði hon at hylja   um hrør fylkis.

13

Svipti hon blæjo   af Sigurði
ok vatt vengi   fyr vífs knjám:
"Líttu á liúfan,   legðu munn við grǫn,
sem þú hálsaðir   heilan stilli."

6

Then Herborg, Lady of the Huns, spoke: "I have a harsher grief to tell. My seven sons fell in battle in a southern land, and my husband the eighth;

7

My father and mother too, and my four brothers, whom the storm sported with at sea when the swelling wave beat against the ship's bulwarks.

8

With my own hands I had to adorn them, bury them, lay them out for their Hel-journey. All that I endured in six months. And no man comforted me.

9

After that, in the same six months, I became a captive and bondwoman. Every morning I had to dress the chieftain's wife and fasten her shoes.

10

Out of jealousy she threatened me, and beat me with hard blows. Never did I find a better master, never a worse mistress."

11

Nevertheless, Guthrun could not weep, so incensed was she at her husband's death, and hard of heart over the prince's body.

12

Then Gullrǫnd spoke, Gjúki's daughter: "Few answers, foster-mother, can you bring to the young woman, though you are wise." She urged them not to keep the prince's body covered.

13

She swept back the sheet from Sigurd, and put his cheek at his wife's knees. "Look on your beloved. Lay your mouth to his lips, as you embraced him while he was still hale."

14

Á leit Guðrún   eino sinni;
sá hon dǫglings skǫr   dreyra runna,
fránar sjónir   fylkis liðnar,
hugborg jǫfurs   hjǫrfi skorna.

15

Þá hné Guðrún   hǫll við bólstri;
haddr losnaði,   hlýr roðnaði,
enn regns dropi   rann niðr um kné.

16

Þá grét Guðrún,   Gjúka dóttir
svá at tár flugo   tresc í gognom,
ok gullo við   gæss í túni,
mœrir fuglar,   er mær átti.

17

Þá kvað þat Gullrǫnd,   Gjúka dóttir:
"Ykrar vissa ek   ástir mestar
manna allra   fyr mold ofan;
undir þú hvárki   úti né inni
systir mín,   nema hjá Sigurði."

18

"Svá var minn Sigurðr   hjá sonom Gjúka,
sem væri geirlaukr   ór grasi vaxinn,
eða væri bjartr steinn   á band dreginn,
jarknasteinn   yfir ǫðlingom.

19

Ek þóttak ok   þjóðans rekkom
hverri hærri   Herjans dísi.
Nú em ek svá lítil,   sem lauf sé
opt í jǫlstrom,   at jǫfur dauðan.

20

Sakna ek í sessi   ok í sæingo
míns málvinar,   valda megir Gjúka.
Valda megir Gjúka   míno bǫlvi
ok systr sinnar   sárom gráti.

14

Only once did Guthrun look. She saw the lord's hair run with blood, the bright eyes of the people's prince, the warrior's breast pierced by the sword.

15

Then Guthrun bent down, leaned on the pillow. Her hair came loose, her cheek grew red, and a tear-drop ran down like rain to her knee.

16

Then Guthrun, Gjúki's daughter, wept, so that the tears flowed through her hair, and the geese in the yard cried out in reply, the beautiful birds which the maiden owned.

17

Then spoke Gullrǫnd, Gjúki's daughter: "I know of no greater love among all men over the world than yours. You were happy neither outdoors nor within, my sister, except with Sigurd."

18

"So was my Sigurd beside the sons of Gjúki as the garlic above the grass, or as a bright stone set in a ring, a precious stone among the princes.

19

And to the ruler's warriors I seemed higher than any of Herjan's maids. Now I am as little as the leaf on the laurel tree, after the prince's death.

20

At bed and board I miss my friend. The sons of Gjúki did that. The sons of Gjúki caused my sorrow, their sister's sore grief.

21

Svá ér um lýða   landi eyðit,
sem ér um unnoð   eiða svarða.
Manu þú, Gunnarr,   gullz um njóta,
þeir muno þér baugar   at bana verða,
er þú Sigurði   svarðir eiða.

22

Opt var í túni   teiti meiri,
þá er minn Sigurðr   sǫðlaði Grana,
ok þeir Brynhildar   biðja fóro,
armrar vættar,   illo heilli."

23

Þá kvað þat Brynhildr,   Buðla dóttir:
"Vǫn sé sú vættr   vers ok barna,
er þik, Guðrún,   gráz um beiddi
ok þér í morgon   málrúnar gaf."

24

Þá kvað þat Gullrǫnd,   Gjúka dóttir:
"Þegi þú, þjóðleið,   þeira orða!
Urðr ǫðlinga   hefir þú æ verið.
Rekr þik alda hverr   illrar skepno,
sorg sára   sjau konunga,
ok vinspell   vífa mest."

25

Þá kvað þat Brynhildr,   Buðla dóttir:
"Veldr einn Atli   ǫllo bǫlvi,
of borinn Buðla,   bróðir minn;

26

þá er við í hǫll   húnskrar þjóðar
eld á jǫfri   ormbeds litom,
þess hefi ek gangs   goldit síðan
þeirar sýnar,   sámk ey."

27

Stóð hon und stoð,   strengði hon elvi;
brann Brynhildi,   Buðla dóttur,
eldr ór augom,   eitri fnæsti,
er hon sár um leit   á Sigurði.

21

Thus you deprive the land of people, as you broke the oaths you had sworn. You will have no joy of the gold, Gunnar, but the rings shall become your bane because you swore false oaths to Sigurd.

22

There was greater joy in the courtyard when my Sigurd saddled Grani, and they went out to ask for Brynhild, miserable creature, with ill fortune."

23

Then Brynhild spoke, Buðli's daughter: "May that creature be without husband and children, she who led you to weep and gave you speech-runes this morning.

24

Then Gullrǫnd, Gjúki's daughter, spoke: "Keep silent of such words, hateful woman. You have always been the death of nobles. Every ill wave drives you on, you cruel sorrow to seven kings, and deadliest to your friend of all women."

25

Then spoke Brynhild, Buðli's daughter: "My brother Atli, born of Buðli, alone caused all this ill,

26

When we saw around the prince in the hall of the Hunnish nation the fiery gold taken from the dragon's lair – I have paid for that visit since; I ever since see that sight."

27

She stood by the pillar and gathered her strength. A fire burned from the eyes of Brynhild, Buðli's daughter; she breathed venom when she saw the wounds on Sigurd.

GUÐRÚNARHVQT*

Guðrún gekk þá til sævar, er hon hafði drepit Atla; gekk út á sæin ok vildi fara sér. Hon mátti eigi søkva. Rak hana yfir fjǫrðinn á land Jónakrs konungs. Hann fekk hennar.

Þeira synir vóro þeir Sǫrli ok Erpr ok Hamðir. Þar fœddiz up Svanhildr, Sigurðar dóttir. Hon var gipt Jǫrmunrekk inum ríkja. Með hánom var Bikki. Han réð þat at Randvér konungs sonr skyldi taka hana. Þat sagði Bikki konungi. Konungr lét hengja Randvé, enn troða Svanhildi undir hrossa fótom. Enn er þat spurði Guðrún, þá kvaddi hon sono sína.

1
Þá frá ek senno   slíðrfengligsta,
trauð mál talið   af trega stórom,
er harðhuguð   hvatti at vígi
grimmon orðom   Guðrún sono.

2
"Hví sitit?   Hví sofit lífi?
Hví tregrað ykr   teitit at mæla?
er Jǫrmunrekkr   yðra systor,
unga at aldri,   jóm of traddi,
hvítom ok svortom,   á hervegi,
grám, gangtǫmom   Gotna hrossom.

3
Urðoa ik glíkir   þeim Gunnari
né in heldr hugðir   sem var Hǫgni;
hennar myndoð iþ   hefna leita,
ef iþ móð ættið   minna brœðra
eða harðan hug   Húnkonunga."

---

* For textual variants of *Guðrúnarhvǫt* (eleventh century?) see Neckel-Kuhn 1983, 263–68, and 1968.

GUTHRUN'S INCITING

Then Guthrun went to the sea, when she had killed Atli. She went out into the water, and wanted to do away with herself, but she could not sink. The water carried her over the fiord to the land of King Jónak, who took her to wife.

Their sons were Sǫrli, Erp, and Hamðir. There Guthrun reared Sigurd's daughter Svanhild. She was given in marriage to the mighty Jǫrmunrekk. In his circle was Bikki, who induced Randver, the king's son, to wish to have her himself. Bikki informed the king about that. Jǫrmunrekk had Randver hanged and Svanhild trampled under the feet of horses. When Guthrun learned that, she spoke to her sons.

1

Then I heard the bitterest words, reluctant speech uttered from great grief, when hard-hearted Guthrun incited her sons to battle with grim words.

2

"Why do you sit? Why do you sleep your lives away? Why does it not grieve you to speak cheerfully? When cruel Jǫrmunrekk has trampled your sister, young in years, with black and white steeds on the battle-way, with grey well-trained horses of the Goths.

3

You have not become like Gunnar, nor in your hearts as was Hǫgni. You would have tried to avenge her, if you had had the spirit of my brothers or a hard heart like the Hunnish kings."

4
Þá kvað þat Hamðir   inn hugomstóri:
"Lítt mundir þú   leyfa dáð Hǫgna
þá er Sigurð vǫkþo   svefni ór;
bœkr vóro þínar   inar bláhvíto
roðnar í vers dreyra   fólgnar í valblóði.

5
Urðo þér   brœðra hefndir
slíðrar ok sárar,   er þú sono myrðir;
knættim allir   Jǫrmunrekki
samhyggjendr   systor hefna.

6
Berið hnossir fram   Húnkonunga!
Hefir þú okr hvatta   at hjorþingi."

7
Hlæjandi, Guðrún   hvarf til skemmo,
kumbl konunga   ór kerom valði,
síðar brynjor   ok sonom fœrði.
Hlóðuz móðgir   á mara bógo.

8
Þá kvað þat Hamðir   inn hugomstóri:
"Sva komaz meirr aptr,   móður at vitja,
geir-Njǫrðr, hniginn   á Goðþjóðo,
at þú erfi   at ǫll oss drykkir,
at Svanhildi   ok sono þína."

9
Guðrún, grátandi,   Gjúka dóttir,
gekk hon tregliga   á tái sitja,
ok at telja,   tárukhlýra,
móðug spjǫll   á margan veg:

10
"Þrja vissa ek elda,   þrjá vissa ek arna;
var ek þrimr verom   vegin at húsi.
Einn var mér Sigurðr   ǫllum betri,
er brœðr mínir   at bana urðo.

11
Svára sára   sákað ek né kunna;
meirr þóttuz   mér um stríða
er mik ǫðlingar   Atla gáfo.

4

Then the great-hearted Hamðir spoke: "Little did you praise the deed of Hǫgni when they awakened Sigurd from sleep. Your snow-white sheets were red with your husband's gore, covered with blood of slaughter.

5

That came to be a vengeance cruel and sore on your brothers, when you murdered your sons; we could all with one mind have avenged our sister on Jǫrmunrekk.

6

Bring out the precious armour of the Hun-kings! You have incited us to sword-dealing."

7

Laughing, Guthrun went to her bower. She got the regal armour of kings, the broad coats of mail, out of her chest, and carried them to her sons. The proud men mounted the backs of their horses.

8

Then the great-hearted Hamðir spoke: "So spear-god Njǫrð [i.e., Hamðir], killed among the Goth-people, will come to visit you hereafter, mother, and you will drink a funeral-draught for us all, for Svanhild and your sons."

9

Weeping, Guthrun, Gjúki's daughter, went sadly to sit in the court, and, with tear-stained cheeks, to relate a passionate tale in many a way:

10

"I have known three fires, three hearths; I was taken to the homes of three husbands. Only Sigurd was better than all to me, he whom my brothers killed.

11

A heavier loss I never saw nor knew, but it seemed to me an even greater affliction when the nobles gave me to Atli.

12

Húna hvassa   hét ek mér at rúnom;
máttigak bǫlva   bœtr um vinna
áðr ek hnóf hǫfuð   af Hniflungom.

13

Gekk ek til strandar,   grǫm vark Nornom,
Vilda ek hrinda   stríð grið þeira.
Hófo mik, né drekþo,   hávar báror,
því ek land um sték,   at lifa skyldak.

14

Gekk ek á beð   – hugðak mér fyrr betra –
þriðja sinni   þjóðkonungi.
Ól ek mér jóð,   erfivorðo Jónakrs sonom.

15

Enn um Svanhildi   sáto þýjar,
er ek minna barna   bazt fullhugðak.
Svá var Svanhildr   í sal mínom,
sem væri sœmleitr   sólar geisli.

16

Gœdda ek gulli   ok guðvefjom
áðr ek gæfak   Goðþjóðar til.
Þat er mér harðast   harma minna
of þann inn hvíta   hadd Svanhildar
auri trǫddo   und jóa fótom.

17

Enn sá sárastr   er þeir Sigurð minn,
sigri ræntan,   í sæing vágo;
enn sá grimmastr   er þeir Gunnari
fránir ormar   til fjǫrs skriðo;
enn sá hvassastr   er til hjarta
konung óblauðan   kvikvan skáro.

18

Fjǫlð man ek bǫlva ...
Beittu, Sigurðr,   inn blakka mar,
hest inn hraðfœra.   Láttu hinig renna!
Sitr eigi hér   snør né dóttir,
sú er Guðrúno   gæfi hnossir.

12

I called the brave boys to me secretly. I could not gain compensation for my woes before I smote off the heads of the Niflungs.

13

In anger against the Fates I went to the sea-shore. I wanted to rid myself of their harsh settlement. But the waves of the sea bore me up instead of drowning me, so that I came to land and must continue living.

14

A third time I bedded with a king – I thought it would turn out better. I bore children, sons as heirs for Jónak.

15

Handmaidens sat around Svanhild, whom I loved best of my children. Like a lovely sunbeam was Svanhild in my hall.

16

I adorned her with gold and costly fabrics before I gave her to the Goths. That was the hardest of my griefs, when the fair hair of Svanhild was trodden in the mud under the feet of stallions.

17

Yet the sorest grief was when they slew my Sigurd, deprived of victory, in his bed; the cruellest when swift-darting snakes made for Gunnar's life; the keenest when they cut the dauntless king [Hǫgni] to the heart while he yet lived.

18

I remember many calamities ... Bridle, Sigurd, your black steed, the swift horse. Let it run hither! There sits here neither daughter-in-law nor daughter to give treasure to Guthrun.

19

Minnztu, Sigurðr,   hvat við mæltom
þá er við á beð   bæði sátom,
at þú myndir mín,   móðugr, vitja
halr ór Heljo,   enn ek þín ór heimi.

20

Hlaðit ér, jarlar,   eikikǫstinn.
Látið þann und hilmi   hæstan verða!
Megi brenna brjóst   bǫlvafult eldr,
... um hjarta   þiðni sorgir!"

21

Jǫrlom ǫllom   óluð batni,
snótom ǫllom   sorg at minni,
at þetta tregróf   um tælið væri.

19

Remember, Sigurd, what we two said when we both sat on the bed, that you, high-hearted man, would seek me from Hell, I you from the world.

20

Pile up, earls, an oak-wood pyre. Let it be the highest ever under a prince. May the fire burn my woeful breast ... melt the sorrows around my heart."

21

May it amend the misery of all nobles, may it lessen the sorrow of all ladies, to have heard this sad tale told.

Bibliography

The bibliography includes all the works referred to in this book, along with a few other relevant items. Frequently cited editions and reference works can also be found listed in the Abbreviations (pp. xi–xv, above). Entries in the bibliography are alphabetized by author or editor, with some cross-referencing, under the following headings:

POETICS AND GENRE THEORY

Chadwick 1932–40
   Chadwick, H.M. and N.K. *The Growth of Literature*. 3 vols. Cambridge 1932, 1936, and 1940.
Culler 1975
   Culler, Jonathan. *Structuralist Poetics*. Ithaca, NY 1975.
Dubrow 1982
   Dubrow, Heather. *Genre*. London 1982.

Elias 1966
Schiller, Friedrich von, transl. Julius A. Elias. *Naive and Sentimental Poetry and On the Sublime*. New York 1966.

Fowler 1982
Fowler, Alastair. *Kinds of Literature: An Introduction to the Theory of Genres and Modes*. Cambridge, Mass. 1982.

Fussell 1979
Fussell, Paul. *Poetic Meter and Poetic Form*. New York 1965; rev. 1979.

Heinzle 1978
Heinzle, Joachim. "Märenbegriff und Novellentheorie." *ZfdA* 107 (1978): 121–38.

Hernadi 1972
Hernadi, Paul. *Beyond Genre: New Directions in Literary Classification*. Ithaca, NY 1972.

Hirsch 1967
Hirsch, E.D., Jr. *Validity in Interpretation*. New Haven, Conn. 1967.

Jauss, transl. Bahti 1982
Jauss, Hans Robert, transl. Timothy Bahti. "Genres and Medieval Literature." In *Toward an Aesthetic of Reception*, Theory and History of Literature 2, pp. 76–109. Minneapolis 1982. First published in *Grundriss der romanischen Literaturen des Mittelalters* 6; Heidelberg 1972.

Lausberg 1973
Lausberg, Heinrich. *Handbuch der Literarischen Rhetorik*. 2. Aufl. 2 Bände. Munich 1973.

Lentricchia 1980
Lentricchia, Frank. *After the New Criticism*. Chicago 1980.

Levi 1978
Levi, Albert William. "Literature and the Imagination: A Theory of Genres." In Strelka 1978, 17–40.

Patterson 1987
Patterson, Lee. *Negotiating the Past: The Historical Understanding of Medieval Literature*. Madison, Wis. 1987.

Potts 1967
Potts, Abbie Findlay. *The Elegiac Mode: Poetic Form in Wordsworth and Other Elegists*. Ithaca, NY 1967

Sacks 1985
Sacks, Peter. *The English Elegy: Studies in the Genre from Spenser to Yeats*. Baltimore 1985.

Schiller 1795
See Wiese and Koopman 1962, and Elias 1966 (transl.).

Sedgwick 1924
Sedgwick, W.B. "The Origin of Rhyme." *Revue bénédictine* 36 (1924): 330–46.
Stahl 1978
Stahl, Ernest L. "Literary Genres: Some Idiosyncratic Concepts." In Strelka 1978, 80–92.
Strelka 1978
Strelka, Joseph P., ed. *Theories of Literary Genre.* Yearbook of Comparative Criticism 3. University Park, Pa. 1978.
Todorov 1970
Todorov, Tzvetan. *Introduction a la littérature fantastique.* Paris 1970.
Todorov transl. Berrong 1976–77
Todorov, Tzvetan, transl. Richard M. Berrong. "The Origin of Genres." *NLH* 8 (1976–77): 159–70.
Weissenberger 1978
Weissenberger, Klaus. "A Morphological Genre Theory: An Answer to a Pluralism of Forms." In Strelka 1978, 229–53.
Wellek and Warren 1948
Wellek, René, and Austin Warren. *Theory of Literature.* New York 1948.
Welsh 1978
Welsh, Andrew. *Roots of Lyric: Primitive Poetry and Modern Poetics.* Princeton 1978.
Wiese and Koopman 1962
Schiller, Friedrich von. "Über naive und sentimentalische Dichtung." In *Schillers Werke: Nationalausgabe,* Band 20; Philosophische Schriften, 1. Teil, hrsg. Benno von Wiese und Helmut Koopman, pp. 413–503. Weimar 1962.

GREEK LITERATURE

Alexiou 1974
Alexiou, Margaret. *The Ritual Lament in Greek Tradition.* Cambridge 1974.
Bowra 1938
Bowra, C.M. *Early Greek Elegists.* London 1938.
Bowra 1961
– *Greek Lyric Poetry.* Oxford 1961.
Bulloch 1985
Callimachus: The Fifth Hymn, ed. and transl. A.W. Bulloch. Cambridge Classical Texts and Commentaries 26. Cambridge 1985.
Dewing 1916
Procopius, ed. and transl. H.B. Dewing. Vol. 2: *Histories of the (Vandal) Wars.* Loeb Classical Library. London 1916.

Hardie 1920
Hardie, W.R. *Res Metrica*. Oxford 1920.

Harvey 1955
Harvey, A.E. "The Classification of Greek Lyric Poetry." *Classical Quarterly* 5 (1955): 157–75.

Murray 1919
Homer. *The Odyssey*, ed. and transl. A.T. Murray. 2 vols. Loeb Classical Library. London 1919.

Page 1936
Page, Denys L. "Elegiacs in Euripides' *Andromache*." In *Greek Poetry and Life*, pp. 206–30. Oxford 1936.

Page 1963
– "Archilochus and the Oral Tradition." In *Fondation Hardt pour L'Étude de l'Antiquité Classique: Entretiens* 10, pp. 117–63. Geneva 1963.

CLASSICAL LATIN LITERATURE

Brink 1971
Horace on Poetry: The Ars Poetica, ed. C.O. Brink. Cambridge 1971.

Butler 1912
Propertius, ed. and transl. H.E. Butler. Loeb Classical Library. London 1912.

Day 1938
Day, Archibald A. *The Origins of the Latin Love-Elegy*. Oxford 1938.

Duff 1970
Lucan. *The Civil War (Pharsalia)*, ed. and transl. J.D. Duff. Loeb Classical Library. London 1928; rev. 1970.

Fairclough 1929
Horace. *Satires, Epistles, and Ars Poetica*, ed. and transl. H.R. Fairclough. Loeb Classical Library. London 1929.

Hutton and Peterson 1970
Tacitus. *Agricola, Germania, Dialogues*, ed. and transl. M. Hutton and W. Peterson. Loeb Classical Library. London 1914; rev. R.M. Ogilvie, E.H. Warmington, and M. Winterbottom, 1970.

Lenz 1938
P. Ovidii Nasonis Epistulae ex Ponto, ed. F.W. Lenz. Turin 1938.

Luck 1959
Luck, Georg. *The Latin Love Elegy*. London 1959.

Luck 1967–77
P. Ovidius Naso: Tristia, ed. Georg Luck. 2 vols. Heidelberg 1967–77.

Owen 1899
P. Ovidi Nasonis Tristium libri V, ed. S.G. Owen. Oxford 1899.

Palmer 1898
P. Ovidi Nasonis Heroides, ed. Arthur Palmer. Oxford 1898; repr. Hildesheim 1967.

Robathan 1973
Robathan, Dorothy. "Ovid in the Middle Ages." In *Ovid*, ed. J.W. Binns, pp. 191–209. London 1973.

Rolfe 1972–82
Ammiani Marcellini rerum gestarum libri qui supersunt, ed. and transl. John C. Rolfe. 3 vols. Loeb Classical Library. London 1935–40; rev. and repr. 1972–82.

Showerman 1921
Ovid. *Heroides and Amores*, ed. and transl. Grant Showerman. Loeb Classical Library. London 1921.

Wheeler 1924
Ovid. *Tristia and Ex Ponto*, ed. and transl. A.L. Wheeler. Loeb Classical Library. London 1924.

CHRISTIAN AND MEDIEVAL LATIN LITERATURE

Bieler 1957
Boethius. *Opera 1: Philosophiae consolatio*, ed. Ludwig Bieler. CCSL 94. Turnhout 1957.

Calder and Allen 1976
Allen, Michael J.B., and Daniel G. Calder. *Sources and Analogues of Old English Poetry: The Major Latin Texts in Translation*. Cambridge 1976.

Chadwick 1955
Chadwick, Nora K. *Poetry and Letters in Early Christian Gaul*. London 1955.

Dreves, Blume, and Bannister 1886–1922
Dreves, G.M., C. Blume, and H.M. Bannister. *Analecta hymnica medii aevi*. 55 vols. Leipzig 1886–1922.

Dronke 1965
Dronke, Peter. "The Beginnings of the Sequence." *BGdSL* (Tübinger Ausgabe) 87 (1965): 43–73.

Dümmler 1881
"Alcuini Carmina." In MGH *Poetae latini aevi carolini* 1.1, ed. Ernst Dümmler, pp. 160–351. Berlin 1881.

Dümmler 1895
"Alcuini sive Albini Epistolae." In MGH *Epistolae* 4, ed. Ernst Dümmler, pp. 18–481. Berlin 1895.

Fontaine 1959
Fontaine, Jacques. *Isidore de Séville et la culture classique dans l'Espagne wisigothique*. 2 tomes. Études augustiniennes. Paris 1959.

Glorie 1968

Variae collectiones aenigmatum merovingicae aetatis, Pars altera, ed. Fr. Glorie. CCSL 133A. Turnhout 1968.

Gneuss 1968

Hymnar und Hymnen im englischen Mittelalter, hrsg. Helmut Gneuss. Buchreihe der Anglia 22. Tübingen 1968.

Herren 1974

The Hisperica Famina: I. The A-Text. Pontifical Institute of Mediaeval Studies: Studies and Texts 31. Toronto 1974.

Kendall 1975

Bede. "De arte metrica et De schematibus et tropis," ed. C.B. Kendall una cum Commentariis et Glossis Remigii autissiodorensis (with Commentaries and Glosses of Remigius of Auxerre), ed. M.H. King. In *Bedae Venerabilis Opera 1: Opera didascalia*, pp. 59–172. CCSL 123A. Turnhout 1975.

Korhammer 1976

Korhammer, Michael. *Die monastischen Cantica im Mittelalter und ihre altenglischen Interlinearversionen*. Texte und Untersuchungen zur englischen Philologie 6. Munich 1976.

Krusch and Levison 1951

Gregorii episcopi turonensis libri Historiarum X, ed. Bruno Krusch and William Levison. 2nd ed. MGH *Scriptores rerum merovingicarum* 1.1. Hanover 1951.

Lapidge 1979

Lapidge, Michael. "Aldhelm's Latin Poetry and Old English Verse." *CL* 31 (1979): 209–31.

Lausberg 1973

See under Poetics and Genre Theory.

Leo 1881

Venanti Fortunati Opera poetica, ed. Friedrich Leo. MGH *Auctores antiquissimi* 4.1. Berlin 1881.

Lindsay 1911

Isidori Hispalensis episcopi Etymologiarum sive Originum libri XX, ed. W.M. Lindsay. 2 vols. Oxford 1911.

McKenna 1963

Saint Augustine on the Trinity, transl. Stephen McKenna. The Fathers of the Church 45. Washington 1963.

Mierow 1908

Jordanes: The Origin and Deeds of the Goths, transl. Charles C. Mierow. Princeton 1908.

Migne 1844–64

Patrologiae cursus completus ..., *series latina, in qua prodeunt patres, doctores scripto-*

resque Ecclesiae Latinae a Tertulliano ad Innocentium III, ed. Jacques Paul Migne. Paris 1844–64.

Mommsen 1882
Jordanis Romana et Getica, ed. Theodor Mommsen. MGH *Auctores antiquissimi* 1.1 Berlin 1882.

Mommsen 1898
Gildas. "De excidio et conquestu Britanniae." In MGH *Auctores antiquissimi* 13, ed. Theodor Mommsen, pp. 25–85. Berlin 1898.

Norberg 1958
Norberg, Dag. *Introduction à l'étude de la versification médiévale*. Studia latina stockholmiensa 5. Uppsala 1958.

Ogilvy 1967
Ogilvy, J.D.A. *Books Known to the English, 597–1066*. Cambridge, Mass. 1967.

Ohl 1928
Symphosius. *The Enigmas of Symphosius*, ed. R.T. Ohl. Philadelphia 1928.

Patrologia Latina (PL)
See Migne 1844–64.

Pertz 1835
"Karoli Magni capitularia." In MGH *Leges* 1, ed. Georg Heinrich Pertz, pp. 32–194. Hanover 1835.

Pertz 1839
"Annales Quedlinburgenses" (to 1025 AD). In MGH *Scriptores* 3, ed. Georg Heinrich Pertz, pp. 22–90. Hanover 1839.

Piper 1882–83
Notker. *Die Schriften Notkers und seine Schule*, ed. Paul Piper. 3 vols. Freiburg 1882–83.

Raby 1934
Raby, F.J.E. *A History of Secular Latin Poetry in the Middle Ages*. Oxford 1934.

Raby 1953
– *A History of Christian-Latin Poetry from the Beginnings to the Close of the Middle Ages*. 2nd ed. Oxford 1953.

Schetter 1970
Schetter, W. *Studien zur Überlieferung und Kritik des Elegikers Maximian*. Klassische-Philologische Studien 36. Wiesbaden 1970.

Stewart, Rand, and Tester 1973
Boethius. *The Theological Tractates and The Consolation of Philosophy*, ed. and transl. H.F. Stewart, E.K. Rand, and S.J. Tester. Loeb Classical Library. London 1973.

Tanenhaus 1962
Tanenhaus, Gussie Hecht. "Bede's *De Schematibus et Tropis*: A Translation." *Quarterly Journal of Speech* 48 (1962): 237–53.

Walpole 1922
  Walpole, A.S. *Early Latin Hymns*. Cambridge 1922.
Winterbottom 1978
  Gildas. *The Ruin of Britain [De excidio et conquestu Britanniae] and Other Works*, ed. and transl. Michael Winterbottom. London 1978.

EARLY WELSH AND IRISH POETRY

Calder et al. 1983
  Calder, Daniel G., Robert E. Bjork, Patrick K. Ford, and Daniel F. Melia. *Sources and Analogues of Old English Poetry 2: The Major Germanic and Celtic Texts in Translation*. Cambridge 1983.
Chadwich 1963
  See under OE Lit.
Ford 1974
  Ford, Patrick. *The Poetry of Llywarch Hen: Introduction, Text, and Translation*. Berkeley and Los Angeles 1974.
Henry 1966
  See under OE Poetry.
Jackson 1935
  Jackson, Kenneth. *Studies in Early Celtic Nature Poetry*. Cambridge, 1935. Repr. with corrections Folcroft, Pa. 1974.
Jackson 1971
  – *A Celtic Miscellany*. Rev. ed. Penguin Classics. Harmondsworth, Middlesex 1971.
Meyer 1901
  King and Hermit, ed. and transl. Kuno Meyer. London 1901.
Rowland 1990
  Rowland, Jenny. *Early Welsh Saga Poetry*. Cambridge 1990.
Williams 1932
  Williams, Ifor. "The Poems of Llywarch Hen." *PBA* 18 (1932): 269–302.
Williams 1953
  Canu Llywarch Hen. 2nd ed. Cardiff 1953.
Williams 1972
  The Beginnings of Welsh Poetry: Studies by Sir Ifor Williams, ed. Rachel Bromwich. 2nd ed. Cardiff 1972.

EARLY GERMANIC LITERATURE AND CULTURE [including Norse]

Bartsch-Stackmann 1965
  Kudrun, hrsg. Karl Bartsch. 5. Aufl. überarb. Karl Stackmann. Wiesbaden 1965.

Beck 1988

Heldensage und Heldendichtung im Germanischen, hrsg. Heinrich Beck. Ergän-zungsbände zum Reallexikon der Germanischen Altertumskunde 2. Berlin and New York 1988.

Bouman 1962

See under OE Elegies.

Brodeur 1929

Snorri Sturluson. *The Prose Edda*, transl. A.G. Brodeur. New York 1929.

Burns 1984

Burns, Thomas S. *A History of the Ostrogoths*. Bloomington 1984.

Calder et al. 1983

See under Early Welsh and Irish Poetry.

Dickins 1915

Dickins, Bruce. *Runic and Heroic Poems of the Old Teutonic Peoples*. Cambridge 1915.

Ebel 1983

Volsunga Saga, hrsg. Uwe Ebel. Frankfurt 1983.

Peter Finch 1979

Saxo Grammaticus. *The History of the Danes*, transl. Peter Finch, ed. Hilda Ellis Davidson. Cambridge 1979.

R.G. Finch 1965

Volsunga saga, ed. R.G. Finch. London 1965.

Gordon 1960

Gordon, C.D. *The Age of Attila: Fifth-Century Byzantium and the Barbarians*. Ann Arbor 1960.

Gordon and Taylor 1957

Gordon, E.V. *An Introduction to Old Norse*. 2nd ed. rev. A.R. Taylor. Oxford 1957.

Grimm 1957

Grimm, Wilhelm. *Die deutsche Heldensage*. 4. Aufl. Darmstadt 1957. (First pub-lished 1829; 2nd ed. rev. Karl Müllenhof 1867; 3rd ed. rev. Reinhold Steig 1889; 4th ed. with Nachwort by Siegfried Gutenbrunner 1957.)

Harris 1988

Harris, Joseph. "Hadubrand's Lament: On the Origin and Age of Elegy in Germanic." In Beck 1988, 81–114.

Heinzel 1889

Heinzel, Richard. *Über die ostgothische Heldensage*. Sitzungsberichte der kaiser-lichen Akademie der Wissenschaften in Wien, Philosophisch-historische Classe 119.3. Vienna 1889.

Helgason 1961

Helgason, Jón, ed. *Skjaldevers*. Copenhagen 1961.

Hollander 1962
The Poetic Edda, transl. Lee M. Hollander. Austin 1962.

Jónsson 1931
Edda Snorra Sturlusonar, ed. Finnur Jónsson. Copenhagen 1931.

Knabe and Hermann 1931
Saxonis Gesta Danorum, ed. C. Knabe and P. Hermann; rev. Jørgen Olrik and Hans Raeder. Copenhagen 1931.

Krusch and Levison 1951
Gregory of Tours. *History of the Franks*. See under Christian and Medieval Latin Lit.

Mierow 1908; Mommsen 1861
Jordanes. *History of the Goths*. See under Christian and Medieval Latin Lit.

Neckel 1908
Neckel, Gustav. *Beiträge zur Eddaforschung, mit Exkursen zur Heldensage*. Dortmund 1908.

Neckel-Kuhn 1968 and 1983
Die Lieder des Codex regius nebst verwandten Denkmälern, hrsg. Gustav Neckel; überarb. H. Kuhn. 2 Bände. Text: 5. Aufl.; Heidelberg 1983. Glossar: 3. Aufl. 1968.

Schröder 1895
Kaiserchronik eines Regensburger Geistlichen, ed. Edward Schröder. MGH *Scriptores qui vernacula lingua usi sunt* 1. Berlin 1895; repr. 1964.

Sprenger 1988
Sprenger, Ulrike. "Zum Ursprung der altnordischen Heroischen Elegie." In Beck 1988, 245–87.

Turville-Petre 1976
Turville-Petre, E.O.G. *Scaldic Poetry*. Oxford 1976

OLD (AND MIDDLE) ENGLISH LITERATURE

Alfred the Great, King, transl.
Augustine: *Soliloquies*. See Carnicelli 1969.
Boethius: *Consolation of Philosophy*. See Sedgefield 1899.
Gregory: *Pastoral Care*. See Sweet 1871.

Assmann 1889
Angelsächsische Homilien und Heiligenleben, hrsg. Bruno Assmann. Bibliothek der angelsächsischen Prosa 3. Kassel 1889; repr. with introd. by P. Clemoes, Darmstadt 1964.

Atwood and Hill 1969
Studies in Language, Literature, and Culture of the Middle Ages and Later, ed. E. Bagby Atwood and Archibald A. Hill. Austin 1969.

Ælfric
> *Grammar* and *Glossary*. See Zupitza 1880.
> Homilies. See Thorpe 1844–46, and Pope 1967–68.
> Lives of Saints. See Skeat 1881–1900.

Bately 1970
> Bately, Janet. "King Alfred and the Old English Translation of Orosius." *Anglia* 88 (1970): 433–60.

Bately 1986
> – "Evidence for a Knowledge of Latin Literature in Old English." In *Sources of Anglo-Saxon Culture*, pp. 35–51. Studies in Medieval Culture 20. Kalamazoo 1986.

Bauer, Stanzel, and Zaic 1973
> *Festschrift Prof. Dr. Herbert Koziol zum siebsigsten Geburtstag*, hrsg. Gero Bauer, Franz K. Stanzel und Franz Zaic. Wiener Beiträge zur englischen Philologie 75. Vienna 1973.

Bede
> *Ecclesiastical History*, OE Version. See Miller 1890–91 and 1898.

Benedictine Office
> See Ure 1957.

Bessinger and Creed 1965
> *Franciplegius: Medieval and Linguistic Studies in Honor of Francis Peabody Magoun, Jr.*, ed. Jess B. Bessinger and Robert P. Creed. New York 1965.

Bethurum 1957
> *The Homilies of Wulfstan*, ed. Dorothy Bethurum. Oxford 1957.

Birch 1885–99
> Birch, Walter de Gray. *Cartularium Saxonicum*. 3 vols. London 1885–99.

Blickling Homilies
> See Morris 1874–80.

Bolton 1963
> Bolton, Whitney F. *An Old English Anthology*. London 1963.

Brandl 1908
> Brandl, Alois H. *Geschichte der altenglischen Literatur*. Strassburg 1908.

Bright 1891
> Bright, James W. *An Anglo-Saxon Reader*. New York 1891.

Brink 1877
> Brink, Bernhard ten. *Geschichte der englischen Litteratur* 1. Berlin 1877.

Brink transl. Kennedy 1883
> – *Early English Literature*, transl. H.M. Kennedy. *History of English Literature* 1. London 1883. (transl. of Brink 1877)

Brown 1932
> Brown, Carleton. *English Lyrics of the Thirteenth Century*. Oxford 1932. Repr. with corrections 1962.

Burlin and Irving 1974
   Old English Studies in Honour of John C. Pope, ed. R.B. Burlin and E.B. Irving.
   Toronto 1974.
Campbell 1974
   The Tiberius Psalter, ed. A.P. Campbell. Ottawa 1974.
Carnicelli 1969
   King Alfred's Version of St. Augustine's Soliloquies, ed. T.A. Carnicelli. Cambridge,
   Mass. 1969.
Chad, Life of St.
   See Vleeskruyer 1953.
Chadwick 1963
   Chadwick, N.K. "The Celtic Background of Early Anglo-Saxon England." In
   Celt and Saxon: Studies in the Early British Border, ed. Kenneth Jackson et al.,
   pp. 323–52. Cambridge 1963.
Christopher, Life of St.
   See Rypins 1924.
Cockayne 1864–66
   Cockayne, Thomas O. *Leechdoms, Wortcunning, and Starcraft of Early England.*
   3 vols. Rolls Series 35. London 1864–66.
Cross 1957
   See under *Wan.*
Cross 1962
   Cross, J.E. "Aspects of Microcosm and Macrocosm in Old English Literature."
   CL 14 (1962): 1–22.
Defensor
   Liber Scintillarum. See Rhodes 1889.
Durham Ritual
   See Thompson and Lindelöf 1927.
Ettmüller 1850
   Ettmüller, Ludwig. *Engla and Seaxna Scôpas and Bôceras.* Quedlinburg and
   Leipzig 1850.
Frantzen 1983
   Frantzen, Allen J. *The Literature of Penance in Anglo-Saxon England.* New Bruns-
   wick, NJ 1983.
Godden 1985
   Godden, Malcolm R. "Anglo-Saxons on the Mind." In Lapidge and Gneuss
   1985, 271–98.
Greenfield 1965
   Greenfield, Stanley B. *A Critical History of Old English Literature.* New York 1965.
Greenfield and Calder 1986
   Greenfield, Stanley B., and Daniel G. Calder. *A New Critical History of Old English*

Literature. With a Survey of the Anglo-Latin Background by Michael Lapidge. New York 1986

Gregory the Great, Pope
Dialogues, OE Version. See Hecht 1900–1907.

Hecht 1900–1907
Bichof Wærferths von Worcester Übersetzung der Dialoge Gregors des Grossen, hrsg. H. Hecht. Bibliothek der angelsächsischen Prosa 5. Leipzig and Hamburg 1900–1907.

Herbst 1975
Die altenglische Margaretenlegende in der HS. Cotton Tiberius A. III, hrsg. Lenore Herbst. Göttingen 1975.

Herzfeld 1900
An Old English Martyrology, ed. G. Herzfeld. EETS 116. London 1900.

Kaiser 1954
Kaiser, R. *Alt- und mittelenglische Anthologie.* Berlin 1954.

Kemble 1849
Kemble, J.M. *The Saxons in England: A History of the English Commonwell till the Norman Conquest.* 2 vols. London 1849.

Kluge 1888, 1897, 1902, 1915
Kluge, Friedrich. *Angelsächsisches Lesebuch.* 4 Auflagen. Halle 1888, 1897, 1902, 1915.

Kuhn 1965
The Vespasian Psalter, ed. Shermann M. Kuhn. Ann Arbor 1965.

Lapidge and Gneuss 1985
Learning and Literature in Anglo-Saxon England: Studies Presented to Peter Clemoes on the Occasion of His Sixty-Fifth Birthday, ed. Michael Lapidge and Helmut Gneuss. Cambridge 1985.

Lee 1977
An English Miscellany Presented to W.S. Mackie, ed. Brian S. Lee. Capetown 1977.

Leechdoms
See Cockayne 1864–66.

Liebermann 1903–16
Die Gesetze der Angelsachsen, hrsg. Felix Liebermann. 3 Bände. Halle 1903–16.

Liggins 1970
Liggins, Elizabeth M. "The Authorship of the Old English *Orosius.*" *Anglia* 88 (1970): 289–322.

Lindelöf 1909–14
Der Lambeth-Psalter, hrsg. Uno Lindelöf. Acta societatis scientiarum fennicae 35, i and 43, iii. Helsinki, 1909–14.

Lindisfarne Gospels
See Skeat 1871–87.

Logeman 1891–93
Logeman, W.S. "De consuetudine monachorum." *Anglia* 13 (1891): 365–454; 15 (1893): 20–40.

Malone 1948
Malone, Kemp. "The Old English Period (to 1100)." In *A Literary History of England*, ed. A.C. Baugh, pp. 1–105. New York 1948.

Margaret, Life of St.
See Herbst 1975.

Medicina de Quadrupedibus
See Vriend 1984.

Miller 1890–91 and 1898
The Old English Version of Bede's Ecclesiastical History of the English People, ed. T. Miller. 2 vols. EETS 95–96: Text; London 1890–91. EETS 110–11: Introduction and Various Readings; London 1898.

Mitchell 1988
Mitchell, Bruce. *On Old English: Selected Papers*. Oxford 1988.

Morris 1874–80
The Blickling Homilies, ed. R. Morris. EETS 58, 63, 73. London 1874–80. Repr. in one vol. 1967.

Napier 1883
Wulfstan: Sammlung der ihm zugeschriebenen Homilien nebst Untersuchungen über ihre Echtheit. Berlin 1883.

Niles 1980
Old English Literature in Context: Ten Essays, ed. John D. Niles. Cambridge 1980.

Oess 1910
Der altenglische Arundel-Psalter, hrsg. G. Oess. Anglistische Forschungen 30. Heidelberg 1910.

Page 1985
Page, R.I. *Anglo-Saxon Aptitudes*. Cambridge 1985 (Inaugural Lecture).

Patterson 1987
See under Poetics and Genre Theory.

Pearsall and Waldron 1969
Mediaeval Literature and Civilization: Studies in Memory of G.N. Garmonsway, ed. Derek A. Pearsall and Ronald A. Waldron. London 1969.

Philpotts 1928
Philpotts, Bertha S. "Wyrd and Providence in Anglo-Saxon Thought." *E and S* 13 (1928): 7–27.

Pope 1967–68
Homilies of Ælfric: A Supplementary Collection, ed. J.C. Pope. 2 vols. EETS 259–60. London 1967–68.

Regularis Concordia
  See Logeman 1891–93.
Rhodes 1889
  Defensor's Liber Scintillarum with an Interlinear Anglo-Saxon Version made Early in the Eleventh Century, ed. E.W. Rhodes. EETS 93. London 1889.
Rieger 1861
  Rieger, Max. *Alt- und angelsächsisches Lesebuch*. Giessen 1861.
Robertson 1956
  Robertson, A.J. *Anglo-Saxon Charters*. 2nd ed. Cambridge 1956.
Robinson 1980
  Robinson, Fred C. "Old English Literature in Its Most Immediate Context." In Niles 1980, 11–29; endnotes pp. 157–61.
Rosier 1962
  The Vitellius Psalter, ed. J.L. Rosier. Cornell Studies in English 42. Ithaca, NY 1962.
Rushworth Gospels
  See Skeat 1871–87.
Rypins 1924
  Rypins, S. *Three Old English Prose Texts*. EETS 161. London 1924.
Sedgefield 1899
  King Alfred's Old English Version of Boethius' De consolatione philosophiae, ed. W.J. Sedgefield. Oxford 1899.
Sisam 1953a
  Sisam, Kenneth. *Studies in the History of Old English Literature*. Oxford 1953.
Skeat 1871–87
  The Four Gospels in Anglo-Saxon, Northumbrian, and Old Mercian Versions, ed. W.W. Skeat. Cambridge 1871–87; repr. Darmstadt 1970.
Skeat 1881–1900
  Ælfric's Lives of Saints, ed. W.W. Skeat. 4 vols. EETS 76, 82, 94, 114. London 1881–1900; repr. in 2 vols. 1966.
Stanley 1987
  Stanley, Eric Gerald. *A Collection of Papers with Emphasis on Old English Literature*. Toronto 1987.
Sweet 1871
  King Alfred's West-Saxon Version of Gregory's Pastoral Care, ed. Henry Sweet. 2 vols. EETS 45 and 50. London 1871.
Sweet 1885
  Sweet, Henry. *The Oldest English Texts*. EETS 83. London 1885.
Sweet 1894
  – *An Anglo-Saxon Reader in Prose and Verse*. 7th ed. Oxford 1894. (This is the first edition of Sweet's *Reader* to contain *Sea*.)

Szarmach 1981
   Vercelli Homilies IX–XXIII, ed. Paul E. Szarmach. Toronto 1981.
Thompson and Lindelöf 1927
   Rituale ecclesiae Dunelmensis, ed. A.H. Thompson and U. Lindelöf. Surtees Society 140. Durham 1927.
Thorpe 1844–46
   Thorpe, Benjamin. *The Homilies of the Anglo-Saxon Church: The First Part, Containing the Sermones Catholici, or Homilies of Ælfric*. 2 vols. London 1844–46.
Timmer 1941
   Timmer, B.J. "Wyrd in Anglo-Saxon Prose and Poetry." *Neophil* 26 (1941):24–33 and 213–28.
Ure 1957
   The Benedictine Office, ed. J.M. Ure. Edinburgh 1957.
Vespasian Psalter
   See Kuhn 1965.
Viebrock and Erzgräber 1961
   Festschrift zum 75. Geburtstag von Theodor Spira, hrsg. H. Viebrock und W. Erzgräber. Heidelberg 1961.
Vleeskruyer 1953
   The Life of St. Chad, ed. R. Vleeskruyer. Amsterdam 1953.
Vriend 1984
   The Old English Herbarium and Medicina de Quadrupedibus, ed. Hubert Jan die Vriend. EETS 286. London 1984.
Wardale 1935
   Wardale, Edith E. *Chapters on Old English Literature*. London 1935.
Warner 1917
   Warner, R.D-N. *Early English Homilies from the Twelfth-Century MS. Vespasian D. XIV*. EETS 152. London 1917.
Wærferth, Bishop of Worcester, transl.
   Gregory: *Dialogues*. See Hecht 1900–1907.
Wrenn 1967
   Wrenn, C.L. *A Study of Old English Literature*. London 1967.
Wulfstan
   Homilies. See Bethurum 1957, and Napier 1883.
Wülker 1885
   Wülker, Richard P. *Grundriss zur Geschichte der angelsächsischen Literatur*. Leipzig 1885.
Zupitza 1880
   Ælfrics Grammatik und Glossar, hrsg. J. Zupitza. Berlin 1880.

OLD ENGLISH POETRY [including individual poems other than the elegies]

Bartlett 1935
Bartlett, Adeline Courtney. *The Larger Rhetorical Patterns in Anglo-Saxon Poetry.* New York 1935.

Bately 1985
Bately, Janet. "Linguistic Evidence as a Guide to the Authorship of Old English Verse: A Reappraisal, with Special Reference to *Beowulf.*" In Lapidge and Gneuss 1985, 409–31. See under OE Lit.

Bessinger and Kahrl 1968
Bessinger, Jess B., and Stanley J. Karl, eds. *Essential Articles for the Study of Old English Poetry.* Hamden, Conn. 1968.

Bloomfield 1968
Bloomfield, Morton W. "Understanding Old English Poetry." *Annuale Medievale* 9 (1968): 5–25. Repr. in *Essays and Explorations: Studies in Ideas, Language, and Literature*, pp. 58–80; Cambridge, Mass. 1970.

Bredley 1982
Bredley, S.J., ed. and transl. *Anglo-Saxon Poetry.* London 1982.

Campbell 1966
Campbell, Jackson J. "Learned Rhetoric in Old English Poetry." *MP* 63 (1966): 189–201.

Chambers 1912
Chambers, R.W. *Widsith: A Study in Old English Heroic Legend.* Cambridge 1912.

Conybeare 1826
Conybeare, J.J. *Illustrations of Anglo-Saxon Poetry*, ed. W.D. Conybeare. London 1826.

Cross 1974
Cross, J.E. "The Poem in Transmitted Text – Editor and Critic." *E and S* 27 (1974): 84–97.

Doubleday 1973
Doubleday, James F. "Two-Part Structure in Old English Poetry." *NDEJ* 8 (1973): 71–79.

Ekwall 1924
Ekwall, Eilert. Review of Kershaw's *Anglo-Saxon and Norse Poems. Anglia Beiblatt* 35 (1924): 133–37.

Fanagan 1978
Fanagan, John M. "An Examination of Tense-Usage in Some of the Shorter Poems of the Exeter Book." *Neophil* 62 (1978): 290–93.

Frey 1963
  Frey, Leonard H. "Exile and Elegy in Anglo-Saxon Christian Epic Poetry."
  JEGP 62 (1963): 293–302.
Fukuchi 1975
  Fukuchi, M.S. "Gnomic Statements in Old English Poetry." *Neophil* 59 (1975):
  610–13.
Gardner 1975
  Gardner, John. *The Construction of Christian Poetry in Old English.* Carbondale
  and Edwardsville 1975.
Gollancz 1895
  The Exeter Book, Part I, ed. Israel Gollancz. EETS 104. London 1895.
Grant 1975
  Grant, Raymond J.S. "*Beowulf* and the World of Heroic Elegy." *Leeds Studies in
  English* 8 (1975): 45–75.
Grave
  See Schröer 1882.
Greenfield 1953
  Greenfield, Stanley B. "The Theme of Spiritual Exile in *Christ I.*" *PQ* 32 (1953):
  321–28.
Greenfield 1972
  – *The Interpretation of Old English Poems.* London 1972.
Grein 1857–58
  Grein, Christian W.M. *Bibliothek der angelsächsischen Poesie.* 2 Bände. Göttingen
  1857–58. (Vols. 3 and 4 form *Sprachschatz*; see under OE Grammar etc.)
Grein 1857–59
  – *Dichtungen der Angelsachsen stabreimend übersetzt.* 2 Bände. Göttingen 1857–59.
Grein 1865
  – "Zur Textkritik der angelsächsischen Dichter." *Germania* 10 (1865): 416–29
  (corrections to *Bibliothek*).
Gribble 1983
  Gribble, Barbara. "Form and Function in Old English Poetry." *Language and
  Style* 16 (1983): 456–67.
Guthlac
  See Roberts 1979.
Halsall 1981
  The Old English Rune Poem, ed. Maureen Halsall. Toronto 1981.
Hansen 1988
  Hansen, Elaine Tuttle. *The Solomon Complex: Reading Wisdom in Old English Poetry.*
  Toronto 1988.
Henry 1966
  Henry. P.L. *The Early English and Celtic Lyric.* London 1966.

Hollowell 1980
    Hollowell, Ida Masters. "Was Widsið a *Scop?*" *Neophil* 64 (1980): 583–91.
Holthausen 1894
    Holthausen, Ferdinand. Review of Grein's *Bibliothek der ags Poesie* rev. Wülker. *Anglia Beiblatt* 5 (1894): 193–98.
Holthausen 1907a and 1912
    – "Zur altenglischen Literatur." *Anglia Beiblatt* 18 (1907): 201–8 (includes textual notes on *Wulf* and *Husb*); 23 (1912): 83–89 (includes textual notes on *Ruin, Husb, Res*).
Holthausen 1920
    – "Zur altenglischen Dichtungen." *Anglia Beiblatt* 31 (1920): 25–32 (includes textual notes on *Sea, Rim, Res*).
Holthausen 1921
    – Review of Schücking's *Kleines ags Dichterbuch. Anglia Beiblatt* 32 (1921): 80–83.
Holthausen 1922
    – "Zur altenglischen Dichtungen." *Anglia* 46 (1922): 52–62 (includes textual notes on *Sea, Husb, Rim*).
Holthausen 1935
    – Review of Mackie's *Exeter Book, Part II. Anglia Beiblatt* 46 (1935): 5–10.
Hume 1974
    Hume, Kathryn. "The Concept of the Hall in Old English Poetry." *ASE* 3 (1974): 63–74.
Hume 1976
    – "The 'Ruin Motif' in Old English Poetry." *Anglia* 94 (1976): 339–60.
Imelmann 1920
    See under OE Elegies.
Isaacs 1968
    Isaacs, Neil D. *Structural Principles in Old English Poetry.* Knoxville 1968.
Jacobs 1981
    Jacobs, Nicholas. "The Old English Heroic Tradition in the Light of Welsh Evidence." *Cambridge Medieval Celtic Studies* 2 (1981): 9–20.
Kershaw 1922
    See under OE Elegies.
Klaeber 1924
    Klaeber, Fr. Review of Sedgefield's *Anglo-Saxon Verse-Book. JEGP* 23 (1924): 121–24.
Klaeber 1950
    – *Beowulf and the Fight at Finnsburg.* 3rd ed. Boston 1950.
Krapp and Dobbie 1931–53
    Krapp, G.P., and E.V.K. Dobbie. *The Anglo-Saxon Poetic Records.* 6 vols. New York 1931–53.

Leslie 1959

Leslie, Roy F. "Analysis of Stylistic Devices and Effects in Anglo-Saxon Literature." In *Stil- und Formprobleme in der Literatur*, pp. 129–36. Proceedings of the Seventh Congress of the International Federation for Modern Language and Literature. Heidelberg 1959. Repr. in Bessinger and Kahrl 1968, 255–63.

Lochrie 1986b

Lochrie, Karma. "Anglo-Saxon Morning Sickness." *Neophil* 70 (1986), 316–18.

Mackie 1925

Mackie, W.S. "Notes on Old English Poetry." *MLN* 40 (1925): 91–93 (includes textual notes on *Ruin, Wan, Rim*).

Mackie 1934

– *The Exeter Book, Part II*. EETS 194. London 1934.

Malone 1959

Studies in Heroic Legend and in Current Speech by Kemp Malone, ed. Stefán Einarrson and Norman E. Eliason. Copenhagen 1959.

Mandel 1987

Mandel, Jerome. *Alternative Readings in Old English Poetry*. New York 1987.

Martin 1969

Martin, B.K. "Aspects of Winter in Latin and Old English Poetry." *JEGP* 68 (1969): 375–90.

Menner 1941

Menner, R.J. *The Poetical Dialogues of Solomon and Saturn*. MLA Monograph Series 13. New York 1941.

Mitchell 1975

Mitchell, Bruce. "Linguistic Facts and the Interpretation of Old English Poetry." *ASE* 4 (1975): 11–28. Repr. in Mitchell 1988, 152–71. See under OE Lit.

Nicholson and Frese 1975

Anglo-Saxon Poetry: Essays in Appreciation for John C. McGalliard, ed. Lewis E. Nicholson and Dolores Warwick Frese. Notre Dame, Ind. 1975.

Opland 1980a

Opland, Jeff. *Anglo-Saxon Oral Poetry: A Study of the Traditions*. New Haven, Conn. 1980.

Opland 1980b

– "From Horseback to Monastic Cell: The Impact on English Literature of the Introduction of Writing." In Niles 1980, 30–43; notes pp. 161–63. See under OE Lit.

Parks 1987

Parks, Ward. "The Traditional Narrator and the 'I Heard' Formulas in Old English Poetry." *ASE* 16 (1987): 45–66.

Pope 1966

Pope, John C. *Seven Old English Poems*. New York 1966.

Pope 1978
See under Manuscripts etc.

Pope 1982
Pope, John C. "The Existential Mysteries as Treated in Certain Passages of our Older Poets." In *Acts of Interpretation*, ed. M.J. Carruthers and E.D. Kirk, pp. 345–62. Norman, Ok. 1982.

Raffel 1964
Raffel, Burton, transl. *Poems from the Old English*. 2nd ed. Lincoln, Neb. 1964.

Raw 1978
Raw, Barbara C. *The Art and Background of Old English Poetry*. London 1978.

Richardson 1987
Richardson, John. "The Critic on the Beach." *Neophil* 71 (1987): 114–19.

Riddles (OE)
See Tupper 1910a, and Williamson 1977.

Rieger 1869
Rieger, Max. "Über Cynewulf." *ZfdP* 1 (1869), 215–26 and 313–34 (includes material on *Wulf, Rim, Sea*).

Roberts 1979
The Guthlac Poems of the Exeter Book, ed. Jane Roberts. Oxford 1979.

Robinson 1985
Robinson, Fred C. *Beowulf and the Appositive Style*. Knoxville 1985.

Rune Poem
See Halsall 1981.

Schaubert 1949
Schaubert, Else von. "Zur Erklärung Schwierigkeiten bietender altenglischer Textstellen." In *Philologica: The Malone Anniversary Studies*, ed. Thomas A. Kirby and Henry B. Woolf, pp. 31–42. Baltimore 1949 (includes notes on *Rim* and *Ruin*).

Schröer 1882
Schröer, Arnold. "The Grave." *Anglia* 5 (1882): 289–90.

Schücking 1919
Schücking, Levin L. *Kleines angelsächsisches Dichterbuch*. Cöthen 1919.

Sedgefield 1922
Sedgefield, Walter J. *An Anglo-Saxon Verse-Book*. Manchester 1922.

Shippey 1972
Shippey, T.A. *Old English Verse*. London 1972.

Solomon and Saturn
See Menner 1941.

Stanley 1955–56
Stanley, Eric Gerald. "Old English Poetic Diction and the Interpretation of *The*

Wanderer, The Seafarer, and *The Penitent's Prayer* [Res]." *Anglia* 73 (1955–56): 413–66. Repr. in Bessinger and Kahrl 1968, 458–514.

Stanley 1964–65
– "The Search for Anglo-Saxon Paganism." *NQ* 209 (1964): 204–9, 242–50, 282–87, 324–31, 455–63; 210 (1965): 9–17, 203–7, 285–93. Repr. as monograph Cambridge 1975.

Stanley 1971
See under OE Grammar etc.

Thorpe 1842
Thorpe, Benjamin. *Codex Exoniensis.* London 1842.

Timmer 1944
Timmer, B.J. "Heathen and Christian Elements in Old English Poetry." *Neophil* 29 (1944): 180–85.

Tupper 1910a
Tupper, Frederick. *The Riddles of the Exeter Book.* Boston 1910.

Widsith
See Chambers 1912.

Williamson 1977
Williamson, Craig. *The Old English Riddles of the Exeter Book.* Chapel Hill 1977.

Wilson 1974
Wilson, James H. *Christian Theology and Old English Poetry.* The Hague 1974.

Wülker 1881–89
Bibliothek der angelsächsischen Poesie von C.W.M. Grein, hrsg. Richard P. Wülker. 3 Bände. Kassel 1881–83, and Leipzig 1888–89.

OLD ENGLISH PROSODY

Bliss 1958
Bliss, Alan J. *The Metre of Beowulf.* Oxford 1958.

Bliss 1962
– "The Appreciation of Old English Metre." In *English and Medieval Studies presented to J.R.R. Tolkien on the Occasion of his Seventieth Birthday,* ed. Norman Davis and C.L. Wrenn, pp. 27–40. London 1962.

Cable 1974
Cable, Thomas. *The Metre and Melody of Beowulf.* Urbana 1974.

Cable 1984
– "Old English Prosody." In *Approaches to Teaching Beowulf,* ed. Jess B. Bessinger and Robert F. Yeager, pp. 173–78. New York 1984.

Guest-Skeat 1882
Guest, Edwin. *A History of English Rhythms.* 2 vols. London 1838. Rev. in one vol. W.W. Skeat; London 1882.

Heusler 1925–29
  Heusler, Andreas. *Deutsche Versgeschichte.* 3 Bände. Berlin 1925–29. (See 1.2, pp. 86–314, on early Gmc. verse.)
Kaluza 1909
  Kaluza, Max. *Englische Metrik in historischer Entwicklung dargestellt.* Berlin 1909.
Kaluza transl. Dunstan 1911
  – *A Short History of English Versification from the Earliest Times to the Present Day,* transl. A.C. Dunstan. London 1911 (transl. of Kaluza 1909).
Kluge 1884
  Kluge, Friedrich. "Zur Geschichte des Reims im Altgermanischen." *BGdSL* 9 (1884): 422–50.
Kuhn 1933
  See under OE Grammar etc.
Lehman 1956
  Lehmann, Winfred P. *The Development of Germanic Verse Form.* Austin 1956.
Pope 1942
  Pope, John C. *The Rhythm of Beowulf.* New Haven, Conn. 1942.
Rankin 1921
  Rankin, J.W. "Rhythm and Rime before the Norman Conquest." *PMLA* 36 (1921): 401–28.
Sedgwick 1924
  See under Poetics and Genre Theory.
Sievers 1885 and 1887
  Sievers, Eduard. "Zur Rhythmik des germanischen Alliterationsverses." *BGdSL* 10 (1885): 209–314 and 451–545; 12 (1887): 454–82.
Sievers 1893
  – *Altgermanische Metrik.* Halle 1893.
Sievers 1905
  – "Altgermanische Metrik." In *Grundriss der germanischen Philologie,* hrsg. Hermann Paul, 2b.1–38. 2. Aufl. Strassburg 1905 (abridgment of Sievers 1893).
Sievers transl. Luster 1968
  – "Old Germanic Metrics and Old English Metrics," transl. G.D. Luster. In Bessinger and Kahrl 1968, 267–88 (transl. of Sievers 1905). See under OE Poetry.

BIBLIOGRAPHY AND SCHOLARSHIP ON OLD ENGLISH STUDIES

Adams 1917
  Adams, Eleanor N. *Old English Scholarship in England from 1566–1800.* New Haven, Conn. 1917.

Berkhout and Gatch 1982
Berkhout, Carl T., and Milton McC. Gatch. *Anglo-Saxon Scholarship: The First Three Centuries*. Boston 1982.

Fry 1982–83
Fry, Donald K. "Old English Reference Books." *ELN* 20, no. 1 (1982–83): 11–20.

Greenfield and Robinson 1980
Greenfield, Stanley B., and Fred C. Robinson. *A Bibliography of Publications on Old English Literature to the End of 1972*. Toronto 1980.

Mitchell, Ball, and Cameron 1975
Mitchell, Bruce, Christopher Ball, and Angus Cameron. "Short Titles of Old English Texts." *ASE* 4 (1975): 207–21.

Mitchell, Ball, and Cameron 1979
– "Short Titles of Old English Texts: Addenda and Corrigenda." *ASE* 8 (1979): 331–33.

OLD ENGLISH GRAMMAR, SYNTAX, VOCABULARY, SEMANTICS

Andrew 1940
Andrew, S.O. *Syntax and Style in Old English*. Cambridge 1940.

Bammesberger 1979
Bammesberger, Alfred. *Beiträge zu einem etymologischen Wörterbuch des Altenglischen*. Anglistische Forschungen 139. Heidelberg 1979.

Bammesberger 1984
– *English Etymology*. Sprachwissenschaftliche Studienbücher, Abt. 1. Heidelberg 1984.

Bammesberger 1985
Problems of Old English Lexicography: Studies in Memory of Angus Cameron, ed. Alfred Bammesberger. Eichstätter Beiträge 15 (Abt. Sprache und Literatur). Regensburg 1985.

Bergman 1985
Bergman, Madeleine M. "Supplement to a Concordance to *The Anglo-Saxon Poetic Records*." *Mediaevalia* 8 (1985 for 1982): 9–52.

Bessinger 1978
Bessinger, Jess B. *A Concordance to the Anglo-Saxon Poetic Records*, programmed by Philip H. Smith. Ithaca, NY 1978.

Bosworth-Toller-Campbell 1898, 1921, 1972
Bosworth, J. *An Anglo-Saxon Dictionary*. Oxford 1898. *Supplement* by T.N. Toller; London 1921. *Addenda* by Alistair Campbell; Oxford 1972.

Brunner 1965

Brunner, Karl. *Altenglische Grammatik nach der angelsächsischen Grammatik von Eduard Sievers.* 3. Aufl. Tübingen 1965.

Cameron and Healey 1979

Cameron, Angus, and A. diPaolo Healey. "The Dictionary of Old English." *Dictionaries* 1 (1979): 87–96.

Cameron, Kingsmill, and Amos 1983

Cameron, Angus, Allison Kingsmill, and Ashley Crandell Amos. *Old English Word Studies: A Preliminary Author and Word Index.* Toronto Old English Series 8. Toronto 1983.

Cameron et al. 1986a

Cameron, Angus, et al. *Dictionary of Old English: Preface.* Toronto 1986 (included in Cameron et al. 1986b).

Cameron et al. 1986b

– *Dictionary of Old English: Preface and List of Texts and Index of Editions* (microfiche). Toronto 1986.

Cameron et al. 1986, 1988, 1991

– *Dictionary of Old English: Æ, B, C, D* (Microfiche). Toronto 1992, 1991, 1988, and 1986, resp.

Campbell 1959

Campbell, Alistair. *Old English Grammar.* Oxford 1959.

Crozier 1986

Crozier, Alan. "Old West Norse *íþrótt* and Old English *indryhtu.*" *SN* 58 (1986): 3–10.

diPaolo

See Healey.

Grein 1880

Grein, Christian W.M. *Kurzgefasste angelsächsische Grammatik.* Kassel 1880.

Grein-Köhler-Holthausen 1861–64, 1912

– *Sprachschatz der angelsächsischen Dichter.* Bibliothek der angelsächsischen Poesie 3–4. Kassel and Göttingen 1861–64. Unter Mitwerkungen von F. Holthausen neu hrsg. von J.J. Köhler; Germanische Bibliothek hrsg. W. Streitberg, 1. Sammlung, 4. Reihe, 4. Band; Heidelberg 1912.

Healey and Venezky 1980

Healey, A. diPaolo, and R.L. Venezky. *A Microfiche Concordance to Old English.* Toronto 1980.

Holthausen 1934

Holthausen, Ferdinand. *Altenglisches etymologisches Wörterbuch.* Germanische Bibliothek, 4. Reihe, Wörterbuch 7. Heidelberg 1934.

Kisbye 1982

Kisbye, T. "A Chronology of Old English Vowel Changes." *OEN* 15, no. 2 (1982): 20–25.

Kuhn 1933

Kuhn, Hans. "Wortstellung und -betonung im Altgermanischen." *BGdSL* 57 (1933): 1–109.

Luick-Wild and Koziol 1914–21,1929–40

Luick, Karl. *Historische Grammatik der englischen Sprache*, Teil 1. Leipzig 1914–21. Teil 2 hrsg. Friedrich Wild und Herbert Koziol; Leipzig 1929–40. Repr. with a word index by Richard Hamer; Stuttgart 1964.

Lutz 1984

Lutz, Angelika. "Spellings of the *Waldend* Group – Again." *ASE* 13 (1984): 51–64.

Meritt 1945

Meritt, Herbert D. *Old English Glosses: A Collection.* New York 1945.

Mitchell 1965

Mitchell, Bruce. "Some Problems of Mood and Tense in Old English." *Neophil* 49 (1965): 44–46.

Mitchell 1980

– "The Dangers of Disguise: Old English Texts in Modern Punctuation." *RES* n.s. 31 (1980): 385–413. Repr. in Mitchell 1988, 172–202. See under OE Lit.

Mitchell 1984

– "The Origin of Old English Conjunctions: Some Problems." In *Historical Syntax*, ed. Jacek Fisiak, pp. 271–99. Berlin 1984. Repr. in Mitchell 1988, 269–95. See under OE Lit.

Mitchell 1985

– *Old English Syntax.* 2 vols. Oxford 1985.

Napier 1900

Napier, Arthur S. *Old English Glosses.* Anecdota Oxoniensa, Mediaeval and Modern Series 11. Oxford 1900.

Searle 1897

Searle, William George. *Onomasticon Anglo-Saxonicum.* Cambridge 1897.

Sievers-Brunner 1965

See Brunner 1965.

Stanley 1969

Stanley, Eric Gerald. "Spellings of the *Waldend* Group." In Atwood and Hill 1969, 38–69. See under OE Lit.

Stanley 1971

– "Studies in the Prosaic Vocabulary of Old English Verse." *NM* 72 (1971): 385–418.

Venezky and Butler 1983

Venezky, R.L., and Sharon A. Butler. *A Microfiche Concordance to Old English: The High-Frequency Words.* Toronto 1983.

Wright-Wülker 1884

Thomas Wright. *Anglo-Saxon and Old English Vocabularies.* 2nd ed. rev. Richard P. Wülker. 2 vols. London 1884.

DATING

Amos 1980
  Amos, Ashley Crandell. *Linguistic Means of Determining the Dates of Old English Literary Texts.* Medieval Academy Books 90. Cambridge, Mass. 1980.
Blake 1977
  Blake, N.F. "The Dating of Old English Poetry." In Lee 1977, 14–27. See under OE Lit.
Boyle 1981
  Boyle, Leonard E., OP. "The Nowell Codex and the Poem of *Beowulf.*" In Chase 1981a, 23–32.
Cable 1981
  Cable, Thomas. "Metrical Style as Evidence for the Date of *Beowulf.*" In Chase 1981a, 77–82.
Cameron et al. 1981
  Cameron, Angus et al. "A Reconsideration of the Language of *Beowulf.*" In Chase 1981a, 33–75.
Chase 1981a
  The Dating of Beowulf, ed. Colin Chase. Toronto 1981.
Chase 1981b
  Chase, Colin. "Opinions on the Date of *Beowulf,* 1815–1980." In Chase 1981a, 3–8.
Chase 1981c
  – "Saints' Lives and Royal Lives." In Chase 1981a, 161–71.
Clemoes 1981
  Clemoes, Peter. "Style as the Criterion for Dating the Composition of *Beowulf.*" In Chase 1981a, 173–85.
Duncan 1986
  Duncan, Edwin. "Chronological Testing and the Scansion of *Frea* in Old English Poetry." *NM* 87 (1986): 92–101.
Frank 1981
  Frank, Roberta. "Skaldic Verse and the Date of *Beowulf.*" In Chase 1981a, 123–39.
Fulk 1989
  Fulk, R.D. "West Germanic Parasiting, Sievers' Law, and the Dating of Old English Verse." *SP* 86 (1989): 117–38.
Fulk 1990
  – "Contraction as a Criterion for Dating Old English Verse." *JEGP* 89 (1990): 1–16.

Goffart 1981
Goffart, Walter. "Hetware and Hugas: Datable Anachronisms in *Beowulf*." In Chase 1981a, 83–100.

Jacobs 1977
Jacobs, Nicholas. "Anglo-Danish Relations, Poetic Archaism and the Date of *Beowulf*: A Reconsideration of the Evidence." *Poetica* 8 (Tokyo 1977): 23–43.

Kiernan 1981a
Kiernan, Kevin. *Beowulf and the Beowulf Manuscript.* New Brunswick, NJ 1981.

Kiernan 1981b
– "The Eleventh-Century Origin of *Beowulf* and the *Beowulf* Manuscript." In Chase 1981a, 9–21.

Kisbye 1982
See under OE Grammar etc.

McTurk 1981
McTurk, R.W. "Variation in *Beowulf* and the Poetic Edda: A Chronological Experiment." In Chase 1981a, 141–60.

Murray 1981
Murray, Alexander Callander. "*Beowulf*, the Danish Invasions, and Royal Genealogy." In Chase 1981a, 101–11.

Page 1981
Page, R.I. "The Audience of *Beowulf* and the Vikings." In Chase 1981a, 113–22.

Pope 1981
Pope, John C. "On the Date of Composition of *Beowulf*." In Chase 1981a, 187–95.

Ricci 1929
Ricci, Aldo. "The Chronology of Anglo-Saxon Poetry." *RES* 5 (1929): 257–66.

Schabram 1965 and 1973
See under Dialects.

Stanley 1981
Stanley, Eric Gerald. "The Date of *Beowulf*: Some Doubts and No Conclusions." In Chase 1981a, 197–211.

Wetzel 1985
Wetzel, Claus-Dieter. "Die Datierung des *Beowulf*: Bemerkungen zur jüngsten Forschungsentwicklung." *Anglia* 103 (1985): 371–400.

DIALECTS

Campbell 1951
Campbell, Jackson J. "The Dialect Vocabulary of the Old English Bede." *JEGP* 50 (1951): 349–72.

Crowley 1986
  Crowley, Joseph P. "The Study of Old English Dialects." *English Studies* 67 (1986): 97–112.
Jordan 1906
  Jordan, Richard. *Eigentümlichkeiten des anglischen Wortschatzes.* Heidelberg 1906.
Schabram 1965
  Schabram, Hans. *Superbia. Studien zum altenglischen Wortschatz, Teil 1: Die dialektale und zeitliche Verbreitung des Wortguts.* Munich 1965.
Schabram 1973
  – "Das altenglische *superbia*-Wortgut. Eine Nachlese." In Bauer, Stanzel, and Zaic 1973, 272–79. See under OE Lit.
Sisam 1953c
  Sisam, Kenneth. "Dialect Origins of the Earlier Old English Verse." In Sisam 1953a, 119–39. See under OE Lit.
Wenisch 1979
  Wenisch, Franz. *Spezifisch anglisches Wortgut in den nordhumbrischen Interlinearglossierungen des Lukasevangeliums.* Anglistische Forschungen 132. Heidelberg 1979.

MANUSCRIPTS, FACSIMILES, AND MANUSCRIPT STUDIES

Blake 1962
  Blake, N.F. "The Scribe of the Exeter Book." *Neophil* 46 (1962): 316–18.
Raymond Chambers 1911–12
  Chambers, Raymond W. "The British Museum Transcript of the Exeter Book." *Anglia* 35 (1911–12): 393–400.
Robert Chambers 1831
  British Library Additional MS 9067. Pen-and-ink facsimile of the Exeter Book, copied by Robert Chambers 1831.
Conner 1986
  Conner, Patrick W. "The Structure of the Exeter Codex." *Scriptorium* 40 (1986): 233–42.
Exeter Book, ca. 970
  The Exeter Book, copied ca. 970. Manuscript in the Library of Exeter Cathedral.
Exeter Book 1933
  The Exeter Book of Old English Poetry. Facsimile with introductory chapters by R.W. Chambers, Max Förster, and Robin Flower. London 1933.
Hill 1986
  Hill, Joyce. "The Exeter Book and Lambeth Palace Library MS. 149: A Reconsideration." *ANQ* 24 (1986): 112–16.

Ker 1933
Ker, N.R. Review of *The Exeter Book*, facsimile ed. *MÆ* 2 (1933): 224–31.
Ker 1957
– *Catalogue of Manuscripts Containing Anglo-Saxon*. Oxford 1957.
Liuzza 1988
Liuzza, Roy Michael. "The Texts of the Old English *Riddle 30*." *JEGP* 87 (1988): 1–15.
Pope 1969
Pope, John C. "The Lacuna in the Text of Cynewulf's *Ascension*." In Atwood and Hill, 210–19. See under OE Lit.
Pope 1974
– "An Unsuspected Lacuna in the Exeter Book: Divorce Proceedings for an Ill-Matched Couple in the Old English Riddles." *Speculum* 49 (1974): 615–22.
Pope 1978
– "Palaeography and Poetry: Some Solved and Unsolved Problems of the Exeter Book." In *Medieval Scribes, Manuscripts, and Libraries: Essays Presented to N.R. Ker*, ed. M.B. Parkes and A.J. Watson, pp. 25–65. London 1978.
Schipper 1874
Schipper, J. "Zum Codex Exoniensis." *Germania* 19 (1874): 327–38.
Sisam 1953b
Sisam, Kenneth. "The Exeter Book." In Sisam 1953a, 97–108. See under OE Lit.
Sisam 1953d
– "The Arrangement of the Exeter Book." In Sisam 1953a, 291–92.
Tupper 1912
Tupper, Frederick. "The British Museum Transcript of the Exeter Book." *Anglia* 36 (1912): 285–88.

OLD ENGLISH ELEGIES

Bessai 1964
Bessai, Frank. "Comitatus and Exile in Old English Poetry." *Culture* 25 (1964): 130–44.
Bouman 1962
Bouman, A.C. *Patterns in Old English and Old Icelandic Literature*. Leidse Germanistische en Anglistische Reeks, Deel 1. Leiden 1962.
Brunner 1921
Brunner, Karl. "Hero and Leander und die altenglischen Elegien." *Archiv* 142 (1921): 258–59.
Campbell 1969
Campbell, Thomas P. "The Treasure Motif in Four Old English Religious Ele-

gies." *Laurentian University Review* 2, no. 2 (1969): 45–58 (on *Wan, Sea, Rim, Res*).

Chadwick 1922

See Kershaw 1922.

Dietrich 1966

Dietrich, Gerhard. "Ursprünge des Elegischen in der altenglischen Literatur." In *Literatur-Kultur-Gesellschaft in England und Amerika: Aspekte und Forschungsbeiträge*, hrsg. Gerhard Müller-Schwefe und Konrad Tuzinski, pp. 3–27. Frankfurt 1966.

Dunleavy 1960

Dunleavy, Gareth W. *Colum's Other Island: The Irish at Lindisfarne*. Madison 1960 (contains discussion of *Ruin, Wife,* and *Sea*).

Elliott 1961

Elliott, Ralph W.V. "Form and Image in the Old English Lyrics." *EIC* 11 (1961): 1–9.

Frey 1963

See under OE Poetry.

Goldman 1979

Goldman, Stephen H. "The Use of Christian Belief in Old English Poems of Exile." *Res Publica Litterarum* 2 (1979): 69–80.

Göller 1964

Göller, Karl H. "Die angelsächsischen Elegien." *Germanisch-romanische Monatsschrift* 14 (1964): 225–41.

Grant 1975

See under OE Poetry.

Green 1983

The Old English Elegies: New Essays in Criticism and Research, ed. Martin Green. Rutherford, Madison, and Teaneck 1983.

Greenfield 1953

See under OE Poetry.

Greenfield 1955

Greenfield, Stanley B. "The Formulaic Expression of the Theme of 'Exile' in Anglo-Saxon Poetry." *Speculum* 30 (1955): 200–206.

Greenfield 1966

– "The Old English Elegies." In *Continuations and Beginnings: Studies in Old English Literature*, ed. E.G. Stanley, pp. 142–75. London 1966.

Grubl 1948

Grubl, Emily D. *Studien zu den angelsächsischen Elegien*. Marburg 1948.

Harris 1983

Harris, Joseph. "Elegy in Old English and Old Norse: A Problem in Literary History." In Green 1983, 46–56.

Henry 1966
See under OE Poetry.

Hicketier 1889
Hicketier, Fritz. *"Klage der Frau, Botschaft des Gemahls* und *Ruine." Anglia* 11 (1889): 363–68.

Holoka 1976
Holoka, James P. "Oral Formula and Anglo-Saxon Elegy." *Neophil* 60 (1976): 570–76.

Idelmann 1932
Idelmann, Theodora. *Das Gefühl in den altenglischen Elegien.* Münster 1932.

Imelmann 1907a
Imelmann, Rudolf. *Die altenglische Odoaker-Dichtung.* Berlin 1907.

Imelmann 1907b
— *Zeugnisse zur altenglischen Odoaker-Dichtung.* Berlin 1907.

Imelmann 1908
— *Wanderer und Seefahrer im Rahmen der altenglischen Odoaker-Dichtung.* Berlin 1908.

Imelmann 1920
— *Forschungen zur altenglischen Poesie.* Berlin 1920.

Irving 1967
Irving, Edward B. "Image and Meaning in the Elegies." In *Old English Poetry: Fifteen Essays*, ed. Robert P. Creed, pp. 153–66. Providence, RI 1967.

Kennedy 1936
Kennedy, Charles W. *Old English Elegies. Translated into Alliterative Verse with a Critical Introduction.* Princeton 1936.

Kershaw 1922
Kershaw, Nora (later Nora K. Chadwick). *Anglo-Saxon and Norse Poems.* Cambridge 1922.

Klaeber 1935
Klaeber, Fr. "Zu altenglischen Dichtungen." *Archiv* 167 (1935): 36–41 (contains textual notes on *Deor, Husb, Res, Wife*).

Klinck 1984
Klinck, Anne L. "The Old English Elegy as a Genre." *English Studies in Canada* 10 (1984): 129–40.

Lally 1980
Lally, Tim D.P. "Synchronic versus Diachronic Popular Culture Studies and the Old English Elegy." In *Five Thousand Years of Popular Culture: Popular Culture before Printing*, ed. Fred E.H. Schroeder, pp. 201–12. Bowling Green, Ohio, 1980.

Lee 1972
Lee, Alvin A. "Hope Has Wandered in Exile: Patterns of Imagery in Old English Lyrics." In *The Guest-Hall of Eden*, pp. 129–70. New Haven, Conn. 1972.

Leslie 1961
   Leslie, Roy F. *Three Old English Elegies*. Manchester 1961. Repr. with corrections 1966.
Pilch 1964
   Pilch, Herbert. "The Elegiac Genre in Old English and Early Welsh Poetry." *ZfcP* 29 (1964): 209–24.
Reuschel 1938
   Reuschel, Helga. "Ovid und die angelsächsischen Elegien." *BGdSL* 62 (1938): 132–42.
Rosteutscher 1938
   Rosteutscher, J.H.W. "Germanischer Schicksalsglaube und angelsächsische Elegiendichtung." *Englische Studien* 73 (1938): 1–31.
Schücking 1908
   Schücking, Levin L. "Das angelsächsische Totenklagelied." *Englische Studien* 39 (1908): 1–13.
Schücking 1917–18
   – *"Die altenglische Elegie"* (review of Sieper's edition). *Englische Studien* 51 (1917–18): 97–115.
Sieper 1915
   Sieper, Ernst. *Die altenglische Elegie*. Strassburg 1915.
Timmer 1942
   Timmer, B.J. "The Elegiac Mood in Old English Poetry." *English Studies* 24 (1942): 33–44.
Tripp 1972
   Tripp, Raymond P. "The Narrator as Revenant: A Reconsideration of Three Old English Elegies." *PLL* 8 (1972): 339–61 (on *Wan, Sea, Wife*).
Tripp 1983
   – "Odin's Powers and the Old English Elegies." In Green 1983, 57–68.
Whitbread 1970
   See under *Deor*.
York 1981
   York, Lamar. "The Early English Lyricist." *Neophil* 65 (1981): 473–79.

DEOR

Anderson 1983
   Anderson, James E. *"Deor, Wulf and Eadwacer,* and *The Soul's Address*: How and Where the Old English Exeter Book Riddles Begin." In Green 1983, 204–30. See under OE Elegies.
Ashdown 1929
   Ashdown, Margaret. "Notes on Two Passages of Old English Verse: II." *RES* 5 (1929): 326–27.

Baesecke 1937

Baesecke, Georg. "Die Herkunft der Wielanddichtung." *BGdSL* 61 (1937): 368–78.

Binz 1895

Binz, Gustav. "Zeugnisse zur germanischen Sage in England." *BGdSL* 20 (1895): 141–223.

Birch 1885–99

See under OE Lit.

Bloomfield 1964

Bloomfield, Morton W. "The Form of *Deor*." *PMLA* 79 (1964): 534–41.

Bloomfield 1986

– "*Deor* Revisited." In *Modes of Interpretation in Old English Literature: Essays in Honour of Stanley B. Greenfield*, ed. P. Brown, G. Crampton, and F.C. Robinson, pp. 273–82. Toronto 1986.

Bolton 1972

Bolton, Whitney F. "Boethius, Alfred, and *Deor* Again." *MP* 69 (1972): 222–27.

Boren 1975

Boren, James L. "The Design of the Old English *Deor*." In Nicholson and Frese 1975, 264–76. See under OE Poetry.

Brandl 1908

See under OE Lit.

Bugge 1897–1900

Bugge, Sophus. "The Norse Lay of Wayland and Its Relation to English Tradition." *Saga-Book of the Viking Club* 2 (1897–1900): 271–312.

Burton 1893

Burton, Richard. "The Oldest English Lyric." *Poet-Lore* 5 (1893): 57–67.

Chadwick 1932

See under Poetics and Genre Theory.

Condren 1981

Condren, Edward I. "Deor's Artistic Triumph." *SP* 78, no. 5 (1981): 62–76.

Dickins 1915

See under Early Gmc. Lt. and Culture.

Ekwall 1934

Ekwall, Eilert. Review of A.H. Smith's *Three Northumbrian Poems* and Malone's *Deor*. *MLR* 29 (1934): 78–82 (80–82 on *Deor*).

Eliason 1965

Eliason, Norman E. "The Story of Geat and Mæðhild in *Deor*." *SP* 62 (1965): 495–509.

Eliason 1966

– "Two Old English Scop Poems." *PMLA* 81 (1966): 185–92.

Eliason 1969
- *"Deor* – A Begging Poem?"* In Pearsall and Waldron 1969, 55–61. See under OE Lit.

Forster 1937
Forster, Leonard. "Die Assoziation in *Deors Klage.*" *Anglia* 61 (1937): 117–21.

Frankis 1962
Frankis, P.J. *"Deor* and *Wulf and Eadwacer*: Some Conjectures." *MÆ* 31 (1962): 161–75.

Frings 1930
Frings, Theodor. "Hilde." *BGdSL* 54 (1930): 391–418 (398–99 on *Deor*).

Grienberger 1921
Grienberger, Theodor. *"Déor."* *Anglia* 45 (1921): 393–407.

Harris 1987
Harris, Joseph. *"Deor* and Its Refrain: Preliminaries to an Interpretation." *Traditio* 43 (1987): 23–53.

Heinzel 1889
See under Early Gmc. Lit. and Culture.

Hill 1983
Hill, Joyce. *Old English Minor Heroic Poems.* Durham and St Andrews Medieval Texts 4. Durham and Fife 1983.

Holthausen 1905–6, 1908–9, 1912–13, 1914–19, 1921–29, 1929, 1938, 1948
Beowulf nebst den kleineren Denkmälern der Heldensage, hrsg. Ferdinand Holthausen. 2 Bände. 8 Auflagen. Heidelberg 1905–6 etc. (includes text of *Deor* from 2nd ed. on).

Jost 1961
Jost, Karl. "Welund und Sampson: Ein Beitrag zur Erklärung der 1. *Deor*-Strophe." In Viebrock and Erzgräber 1961, 86–87. See under OE Lit.

Kaske 1963
Kaske, Robert E. "Weland and the *wurmas* in *Deor.*" *English Studies* 44 (1963): 190–91.

Kemble 1849
See under OE Lit. Vol. 1, pp. 370–72 and 421–24 on *Deor*.

Kiernan 1975
Kiernan, Kevin. "A Solution to the Mæthhild-Geat Crux in *Deor.*" *English Studies* 56 (1975): 97–99.

Kiernan 1978
- *"Deor*: The Consolations of an Anglo-Saxon Boethius." *NM* 79 (1978): 333–40.

Klaeber 1906
Klaeber, Fr. "Zu *Deors Klage* 15 f." *Anglia Beiblatt* 17 (1906): 283–84.

Klaeber 1921
- "The First Line of *Deor*." *Anglia Beiblatt* 32 (1921): 38–40.
Klaeber 1935
See under OE Elegies. Pp. 40–41 on *Deor*.
Klaeber 1948
Klaeber, Fr. "Ein paar Anmerkungen zu den altenglischen *Deor*-Versen." *Archiv* 185 (1948): 124–26.
Kluge 1895
Kluge, Friedrich. "Zeugnisse zur germanischen Sage in England." *Englische Studien* 21 (1895): 446–48.
Kock 1921
Kock, Ernst A. "Interpretations and Emendations of Early English Texts." *Anglia* 45 (1921): 105–31 (123–24 on *Deor*).
Kögel 1894
Kögel, Rudolf. *Geschichte der deutschen Litteratur bis zum Ausgange des Mittelalters* 1.1. Strassburg 1894 (pp. 101–2 on *Deor*).
Kossick 1972
Kossick, Shirley G. "The Old English *Deor*." *Unisa English Studies* 10 (1972): 3–6.
Kuhn 1963
Kuhn, Hans. "Dietrichs dreissig Jahre." In *Märchen, Mythos, Dichtung. Festschrift zum 90. Geburtstag Friedrich von der Leyens am 19. August 1963*, pp. 117–20. Munich 1963. Repr. in Hans Kuhn, *Kleine Schriften. Aufsätze und Rezensionen aus den Gebieten der germanischen und nordischen Sprach-, Literatur-, und Kulturgeschichte* 2: 135–37; Berlin 1969–72.
Lawrence 1911–12
Lawrence, W.W. "The Song of Deor." *MP* 9 (1911–12): 23–45.
Magoun 1942
Magoun, Francis Peabody. "*Deors Klage* und *Guðrúnarkviða I*." *Englische Studien* 75 (1942): 1–5.
Malone 1933, 1949, 1961, 1966, 1977
Deor, ed. Kemp Malone. 5 eds. London 1933, 1949, 1961, 1966. Exeter 1977
Malone 1934a
Malone, Kemp. "Secca and Becca." In *Studia Germanica tillägnade Ernst Albin Kock*, pp. 192–99. Lund 1934. Repr. in Malone 1959, 158–63. See under OE Poetry.
Malone 1934b
- "The Theodoric of the Rök Inscription." *Acta Philolologica Scandinavica* 9 (1934): 76–84. Repr. in Malone 1959, 116–23.
Malone 1936
- "Mæðhild." *Journal of English Literary History* 3 (1936): 253–56.

Malone 1937a
- "The Tale of Geat and Mæðhild." *English Studies* 29 (1937): 193–99.
Malone 1939
- "Becca and Seafola." *Englische Studien* 73 (1939): 180–84. Repr. in Malone 1959, 164–67.
Malone 1942
- "On *Deor* 14–17." *MP* 40 (1942): 1–18.
Malone 1964
- "An Anglo-Latin Version of the 'Hjaðningavíg.'" *Speculum* 39 (1964): 35–44.
Malone 1974
- "The Rhythm of *Deor*." In Burlin and Irving 1974, 165–69. See under OE Lit.
Mandel 1977
Mandel, Jerome. "Exemplum and Refrain: The Meaning of *Deor*." *YES* 7 (1977): 1–9.
Mandel 1982
- "Audience Response Strategies in the Opening of *Deor*." *Mosaic* 15, no. 4 (1982): 127–32.
Markland 1968
Markland, Murray F. "Boethius, Alfred, and *Deor*." *MP* 66 (1968): 1–4.
Markland 1972–73
- "*Deor*: þæs ofereode; þisses swa mæg." *ANQ* 11 (1972–73): 35–36.
Maurus 1902
Maurus, Peter. *Die Wielandsage in der Literatur*. Münchener Beiträge zur romanischen und englischen Philologie 25. Erlangen and Leipzig 1902 (pp. 8–9 on *Deor*).
Müllenhoff 1849
Müllenhoff, Karl. "Sängernamen." *ZfdA* 7 (1849): 530–31.
Müllenhoff 1859
- "Zur Kritik des angelsächsischen Volksepos." *ZfdA* 11 (1859): 272–75.
Müllenhoff 1860–65
- "Zeugnisse und Excurse zur deutschen Heldensage." *ZfdA* 12 (1860–65): 253–386 and 413–36 (261–62 on *Deor*). Repr. in Grimm 1957 [1867], 533–696. See under Early Gmc. Lit. and Culture.
Norman 1937
Norman, Frederick. "*Deor*: A Criticism and an Interpretation." *MLR* 32 (1937): 374–81.
Norman 1937–39
- "*Deor* and Modern Scandinavian Ballads." *London Medieval Studies* 1 (1937–38): 165–78.

Norman 1965
- "Problems in the Dating of *Deor* and Its Allusions." In Bessinger and Creed 1965, 205–13. See under OE Lit.

North 1988
"Jeux d'esprit in *Deor*: Geat and Mæðhild." In Beck 1988, 11–24. See under Early Gmc. Lit. and Culture.

Pertz 1839
See under Christian and Medieval Latin Lit.

Raffel 1964
See under OE Poetry.

Raffel 1972
Raffel, Burton. "Scholars, Scholarship, and the Old English *Deor*." *NDEJ* 8 (1972): 3–10.

Rieger 1861
See under OE Lit.

Schibsbye 1969
Schibsbye, Knud. *"Þæs oferēode, þisses swā mæg." English Studies* 50 (1969): 380–81.

Schücking 1919
See under OE Poetry.

Searle 1897
See under OE Grammar etc.

Sedgefield 1910, 1913, 1935
Beowulf, ed. Walter J. Sedgefield. 3 eds. Manchester 1910, 1913, 1935 (includes text of *Deor*).

Sedgefield 1922
See under OE Poetry.

Stefanovíc 1910
Stefanovíc, Svetislav. "Zu *Deor* v. 14–17." *Anglia* 33 (1910): 397–402.

Stefanovíc 1912
- "Zur Geat-Hilde-Episode im *Deor*." *Anglia* 36 (1912): 383–88.

Stefanovíc 1913
- "Zur dritten Strophe des *Deor*." *Anglia* 37 (1913): 533–38.

Stephens 1969
Stephens, John. "Weland and a Little Restraint: A Note on *Deor* 5–6." *SN* 41 (1969): 371–74.

Tuggle 1977
Tuggle, Thomas T. "The Structure of *Deor*." *SP* 74 (1977): 229–42.

Frederick Tupper 1911–12
Tupper, Frederick. "The Song of Deor." *MP* 9 (1911–12): 265–67.

Frederick Tupper 1913
- "The Third Strophe of *Deor*." *Anglia* 37 (1913): 118–24.

James Tupper 1895
  Tupper, James W. "Deor's Complaint." *MLN* 10 (1895): 63–64.
Whitbread 1940
  Whitbread, Leslie. "Four Text-Notes on *Deor*," *MLN* 55 (1940): 204–7.
Whitbread 1940–41
  – "The Third Section of *Deor*." *MP* 38 (1940–41): 371–84.
Whitbread 1942
  – "An Allusion in *Deor*." *JEGP* 41 (1942): 368–69.
Whitbread 1943
  – "More Text-Notes on *Deor*." *MLN* 58 (1943): 367–69.
Whitbread 1947
  – "Text-Notes on *Deor*." *MLN* 62 (1947): 15–20.
Whitbread 1956
  – "The Binding of Weland." *MÆ* 25 (1956): 13–19.
Whitbread 1963
  – "Four Notes on Old English Poems." *English Studies* 44 (1963): 187–90
  (pp. 188–89 on *Deor*).
Whitbread 1970
  – "The Pattern of Misfortune in *Deor* and Other Old English Poems." *Neophil* 54
  (1970): 167–83.
Wienold 1972
  Wienold, Götz. "*Deor*. Über Offenheit und Auffüllung von Texten."
  Sprachkunst 3 (1972): 285–97.

THE HUSBAND'S MESSAGE [including pertinent material on *Riddle 60*]

Earl Anderson 1973
  Anderson, Earl R. "Voices in *The Husband's Message*." *NM* 74 (1973): 238–
  46.
Earl Anderson 1975
  – "*The Husband's Message*: Persuasion and the Problem of *Genyre*." *English
  Studies* 56 (1975): 289–94.
James Anderson 1974
  Anderson, James E. "Die Deutungmöglichkeiten des altenglischen Gedichtes
  The Husband's Message." *NM* 75 (1974): 402–7.
Blackburn 1901
  Blackburn, F.A. "*The Husband's Message* and the Accompanying Riddles of the
  Exeter Book." *JEGP* 3 (1901): 1–13.
Bolton 1969
  Bolton, Whitney F. "*The Wife's Lament* and *The Husband's Message*: A Reconsi-
  deration Revisited." *Archiv* 205 (1969): 337–51.

Bouman 1962
See under OE Elegies.

Derolez 1954
Derolez, René L.M. *Runica Manuscripta: The English Tradition.* Bruges 1954 (pp. 396–99 on *Husb*).

Dietrich 1859
Dietrich, Franz. "Die Räthsel des Exeterbuchs: Würdigung, Lösung und Herstellung." *ZfdA* 11 (1859): 448–90 (477 on *Rid 60*).

Elliott 1955
Eliott, Ralph W.V. "The Runes in *The Husband's Message.*" *JEGP* 54 (1955): 1–8.

Goldsmith 1975
Goldsmith, Margaret E. "The Enigma of *The Husband's Message.*" In Nicholson and Frese 1975, 242–63. See under OE Poetry.

Greenfield 1972
See under OE Poetry. Pp. 145–54 on *Husb*.

Grein 1880
See under OE Grammar etc.

Holthausen 1907a and 1912
See under OE Poetry. Pp. 207 and 86–87, resp., on *Husb*.

Holthausen 1922
See under OE Poetry. P. 56 on *Husb*.

Holthausen 1923
— "Zu altenglischen Dichtungen." *Anglia Beiblatt* 34 (1923): 89–91 (90 on *Husb*).

Howlett 1978
Howlett, D.R. "*The Wife's Lament* and *The Husband's Message.*" *NM* 79 (1978): 7–10.

Imelmann 1907a
See under OE Elegies.

Kaske 1964
Kaske, Robert E. "The Reading *Genyre* in *The Husband's Message*, line 49 [50]." *MÆ* 33 (1964): 204–6.

Kaske 1967
— "A Poem of the Cross in the Exeter Book: *Riddle 60* and *The Husband's Message.*" *Traditio* 23 (1967): 41–71.

Klaeber 1935
See under OE Elegies. Pp. 38–39 on *Husb*.

Kluge 1897, 1902
See under OE Lit.

Kock 1921
See under *Deor*. Pp. 122–23 on *Husb*.

Leslie 1961
See under OE Elegies.
Leslie 1968
Leslie, Roy F. "The Integrity of *Riddle 60*." *JEGP* 67 (1968): 451–57.
Nicholson 1982
Nicholson, Peter. "The Old English Rune for *S*." *JEGP* 81 (1982): 313–19.
Orton 1981
Orton, Peter. "The Speaker in *The Husband's Message*." *Leeds Studies in English* 12 (1981): 43–56.
Pope 1978
See under Manuscripts etc. Pp. 42–63 on *Husb*.
Renoir 1981
Renoir, Alain. "The Least Elegiac of the Elegies: A Contextual Glance at *The Husband's Message*." *SN* 53 (1981): 69–76.
Schofield 1906
Schofield, W.H. *English Literature from the Norman Conquest to Chaucer*. London 1906 (pp. 201–2 allude briefly to *Husb*).
Schubel 1973
Schubel, Friedrich. "Der angelsächsische 'klagende' Kuckuck." In Bauer, Stanzel, and Zaic 1973, 280–96. See under OE Lit.
Strobl 1887
Strobl, Joseph. "Zur Spruchdichtung bei den Angelsachsen." *ZfdA* 31 (1887): 54–64 (55–56 and n. 1 on *Husb*).
Swanton 1964
Swanton, Michael J. "*The Wife's Lament* and *The Husband's Message*: A Reconsideration." *Anglia* 82 (1964): 269–90.
Trautmann 1894
Trautmann, Moritz. "Zur Botschaft des Gemahls." *Anglia* 16 (1894): 207–25.
Williamson 1977
See under OE Poetry.
Wülker 1879
See under *Ruin*. Pp. 381–85 on *Husb*.

RESIGNATION

Berkhout 1974
Berkhout, Carl T. "The Speaker in *Resignation*: A Biblical Note." *NQ* 219 (1974): 122–23.
Bestul 1977
Bestul, Thomas H. "The Old English *Resignation* and the Benedictine Reform." *NM* 78 (1977): 18–23.

Bliss and Frantzen 1976
   Bliss, Alan, and Allen J. Frantzen. "The Integrity of *Resignation*." *RES* n.s. 27 (1976): 385–402.
Brandl 1908
   See under OE Lit.
Cross 1974
   See under OE Poetry.
Henry 1966
   See under OE Poetry.
Holthausen 1894
   See under OE Poetry.
Holthausen 1907b
   Holthausen, Ferdinand. "Zur Textkritik altenglischer Dichtungen." *Englische Studien* 37 (1907): 198–211 (201–2 on *Res*).
Holthausen 1912
   See under OE Poetry. Pp. 88–89 on *Res*.
Holthausen 1920
   See under OE Poetry. Pp. 28–29 on *Res*.
Holthausen 1935
   See under OE Poetry.
Klaeber 1935
   See under OE Elegies. Pp. 36–38 on *Res*.
Klinck 1987b
   Klinck, Anne L. "*Resignation*: Exile's Lament or Penitent's Prayer?" *Neophil* 71 (1987): 423–30.
Kock 1920
   Kock, Ernst A. "Interpretations and Emendations of Early English Texts." *Anglia* 44 (1920): 245–60 (255–56 on *Res*).
Lochrie 1986a
   Lochrie, Karma. "*Wyrd* and the Limits of Human Understanding: A Thematic Sequence in the Exeter Book." *JEGP* 85 (1986): 323–31.
Malmberg 1979
   Malmberg, Lars. *Resignation*. Durham and St Andrews Medieval Texts 2. Durham and Fife 1979.
Nelson 1983
   Nelson, Marie. "On *Resignation*." In Green 1983, 133–47. See under OE Elegies.
Prins 1964
   See under *Wan*.
Schücking 1917
   See under OE Elegies.

Schücking 1919
    See under OE Poetry.
Stanley 1955–56
    See under OE Poetry.

THE RIMING POEM

Brandl 1908
    See under OE Lit.
Cross 1962
    See under OE Lit.
Earl 1985
    Earl, James W. "A Translation of The Rhyming Poem." *OEN* 19, no. 1 (1985): 31–33.
Earl 1987
    Earl, James W. "Hisperic Style in the Old English *Rhyming Poem*." *PMLA* 102 (1987): 187–96.
Goldsmith 1967
    Goldsmith, Margaret E. "Corroding Treasure: A Note on the Old English *Rhyming Poem*, lines 45–50." *NQ* 212 (1967): 169–71.
Grein 1865 transl.
    Grein, Christian W.M. "Das Reimlied des Exeterbuchs." *Germania* 10 (1865): 305–7 (Latin translation).
Holthausen 1909
    Holthausen, Ferdinand. "Zum Reimlied." *Anglia Beiblatt* 20 (1909): 313–14.
Holthausen 1910a
    – "Zum Reimlied." *Anglia Beiblatt* 21 (1910): 12–13.
Holthausen 1910b
    – "Nochmals das Reimlied." *Anglia Beiblatt* 21 (1910): 155–56.
Holthausen 1913
    – "Das altenglische Reimlied." In *Festschrift für Lorenz Morsbach*, hrsg. F. Holthausen und H. Spies, pp. 190–200; Nachtrag, p. 722. Studien zur englischen Philologie 50. Halle 1913 (an edition of *Rim*).
Holthausen 1920
    See under OE Poetry. Pp. 25–27 on *Rim*.
Holthausen 1922
    See under OE Poetry. Pp. 57–60 on *Rim*.
Holthausen 1930
    Holthausen, Ferdinand. "Zum altenglischen Reimliede." *Anglia Beiblatt* 41 (1930): 39–40.

Holthausen 1930–31
  – "Das altenglische Reimlied." *Englische Studien* 65 (1930–31): 181–89 (an edition of *Rim*).
Holthausen 1953a
  – "Das altenglische Reimlied." *Germanisch-romanische Monatsschrift* 34 (1953): 148–52 (an edition of *Rim*).
Howlett 1978
  Howlett, D.R. "The Structure of *The Riming Poem*." *NM* 79 (1978): 330–32.
Klinck 1985–86
  Klinck, Anne L. "Growth and Decay in *The Riming Poem*, Lines 51–54." *ELN* 23, no. 3 (1985–86): 1–3.
Klinck 1988
  – "*The Riming Poem*: Design and Interpretation." *NM* 89 (1988): 266–79.
Kluge 1897
  See under OE Lit.
Lee 1972
  See under OE Elegies.
Lehmann 1970
  Lehmann, Ruth P.M. "The Old English *Riming Poem*: Interpretation, Text, and Translation." *JEGP* 69 (1970): 437–49.
Mackie 1922
  Mackie, W.S. "The Old English *Rhymed Poem*." *JEGP* 21 (1922): 507–19.
Macrae-Gibson 1973
  Macrae-Gibson, O.D. "The Literary Structure of *The Riming Poem*." *NM* 74 (1973): 62–84.
Macrae-Gibson 1983
  – *The Old English Riming Poem*. Cambridge 1983.
Olsen 1979
  Olsen, Alexandra Hennessy. "The Heroic World: Icelandic Sagas and the Old English *Riming Poem*." *Pacific Coast Philology* 14 (1979): 51–58.
Rieger 1869
  See under OE Poetry. Pp. 321–22 on *Rim*.
Schaar 1962
  Schaar, Claes. "*Brondhord* in the Old English *Rhyming Poem*." *English Studies* 43 (1962): 490–91.
Schücking 1919
  See under OE Poetry.
Sedgefield 1921
  Sedgefield, Walter J. "Suggested Emendations in Old English Poetical Texts." *MLR* 16 (1921): 59–61 (61 on *Rim*).

Sievers 1884
Sievers, Eduard. "Miscellen zur angelsächsischen Grammatik." *BGdSL* 9 (1884): 197–300 (235–36 on *Rim*).
Sievers 1886
– "Zum angelsächsischen Reimlied." *BGdSL* 11 (1886): 345–54.
Stanley 1984a
Stanley, Eric G. "Notes on the Text of *Christ and Satan*; and on *The Riming Poem* and *The Rune Poem*, Chiefly on *wynn, wēn* and *wenne*." *NQ* 229 (1984): 443–53 (450–52 on *Rim*).
Stanley 1984b
– Review of Macrae-Gibson's *OE Riming Poem*. *NQ* 229 (1984): 526–28.
Wentersdorf 1985
Wentersdorf, Karl P. "The Old English *Rhyming Poem*: A Ruler's Lament." *SP* 82 (1985): 265–94.

THE RUIN

Baker 1963
Baker, Stewart A. "*Weal* in the Old English *Ruin*." *NQ* 208 (1963): 328–29.
Bately 1984
See under *Wan*.
Brandl 1919
Brandl, Alois. "Venantius Fortunatus und die angelsächsischen Elegien *Wanderer* und *Ruine*." *Archiv* 139 (1919): 84.
Calder 1971
Calder, Daniel G. "Perspective and Movement in *The Ruin*." *NM* 72 (1971): 442–45.
Cross 1954
Cross, James E. "Notes on Old English Texts." *Neophil* 39 (1954): 203–6 (204–5 on *Rim*).
Cross 1957
– "On Sievers-Brunner's Interpretation of *The Ruin*, Line 7, *Forweorone, Geleorene*." *English and Germanic Studies* 6 (1957): 104–6.
Doubleday 1971
Doubleday, James F. "*Ruin* 8b–9a." *NQ* 216 (1971): 124.
Doubleday 1972
– "*The Ruin*: Structure and Theme." *JEGP* 71 (1972): 369–81.
Dunleavy 1959
Dunleavy, Gareth W. "A 'De Excidio' Tradition in the Old English *Ruin*?" *PQ* 38 (1959): 112–18.

Earle 1870–73
Earle, John. "An Ancient Saxon Poem of a City in Ruins, Supposed to be Bath." *Proceedings of the Bath Natural History and Antiquities Field Club* 2 (1870–73): 259–70 (paper delivered to the Field Club, 15 March 1871).

Earle 1884
– "The Ruined City." *Academy* 26 (1884): 29.

Förster 1923
Förster, Max. Review of G. Ehrismann's *Geschichte der deutschen Literatur*, 1. Teil. *Anglia Beiblatt* 34 (1923): 100–104 (includes discussion of *teafor*, as in *Ruin* 30).

Herben 1939
Herben, Stephen J. "The Ruin." *MLN* 54 (1939): 37–39.

Herben 1944
– *The Ruin* Again." *MLN* 59 (1944): 72–74.

Holthausen 1907b
See under *Res.* P. 200 on *Ruin*.

Holthausen 1912
See under OE Poetry. Pp. 85–96 on *Ruin*.

Holthausen 1935
See under OE Poetry.

Hotchner 1939
Hotchner, Cecilia A. *Wessex and Old English Poetry, with Special Consideration of The Ruin*. Lancaster, Pa. 1939.

Johnson 1980
Johnson, William. "*The Ruin* as Body-City Riddle." *PQ* 59 (1980): 397–411.

Jordan 1906
See under Dialects.

Keenan 1966
Keenan, Hugh T. "The Ruin as Babylon." *TSL* 11 (1966): 109–17.

Kirkland 1886
Kirkland, J.H. "A Passage in the Anglo-Saxon Poem *The Ruin*, Critically Discussed." *American Journal of Philology* 7 (1886): 367–69.

Klinck 1986b
Klinck, Anne L. "A Damaged Passage in the Old English *Ruin*." *SN* 58 (1986): 165–68.

Kluge 1897
See under OE Lit.

Lee 1973
Lee, Anne Thompson. "*The Ruin*: Bath or Babylon? A Non-archaeological Investigation." *NM* 74 (1973): 443–55.

Leo 1865

Leo, Heinrich. *Carmen anglo-saxonicum in Codice Exoniensi servatum quod vulgo inscribitur 'Ruinae.'"* Halle 1865.

Leslie 1961
See under OE Elegies.

Mackie 1925
See under OE Poetry.

Meritt 1941
Meritt, Herbert D. "Three Studies in Old English. II: An Old English Term for Waled Ornamentation." *American Journal of Philology* 62 (1941): 331–39.

Meritt 1945
See under OE Grammar etc.

Meritt 1957
Meritt, Herbert D. "Old English Glosses to Gregory, Ambrose, and Prudentius." *JEGP* 56 (1957): 65–68 (p. 65 *gebregde*, as in *Ruin* 18).

Mitchell 1965
See under OE Grammar etc.

Napier 1900
See under OE Grammar etc.

Nenninger 1938
Nenninger, Julius. *Die altenglische Ruine textkritisch und literarhistorisch untersucht.* Limburg 1938.

Page 1985
See under OE Lit.

Renoir 1983
Renoir, Alain. "The Old English *Ruin*: Contrastive Structure and Affective Impact." In Green 1983, 148–73. See under OE Elegies.

Robinson 1966
Robinson, Fred C. "Notes and Emendations to Old English Poetic Texts." *NM* 67 (1966): 356–64 (363 on *Ruin*).

Rubin 1979
Rubin, Gary. "MS. Integrity: Lines 3a–4b of *The Ruin*." *Neophil* 63 (1979): 297–99.

Stanley 1963
Stanley, Eric G. "Weal in the Old English *Ruin*: A Parallel?" *NQ* 208 (1963): 405.

Talentino 1978
Talentino, Arnold V. "Moral Irony in *The Ruin*." *PLL* 14 (1978): 3–11.

Timmer 1941
See under OE Lit.

Wenisch 1979
See under Dialects.

Wentersdorf 1977
   Wentersdorf, Karl. "Observations on *The Ruin*." *MÆ* 46 (1977): 171–80.
Wülker 1879
   Wülker, Richard P. "Aus englischen Bibliotheken II: Exeter." *Anglia* 2 (1879): 374–87.

THE SEAFARER

Anderson 1937–38
   Anderson, O.S. (later Arngart). "*The Seafarer*: An Interpretation." *Kungl. Humanistika Vetenskapssamfundets i Lund Årsberättelse* 1 (1937–38): 1–50.
Andrew 1940
   See under OE Grammar etc.
Arngart 1979
   Arngart, O.S. (previously Anderson). "*The Seafarer*: A Postscript." *English Studies* 60 (1979): 249–53.
Bately 1984
   See under *Wan*.
Bessai 1971
   Bessai, Frank. "The Two Worlds of the Seafarer." *Peregrinatio* 1 (1971): 1–8.
Blake 1962
   Blake, Norman F. "*The Seafarer*, Lines 48–49." *NQ* 207 (1962): 163–64.
Boer 1903
   Boer, R.C. "*Wanderer* und *Seefahrer*." *ZfdP* 35 (1903): 1–28.
Bolton 1960
   Bolton, Whitney F. "Connectives in *The Seafarer* and *The Dream of the Rood*." *MP* 57 (1960): 260–62.
Bosse 1973
   Bosse, Roberta B. "Aural Aesthetic and the Unity of *The Seafarer*." *PLL* 9 (1973): 3–14.
Calder 1971
   Calder, Daniel G. "Setting and Mode in *The Seafarer* and *The Wanderer*." *NM* 72 (1971): 264–75.
A.P. Campbell 1973
   Campbell, A.P. "*The Seafarer*: Wanderlust and Our Heavenly Home." *Revue de l'Université d'Ottawa* 43 (1973): 235–47.
Jackson Campbell 1960
   Campbell, Jackson J. "Oral Poetry in *The Seafarer*." *Speculum* 35 (1960): 87–96.
Cherniss 1968–69
   Cherniss, Michael D. "The Meaning of *The Seafarer*, Lines 97–102." *MP* 66 (1968–69): 146–49.

Clemoes 1969

Clemoes, Peter. "*Mens absentia cogitans* in *The Seafarer* and *The Wanderer.*" In Pearsall and Waldron 1969, 62–77. See under OE Lit.

Cornell 1981

Cornell, Muriel. "Varieties of Repetition in Old English Poetry, especially in *The Wanderer* and *The Seafarer.*" *Neophil* 65 (1981): 292–307.

Craigie 1923–24

Craigie, W.A. "Interpolations and Omissions in Anglo-Saxon Poetic Texts." *Philologica* 2 (1923–24): 5–19.

Cross 1957

See under *Wan.*

Cross 1959

Cross, James E. "On the Allegory in *The Seafarer* – Illustrative Notes." *MÆ* 28 (1959): 104–6.

Cross 1961a

See under *Wan.*

Cross 1961b

Cross, James E. Review of Gordon's *Seafarer*. *JEGP* 60 (1961): 545–49.

Cross 1962

See under OE Lit.

Dahlberg 1982

Dahlberg, Charles. "*The Seafarer*: The Weir-Metaphor and Benedictine Silence." *Mediaevalia* 6 (1982 for 1980): 11–35.

Daunt 1916

Daunt, Majorie. "*The Seafarer*, Lines 97–102." *MLR* 11 (1916): 337–38.

Daunt 1918

– "Some Difficulties of *The Seafarer* Reconsidered." *MLR* 13 (1918): 474–79.

Davenport 1974

Davenport, W.A. "The Modern Reader and the Old English *Seafarer.*" *PLL* 10 (1974): 227–40.

Diekstra 1971

Diekstra, F.N.M. "*The Seafarer* 58–66a. The Flight of the Exiled Soul to its Fatherland." *Neophil* 55 (1971): 433–46.

Dietrich 1966

See under OE Elegies

Ehrismann 1909

Ehrismann, Gustav. "Religionsgeschichtliche Beiträge zum germanischen Frühchristentum." *BGdSL* 35 (1909): 209–39.

Ekwall 1924

See under OE Poetry.

Empric 1972
　　Empric, Julienne H. "*The Seafarer*: An Experience in Displacement." *NDEJ* 7 (1972): 23–33.

Ferrell 1894
　　Ferrell, C.C. "Old Germanic Life in the Anglo-Saxon *Wanderer* and *Seafarer*." *MLN* 9 (1894): 402–7.

Galloway 1988
　　Galloway, Andrew. "1 Peter and *The Seafarer*." *ELN* 25, no. 4 (1988): 1–10.

Godden 1985
　　See under OE Lit.

Goldsmith 1954
　　Goldsmith, Margaret E. "The Seafarer and the Birds." *RES* n.s. 5 (1954): 225–35.

Gordon 1954
　　Gordon, Ida L. "Traditional Themes in *The Wanderer* and *The Seafarer*." *RES* n.s. 5 (1954): 1–13.

Gordon 1960
　　– *The Seafarer*. London 1960.

Brian Green 1977
　　Green, Brian. "*Spes viva*: Structure and Meaning in *The Seafarer*." In Lee 1977, 28–45. See under OE Lit.

Martin Green 1975
　　Green, Martin. "Man, Time, and Apocalypse in *The Wanderer*, *The Seafarer*, and *Beowulf*." *JEGP* 74 (1975): 502–18.

Greenfield 1954
　　Greenfield, Stanley B. "Attitudes and Values in *The Seafarer*." *SP* 51 (1954): 15–20.

Greenfield 1966
　　See under OE Elegies.

Greenfield 1969
　　Greenfield, Stanley B. "*Mīn*, *Sylf*, and 'Dramatic Voices in *The Wanderer* and *The Seafarer*.'" *JEGP* 68 (1969): 212–20.

Greenfield 1981
　　– "*Sylf*, Seasons, Structure and Genre in *The Seafarer*." *ASE* 9 (1981): 199–211.

Gribble 1983
　　See under OE Poetry.

Holthausen 1908
　　Holthausen, Ferdinand. "Zur altenglischen Literatur." *Anglia Beiblatt* 19 (1908): 248–49.

Holthausen 1920
　　See under OE Poetry. P. 25 on *Sea*.

Holthausen 1921

See under OE Poetry.

Holthausen 1922

See under OE Poetry. Pp. 55–56 on *Sea*.

Holthausen 1935

See under OE Poetry.

Holton 1982

Holton, Frederick S. "Old English Sea Imagery and the Interpretation of *The Seafarer*." *YES* 12 (1982): 208–17.

Hönncher 1886

Hönncher, Erwin. "Zur Dialogeinteilung im *Seefahrer* (A) und zur zweiten homiletischen Partie (B) dieses Gedichtes." *Anglia* 9 (1886): 435–46.

Horgan 1979

Horgan, A.D. "The Structure of *The Seafarer*." *RES* n.s. 30 (1979): 41–49.

Howlett 1975

Howlett, D.R. "The Structures of *The Wanderer* and *The Seafarer*." *SN* 47 (1975): 313–17.

Hultin 1977

Hultin, Neil. "The External Soul in *The Seafarer* and *The Wanderer*." *Folklore* 88 (1977): 39–45.

Hume 1974

See under OE Poetry.

Isaacs 1966

Isaacs, Neil D. "Image, Metaphor, Irony, Allusion, and Moral: The Shifting Perspective of *The Seafarer*." *NM* 67 (1966): 266–82. Repr. in Isaacs 1968, 19–34. See under OE Poetry.

Jacobs 1989

Jacobs, Nicholas. "Syntactical Connection and Logical Disconnection: The Case of *The Seafarer*. *MÆ* 58 (1989): 105–13.

Klaeber 1924

See under OE Poetry.

Klaeber 1927

Klaeber, Fr. "Weitere Randglossen zu Texterklärungen." *Anglia Beiblatt* 38 (1927): 354–60 (354–55 on *Sea*).

Klaeber 1932–33

– "Three Textual Notes." *Englische Studien* 67 (1932–33): 340–43 (341–42 on *Sea*).

Klein 1975

Klein, W.F. "Purpose and the 'Poetics' of *The Wanderer* and *The Seafarer*." In Nicholson and Frese 1975, 208–23. See under OE Poetry.

Kluge 1883

Kluge, Friedrich. "Zu altenglischen Dichtungen:1. Der *Seefahrer*." *Englische Studien* 6 (1883): 322–27.

Kluge 1885
- "Zu altenglischen Dichtungen:2. Nochmals der *Seefahrer*." *Englische Studien* 8 (1885): 472–74.

Kluge 1888
See under OE Lit.

Kock 1918
Kock, Ernst A. "Jubilee Jaunts and Jottings: Two Hundred and Fifty Contributions to the Interpretation and Prosody of Old West Teutonic Alliterative Poetry." *Lunds Universitets Årsskrift* n.s. 1, 14, no. 26 (1918): 1–82 (75–77 on *Sea*).

Kock 1920
See under *Res*. P. 257 on *Sea*.

Lawrence 1902b
Lawrence, W.W. "The Wanderer and The Seafarer." *JEGP* 4 (1902): 460–80.

Leslie 1959
See under OE Poetry.

Leslie 1983
Leslie, Roy F. "The Meaning and Structure of *The Seafarer*." In Green 1983, 96–122. See under OE Elegies.

Liljegren 1942
Liljegren, S.B. "Some Notes on the Old English Poem *The Seafarer*." *SN* 14 (1942): 145–59.

Malmberg 1973
Malmberg, Lars. "Poetic Originality in *The Wanderer* and *The Seafarer*." *NM* 74 (1973): 220–28.

Malone 1937b
Malone, Kemp. "*The Seafarer*, 111–116." *MÆ* 6 (1937): 214–15.

Mandel 1976
Mandel, Jerome. "The Seafarer." *NM* 77 (1976): 538–51.

Mitchell 1968a
Mitchell, Bruce. "More Musings on Old English Syntax." *NM* 69 (1968): 53–63. Repr. in Mitchell 1988, 126–33. See under OE Lit.

Mitchell 1985
- "The Syntax of *The Seafarer*, Lines 50–52." *RES* n.s. 36 (1985): 535–37. Repr. in Mitchell 1988, 203–6.

O'Neil 1960
O'Neil, W.A. "Another Look at Oral Poetry in *The Seafarer*." *Speculum* 35 (1960): 596–600.

Orton 1982a
Orton, Peter R. "*The Seafarer* 6b–10a and 18–22." *NM* 83 (1982): 255–59.

Orton 1982b
- "*The Seafarer* 58–64a." *Neophil* 66 (1982): 450–59.

Osborn 1978
 Osborn, Marijane. "Venturing upon Deep Waters in *The Seafarer*." *NM* 79 (1978): 1–6.
Pheifer 1965
 Pheifer, J.D. "*The Seafarer* 53–55." *RES* n.s. 16 (1965): 282–84.
Pope 1965
 Pope, John C. "Dramatic Voices in *The Wanderer* and *The Seafarer*." In Bessinger and Creed 1965, 164–93. See under OE Lit. Repr. in Bessinger and Kahrl 1968, 533–70. See under OE Poetry.
Pope 1974
 – "Second Thoughts on the Interpretation of *The Seafarer*." *ASE* 3 (1974): 75–86.
Prins 1964
 See under *Wan*.
Richardson 1983
 Richardson, John. "On *The Seafarer*, Line 34b." *MP* 81 (1983): 168–69.
Rieger 1869
 See under OE Poetry. Pp. 330–39 on *Sea*.
Rigby 1962
 Rigby, Marjorie. "*The Seafarer, Beowulf*, l. 769 and a Germanic Conceit." *NQ* 207 (1962): 246.
Robinson 1982
 Robinson, Fred C. "'The Might of the North': Pound's Anglo-Saxon Studies and *The Seafarer*." *Yale Review* 71 (1982): 199–224.
Salmon 1960
 Salmon, Vivian. "*The Wanderer* and *The Seafarer* and the Old English Conception of the Soul." *MLR* 55 (1960): 1–10.
Schubel 1973
 See under *Husb*.
Schücking 1917
 See under OE Poetry.
Schücking 1936
 Schücking, Levin L. "Heroische Ironie im angelsächsischen *Seefahrer*." In *Englische Kultur in sprachwissenschaftlicher Deutung: Max Deutschbein zum 60. Geburtstag*, hrsg. Wolfgang Schmidt, pp. 72–74. Leipzig 1936.
Serio 1973
 Serio, John N. "Thematic Unity in *The Seafarer*." *Gypsy Scholar* 1 (1973): 16–21.
Shields 1980
 Shields, John C. "*The Seafarer* as a *Meditatio*." *Studia Mystica* 3 (1980): 29–41.
Sisam 1912–13
 Sisam, Kenneth. "To *Seafarer* ll. 72ff." *Englische Studien* 46 (1912–13): 336.

Sisam 1945
 – *"The Seafarer*, lines 97–102." *RES* 21 (1945): 316–17.
Sisam 1962
 – "Old English *Stefn, Stefna,* 'Stem.'" *RES* n.s. 13 (1962): 282–83.
Smithers 1957 and 1959
 Smithers, G.V. "The Meaning of *The Seafarer* and *The Wanderer*." *MÆ* 26 (1957):
 137–53; 28 (1959): 1–22.
Stanley 1955–56
 See under OE Poetry.
Stanley 1962
 Stanley, Eric G. Review of Gordon's *Seafarer*. *MÆ* 31 (1962): 54–60.
Stevick 1965
 Stevick, Robert D. "The Text and the Composition of *The Seafarer*." *PMLA* 80
 (1965): 332–36.
Strunk 1903
 Strunk, William. "Notes on the Shorter Old English Poems." *MLN* 18 (1903):
 72–73.
Swaen 1907
 Swaen, A.E.H. "Some Old English Bird Names." *Archiv* 118 (1907): 387–89.
Sweet 1894
 See under OE Lit.
Timmer 1941
 See under OE Lit.
Tripp 1972
 See under OE Elegies.
Vickrey 1982
 Vickrey, John F. "Some Hypotheses Concerning *The Seafarer*, Lines 1–47."
 Archiv 219 (1982): 57–77.
Vickrey 1989
 – "*The Seafarer* 12–17, 25–30, 55–70: *Dives* and the Fictive Speaker." *SN* 61
 (1989): 145–56.
Wardale 1935
 See under OE Lit.
Whitelock 1950
 Whitelock, Dorothy. "The Interpretation of *The Seafarer*." In *The Early Cultures
 of Northwest Europe*, ed. Sir Cyril Fox and Bruce Dickens, pp. 259–72. Cambridge
 1950. Repr. in Bessinger and Kahrl 1968, 442–57. See under OE Poetry.
Whittier 1968
 Whittier, Phyllis Gage. "Spring in *The Seafarer* 48–50." *NQ* 213 (1968): 407–9.
Williams 1989

Williams, Douglas. "*The Seafarer* as an Evangelical Poem." *Lore and Language* 8, no. 1 (1989): 19–30.

Woolf 1975
    Woolf, Rosemary. "*The Wanderer, The Seafarer*, and the Genre of *Planctus*." In Nicholson and Frese 1975, 192–207. See under OE Poetry.

Wülker 1885
    See under OE Lit.

THE WANDERER

Alfred 1982
    Alfred, William. "The Drama of *The Wanderer*." In *The Wisdom of Poetry: Essays in Early English Literature in Honor of Morton W. Bloomfield*, ed. Larry Benson and Siegfried Wenzel, pp. 31–44 and 268–70. Kalamazoo 1982.

Bately 1984
    Bately, Janet. "Time and the Passing of Time in *The Wanderer* and Related Old English Texts." *E and S* n.s. 37 (1984): 1–15.

Bjork 1989
    Bjork, Robert E. "*Sundor æt rune*: The Voluntary Exile of the Wanderer." *Neophil* 73 (1989): 119–26.

Boer 1903
    See under *Sea*.

Bolton 1969
    Bolton, Whitney F. "The Dimensions of *The Wanderer*." *Leeds Studies in English* n.s. 3 (1969): 7–34.

Brandl 1919
    See under *Ruin*.

Breuer 1974
    Breuer, Rolf. "Vermittelte Unmittelbarkeit: zur Struktur des altenglischen *Wanderer*." *NM* 75 (1974): 552–67.

Brewer 1952
    Brewer, D.S. "*Wanderer*, lines 50–57." *MLN* 67 (1952): 398–99.

Bright 1891
    See under OE Lit.

Bright 1893
    Bright, James W. "The *ubi sunt* Formula." *MLN* 8 (1893): 94.

Bright 1898
    – "*The Wanderer* 78–84." *MLN* 13 (1898): 176–77.

Brink 1877
    See under OE Lit.

Brooks 1968
  Brooks, K.R. Review of Leslie's *Wanderer*. *MLR* 63 (1968): 157–59.
Brown 1978
  Brown, George Hardin. "An Iconographic Explanation of *The Wanderer*, Lines 81b–82a." *Viator* 9 (1978): 31–38.
Burrow 1965
  Burrow, John. "*The Wanderer*, Lines 73–87." *NQ* 210 (1965): 166–68.
Calder 1971
  See under *Sea*.
Clark and Wasserman 1979
  Clarke, S.L., and Julian N. Wasserman. "The Imagery of *The Wanderer*." *Neophil* 63 (1979): 291–96.
Clemoes 1969
  See under *Sea*.
Cornell 1981
  See under *Sea*.
Craigie 1923–24
  See under *Sea*.
Crawford 1931
  Crawford, D.H. "The Wanderer." *Times Literary Supplement*, 23 July 1931, 583.
Cross 1956
  Cross, James E. "*Ubi Sunt* Passages in Old English – Sources and Relationships." *Vetenskaps-Societeten i Lund Årsbok* (1956): 23–44.
Cross 1958–59
  – "On *The Wanderer* lines 80–84: A Study of a Figure and a Theme." *Vetenskaps-Societeten i Lund Årsbok* (1958–59): 75–110.
Cross 1961a
  – "On the Genre of *The Wanderer*." *Neophil* 45 (1961): 63–75.
Cunningham 1979
  Cunningham, J.S. "'Where Are They?': The After-Life of a Figure of Speech." *PBA* 65 (1979): 369–94.
Dean 1965
  Dean, Christopher. "*Weal wundrum heah, wyrmlicum fah* and the Narrative Background of *The Wanderer*." *MP* 63 (1965): 141–43.
Diekstra 1971
  Diekstra, F.N.M. "*The Wanderer*, 65b–72. The Passions of the Mind and the Cardinal Virtues." *Neophil* 55 (1971): 73–88.
Doubleday 1969
  Doubleday, James F. "The Three Faculties of the Soul in *The Wanderer*." *Neophil* 53 (1969): 189–94.

Doubleday 1972
– "The Limits of Philosophy: A Reading of *The Wanderer*." NDEJ 7 (1972): 14–22.

Dunning and Bliss 1969
Dunning, T.P., and Alan J. Bliss. *The Wanderer*. London 1969.

Ekwall 1924
See under OE Poetry.

Elliott 1958
Elliott, Ralph W.V. "The Wanderer's Conscience." *English Studies* 39 (1958): 193–200.

Engberg 1984
Engberg, Norma. "*Mod-Mægen* Balance in *Elene, The Battle of Maldon* and *The Wanderer*." *NM* 85 (1984): 212–26.

Erzgräber 1961
Erzgräber, Willi. "*Der Wanderer*: Eine Interpretation von Aufbau und Gehalt." In Viebrock and Erzgräber 1961, pp. 57–85. See under OE Lit.

Faraci 1982
Faraci, Mary. "Phenomenology: Good News for Old English Studies." *Language and Style* 15 (1982): 219–24.

Ferrell 1894
See under *Sea*.

Fichte 1985
Fichte, Jörg O. "Altenglische Mystik: Sackgasse der neohistorischen Literaturkritik." In *Mittelalterbilder aus neuer Perspektive*, pp. 392–403. Beiträge romanischen Philologie des Mittelalters 14. Munich 1985.

Fischer 1935
Fischer, Walther. "*Wanderer* v. 25 und v. 6–7." *Anglia* 59 (1935): 299–302.

Fowler 1967
Fowler, Roger. "A Theme in *The Wanderer*." *MÆ* 36 (1967): 1–14.

Frankis 1973
Frankis, P.J. "The Thematic Significance of *enta geweorc* and Related Imagery in *The Wanderer*." *ASE* 2 (1973): 253–69.

French 1952
French, Walter Hoyt. "*The Wanderer* 98: *wyrmlicum fāh*." *MLN* 67 (1952): 526–29.

Godden 1985
See under OE Lit.

Gollancz 1895
See under OE Poetry.

Gordon 1954
See under *Sea*.

Gottlieb 1965
Gottlieb, Stephen A. "The Metaphors of *Wanderer*, lines 53a–55a." *NM* 66 (1965): 145–48.

Brian Green 1976
Green, Brian K. "The Twilight Kingdom: Structure and Meaning in *The Wanderer*." *Neophil* 60 (1976): 442–51.

Martin Green 1975
See under *Sea*.

Greenfield 1951
Greenfield, Stanley B. "*The Wanderer*: A Reconsideration of Theme and Structure." *JEGP* 50 (1951): 451–65.

Greenfield 1963
– "Syntactic Analysis and Old English Poetry." *NM* 64 (1963): 373–78. Repr. in *Old English Literature: Twenty-two Analytical Essays*, ed. M. Stevens and J. Mandel, pp. 82–86; Lincoln, Neb. 1968.

Greenfield 1970
– Review of Dunning and Bliss's *Wanderer*. *NQ* 215 (1970): 113–16.

Greenfield and Calder 1986
See under OE Lit.

Gribble 1983
See under OE Poetry

Gruber 1972
Gruber, Loren C. "The Wanderer and Arcite: Isolation and the Continuity of the English Elegiac Mode." In *Four Papers for Michio Masui*, ed. Raymond Tripp, pp. 1–9. Denver 1972.

Hait 1984
Hait, Elizabeth A. "The Wanderer's Lingering Regret: A Study of Patterns of Imagery." *Neophil* 68 (1984): 278–91.

Hollowell 1983
Hollowell, Ida Masters. "On the Identity of the Wanderer." In Green 1983, 82–95. See under OE Elegies.

Holthausen 1891
Holthausen, Ferdinand. "Zu alt- und mittelenglischen Dichtungen." *Anglia* 13 (1891): 357–62 (357 on *Wan*).

Holthausen 1934
See under OE Grammar etc.

Holthausen 1953b
– "Altenglische Kleinigkeiten." *Germanisch-romanische Monatsschrift* 34 (1953): 345.

Horgan 1987
Horgan, A.D. "*The Wanderer*: A Boethian Poem?" *RES* n.s. 38 (1987): 40–46.

Howlett 1975
  See under *Sea.*
Hultin 1977
  See under *Sea.*
Huppé 1943
  Huppé, Bernard F. "The *Wanderer*: Theme and Structure." *JEGP* 42 (1943): 516–38.
Jacobsen 1901
  Jacobsen, Rudolf. *Darstellung der syntaktischen Erscheinungen im angelsächsischen Gedichte vom Wanderer.* Rostock 1901.
Kintgen 1975
  Kintgen, Eugene R. "Wordplay in *The Wanderer*." *Neophil* 59 (1975): 119–27.
Klaeber 1906
  Klaeber, Fr. "*Wanderer* 44; *Rätsel XII* 3f." *Anglia Beiblatt* 17 (1906): 300–301.
Klaeber 1909
  – "Textual Notes on the *Beowulf*." *JEGP* 8 (1909): 254–59 (254–55 on *myne wisse*, as in *Wan* 27).
Klaeber 1913
  – "Notes on Old English Poems." *JEGP* 12 (1913): 259–60.
Klaeber 1929
  – "Jottings on Old English Poems." *Anglia* 53 (1929): 225–34 (229 on *Wan*).
Klein 1975
  See under *Sea.*
Kluge 1888 and 1902
  See under OE Lit.
Kock 1904
  Kock, Ernst A. "Interpretations and Emendations of Early English Texts." *Anglia* 27 (1904): 218–37 (227 on *Wan*).
Kock 1918
  See under *Sea.* Pp. 78–79 on *Wan.*
Kock 1922
  Kock, Ernst A. "Plain Points and Puzzles, Sixty Notes on Old English Poetry." *Lunds Universitets Årsskrift* n.F. 1, 17, no. 7 (1922): iii–iv, 1–26 (25–26 on *Wan*).
Larson 1908
  Larson, L.M. "The Household of the Norwegian Kings." *American Historical Review* 13 (1908): 439–79 (461, n. 11 on *Wan*).
Lawrence 1902b
  See under *Sea.*
Leslie 1966
  Leslie, Roy F. *The Wanderer.* Manchester 1966. Repr. with additional bibliography. Exeter 1985.

Lumiansky 1950
  Lumiansky, R.M. "The Dramatic Structure of the Old English *Wanderer*." *Neophil* 34 (1950): 104–12.
Malmberg 1970
  Malmberg, Lars. "*The Wanderer*: *waþema gebind*." *NM* 71 (1970): 96–99.
Malmberg 1973
  See under *Sea*.
Midgely 1959
  Midgely, Graham. "*The Wanderer*, Lines 49–55." *RES* n.s. 10 (1959): 53–54.
Millns 1977
  Millns, Tony. "*The Wanderer* 98: *weal wundrum heah wyrmlicum fah*." *RES* n.s. 28 (1977): 431–38.
Mitchell 1967
  Mitchell, Bruce. "An Old English Syntactical Reverie: *The Wanderer*, Lines 22 and 34–36." *NM* 68 (1967): 139–49. Repr. in Mitchell 1988, 118–25. See under OE Lit.
Mitchell 1968a
  See under *Sea*.
Mitchell 1968b
  Mitchell, Bruce. "Some Syntactical Problems in *The Wanderer*." *NM* 69 (1968): 172–98. Repr. in Mitchell 1988, 99–117.
Mitchell 1975
  See under OE Poetry.
Mullen 1974
  Mullen, Karen A. "*The Wanderer*: Considered Again." *Neophil* 58 (1974): 74–81.
O'Faolàin 1931
  O'Faolàin, Seàn. "The Wanderer." *Times Literary Supplement*, 9 July 1931, 547.
Osborn 1974
  Osborn, Marijane. "The Vanishing Seabirds in *The Wanderer*." *Folklore* 85 (1974): 122–27.
Osborn 1975
  – "Classical Meditation in *The Wanderer*." *Comparison* 1 (Warwick 1975): 67–101.
Osborn 1978
  – "Towards the Contemplative in *The Wanderer*." *Studia Mystica* 1 (1978): 53–69 (shorter version of Osborn 1975).
Owen 1950 and 1953
  Owen, W.J.B. "*Wanderer*, Lines 50–57." *MLN* 65 (1950): 161–65; 67 (1953): 214–16.

Peters 1981
Peters, R.A. "Philosophy and Theme of the Old English Poem 'The Exile.'" *Neophil* 65 (1981): 288–91.

Pope 1965
See under *Sea*.

Pope 1966
See under OE Poetry.

Pope 1967–68
See under OE Lit.

Prins 1964
Prins, A.A. "The *Wanderer* (and the *Seafarer*)." *Neophil* 48 (1964): 237–51.

Ray 1978
Ray, T.J. "*The Wanderer* 78–84." *South Central Bulletin* 38 (New Orleans 1978): 157–59.

Richardson 1988
Richardson, John. "The Hero at the Wall in *The Wanderer*." *NM* 89 (1988): 280–85.

Richardson 1989
– "Two Notes on the Time Frame of *The Wanderer* (Lines 22 and 73–87)." *Neophil* 73 (1989): 158–59.

Richman 1982
Richman, Gerald. "Speaker and Speech Boundaries in *The Wanderer*." *JEGP* 81 (1982): 469–79.

Robertson 1951
Robertson, D.W. "Historical Criticism." *English Institute Essays*, 1950 (1951): 3–31 (18–22 on *Wan*).

Rosier 1964
Rosier, James L. "The Literal-Figurative Identity of *The Wanderer*." *PMLA* 79 (1964): 366–69.

Rumble 1958
Rumble, T.C. "From *Eardstapa* to *Snottor on Mode*: The Structural Principle of *The Wanderer*." *MLQ* 19 (1958): 225–30.

Salmon 1960
See under *Sea*.

Schücking 1915
Schücking, Levin L. *Untersuchung zur Bedeutungslehre der angelsächsischen Dichtersprache.* Germanische Bibliothek, Abt. 2, Band 11. Heidelberg 1915 (pp. 91–98 on *woma*, as in *Wan* 103).

Sedgefield 1922
See under OE Poetry.

Selzer 1983
  Selzer, John L. "*The Wanderer* and the Meditative Tradition." *SP* 80 (1983): 227–37.
Sievers 1885
  See under OE Prosody. P. 516 on *Wan.*
Smithers 1951–52
  Smithers, George V. "Five Notes on Old English Texts." *English and Germanic Studies* 4 (1951–52): 84–85.
Smithers 1957 and 1959
  See under *Sea.*
Spolsky 1974
  Spolsky, Ellen. "Semantic Structure of *The Wanderer.*" *Journal of Literary Semantics* 3 (1974): 101–19.
Stanley 1955–56
  See under OE Poetry.
Strunk 1903
  See under *Sea.*
Suddaby 1954
  Suddaby, Elizabeth. "Three Notes on Old English Texts." *MLN* 69 (1954): 465–66.
Taylor 1972
  Taylor, Paul B. "Charms of *Wynn* and Fetters of *Wyrd* in *The Wanderer.*" *NM* 73 (1972): 448–55.
ten Brink 1877
  See Brink under OE Lit.
Tripp 1972
  See under OE Elegies.
Tucker 1958
  Tucker, Susie. "Return to *The Wanderer.*" *EIC* 8 (1958): 229–37.
Tupper 1912a
  Tupper, Frederick. "Notes on Old English Poems V: *Hand ofer Heafod.*" *JEGP* 11 (1912): 97–100.
Tupper 1912b
  – "'Commendation' in the *Wanderer.*" *JEGP* 11 (1912): 292.
Wentersdorf 1975
  Wentersdorf, Karl P. "*The Wanderer*: Notes on Some Semantic Problems." *Neophil* 59 (1975): 287–92.
Woolf 1975
  See under *Sea.*
Wülker 1885

See under OE Lit.

Zupitza 1890

Zupitza, Julius. "Zu *Wanderer* 31." *Archiv* 86 (1890): 279–80.

THE WIFE'S LAMENT

Bambas 1963

Bambas, Rudolf C. "Another View of the Old English *Wife's Lament.*" *JEGP* 62 (1963): 303–9.

Bately 1984

See under *Wan.*

Böker 1982

Böker, Uwe. "The Non-Narrative Structure of *The Wife's Lament*: A Reconsideration of Its Lyric Elements." In *Festschrift für Karl Schneider*, ed. Kurt R. Jankowsky and Ernst S. Dick, pp. 417–29. Amsterdam 1982.

Bolton 1969

See under *Husb.*

Bouman 1962

See under OE Elegies.

Bragg 1989

Bragg, Lois. "*Wulf and Eadwacer, The Wife's Lament*, and Women's Love Lyrics of the Middle Ages." *Germanisch-romanische Monatsschrift* n.s. 39 (1989): 257–68.

Curry 1966

Curry, Jane L. "Approaches to a Translation of the Anglo-Saxon *The Wife's Lament.*" *MÆ* 35 (1966): 187–98.

Davidson 1975

Davidson, Clifford. "Erotic 'Women's Songs' in Anglo-Saxon England." *Neophil* 59 (1975): 451–62.

Davis 1965

Davis, Thomas M. "Another View of the *Wife's Lament.*" *PLL* 1 (1965): 291–305.

Desmond 1990

Desmond, Marilynn. "The Voice of Exile: Feminist Literary History and the Anonymous Anglo-Saxon Elegy." *Critical Inquiry* 16 (1990): 572–90.

Doane 1966

Doane, A.N. "Heathen Form and Christian Function in *The Wife's Lament.*" *MS* 28 (1966): 77–91.

Dunleavy 1956

Dunleavy, Gareth W. "Possible Irish Analogues for *The Wife's Lament.*" *PQ* 35 (1956): 208–13.

Fitzgerald 1963
Fitzgerald, Robert P. "*The Wife's Lament* and 'The Search for the Lost Husband.'" *JEGP* 62 (1963): 769–77.

Greenfield 1953
Greenfield, Stanley B. "*The Wife's Lament* Reconsidered." *PMLA* 68 (1953): 907–12.

Greenfield and Calder 1986
See under OE Lit. Pp. 292–94 and 301 (notes) on *Wife*.

Grein 1857–59
See under OE Poetry.

Harris 1977
Harris, Joseph. "A Note on *eorðscræf/eorðsele* and Current Interpretations of *The Wife's Lament*." *English Studies* 58 (1977): 204–8.

Holthausen 1908
See under *Sea*.

Howlett 1978
See under *Husb.*

Imelmann 1907a
See under OE Elegies.

Lee Ann Johnson 1971
Johnson, Lee Ann. "The Narrative Structure of *The Wife's Lament*." *English Studies* 52 (1971): 497–501.

William Johnson 1983
Johnson, William C. "*The Wife's Lament* as Death-Song." In Green 1983, 69–81. See under OE Elegies.

Klaeber 1935
See under OE Elegies.

Lawrence 1907–8
Lawrence, W.W. "The Banished Wife's Lament." *MP* 5 (1907–8): 387–405.

Lench 1970
Lench, Elinor. "*The Wife's Lament*: A Poem of the Living Dead." *Comitatus* 1 (1970): 3–23.

Leslie 1961
See under OE Elegies.

Lucas 1969
Lucas, Angela M. "The Narrator of *The Wife's Lament* Reconsidered." *NM* 70 (1969): 282–97.

Malone 1962
Malone, Kemp. "Two English *Frauenlieder*." *CL* 14 (1962): 106–17.

Mandel 1987
See under OE Poetry.

Mitchell 1972
Mitchell, Bruce. "The Narrator of *The Wife's Lament*: Some Syntactical Problems Reconsidered." *NM* 73 (1972): 222–34. Repr. in Mitchell 1988, 134–45. See under OE Lit.

Mitchell 1975
See under OE Poetry.

Renoir 1975
Renoir, Alain. "A Reading Context for *The Wife's Lament*." In Nicolson and Frese 1975, 224–41. See under OE Poetry.

Renoir 1977a
– "A Reading of *The Wife's Lament*." *English Studies* 58 (1977): 4–19.

Renoir 1977b
– "Christian Inversion in *The Wife's Lament*." *SN* 49 (1977): 19–24.

Rickert 1904–5
Rickert, Edith. "The Old English Offa Saga." *MP* 2 (1904–5): 29–76 and 321–76.

Rissanen 1969
Rissanen, Matti. "The Theme of 'Exile' in *The Wife's Lament*." *NM* 70 (1969): 90–104.

Roeder 1899
Roeder, Fritz. *Die Familie bei den Angelsachsen. 1: Mann und Frau.* Studien zur englischen Philologie 4. Halle 1899.

Schaefer 1986
Schaefer, Ursula. "Two Women in Need of a Friend: A Comparison of *The Wife's Lament* and Eangyth's Letter to Boniface." In *Germanic Dialects: Linguistic and Philological Investigations*, ed. Bela Brogyanyi and Thomas Krömmelbein, pp. 491–524. Amsterdam 1986.

Schücking 1906
Schücking, Levin L. "Das angelsächsische Gedicht von der *Klage der Frau*." *ZfdA* 48 (1906): 436–49.

Schulze 1969
Schulze, Fritz. "Die altenglische *Klage der Frau*." In *Festschrift für Edgar Mertner*, hrsg. Bernhard Fabian und Ulrich Suerbaum, pp. 65–88. Munich 1969.

Short 1970
Short, Douglas D. "The Old English *Wife's Lament*: An Interpretation." *NM* 71 (1970): 585–603.

Sievers 1885
See under OE Prosody. P. 516 on *Wife*.

Stefanovíc 1909
Stefanovíc, Svetislav. "Das angelsächsische Gedicht *Die Klage der Frau*." *Anglia* 32 (1909): 399–433.

Stevens 1968
   Stevens, Martin. "The Narrator of *The Wife's Lament*." *NM* 69 (1968): 72–90.
Stevick 1960
   Stevick, Robert D. "Formal Aspects of *The Wife's Lament*." *JEGP* 59 (1960): 21–25.
Straus 1981
   Straus, Barrie Ruth. "Women's Words as Weapons: Speech as Action in *The Wife's Lament*." *Texas Studies in Literature and Language* 23 (1981): 268–85.
Swanton 1964
   See under *Husb*.
Trautmann 1894
   See under *Husb*.
Trautmann 1910
   Trautmann, Moritz. "Beiträge zu einem künftigen 'Sprachschatz der alten-glischen Dichter.'" *Anglia* 33 (1910): 276–82 (276–79 on *gedreag* and *gedræg*, as in *Wife* 45).
Tripp 1972
   See under OE Elegies.
Ward 1960
   Ward, J.A. "*The Wife's Lament*: An Interpretation." *JEGP* 59 (1960): 26–33.
Wentersdorf 1970
   Wentersdorf, Karl P. "The Situation of the Narrator's Lord in *The Wife's Lament*." *NM* 71 (1970): 604–10.
Wentersdorf 1981
   – "The Situation of the Narrator in the Old English *Wife's Lament*." *Speculum* 56 (1981): 492–516.
Wülker 1885
   See under OE Lit.

WULF AND EADWACER

Adams 1958
   Adams, John F. "*Wulf and Eadwacer*: An Interpretation." *MLN* 73 (1958): 1–5.
Anderson 1983
   See under *Deor*.
Baker 1981
   Baker, Peter S. "The Ambiguity of *Wulf and Eadwacer*." *SP* 78, no. 5 (1981): 39–51.
Baker 1983
   – "*Wulf and Eadwacer*: A Classroom Edition." *OEN* 16, no. 2 (1983): appendix, 1–8.

Bouman 1949
   Bouman, A.C. "*Leodum is Minum*: Beadohild's Complaint." *Neophil* 33 (1949): 103–13. Repr. in Bouman 1962, 93–106.
Bouman 1962
   See under OE Elegies.
Bradley 1888
   Bradley, Henry. "The First Riddle of the Exeter Book." *Academy* 33 (1888): 197–98.
Bradley 1893
   – Letter to the editors. *Anglia* 15 (1893): 390.
Bradley 1902
   – "The Sigurd Cycle and Britain." *Athenaeum* 1902 (2): 758.
Bragg 1989
   See under *Wife*.
Budjuhn 1916
   Budjuhn, Gustav. "*Lēodum is mīnum* – ein altenglischer Dialog." *Anglia* 40 (1916): 256–59.
Bülbring 1891
   Bülbring, Karl D. Review of Georg Herzfeld's *Die Räthsel des Exeterbuches. Literaturblatt für germanische und romanische Philologie* 12 (1891): 155–58.
Cameron and Healy 1979
   See under OE Grammar etc.
Arnold Davidson 1975
   Davidson, Arnold E. "Interpreting *Wulf and Eadwacer*." *Annuale Mediaevale* 16 (1975): 24–32.
Clifford Davidson 1975
   See under *Wife*.
Desmond 1990
   See under *Wife*.
Eliason 1974
   Eliason, Norman E. "On *Wulf and Eadwacer*." In Burlin and Irving 1974, 225–34. See under OE Lit.
Fanagan 1976
   Fanagan, John M. "*Wulf and Eadwacer*: A Solution to the Critics' Riddle." *Neophil* 60 (1976): 130–37.
Frankis 1962
   See under *Deor*.
Frese 1983
   Frese, Dolores Warwick. "*Wulf and Eadwacer*: The Adulterous Woman Reconsidered." *NDEJ* 15, no. 1 (1983): 1–22.
Fry 1971

Fry, Donald K. "*Wulf and Eadwacer*: A Wen Charm." *Chaucer Review* 5 (1971): 247–63.

Giles 1981

Giles, Richard R. "*Wulf and Eadwacer*: A New Reading." *Neophil* 65 (1981): 468–72.

Gollancz 1893

Gollancz, Sir Israel. "*Wulf and Eadwacer*: An Anglo-Saxon Monodrama in Five Acts." *Athenaeum* 1893 (2): 883.

Gollancz 1902

– "The Sigurd Cycle and Britain." *Athenaeum* 1902 (2): 551–52.

Greenfield 1986

Greenfield, Stanley B. "*Wulf and Eadwacer*: All Passion Pent." *ASE* 15 (1986): 5–14.

Herzfeld 1890

Herzfeld, Georg. *Die Räthsel des Exeterbuches und ihr Verfasser*. Berlin 1890 (pp. 68–70 on *Wulf*).

Hicketier 1888

Hicketier, Fritz. "Fünf Rätsel des Exeterbuches." *Anglia* 10 (1888): 564–600 (564–82 on *Wulf*).

Holthausen 1893

Holthausen, Ferdinand. "Zu alt- und mittelenglischen Denkmälern." *Anglia* 15 (1893): 187–203 (188–89 on *Wulf*).

Holthausen 1907a

See under OE Poetry. Pp. 206–7 on *Wulf*.

Holthausen 1914

Holthausen, Ferdinand. "Nochmals die altenglischen Rätsel." *Anglia* 38 (1914): 77–82 (77 on *Wulf*).

Holthausen 1919

– "Zu den altenglischen Rätseln." *Anglia Beiblatt* 30 (1919): 50–55 (54–55 on *Wulf*).

Imelmann 1907a, 1907b, 1908, 1920

See under OE Elegies.

Jensen 1979

Jensen, Emily. "Narrative Voice in the Old English *Wulf*." *Chaucer Review* 13 (1979): 373–83.

Jones 1985

Jones, F. "A Note on the Interpretation of *Wulf and Eadwacer*." *NM* 86 (1985): 323–27.

Kavros 1977–78

Kavros, Harry E. "A Note on *Wulf and Eadwacer*." *ELN* 15 (1977–78): 83–84.

Keough 1976
  Keough, Terrence. "The Tension of Separation in *Wulf and Eadwacer*." *NM* 77 (1976): 552–60.
Kerling 1980
  Kerling, Johan. "Another Solution to the Critics' Riddle: *Wulf and Eadwacer* Revisited." *Neophil* 64 (1980): 140–43.
Klinck 1984
  See under OE Elegies.
Klinck 1987a
  Klinck, Anne L. "Animal Imagery in *Wulf and Eadwacer* and the Possibilities of Interpretation." *PLL* 23 (1987): 3–13.
Lawrence 1902a
  Lawrence, W.W. "The First Riddle of Cynewulf." *PMLA* 17 (1902): 247–61.
Lehmann 1969
  Lehmann, Ruth P.M. "The Metrics and Structure of *Wulf and Eadwacer*." *PQ* 48 (1969): 151–65.
Leo 1857
  Leo, Heinrich. *Quae de se ipso Cynevulfus (sive Cenevulfus sive Coenevulfus) poeta Anglosaxonicus tradiderit.* Halle 1857 (pp. 21–27 on *Wulf*).
Luecke 1983
  Luecke, Jane Marie. "*Wulf and Eadwacer*: Hints for Reading from *Beowulf* and Anthropology." In Green 1983, 190–203. See under OE Elegies.
Malone 1962
  See under *Wife*.
Mattox 1975
  Mattox, Wesley S. "Encirclement and Sacrifice in *Wulf and Eadwacer*." *Annuale Mediaevale* 16 (1975): 33–40.
Morley 1888
  Morley, Henry. *English Writers.* 2 vols. London 1888 (2:224–26 on *Wulf*).
Nuck 1888
  Nuck, R. "Zu Trautmanns Deutung des ersten und neunundachtzigsten Rätsels." *Anglia* 10 (1888): 390–94.
Nutt 1902
  Nutt, Alfred. "The Sigurd Cycle and Britain." *Athenaeum* 1902 (2): 521–22.
Orton 1985
  Orton, Peter. "An Approach to *Wulf and Eadwacer*." *Proceedings of The Royal Irish Academy* 85c (1985): 223–58.
Osborn 1983
  Osborn, Marijane. "The Text and Context of *Wulf and Eadwacer*." In Green 1983, 174–89. See under OE Elegies.

Patzig 1923
Patzig, H. "Zum ersten Rätsel Des Exeterbuchs." *Archiv* 145 (1923): 204–7.

Pulsiano and Wolf 1990–91
Pulsiano, Philip, and Kirsten Wolf. "The 'Hwelp' in *Wulf and Eadwacer*." *ELN* 28, no. 3 (1990–91): 1–9.

Renoir 1965
Renoir, Alain. "*Wulf and Eadwacer*: A Non-Interpretation." In Bessinger and Creed 1965, 147–63. See under OE Lit.

Rieger 1869
See under OE Poetry. Pp. 215–19 on *Wulf*.

Schofield 1902
Schofield, W.H. "Signy's Lament." *PMLA* 17 (1902): 262–95.

Searle 1897
See under OE Grammar etc.

Sedgefield 1931
Sedgefield, W.J. "Wulf and Eadwacer." *MLR* 26 (1931): 74–75.

Spamer 1978
Spamer, James B. "The Marriage Concept in *Wulf and Eadwacer*." *Neophil* 62 (1978): 143–44.

Suzuki 1987
Suzuki, Seiichi. "*Wulf and Eadwacer*: A Reinterpretation and Some Conjectures." *NM* 88 (1987): 175–85.

Trautmann 1883
Trautmann, Moritz. "Cynewulf und die Rätsel." *Anglia* 6 (1883): Anzeiger 158–69.

Trautmann 1912
– "Das sogenannte erste Rätsel." *Anglia* 36 (1912): 133–38.

Tupper 1910a
See under OE Poetry.

Tupper 1910b
Tupper, Frederick. "The Cynewulfian Runes of the First Riddle." *MLN* 25 (1910): 235–41.

Whitbread 1941
Whitbread, Leslie. "A Note on *Wulf and Eadwacer*." *MÆ* 10 (1941): 150–54.

Glossary and Word-Index

T he words in the Glossary are defined in terms of their uses in the present Texts rather than of their general reference in OE. More than one of the meanings given may be present in a particular usage. All occurrences of all complete words are recorded (in their various forms), including restorations and emendations, but expansions of MS abbreviations are not indicated (see p. 72, above). To simplify the entries, a few high-frequency forms and uses are given complete citation at the end of the Glossary.

In the alphabetization, *æ* is treated as a separate letter following *a*, and *þ/ð* as one letter following *t*. Words beginning with the prefix *ge* are included under *g* and referred to the simplex if this appears in the same meaning. Verbs are normally cited under the infinitive, nouns under the nom. (or nom.-acc.) sg., pronouns and adjectives under the nom. sg. masc. The sg. and pl. of the first- and second-person pronouns are treated separately. Comparatives and superlatives are cited under the positive if that occurs in the Texts.

Verbs are marked *strong, weak, preterite-present,* or *anomalous* – without division into classes. Similarly, nouns are classified by gender only. Emendations are indicated by italics, restorations by square brackets, comments in the Textual Notes by n superscript. The grammatical abbreviations used should be self-explanatory.

GLOSSARY AND WORD-INDEX TO THE OLD ENGLISH TEXTS (INCLUDING PROPER NAMES)

ā, *adv* always, forever
Sea 42, 47, *Wife* 5, 42, *Res* 85, 95,
115; **āa** *Rim* 87

ābēodan, *v str* announce
Rid 60 16

ābīdan, *v str* (+ *gen*) wait for
Wife 53

ābolgen, *past partic* (+ *dat*) angered; vexed, distressed
Res 79, 110

ac *conj* but
Sea 47, Rim 27, 76, Rid 60 6

āctrēo, *n neut* oak-tree
dat sg Wife 28[n], 36

ācweðan, *v str* utter
pres 3 sg **ācwið** Wan 91

ācȳþan, *v wk* reveal
Wan 113

ādl, *n fem or neut*　disease
　Sea 70

ādrēogan, *v str*　perform, put into action; suffer, bear
　Res 104. *pres 1 sg* **ādrēoge**
　Res 82

ādrīfan, *v str*　drive away
　pret 3 sg **ādrāf** *Husb* 19

ādroren, *past partic*　declined
　Rim 79^n

āfȳsed, *past partic*　sent in haste
　Res 88^n

āgan, *v pret-pres*　own, possess
　pres 1 & 3 sg **āh** *Sea* 27^n; *neg* **nāh** *Res*
　101. *subjunct sg* **āge** *Wan* 64, *Res* 1.
　subjunct pl **āgen** *Sea* 117. *pret 1 & 3*
　sg **āhte** *Rim* 23, *Deor* 18^n, 22, 38,
　Wife 16

āgrafan, *v str*　engrave, incise
　pret 3 sg **āgrōf** *Husb* 13

alan, *v str*　bring forth, produce
　pret 3 sg **ōl** *Rim* 23^n

ald *see* **eald**

ālibban, ālifian, *v wk*　live
　pret 1 sg **ālifde**, "have been living,"
　Res 116

ālicgan, *v str*　fail, come to an end
　pret pl **ālēgon** *Rim* 5

alwaldend, *adj*　all-ruling
　Husb 32

ālȳfan, *v wk*　allow, grant
　pres sg subjunct **ālȳfe** *Res* 34

ān, *num & adj*　one; alone, only
　Rim 77^n? Husb 18^n. *wk* **āna** *Wan* 8,
　Wife 22, 35^n, [Husb 42^n]. *dat pl* **ānum**
　Rid 60 15

ānad, *n neut*　solitary place, wilderness
　dat sg **ānæde** *Rid* 60 5

anda, *n masc*　hostility
　dat sg **andan** *Wan* 105

ānfloga, *n masc*　solitary flier
　Sea 62^n

ānhaga, *n masc*   solitary
  Wan 1[n]; **ānhoga** *Res* 89. *acc sg*
  ānhogan *Wan* 40
ānhȳdig, *adj*   resolute
  Deor 2
ār, *n fem*   grace, mercy, favour
  Sea 107. *acc sg* **āre** *Wan* 1 (*gen?*), 114,
  Deor 33. *gen pl wk* **ārna** *Res* 49[n], 67
ārǣd, *adj*   resolute, unrelenting; appointed
  Wan 5[n]
ārǣran, *v wk*   raise up, set
  pres sg subjunct **ārǣre** *Res* 15
āreaht, *past partic*   extended
  Rim 10
ārfæst, *adj*   gracious
  Res 33
asca *see* **æsc**
āsecgan, *v wk*   say, tell
  Wan 11
āsettan, *v wk*   set up, initiate, make
  Res 73
atol, *adj*   horrible, dreadful
  Sea 6
āð, *n masc*   oath
  Rim 64. *dat sg* **āþe** *Husb* 51
āþecgan, *v wk*   take (as food or an offering),
  Wulf 2[n], 7   consume
āþringan, *v str*   urge
  pret 3 sg **āþrong** *Husb* 41
āwa, *adv*   always, eternally
  Sea 79
āweaht, *past partic*   awakened
  Rim 9
āweaxan, *v str*   grow up
  pret 1 sg **āwēox** *Husb* 2[n]

æfest, *n neut*   envy, spite
  dat pl as adv **æfestum,** "maliciously,"
  Res 47[n]?
æfest, *adj*   pious, righteous
  dat pl **æfestum** *Res* 47[n]?

æfre, *adv*   ever
  Deor 11, *Wife* 39, *Rid 60* 8
æfter, *adv*   afterwards
  Sea 77
æfter, *prep*
  (1) + *acc*   after, in relation to, because of
      Wan 50
  2) + *dat*   after; during
      Res 31, 52^n, 111, *Ruin* 10
æftercweþende, *pres partic*   speaking afterwards
  gen pl **æftercweþendra**, "those who
  speak of a man after his death," *Sea* 72
æht, *n fem*   possessions, riches
  Ruin 36
ælc, *adj*   every
  instr sg **ælce** *Res* 93
ælde, *n masc pl*   men
  gen pl **ælda** *Wan* 85, *Sea* 77, *Husb* 3^n?
ældo *see* **yldo**
ælmihtig, *adj*   almighty
  wk *ælmihtga* *Res* 1^n
ænig, *pron* (+ *gen*)   any
  Rid 60 3. *acc sg masc* **ænigne** *Res* 107.
  gen sg masc-neut **ænges** *Sea* 116,
  Husb 47^n. *instr sg* **ænge** *Res* 112. *nom
  pl fem* **ænige** *Res* 69
ær, *adv*   previously, before; early
  Wan 43, 113, *Sea* 102, *Rim* 45, 80,
  Deor 41, *Res* 48; ~ **oþþe sīð**, "early
  or late," *Rid 60* 8. *superl* **ærest**, "first,"
  Wife 6
ær, *prep* (+ *dat*)   before
  Sea 69
ær, *conj*   before
  Wan 64, 69, *Sea* 74
ærdæg, *n masc*   former day
  dat pl **ærdagum** *Husb* 16, 54
ærendspræc, *n fem*   message
  acc sg **ærendspræce** *Rid 60* 15
ærsceaft, *n fem*   ancient work
  Ruin 16^n

æsc, *n masc*   ash-wood spear
  gen pl **asca** *Wan* 99
æt, *prep* (+ *dat*)   at, in; near; with; from
  Wan 111, *Sea* 7, *Rim* 78, *Wife* 45,
  Res 48, 57, 110, *Rid 60* 2
ætgædre, *adv*   together
  Wan 39
ætsomne, *adv*   together
  Husb 33, 50
æþeling, *n masc*   noble, prince
  gen pl **æþelinga** *Sea* 93

bald, *adj as n*   bold(ness)
  Rim 63[n]
bān, *n neut*   bone
  pl *Rim* 77
bāt, *n masc*   boat, ship
  Res 100. gen sg **bātes** *Husb* 6
baþian, *v wk*   bathe
  Wan 47
bǣl, *n neut*   pyre
  dat sg **bǣle** *Sea* 114[n]
bæð, *n neut*   bath
  pl **baþu** *Ruin* 40, 46
be, *prep* (+ *dat*)   beside, by, among; about,
  Sea 1, 8, 98, *Deor* 1, *Rid 60* 1,   concerning; during
  Husb 53; **bi** *Wan* 80, *Deor* 35, *Wife* 1,
  Res 96[n]
bēacnian, *v wk*   be a beacon, be prominent
  pret 3 sg **bēacnade** *Rim* 31[n]
Beadohild   *daughter of Niðhad*
  dat **Beadohilde** *Deor* 8[n]
beaducāfa, *n masc or adj wk* one bold in battle
  Wulf 11[n]
bēag, *n masc*   ring, circlet
  pl **bēagas** *Husb* 35[n]
bēag, *v see* **būgan**, *v str*
bealdlīce, *adv*   boldly
  Rid 60 16
bealo, *n neut*   harm, destruction, disaster
  Sea 112

bealodǽd, *n fem* wicked deed
  pl **bealodǽde** *Res* 20, 35
bealofūs, *adj* disastrous, murderous
  Rim 50
bealosīð, *n masc* terrible journey; terrible experience
  gen pl **bealosīþa** *Sea* 28
bēam, *n masc* wood, piece of wood
  Husb 13
bearn, *n neut* son
  pl Sea 77, 93
bearo, *n masc* grove
  dat sg **bearwe** *Wife* 27, *Husb* 23. *nom*
  pl **bearwas** *Sea* 48
bēatan, *v str* beat
  pret pl **bēotan** *Sea* 23
bebēodan, *v str* offer
  pres 1 sg **bebēode** *Res* 6
becuman, *v str* arrive
  pres 3 sg **becymeð** *Rim* 73
befealdan, *v str* surround
  pret 3 sg **befēold** *Rim* 21
beflōwen, *past partic* flowed around, surrounded
  Wife 49
befōn, *v str* hold in, encompass
  pret 3 sg **befēng** *Ruin* 39
begietan, *v str* take hold of; come upon, assail (*fig.*)
  pret 3 sg **begeat** *Wife* 32[n], 41; **bi~**
  Sea 6[n]
behealdan, *v str* look upon
  pret sg subjunct **behēolde** *Rid* 60 5
behrīmed, *past partic* frosted
  Wife 48
belācan, *v str* play around, move around
  pret 3 sg **belēolc** *Rid* 60 7
benemnan, *v wk* affirm
  Husb 51
benn, *n fem* wound
  pl **benne** *Wan* 49
benugan, *v pret-pres* (+ *gen*) enjoy
  pres 3 sg **beneah** *Husb* 48[n]

bēodan, *v str*
  pres 3 sg **bēodeð** *Sea* 54
beofode *see* **bifian**
bēon, *v anom (no pret)*
  pres 3 sg **bið** *Wan* 5, 30, 50, 55, 73,
  108 (2), 109 (2), 114, *Sea* 107,
  Wife 52ⁿ, *Res* 95; **biþ** *Wan* 12, 112,
  Sea 44, 100, 103, 106, 115, *Rim* 79,
  Res 117. *pl* **bēoð** *Wan* 49; **bēoþ**
  Rim 77
beorg, *n masc*
  dat pl **beorgum** *Ruin* 32ⁿ
beorgan, *v str*
  pres 3 sg **byrgeð** *Rim* 81
beorht, *adj*
  Wan 94, *Rim* 30. *acc-dat sg wk*
  beorhtan *Ruin* 37, 40 (*or dat sg strong*
  = *beorhtum*). *neut pl* **beorht** *Ruin* 21
beorn, *n masc*
  Wan 70, 113, *Sea* 55, *Ruin* 32. *gen pl*
  beorna *Rid 60* 16
bēot, *n neut*
  Wan 70; **gebēot** *Husb* 49ⁿ
bēotan *see* **bēatan**
bēotian, *v wk*
  pret pl **bēotedan** *Wife* 21ⁿ
bēoð/-þ *see* **bēon**
beran, *v str*
  pres 3 sg **bireð** *Wulf* 17. *past partic dat*
  sg masc **geborenum**, "fellow-born
  (brother)," "brother by birth," *Sea* 98
berofen, *past partic*
  Ruin 4
berstan, *v str*
  pret pl **burston** *Ruin* 2
bescær *see* **biscyran**
bētan, *v wk*
  pret sg subjunct **bētte** *Res* 35
bētend, *n masc*
  pl Ruin 28ⁿ

announce, presage, bode

be (*of repeated action; in gnomic and
proverbial utterances; with future
sense*)

hill; heap, mound

keep off from, protect

bright

man, warrior

vaunt, boast; vow

vow

bear

taken away, missing

burst, break apart

make better, amend; atone for

repairer

betran, betst *see* **gōd**

beweaxen, *past partic*   overgrown
 masc pl **beweaxne** *Wife* 31

bi *see* **be**

bibod, *n neut*   command
 pl **bibodu** *Res* 35

bīdan, *v str* (+ *acc or gen*) wait, stay; wait for; live to see; re-
 Sea 30, *Res* 105; **gebīdan** *Wan* 70ⁿ. ceive; endure, survive through
 pres 3 sg **gebīdeð** *Wan* 1ⁿ. *pret 1 & 3*
 sg **gebād** *Rim* 16, *Wife* 3, *Ruin* 9. *past*
 partic **gebiden** *Sea* 4, 28

bidǣled, *past partic* (+ *dat*) separated from, deprived of
 Wan 20, *Deor* 28

biddan, *v str*   bid
 Husb 13

bidroren, *past partic* (+ *dat*) deprived of, having lost
 Sea 16. *masc pl* **bidrorene** *Wan* 79

bifian, *v wk*   tremble; vibrate
 pret 3 sg **beofode** *Rim* 30

bifōran, *prep* (+ *dat*)   before, in front of
 Wan 46

bigeat *see* **begietan**

bigiellan, *v str*   cry out against; cry out in
 pret 3 sg **bigeal** *Sea* 24   response to

biglīdan, *v str* (+ *dat*)   deceive; let down
 pret 3 sg **biglād** *Rim* 14

bihongen, *past partic*   hung about with
 Sea 17

bihroren, *past partic*   fallen upon; covered with (what has
 masc pl **bihrorene** *Wan* 77 fallen)

bilecgan, *v wk*   place around
 pret 3 sg **bilegde** *Wulf* 11

bindan, *v str*   bind
 pres 3 sg **bindeð** *Wan* 102. *subjunct sg*
 binde *Wan* 13. *indic pl* **bindað**
 Wan 18; **gebindað** *Wan* 40. *pret 3 sg*
 bond *Sea* 32; **gebond** *Ruin* 19. *past*
 partic **gebunden** *Sea* 9, *Deor* 24; "obli-
 gated," "committed" *Res* 75ⁿ

biniman, *v str* (+ *dat/instr*) deprive, take away (*of thing taken*)
 pret 3 sg **binōm** *Deor* 16ⁿ

bireð *see* **beran**

biscyran, *v wk* cut short; cut off (from)
  pret 3 sg **bescær** *Rim* 26[n]? *past partic*
  masc pl **biscyrede** *Rim* 84

bisgo, *n fem* labour, toil
  Sea 88

bītan, *v str* bite; (*fig*) gnaw, fret
  pres 3 sg **bīteð** *Rim* 63

bit(t)er, *adj* bitter; severe; oppressive
  acc sg fem **bitter'** (=. *bittere*) *Sea* 55;
  bitre *Sea* 4. *wk* **bitran** *Rim* 81. *masc-*
  fem pl **bitre** *Wife* 31, *Res* 20

bittre, *adv* bitterly, harshly
  Rim 50, *Res* 79, 110

bið/-þ *see* **bēon**

biwāwen, *past partic* blown upon
  masc pl **biwāune** *Wan* 76

biwerian, *v wk* (+ *dat*) protect against
  pret pl **biweredon** *Rim* 20. *past partic*
  masc pl **biwerede** *Rim* 85

biworpen, *past partic* surrounded
  Wulf 5

biwrēon, *v str* cover
  pret 1 sg **biwrāh** *Wan* 23

blācian, *v wk* grow pale
  pres 3 sg **blācað** *Sea* 91

blǣd, *n masc* prosperity; riches; glory
  Wan 33, *Sea* 79, 88, *Rim* 35, 53,
  Deor 34

blēo, *n neut* colour
  dat pl **blēoum** *Rim* 4

blinnan, *v str* cease, come to an end
  pres 3 sg **blinnið** *Rim* 53

bliss, *n fem* joy
  dat sg **blisse** *Rim* 53. *nom pl Rim* 82.
  gen pl **blissa** *Rim* 4

blissian, *v wk* be joyful
  pret 3 sg **blissade** *Rim* 35

blīþe, *adj* joyful
  acc sg fem (or *pl neut*) *Wife* 21[n], 44.
  instr sg Res 75

blōstm, blōstma, *n masc*　　　　　blossom, flower
　gen pl **blōstma** *Rim* 4. *dat pl* **blōst-**
　mum *Sea* 48
bōg, bōh, *n masc*　　　　　branch; shoulder (of a quadruped)
　dat pl **bōgum,** "forequarters," "arms,"
　Wulf 11[n]
bond *see* **bindan**
bōsm, *n masc*　　　　　bosom
　dat sg **bōsme** *Ruin* 40
bōt, *n fem*　　　　　remedy; amelioration
　Res 110. *acc sg* **bōte** *Wan* 113, *Res* 20[n]
brād, *adj*　　　　　broad
　neut as n, "open space," *Rim* 13. *gen*
　sg wk **brādan** *Ruin* 37[n]
brǣdan, *v wk*　　　　　spread out
　Wan 47
brēac *see* **brūcan**
breahtm, *n masc*　　　　　noise
　gen pl **breahtma** *Wan* 86
(ge)brecan, *v str*　　　　　break
　pret pl **gebrǣcon** *Ruin* 1[n]. *past partic*
　gebrocen *Ruin* 32
brego, *n masc*　　　　　ruler
　Res 79
brēost, *n neut*　　　　　breast
　dat pl (for sg) **brēostum** *Wan* 113,
　Rim 46
brēostcearu, *n fem*　　　　　care in the breast; anxiety
　acc sg **brēostceare** *Sea* 4, *Wife* 44
brēostcofa, *n masc*　　　　　(repository of the) breast
　dat sg **brēostcofan** *Wan* 18
brēosthord, *n masc or neut*　　　　　(what is stored in the) breast
　Sea 55
brēr, *n fem*　　　　　briar, bramble
　dat pl **brērum** *Wife* 31
brimfugel, *n masc*　　　　　seabird
　pl **brimfuglas** *Wan* 47
brimlād, *n fem*　　　　　sea-path, pathway of the sea
　dat sg **brimlāde** *Sea* 30
bringan, *v wk*　　　　　bring
　pres 3 sg **bringeð** *Wan* 54

brondhord, *n masc or neut* — hoard of fire, hidden fire
Rim 46^n

brosnian, *v wk* — decay, crumble
pres 3 sg **brosnað** Ruin 2. *pret 3 sg*
brosnade Ruin 28

brōþor, *n masc* — brother
Sea 98. *gen pl* **brōþra** Deor 8

brūcan, *v str* (+ *gen*) — enjoy
pres pl **brūcað** Sea 88. *pret 3 sg* **brēac**
Wan 44^n

brūn, *adj* — dark, brown; shining
fem wk **brūne** Rid 60 6

brytta, *n masc* — dispenser, distributer
acc sg **bryttan** Wan 25

būgan, *v str* — bend
pret 3 sg **bēag** Ruin 17^n

būgan, *v wk* — inhabit
Husb 18

būne, *n fem* — cup
Wan 94

burg, *n fem* — fortress, city
Rim 63^n, Deor 19, Ruin 37, 49^n. *nom*
pl **byrig** Sea 48. *dat pl* **burgum** Sea 28

burgreced, *n neut* — dwelling in a fortress or city
pl **burgræced** Ruin 21

burgsele, *n masc* — hall in a fortress
Rim 30

burgsteall, *n neut* — city site
Ruin 28

burgstede, *n masc* — fortified place
pl Ruin 2

burgtūn, *n masc* — fortified enclosure
pl **burgtūnas** Wife 31^n

burgware, *n masc pl* — inhabitants of a fortress or city
gen pl **burgwara** Wan 86^n

burnsele, *n masc* — bath-house
pl Ruin 21^n

burston *see* **berstan**

būtan, *prep* — except; without
(1) + *acc* Sea 18
(2) + *dat* Res 112

byrgan, *v wk*   bury
  Sea 98
byrgeð *see* **beorgan**
byrig *see* **burg**
byrnan, *v str*   burn
  pres 3 sg **byrneð** *Rim* 50
byrnwiga, *n masc*   mail-clad warrior
  Wan 94

cald, *n neut*   cold
  dat sg **calde** *Sea* 8[n]
cald, *adj*   cold
  dat pl **caldum** *Sea* 10. *superl nom sg*
  caldast *Sea* 33
cāsere, *n masc*   emperor
  pl **cāseras** *Sea* 82
cealdian, *v wk*   grow cold
  pres 3 sg *cealdað* *Rim* 69[n]
cearseld, *n neut*   abode of care
  gen pl **cearselda** *Sea* 5[n]
cearu, *n fem*   care, sorrow
  Res 115; **cearo** *Wan* 55. *acc sg* **ceare**
  Wan 9. *nom pl* **ceare** *Sea* 10
cēol, *n masc*   boat, ship
  dat sg **cēole** *Sea* 5
cēolþel, *n neut*   deck of a ship; ship
  dat sg **cēolþele** *Husb* 9
cinnan, *v str?*   grow, increase
  pres 3 sg **cinnið** *Rim* 52[n]
clǣne, *adj*   clean, pure
  Sea 110
clif, *n neut*   cliff
  dat pl **clifum** *Sea* 8
clom(m), *n masc or fem*   bond
  dat pl **clommum** *Sea* 10
clyppan, *v wk*   embrace
  pres sg subjunct **clyppe** *Wan* 42
cnēo(w), *n neut*   knee; generation
  Wan 42. *gen pl* **cnēa** *Ruin* 8[n]
cnossian, *v wk*   beat, crash
  pres 3 sg **cnossað** *Sea* 8[n]

cnyssan, *v wk*   beat upon; afflict, agitate
   pres pl **cnyssað** *Wan* 101, *Sea* 33[n]

cōlian, *v wk*   grow cool
   pres 3 sg **cōlað** *Rim* 67

collenferð, *adj*   high-hearted
   Wan 71[n]

conn, const *see* **cunnan**

corn, *n neut*   grain
   gen pl **corna** *Sea* 33

cringan, *v str*   fall; die in battle
   pret 3 sg **gecrong** *Wan* 79, *Ruin* 31[n].
   pret pl **crungon** *Ruin* 25[n], 28

Crist   Christ
   Res 56

cuman, *v str*   come
   infin (or pres sg subjunct) **cume**
   Res 21[n]. *pres 3 sg* **cymeð** *Wan* 103,
   Sea 61, 106, 107, *Wulf* 2, 7. *subjunct*
   sg **cyme** *Res* 59. *subjunct pl* **cumen**
   Sea 118. *pret 3 sg* **cwōm** *Wan* 92 (3),
   93[n]. *pl* **cwōman** *Ruin* 25. *past partic*
   cumen *Husb* 8

cunnan, *v pret-pres*   know; know how to; be acquainted
   Husb 9. *pres 1 & 3 sg* **conn** *Res* 77,   with
   Rid 60 11. 2 sg **const** *Res* 25. *subjunct*
   sg **cunne** *Wan* 69[n], 71, 113

cunnian, *v wk* (+ *acc or gen*)   try, try out, have experience of
   pres 1 sg **cunnige** *Sea* 35. *3 sg* **cunnað**
   Wan 29. *pret 3 sg* **cunnade** *Deor* 1.
   past partic **gecunnad** *Sea* 5

cunnung, *n fem*   trial
   dat sg **cunnunge** *Res* 25[n]

cūþ, *adj*   well-known; familiar; intelligible?
   Deor 19. *gen pl* **cūðra**
   Wan 55

cweðan, *v str*   speak, say
   pret 3 sg **cwæð** *Wan* 6, 111

cwic(u), *adj*   alive, living
   gen pl **cwicra** *Wan* 9

cwidegiedd, *n neut*   utterance in words
   gen pl **cwidegiedda** *Wan* 55[n]

cwīþan, *v wk*   lament, bewail
    Wan 9
cwōm, cwōman, cyme, cymeð *see*
    cuman
cyn(n), *n neut*   kind; race
    gen sg **cynnes** *Rid 60* 4
cynelic, *adj*   royal; splendid
    Ruin 48
cynerīce, *n neut*   kingdom; kingly power
    gen sg **cynerīces** *Deor* 26[n]
cyning, *n masc*   king
    Deor 23, *Res* 14, 24, 40, 50. *nom pl*
    cyningas *Sea* 82. *gen pl* **cyninga**
    Res 21
cyssan, *v wk*   kiss
    pres sg subjunct **cysse** *Wan* 42
cyðþu, *n fem*   intimacy; home and kin
    Res 115[n]

dǣd, *n fem*   deed
    dat pl **dǣdum** *Sea* 41, 76
dæg, *n masc*   day
    Rim 72, *Wife* 37. *dat sg* **dæge** *Rim* 45.
    nom pl **dagas** *Sea* 80. *dat pl* **dagum**
    Res 31
dǣl, *n masc*   portion; (large) number or amount
    Wan 65, *Deor* 30, 34, *Rid 60* 10
dēad, *adj*   dead
    neut wk **dēade** *Sea* 65. *dat pl* **dēadum**
    Sea 98
dear *see* **durran**
dēað, *n masc*   death
    Sea 106, *Wife* 22; **dēaþ** *Deor* 8. *dat sg*
    dēaðe *Wan* 83
dēma, *n masc*   judge
    Res 82
dene, *n fem*   valley
    pl **dena** *Wife* 30
dēofol, *n masc (sg) & neut (pl)*   the Devil
    pl Res 52. *dat sg* **dēofle** *Sea* 76
dēop, *adj*   deep
    Rim 45. *acc sg masc* **dēopne** *Res* 82

dēope, *adv*
  Wan 89

deeply

dēor, *adj*
  Sea 41, *Deor* 37[n] *(as proper name). dat*
  pl **dēorum** *Sea* 76

brave

deorc, *adj*
  neut wk **deorce** *Wan* 89[n]

dark

dim(m), *adj*
  fem pl **dimme** *Wife* 30

dark

dogian, *v wk*
  pret 1 sg **dogode** *Wulf* 9[n]

dog, pursue like a dog?

dōgor, *n masc*
  gen pl **dōgra** *Wan* 63. *dat pl* **dōgrum**
  Res 52

day

dohtor, *n fem*
  Husb 48

daughter

dol, *adj*
  Sea 106

foolish

dōm, *n masc*
  dat sg **dōme** *Sea* 85

glory

dōmgeorn, *adj*
  masc pl **dōmgeorne** *Wan* 17

eager for good fame

dōn, *v anom*
  gedōn *Sea* 43. *pret 1 sg* **dyde** *Sea* 20,
  Res 52. *pret pl* **gedydon** *Wulf* 13

do, commit; make; put (in a situation), bring (to)

drēam, *n masc*
  Sea 80, *Rim* 39. *gen sg* **drēames**
  Res 33. *dat sg* **drēame** *Wan* 79. *nom pl*
  drēamas *Sea* 65, 86, *Rim* 55

joy; (sound of) merry-making or celebration

drēfan, *v wk*
  pret sg subjunct **drēfde** *Husb* 21

stir up

drēogan, *v str*
  Wife 26. *pres 3 sg* **drēogeð** *Wife* 50.
  pres pl **drēogað** *Sea* 56. *pret 3 sg*
  drēag *Deor* 2

endure, suffer

drēor(i)gian, *v wk*
  pres pl **drēorgiað** *Ruin* 29[n]

be or grow dismal

drēorig, *adj*
  Wan 25. *acc sg masc* **drēorigne**
  Wan 17[n]

distressed, sad

drēorighlēor, *adj*
  Wan 83[n]

sad-faced, with grief-stricken face

drēorsele, *n masc*　　　　dismal hall
　dat sg Wife 50[n]

drēosan, *v str*　　　　fall, decline
　pres 3 sg **drēoseð** *Wan* 63. *pl*
　gedrēosað *Rim* 55. *pret 3 sg* **gedrēas**
　Wan 36, *Ruin* 11. *past partic* **gedroren**
　Sea 86. *fem pl* **gedrorene** *Ruin* 5.

drohtað, *n masc*　　　　condition of life
　Rim 39

drohtian, *v wk*　　　　live, carry on
　Res 90

dryhten, *n masc*　　　　lord; the Lord
　Sea 41, 43, 106, 124, *Deor* 32, *Res* 2,
　4, 7, 45, 61, 108. *gen sg* **dryhtnes**
　Sea 65, 121. *dat sg* **dryhtne** *Deor* 37,
　Res 18

dryhtlic, *adj*　　　　noble
　Rim 39. *superl dat sg* **dryhtlicestum**
　Sea 85

dryhtscype, n *masc*　　　　lordly power; nobility
　Rim 55

duguþ, *n fem*　　　　band of seasoned warriors, noble
　Wan 79; **duguð** *Sea* 86. *gen sg*　　　band
　duguþe *Wan* 97. *dat pl* **dugeþum**
　Sea 80

dūn, *n fem*　　　　hill
　pl **dūna** *Wife* 30

durran, *v pret-pres*　　　　dare
　pres 1 sg **dear** *Husb* 11. *subjunct sg*
　durre *Wan* 10

dyde *see* **dōn**

dynian, *v wk*　　　　resound, re-echo
　pret 3 sg **dynede** *Rim* 28

dȳre, *adj*　　　　dear, precious, valued; illustrious
　Rim 45, *Deor* 37

dyrne, *adj*　　　　secret
　Wife 12

ĒA *for runic letter, see* **ēar**

ēac, *adv*　　　　also
　Sea 119, *Wulf* 12

Res 67, 86. *instr sg* **ealle** *Deor* 16[n]?
nom pl masc **ealle** *Wan* 74[n]?, *Sea* 50,
81. *acc pl neut* **eall** *Res* 3; **eal** *Res* 8.
gen pl **ealra** *Wan* 63

ealle, *adv*   entirely
Wan 74[n]?, *Deor* 16[n]?

ēar, *n masc*   earth; name of runic letter ᛠ (*ĒA*)
Husb 51[n] (*rune*)

eard, *n masc*   country, home
Sea 38, *Rid* 60 5, *Husb* 18. *gen sg*
eardes, "(in my) home," *Rim* 74[n]

eardgeard, *n masc*   dwelling-place
Wan 85

eardstapa, *n masc*   land-stepper, wanderer
Wan 6

earfoðe, *n neut*   hardship, distress
nom-acc-gen pl **earfoþa** *Deor* 2,
Wife 39; **earfoða** *Deor* 30; **earfeþa**
Wan 6. *dat pl* **earfoþum** *Res* 112

earfoðhwīl, *n fem*   time of hardship
acc sg **earfoðhwīle** *Sea* 3[n]

earfoðlic, *adj*   fraught with hardship or affliction
Wan 106

earm, *adj*   poor, wretched
Res 89[n]. *acc sg masc* **earmne** *Wan* 40,
Wulf 16[n]

earmcearig, *adj*   wretched and sad
Wan 20[n], *Sea* 14

earn, *n masc*   eagle
Sea 24

earnian, *v wk*   earn, merit
pret sg subjunct **earnode** *Res* 49

earning, *n fem*   desert, merit
pl **earninga** *Res* 69

ēaþe, *adv*   easily
Wulf 18

ēaþmōd, *adj*   humble
Sea 107

ēce, *adj*   eternal
Sea 67, 124, *Res* 4, 56, 63. *acc-gen sg*
wk **ēcan** *Sea* 79[n], 120, *Res* 33

ecghete, *n masc*
  Sea 70

sword-hate; attack by the sword

edor, *n masc*
  pl **ederas** *Wan* 77[n]

enclosure; dwelling-place

eft, *adv*
  Wan 45, *53*[n], *Sea* 61, *Wife* 23

afterwards, subsequently; again, back
  again

eglond, *n neut*
  Wulf 5

island

egsa, *n masc*
  Sea 103. *dat sg* **egsan** *Sea* 101[n]

fear

ellen, *n masc or neut*
  Rim 31, 69, *Res* 70. *dat sg* **elne**
  Wan 114

courage

elles, *adv*
  Sea 46, *Wife* 23

else

ellor, *adv*
  Husb 3

elsewhere

elþēod, *n fem*
  acc or dat sg? **elþēode** *Husb* 37

foreign nation

elþēodig, *adj*
  gen pl **elþēodigra**, "those living in a
  foreign land," *Sea* 38[n]

foreign, strange

endelēas, *adj*
  Deor 30

endless

engel, *n masc*
  nom-acc pl **englas** *Res* 49, 56. *dat pl*
  englum *Sea* 78

angel

ent, *n masc*
  gen pl **enta** *Wan* 87, *Ruin* 2

giant

eom *see* **wesan**

eorcanstān, *n masc*
  sg for pl Ruin 36[n]

precious stone

eorl, *n masc*
  Wan 84, 114, *Deor* 2, *Res* 108. *gen sg*
  eorles *Rid* 60 13. *dat sg* **eorle** *Wan* 12,
  Deor 33. *acc pl* **eorlas** *Wan* 99.
  gen pl **eorla** *Wan* 60, *Sea* 72, *Deor* 41

man (of the upper class)

eorlgestrēon, *n neut*
  gen pl **eorlgestrēona** *Husb* 47

noble treasure

Eormanrīc
  gen **Eormanrīces** *Deor* 21[n]

Ermanaric (*king of the Goths*)

eorþe, *n fem*   earth
  Rim 23. *acc-gen-dat sg* **eorþan**
  Wan 106, 110, *Sea* 32, 39, 61, 81, 89,
  93, 105, *Wife* 33^n, *Res* 2, 67, 85,
  Husb 47

eorðgrāp, *n fem*   clutches of the earth
  Ruin 6

eorðmægen, *n neut*   might of the earth
  Rim 69

eorðscræf, *n neut*   hole or cave in the earth
  dat sg **eorðscræfe** *Wan* 84, *Wife* 28^n.
  acc pl **eorðscrafu** *Wife* 36^n

eorðsele, *n masc*   hall or cavity in the earth
  Wife 29^n

eorðwela, *n masc*   riches of the earth
  pl **eorðwelan** *Sea* 67

ēstēadig, *adj*   blessed with bounty or luxury
  Sea 56^n

ēþel, *n masc or neut*   home, native land
  Sea 60, *Husb* 26, 37. *gen sg* **ēðles**
  Rim 74. *dat sg* **ēðle** *Wan* 20; **ēþle**
  Res 89, 108

faca *see* **fæc**

fāh[1], *adj*   marked, patterned; stained
  Wan 98, *Res* 65

fāh[2], *adj*   outlawed, proscribed
  Wife 46

faran, *v str*   travel
  Husb 43

faroð, *n masc*   water, sea
  dat sg **faroðe** *Res* 101

fæc, *n neut*   space of time, time
  gen pl **faca** *Res* 43

fǣd, *past partic*   adorned, decorated
  gen sg wk **fǣdan** *Husb* 36^n

fæder, *n masc*   father
  Res 41, 62. *dat sg Wan* 115

fǣge, *adj*   doomed to die
  dat sg masc **fǣgum** *Sea* 71

fægen, *adj*   cheerful, sanguine
  Wan 68^n

fæger, *adj*
  acc sg fem **fægre** *Husb* 38
fægnian, *v wk*
  pret 3 sg **fægnade** *Rim* 33
fægre, *adv*
  Rim 20. *superl* **fægrost** *Sea* 13
fægrian, *v wk*
  pres pl **fægriað** *Sea* 48[n]
fæhðu, *n fem*
  Wife 26[n]; **fæhþo** *Husb* 19[n]
færlīce, *adv*
  Wan 61.
fæst, *adj*
  Wulf 5[n], *Rid* 60 3
fæste, *adv*
  Wan 13, 18, *Res* 76
fæstlīce, *adv*
  Res 38
fæstnung, *n fem*
  Wan 115[n]
fēa, *adj*
  Rid 60 3. *dat pl* **fēam** *Res* 66[n]
feallan, *v str*
  pres 3 sg **fealleþ** *Wan* 63; **fealleð**
  Rim 68. *pret 3 sg* **fēol** *Sea* 32
fealu, *adj*
  masc pl **fealwe** *Wan* 46
fēasceaft, *adj*
  Res 113
fēasceaftig, *adj*
  Sea 26
fela, *indecl n as adj* (+ *gen*)
  Wan 54, *Sea* 5, *Deor* 38, *Wife* 39,
  Res 26, 36, 46, 51, 66, 101
felalēof
  gen sg wk **felalēofan** *Wife* 26
fenn, *n masc or neut*
  dat sg **fenne** *Wulf* 5
feoh, *n neut*
  Wan 108
feohgīfre, *adj*
  Wan 68

fair

be joyful

fairly, fittingly

grow fair

enmity; feud

suddenly

fast, fixed, secure

fast, securely

firmly

stability, fastness

few, a few; rare, infrequent

fall, decline

tawny; dun-coloured, dull

destitute

destitute; desolate

much, many

very dear, beloved

fen, marsh

money, wealth

eager for wealth

fēol *see* **feallan**

fēolan, *v str* reach; adhere; persist
  pret pl **fēlon** *Ruin* 13[n]

fēond, *n masc* enemy; fiend
  gen pl **fēonda** *Sea* 75. *dat pl* **fēondon**
  (= *fēondum*) *Rim* 20

fēondscipe, *n masc* hostility, enmity
  Rim 68

feor, *adj* far, far-off
  Wan 21. *gen sg neut* **feorres**
  Wife 47[n]

feor, *adv* far, from afar
  Wan 26, 90, *Sea* 37, 52, *Rim* 65[n],
  Wife 25

feorh, *n neut* life
  Sea 71; **feorg** *Sea* 94. *dat sg* **fēore**
  Rim 45[n]

feorhgiefu, *n fem* gift of life
  dat sg **feorhgiefe** *Rim* 6

feormian, *v wk* support, sustain; receive
  imperat **feorma** *Res* 26[n], 43[n];
  gefeorma *Res* 62

fēran, *v wk* travel
  Sea 37, *Wife* 9

ferian, *v wk* carry, convey
  pret 3 sg **ferede** *Wan* 81. *pret pl* **fere-**
  don *Rim* 20

ferð, *n fem* host, troop
  Wan 54[n]

ferð, *n neut* spirit, heart
  Sea 26, 37. *dat sg* **ferðe** *Wan* 90;
  ferþe *Res* 76, 84

ferðloca, *n masc* container of the spirit, breast
  Wan 33. *acc sg* **ferðlocan** *Wan* 13

ferðweg, *n masc* way of the spirit, soul's road
  Res 72[n]

fēt *see* **fōt**

feter, *n fem* fetter
  dat pl **feterum** *Wan* 21

feþer, *n fem* feather; wing
  pl **feþra** *Wan* 47

fierst *see* **fyrst**

findan, *v str* find
  Wan 26. *pres 2 sg* **findest** *Husb* 12[n],
  28[n]. *pret 1 sg* **funde** *Wife* 18[n]

firendǣd, *n fem* wicked deed
  gen pl **firendǣda** *Res* 26

flāh, *n (neut?)* hostility, malice
  Rim 47

flāhmāh, *adj* treacherously or maliciously evil
  Rim 62[n]

flān, *n masc* arrow
  Rim 62

flānhred, *adj* arrow-swift
  Rim 72

flǣsc, *n neut* flesh
  dat sg **flǣsce** *Rim* 72

flǣschoma, *n masc* covering of flesh, body
  Sea 94

flēah, *n (neut?)* flight
  Rim 44[n]

flēan (= *flēon*), *v str* flee, escape
  Rim 72

flēogan, *v str* fly
  pret 3 sg **flēag** *Sea* 17

flēot, *n masc* vessel, ship
  Res 101

flēotende, *pres partic* floating
  gen pl **flēotendra** *Wan* 54[n]

flēt, *n neut* floor of a hall; hall
  Wan 61

flītan, *v str* dispute, contend
  pres 3 sg **flīteþ** *Rim* 62

flōdweg, *n masc* path of the flood
  pl **flōdwegas** *Sea* 52

flotweg, *n masc* path of the sea
  Husb 43

flyht, *n masc* flight
  dat pl **flyhtum** *Rim* 47

folc, *n neut* people
  Deor 22. *dat sg* **folce** *Res* 88. *dat pl*
  folcum *Rim* 40

folclond, *n neut* land that reverts to the community;
  gen sg **folclondes** *Wife* 47[n] country

folde, *n fem*
  acc-gen-dat sg **foldan** *Wan* 33, *Sea* 13,
  75, *Rim* 40, *Res* 113, [*Husb* 38[n]]
      earth, world, land

foldwela, *n masc*
  Rim 68
      riches of the earth

folgað, *n masc*
  Deor 38, *Wife* 9[n]
      position in someone's service

for, *prep* (+ *dat*/*instr*)
  Sea 101[n], *Rim* 86, *Wife* 10, *Res* 27, 51,
  74, 80, 106, *Rid 60* 15; ~ **þon**, "before which," *Sea* 103[n]; **fore** *Sea* 21
  (+ *acc*?), 22, *Res* [80[n]], 81, 83, 104
      before, in the sight of; because of,
        for the sake of; instead of

forbærned, *past partic*
  acc sg masc **forbærnedne** *Sea* 114
      burned up

foreþonc, *n masc*
  Res 54. *pl* **foreþoncas** *Res* 38
      thought entertained previously;
        thought about the future

forgiefan, *v str*
  imperat **forgif** *Res* 19[n], 22. *pret 2 sg*
  forgēafe *Res* 37. *pret 3 sg* **forgeaf**
  Rim 70. *past partic masc pl* **forgiefene**
  Sea 93[n]
      grant, consign to; ordain; forgive

forgrōwen, *past partic*
  Rim 46
      grown to excess, grown perversely

forht, *adj*
  Wan 68, *Res* 66. *masc pl* **forhte** *Res* 38
      afraid, fearful

forhwan, *conj*
  Wan 59
      why, for what reason

forlætan, *v str*
  imperat **forlæt** *Res* 49
      let, allow

forlēosan, *v str*
  pres pl **forlēosað** *Rim* 56
      lose; throw away

forniman, *v str*
  pret 3 sg **fornōm** *Wan* 80, *Ruin* 26.
  pl **fornōman** *Wan* 99
      take away

forst, *n masc*
  dat sg **forste** *Sea* 9
      frost

forstondan, *v str*
  imperat **forstond** *Res* 59
      stand before, protect

forswelgan, *v str*
  Sea 95
      swallow

forþolian, *v wk* (+ *dat*)
  Wan 38
      endure without

forþon, *adv*
  Wan 37, 58, 64, *Sea* 27ⁿ, 33, 58, 72,
  Wife 17ⁿ, *Res* 57, 79, 83, 88ⁿ,
  Ruin 29; **forðon** *Wan* 17ⁿ

therefore; for the following reason;
  accordingly, indeed

forþon, *conj*
  Sea 38, 64ⁿ, 108, *Wife* 39ⁿ

because; in that

forþsīþ, *n masc*
  gen sg **forþsīþes** *Husb* 43

journey forth or away

forðweg, *n masc*
  dat sg **forðwege**: **in** ~, "away,"
  Wan 81

way off or hence

forworen, *past partic*
  masc pl **forweorone** *Ruin* 7ⁿ

decayed

fōt, *n masc*
  pl **fēt** *Sea* 9

foot

frætwe, *n fem pl*
  dat pl **frætwum** *Rim* 38

adornments, trappings; armour

frætwian, *v wk*
  Res 72ⁿ. *past partic* **gefrætwed** *Ruin*
  33ⁿ; *neut pl* **frætwed** *Rim* 6

adorn; dress, equip

frēa, *n masc*
  Res 22. *gen-dat sg* **frēan** *Wife* 33,
  Res 48, *Husb* 10ⁿ

lord; the Lord

frēfran, *v wk*
  Wan 28, *Sea* 26ⁿ

comfort

fremman, *v wk*
  Sea 75ⁿ, *Husb* 19; **gefremman**
  Wan 16, 114. *pret pl* **gefremedon**
  Sea 84. *pret sg subjunct* **fremede**
  Res 27

perform, commit, achieve; put into
action; show

fremþe, *adj*
  dat pl **fremþum** *Res* 114

strange, foreign

frēo, *adj*
  dat pl **frēaum** (= *frēom*) *Rim* 32

noble

frēod, *n fem*
  acc sg **frēode** *Res* 114ⁿ

friendship, affection

frēolic, *adj*
  Rim 38

noble; fair, handsome

frēomæg, *n masc*
  dat pl **frēomægum** *Wan* 21

noble kinsman

frēond, *n masc*
  Wan 108, *Wife* 47. *gen sg* **frēondes**

loved one, friend; relative

Res 102. *nom pl* **frȳnd** *Wife* 33. *gen pl*
frēonda *Wife* 17

frēondlēas, *adj* · friendless
acc sg masc **frēondlēasne** *Wan* 28[n]

frēondscipe, *n masc* · friendship; close relationship; love
Wife 25; **frēondscype** *Husb* 19

frēorig, *adj* · cold, icy
Wan 33

fretan, *v str* · eat up; eat at, gnaw
pres 3 sg **friteð** *Rim* 75

frige, *n fem pl* · embraces; love
Deor 15[n]

friþian, freoþian, *v wk* (+ *acc or dat*) · protect; keep the peace among
imperat **gefreoþa** *Res* 62. *pret 1 sg*
freoþode *Rim* 40

frōd, *adj* · (old and) wise
Wan 90

frōdian, *v wk* · be wise
pret 3 sg impers **frōdade**, "there was
wisdom," *Rim* 32[n]

frōfor, *n fem* · comfort
acc sg **frōfre** *Wan* 115, *Res* 48

from, *adj* · strong
Rim 38. *dat pl* **fromum** *Rim* 32

fromsīþ, *n masc* · journey away, departure
Wife 33

fromweard, *adj* · departing, on one's way hence
dat sg masc **fromweardum** *Sea* 71[n]

frumstaþol, *n masc* · first resting-place
dat sg **frumstaþole** *Rid* 60 3

frymð, *n fem* · beginning
dat sg **frymðe** *Res* 84

frȳnd *see* **frēond**

fugel, *n masc* · bird
Wan 81[n]

ful, *adv* · very, extremely
Wan 5, *Sea* 24, *Wife* 1, 18, 21, 32, 46,
Res 43, *Husb* 6

full, *adj* (+ *gen*) · full
Ruin 23; **ful** *Sea* 100. *acc sg masc*
fulne *Sea* 113

fullēstan, *v wk* (+ *dat*) support, give assistance to
    pres pl **fullēstað** *Res* 93[n]. *pret sg*
    subjunct **gefylste** *Res* 102[n]
funde *see* **findan**
fundian, *v wk* hasten; set out eagerly or urgently
    Res 72. *pres 1 sg* **fundige** *Res* 41. *3 sg*
    fundað *Sea* 47
fūs, *adj* eager to depart, ready to depart
    Res 84, 98. *acc sg masc* **fūsne** *Sea* 50[n]
fȳr, *n neut* fire
    gen sg **fȳres** *Sea* 113
fyrhto, *n fem* fear
    Res 88
fyrst, *n masc* time, space of time
    fierst *Res* 22. *dat sg* **fyrste** *Res* 48

gād, *n neut* lack
    Rim 15, *Husb* 45
galan, *v str* sing
    Husb 23. *pret 1 sg* **gōl** *Rim* 24
galdorword, *n neut* word of an incantation or charm
    dat pl **galdorwordum** *Rim* 24
ganot, *n masc* gannet
    gen sg **ganetes** *Sea* 20
gǣst, *n masc* spirit, soul
    Res 74. *gen sg* **gǣstes** *Res* 46. *dat sg*
    gǣste *Res* 60. *gen pl* **gǣsta** *Res* 40
gǣstlic, *adj* spiritual; eerie
    Wan 73[n]
ge, *conj* and, or
    Wife 25[n]
gēac, *n masc* cuckoo
    Sea 53[n], *Husb* 23[n]
geador, *adv* together
    Wulf 19, *Husb* 50
gēap, *adj* curved; arched
    Ruin 11[n]
gēar, *n neut* year
    Rim 25. *gen pl* **gēara** *Wan* 22, *Res* 86
gēardæg, *n masc* day of old
    dat pl **gēardagum** *Wan* 44

gearo, *adj*
  acc sg masc **gearone** *Res* 40

ready, prepared

gearolīce, *adv*
  Deor 10

certainly, clearly

gearwe, *adv*
  Wan 71. *Wan* 69 **geare**

well, certainly

gearwian, *v wk*
  Res 74. *pret 3 sg* **gearwade**, "was
ready," "was at hand," *Rim* 36[n]

make ready

geascian, *v wk*
  pret pl **geascodan** *Deor* 21

find out about (by asking), hear of

Geat
  gen **Geates** *Deor* 15[n]

lover of Mǣðhild

geatwe, *n fem pl*
  dat pl **geatwum** *Rim* 38

trappings, ornaments

gebād, gebīdan, gebiden, gebīdeð *see*
  bīdan

gebǣded, *past partic*
  Husb 41

compelled, constrained

gebǣro, *n fem (or neut pl)*
  acc sg (or pl) Wife 21[n], 44

demeanour

gebēot *see* **bēot**

gebind, *n neut*
  Wan 24[n], 57

a gathering together, body (of water)

gebindað, gebond, gebunden *see*
  bindan

geblōwen, *past partic*
  Rim 46, 47

flourishing; spreading

geborenum *see* **beran**

gebrǣcon, gebrocen *see* **brecan**

gebrægd, *n masc*
  Ruin 18[n]

sharp movement; mental quickness;
  clever idea

gebycgan, *v wk*
  pres 1 sg subjunct **gebycge** *Res* 100[n]

buy

gecēosan, *v str*
  pres pl **gecēosað** *Rim* 56

choose

gecrong *see* **cringan**

gecunnad *see* **cunnian**

[gecwēme], *adj*
  [Res 115[n]*]*

pleasant

gecynd, *n fem*
  acc sg **gecynde** *Rim* 48[n]

nature, condition

gedǣlan, *v wk*   divide; dispense; distribute
  [*Husb* 34^n]. *pret 3 sg* **gedǣlde**
  Wan 83^n. *subjunct Wife* 22
gedōn, gedydon *see* **dōn**
gedreag, *n neut*   multitude; tumult
  Wife 45
gedrēas, gedrēosað, gedroren, -e *see*
  drēosan
gefēlan, *v wk*   feel
  Sea 95
gefēon, *v str*   rejoice
  Res 54; **gefēan** *Rim* 87. *pret pl* **gefē-**
  gon *Rim* 6
gefeorma *see* **feormian**
gefēra, *n masc*   companion
  dat sg **gefēran** *Wan* 30
gefest (= *gieffæst*), *adj*   secure in gifts
  Rim 25^n
gefrætwed *see* **frætwian**
gefremedon, gefremman *see* **fremman**
gefreoþa *see* **friþian**
gefrignan, *v str*   hear about
  pret pl **gefrugnon** *Deor* 14
gefylste *see* **fullēstan**
gegrunden, *past partic*   ground
  Ruin 14^n
gehātan *see* **hātan**
gehealdeþ *see* **healdan**
gehēapen, *past partic*   piled high
  Ruin 12^n
gehloten, *past partic*   allotted
  Rim 79^n
gehnǣged, *past partic*   brought low
  Sea 88
gehnīgan, *v str*   decline
  pret 3 sg **genāg** (= *gehnāg*) *Rim* 57,
  58
gehogode *see* **hycgan**
gehola, *n masc*   confidant
  gen pl **geholena** *Wan* 31^n
gehonge, *adj*   hung about with; adorned
  Rim 42^n

gehrēosaðˍ, gehrorene *see* **hrēosan**
gehwā, *pron (+ gen)*   each
  dat sg **gehwām** *Wan* 63, *Sea* 72,
  Rid 60 6
gehwylc, *pron (+ gen)*   each
  Sea 90, 111. *acc sg fem* **gehwylce**
  Wan 8. *gen sg neut* **gehwylces** *Res* 23.
  instr sg **gehwylce: mæla** ~, "at all
  times," "constantly," *Sea* 36; **þinga** ~,
  "in every case," "in every respect,"
  Sea 68, *Res* 13; **gēara** ~, "every
  year," *Res* 86
gehwyrft, *n masc*   turn; cycle of time
  Rim 70^n
gehȳdde *see* **hȳdan**
gehygd, *n fem*   thought(s)
  Wan 72, *Sea* 116
gehȳrde, gehȳre, gehȳrest *see* **hȳran**
gelāc, *n neut*   tossing, movement, play
  Sea 35, *Wife* 7
gelæg, *n neut*   stretch of water
  pl **gelagu** *Sea* 64
gelēafa, *n masc*   belief
  dat sg **gelēafan** *Res* 57
gelēogan, *v str*   deceive
  pret pl **gelugon** *Res* 57
gelēoran, geleorene *see* **lēoran**
gelettan, *v wk (+ gen)*   hinder from
  Husb 25
gelīc *adj (+ dat)*   like
  masc pl **gelīce** *Rim* 83
gellende *see* **giellan**
gelimpan, gelomp *see* **limpan**
gelong, *adj*   dependent on, to be obtained from
  Sea 121, *Wife* 45^n, *Res* 111
gelufian, *v wk*   love
  Res 107
gelugon *see* **gelēogan**
gelȳfan, *v wk*   believe
  pres 1 sg **gelȳfe** *Sea* 66. *3 sg* **gelȳfeðˍ**
  Sea 27, 108

gemæc, *adj*   suited
  acc sg masc **gemæcne** *Wife* 18
gemearcian, *v wk*   point out
  inflect infin **gemearcenne**
  Res 12[n]
gemenged *see* **mengan**
gemet, *n neut*   moderation
  dat sg **gemete** *Sea* 111
gemong, *n neut*   company, throng
  dat sg **gemonge**: **in** ~, "among,"
  Rim 41
gemoniað *see* **monian**
gemunan, *v pret-pres*   be mindful of, remember
  pres 1 & 3 sg **gemon** *Wan* 34, 90,
  Rim 82, *Wife* 51, *Res* 20. *pret sg sub-*
  junct **gemunde** *Husb* 14
gemynd, *n fem or neut*   memory, remembrance; mind
  Wan 51, *Res* 23. *dat sg* **gemynde**
  Rim 48. *dat pl (for sg)* **gemyndum**
  Husb 31
gemyndig, *adj* (+ *gen, dat?*)   mindful of
  Wan 6 (*see note on line 7b*)
genāg *see* **gehnīgan**
genāp *see* **genīpan**
geneahhe, *adv*   often
  Wan 56, *Deor* 25, 32
generede, generedon *see* **nerian**
gengan, *v wk*   go; come
  pret pl **gengdon** *Rim* 11
geniman *see* **niman**
genīwad, *past partic*   renewed
  Wan 50, 55
genōh, *indecl n neut* (+ *gen*)   enough; plenty
  Husb 35
gēoc, *n fem*   help
  dat sg **gēoce** *Sea* 101
gēocian, *v wk* (+ *gen or dat*)   save
  imperat **gēoca** *Res* 46, 60
geoguþ, *n fem*   youth
  dat sg **geoguþe** *Sea* 40; **geoguðe**
  Wan 35

geohþu, *n fem*　　　　　　　　　　　　sorrow, care
　dat sg **geohþe** *Res* 92^n
gēomor, *adj*　　　　　　　　　　　　　sad, mournful
　Wife 17, *Res* 95. *acc sg masc* **gēo-**
　morne *Husb* 23^n. *dat sg fem* **gēomorre**
　Wife 1^n. *wk dat (instr) sg fem or neut*
　gēomran *Sea* 53^n
gēomormōd, *adj*　　　　　　　　　　sad-minded, with sad thoughts
　Wife 42
geond, *prep* (+ *acc*)　　　　　　　　throughout
　Wan 3, 58, 75, *Sea* 90, *Deor* 31,
　Wife 36
geondhweorfan, *v str*　　　　　　　move through
　pres 3 sg **geondhweorfeð** *Wan* 51^n
geondscēawian, *v wk*　　　　　　　scan, look all over
　pres 3 sg **geondscēawað** *Wan* 52
geondþencan, *v wk*　　　　　　　　consider, ponder, examine (mentally)
　pres 1 sg **geondþence** *Wan* 60. *3 sg*
　geondþenceð *Wan* 89
geong, *adj*　　　　　　　　　　　　　young
　Wife 42
georn, *adj* (+ *gen*)　　　　　　　　eager (for)
　Wan 69, *Husb* 43
georne, *adv*　　　　　　　　　　　　eagerly, earnestly
　Wan 52
gēotan, *v str*　　　　　　　　　　　gush
　Ruin 42
gerestan, *v wk* (+ *gen*)　　　　　　have rest from, cease from
　Wife 40
gerscype, *n masc*　　　　　　　　　noisy conversation
　Rim 11^n
gesæt *see* **sittan**
gescād, *n neut*　　　　　　　　　　　discernment, correct judgment
　Rim 13^n
gesceaft, *n neut*　　　　　　　　　　decree, ordinance
　Wan 107
gescēawian, *v wk*　　　　　　　　　show
　pres 3 sg **gescēawað** *Deor* 33
gescyppan, *v str*　　　　　　　　　create
　pret 2 sg **gescēope** *Res* 2
gesealde *see* **syllan**

gesēce *see* **sēcan**

geselda, *n masc*   companion
  pl **geseldan** *Wan* 53[n]

gesēo, gesēon, gesihð *see* **sēon**

gesetu, *n neut pl* **seats**
  Wan 93

gesette *see* **settan**

gesīþ, *n masc*   companion; retainer
  dat sg masc **gesīþþe** *Deor* 3. *dat pl*
  gesīþum *Husb* 34

gesōhte *see* **sēcan**

gesomnad, *past partic*   united, joined
  Wulf 18[n]

gespræcon(n) *see* **sprecan**

gestaðelad, gestaþelade, gestaþelað *see*
  staðelian

gesteal, *n neut*   framework
  Wan 110[n]

gestȳr *see* **stīeran**

gesweorce *see* **sweorcan**

geswincdæg, *n masc*   day of toil
  dat pl **geswincdagum** *Sea* 2

getācnian, *v wk*   show, indicate, point out
  imperat **getācna** *Res* 10

getēon, *v str*   draw forth
  pret 3 sg **getēoh** (= *getēah*) *Rim* 2[n]

getilge *see* **tilian**

getong, *n*   hastening
  dat pl **getongum** *Rim* 8[n]

getonge, *adj* (+ *dat*)   associated with
  Rim 42[n]

getwǣfan, *v wk* (+ *gen*)   separate, keep from
  Husb 24

geþencan, *v wk*   consider; discover by thinking
  Wan 58, *Sea* 118, *Deor* 12, 31. *pres 3*
  sg **geþenceð** *Rim* 80

geþēon, *v str* (+ *dat*)   prosper before
  pres sg subjunct **geþēo** *Res* 13[n]

geþicgan, *v str*   take, receive; eat
  pres 3 sg **geþygeð** *Rim* 76. *pret 3 sg*
  geþāh *Deor* 40

geþōht, *n masc* — thought
Deor 22, Wife 12, 43. *dat sg* **geþōhte**
Wan 88ⁿ. *nom-acc pl* **geþōhtas** Sea 34,
Res 9

geþrungen, *past partic* — oppressed, afflicted
Sea 8ⁿ

geþwǣre, *adj* (+ *dat*) — mild; in harmony with
Rim 18ⁿ

geþyld, *n fem* — patience
Res 23

geþyldig, *adj* — patient
Wan 65

geþȳwan, *v wk* — compel
pret pl **geþȳdan** Rid 60 14ⁿ

geunne *see* **unnan**

gewāt *see* **gewītan**

gewealc, *n neut* — tossing
Sea 6, 46

gewefan, *v str* — weave
pret 3 sg **gewæf** Rim 70

geweorc *see* **weorc**

geweorþian, *v wk* — honour
pret 3 sg **geweorþade** Sea 123

gewīdost *see* **wīde**

gewigeð *see* **wegan**

gewis, *adj* — certain, unfailing, reliable
Sea 110

gewītan, *v str* — depart
3 sg pres **gewīteð** Rim 44, 61;
gewītað Sea 52ⁿ. *pret 1 & 3 sg* **gewāt**
Wan 95, Wife 6, 9. *pret pl* **gewitan**
Ruin 9ⁿ. *past partic masc pl* **gewitene**
Sea 80, 86

gewitloca, *n masc* — seat of thought, mind
dat sg **gewitlocan** Husb 15

gewītnad, *past partic* — punished
Res 80

gewunade *see* **wunian**

gewyrcan *see* **wyrcan**

gewyrht(u), *n fem or neut* — deed
pl **gewyrhto**, "transgressions," Res 80ⁿ

giedd, *n neut* tale
  Wulf 19ⁿ, *Wife* 1. *See also*
  p. 245
giefan, *v str* give
  pres sg subjunct **gife** *Wulf* 1
giefstōl, *n masc* seat from which gifts are distributed,
  gen sg **giefstōlas** (= *giefstōles*) gift-throne
  Wan 44ⁿ
giellan, *v str* cry; make a shrill sound
  pres 3 sg **gielleð** *Sea* 62ⁿ. *pres partic*
  gellende *Rim* 25
gielp, *n masc* boast, vaunt
  gen sg **gielpes** *Wan* 69
giest, *n masc* visitor, guest
  pl **giestas** *Rim* 11
giet, *adv* still, yet
  Res 117, *Ruin* 12ⁿ
gif, *conj* if
  Wulf 2, 7, *Res* 21, *Husb* 48
gife (= *gifu*), *n fem* gift
  gen pl **gifena** *Sea* 40ⁿ
gife, *v see* **giefan**
gīfre, *adj* eager, greedy
  Sea 62
gim, *n masc* jewel, jewelled ornament
  Rim 36 (*sg for pl*)
git, *2-pers-dual pron* you two
  Husb 16, 17, 54. *gen* **incer** *Husb* 49.
  dat **inc** *Husb* 32
glād *see* **glīdan**
glæd, *adj* bright, joyful
  Rim 3
glædmōd, *adj* joyful-hearted
  Ruin 33
glēam, *n masc* (or **gleomu**, *fem*) brightness, joyfulness
  gen pl as adv **glĕoma**, "brightly,"
  Ruin 33ⁿ
glēaw, *adj* wise, well instructed
  Wan 73, *Res* 82
glēawlīce, *adv* wisely
  Res 78

glengan, *v wk* — adorn
   pret pl **glengdon**, "were adorned,"
   Rim 12^n. *past partic* **glenged** *Rim* 3

glīdan, *v str* — glide; move imperceptibly
   pres 3 sg **glīdeþ** *Rim* 65^n. *pret 3 sg*
   glād *Rim* 13

glīw, *n neut* — music; entertainment; mirth
   dat pl **glīwum** *Rim* 3

glīwstæf, *n masc* — mark or indication of joy
   dat pl **glīwstafum** *Wan* 52^n

gnornian, *v wk* — lament
   pres 3 sg **gnornað** *Sea* 92, *Res* 92

god, *n masc* — God
   Rim 87, *Res* 1, 5, 19, 28, 33, 63,
   Husb 32. *gen sg* **godes** *Sea* 101. *dat sg*
   gode *Res* 74, 78, 86

gōd, *adj* — good; fortunate
   Sea 40^n, *Res* 40. *compar dat sg* **betran**
   Rim 81. *compar acc sg* **sȳllan** *Deor* 6.
   nom pl **sēllan** *Res* 55. *superl nom sg*
   betst *Sea* 73; **sēlast** *Res* 11, 117^n

gōdian, *v wk* — make wealthy
   pret 3 sg impers **gōdade**, "there was
   wealth," *Rim* 32^n

gōl *see* **galan**

gold, *n neut* — gold
   Wan 32, *Sea* 101, *Rim* 36. *gen sg*
   goldes *Res* 101, [*Husb* 36^n]. *dat sg*
   golde *Sea* 97^n

goldbeorht, *adj* — bright with gold
   Ruin 33

goldgiefa, *n masc* — lord who gives gold
   pl **goldgiefan** *Sea* 83

goldwine, *n masc* — gold-friend, gold-giving lord
   Wan 22, 35

gomelfeax, *adj* — old-haired, grey-haired
   Sea 92

gomelsibb, *n fem* — ancient friendship or peace
   dat sg **gomelsibbe** *Rim* 24^n

gomen, *n neut* — enjoyment; entertainment
   dat sg **gomene** *Sea* 20

gong, *n masc* — going, journey
   dat pl **gongum** *Rim* 7

gongan, *v str* — go, walk
   pres 1 sg **gonge** *Wife* 35

Gota, *n masc* — Goth
   gen pl **Gotena** *Deor* 23 *(see note on lines 18–22)*

grafan, *v str* — burrow, dig
   pres 3 sg **græfeþ** *Rim* 66. *pret sg subjunct* **grōfe** *Rim* 71

grǣdig, *adj* — greedy; fierce
   Sea 62

græf, *n neut* — grave
   Sea 97, *Rim 66ⁿ*, 71 (2)

grētan, *v wk* — greet; assail
   pres 3 sg **grēteð** *Wan* 52, *Rim* 49

grim, *adj* — grim, fierce, savage; dire
   Deor 23. *neut wk* **grimme** *Rim* 71. *gen pl* **grimra** *Res* 28

grimme, *adv* — harshly, direly
   Ruin 14ⁿ

gripe, *n masc* — grip
   Ruin 8

grōfe *see* **grafan**

grom, *adj* — hostile; *as n*, enemy
   gen pl **gromra** *Res* 46

gromtorn, *n neut* — angry resentment
   Rim 66ⁿ

grorn, *adj as n* — trouble(d), bitter(ness)
   Rim 49ⁿ

grund, *n masc* — foundation
   pl **grundas** *Sea* 104

grundlēas, *adj* — bottomless
   fem pl **grundlēase** *Deor* 15ⁿ

guma, *n masc* — man
   Wan 45

gylt, *n masc* — crime
   gen pl **gylta** *Res* 28

habban, *v wk* — have
   Wife 43, *Res* 71. *pres 1 sg* **hæbbe**

Sea 4, *Res* 29, 47, 78. *3 sg* **hafað**
Wan 31, *Sea* 47, *Rim* 66, *Husb* 35, 44,
Ruin 6. *pres sg subjunct neg* **næbbe**
Sea 42. *pret 1 & 3 sg* **hæfde** *Rim* 15,
Deor 3, 10, *Wife* 7, *Res* 114

hād, *n masc*   condition, position, status
   Rim 15
hafu *see* **hæf**
hagle *see* **hægl**
hālig, *adj*   holy
   wk **hālga** *Res* 2. *gen sg masc* **hālges**
   Res 30. *wk gen-dat sg* **hālgan** *Sea* 122,
   Res 36. *dat pl* **hālgum** *Rim* 83
hām, *n masc*   home
   Sea 117
hār, *adj*   grey
   wk **hāra** *Wan* 82. [*acc sg masc* **hārne**
   Ruin 43^n]
hāt, *adj*   hot
   hāte *Ruin* 45^n (*context unclear*). *masc-*
   fem pl **hāte** *Ruin* 43; **hāt'** *Sea* 11^n.
   neut pl **hāt** *Ruin* 41. *compar pl* **hātran**
   Sea 64
hātan, *v str*   command, bid; promise
   gehātan *Husb* 11. *pret 3 sg* **heht**
   Wife 27, *Husb* 20; **hēt** *Wife* 15^n,
   Husb 13
hāte, *adv*   with heat, hotly
   Ruin 38^n
hātheort, *adj*   irascible
   Wan 66
hæbbe, hæfde *see* **habban**
hædre, *adv*   brightly, clearly; purely
   Res 63^n
hæf, *n neut*   sea
   pl **hafu** *Husb* 8^n
hæft, *n masc*   bond; bondage; prisoner
   Rim 66^n
hægl, *n masc*   hail
   Sea 17, 32. *dat sg* **hagle** *Wan* 48
hæglfaru, *n fem*   hail-storm
   acc sg **hæglfare** *Wan* 105

hǣlan, *v wk*   save
   imperat **hǣl** *Res* 63[n]
hæle, *n masc*   man, hero
   Wan 73, *Res* 113. *acc pl* **hæleþe**
   Rim 60. *gen pl* **hæleþa** *Husb* 39. *dat pl*
   hæleþum *Wan* 105, *Rim* 79[n]
hē, *3-pers pron*
   1   *masc sg*
   nom **hē**, "he," (29) *Wan* 2, *etc*; "it" (*for*
   masc n) *Sea* 8. *acc* **hine**, "him," (10)
   Wan 32, *etc*; *reflex* "himself" *Rim* 80.
   gen **his**, "of him," "his," (23) *Wan* 13,
   etc. dat **him**, "him," (15) *Wan* 10, *etc*;
   reflex "himself" (14) *Wan* 1, *etc*; "itself" *Rim* 76, *Res* 105
   2   *fem sg*
   nom **hēo**, "she," *Deor* 10, 11; "it" (*for*
   fem n) *Wan* 96. *acc* **hī**, "her,"
   Deor 16[n]?; **hȳ**, "it," *Res* 62; *reflex* **hī**,
   "itself," *Sea* 103. *gen* **hyre**, "of her,"
   "her," *Deor* 8, 9. *dat* **hyre**, "it," *Res* 62
   3   *neut sg*
   nom-acc **hit**, "it," *Sea* 102, *Wulf* 10,
   Wife 24, *Rid 60* 16
   4   *pl*
   nom **hī**, "they," *Wan* 61, *Sea* 84,
   Res 54; **hȳ** *Wulf* 2, 7, *Wife* 12, *Res* 55,
   57 (2); **hīo** *Res* 38[n]. *acc* **hī**, "them,"
   Deor 16[n]? *gen* **hyra**, "of them,"
   "their," *Wan* 18, *Ruin* 27. *dat* **him**,
   "them," *Sea* 23, *Wulf* 1, *Res* 59; *reflex*
   "themselves" *Sea* 67, 84, *Res* 57; ~
   sylfum *Res* 55
hēafod, *n neut*   head
   Wan 43
hēah, *adj*   high; deep
   Wan 98, *Ruin* 22. *acc sg masc* **hēanne**
   Wan 82, *Rim* 15. *pl wk* **hēan** *Sea* 34[n].
   neut pl **hēah** *Husb* 8
healdan, *v str*   hold, keep, possess, occupy
   Sea 109, 111. *pres 3 sg* **gehealdeþ**
   Wan 112. *pres sg subjunct* **healde**

Wan 14[n], Husb 37. *pl indic* **healdaþ**
Sea 87. *pret 3 sg* **hēold** *Rim* 21

heall, *n fem*	hall
dat sg **healle** *Rim* 15	
hēan, *adj*	wretched, abased
Wan 23	
heard, *adj*	hard; cruel
Wife 15[n], 43, *Ruin* 8	
heardsǽlig, *adj*	hard in one's fortune
acc sg masc **heardsǽligne**	
Wife 19	
hearpe, *n fem*	harp
Rim 27. *dat sg* **hearpan** *Sea* 44	
hefig, *adj*	heavy; painful
compar pl **hefigran** *Wan* 49	
heht *see* **hātan**	
help, *n fem*	help
acc sg **helpe** *Wan* 16	
helpan, *v str* (+ *gen*)	help
pres sg subjunct **helpe** *Res* 2	
hentan, *v wk*	get at; seize
pres 3 sg **henteð** *Rim* 60[n]	
hēo *see* **hē**	
Heodeningas	Heodenings, *ON* Hjaðningar
gen pl **Heodeninga** *Deor* 36[n]	
heofon, *n masc*	heaven
Res 2. *gen pl* **heofona** *Rim* 83. *dat pl*	
heofonum *Wan* 107, 115, *Sea* 107,	
122	
heofoncyning, *n masc*	heavenly king
gen sg **heofoncyninges** *Res* 30	
heofonmægen, *n neut*	heavenly power
gen sg **heofonmægnes** *Res* 36	
hēofsīþ, *n masc*	unhappy journey; sad experience
dat pl *hēofsīþum Rim 43[n]*	
hēold *see* **healdan**	
heolstor, *n neut*	darkness
dat sg **heolstre** *Wan* 23[n]	
heonan, *adv*	hence, from here
Sea 37, *Wife* 6, *Husb* 27	
Heorrenda	*the bard* Heorrenda, *ON* Hjarrandi
Deor 39[n]	

heorte, *n fem*   heart
  acc-gen sg **heortan** *Wan* 49, *Sea* 11,
  34[n], *Wife* 43
hēr, *adv*   here
  Wan 108 (2), 109 (2), *Sea* 102,
  Rim 55, 56, 74, 79, *Wife* 15[n], 32,
  Res 36, *Husb* 8, 39
here, *n masc*   army
  pl **hergas** *Ruin* 29
heresweg, *n masc*   sound of a company of warriors
  Ruin 22
herian, *v wk*   praise
  pres pl subjunct **hergen** *Sea* 77. *pret pl*
  indic **heredon** *Rim* 19
hēt *see* **hātan**
hete, *n masc*   hate
  gen sg as adv **hetes**, "with hate,"
  Rim 60
hī, him, hine, hīo, his, hit *see* **hē**
hige *see* **hyge**
hild, *n fem*   battle
  dat sg **hilde** *Rim* 19
hīw, *n neut*   colour
  dat pl **hīwum** *Rim* 3, 4
hlāford, *n masc*   lord
  Deor 39, *Wife* 6[n], 15
hleahtor, *n masc*   laughter
  acc (dat?) sg *Sea* 21
hlēo, *n neut*   protection; protector
  Deor 41
hlēomǣg, *n masc*   supportive kinsman
  gen pl **hlēomǣga** *Sea* 25
hlēoþor, *n neut*   sound; voice
  Sea 20, *Rim* 28
hlifian, *v wk*   tower
  pret 3 sg **hlifade** *Rim* 30
hlimman, *v str*   roar
  Sea 18
hlīsa, *n masc*   fame
  Rim 79
hliþ, *n neut*   cliff; slope
  gen sg **hliþes** *Husb* 22

hlūde, *adv*   loud
  Rim 28
hlyhhan, *v str*   laugh
  Res 71
hlynnan, *v wk*   resound
  pret 3 sg **hlynede** *Rim* 28
hof, *n neut*   dwelling
  pl **hofu** *Ruin* 29
hogaþ *see* **hycgan**
hold, *adj*   gracious, kind; loyal
  Sea 41. *acc sg masc* **holdne**
  Deor 39. *gen pl* **holdra** *Wife* 17,
  [*Husb* 39ⁿ]
holm, *n masc*   sea
  Wan 82. *gen pl* **holma** *Sea* 64
hond, *n fem*   hand
  Sea 96, *Rid* 60 12. *acc pl* **honda**
  Wan 43. *dat pl* **hondum** *Wan* 4
hordcofa, *n masc*   repository, treasury (of thoughts)
  acc sg **hordcofan** *Wan* 14
horngestrēon, *n neut*   abundance of arched structures
  Ruin 22ⁿ
horsc, *adj*   bold, keen
  masc pl **horsce** *Rim* 19
hrædwyrde, *adj*   hasty of speech
  Wan 66ⁿ
hrēoh, *adj*   fierce; troubled
  Rim 43. **hrēo** *Wan* 16ⁿ, 105
hrēorig, *adj*   collapsing
  masc pl **hrēorge** *Ruin* 3
hrēosan, *v str*   fall
  Wan 48. *pres pl* **gehrēosað** *Rim* 55.
  pres partic **hrēosende** *Wan* 102. *past*
  partic masc pl **gehrorene** *Ruin* 3
hrēran, *v wk*   stir, move
  Wan 4
hreþer, *n masc*   breast, bosom; spirit
  Sea 63, *Rim* 43. *dat sg* **hreþre**
  Ruin 41. *gen pl (for sg)* **hreþra**
  Wan 72
hreþerloca, *n masc*   confines of the breast
  acc sg **hreþerlocan** *Sea* 58

hrīm, *n masc*
　Wan 48, *Sea* 32, *Ruin* 4. *dat sg* **hrīme**,
　Wan 77

hoar-frost

hrīmceald, *adj*
　acc sg fem **hrīmcealde** *Wan* 4

cold as hoar-frost, icy-cold

hrīmgicel, *n masc*
　dat pl **hrīmgicelum** *Sea* 17^n

icicle

hring, *n masc*
　pl **hringas** *Ruin* 19

ring, circular structure

hringeat (= *hring-geat*)
　Ruin 4^n

archway-gate

hringmere, *n masc*
　Ruin 45^n

circular pool

hringþegu, *n fem*
　dat sg **hringþege** *Sea* 44

receiving of rings

hrīð, *n fem*
　Wan 102^n

snowstorm

hrōf, *n masc*
　rōf *Ruin* 31^n. *pl* **hrōfas** *Ruin* 3

roof; ceiling

hrostbēam, *n masc*
　gen sg **hrostbēames** *Ruin* 31^n

support for the inner framework of a
　roof, pillar of a vault

hrūse, *n fem*
　acc-gen-dat sg **hrūsan** *Wan* 23^n, 102^n,
　Sea 32, *Ruin* 8, 29

ground, earth

hryre, *n masc*
　dat sg Wan 7^n, *Ruin* 31^n

fall; ruin

hrȳðig (= *hrīðig*)
　pl **hrȳðge** *Wan* 77^n

snow-swept

hū, *excl*
　Wan 95

how!

hū, *adv*
　Wan 30, 73

how

hū, *conj*
　Wan 35, 61, *Sea* 2, 14, 29, 118,
　Deor 12, *Rid* 60 12, *Husb* 10,
　Ruin 49^n

how

huilpa (= *hwilpa*), *n masc*
　gen sg **huilpan** *Sea* 21^n

curlew

hund, *num as neut n* (+ *gen*)
　Ruin 8

hundred

hungor, *n masc*
　Sea 11

hunger

hūru, *excl* — indeed!
 Res 76, 102

hwæl, *n masc* — whale
 gen sg **hwæles** *Sea* 60

hwælweg, *n masc* — whale's path
 Sea 63[n]

hwǣr, *interrog adv* — where
 Wan 92 (3)[n], 93 (2)

hwǣr, *interrog conj* — where
 Wan 26, *Sea* 117, *Wife* 8

hwæt, *excl* — oh!, how!, now!
 Res 36, *Husb* 13[n]

hwæt, *interrog pron neut* — what
 Sea 56, *Wife* 3. instr sg **hwon** *Sea* 43;
 hwȳ, "with what," *Res* 100

hwæt, *adj* — keen
 Sea 40

hwætrēd (= *hwætrǣd*), *adj* — of vigorous intellect, acute in thought
 Ruin 19

hwæþre, *adv* — nevertheless
 Wulf 12, *Res* 26, 70

hwearfian, *v wk* — turn around, move about, pass
 pret 3 sg **hwearfade** *Rim* 36   around

hwelp, *n masc* — whelp, young of a beast
 Wulf 16[n]

hweorfan, *v str* — turn, move, go
 Wan 72. pres 3 sg **hweorfeð** *Sea* 58,
 60

hwettan, *v wk* — urge, whet, make keen
 pres 3 sg **hweteð** *Sea* 63

hwider, *adv* — whither, in what direction
 Wan 72

hwīl, *n fem* — time, space of time, occasion
 acc sg **hwīle**, "for a time," *Deor* 36.
 dat pl **hwīlum**, "at times," *Wan* 43,
 Sea 19

hwītan, *v wk* — whiten
 pres 3 sg **hwīteð** *Rim* 62[n]

hwōn, *indecl n* (+ *gen*) — few
 Sea 28

hwon, hwȳ *see* **hwæt**, *pron*
hȳ *see* **hē**

hycgan, *v wk*   think
  Sea 117, *Wife* 11. *pres 3 sg* **hogaþ**
  Rim 81. *pres sg subjunct* **hycge**
  Wan 14, *Husb* 11. *pres partic*
  hycgende, "thinking of," "contemplating," *Wife* 20ⁿ. *past partic acc sg*
  fem **gehogode**, "thinking," "minded,"
  Res 63ⁿ
hȳdan, *v wk*   hide, cover up
  pres 3 sg **hȳdeð** *Sea* 102. *pret 3 sg*
  gehȳdde *Wan* 84
hyge, *n masc*   mind, thoughts
  Wan 16, *Sea* 44, 58, *Wife* 17. *acc sg*
  hige *Res* 39. *dat sg* **hyge** *Sea* 96,
  Husb 11
hȳgedryht (= *hī-gedryht*), *n fem*   band of household retainers
  Rim 21ⁿ
hygegēomor, *adj*   sad-hearted
  acc sg masc **hygegēomorne**
  Wife 19
hygerōf, *adj*   stout-hearted
  Ruin 19
hyht, *n masc*   hope; joyful expectation, joy
  Sea 45, 122, *Res* 37
hyhtan, *v wk*   hope
  Res 71
hyhtgiefu, *n fem*   joyful gift, blessing
  Rim 21
hyhtlic, *adj*   joyful, delightful
  Rim 39. *fem pl* **hyhtlice** *Rim* 83
hyldo, *n fem*   favour
  Res 30
hyra, hyre *see* **hē**
hȳran, *v wk*   hear; (+ *dat*) listen to, obey
  pres 1 sg [**gehȳre** *Husb* 50ⁿ]. *2 sg*
  gehȳrest *Wulf* 16. *pret 1 sg* **gehȳrde**
  Sea 18. *pret sg subjunct* **hȳrde** *Res* 17;
  gehȳrde *Husb* 22
hyrde, *n masc*   keeper
  Res 8, 10
hȳðelic, *adj*   convenient
  Ruin 41

ic, *1-pers-sg pron* I
  nom **ic** (90) *Wan* 8, *etc. acc* **mec**,
  "me," (24) *Wan* 28, *etc*; **mē** *Rim* 74,
  Wulf 13, *Res* 43, 49. *gen* **mīn**, "me,"
  Res 2. *dat* **mē**, "me," (24) *Sea* 61, *etc*;
  reflex "myself" (14) *Sea* 1, *etc*

īdel, *adj* empty; useless
  Wan 110. *neut pl* **īdlu**
  Wan 87

īg, *n fem* island
  dat sg **īge** *Wulf* 6; **īege** *Wulf* 4[n]

in, *prep*
  1 + *acc* in, into; for
  (9) *Sea* 55, *etc*
  2 + *dat* in; on
  (31) *Wan* 12, *etc*

inc, incer *see* **git**

indryhten, *adj* noble
  Wan 12[n]

indryhto, *n fem* nobility
  Sea 89

ingeþonc, *n masc or neut* intellect; intention
  Rid 60 13

innan, *adv* within
  Sea 11

is *see* **wesan**

īscald, *adj* ice-cold
  acc sg masc **īscaldne** *Sea* 19;
  īscealdne *Sea* 14

īsigfeþera, *adj* icy-feathered
  Sea 24

īþan, *v wk* lay waste
  pret 3 sg **ȳþde** *Wan* 85

iū, *adv* (+ *gen*) long ago
  Wan 22, *Sea* 83, *Ruin* 32

iūwine, *n masc* friend of old, lord of old
  pl Sea 92[n]

lāc, *n neut* gift, offering
  Wulf 1[n]

lād, *n fem* way, path, journey
  Rim 14. *gen sg* **lāde** *Husb* 25

lagu, *n masc* — water, ocean
  Sea 47, *Res* 98, *Husb* 21

lagufæðm, *n masc* — embrace of water
  dat sg **lagufæðme** *Rid* 60 7

lagulād, *n fem* — path across water, ocean path
  acc sg **lagulāde** *Wan* 3

lagustrēam, *n masc* — ocean stream
  dat sg **lagustrēame** *Rim* 14

lāmrind, *n fem* — clay coating, tile
  dat pl **lāmrindum** *Ruin* 17[n]

langoþe *see* **longaþ**

lārcwide, *n masc* — word of counsel or instruction
  dat pl **lārcwidum** *Wan* 38

lāst, *n masc* — trace; track, path
  dat sg **lāste** *Wan* 97. *dat pl* **lāstum**:
  wræccan ~, "paths of exile," *Sea* 15

lāstword, *n neut* — word left behind, word pronounced
  gen pl **lāstworda** *Sea* 73 — on a man after his death

lāð, *adj* — hateful; hostile
  Wulf 12[n] (*as n,* "hateful thing"?).
  acc sg masc **lāðne** *Res* 53; *as n* **lāþne**,
  "foe," *Sea* 112

lāðlīcost, *adv superl* — most hatefully
  Wife 14[n]

lǣdan, *v wk* — lead; (+ *dat*) produce, bring forth
  Res 53, 106

lǣne, *adj* — loaned; temporary, fleeting
  Wan 108 (2), 109 (2), *Sea* 66

lǣran, *v wk* (+ *dat*) — direct, instruct
  Husb 21

lǣs *see* **lȳt,** *adv*

lǣstan, *v wk* — perform, carry out
  Husb 53

lǣtan, *v str* — let
  imperat **lǣt** *Res* 15, 45, 52, *Husb* 24.
  pret pl **lēton** *Ruin* 42

lǣtlīcor, *adv compar* — more tardily
  Res 34

leahter, *n masc* — vice
  pl **leahtras** *Rim* 56

lēan, *n neut* — reward
  dat sg **lēane** *Res* 116

lēas, *adj* (+ *gen*) without, devoid of, deprived of
Wife 32 (*neut pl*?), *Res* 90. *neut pl*
lēase *Wan* 86

lecgan, *v wk* lay
pres sg subjunct **lecge** *Wan* 42. *pres pl*
indic **lecgað: wræclāstas** ~, "travel
the paths of exile," *Sea* 57. *pret 3 sg*
legde *Deor* 5

leger, *n neut* place to lie, bed
Wife 34[n]

leng *see* **longe**

lengan, *v wk* protract; linger over
pret pl **lengdon** *Rim* 12

lēode, *n masc pl* people, (members of a) tribe
dat pl **lēodum** *Rim* 41, *Wulf* 1, *Wife* 6

lēodfruma, *n masc* leader of the people
Wife 8[n]

lēodwynn, *n fem* joy of a people or country;
gen pl **lēodwynna** *Res* 90[n] communal joy

lēof, *adj* dear; (*as n*) friend, loved one
acc sg masc **lēofne** *Sea* 112. *gen sg*
masc **lēofes** *Wan* 38, *Wife* 53. *gen sg*
fem **lēofre** *Wan* 97. *nom pl masc* **lēofe**
Wife 34. *gen pl* **lēofra** *Wan* 31,
Wife 16, *Res* 45[n]

leofað/-þ *see* **lifian**

lēoht, *n neut* light
Rim 1. *gen sg* **lēohtes** *Res* 8. *dat sg*
lēohte *Res* 111[n]

leoma *see* **lim**

lēoran, *v wk* pass away
gelēoran *Res* 45. *pres partic dat pl* **lēo-**
rendum *Res* 31[n]. *str past partic masc pl*
geleorene *Ruin* 7[n]

lēoðcræftig, *adj* skilled in songs
Deor 40

leoþo *see* **liþ**

leoþode *see* **liþian**

leoþu, *n fem* ship?; voyage?
Rim 14[n]

lēton *see* **lǣtan**

līc, *n neut* body
  Res 6

licgan, *v str* lie; lie still, be dead
  pres 3 sg **ligeð** *Rim* 75. *pres pl* **licgað**
  Wan 78

līchoma, *n masc* bodily frame, body
  Rim 75

līf, *n neut* life
  Wan 60, 89, *Sea* 65, 121, *Rim* 41, 56,
  Res 31[n], 34. *gen sg* **līfes** *Sea* 27, 79,
  Rim 1. *dat sg* **līfe** *Wife* 41, [*Res* 111[n]]

lifian, *v wk* live
  pres 3 sg **leofað** *Sea* 102; **leofaþ**
  Sea 107. *pres sg subjunct* **lifge** *Sea* 78.
  pret pl **lifdon** *Sea* 85, *Wife* 14[n]. *pres*
  partic **lifgende** *Res* 19. *acc sg masc*
  lifgendne *Husb* 25. *nom pl* **lifgende**
  Wife 34[n]. *gen pl* **lifgendra** *Sea* 73. *dat*
  pl **lifgendum** *Husb* 53

līm, *n masc* mortar
  dat sg **līme** *Ruin* 4

lim, *n neut* limb, member
  Res 53. *acc pl* **lima** (= *limu*) *Rim* 75[n].
  gen pl **leoma** *Rim* 8

limpan, *v str* (+ *dat*) happen to, befall
  gelimpan *Husb* 30. *pres 3 sg impers*
  limpeð *Sea* 13. *pret 3 sg* **gelomp**
  Res 84

linnan, *v str* (+ *dat*) desist from; lose
  pres 3 sg **linneð** *Rim* 54; **linnað**
  Rim 53[n]

liss, *n fem* delight; mercy, remission (of sins)
  acc sg **lisse** *Rim* 82. *dat sg Res* 19[n]; *as*
  adv, "pleasantly," *Rim* 8, 12

list, *n masc or fem* craft, cunning
  dat pl as adv **listum,** "cunningly," "by
  craft," *Rim* 54

liþ, *n neut* joint; limb
  pl **leoþo** *Res* 8

liþian, *v wk* (+ *dat*) be mild to, comfort
  pret 1 sg **leoþode** *Rim* 40[n]

lof, *n masc or neut*   praise
   Sea 73[n], 78
lond, *n neut*   land; earth
   Husb 18. *gen sg* **londes**, "in the/a
   land," "on the earth," *Wife* 8, *Husb* 3.
   dat sg **londe** *Sea* 66[n]
londryht, *n neut*   rights to an estate
   Deor 40
londstede, *n masc*   territory
   dat sg Wife 16
long, *adj*   long
   dat pl **longum** *Rim* 8[n]
longaþ, *n masc*   longing; sadness
   Deor 3. *gen sg* **longaþes** *Wife* 41. *dat
   sg* **langoþe** *Wife* 53
longe, *adv*   for a long time
   Wan 3, 38, *Rim* 41[n], *Res* 57. *compar*
   leng *Res* 90
longian, *v wk*   long, pine
   pret 3 sg impers **longade**, "yearning or
   anxiety occupied (me)," *Wife* 14[n]
longung, *n fem*   yearning; anxiety
   acc-dat sg **longunge** *Sea* 47[n], *Res* 98
lōsian, *v wk*   be lost, escape
   pres 3 sg **lōsað** *Sea* 94
lufe (*wk form of lufu*), *n fem*   love
   dat sg **lufan** *Sea* 121
lufen, *n fem*   hope
   gen pl **lufena** *Res* 116[n]
lust, *n masc*   desire
   Sea 36. *dat pl as adv* **lustum**,
   "joyfully," *Rim* 12, 54, *Husb* 21
lȳfan, *v wk*   allow
   pret 3 sg **lȳfde** *Res* 28
lȳt, *indecl n as adj* (+ *gen*)   few
   Wan 31, *Wife* 16[n], *Res* 48
lȳt, *adv*   little
   Sea 27, *Rid* 60 7. *compar* **læs** *Res* 54

M *for runic letter, see* **monn**
mā, *indecl n as adj* (+ *gen*)   more
   Res 27[n], 87, *Rid* 60 16

mā, *adv*   more
   Wife 4. *superl* **mǣst**, "most,"
   Sea 84
māga, māgas *see* **mǣg**, *n masc*
magan, *v pret-pres*   be able
   pres 1 & 3 sg **mæg**, "can," (23)
   Wan 15, *etc. pret 3 sg* **meahte**,
   "might," "could," *Sea* 26, *Deor* 11. *pret*
   sg subjunct **meahte**, "might," "would
   be able to," *Wan* 26
mago, *n masc*   young man, retainer
   Wan 92
maguþegn, *n masc*   retainer
   pl **maguþegnas** *Wan* 62
mān, *n neut*   crime, sin, evil
   Rim 62[n]. *gen pl* **māna** *Res* 51
manigfeald, *adj*   manifold, many
   neut pl Res 5. *masc pl wk* **manigfeal-**
   dan *Res* 9
māra *see* **micel**
martirdōm, *n masc*   martyrdom; suffering
   [*Res* 81[n]]
māþþum, *n masc*   treasure, valuable, heirloom
   gen pl **māðma** *Husb* 46. *dat pl*
   māþmum *Sea* 99
māþþumgyfa, *n masc*   treasure-giver (lord)
   Wan 92
mǣg, *n masc*   kinsman
   nom pl **māgas** *Wife* 11[n]. *gen pl* **māga**
   Wan 51
mǣg, *n fem*   maid, woman
   Wan 109[n]
mæg, *v see* **magan**
mǣgnian, *v wk*   be strong
   pret 3 sg **mægnade** *Rim* 33
mǣl, *n masc or neut*   time; meal
   dat sg **mǣle** *Res* 93[n]. *gen pl* **mǣla**
   Sea 36
mǣnan, *v wk*   tell, relate
   pret pl subjunct **mǣnden** *Rid 60* 17
mǣre, *adj*   renowned
   Rim 18[n], *Res* 5. *fem wk Wan* 100[n]

Mǣringas   *the Ostrogoths?*
  gen **Mǣringa** *Deor* 19[n]

mǣrþu, -o, *n fem*   glory, honour
  pl **mǣrþa,** "glorious deeds," *Sea* 84

mǣst *see* **mā,** *adv*

Mǣðhild   *woman loved by Geat*
  gen **Mǣðhilde** *Deor* 14[n]

mǣw, *n masc*   seagull
  Sea 22. *gen sg* **mǣwes** *Husb* 26

mē, mec *see* **ic**

meaht, *n fem*   might, power
  dat sg **meahte** *Sea* 108. *dat pl*
  meahtum *Res* 64

meahte, *v see* **magan**

meahtig, *adj*   mighty
  Res 109; **mihtig** *Res* 61. *compar*
  meahtigra *Sea* 116

mearg, *n masc*   horse, steed
  Wan 92. *gen pl* **mēara** *Husb* 46

medodrinc, *n masc*   mead-drink; drinking of mead
  dat sg **medodrince** *Sea* 22

men *see* **monn**

mengan, *v wk*   mingle, stir up; exchange
  Husb 44. *pret pl* **mengdon** *Rim* 11.
  past partic (pl) **gemenged** *Wan* 48

meododrēam, *n masc*   joy of the mead
  gen pl **meododrēama** *Husb* 46

meodoheall, *n fem*   mead-hall
  Ruin 22. *dat sg* **meoduhealle** *Wan* 27

meodu, *n masc or neut*   mead
  Rid 60 9[n]

meoduburg, *n fem*   city or fortress where mead is drunk
  dat pl **meoduburgum** *Husb* 17

meord, meorð, *n fem*   reward
  gen pl **meorda** *Res* 68; **morþa**
  Rim 82[n]

meotod, *n masc*   the Ordainer, God
  Sea 108, *Res* 27, 64. **meotud** *Sea* 116,
  Res 51, 91. *gen sg* **meotudes** *Sea* 103,
  Res 12; **metudes** *Wan* 2. *dat sg*
  meotude *Rim* 86

mere, *n masc*   sea
  Husb 26
merefaroð, *n masc*   ocean stream
  dat sg **merefaroðe** *Rid 60* 2[n]
mereflōd, *n masc or neut*   sea-flood, ocean
  dat sg **mereflōde** *Sea* 59
merelād, *n fem*   sea-path
  acc sg **merelāde** *Husb* 28
merestrēam, *n masc*   sea-stream
  pl **merestrēamas** *Husb* 44
merewērig, *adj*   sea-weary, worn out by the sea
  gen sg masc **merewērges**
  Sea 12
metelēast, *n fem*   lack of food
  dat sg or nom pl (for sg) **metelīste**
  Wulf 15[n]
metudes *see* **meotod**
micel, *adj*   great
  Sea 103, *Ruin* 22. *acc sg fem* **micle**
  Wife 51. *nom pl neut* **micel** *Res* 5. *neut*
  or fem pl **micle** *Res* 81. *dat pl as adv*
  miclum, "greatly," *Rim* 48. *compar*
  nom sg masc **māra**, "more," "greater,"
  Husb 31
mid, *adv*   with
  "with (me)" *Res* 69[n]
mid, *prep*
  (1)   + *acc*   with
  Sea 99
  (2)   + *dat*   with; by means of; in proximity to;
  Wan 4, 29, 114, *Sea* 59, 78, 80, 84,   in company with
  96, 111, *Rim* 8
middangeard, *n masc*   middle-earth, the earth, the world
  Wan 62, 75 *Sea* 90
mihtig *see* **meahtig**
milts, *n fem*   mildness, mercy, favour
  gen-dat sg **miltse** *Wan* 2, *Res* 27, 51.
  gen pl **miltsa** *Rim* 82, *Res* 68
mīn, *possess adj*   my, mine
  (21) *Wan* 59, *etc. acc sg masc* **mīnne**
  Wan 10, 19, 22[n], *Res* 37, 39,

Rid 60 4. *acc sg fem* **mīne** *Wan* 9,
Res 6. *gen sg masc* **mīnes** *Wulf* 9,
Wife 26, *Res* 6, 46, *Husb* 10. *gen-dat sg*
fem **mīnre** *Wife* 2ⁿ, 10, 40, *Res* 11,
61. *dat sg masc-neut* **mīnum** *Res* 60,
76, 89, *Rid* 60 2. *nom-acc pl masc*
mīne *Sea* 9ⁿ, *Wife* 38, *Res* 9. *nom-acc*
pl neut **mīn** *Res* 7 (2), 8, 80. *gen pl*
mīnra *Wife* 5. *dat pl* **mīnum** *Wulf* 1,
Res 104

mine (= *myne*), *n masc* *Wan* 27ⁿ, *Rim* 33	concern, care, love
minsian, *v wk* *pret 3 sg* **minsade** *Rim* 29	diminish
mislic, *adj* *dat pl* **mislicum** *Sea* 99	various
missenlīce, *adv* *Wan* 75	variously
misþēon, *v str* *pret 3 sg impers* (+ *dat*) **misþāh** *Rim* 58ⁿ	go ill
mīþende, *pres partic* *acc sg masc* **mīþendne** *Wife* 20	concealing
mōd, *n neut* *Wan* 15, 51, *Sea* 12, 108, *Rim* 33, *Wulf* 15, *Wife* 20, *Res* 96, *Ruin* 18. *gen sg* **mōdes** *Sea* 36, 50, *Rim* 48. *dat sg* **mōde** *Wan* 41, 111, *Sea* 109, *Res* 75, 107, 109	mind, heart, spirit; courage
mōdcearig, *adj* *Wan* 2	sad at heart
mōdcearu, *n fem* *acc-gen sg* **mōdceare** *Wife* 40, 51	sadness of heart
mōdearfoþe, *n neut* *gen pl* **mōdearfoþa** *Res* 87ⁿ	distress of mind
mōdig, *adj* *pl* **mōdge** *Wan* 62	brave, high-spirited, high-hearted
mōdlufe (*wk form of mōdlufu*), *n fem* *acc sg* **modlufan** *Husb* 10	heart's love
mōdsefa, *n masc* *Wan* 59ⁿ, *Sea* 59. *acc sg* **mōdsefan** *Wan* 10, 19	thoughts of the mind, state of mind, spirit

mōdwlonc, *adj*
  Sea 39

proud-hearted, high-hearted

molde, *n fem*
  Sea 103

world, earth

mon *see* **monn**

moncyn, *n neut*
  Rim 86. *gen sg* **moncynnes** *Res* 41,
  62, 79, 107

mankind

mondrēam, *n masc*
  gen pl **mondrēama** (*M-rune* +
  dreama) *Ruin* 23[n]

mirth or celebration of men

mondryhten, *n masc*
  Wan 41, *Husb* 7

lord

monian, *v wk*
  pres 3 sg **monað** *Sea* 36, 53. *pres pl*
  gemoniað *Sea* 50. *pret 3 sg* [**monade**
  Ruin 18[n]]

admonish, prompt

monig, *adj*
  Deor 24, *Ruin* 23, 32. *dat sg masc*
  monegum *Deor* 33. *nom pl masc*
  monige *Ruin* 21; **monge** *Deor* 14[n].
  dat pl **monegum** *Deor* 19

many a, many

monn, *n masc*
  Deor 6, 40, *Husb* 25; **mon** *Wan* 109,
  Sea 12, 39, *109*[n], *Wulf* 1, 18,
  Wife 27[n], 42[n], *Res* 117, *Husb* 44;
  runic M *Husb* 51[n], *Ruin* 23 (*rune* +
  drēama; *see* **mondrēama**). *gen sg*
  monnes *Sea* 116, *Wife* 11. *nom pl*
  men *Rim* 56, *Res* 93. *gen pl* **monna**
  Sea 90, 111, *Rid 60* 4. *dat pl* **monnum**
  Res 81

man; person, someone; name of
runic letter ᛗ (*M*)

monna, *n masc*
  acc sg **monnan** *Wife* 18, *Husb* 28

man

morgensēoc, *adj*
  Res 96

sick or sad in the morning

morþa *see* **meord**

morþor, *n masc or neut*
  Wife 20[n]

violent death; violent crime; wicked-
ness

mōtan, *v pret-pres*
  pres 1 & 3 sg **mōt**, "may," "have the
  opportunity to," *Rim* 86, *Wife* 37,

be permitted to

Res 21, 105. *pres pl* **mōtan** *Res* 54,
Husb 33. *subjunct pl* **mōten** *Sea* 119.
pret pl indic **mōston** *Husb* 17

mundbora, *n masc*   protector, guardian
Res 109
murnende, *pres partic*   mourning
Wulf 15
mūðlēas, *adj*   without a mouth
Rid 60 9
[**myneswift**], *adj*   quick-minded, keen-minded
acc sg [**myneswiftne** *Ruin* 18[n]]

naca, *n masc*   ship
acc-gen sg **nacan** *Sea* 7, *Husb* 41
nāh *see* **agan**
nālæs, *adv*   by no means, not at all
Wan 32, 33; **nāles** *Wan* 32,
Wulf 15
nān, *pron* (+ *gen*)   not one, none; nothing
Wan 9, *Rim* 78
nāp *see* **nīpan**
nāt *see* **witan**
næbbe *see* **habban**
næfre, *adv*   never
Wan 69, 112, *Wulf* 18, *Res* 52
nægled, *past partic*   studded
masc pl **næglede** *Husb* 35[n]
nænig, *pron* (+ *gen*)   not one, not any
Sea 25
næron *see* **wesan**
ne, *adv*   not
(41) *Wan* 15, *etc*
ne, *conj*   nor
(25) *Wan* 16, *etc*
nēah, *adv*   near
Wan 26, *Wife* 25[n]
nēah, *prep* (+ *dat*)   near
Rim 44, *Rid* 60 1
neaht *see* **niht**
nearo, *adj*   perilous
Sea 7

nearwian, *v wk*   be close
 þret 3 sg **nearwade** *Rim* 37[n]

nēawest, *n masc*   nearness, presence
 Res 50

nēda, nēde *see* **nȳd**

nefne, *conj*   unless, except
 Sea 46, *Rim* 78; **nemne** *Wife* 22;
 nemþe *Wan* 113

nerian, *v wk*   save
 pres partic **nergende** *Res* 50. *pret pl*
 generedon *Rim* 19. *past partic masc pl*
 generede *Rim* 84, 85

niht, *n fem*   night
 neaht *Rim* 73[n]. *gen sg as adv* **nihtes,**
 "by night," *Rim* 44

nihthelm, *n masc*   cover of night
 Wan 96

nihtscūa, *n masc*   shadow of night
 Wan 104, *Sea* 31

nihtwaco, *n fem*   night-watch
 Sea 7

niman, *v str*   take, seize
 Wife 15; **geniman** *Res* 50. *pres 3 sg*
 nimeð *Rim* 73. *pres pl* **nimað**
 Sea 48[n]

nīpan, *v str*   grow dark
 pres 3 sg **nīpeð** *Wan* 104. *pret 3 sg*
 nāp *Sea* 31; **genāp** *Wan* 96

nis *see* **wesan**

nīþ, *n masc*   malice, hostility
 Sea 75

Nīðhād   *captor of Weland*
 Deor 5[n]

nīwe, *adj*   new; recent
 gen sg neut as adv **nīwes,** "recently,"
 Wife 4

nō, *adv*   not at all; never
 Wan 54, 66, 96, *Sea* 66, *Wife* 4, 24
 Res 69

noma, *n masc*   name
 Deor 37

norþan, *adv* — from the north
    Wan 104, *Sea* 31

nū, *adv* — now
    (26) *Wan* 9, *etc*

nȳd, *n fem* — necessity
    dat sg **nȳde** *Husb* 41. *acc pl* **nēde**,
    "constraints," *Deor* 5[n]. *gen pl (for sg)*
    nēda, "of necessity," "inevitable"
    Rim 78

nȳdbysgu, *n fem* — trouble; toil
    dat pl **nȳdbysgum** *Rim* 44

nȳdgrāp, *n fem* — inescapable clutch
    dat pl **nȳdgrāpum** *Rim* 73

nȳhst, *adj superl* — nearest; latest, last
    dat sg neut wk **nȳhstan:** **æt** ~, "at
    last," *Rim* 78

of, *prep* (+ *dat*) — from
    Wan 113, *Sea* 107, *Wife* 6, 53[n],
    Res 42, 89, *Husb* 20

ofer, *prep*
    1   + *acc* — over, across, throughout; in addition
    Wan 24, 57, 82, *Sea* 39, 58, 60, 64,   to; according to; concerning
    Wife 7, *Res* 85, *Rid* 60 9, *Husb* 8, 28,
    47, 49[n], *Ruin* 43
    2   + *dat* — over, throughout
    Rim 7, [*Husb* 30[n]]

ofercumen, *past partic* — overcome
    Deor 26[n] (*impers* + *gen*)

ofergān, *v anom* — get over, pass over
    pret 3 sg impers (+ *gen*) **oferēode**
    Deor 7[n], 13, 17, 20, 27, 42

oferhȳdig, *adj* — arrogant
    masc pl **oferhȳdige** *Res* 56[n]

oferþeaht, *past partic* — covered over
    Rim 10[n]

oferwunnen, *past partic* — overcome
    Husb 45

offeallan, *v str* — decline
    pret 1 sg **ofēoll** (= *offēoll*) *Rim* 24[n]

ofgiefan, *v str* — give up, leave
  pret pl **ofgēafon** *Wan* 61

oflongad, *past partic* — worn out with yearning or anxiety
  Wife 29

ofstonden, *past partic* — having withstood, enduring
  Ruin 11[n]

oft, *adv* — often
  Wan 1, 8, 17, 20, 40, 90, *Sea* 3, 6, 29,
  Rim 16, 56, *Deor* 4, *Wife* 21, 32, 51,
  Husb 6, 16, 54, *Ruin* 9. *compar* **oftor**
  Rim 80

ofunnan, *v pret-pres* (+ *gen*) — deny, deprive
  pres 3 sg **ofonn** *Rim* 74[n]

ōl *see* **alan**

on, *adv* — on
  Res 4

on, *prep*
  1   + *acc* — in, into; on, onto; towards; for
  (25) *Wan* 42, *etc*
  2   + *dat* — in, on
  (52) *Wan* 35, *etc*

oncunnan, *v pret-pres* — attack, assail
  pres 3 sg **onconn** *Rim* 74[n]

oncweðan, *v str* (+ *dat*) — address, call out to
  pret 3 sg **oncwæð** *Sea* 23

oncyrran, *v wk* — turn; change
  pres 3 sg **oncyrreð** *Sea* 103[n]

ond, *conj* — and
  (74) *Wan* 23, *etc* (*written* 7 *except at*
  Rim 58)

ondgiet, *n neut* — understanding, perception
  Res 22

ondrǣdan, *v str or wk* — fear
  pres 3 sg **ondrǣdeþ** *Sea* 106

onettan, *v wk* — hasten
  pres 3 sg **onetteð** *Sea* 49[n]

onfaran, *v str* (+ *dat*) — move on, approach
  pret 3 sg **onfareð** *Sea* 91

onfindan, *v str* — find, encounter
  pret 3 sg **onfond** *Deor* 4

ongegn, *prep* (+ *dat*)   against
   Res 60

ongietan, *v str*   perceive
   Wan 73, *Res* 78. *past partic* **ongieten**
   Deor 10

onginnan, *v str*   begin, set about
   pres 3 sg **onginneð** *Rim* 51. *imperat*
   ongin *Husb* 26. *pret pl* **ongunnon**
   Wife 11[n]

onhrēran, *w wk*   stir, move
   Sea 96

onhworfen, *past partic*   turned around, changed, reversed
   Wife 23

onlēon, *v str* (+ *gen*)   grant, loan
   pret 3 sg **onlāh** *Rim* 1

onmedla, *n masc*   pomp
   pl **onmedlan** *Sea* 81

onsendan, *v wk*   send against
   pres 3 sg **onsendeð** *Wan* 104

onsittan, *v str*   sit in; get into; occupy
   wk imperat **onsite** *Husb* 27

onspreht, *past partic*   enlivened, full of growth
   Rim 9[n]

onstēpan, *v wk*   raise
   imperat **onstēp** *Res* 39[n]

onsundran (= *onsundrum*), *adv*   apart; especially
   Husb 1

onsȳn, *n fem*   appearance; face
   Sea 91

onwæcnan, *v wk*   awaken
   pres 3 sg **onwæcneð** *Wan* 45

onweg, *adv*   away
   Wan 53, *Sea* 74

onwendan, *v wk*   change
   Res 118. *pres 3 sg* **onwendeð**
   Wan 107. *pret 3 sg* **onwende**
   Ruin 24

onwrēon, *v str*   reveal
   pret 3 sg **onwrāh** *Rim* 1[n], 2

ōra, *n masc*   edge
   dat sg **ōran** *Husb* 22

106b, *Rim* 78, 79, *Wulf* 11, *Wife* 50,
Res 1, 2, *Husb* 29, 44, *Ruin* 49[n]. *fem*
sēo *Wan* 95, 100, 115, *Sea* 103, 107,
Rim 57, 73, *Deor* 16, *Res* 110, *Rid 60*
12, *Ruin* 12[n]?, 24; **sīo** *Rid 60* 6. *nom-
acc neut* **þæt** *Sea* 94, 108, *Rim* 2, 71,
Wulf 5. *acc sg masc* **þone** *Res* 54. *acc
sg fem* **þā** *Wan* 113, *Sea* 120, *Rim* 76,
81, *Res* 20, *Husb* 52 (2). *gen sg masc-
neut* **þæs** *Deor* 26, *Wife* 11, 41, *Res*
102. *gen-dat sg fem* **þære** *Sea* 100,
Rim 81, *Wife* 40. *dat sg masc-neut* **þām**
Sea 122, *Wife* 28, *Res* 57, 73, 103.
nom-acc pl **þā** *Wan* 77, 78, *Sea* 10, 56,
57, 87, *Rim* 77, *Ruin* 40, 46. *gen pl*
þāra *Res* 77

sē þe, *masc pron + indecl relat*   (the) one who, one that
Wan 29, 37, 112, *Sea* 27, 47, 106a,
107. *acc sg* **þone** ~ *Wan* 27. *dat sg*
þām ~ *Wan* 31, 56, 114, *Sea* 51,
Wife 52, *Rid 60* 11

seah *see* **sēon**

sealde, sealdest *see* **syllan**

sealt, *adj*   salt, salty
masc pl **sealte** *Husb* 5

sealtȳþ, *n fem*   salt-wave
gen pl **sealtȳþa** *Sea* 35

sēarian, *v wk*   wither
pres 3 sg **sēarað** *Sea* 89

searo, *n fem*   craft; cunning
Rim 65[n]

searogimm, *n masc*   cunningly wrought jewel
pl **searogimmas** *Ruin* 35

searohwīt, *adj*   cunningly white
neut as n Rim 67[n]

searolic, *adj*   cunning, marvellous
Rid 60 11

searwian, *v wk*   use craft; be cunning
pret 3 sg **searwade**, "was cunningly
made," *Rim* 37[n]

seax, *n neut*   knife
gen sg **seaxes** *Rid 60* 12

sēcan, *v wk* seek; make for
  Wife 9, *Husb* 26. *pres 3 sg* **sēceð**
  Wan 114. *pres sg subjunct* **gesēce**
  Sea 38, *Res* 32. *pret 1 sg* **sōhte**
  Wan 25; **gesōhte** *Husb* 6
secg, *n masc* man
  Sea 56, *Deor* 24. *nom pl* **secgas** *Rim* 5.
  gen pl **secga** *Wan* 53, *Res* 95. *dat pl*
  secgum *Husb* 34
secgan, *v wk* say, tell
  Sea 2, *Deor* 35, *Wife* 2, *Husb* 1. *pres 1*
  sg **secge** *Res* 97. *pret 3 sg* **sægde**
  Husb 31
secgrōf, *adj* brave with the sword
  gen pl **secgrōfra** *Ruin* 26ⁿ
sefa, *n masc* mind, spirit
  Res 65, 95. *acc-dat sg* **sefan** *Wan* 57,
  Sea 51, *Deor* 9, 29, *Rid 60* 11
sēgon *see* **sēon**
sēlast, **sēllan** *see* **gōd**
seldcyme, *n masc* rare visit
  pl **seldcymas** *Wulf* 14ⁿ
sele, *n masc* hall
  acc-dat sg *Wan* 25, *Rim* 17
seledrēam, *n masc* joy of the hall; joyful sound of the
  pl **seledrēamas** *Wan* 93ⁿ hall
seledrēorig, *adj* sad or distressed at the loss of a hall
  Wan 25ⁿ
selesecg, *n masc* man of the hall, retainer
  pl **selesecgas** *Wan* 34ⁿ
sendan, *v wk* send
  Wan 56, *Res* 24. *pres 3 sg* **sendeþ**
  Rim 59
sēo *see* **sē**, *pron & adj*
sēoc, *adj* sick
  [*Res* 109ⁿ]. *acc sg fem* **sēoce** *Wulf* 13
sēofian, *v wk* lament
  pret pl **sēofedun** (= *sēofedon*) *Sea* 10ⁿ
sēon, *v str* see; look upon
  gesēon *Rim* 87. *pres 3 sg* **gesihð**
  Wan 46. *pres sg subjunct* **gesēo** *Res* 32.

pret 3 sg **seah** *Ruin* 35. *pret sg subjunct*
sǣge *Rim* 17. *pret pl indic* **sēgon**
Rim 5

seonobend, *n fem*   sinew-bond
  pl **seonobende** *Deor* 6ⁿ

settan, *v wk*   set
  [*Husb* 4ⁿ]. *pres 1 sg* **gesette**
  Res 37

seþēah (= *swāþēah*), *adv*   nevertheless
  Res 29ⁿ, 49, 52

sib, *n fem*   kinship; friendship; peace
  Rim 37. *dat sg* **sibbe** *Rim* 87

sīdian, *v wk*   spread wide
  pres 3 sg **sīdaδ** *Rim* 65ⁿ

sīe *see* **wesan**

sigel, *n neut*   sun; name of runic letter ᚻ (*S*)
  Husb 50ⁿ (*rune*)

sigeþēod, *n fem*   victorious people
  dat sg **sigeþēode** *Husb* 20

simle, *adv*   always; constantly
  Sea 68; **symle** *Res* 115

sinc, *n neut*   treasure
  Rim 37, [*Husb* 34ⁿ], *Ruin* 35. *gen sg*
  sinces *Wan* 25

sincgewǣge, *n neut*   weight of treasure
  Rim 17

sinchroden, *adj*   adorned with precious ornaments
  Husb 14

sincþegu, *n fem*   receiving of treasure
  acc sg **sincþege** *Wan* 34

sind, sindon *see* **wesan**

singan, *v str*   sing
  pres 3 sg **singeδ** *Sea* 54. *pres partic*
  singende *Sea* 22

singryn, *n fem or neut*   net of sin
  Rim 65ⁿ

sinnan, *v str*   have consideration for; give respite
  pret 3 sg **sinniþ** *Rim* 52ⁿ   to; cease

sinsorg, *n fem*   perpetual sorrow or care
  gen pl wk **sinsorgna** *Wife* 45ⁿ

sīo *see* **se**, *adj*

sittan, *v str* — sit
    Wife 37. *pres 3 sg* **siteð** *Deor* 28,
    Wife 47. *pret 1 & 3 sg* **sæt** *Deor* 24,
    Wulf 10; **gesæt** *Wan* 111

sīð, *n masc* — journey; experience; time
    Wife 2ⁿ, *Res* 53; **sīþ** *Res* 97. *gen sg*
    sīþes *Husb* 24. *dat sg* **sīþe** *Sea* 51,
    Res 73. *acc pl* **sīþas** *Sea* 2. *dat pl*
    sīþum *Res* 66

sīð, *adv* — late
    ær oþþe ~, "early or late," *Rid 60* 8

sīðfæt, *n masc* — journey; way
    dat sg **sīðfate** *Res* 103

siþþan, *adv* — afterwards; then
    Sea 78, *Res* 32, *Husb* 24, 33

siþþan, *conj* — when; since
    Wan 22, *Deor* 5, *Wife* 3, *Husb* 22

slǣp, *n masc* — sleep
    Wan 39. *dat sg* **slǣp'** (= *slǣpe*)
    Deor 16ⁿ

slītan, *v str* — cut, tear
    pres 3 sg **slīteð** *Rim* 61. *pret 3 sg* **slāt**
    Sea 11

slīþen, *adj* — cruel
    Wan 30

smītan, *v str* — smear; smite
    pres 3 sg **smīteþ** *Rim* 64ⁿ

snāw, *n masc* — snow
    Wan 48

snēr, *n fem* — harpstring
    Rim 25

snīwan, *v wk* — snow
    pret 3 sg **snīwde** *Sea* 31

snottor, *adj* — wise
    Wan 111

sōhte *see* **sēcan**

sōlian, *v wk* — become soiled
    pres 3 sg **sōlað** *Rim* 67ⁿ

somod, *adv* — together
    Wan 39, *Rid 60* 13

sond, *n neut* — sea-shore
    dat sg **sonde** *Rid 60* 1

song, *n masc*   song
    Sea 19[n]

sorg, *n fem*   sorrow, care
    Wan 30, 39, 50, *Rim* 63[n]. *acc sg* **sorge**
    Sea 42, 54, *Deor* 3. *dat pl* **sorgum**
    Deor 24; *as adv,* "sorrowfully,"
    Rim 52

sorgcearig, *adj*   filled with anxiety and care
    Deor 28

sorglufu, *n fem*   troubled love, anxious love
    Deor 16

sōþ, *n neut*   truth
    dat sg (or instr sg of adj) **sōþe** *Wan* 11

sōð, *adj*   true
    acc sg masc **sōðne** *Rim* 87. *instr sg neut*
    (or dat sg of n) **sōþe** *Wan* 11

sōðfæst, *adj*   true; righteous
    Res 14, 24

sōðgied, *n neut*   true tale
    Sea 1

sprecan, *v str*   speak, utter, say
    Rid 60 9. *pres 1 sg* **spræce** *Res* 83, 97.
    3 sg **spriceð** *Wan* 70. *pret pl* **gespræ-**
    con *Husb* 16; **-nn** *Husb* 54[n]

stān, *n masc*   stone
    Ruin 43

stānclif, *n neut*   rocky cliff
    pl **stānclifu** *Sea* 23

stānhliþ, *n neut*   rocky slope; rocky cliff; stone ram-
    dat sg **stānhliþe** *Wife* 48. *acc pl* **stān-**   part
    hleoþu *Wan* 101[n]

stānhof, *n neut*   stone dwelling, stone building
    pl **stānhofu** *Ruin* 38

(ge)staðelian, *v wk*   establish, make firm
    pres 3 sg **gestaþelað** *Sea* 108. *pret 3 sg*
    gestaþelade *Sea* 104. *past partic*
    gestaðelad *Res* 39

staþol, *n masc*   fixed place; station in life; seat (of
    dat sg **steaðole** (= *staðole*) *Rim* 58[n]. *dat*   power)
    pl (for sg) **staþelum** *Sea* 109

staþolæht, *n fem*   landed estate
    dat pl **staþolæhtum** *Rim* 22[n]

stealdan, *v str* (+ *dat*)   possess?
  pret 1 sg **stēald** (= *stēold*) *Rim* 22[n]
stēap, *adj*   high, prominent
  Ruin 11[n]. *dat sg masc* **stēapum** *Rim* 58
stearn, *n masc*   tern
  Sea 23[n]
steaðole *see* **staþol**
stefna, *n masc*   prow
  dat sg **stefnan** *Sea* 7
stepegong (= *stæpegong*), *n masc*   going, step
  dat pl **stepegongum** *Rim* 22
stīeran, *v wk* (+ *dat*)   control, direct; restrain
  Sea 109. *imperat* **gestȳr** *Res* 59
stīþ, *adj*   solid, hard, firm
  masc pl **stīþe** *Sea* 104
stondan, *v str*   stand
  pres 3 sg **stondeð** *Wan* 74, 97, 115.
  pres pl **stondaþ** *Wan* 76; **stondeð**
  Sea 67[n]. *subjunct pl* **stonde** (= *ston-*
  den) *Res* 39[n]. *pret pl indic* **stōdon**
  Wan 87; **stōdan** *Ruin* 38
storm, *n masc*   storm; assault
  Res 59. *dat sg* **storme** *Wife* 48. *nom pl*
  stormas *Wan* 101, *Sea* 23. *dat pl*
  stormum *Ruin* 11
strēam, *n masc*   stream, moving water, sea
  Ruin 38. *pl* **strēamas** *Sea* 34,
  [*Husb* 5[n]], *Ruin* 43
strēgan, *v wk*   strew
  Sea 97
strong, *adj*   vehement; unruly
  dat sg neut **strongum** *Sea* 109
stund, *n fem*   time, hour, appointed time
  Rim 58
sum, *adj*   one, a certain; (*in pl*) some
  Sea 68. *acc sg masc* **sumne** *Wan* 81[n],
  82, 83. *nom-acc pl masc-fem* **sume**
  Wan 80[n], *Sea* 56, *Res* 77. *dat pl*
  sumum *Deor* 34
sumer, *n masc*   summer
  gen sg **sumeres** *Sea* 54

sumorlang, *adj*
  acc sg masc **sumorlangne**
  Wife 37[n]
                           long as in summer

sumurhāt, *n neut*
  Rim 67
                           summer heat

sundor, *adj*
  Wan 111
                           apart, separate

sūð, *adv*
  Husb 27
                           south

swā, *adv*
  Wan 6, 19, 62, 85, 111, *Sea* 51,
  Rim 21, 55, 59, *Deor* 7, 9a (*see* **swā**,
  conj), 13, 17, 20, 27, 42, *Res* 116
                           thus, so, as

swā, *conj*
  Wan 14, 43[n], 75, 96, *Sea* 90, *Wife* 24,
  Res 80, 84, *Rid 60* 16 ~ **sār** ~, "as
  sore as," *Deor* 96
                           as, just as, according as; in whatever
                             way that; as if; in such a way that

swǣs, *adj*
  acc sg masc **swǣsne** *Wan* 50
                           dear, sweet

swēg, *n masc*
  Sea 21
                           sound

sweglrād, *n fem*
  Rim 29[n]
                           path of music, musical instrument

swencan, *v wk*
  pres 3 sg **swenceð** *Rim* 80
                           afflict, tax

sweorcan, *v wk*
  pres 3 sg impers **sweorceð** *Deor* 29.
  subjunct sg **gesweorce** *Wan* 59[n]
                           grow dark

sweotule, *adv*
  Wan 11
                           clearly

swēte, *adj*
  as neut n, "sweet-tasting thing,"
  Sea 95
                           sweet

swimman, *v str*
  pres pl **swimmað** *Wan* 53[n]
                           swim

swinsian, *v wk*
  pret 3 sg **swinsade** *Rim* 29
                           sound sweetly, make music

swīþ, *adj*
  Res 64. *fem wk* **swīþe** *Ruin* 24. *compar*
  fem **swīþre** *Sea 115*; "more powerful,"
  i.e. "right (hand)," *Rid 60* 12
                           great, strong

swīþe, *adv* — very, greatly
  Wan 56, *Rim* 29

swoncor, *adj* — supple
  fem pl **swoncre** *Deor* 6[n]

swylc, *adj* — such, like
  Rid 60 11

swylce, *adv* — likewise
  Sea 53, *Wife* 43

swylce, *conj* — as, such as, according as; as if
  Sea 83, *Rim* 23, *Wulf* 1

swylt, *n masc* — death
  Ruin 26

sȳ *see* **wesan**

sylf, *pron* — self
  Sea 35[n], *Res* 73, 77, 103, 117,
  Husb 14. *wk* **sylfa** *Husb* 20[n]. *gen sg*
  masc **sylfes**: **mīnes** ~, "my own,"
  Res 6. *gen sg fem* **sylfre**: **hyre** ~, "her
  own," *Deor* 9; **mīnre** ~, "my own,"
  Wife 2[n]. *dat sg masc* **sylfum** *Sea* 1,
  Deor 29, 35, *Wife* 45, *Res* 14. *dat pl*
  Res 55

sylfor, *n neut* — silver
  Ruin 35

sȳllan, *adj see* **gōd**

syllan, *v wk* — give
  pret 2 sg **sealdest** *Res* 68. *3 sg* **ge-**
  sealde *Deor* 41. *pret sg subjunct* **sealde**
  Res 66

symbel, *n neut* — feast
  nom pl Rim 5. *gen pl* **symbla** *Wan* 93

symle *see* **simle**

syn(n), *n fem* — sin
  acc sg fem **synne** *Rim* 81. *gen pl* **synna**
  Sea 100, *Res* 77. *dat pl* **synnum**
  Res 65

tān, *n masc* — twig, branch; lot
  Rim 78. *dat pl* **tānum** *Res* 106

tǣl, *n fem* — calumny, abuse
  dat sg **tǣle** *Res* 106[n]

tēaforgēap, *adj*
  wk **tēaforgēapa** *Ruin* 30[n]

red-arched

teala, *adv*
  Rim 42[n]

well

telgian, *v wk*
  pret 3 sg **telgade** *Rim* 34

put forth shoots, flourish

tīd, *n fem*
  Sea 124[n]

time

tīdeg (= *tīddæg*)
  dat sg **tīdege** *Sea* 69[n]

appointed time, final day

tigel, *n fem*
  dat pl **tigelum** *Ruin* 30

tile

til, *adj*
  Wan 112. *acc sg masc* **tilne**
  Deor 38

good, practical, advantageous

tilian, *v wk*
  pres sg subjunct **getilge** *Res* 30. *subjunct pl* **tilien** *Sea* 119

strive after; obtain

tillīce, *adv*
  Rim 2

beneficently

tinnan, *v wk*
  pres 3 sg **tinneð** *Rim* 54[n]

grow, extend

tīr, *n masc*
  Rim 34. *dat pl* **tīrum** *Rim* 42

glory, honour

tīrfæst, *adj*
  acc sg fem **tīrfæste** *Husb* 12[n]

firm in glory, gloriously assured

tō, *adv*
  1
  Sea 119[n], *Res* 21[n], 71[n]
  2
  Wan 66 (2), 67 (2), 68 (3), 69, 112,
  Rim 57, *Wife* 51, *Res* 46

to that place; in a forward direction, forward

too

tō, *prep*
  1   + *dat/instr*
  (27) *Wan* 11, *etc*
  2   + *infin*
  Sea 37, *Res* 11

to, towards, into, with regard to; for, as; from, at the hands of

to

tō ealdre, *adv*
  Sea 79

forever

tō þæs, *adv*
  Sea 40b, 41 (2)

to the extent (that), so ... (that)

tōdǣlan, *v wk*
  pret pl subjunct **tōdǣlden**
  Wife 12
separate

tōflōwen, *past partic*
  Rim 47
spread, dispersed

tōgædre, *adv*
  Ruin 20
together

tōgēanes, *prep* (+ *dat*)
  Sea 76
against

torht, *adj*
  neut wk **torhte** *Rim* 2
bright

tōirnan, *v str*
  pres 3 sg **tōyrneð** *Rim* 50
run, spread

torn, *n neut*
  Wan 112
anger, resentment

torr, *n masc*
  pl **torras** *Ruin* 3
tower

tōslītan, *v str*
  pres 3 sg **tōslīteð** *Wulf* 18[n]
rend apart

trāg, *adj*
  Rim 57[n]
worthless, without substance

trēocyn, *n neut*
  Husb 2[n]
species of tree; kind of wood

trēow, *n fem*
  Rim 34. *acc sg* **trēowe** *Wan* 112,
  Husb 12[n]
loyalty, commitment, good faith

trēowþrāg, *n fem*
  Rim 57
time of good faith

tūdor, *n neut*
  dat sg **tūdre** *Husb* 2
progeny; young offspring; breed or
  kind

tungol, *n neut*
  gen pl **tungla** *Res* 10
heavenly body

twēgen, *num*
  gen pl **twēga** *Husb* 49. *dat pl* **twām**
  Rid 60 15
two

twēo, *n masc*
  dat sg **twēon** *Sea* 69[n]
doubt, uncertainty, hazard

tylgust, *adv superl*
  Res 96
chiefly

þā, þām, þāra, *pron & adj see* **sē**

þā, *adv*   then, next; at that time; at this time
   Rim 9, *Res* 64 (**nū** ~, *emphatic*); **ðā**
   Wife 9[n]
ðā, *conj*   since
   Wife 18[n]
þās *see* þes
þǣr, *adv*   there
   Wan 54, *Sea* 18, 23a, *Rim* 16 (2),
   Wulf 6[n], *Res* 4, 32, *Rid* 60 4, *Husb* 12
þǣr, *conj*   where
   Wan 115, *Sea* 6[n], 10, 23b[n], 121,
   Rim 14, *82*[n], 86, *Wife* 37, 38, *Res* 11,
   Husb 7, 29, *Ruin* 32, 40, 46
þǣre, þæs (*gen*), þæt, *pron & adj see* **sě**
þæs (*nom*) *see* þes
þæs, *pron gen sg neut as adv* (*see also* **tō**   for that reason, with regard to that;
  þæs, þæs þe)   to that extent, so ... (that)
   Sea 39, 40a, 122, *Deor* 7[n], 13, 17, 20,
   27, 42[n], *Res* 70; **ðæs** *Res* 69
þæs þe, *conj*   according to that which, as
   Husb 31
þæt, *excl*   how!
   Res 109
þæt, *conj*   that, in that; in order that, until;
   (40) *Wan* 12, *etc*   with the result that
þætte (= *þæt þe*) *relat pron neut*   which
   Wulf 18
þē, þec, *2-pers-sg pron see* **þū**
þē, *pron instr as adv see* **þȳ**
þe, *indecl relat*   who, that, such that
   (*see also* **sē þe, þæs þe, þēah þe, þȳ**
   þe) (24) *Wan* 10, *etc*
þēah, *conj*   although
   Res 66
þēah þe, *conj*   although
   Wan 2, *Sea* 97, 113, *Res* 16, 27, 34,
   48, *Husb* 39; **þēah ðe** *Res* 51
þearf, *n fem*   need
   acc sg **þearfe** *Res* 29
þēaw, *n masc*   custom
   Wan 12

þegn, *n masc*
  dat pl **þegnum** *Rim* 18
thane, retainer

þencan, *v wk*
  Sea 96. *pres 1 sg* **þence** *Res* 98. *3 sg*
  þenceð *Sea* 51
think, intend, be minded, incline towards

þenden, *conj*
  Sea 102, *Husb* 17
while

þēoden, *n masc*
  Rim 18ⁿ, *Husb* 29. *gen sg* **þēodnes**
  Wan 95, *Husb* 48
ruler, king, prince

Ðēodric,
  Deor 18ⁿ
Theodoric (*the Goth*)

þes, *demst adj*
  Wan 62, *Wife* 29, *Ruin* 1ⁿ; **þæs**
  Res 89ⁿ, *Ruin* 9ⁿ, 30ⁿ. *fem* **þēos**
  Sea 86. *nom-acc neut* **þis** *Wan* 89, 110,
  Sea 65, *Rim* 1, *Wife* 1, *Res* 97. *acc sg*
  masc **þisne** *Wan* 75, 85, 88, *Husb* 13.
  acc sg fem **þās** *Wan* 58, *Sea* 87,
  Deor 31, *Ruin* 37. *gen sg neut* **þisses**,
  "with regard to this," *Deor* 7ⁿ, 13, 17,
  20, 27, 42. *gen-dat sg fem* **þisse**
  Wan 74, *Res* 42, 67, 80. *dat sg masc-
  neut* **þissum** *Wife* 16, 41. *nom-acc pl*
  þās *Wan* 91, 101, *Wife* 36, *Res* 83,
  Ruin 29
this

þider, *adv*
  Sea 118
thither, to that place

þīn, *pron gen see* **þū**

þīn, *possess adj*
  Res 53. *acc sg masc* **þīnne** *Res* 44, 50.
  acc sg fem **þīne** *Res* 29. *dat sg fem*
  þīnre *Res* 27, 51. *nom pl* **þīne** *Wulf*
  13, 14
thy, thine, your

þinceð *see* **þyncan**

þing, *n neut*
  Deor 9, *Ruin* 48. *gen pl* **þinga**: ~ **gehwylce**, "in every case," "in every respect," *Sea* 68, *Res* 13; ~ **gehwylces**,
  "in everything," *Res* 23; **ænge** ~, "in
  any respect," "in any way," *Res* 112.
  dat pl **þingum** *Rid 60* 14ⁿ
thing; case; affair; purpose

þis, þisne, þisse, þisses, þissum *see* þes

þolian, *v wk*   endure
   Res 74. *pres 3 sg* þolað *Res* 94. *pres sg*
   subjunct þolige *Res* 118. *pret 1 sg*
   þolade *Res* 85

þon *see* sē, *pron*

þonan, *adv*   thence, from there
   Wan 23

þonc, *n masc*   thanks
   Sea 122, *Res* 67, 86[n]

þone *see* se *(adj) and* sē þe

þonne, *adv*   then; therefore
   Wan 49[n], 88, *Sea* 94a, 118, 119,
   Deor 31, *Res* 29, 43, 47, 60, 118[n],
   Husb 13, *Ruin* 42, 47; ðonne
   Wan 45[n]

þonne, *conj*
   1   when, whenever
   Wan 51[n], 60, 70, 74, 103, *Sea* 8, 84,
   94b, 102, *Rim* 72, 73, 75, *Wulf* 10[n],
   11, *Wife* 35, *Res* 46, 59, 114, 117;
   ðonne *Wan* 39[n]
   2   than
   Sea 65, 116, *Wife* 4, *Res* 18, 28, 35,
   56, 87, *Husb* 32

þrāg, *n fem*   time
   Wan 95

þrēat, *n masc*   troop, host; violence
   Wulf 2[n], 7

þrēo, *num*   three
   gen pl þrēora *Sea* 68

þrīste, *adv*   boldly, confidently, without fear
   Deor 12

þrītig, *num* (+ *gen*)   thirty
   Deor 18

þrōwian, *v wk*   endure, suffer
   Res 58. *pret 1 sg* þrōwade
   Sea 3

þrym, *n masc*   glory, splendour
   Wan 95

þrȳþe, *n fem pl*   might
   Wan 99

þū, *2-pers-sg pron*   thou, you
   Wulf 16, *Res* 2, 22, 24, 25, 36, 52, 59,
   66, 68, *Husb* 10, 12, 14, 21, 22, 24,
   27. *acc* þec *Res* 37, *Husb* 13, 24. *gen*
   þīn, "(of) thee," "(of) you," *Husb* 29,
   48. *dat* þē *Res* 5, 13, 41, 67, 110,
   Rid 60 14, *Husb* 1, 20
þūhten *see* þyncan
þurh, *prep* (+ *acc*)   through, by means of
   Sea 88, *Rim* 13, *Wife* 13
þus, *adv*   thus
   Res 79
þwītan, *v str*   cut off
   pres 3 sg þwīteþ *Rim* 63
þȳ, *pron instr as adv (with compar)*   the, by that much
   Wan 49, *Res* 54; þē *Rim* 80
þȳ þe, *conj*   inasmuch as, because
   Res 55
þyncan, *v wk*   seem
   pres 3 sg impers þinceð *Wan* 41,
   Deor 29. *pret pl subjunct* þūhten
   Res 55

ūhtcearu, *n fem*   care or anxiety in the small hours of
   acc sg ūhtceare *Wife* 7[n]   the morning
ūhte, *n fem*   the small hours of the morning
   dat sg ūhtan *Wife* 35[n]. *gen pl* ūhtna
   Wan 8, *Rid* 60 6
unc *see* wit
uncer, *possess adj*   of us two, our
   Wulf 19, *Wife* 25. *acc sg masc* uncerne
   Wulf 16[n]. *acc pl* uncre *Rid* 60 17
under, *prep*   under
   1 + *acc*
   Wan 96
   2 + *dat*
   Wan 107, *Rim* 10, *Wife* 28, 36, 48,
   Ruin 11
undereten, *past partic*   eaten away
   fem pl undereotone *Ruin* 6[n]
unfyr (= *unfyrn*), *adv*   not long (in time), before long
   Res 43[n]

ungelīc, *adj* unalike
  Wulf 3[n]
ungelīce, *adv* unalike
  Wulf 8[n]
ungeþynde, *adj* unpenned, unrestrained
  Rim 49[n]
ungrynde, *adj* bottomless
  Rim 49
unnan, *v pret-pres* (+ *gen*) grant
  pres sg subjunct **unne** *Res* 33; **geunne**
  Husb 32
untrum, *adj* infirm, feeble
  fem wk **untrume** *Rim* 57
unþinged, *adj* unprepared for; unbargained for,
  Sea 106 unreconciled
unwearnum, *adv* irresistibly
  Sea 63
up, *adv* up
  Wife 3
uphēah, *adj* high, steep
  fem pl **uphēa** *Wife* 30
uprodor, *n masc* sky above
  Sea 105
ūrigfeþra, *adj* wet-feathered
  Sea 25[n]
ūs, ūsic *see* **wē**
ūt, *adv* out
  Husb 41
uton, *v, 1 pl imperat* let us
  Sea 117[n], *Rim* 83

W *for runic letter, see* **wynn**
wā, *indecl n* woe
  Wife 52
wāc, *adj* weak, timorous, yielding
  Wan 67. *compar pl* **wācran**, "inferior,"
  Sea 87
wāccor (= *wācor*), *adv compar* more feebly
  Res 17[n]
wadan, *v str* go across or through, make one's way
  Wan 5. *pret 1 sg* **wōd**
  Wan 24

wāg, *n masc*   wall
  Ruin 9
walanwīr, *n masc*   strip of metal, cramp
  dat pl **walanwīrum** *Ruin* 20^n
waldend, *n masc*   ruler; owner
  Res 44 (of God). *pl Wan* 78
waldendwyrhta, *n masc*   owner-builder; powerful maker
  pl **waldendwyrhtan** *Ruin* 7^n
walo *see* **wæl**
wānhȳdig, *adj*   reckless
  Wan 67
warian, *v wk*   occupy (the attention of)
  pres 3 sg **warað** *Wan* 32^n
wāt *see* **witan**
waþem, *n masc*   wave
  gen pl **waþema** *Wan* 24^n, 57
wæg, *n masc*   wave
  Sea 19. *pl* **wēgas** *Wan* 46^n
wǣgon *see* **wegan**
wæl, *n neut*   the slain in battle
  pl **walo** *Ruin* 25^n
wælgār, *n masc*   slaughtering spear
  Rim 61
wælgīfre, *adj*   eager for slaughter
  neut pl **wælgīfru** *Wan* 100
wælhrēow, *adj*   bloodthirsty, ferocious
  masc pl **wælrēowe** *Wulf* 6
wælsleaht, *n masc*   slaughter in battle
  gen pl **wælsleahta** *Wan* 7, 91
wǣpen, *n neut*   weapon
  pl Wan 100
wǣr, *n fem*   pledge, contract; peace
  Rim 26. *acc sg* **wǣre** *Husb* 52. *dat pl*
  wērum *Sea* 110^n
wǣre, wǣron, wæs, *v see* **wesan**
wæstm, *n masc*   fruit, produce, abundant growth
  dat pl **wæstmum** *Rim* 9
wæter, *n neut*   water
  dat sg **wætre** *Wife* 49
wē, *1-pers-pl pron*   we
  Sea 117a, 117b, 118, 119 (2),

Deor 14, 21. *acc* **ūsic** *Sea* 123. *dat* **ūs**
Wan 115, *Wulf* 3[n], 8

wēa, *n masc* — woe, trouble
acc sg or pl **wēan** *Deor* 4, *Husb* 45. *gen*
sg Deor 25. *gen pl* **wēana** *Deor* 34

weal, *n masc* — wall; rampart
Wan 98, *Ruin* 39[n]; **weall** *Ruin* 20. *dat*
sg **wealle** *Wan* 80. *nom pl* **weallas**
Wan 76

wealdan, *v str* (+ *dat*) — have control over
pret 1 sg **wēold** *Rim* 22

weallan, *v str* — surge, seethe
pres 3 sg **wealleð** *Rim* 68

wealstān, *n masc* — construction made of stone
Ruin 1

wealsteal, *n masc* — walled place, fortress
Wan 88

weard, *n masc* — keeper, watchman
Sea 54

weardian, *v wk* — keep, occupy
weardigan *Husb* 18. *pres pl* **weardiað**
Wife 34

wearp *see* **weorpan**

wearð, **wearþan** *see* **weorþan**

wēaþearf, *n fem* — woeful need
dat sg **wēaþearfe** *Wife* 10

weaxan, *v str* — grow
Res 105. *pret 1 sg* **wēox**
Wife 3[n]

weder, *n neut* — weather
Wulf 10

wegan, *v str* — carry; go, proceed
pres 3 sg **gewigeð** *Rim* 76. *pret pl*
wǣgon Rim 6[n]

wēgas *see* **wǣg**

wel, *adv* — well
Wan 114, *Res* 118

wēla, *n masc* — riches
Wan 74

welgian, *v wk* — be rich, abound
pret 3 sg **welgade** *Rim* 34

Wēlund Weland, *the legendary smith*
   Deor 1[n] (*see also notes on lines 5–6 and 8–13*)

wēman, *v wk* entice
   Wan 29[n]

wēn, *n fem* hope; expectation
   nom pl **wēna** *Wulf* 13. *dat pl* **wēnum**
   Wulf 9, *Husb* 29; **wēnan** *Deor* 25

wēnan, *v wk* think, expect
   pret 1 sg **wēnde** *Rid 60* 7

wendan, *v wk* turn, change
   pres 3 sg **wendeþ** *Rim* 59,
   Deor 32

wenian, *v wk* accustom
   pret 3 sg **wenede** *Wan* 36

wennan, wenne *see* **wynn**

wēold *see* **wealdan**

weorc, *n neut* work, thing made or done
   geweorc *Ruin* 2. *pl* **weorc** *Res* 7;
   geweorc *Wan* 87

weorod, *n neut* company, throng, retinue
   weord *Rim* 16[n]. *dat sg* **weorude**
   Res 83

weorpan, *v str* throw, throw up; gush
   pret 3 sg **wearp** *Ruin* 38[n]

weorþan, *v str* become, turn into; (*in passive con-*
   wearþan *Wan* 64[n]. *pres 3 sg* **weorþeð** *structions*) be
   Wan 110, *Sea* 69. *pret 1 sg* **wearð**
   Res 79. *pret pl* **wurdon** *Deor* 15,
   Ruin 27

weoruld *see* **woruld**

wēox *see* **weaxan**

wēpan, *v str* weep, bewail
   Wife 38

wer, *n masc* man
   Wan 64. *nom pl* **weras** *Wulf* 6. *gen pl*
   wera *Sea* 21, *Ruin* 26

wercyn, *n neut* race of men
   Rim 61[n]

werg, werig (= *wearg*), *adj* cursed
   pl **werge** *Res* 58

wērig, *adj*
  Wan 15^n, *Sea* 29, *Rim* 51. *acc sg masc*
  wērigne *Wan* 57

weary, depressed, afflicted

wērigmōd, *adj*
  Wife 49^n

sad at heart, dejected

werþēod, *n fem*
  gen pl **werþēoda** *Ruin* 8

nation of men

wērum *see* **wǣr**

wesan, *v anom*
  Wife 42. *pres 1 sg* **eom** *Wife* 29,
  Res 65, 75, 82, 88, 109, *Husb* 8. *3 sg*
  is (25) *Wan* 106, *etc*; *neg* **nis** *Wan* 9,
  Sea 39, *Husb* 45. *pres pl* **sind** *Sea* 64,
  80, 86, *Wife* 33, *Ruin* 3; **sindon**
  Wan 93, *Rim* 82, *Res* 4; "there are"
  Wulf 6, *Wife* 30. *neg pl* **nǣron** (= *ne*
  earon) *Sea* 82^n. *pres sg subjunct* **sȳ**
  Sea 122, *Deor* 30, *Res* 11; **sȳ** ... **sȳ**,
  "whether it be ... or whether it be
  that," *Wife* 45 & 46^n; **sīe** *Res* 67. *pret*
  1 & 3 sg **wæs** (25) *Rim* 3, *etc*. *pret pl*
  wǣron *Sea* 9, 83, *Rim* 27, *Res* 35 (*subjunct?*), 69, 80, *Ruin* 21, [40^n], 46.
  pret sg subjunct **wǣre** *Wan* 96,
  Deor 26, *Wife* 8, 24, *Res* 18

be

wēste, *adj*
  Wan 74

desolate, waste

wēstenstaþol, *n masc*
  pl **wēstenstaþolas** *Ruin* 27^n

deserted site

wīc, *n neut*
  Wife 32 (*pl?*). *pl (for sg)* *Wife* 52

dwelling-place

wicg, *n neut*
  pl Rim 7^n

horse, steed

wīd, *adj*
  dat sg masc wk **wīdan** *Ruin* 39 (*or
  dat sg str* = *wīdum*)

wide

wīde, *adv*
  Sea 60, *Deor* 22, *Wife* 46, *Ruin* 25.
  compar **wīddor** *Rid* 60 17^n. *superl*
  wīdost *Sea* 57; **gewīdost**, "farthest
  apart," *Wife* 13

widely, far and wide

wīdlāst, *n masc*
  dat pl **wīdlāstum** *Wulf* 9[n]

wide track, wandering far and wide

wīdsīð, *n masc*
  Rim 51

wide journey, long journey (*perhaps fig*)

wīf, *n neut*
  dat sg **wīfe** *Sea* 45[n]

woman

wīg, *n neut*
  Wan 80

battle

wiga, *n masc*
  Wan 67

warrior

wīghyrst, *n fem*
  dat pl **wīghyrstum** *Ruin* 34

war-trappings

wīgsteal, *n neut*
  pl Ruin 27[n]

bastion

wiht, *n fem*
  pl **wihta** *Res* 58

creature

wīlbec? *n*
  Rim 26[n]

stream of misery

willa, *n masc*
  Husb 30. *acc sg* **willan** *Res* 12, 104.
  gen pl **wilna** *Husb* 45

desire; joy

willan, *v anom*
  pres 1 & 3 sg **wille** *Deor* 35, *Husb* 1;
  wylle *Res* 70. *subjunct sg* **wille**
  Wan 14, 72, *Sea* 43, 97, 99 (*indic?*),
  113; **wylle** *Res* 24. *pres pl indic* **willað**
  Wulf 2[n], 7. *pret sg subjunct* **wolde**,
  "would," *Wan* 28, *Husb* 53

will, wish

wind, *n masc*
  dat sg **winde** *Wan* 76

wind

wine, *n masc*
  Sea 115, *Wife* 49, 50, [*Husb* 39[n]]

friend; lord

winedryhten, *n masc*
  gen sg **winedryhtnes** *Wan* 37

dear lord

winelēas, *adj*
  Wan 45, *Wife* 10, *Res* 91

friendless

winemǣg, *n masc*
  gen pl **winemǣga** *Wan* 7. *dat pl*
  winemǣgum *Sea* 16

dear kinsman

winetrēow, *n fem*
  acc sg **winetrēowe** *Husb* 52

pledge of friendship

wīngāl, *adj*   elated with wine
  Sea 29ⁿ, *Ruin* 34
winnan, *v str*   struggle; suffer
  pres 3 sg **winneð** *Rim* 51. *pret 1 sg*
  wonn *Wife* 5ⁿ
wīnsæl, *n neut*   wine-hall
  pl **wīnsalo** *Wan* 78
winter, *n masc*   winter; year
  Sea 15. *gen sg* **wintres** *Wan* 103.
  gen pl **wintra** *Wan* 65, *Deor* 18, 38
winterceald, *adj*   cold as winter, wintry-cold
  acc sg fem **wintercealde** *Deor* 4
wintercearig, *adj*   sad as winter
  Wan 24ⁿ
wīs, *adj*   wise
  Wan 64, *Res* 83. *instr sg* **wīse**
  Wan 88ⁿ
wīse, *n fem*   way, manner, habit
  dat pl **wīsum** *Sea* 110
wislic, *adj*   certain, established
  acc sg masc **wislicne** *Deor* 34
wist, *n fem*   food, feast
  Rim 76. *dat sg* **wiste** *Wan* 36
wit, *1-pers-dual pron*   we two
  Wife 13, 21. *acc-dat* **unc** *Wife* 12, 22,
  Rid 60 15
wita, *n masc*   wise man
  Wan 65
wītan, *v str* (+ *dat of pers*)   lay to one's charge, accuse of
  pres 3 sg **wīteð** *Res* 76
witan, *v pret-pres*   know; feel, show
  pres 1 & 3 sg **wāt** *Wan* 11, 29, 37ⁿ,
  Sea 12, 55, 92, *Res* 42; *neg* **nāt**
  Res 99. *pret sg subjunct* **wisse** *Wan* 27
wīte, *n neut*   punishment; pain, suffering
  Wife 5ⁿ
witig, *adj*   wise
  Deor 32, *Res* 7
wiþ, *prep*
  1   + *acc*   against; towards
  Sea 112; **wið** *Sea* 75, 112

2   + dat   beside, over against; to
 Rid 60 14

wiðstondan, *v str* (+ *dat*)   withstand
 Wan 15

wlitian, *v wk*   grow beautiful
 pres pl **wlitigað** *Sea* 49[n]

wlonc, *adj*   proud, splendid
 Wan 80, *Sea* 29, *Ruin* 34

wōd *see* **wadan**

wōldæg, *n masc*   day of pestilence
 pl **wōldagas** *Ruin* 25[n]

wolde *see* **willan**

wōma, *n masc*   roaring, tumult
 Wan 103[n]

womm, *n masc or neut*   stain; sin
 dat pl **wommum** *Rim* 85

won, *adj*   dark
 Wan 103

wonǣht, *n fem*   lack of possessions, poverty
 dat pl (for sg) **wonǣhtum** *Res* 104

wong, *n masc*   plain; place
 Ruin 31[n]. *nom pl* **wongas** *Sea* 49.
 dat pl **wongum** *Rim* 7

wonn *see* **winnan**

word, *n neut*   word
 acc pl *Wan* 91, *Res* 7, 83. *dat pl*
 wordum *Rid* 60 10

wordbēotung, *n fem*   promise, vow
 pl **wordbēotunga** *Husb* 15

wordcwide, *n masc*   utterance, words
 pl **wordcwidas** *Rid* 60 17

wōrian, *v wk*   wander about; totter
 pres pl **wōriað** *Wan* 78[n]

worn, *indecl n* (+ *gen*)   many
 Wan 91

woruld, *n fem*   world
 Wan 58, *Sea* 49, 87, *Deor* 31;
 weoruld *Wan* 107; *world* *Rim* 9, 59.
 gen-dat sg **worulde** *Wan* 74, *Sea* 45,
 Wife 46, *Res* 42, 80, *Husb* 30

woruldrīce, *n neut*   the kingdom of this world
 dat sg *Wan* 65, *Wife* 13

wracu, *n fem* — pain; punishment; persecution;
  acc sg **wræce** *Deor* 4, *Res* 58 — vengeance

wrāþ, *n neut* — cruelty, savagery
  Rim 64

wrāþ, *adj* — angry; rough, cruel
  Res 91. *gen pl* **wrāþra** *Wan* 7

wrāþe, *adv* — cruelly
  Wife 32

wræc, *n neut* — misery; exile
  gen sg **wræces** *Deor* 1[n]

wræcca, *n masc* — exile; wretched person
  Wife 10, *Res* 91. *gen sg* **wræccan**:
  ~ **lastum,** "paths of exile," *Sea* 15

wræcfæc, *n neut* — time of misery
  Rim 64[n]

wræclāst, *n masc* — exile-track, path of exile
  Wan 32. *pl* **wræclāstas** *Wan* 5, *Sea* 57

wræcsīþ, *n masc* — journey of exile; painful experience
  acc pl **wræcsīþas** *Wife* 38. *gen pl*
  wræcsīþa *Wife* 5

wrǣtlic, *adj* — artfully made, wonderful
  Ruin 1

wrecan, *v str* — recount, narrate, tell
  Sea 1. *pres 1 sg* **wrece** *Wife* 1

wrīþian (= *wrīdian*), *v wk* — flourish
  pres 3 sg **wrīþað** *Rim* 64[n]

wrixlan, *v wk* (+ *dat*) — exchange
  Rid 60 10

wudu, *n masc* — tree; forest
  Res 105. *gen-dat sg* **wuda** *Wulf* 17,
  Wife 27 (or *gen pl*)

wuldor, *n neut* — glory
  Res 21. *gen sg* **wuldres** *Sea* 123. *dat sg*
  as adv **wuldre,** "gloriously," *Rim* 85

wuldorcyning, *n masc* — king of glory
  dat sg masc **wuldorcyninge**
  Res 17

wuldordrēam, *n masc* — glorious joy
  Res 44

wulf, *n masc* — wolf
  Wan 82. *proper name*: *Wulf* 4[n], 13 (2),
  17[n]; *gen* **wulfes** *Wulf* 9

wunden, *past partic*
  Wan 32

twisted (into rings and circular ornaments)

wundor, *n neut*
  gen sg **wundres** *Rid 60* 10. *acc pl*
  wundor *Res* 3. *dat pl as adv*
  wundrum, "wonderfully," *Wan* 98,
  Ruin 20

wonder, marvel

wundorcyning, *n masc*
  Res 3^n

king of wonders

wunian, *v wk*
  Wife 27, [*Res* 113^n]. *pres 3 sg* **wunað**
  Ruin 12^n. *pres pl* **wuniað** *Sea* 87. *pres*
  partic nom sg fem **wuniendo** *Rim* 26.
  pret 1 sg **wunade** *Sea* 15; **gewunade**
  Rid 60 2

remain, last; dwell; inhabit

wurdon *see* **weorþan**

wurman *see* **wyrm**

wylfen, *adj*
  acc sg masc **wylfenne** *Deor* 22

wolfish, savage

wylle *see* **willan**

wylm, *n masc*
  dat sg **wylme** *Ruin* 39

surging

wynlicra, *adj compar*
  neut pl **wynlicran** *Wife* 52

more joyful

wynn, *n fem*
  Husb 51^n (rune); **wyn** *Wan* 36,
  Sea 27, 45, *Wulf* 12, *Wife* 46. *dat sg*
  wynne *Rim* 81; *as adv* **wenne**,
  "joyfully," *Rim* 76^n. *gen pl* **wynna**
  Wife 32. *dat pl* **wynnum** *Wan* 29; *as*
  adv **wennan** *Rim* 7^n

joy; name of runic letter ᚹ (W)

(ge)wyrcan, *v wk*
  pres sg subjunct **gewyrce** *Sea* 74. *past*
  partic acc sg masc **geworhtne**
  Sea 115

make, accomplish, achieve

wyrd, *n fem*
  Wan 5^n, 100^n, *Sea* 115, *Rim* 70,
  Res 118, *Ruin* 24^n. *gen-dat sg* **wyrde**
  Wan 15, *Res* 105. *nom-acc pl* **wyrde**
  Rim 59, *Ruin* 1^n. *gen pl* **wyrda**
  Wan 107^n, *Res* 44

fate; accident; (disastrous) event

wyrm, *n masc*   worm; serpent, snake
   Rim 75, *dat pl* **wurman** (= *wyrmum*)
   Deor 1[n]

wyrmlīc, *n neut*   serpent form
   dat pl **wyrmlīcum** *Wan* 98[n]

wȳscan, *v wk*   wish
   pret 3 sg **wȳscte** *Deor* 25

ȳcan, *v wk*   increase
   pres pl **ȳcað** *Res* 94[n]

yldo, *n fem*   age; old age
   Sea 70, 91. *dat sg* **ældo** *Ruin* 6[n]

ylfetu, *n fem*   swan
   gen sg **ylfete** *Sea* 19[n]

ymb, *prep* (+ *acc*)   around; about, concerning
   Sea 11, 46, *Deor* 12, *Res* 65, 97,
   Husb 10; **ymbe** *Sea* 46

yrmþu, *n fem*   misery
   Res 85. *nom pl Res* 94[n]. *gen pl* **yrmþa**
   Wife 3

ȳð, *n fem*   wave
   Rid 60 6. *gen pl* **ȳþa** *Sea* 6, *Wife* 7,
   Husb 42; **ȳða** *Sea* 46

ȳþde *see* **īþan**

HIGH-FREQUENCY FORMS AND USES

See Glossary for further information on these words

hē

nom **hē**: *Wan* 2, 13, 14, 34, 41, 43, 64, 69, 70, 113, *Sea* 42, 74 (2), 102 (2), 108,
   113, 123, *Rim* 17, 80, *Wulf* 2, 7, *Wife* 51, *Res* 94, 118, *Husb* 31, 35, 48, 52

acc **hine**: *Wan* 32, 35, *Sea* 43, 77, 99, 113, *Deor* 5, *Wulf* 2, 7, *Husb* 19

gen **his**: *Wan* 13, 14, 35, 37, 41, 112 (2), 113, *Sea* 40, 41 (2), 43, 69, 78, 92, 98,
   106, 108, 115, *Rim* 53, *Wife* 46, *Res* 92, 94

dat **him**

1 *non-reflex*: *Wan* 10, 41, *Sea* 41, 44, 91, 94 (2), 106b, 107, 108, *Res* 91, 93, 95,
   Husb 30, 45

2 *reflex*: *Wan* 1, 31, 46, 111, 114, *Sea* 13, 27, 106a, *Rim* 81, *Deor* 1, 3, *Res* 117,
   Husb 53; ~ **sylfum** *Wife* 45

ic

nom **ic**: *Wan* 8, 10, 11, 19, 23, 26, 58, 60, *Sea* 1, 2, 14, 18, 20, 29, 34, 37, 66, *Rim*
3, 15, 18, 23, 38, 40 (2), 71, *Deor* 35, 36, 38, *Wulf* 4, 9, 10, *Wife* 1, 2, 3 (2), 5,
7, 9, 16, 18, 25, 29, 35, 37, 38, 39, *Res* 5, 13, 16, 20, 21, 27, 29 (2), 41, 42 (2),
47, 48, 51, 65, 70, 73, 75, 77, 78, 79, 81, 82, 83, 85, 88, 96^n, 100, 101, 103,
106, 109, 111, 114, 116, *Rid 60* 1, 7, 8, 14, *Husb* 1, 2, 6, 11, 50

acc **mec**: *Wan* 28, *Sea* 6, *Rim* 5, 19, 21, 74, *Wulf* 11, *Wife* 14, 15, 27, 32, 41, *Res*
1, 25, 26, 45, 49, 52, 59, 72, *Rid 60* 6, 12, *Husb* 3, 7

dat **mē**

1   *non-reflex*: *Sea* 61, 64, *Rim* 1, 14, 15, 70, *Deor* 37, 41, *Wulf* 12 (2), *Res* 10, 19,
22, 24, 28, 32, 36, 66, 68, 76, 84, 102, 115, *Husb* 31

2   *reflex*: *Sea* 20, *Wife* 1, 9, 18, *Res* 70, 71^n, 74, 77, 96, 103, 114; ~ **sylfum** *Sea* 1,
Deor 35, *Res* 14

in, *prep*

1   + *acc*: *Sea* 55, 120, 124, *Rim* 13, 44, *Res* 40, 44, [*Husb* 3^n], *Ruin* 19

2   + *dat*: *Wan* 12, 18, 27, 44, 65, 81, 84, 90, *Sea* 5, 28, 30, 40, 41, 108, 121, 122,
Rim 15, 17, 38 (2), 41, 45a, *45b^n*, 46, 48, 83, 87, *Wife* 13, 28, *Res* 76, 88

magan

pres 1 & 3 sg **mæg**: *Wan* 15, 58, 64, *Sea* 1, 94, 100, *Rim* 72, *Deor* 7^n, 13, 17, 20,
27, 31, 42, *Wife* 2, 38, 39, *Res* 89, 103, 106, 111, 117, *Husb* 30

mīn

nom (& neut acc) sg: *Wan* 59, *Sea* 58, 59, *Rim* 39, 41, 43, *Wulf* 13, *Wife* 6, 8, 15,
17, 47, 50, *Res* 3, 18, 22, 64, 99, 108, *Husb* 7, 39

ne

adv: *Wan* 15, 58, 59, 64, 66a, 112, *Sea* 12, 18, 44a, 55, 94, 95a, 100, 106, *Rim* 5,
14, 15, 24, 29, 52, 54, 72, 79, *Deor* 8, 11, *Wife* 22, 39, *Res* 15, 52, 77, 82, 89,
103, 106, 111, 117, *Rid 60* 11, 17, *Husb* 24, 30, 46a

conj: *Wan* 16, 66b, 67 (2), 68 (3), 69, *Sea* 40 (2), 41 (2), 44b, 45 (2), 46, 82, 83,
95b, 96 (2), *Wife* 41, *Res* 102, *Husb* 46 (2)

nū

Wan 9, 75, 97, *Sea* 33, 58, 82, 90, *Rim* 43, 45, 59, 83, *Deor* 39, *Wife* 4, 24, *Res*
25, 41, 42, 64 (~ **þā**), 75, 103, 116, *Husb* 1, 8, 9, 20, 44

on

1   + *acc*: *Wan* 42, *Sea* 32, 47, 52, 63, *Deor* 5^n, 6, *Wulf* 2^n, 7, *Res* 25, 37, 50, 53,
54, 72, 98, *Husb* 42, 43, *Ruin* 35 (3), 36 (3), 37

2 + *dat*: *Wan* 35, 41, 97, 105, 111, 115, *Sea* 13, 66, 75, 85, 109, 114, *Rim* 14, *Deor* 9, 25, 29, *Wulf* 4 (2), 6, *Wife* 16, 27, 33^n, 35, 41, 50, *Res* 14, 16, 48, 67, 84 (2), 87, 92, 100, 101, 108, 111, *Rid 60* 5, 11 *Husb* 6^n, 9, 11, 15, 16, 17, 22, 23, 29, 31, 54, *Ruin* 4, 41

ond

Wan 23, 34, 39, 42 (2), 43, 48, 63, 89, 91, 101, *Sea* 21, 29, 62, 78, 85, 87, 89, 105, 109, 110, 112, 118, 119, *Rim* 2, 58, 60, 70, 71, 74, 76, 78, 87, *Deor* 3, *Wulf* 10, *Wife* 14, *Res* 2, 3, 5, 6, 7 (2), 8, 9, 14, 22, 23 (2), 32, 45, 59, 62, 65, 68, 71 (2), 72, 74, 93, 94, 95, 97, 98, *Rid 60* 12, 13, *Husb* 9, 34, 42, 51, 52, *Ruin* 10, 30, 33, 34

tō, *prep* + *dat*

Wan 11, 30, 36, 115, *Sea* 20, 43, 44 (2), 45 (2), 51, 61, 69, 101, *Rim* 81, *Deor* 3, *Wulf* 12^n, 17, *Res* 19^n, 25, 41, 73, 103, 114^n, 116, *Ruin* 29, 32^n

þæt

demst pron: *Sea* 12, 24^n, 55, 72^n, 109, *Rim* 70, 80, *Deor* 12, 14^n, 19, 23, 35, *Wulf* 18, *Wife* 2, 11, 23, *Res* 74, 94, 117^n, *Rid 60* 10, *Ruin* 24, 41, 48

conj: *Wan* 12, 13, 41, *Sea* 34^n, 37, 42, 67, 74, 77, 119, 123, *Rim* 16, 17, 71, *Deor* 10, 11, 16, 26, 30, 31, 36, *Wife* 12, 13, 22, 47, *Res* 13, 29, 32, 38, 42, 81, 85, 118, *Rid 60* 8, 14, *Husb* 12, 14, 21, 27, 52

þe (*occurrences in compounds not included*)

Wan 10, 27, 29, 31, 37, 56, 112, 114, *Sea* 13, 27, 51, 57, 100, 106, 107, *Wife* 41, 52, *Res* 4, 73, 77, 102, *Rid 60* 11, *Husb* 16, 54

wesan

pres 3 sg **is**: *Wan* 106, *Sea* 86, 88, 121, *Rim* 43, 47, 57, *Wulf* 1, 3, 4, 5, 8, *Wife* 17, 23, 24, 29, *Res* 46, 64, 91, 110 *Rid 60* 10, *Husb* 29, *Ruin* 1, 47, 48

pret 1 & 3 sg **wæs**: *Rim* 3, 9, 14, 15, 18, 25, 27, 38, 39, 41, 45, *Deor* 8, 11, 19, 23, 36, 37, *Wulf* 10, 12 (2), 18, *Res* 115, *Rid 60* 1, 3, *Ruin* 41